Howard Sounes was born in 1965 and lives in London. He is the author of four books, including the biography of American writer Charles Bukowski – *Charles Bukowski: Locked in the Arms of a Crazy Life*: 'Wonderful – the first such serious and thorough Bukowski biography . . . an excellent book about a remarkable man' *Time Out*

Acclaim for *Down the Highway:*

'Must stand as the definitive work [and] might be the best psychological profile of Dylan that anyone is likely to produce' Rick Shefchik, *St. Paul Pioneer Press*

'A judicious portrait of Dylan's foibles and virtues [and] aptly captures the contradictory facets of an American folk legend' *Publishers Weekly*

'Lively and readable' Bob Eggington, *BBC News Online*

'The portrait drawn in *Down the Highway* is mesmerizing as we watch the trajectory of Dylan's life from young upstart to Grand Old Man of rock 'n' roll' William McKeen, *Orlando Sentinel*

'[Dylan] has always ensured his life is obscured in mystery [but] Howard Sounes's new biography, *Down the Highway*, blows away more of the fog than anyone else has managed to do' Barney Hoskyns, *Independent on Sunday*

'Thoughtful and shrewd' Mark Ford, (London) *Evening Standard*

'The first truly complete [Dylan] biography likely to satisfy the intelligent general reader' *Publishing News*

'Dylan comes alive . . . a vivid account' Perry Meisel, *New York Times*

'[This] fast-paced book has a fine interest in details [and is] rich with the observations of new witnesses' Sheri Linden, *Variety*

'Revealing' Robert Levine, *New York Magazine*

'The most definitive Dylan biography to be published so far . . . an essential book for anyone who has enjoyed Dylan's music' Donia Clark, *The Buffalo News*

'Engrossing' Carlo Wolff, *Kansas City Star*

'The inscrutable and intensely private Dylan is dissected, measured and categorized' *Esquire*

'A treasure-trove for Dylan fans' John Valentine, *Independent Weekly*

'Thoroughly researched' Al Brumley, *The Dallas Morning News*

'Howard Sounes [is] a master of the facts. The way he accumulates them, logically, almost kaleidoscopically, amounts to one of the clearest, least agenda-ridden biographies of Bob Dylan ever written' Robert Hudson, *Gadflyonline*

'Accurate and well-written' Christopher Gray, *The Oxford Times*

'Fast-paced [and] readable' Andy Dougan, *Glasgow Evening Times*

'Every page contains some gem' Mike Cohen, *Jewish Telegraph*

'This extraordinary biography [covers] much new ground' Charles Barker, *Coventry Evening Telegraph*

'[Sounes] keeps his pace quick, tossing out nugget after nugget' Gina Vivinetto, *St. Petersburg Times*

'Well-written, hugely detailed and often intriguing . . . impressive' Ross Reyburn, *The Birmingham Post*

'Sounes [writes] in great detail and with a good deal of quiet authority' Thomas Goldsmith, *The (*Nashville*) Tennessean*

DOWN THE HIGHWAY

THE LIFE OF BOB DYLAN

HOWARD SOUNES

BLACK SWAN

DOWN THE HIGHWAY
A BLACK SWAN BOOK : 0 552 99929 6

Originally published in Great Britain by Doubleday
a division of Transworld Publishers

PRINTING HISTORY
Doubleday edition published 2001
Black Swan edition published 2002

5 7 9 10 8 6 4

Set in 10.5/11.5 Melior by
Falcon Oast Graphic Art Ltd.

Black Swan Books are published by Transworld Publishers,
61–63 Uxbridge Road, London W5 5SA,
a division of The Random House Group Ltd,
in Australia by Random House Australia (Pty) Ltd,
20 Alfred Street, Milsons Point, Sydney, NSW 2061, Australia,
in New Zealand by Random House New Zealand Ltd,
18 Poland Road, Glenfield, Auckland 10, New Zealand
and in South Africa by Random House (Pty) Ltd,
Endulini, 5a Jubilee Road, Parktown 2193, South Africa.

Printed and bound in Great Britain by
Clays Ltd, St Ives plc.

For Jane Sounes and Claire Weaver

CONTENTS

AUTHOR'S NOTE AND ACKNOWLEDGMENTS

Bob Dylan is an artist of almost unrivaled importance in modern, popular music. He is a great recording star, an extraordinary live performer, an iconic figure of popular culture, and, most important, he is the preeminent songwriter of his time.

His reputation does not rest on commercial success. During his forty-year career Dylan has sold, throughout the world, in excess of fifty-six million records, including more than twenty-three million albums in the United States. Although these figures might seem enormous, they are much less impressive when one considers that The Beatles, his near contemporaries, have estimated worldwide sales of more than six hundred million, including more than a hundred and nine million albums in the United States. Dylan has had surprisingly few hit singles, never achieving a number-one single in America, and not placing one in the top forty since 1979.* He has always been considered more of an album artist. Yet as of September 2000 he languished at fifty-sixth place in the table of lifetime album sales compiled by the Recording Industry Association of America (R.I.A.A.), far behind younger artists like Madonna and Prince, and outsold even by such acts as Ozzy Osbourne and The Carpenters. Still, Bob Dylan's greatest albums, such as *Blonde on Blonde* and *Blood on the Tracks*, are touchstones of popular culture, works of such depth and quality that they place him in the front rank of entertainers.

**Billboard* Hot 100 chart.

Dylan tours the world relentlessly, and is one of the hardest-working live performers in music. On stage, he is truly dynamic, exuding a palpable charisma comparable to the likes of Elvis Presley and Frank Sinatra. But he stands apart from these great artists because – aside from a limited number of cowriting credits given to Presley – they did not write their own material. In addition to being a performer, Dylan is the author of more than 450 original compositions, including popular classics like 'Blowin' in the Wind', 'The Times They Are A-Changin'', 'Like a Rolling Stone', 'Forever Young', 'Knockin' on Heaven's Door', and 'Tangled Up in Blue'. These songs are as diverse in subject matter and as rich in imagery as the work of a major poet or novelist. For the most part, they were written with ease. Dylan has always felt he is a channel for divine inspiration, and has said that the words stream through him. The ability to create brilliant work over a long period of time, without straining for ideas, is the signal characteristic of his genius.

Bob Dylan changed music in the 1960s by bringing poetic lyrics to popular song. He was not afraid to say serious things in a medium that had never been taken particularly seriously, and did so with such deftness, wit and élan that he inspired others to follow. Almost every singer-songwriter of recent times owes him a debt, including John Lennon and Paul McCartney. The Beatles were greatly influenced by Dylan, who was a star before they were and who has long outlasted them. Indeed, his longevity in the front rank of popular music is another achievement that sets him apart.

Lennon and McCartney were a songwriting team, like the teams of Goffin and King, Jagger and Richards, and Leiber and Stoller. Collaboration is commonplace in songwriting because few artists have both a talent for melody and a facility for language. For the most part, however, Dylan has written on his own, just as he has built his live shows on solo performances. He is a fundamentally self-contained man. 'He walks out there alone.

He comes back off that stage alone. He writes those songs alone. He is his own man. He stands proud in his shoes. He don't need nobody to do nothin',' says former girlfriend Carole Childs. 'He's that gifted and that talented.'

Such is the power of his work that Dylan has become more than an entertainer. He is a minstrel guru to millions who hear their deepest thoughts and feelings expressed in his songs, an artist who is perceived to be an original thinker, whose work encapsulates wisdom. Bob Dylan lyrics have become figures of speech. 'Blowin' in the Wind' may be the best-known example. Others are 'money doesn't talk, it swears' and 'to live outside the law, you must be honest'. His quips are included in compendiums of modern quotations, including his reply to a question from *Playboy* magazine in 1966 about whether he knew what his songs were about: 'Oh, some are about four minutes; some are about five, and some, believe it or not, are about eleven or twelve.' Once again, this makes him a very unusual entertainer; however great Elvis Presley was, few would consider him a source of wit and wisdom. In his youth, as a folksinger, Dylan was also closely associated with movements for social change, an icon of the early 1960s alongside Martin Luther King Jr. and President John F. Kennedy. In the mid-1960s he rebelled against categorization by setting his poetic lyrics to the sound of amplified rock 'n' roll. In his maturity, he has written eloquently of love, faith, marriage, parenthood, and aging.

It is remarkable that Dylan's best work is not limited to a single period. After the glory years of the 1960s, he came back in 1975 with the outstanding *Blood on the Tracks*, an album as good as anything he had recorded before, and one that many consider to be his best. He surprised again in the mid-1980s with major new songs like 'Blind Willie McTell' (recorded in 1983, but not released until 1991) and the triple Grammy Award-winning *Time Out of Mind*. In between there have been remarkable concert tours, like the celebrated Rolling Thunder Revue of 1975–76. Few major artists have produced so much first-class material, and given so many compelling concerts, over such a long period. The undeniable fact that there has also been disappointing work – shambolic concert appearances and lackluster albums – has not detracted from his ability to surge back. Successive generations have grown up to appreciate his achievement, and teenagers are found next to parents, and even grandparents, at the hundred or so concerts he gives each year. It seems 'A Hard Rain's A-Gonna Fall' is still as relevant in an age of ecological concerns and flashpoint wars as it was during the Cuban Missile Crisis; the excitement of 'All Along the Watchtower' has not faded; the romance of 'Lay, Lady, Lay' has endured; and a recent song like 'Love Sick' can hold its own alongside songs of the past.

As a man, Dylan has always been contradictory and mercurial. He is one of the most famous people in the Western world and yet, when he is not on stage, he is reclusive. He is also extremely secretive. It is remarkable, considering he has been scrutinized by the world's press all his adult life, that large areas of that life have remained clouded with mystery. In this book, much that was mysterious becomes clear. For example, although it is well known that Dylan married former model Sara Lownds in 1965, and that they divorced in 1977, the fact that he married a second time in 1986, to backing singer Carolyn Dennis, and had a second family, has been hidden from press and public. There has been a great deal of speculation about this part of Dylan's life – including estimates of how many children he has fathered and by whom – but most of what has been written is wrong. The fully story, based on documented fact and the firsthand accounts of intimate friends and family, appears here for the first time.

Bob Dylan has long been a figurehead for the counterculture, yet paradoxically he takes little or no active interest in politics or social causes, going so far as to denounce politics as the 'instrument of the devil.' His mind is elsewhere – in the language and ancient morality of the Bible and in the ghostly heritage of American folk music. He is a deeply serious person, refusing to smile for cameras and refusing to talk on television shows. At the same time, he is renowned for his sense of humour; he can surprise with childish jokes, even card tricks, and takes impish delight in mind games. He is extremely wealthy, but chooses to live like a gypsy, spending more time on his tour bus than in any of the seventeen properties he owns around the world. Eccentricity has enhanced the legend. It is one thing to be a genius; it is better still to be an eccentric genius.

It is not surprising that more has been written about Dylan than almost any popular music artist; there would be something amiss if he had not been studied extensively. There have been dozens of books over the past forty years, including picture books, books analyzing lyrics, and four previous biographies of note: *Bob Dylan: An Intimate Biography* (Grosset & Dunlap, 1971) by Anthony Scaduto; *No Direction Home: The Life and Music of Bob Dylan* (New English Library, 1986) by Robert Shelton; *Dylan: A Biography* (McGraw-Hill, 1989) by Bob Spitz; and *Dylan: Behind the Shades* (Viking, 1991) by Clinton Heylin (revised as *Bob Dylan: Behind the Shades – Take Two* [Viking, 2000]. While good work has been done, the challenge of writing a major biography that conveys the full grandeur of Bob Dylan's artistic achievement, and also reveals the true life of this fascinating and elusive man, has remained.

This biography is based on painstaking new research. As a solid foundation to the book, I obtained a considerable amount of previously unseen documentary evidence about Bob Dylan's professional and family life. This includes birth, marriage, and death certificates, court papers, and real estate and property tax records. These documents have enabled me, in many cases, to pin down precise details in areas where there has been widespread, and often erroneous, speculation. Nearly everyone of significance in Dylan's life was contacted and new interviews were conducted with most of these people. Subjects who had never previously given interviews shared their experiences, and a surprising amount of new information was revealed that illuminates almost every aspect of the life. It includes, but is not limited to, the first full picture of Dylan's family life (for instance, the full names and the dates of birth of his first five children have been only sketchily understood until now). It also includes the inside story of his years of seclusion in Woodstock; stories behind the making of albums like *Blonde on Blonde*; his life on the road; his secret second marriage; his wealth; his legal battles; his unexpected property interests; and how the obsessive behavior of deranged fans, over many years, has caused him to fear for his safety.

Direct quotations have been taken only from previously published interviews in the case of Bob Dylan himself, who chose not to contribute to this biography, and where subjects have died or were otherwise unavailable for interview. All such quotations are attributed in the comprehensive source notes at the end of the book, together with explanations of background material used. More than 250 people helped me in this project, most by granting formal interviews, some by answering questions by letter or e-mail, and others by engaging in general discussions. These sources include relatives, childhood friends and teachers, girlfriends, neighbors, religious confidants, former employees, band members, poets, filmmakers, painters, and fellow musicians. Key sources include members of Bob Dylan's family and his closest male and female friends. Many of these people – including longtime girlfriend Carole Childs; Woodstock neighbor Bruce Dorfman; Albert Grossman's widow, Sally; and Dylan's oldest friend, Larry Kegan – have not spoken to previous biographers. Girlfriends Echo Helstrom and Bonnie Beecher have given their first interviews in many years. Many distinguished musicians with close associations with Bob Dylan have contributed to the book, including Rick Danko, Levon Helm, Garth Hudson, and Robbie Robertson of The Band; also, Tim Drummond, Ramblin' Jack Elliott, Arlo Guthrie, Richie Havens, Carolyn Hester, John Lee Hooker, Jim Keltner, Al Kooper, Mark Knopfler, Roger McGuinn, Maria Muldaur, Tom Paxton, Pete Seeger, Mick Taylor, Bob Weir of The Grateful Dead, and Peter Yarrow and Noel Paul Stookey of Peter, Paul and Mary. Some key people, including members of the Dylan family, helped on the understanding that they would not be named. A handful of others asked not to be quoted directly.

I am particularly grateful to the following individuals:

Kenny Aaronson, the late Steve Allen, David Amram, Al Aronowitz, Mary Alice Artes, Arthur Baker, Eve Baer, Stanley Bard, 'Bucky' Baxter, Danielle Beeh, Joel Bernstein, Louise Bethune, Theodore Bikel, Ronee Blakley, Peggi Blu, Oscar Brand, Marshall Brickman, Bob Britt, John Bucklen, Joanna Bull, Henry 'T-Bone' Burnett, Wayne Butler, Kenny Buttrey, Hamilton Camp (aka Bobby Camp), Nancy Carlen, Cindy Cashdollar, Anna L. Chairetakis (née Lomax), Carole Childs, Liam Clancy, John Cohen, Paul Colby, Walt Conley, Ron Cornelius, Billy Cross, Jones Cullian (née Alk), Ethel Crystal, Charlie Daniels, the late Rick Danko, Erik Darling, Luke Davich, Bruch Dorfman, Tim Drummond, Sly Dunbar, Manny Dworman, Pastor Bill Dwyer, Debi Dye-Gibson, Delores Edgin, Bob Engelhardt, Ramblin' Jack Elliott, Mimi Fariña (née Baez), Barry Feinstein, Lawrence Ferlinghetti, Anton Fig, Ray Foulk, Erik Frandsen, Dottie Gardner, Dana Gillespie, Tony Glover, Robert F. Goheen, Harvey Goldsmith, Dennis A. Good, Nick Gravenites, Wavy Gravy (aka Hugh Romney), 'Mean' Willie Green III, Marlie Griffiths (née Helstrom), Sally Grossman, Pastor Kenn Gullikson, Arlo Guthrie, Nora Guthrie, George

Haidos, Bobbye Hall, Tova Hammerman, John Hammond Jr., Jo Ann Harris, Richie Havens, Ronnie Hawkins, Bill HeckeRoth, Levon Helm, Echo Helstrom, John Herald, Carolyn Hester, LeRoy Hoikkala, J. J. Holiday, John Lee Hooker, Jim Horn, Neil Hubbard, Garth Hudson, Gayle Jamison, Bob Johnston, Mickey Jones, Steve Jones, Horace Judson, Pete Karman, Robert J. Karon, Larry Keenan, Larry Kegan, Jim Keltner, Doug Kershaw, Millie Kirkham, Mark Knopfler, 'Spider' John Koerner, Sandy Konikoff, Al Kooper, Danny Kortchmar, Daniel Kramer, Tony Lane, Bruce Langhorne, Harold Leventhal, Jacques Levy, George Lois, Alan Lomax, Peter Lownds, Rory Makem, Tommy Makem, Gerard Malanga, David Mansfield, Angel Marolt, Paul Martinson, Charlie McCoy, Michael McClure, Martha McCrory, Faridi McFree, Roger McGuinn, Augie Meyers, Marvin Mitchelson, Bob Moore, Dave Morton, Wayne Moss, Maria Muldaur, Jim Mullen, Shawn Nadery, Gloria Naftali, Bobby Neuwirth, Anne Noznisky, Jeffrey Noznisky, Odetta, 'Spooner' Oldham, Tony O'Malley, Richard Ostrander, Peter Ostroushko, Jon Pankake, Graham Parker, Alan Pasqua, Bernard Paturel, Mary Lou Paturel, Tom Paxton, the late Kenneth Pederson, Gretel Pelto (née Whitaker), D. A. Pennebaker, Regina Peoples, Ted Perlman, Billy Peterson, Chuck Plotkin, Larry Poons, Charlie Quintana, Kenny Rankin, Jean Ritchie, Scarlet Rivera, Hargus 'Pig' Robbins, Robbie Robertson, 'Duke' Robillard, B. J. Rolfzen, Jahanara Romney (née Bonnie Beecher), Dave Van Ronk, Arthur Rosato, Susan Ross, Carla Rotolo, Suze Rotolo, Bruce Rubenstein, Howard Rutman, Carole Bayer Sager, Monique Sampas (née Paturel), Ed Sanders, Philip Saville, Paul Schrader, Tim Schussler, John Sebastian, Mike Seeger, Peggy Seeger, Pete Seeger, Sam Shepard, Janine Signorelli, Roy Silver, P. F. Sloan, Larry 'Ratso' Sloman, Steven Soles, Mark Spoelstra, Patrick Stansfield, Yvonne Staples, Maeretha Stewart, Brian Stoltz, Lewis Stone, Rob Stoner, Noel Paul Stookey, Henry Strzelecki, Jonathan Taplin, Mick Taylor,

Dr. Ed Thaler, Selma Thaler, David C. Towbin, Adam Traum, Happy Traum, Jane Traum, Matt Umanov, Bill Walker, Ian Walker, Jennifer Warnes, Bill Waterous, Winston Watson, Harry Weber, A. J. Weberman, Bob Weir, Dave Whitaker, Ubi Whitaker, Josh White Jr., Steve Wiese, Charlie Wolven, Peter Yarrow, Israel 'Izzy' Young, Monalisa Young, Terry Young, William Zantzinger, and Jack Zimmerman.

Thank you to Russell Galen, of the Scovil Chichak Galen Literary Agency, Inc., whose judicious advice made this biography possible. Thank you to publisher Morgan Entrekin, who commissioned the book for Grove/Atlantic, Inc. Thank you also to Grove editor Andrew Miller; Jo Goldsworthy at Transworld Publishers in London; Sheila Lee, who researched the photographs; and Jonathan Lloyd at Curtis Brown Ltd.

PROLOGUE

YESTERDAY IS GONE, BUT THE PAST LIVES ON

The man's walk was weirdly jaunty, like a puppet on invisible strings. His head seemed to move to its own rhythm. He wore ill-fitting clothes, which made him look out of place in a fashionable district of Manhattan, almost the garb of a homeless person. If one looked closely, however, the clothes appeared new. If one looked closer still at the sallow, half-bearded face, this slightly built, middle-aged man seemed familiar. Under the hat there was the distinctive hooked nose, the delicate features framed with wisps of beard. When he went to scratch his nose, his fingernails were very long and dirty. When he looked to cross the street, his eyes were seen to be vivid blue, bluer than robins' eggs.

'You're Bob Dylan!'

People often recognized him, yelling out excited greetings, not quite believing they were seeing a legend on the street. Bob hated it when they grabbed at him, but he was at heart a polite Midwesterner and he did not mind saying hello. When he spoke – just to say, perhaps, 'Hey, man, how are ya *doin'*?' – his voice was so distinctive, with words pushed up from his diaphragm in bursts and then seemingly squeezed out through his almost comical nose, emphasizing the *wrong word* in a sentence and clipping other words short, it could be only Bob Dylan.

Bob came to the corner of 57th Street and Lexington Avenue and entered a small club, Tommy Makem's Irish Pavilion. Tommy Makem was an old friend from the early 1960s when Bob was learning his trade, a soft-spoken Irishman who had performed traditional folk songs with The Clancy Brothers in the clubs of Greenwich Village, New York. Makem had not seen Bobby – as he knew him – in many years. 'There was no one with him, no driver, no companion, no nothing. He was just on his own,' he recalls.

Makem settled Bob at a quiet table, where he would not be seen by other patrons. Then Makem fetched his banjo and got on stage for the show. He performed the old ballads Bob loved, hearty songs like 'Brennan on the Moor' and the wistful 'Will You Go, Lassie, Go.' There was a break before the second set and Makem went over to where Bob was having something to eat and drink. 'If you feel like singing a song, let me know,' he said. But Bob preferred to sit quietly alone. He was enjoying himself greatly. The Irish Pavilion reminded him of his early days in New York and the people he had met there, artists like John Lee Hooker, 'Cisco' Houston, and 'Big' Joe Williams. These men were monumental in his mind; they had informed and influenced his entire career.

After the audience drifted away, Makem pulled up a chair and he and Bob talked as the staff swept up around their chairs. It was the past Bob wanted to discuss – old friends from the old clubs, people he had not seen in thirty years, and old memories like the evening he ran up to the Irishman on Sixth Avenue excited about a song he had written. 'God it must have been 2:30 or 3 o'clock in the morning,' says Makem. 'Stopping [to] sing me a long murder ballad that he had written to the tune of some song he had heard Liam [Clancy] and myself singing. There would be twenty verses in it, and he would sing the whole lot for you. I thought, God, it's a very interesting thing this young fella's doing.'

A few weeks after Bob's unexpected visit to the Irish Pavilion, in the spring of 1992, Tommy Makem received a letter from Bob's record company, Sony Music. Makem was invited to perform at a concert celebrating Bob's thirty years as a recording artist (although, in fact, he had been making records for thirty-one). Bob had not said a word about it when they met, but that was typical of him; he was never much of a talker. Makem was not sure at first what sort of show this would be. From the low-key way in which Bob padded around town on his own, dressed like a bum, one might think his days as a major star were over, and that a celebration of his career would be held in a modest theater somewhere with a few old friends. 'It was extremely glamorous and much more of a huge event than I realized,' says Makem. 'It was gigantic.'

The venue for Bob's 'Thirtieth Anniversary Concert Celebration,' as it was called, was Madison Square Garden, the huge sports arena in Manhattan. When it was announced that Bob would appear with some of the most famous names in music, eighteen thousand seats sold within an hour. This was despite the fact promoters were charging between $50 and $150 a seat, record prices for a concert of its kind. When Makem arrived at the Rihga Royal Hotel, where the musicians were staying, he discovered that the guest list included not only old folkies but superstars such as Eric Clapton and George Harrison, who were devoted friends of Bob. For ten days prior to the show, limousines ferried the artists between the hotel and the Kaufman Astoria Studios for rehearsals. Bob dressed down, for rehearsals, his sweatshirt hood over his head, muttering that he was not sure the concert was a good idea: 'It'll be like goin' to my own *funeral*.'

Still, there was great excitement on the evening of Friday October 16, 1992, as the lights in the Garden came up to reveal a huge stage in the shape of a Mexican hacienda. The house band, Booker T. and the M.G.s, began the show with one of Bob's songs of Christian faith, 'Gotta Serve Somebody.' Then, for more than three hours, they backed a succession of stars selected to represent the range of Dylan's influence, from folk artists; country artists, such as Willie Nelson and Johnny Cash; African-American stars who had covered his songs, like Stevie

Wonder and the O'Jays; and younger rockers, including Eddie Vedder and Tom Petty and The Heartbreakers, who toured with Bob in the 1980s. All performed Bob Dylan songs.

At times the concert was a salutary reminder of how many years had passed since the salad days of Dylan and his contemporaries. Carolyn Hester – one of the beauties of the folk revival – now had the white hair of a grandmother. The Band, the extraordinary group Bob toured with in 1965–66, and again in 1974, had been five rugged young men with full, dark beards. In the intervening years, guitarist Robbie Robertson had become estranged from the group, and pianist Richard Manuel had killed himself. The remaining three members now appeared much changed as they walked on stage to perform the song 'When I Paint My Masterpiece.' The beards of drummer Levon Helm and keyboardist Garth Hudson were gray, and Helm looked frail. Rick Danko, the once skinny bass guitarist, was bloated after years of drug abuse. 'It was a shock,' says Joel Bernstein, who had worked for Bob and The Band in their heyday. 'When the lights came up [you] could hear people go, "Uh!"'

In comparison, Richie Havens looked much like he had years ago when he and The Band were among the stars of the original Woodstock Festival. He brought the audience to its feet with a tremendous cover of 'Just Like a Woman'. 'I was greatly pleased to be invited and to be able to sing a song I still do on stage,' he says. 'Bob is one of my mental mentors – an utterly shy person, except on stage [which] is what most people perceive as [his] mysteriousness.'

True to form, Bob was secreted in his dressing room, watching the show on closed-circuit television. Numerous celebrities, including John McEnroe, Martin Scorsese, and Carly Simon, were drifting around backstage, craning their necks to catch sight of one of the few people in the world more famous than themselves. Ronnie Wood of The Rolling Stones passed around a

180-proof bottle of vodka. Liam Clancy took a swig. He had flown in from Ireland with his brothers to perform 'When the Ship Comes In' with Tommy Makem. 'Christ, if we have any more of that we'll never sing tonight,' he said.

Outside in the auditorium members of the audience were expressing themselves in a forthright way if anybody came on stage that they did not like. Singer Sophie B. Hawkins got short shrift. The president of Sony Music was booed. Kris Kristofferson nervously introduced an artist whose name, he said, was synonymous with courage. Irish singer Sinead O'Connor, stick-thin with head shaved, stepped up to the microphone. She had recently been embroiled in controversy over a television appearance during which she denounced the Pope. There was fierce booing. Booker T. repeatedly played the opening chords of 'I Believe in You', the song she had rehearsed, but she froze.

'Get off!' people shouted.

O'Connor made a cutting motion with her hand, ordered her microphone turned up, and spat out the words of the song 'War.' It was a genuine act of protest and, for a few moments, she silenced the hecklers. Then it dawned on the audience that she was not singing a Bob Dylan song at all. 'War' was by Bob Marley. She was howled off stage; she was so upset she threw up. Artists watched her humiliation with surprise. 'It was outrageous,' says blues artist John Hammond Jr., son of Bob's first record producer. 'I couldn't believe the New York audience would be so unopen to her view.'

Neil Young came on after the Sinead O'Connor debacle, seeming a bit nervous. But the crowd loved him, especially when he performed 'All Along the Watchtower' in the incandescent style of Jimi Hendrix, who had had a hit with it in 1968. (Curiously, many of Bob's songs were more familiar to a mass audience as cover versions than in their original recordings.) 'This song's for you, Bob,' shouted Young. 'Thanks for having

Bobfest.' Roger McGuinn of The Byrds also received a warm reception when he performed 'Mr. Tambourine Man.' The Byrds had a number-one hit with the song in the summer of 1965, and the distinctive sound of McGuinn's twelve-string guitar and his tremulous, slightly spacey vocal invoked a profound nostalgia. He sounded just like he had all those years ago. 'It was joyful,' he says. 'I was singing to God.'

When the stage was cleared, George Harrison made a long-overdue announcement. 'Some of you may call him Bobby. Some of you may call him Zimmy. *I* call him Lucky,' he said in his distinctive Liverpudlian accent, recalling their brief-lived band, The Traveling Wilburys. 'Ladies and gentlemen, please welcome BOB DYLAN!'

The audience shrieked and whistled, straining to catch their first glimpse of the legend. A little man trotted out into the converging violet spotlights, appearing to many surprisingly short and skinny. The applause grew even louder. Dressed in a black silk suit, his white shirt done up tight, Bob looked like a disheveled waiter. He had not shaved, or maybe even slept, for several days. His skin was pale and his face was deeply lined. His once luxuriant curly hair was lank against his sweaty forehead. He moved to the microphone and began strumming his acoustic guitar with his long, nicotine-yellow fingernails. It might be a $5 million show, but he was going to perform solo, as he'd done in coffeehouses decades ago. The tune he strummed was rudimentary and he did not attempt to converse with his audience, other than to say a casual 'Thanks everybody.' When he started playing, though, the attention of all eighteen thousand people was locked onto this extraordinarily charismatic man. Beyond the front rows of special guests – which were all the nearsighted singer could make out – was a vast cavern of people, a cavern studded with the rapid flashing of camera bulbs.

He began with 'Song to Woody,' the first important

song he wrote. It was a tribute to his first hero, Woody Guthrie, the father of American folk music. When he wrote it, Bob was nineteen, affecting a world-weariness beyond his years. At fifty-two, his battered features and weary voice betrayed a man who had been on an extraordinary journey. Woody's daughter, Nora, sat in front. She began to weep as Bob sang about her father, who died in 1967, worn away by Huntington's chorea. 'If Dad was on a river, there were a lot of streams and estuaries coming in and out of that river. That was a very big river that he was on,' she explains. 'Bob went right in and he then became captain of that same river. My father faded, and Bob took it over, and I've always felt that he's always been a pretty true captain.'

After 'Song to Woody,' Bob ripped into 'It's Alright, Ma (I'm Only Bleeding),' bending at the knees and twisting his body as he thrashed the steel strings of his guitar. Guest artists crowded around the perimeter of the stage to watch him. Ronnie Wood and drummer Anton Fig peeped from behind the drum riser. 'He was just on fire,' says Fig.

Roger McGuinn, Tom Petty, Eric Clapton, Neil Young, and George Harrison joined Bob for a singalong version of 'My Back Pages.' Then everybody crowded onto the stage for 'Knockin' on Heaven's Door,' recently a hit for Guns N' Roses. At the end, Bob stood center stage, applauded not only by the audience but also by the great stars clustered around him. Ronnie Wood and George Harrison sang 'For He's a Jolly Good Fellow.' Bob stood awkwardly, apparently not knowing quite what to do with his hands, not knowing what words to say. Carolyn Hester picked up a small spray of flowers that had been thrown on stage and, encouraged by Neil Young, gave them to Bob, hugging him quickly and pecking him on the cheek. She feared he might not like it, even though they were old friends. 'I thought, I'll be thrown out for that, but nobody threw me out. I was so glad. And he smiled. He gave a little smile. Everybody was amazed.' It was the first time Bob had smiled all evening.

* * *

It was clear during the planning of the event that there had to be an after-show party, somewhere Sony could entertain Bob, celebrity guests, and music-industry people. The Waldorf-Astoria hotel had been a possibility early on. But then Bob said, 'I don't want to go there. I'm going to Tommy Makem's place.' So plans were changed and the little folk club was hired for the night. It held only a hundred and fifty people, and first priority went to Bob's friends and notable guest stars. Fans and press watched them arrive. Then there were the band musicians, their wives and girlfriends. There was little room left for record-company executives and the remaining celebrities who wanted to get in. In fact, there was no room for anybody else. 'You can't come in unless you have a ticket,' Tommy Makem was told when he returned from the show.

'I own this pub,' Makem informed the security man. But he still had to find his ticket.

Inside, Bob was ensconced like a gypsy king at a long rectangular table in a corner of the Irish Pavilion, a glass of white wine in front of him. Around him, at smaller tables, sat his courtiers – close friends including George Harrison, who was drinking tea, Ronnie Wood, and Eric Clapton, who was learning to play the Irish tin whistle. Others were escorted to Bob's table one at a time to pay their respects. 'Bob Dylan, King of Rock 'n' Roll, was what was going on that night,' says Carolyn Hester. 'He would summon various ones of us.'

When Liam Clancy came up to thank Bob for inviting The Clancy Brothers to perform, Bob asked him to sit awhile. Clancy said he and his brothers were thinking of making an album of Bob's songs, in traditional Irish folk style. It would be a way of giving the songs back to him. 'Man, would you do that? *Would* you?' asked Bob.

'Would you object?'

'Liam, you don't realize, do you, man?' asked Bob, who

had relaxed a good deal. He was alternating white wine with Guinness, and was drinking steadily. 'You're my fucking hero, man.' Bob's acceptance by the folk artists he looked up to when he first came to New York from Minnesota was the fulfillment of a lifelong dream, and he beamed at the portly, fifty-six-year-old Irishman. 'He ceased being the star and he was the insecure little boy I first knew,' says Clancy. 'He was looking for affirmation [then], and he was still looking after all these years, after all the stardom and acclaim and everything . . . I thought it was lovely that, at that stage of his life, he could admit it.'

Clancy told Bob he had not looked comfortable on stage. He had heard persistent rumors that Bob had a drug problem. Bob's strange behavior in recent years – performing in hooded sweatshirts and hats that hid his face, and singing songs in ways that made them almost unrecognizable – seemed to indicate something was wrong. But his reply was surprising. 'Hey, man, I suffer from claustrophobia,' he said. 'I just wanted to be out [of there]. I can't stand that much time indoors anymore.'

'You were breaking out in a cold sweat.'

'I don't want to be in that situation anymore, but I have to do it.'

Clancy then plucked up the courage to ask a question that had bothered him for years. When they were young men in Greenwich Village, the Irishman had a girlfriend named Cathy. He suspected Cathy had had an affair with Bob, who had always been an incorrigible womanizer. 'Bobby, were you screwing Cathy?' he asked.

Bob looked at him and Clancy knew he was going to get the truth at last. 'Man, she loved you,' he replied, apparently unable to tell a lie. 'But she was so lonesome. I gotta admit, man, I did comfort her.'

Clancy was hurt. It was painful to think that the love letters Cathy had sent him when he was on the road with his brothers were written when she was snuggled up in New York with baby-faced Bobby Dylan. But they were both too old to fight. Instead, Clancy picked up a guitar and thrust it at Bob, reminding him that in the old days, at the Lion's Head or the White Horse Tavern, they always passed a guitar at the end of an evening. 'Come on, here's a guitar. Sing me a song.'

'I can't do that anymore, man.'

'Are you too big a fucking star for that? Don't pull that shit with me, Bobby. Sing a fuckin' song now, because that's what we've done, always.'

Reluctantly, Bob took the guitar and began singing 'Roddy McCorley,' a traditional song he had learned from The Clancy Brothers. But when it came to his friend's turn to sing a verse, he dried. 'Jesus, would you believe it, I was so drunk I couldn't remember it?' From the other end of the table, Ronnie Wood piped up:

Up the narrow street he stepped
Smiling, proud and young

The guitar was passed to George Harrison who sang the next verse. Keyboard player Ian McLagan, who toured with Bob in 1984, jerked awake and contributed a lewd ditty he had learned from Steve Marriott, of The Faces, when they were playing pubs in London:

I love my wife
I love her dearly
I love the hole she pisses through

Before long, everybody was laughing, singing songs, reciting snatches of poetry, and slapping one another on the back. 'Drink is a great leveler and we all had our arms around each other, and we were in a huddle, like we were when we were young,' says Clancy. 'We could have been a rugby team at the end of the evening.' They drank until morning light came through the windows. At seven A.M. Tommy Makem's sons announced it was time they were all off home to their beds. Fans and press were gone. So were the limousines, the chauffeurs sent home hours ago. They would have to get taxis.

With his custom-made stage suit crumpled and smelling of beer and cigarettes, Bob looked relaxed, much happier than the embarrassed figure on stage at the Garden. When the cabs came, he hugged his friends, thanked them for coming, and allowed himself to be guided to a car. He was smiling broadly as he was driven away into the early morning traffic.

He would sleep until late afternoon. When he woke, in the dusk of a missed day, he would have to turn his mind back to his tour, the so-called Never-Ending Tour of a hundred or so shows a year. He was due to give a concert at the University of Delaware in a couple of days. After that, there were concerts booked until Christmas. They were mostly small theaters, and the people who came to see him probably would not buy his new album; nowadays people came to the shows, like they visited museums, to experience history. His personal life was in ruins. He was getting divorced for the second time, from a marriage he had managed to keep hidden. He was concerned for the future of the daughter he had fathered by his secret, second wife, and mindful of the large sums of money he would have to hand over for the settlement. The show at the Garden would help, but there was a massive overhead and he was not sure how the CD and video spin-offs would sell. Judging by the performance of his recent albums, they might sink without a trace. Maybe it would help if he could talk about his problems, but he was an inward man, with no confidants. Having been famous all his adult life, he felt he could trust only himself.

These were the peculiar pressures of being Bob Dylan. Yet for one night he had been Bobby again, the carefree boy who had come out of the Midwest to make his fortune in New York, the boy who had hung out in the Village with Tommy Makem, Liam Clancy, and Carolyn Hester. He had been happy then, as happy as he has ever been. 'A very lonely man,' says Clancy, of his old friend. 'So few people left in the world, I suppose, that he [can] talk to.'

CHAPTER 1

NORTH COUNTRY CHILDHOOD

Duluth is an iron-ore shipping town in northern Minnesota, built on a rocky cliff on the western shore of Lake Superior. Bob Dylan was born here as Robert Allen Zimmerman in May 1941. In a 1998 magazine article, Elvis Costello asked, '. . . what's Robert Zimmerman doing living in Duluth? That's in itself a story. His family had to get there from somewhere. There's folk music explained right there.'

Bob's father, Abe Zimmerman, was the son of Zigman and Anna Zimmerman, Jewish immigrants from eastern Europe. Zigman was born in 1875 in the Black Sea port of Odessa and grew up in desperate times. As the power of Czar Nicholas II faltered, he blamed Jews for the problems besetting the Russian empire, and thousands were murdered by mobs. Anti-Semitic hysteria reached Odessa in November 1905. Fifty thousand Czarists marched through the streets, screaming 'Down with the Jews,' and shot, stabbed, and strangled a thousand to death. In the wake of the massacre Bob's paternal grandfather fled the country, telling his wife and children he would send for them when he had found a place to settle.

Zigman Zimmerman caught a ship to the United States and found his way to Duluth, one hundred and fifty-one miles north of the Twin Cities of Minneapolis and St. Paul. Like many émigrés, Zimmerman gravitated to a place similar to the land where he was born. Duluth was a small but bustling port, like Odessa, with an almost Russian climate of short summers and long, bitter winters. Duluth was a fishing port, but its main trade was in the iron ore from the Iron Range, a necklace of mining towns to the northwest. The ore was transported by train to Duluth and transferred to ships that carried it to iron and steel works in Chicago and Pittsburgh. Zimmerman worked as a street peddler, repairing shoes. When he was established he sent for his Russian wife, Anna. She came with three children, Marion, Maurice, and Paul. Three more boys – Jack, Abram (also known as Abe), and Max – were born after the couple was reunited in America.

Abe Zimmerman was born in 1911. By the age of seven, he was selling newspapers and shining shoes to help the family. Although Abe was not tall and wore glasses, he was an athletic boy. He was also a musician, and the Zimmerman children formed a little band. 'Abe played violin. I played violin [and] Marion played piano,' says Abe's brother Jack. 'We had pretty good talent and played together at some high schools.' Abe graduated high school in 1929, a few months before the Wall Street stock market crash, and went to work for Standard Oil.

Bob Dylan's mother, Beatrice Stone – whom everybody called Beatty, pronounced Bee-tee, with emphasis on the second syllable – was from a prominent Jewish family in the Iron Range town of Hibbing. Her maternal grandparents, Benjamin and Lybba Edelstein, were Lithuanian Jews who had arrived in America with their children in 1902, and came to Hibbing two years later. Her grandfather, known as B. H., operated a string of movie theaters. B.H.'s eldest daughter, Florence, who was born in Lithuania, married Ben Stone, also born in Lithuania, and they ran a clothing store in Hibbing, selling to the families of miners, most of whom were also immigrants. Beatty was born in 1915, the second of Ben and Florence's four children. Her siblings were named Vernon, Lewis, and Irene. Like the Zimmermans, the Stones were a musical family and Beatty learned to play the piano.

Although Hibbing was the largest of the Iron Range towns, the population was only ten thousand, and the Jewish community was small. 'It was quite difficult for us because there weren't too many young Jewish people,' says Beatty's aunt, Ethel Crystal, who was like a sister to Beatty because they were close in age. 'So we used to go to Duluth to visit our relatives.' They were in Duluth, at a New Year's party, when Ethel introduced Beatty to Abe Zimmerman. 'He was a doll,' says Ethel Crystal. 'Everybody liked him.' Abe was a quiet, almost withdrawn, young man, and Beatty was vivacity itself, but their differences were complementary.

Abe and Beatty married at her mother's home on June 10, 1934, three days after her nineteenth birthday. Abe was twenty-two at the time. The country was still gripped by the Depression. Sharecroppers from the Midwest were migrating to California. Newspapers reported the desperate crimes of gangsters like Bonnie and Clyde, who were involved in a shoot-out in St. Paul in March. John Dillinger was shot dead in Chicago a couple of weeks after Abe and Beatty honeymooned in the city. It was a strange, hard time, and it would be six years before they could afford to start a family. In the meantime, they lived with Abe's mother in Duluth.

It took the Second World War, and President Franklin D. Roosevelt's New Deal, to pull America out of the Great Depression. By 1941, Abe had been promoted to management level at Standard Oil, and he and Beatty had enough money to get their own apartment. Beatty was pregnant when they moved to 519 North 3rd Avenue East, a clapboard house with a steeply pitched roof and verandah, built on a hill above Duluth. They rented the two-bedroom top duplex. At five past nine on the evening of May 24, 1941, Beatty gave birth to baby boy at nearby St. Mary's Hospital. He weighed seven pounds and one ounce. Four days later when the child was registered and circumcised he had a name. In fact, he had two. In Hebrew he was called Shabtai Zisel ben Avraham. In the wider world he would be known as Robert Allen Zimmerman. Robert was the most popular name for boys in the country at the time. Almost immediately he was known as Bob, or Bobby. His mother said he was so beautiful he should have been a girl.

The central hillside district of Duluth was predominantly Jewish and Polish, with a synagogue at the end of the road. There was a general store, a European bakery, the Loiselle liquor store, and a Sears Roebuck at the bottom of the hill. The weather was determined by Lake Superior, so vast and deep it remained icy cold throughout the year. Even in mid-summer, Duluth could be shrouded in frigid fog. There was a fresh ocean smell and the cry of seagulls. Ships approaching the landmark Ariel Bridge sounded their horns and a horn on the bridge blasted in reply. These were the sights and sounds Bob grew up with as the Second World War raged to its end.

In 1946, a year after the war ended, Bob enrolled at the Nettleton elementary school two blocks from his home. The same year he gave his singing debut at a family party. Children were encouraged to perform for the entertainment of the adults. When it was his turn, four-year-old Bob stamped his foot for attention. 'If everybody in this room will keep quiet,' he said, 'I will sing for my grandmother. I'm going to sing "Some Sunday Morning."' It was such a success the audience demanded an encore. Bob obliged with 'Accentuate the Positive.' These were popular tunes on the radio at the time. 'Our phone never stopped ringing with people congratulating me,' said the proud Beatty.

Not long after, Bob had a second opportunity to perform, at the wedding of Beatty's sister, Irene. The relatives wanted Bob to sing again. Bob was reluctant, even when an uncle offered him money, but Abe persuaded him. Once again he prefaced his performance by telling the excited relatives, 'If it's quiet, I will sing.' It was another great success. Everybody cheered and clapped and one of Bob's uncles pressed money into his hand. With instinctive showmanship, Bob turned to his mother and said, 'Mummy, I'm going to give the money back.' It brought the house down. 'People would laugh with delight at hearing him sing. He was, I would say, a very lovable, a very unusual child,' Abe remembered. 'I think we were the only ones who would *not* agree that he was going to be a very famous person some day . . . When he sang 'Accentuate the Positive' the way other children his age sang 'Mary Had a Little Lamb' people said he was brilliant.' As Beatty said, it was amazing her son was not spoiled by so much attention.

In February 1946 Bob was joined by a baby brother, David Benjamin. Around the same time Abe was stricken with polio, which had reached the level of an epidemic by that year. After a week in the hospital he came home and crawled up the front steps of the house 'like an ape,' as he described it. He stayed home for six months, and then lost his job at Standard Oil. Although Abe suffered his misfortunes manfully, the illness had a marked effect. He had been an active, even athletic young man. Now he had to learn to walk again. 'My father never walked right again and suffered much pain his whole life,' said Bob. 'I never understood this until much later but it must have been hard for him.' Without work, short of money, and needing relatives around to help them, the Zimmermans moved to Hibbing, where Beatty's family lived and where two of Abe's brothers ran a business.

Seventy-five miles northwest of Duluth, and separated from Canada by a hundred miles of forest and lake country, Hibbing had greatly expanded with the demand for iron during the Second World War. The population swelled to eighteen thousand and there was a busy downtown district around Howard Street and 1st Avenue. Mining dominated the town. The Hull-Rust-Mahoning mine was a gash in the earth three miles wide and more than five hundred feet deep. Local people called it 'the man-made Grand Canyon of the North.' They had good reason to look kindly upon the mine, for the prosperity of Hibbing correlated directly with the fortunes of the Oliver Mining Company. When demand for ore was high, as it was during and just after the war, Hibbing enjoyed better than average standards of living and full employment. It was said everybody who could breathe could get a job. The mine itself was a mile and a half north of town, but iron ore was everywhere. The town was surrounded by hills of red overburden, some large enough for houses to be built on, and cars coming back from the mine were covered in iron oxide, as were the nearest buildings. There was a saying in Minnesota that one should wash out one's ears after visiting Hibbing.

Hibbing was the quintessential small town, where American flags hung from every building on Independence Day and where virtually everybody knew one another, and probably knew their parents, too. People did not like to stand out or appear special. It was important to get on with one's neighbors; they were the same people who worked in Feldman's department store, taught at Hibbing High School, and sat at the next table in Sammy's Pizza restaurant. The feeling of community was perhaps stronger than normal because Hibbing was so remote, lying closer to Canada than to any major U.S. city. There were bears in the pine forests. The northern lights could be seen flashing across the bleak horizon. In mid-winter people had to dig through deep snow drifts to their cars. 'In the winter everything was still, nothing moved,' Bob has reminisced. 'Eight months of that . . . you can have some amazing hallucinogenic experiences doing nothing but looking out your window.'

Originally, the town was established farther north. But when the Oliver Mining Company decided to expand in 1912, everybody had to move, jacking their houses onto wheels and rolling them down the road. They left behind a ghost town known as North Hibbing. To partially compensate the citizens for this upheaval, the mining company invested in grand civic building schemes including a new business district, the Androy Hotel, and a City Hall. The scale of these projects lent Hibbing a feeling of affluence. Many of the town folk had come to America as semiliterate immigrants and they wanted something better for their children, so the Oliver Company also raised an opulent high school as part of the rebuilding, complete with a luxuriously appointed auditorium copied from the Capitol Theater in New York.

The move from North Hibbing was still in progress when the Zimmermans moved to town. There was a temporary shortage of housing, so they lived initially with Beatty's mother, Florence Stone, who had been widowed in 1945. She became like a second mother to Bob and David. Abe went into partnership with his two electrician brothers, Maurice and Paul, at Micka Electric on 5th Avenue. The brothers sold a range of household appliances and carried out wiring and electrical repair work.

In 1948 Abe moved his family to 2425 7th Avenue, Bob's primary childhood home. This was a two-story detached house two blocks from Hibbing High, where Bob and David enrolled, and a ten-minute walk from downtown where Abe worked. Entering the house, one walked directly into the living room. There was a central, two-way staircase that led to three bedrooms. The house was connected to 'city heat,' steam heat pumped underground to houses near downtown, so there was no need for a furnace. Abe converted the basement into a recreation room, cladding the walls in pine paneling. Bob carved his initials, B. Z., next to the wall-mounted telephone. He and David shared a bedroom at the back of the house with two windows, one looking south down 7th Avenue and one looking west on 25th Street. Under the window was situated a flat-roofed garage. The Zimmermans also owned a second garage, which they rented to a bakery as storage space. When the bread truck came in the late afternoon kids would gather around for leftover buns.

There were several boys of Bob's age in the neighborhood and, from the time they first moved to Hibbing, Beatty helped Bob make friends by organizing enjoyable parties for him. Children were invited to the house, or to outings to Side Lake, a picturesque spot outside of town. The friends Bob made in this way included the Furlong brothers; Bill Marinac, who later played bass in one of Bob's high school bands; and Luke Davich. The children played together in the playground adjacent to the high school and, when they got older, they rode their bikes to Bennett Park, or out to the manmade hills, skidding and sliding on the red overburden. In the summer there was fishing and swimming; ice-skating and hockey in winter. Sometimes it was fun to ride to the mine and peer over the edge at the trucks so far below they looked like toys.

In September 1949 the steam locomotives that worked day and night in the mine fell silent. There were no more horn blasts, or explosions. Miners across the northern states were striking for pensions and insurance rights from United Steel. This strike lasted two months; the miners struck again in 1952. The strikes were hard on Hibbing, but they created a feeling of solidarity. Shopkeepers knew their prosperity depended on the miners having money to spend and, with the support of the community, the miners got their demands. For Bob, it was an early firsthand experience of people pulling together to achieve justice.

When the strikes were won, the town boomed. A new consumer age was beginning and a large proportion of the iron for America's skyscrapers, automobiles, and domestic appliances was dug out of the mines outside Hibbing. There were few rich people in town, but there were not many poor people, and most citizens were slightly better off than the national average. Micka Electric was enjoying success and the Zimmermans became fairly comfortable. Abe and Beatty were soon prominent in various social groups and organizations. The family home had good-quality furniture and fitted carpeting. They ate from expensive china, had crystal glass, and sterling silver cutlery. A small chandelier hung over the dining table.

Bob flourished in a stable home where he was denied almost nothing and yet was not spoiled. He was particularly lucky to have such a loving mother. Beatty was a popular personality in Hibbing, where she worked part-time at Feldman's department store. 'I think one of the reasons he did have a pretty decent childhood was because of Beatty,' says boyhood friend John Bucklen. 'She was a very good mother, a very likable woman.' Around his tenth birthday, Bob wrote a poem for Mother's Day. It was an unequivocal statement of love for his mother. He wrote that he hoped she would never grow old. With a touch of melodrama, Bob added that without her love he would be dead and buried. Beatty was delighted with the poem, and showed all her friends. She kept it, together with other poems Bob and David gave her, in a footstool with a hinged lid.

The following year Bob wrote a Father's Day poem. This was slightly different. Bob's relationship with his father was not as close as that with his mother. Abe was a reserved man, very quiet, authoritarian and hard to know. He was articulate and could be witty, in a dry way, but he generally said little, being shy of company, and preferred to sit with the *New York Times* crossword rather than make conversation. While Bob's school friends remember Beatty as a radiant presence, Abe could seem disdainful. In his Father's Day poem, Bob affirmed his respect for his father, stating that he tried his best to please him. He added that maybe this was hard for his father to believe. There were times when Abe got 'real mad.' At these times Bob found it was best to keep quiet in case his father became even angrier.

It was around this time that Bob began playing music, for the Zimmermans had acquired a Gulbranson spinet piano. Beatty had played when she was young and Abe could pick out a tune, but the piano was bought mostly in the hope that the boys might show an interest. A cousin named Harriet Rutstein gave Bob and his six-year-old brother initial tutoring. 'David, who was a very, very smart boy, took it all in . . . and he could play better than Bob,' says his uncle, Lewis Stone. 'He was very musically inclined.' Bob became frustrated and dispensed with his cousin's help, announcing, 'I'm going to play the piano the way I want to.' He proceeded to teach himself, and without ever learning how to read music. The boys were encouraged to take up other instruments, too. Bob tried the trumpet and saxophone before settling on acoustic guitar, working with the *Nick Manoloff Basic Spanish Guitar Manual*.

After the Zimmermans bought a television set in 1952 – one of the first in town – Bob and David watched comedies and Westerns. But reception was poor in remote northern Minnesota and there was only a short period each day when programs for children were broadcast. There was still plenty of time to be alone and think and Bob was by nature a solitary, contemplative child. He did have a brother, but friends do not remember Bob and David as being particularly close. Indeed, when Bob invited friends home he would shoo David out of the way. Bob loved to read adventure books, and he liked to paint and make up stories of his own. He would sometimes sit beside the railroad tracks watching the cars filled with iron ore rattling down the line to Duluth. He would wave shyly at the engine driver, count the cars, and listen as the wheels receded. As he did so, he later recalled, he absentmindedly uprooted hunks of grass or tossed rocks across the tracks. He did some light work at Micka Electric, sometimes going out on the truck with his uncles to do wiring jobs, or sweeping up at the store for pocket money. But he did not like the work, and seems to have been disturbed by the brisk way his family did business with people who owed them money. Bob usually had plenty of pocket money nonetheless, enough to buy cigarettes, a habit he took up furtively at an early age, and cokes and pie at one of the downtown luncheonettes.

There was a European flavor to downtown Hibbing. The town was built by woodsmen and miners drawn to northern Minnesota from all over Europe, but particularly eastern Europe and Scandinavia. Practically every kid in Hibbing had some European ancestry and most of the older people spoke with accents. Vowels were commonly pronounced in a Germanic way, most noticeably when people said 'yar' for 'yeah.' When they agreed strongly, they exclaimed, 'Yaarrr!' At the Sunrise Bakery on Saturday mornings, with customers *oh-yaarring* over purchases of potica cake and other European delicacies, one would almost be in the Rhineland. Despite the prevalence of immigrants, there was some degree of anti-Semitism. The Jews of Hibbing were not Orthodox; the men, including Abe, were clean-shaven and the Sabbath did not prevent them working. Still, Jews were not allowed to join the Mesaba Country Club. Bob was known as Zimbo to some children, and although there is no evidence he was bullied or picked on, his Jewishness was a factor that set him apart.

The Jewish community was so small that Hibbing did not have a rabbi. When it came time for Bob to study for his bar mitzvah a rabbi arrived by bus from New York. The rabbi was a very old man, with black robes and a white beard, like a character from the Old Testament. The Jewish community found him a room downtown and, every day after school, Bob went there and studied with him. Bob had his bar mitzvah in May 1954. There was a party at the Androy Hotel, with relatives driving in from Duluth and beyond. Afterward, the Jews did not want to keep the Orthodox rabbi on – he looked too old-fashioned in go-ahead 1954 Hibbing – and so he went back to New York.

While Bob was not brought up in an Orthodox home,

he did receive a grounding in the Bible – an important source of imagery for his song lyrics long before his Christian conversion of the 1970s – and his father instilled a stern ethical code in the boy. As Bob later recalled, Abe once told him it was possible to become so 'defiled' that his own mother and father would abandon him. 'If that happens, God will always believe in your own ability to mend your own ways.' Although from the outside Bob might seem manipulative, egocentric, and amoral in later life – especially during the first years of his success when he was showered with adulation and money – something of his father's Midwestern values always remained with him. As he grew up, Bob rarely swore; he was never in trouble with the police; he was close to his parents; he was loyal to friends for long periods of time; he was, in many ways, a person of strongly held moral principles; and he worked hard at his music, which increasingly seemed to be his vocation in life.

As he became more interested in music, the artists he liked tended to write and sing lyrics with a serious core, and performed with a sense that they were singing about something important. Popular music first reached Bob via the radio. Years later he identified Johnnie Ray as someone whom he heard very early on. Ray, who wept as part of his stage act, was one of the big stars of the early 1950s. 'He was popular and we knew he was . . . dynamic and different and really had heart and soul,' said Bob. 'He was an anomaly. He was stuck in there with Perry Como and Patti Page. I remember thinking he could really make you feel something.' Then there was Hank Williams, who wrote and sang deceptively simple songs in a voice that was not pretty, nor particularly musical, but had abundant conviction. The son of dirt-poor parents from the backwoods of southern Alabama, Williams was an unhealthy, unhappy alcoholic. Many of his songs were about the heartbreak of being in love with faithless women, which seemed to reflect his own marriage. In the last years of his short life he was one of the stars of the Grand Ole Opry, a variety show broadcast each Saturday night from Nashville, Tennessee. Bob heard Hank Williams on the Opry, introduced as 'the ol' Lovesick Blues boy,' and the sad songs sank into his heart. To Bob, Hank Williams would always be the greatest American songwriter.

Late at night Bob picked up radio stations from Little Rock, Arkansas, Chicago, Illinois, and way down south in Shreveport, Louisiana. What these stations played was mostly the blues, particularly on disc jockey Frank 'Brother Gatemouth' Page's show, *No-Name Jive*. 'Late at night I used to listen to Muddy Waters, John Lee Hooker, Jimmy Reed, and Howlin' Wolf blastin' in from Shreveport,' Bob has said. 'I used to stay up till two, three o'clock in the morning. Listened to all those songs, then tried to figure them out. I started playing myself.' Bob had stumbled upon the basic forms of American popular music, before the explosion of rock 'n' roll, before Chuck Berry, Little Richard, or Elvis Presley. The hillbilly songs and heartbreak lyrics of Hank Williams made him think. The libidinous riffs of Jimmy Reed and Howlin' Wolf inspired him to play. The combination of words and sounds was intoxicating. Indeed, it was a life-changing experience. 'The reason I can stay so single-minded about my music is because it affected me at an early age in a very, very powerful way and it's all that affected me. It's all that ever remained true for me,' Bob has said. 'And I'm very glad this particular music reached me when it did because frankly, if it hadn't, I don't know what would have become of me.'

Gripped with a passion for music – particularly the blues – Bob wrote off for records he heard advertised on the radio. 'Brother Gatemouth' Page sold records for Stan's Rockin' Record Shop in Shreveport, huckstering special $3.49 deals for six recordings. There was no way to buy this so-called race music in Hibbing as the assistant in Crippa's music store downtown had never heard of the artists Bob liked.

Bob practiced piano and acoustic guitar constantly and talked about music all the time. He sought out the company of the few children in town who shared his interest. One of these was John Bucklen, a boy Bob had known from around Hibbing but had not spoken to much before now. One day they were walking along the road with some friends when the subject of music came up. Bucklen revealed he knew and liked the same songs Bob did. 'Do you sing?' Bob asked.

'Yeah.'

'Okay, sing something.'

Finding himself on the spot, Bucklen began a tune. 'Oh, that's really great, man,' said Bob, who was beginning to affect hipster expressions he had heard on the radio. Bucklen continued singing, even though he was shy. 'Oh gee! Did you hear that guy?' asked Bob, turning to their friends. 'That guy's really good. Sing some more.' All of a sudden it dawned on Bucklen that Bob was putting him on.

John Bucklen soon became the closest friend Bob had in Hibbing. He was six months younger than Bob, and a year below him in high school. His father, a disabled mine worker, was an accomplished musician who enjoyed a wide variety of music. His sister, Ruth, had a record player. The boys began to spend a lot of time at each other's houses, although Bucklen got the impression Abe may not have approved of the friendship as he seemed to frown upon most of Bob's friends.

During jam sessions with Bucklen, Bob mixed up snatches of pop tunes with song ideas of his own. The first song Bob invented was about actress Brigitte Bardot. Bob played his parents' white baby grand, and Bucklen accompanied him on guitar. Bucklen had a tape recorder and they recorded the sessions, interjecting juvenile humor and bits of hipster slang, as if making their own radio show. When they got tired of the game, they headed over to Crippa's where they could listen to records in the sound booths. On visits to see his relatives in Duluth and the Twin Cities Bob was able to visit bigger stores that stocked the race records he liked.

Bucklen noticed that when he visited the Zimmerman house there was little interaction between Bob and his brother, David. 'I don't recall him having a very warm, friendly discussion with David. David was just his little brother,' says Bucklen. 'And David was so radically different to Bob in his personality. He was probably the type of kid that any parent would like to raise – he was studious, and [he] wasn't wild at all.' Although from the outside Bob did not seem to be particularly wild himself, he was a strong-minded, independent boy who, as his teenage years progressed, would become more involved in a rebellious teen culture of raucous music, motorcycles, and girlfriends his father considered unsuitable. He always kept a surprisingly eclectic circle of acquaintances. In Hibbing, he was an active member of a bowling team, called the Gutter Boys, who won the 1955–56 Teen-Age Bowling League. Conversely, he also knew tough kids, like LeRoy Hoikkala, whose hair was slicked back DA-style, and who wore a leather jacket, jeans, and engineer boots like Marlon Brando in *The Wild One*. Bob also made friends at a coeducational Jewish summer camp, Camp Herzl, in Webster, Wisconsin. He did not want to go to camp at first, but his mother was set on the idea. 'She wanted to send him there so he could meet Jewish kids and maybe meet some Jewish girls,' says Howard Rutman, one of the friends Bob made at camp, which he began to attend for three weeks each August. Bob slept in a cabin along with seven other boys, and went swimming and canoeing. Often he could be found pounding the piano in the lodge building.

In August 1954, the second year he was at summer camp, Bob was playing piano when twelve-year-old Larry Kegan walked into the lodge. 'How do you know this song?' asked Kegan, recognizing a bluesy tune from the radio.

'Well, late at night up north where I live you get this [radio] station,' said Bob.

'Well, I've been listenin' to the same stuff.'

Although Kegan was a year younger than Bob, they formed a close friendship based on their mutual love of music. Kegan was an accomplished singer, and home in St. Paul he had a high school doo-wop group, including three African-American boys whom he introduced to Bob when Bob visited St. Paul. This was something new. There were virtually no black people on the Iron Range. (Bob and John Bucklen later sought out one of the few African Americans, disc jockey Jim Dandy, who broadcast a show from nearby Virginia, Minnesota.) Bob respected African-American people from the start, partly because they were the originators of much of the music he loved, and was no doubt impressed that Larry Kegan was connected to this community.

Bob knew every song Kegan named, and what was on the flip side. They formed a double act at camp, Bob playing the piano and both boys singing. Girls soon came around and Bob struck up a friendship with Judy Rubin, a girl he saw on and off for several years. He was also keen on Harriet Zisson. But it was the buddies he made at camp that were most important to him. Apart from Larry Kegan and Howard Rutman, Louis Kemp also became a lifelong friend.

When Bob traveled down to St. Paul he stayed with the parents of his new friends. Howard Rutman's family had a piano in their basement. 'He would bang the shit out of the piano,' says Rutman. 'He would get up there and dance on the damn thing . . . Ah God, he just ruined it.' They went driving and parked in front of the house to talk late into the night, whiling away time until their favorite radio program, *Lucretia the Werewolf*, came on. 'We were a real close-knit group,' says Rutman, who recalls discussing big subjects like war and man's inhumanity to man. Still, Bob stayed very much to himself. 'A great deal he kept to himself because he was a very, very inward type,' says Rutman. 'He's always been that way.' Music was Bob's preferred form of expression. In everyday life he was a quiet kid. When he sang and played music he became somebody else altogether, a complete extrovert. He also lost himself in films.

Bob spent many hours in the Hibbing movie houses, including the Lybba Theater, owned by his relatives and named after his maternal great-grandmother, Lybba Edelstein. His favorites included *The Blackboard Jungle*, which featured Bill Haley's 'Rock Around the Clock.' Bob also loved any movie with Brigitte Bardot or Marlon Brando. But one star overshadowed all others in his eyes.

Before he died in a car crash, on September 30, 1955, the only James Dean film that had been released was *East of Eden*. It was the tragic death of James Dean that made him special to Bob and other teenagers. *Rebel Without a Cause* opened four days after the fatal accident and reached the Lybba Theater that winter. Bob and John identified strongly with Jimmy Dean, as they called him, and with Jim Stark, the character Dean played in the film. Jim Stark was a teenager torn apart by battling parents and the need to prove himself. Like Bob, Stark was not very articulate, but he was goodhearted. 'He doesn't say much, but when he does you know he means it,' said Sal Mineo's character. 'He's sincere.' Bob could see himself described in the same way, and the similarity went further. Bob's family was comfortable, middle class, like Stark's. 'Don't I buy you everything you want?' asked Stark's father. Abe might have asked the same. When Stark was challenged to take part in a test of courage, a 'chickie run' in which he would race another boy toward a cliff, leaping free of his car at the last minute, Stark tried to ask his father for advice. In reply, he received a waffled admonition that in ten years he would see things differently. 'Ten years?' asked Stark in anguish. 'I want an answer now. I *need* one.' Bob and John Bucklen memorized many lines from *Rebel Without a Cause*, but this was a favorite. 'I don't want an answer in ten years,' they would tell each other, as they went about town. 'I want an answer *now*.' Bob and his Hibbing friends went into Steven's Confectionery store almost daily to look through the movie magazines for anything about Dean. Bob bought a red biker jacket like the one his idol wore. Although James Dean was an actor playing a character, Jimmy Dean *was* Jim Stark in their minds.

Another very exciting figure was Elvis Presley. 'When I first heard Elvis's voice I just knew that I wasn't going to work for anybody and nobody was gonna be my boss,' said Bob. 'Hearing him for the first time was like busting out of jail.' It was the very early Elvis Presley that Bob loved, the recordings made at Sun Records in Memphis, Tennessee, in 1954–55. Bob learned to play 'Blue Moon of Kentucky' soon after it was released in July 1954, and he performed the song in concert as late as 1999. The primitive, exciting sound of these early Sun sessions would be a recording ideal throughout Bob's career. 'We started losing interest in Elvis after he started becoming popular,' says Bucklen. Little Richard became a favorite instead. He was fun to watch on television, his music was tremendously exciting, and he was a quintessential nonconformist, a quality that appealed strongly to Bob. Richard's driving piano riffs were also something Bob learned to copy, playing his parents' baby grand standing up. As Bob pointed out to Bucklen, even Presley copied Little Richard. Bob began to grow his hair longer and tried to comb it into an imitation of Little Richard's pompadour.

The first band Bob was associated with was an a cappella group formed by his summer-camp buddies Larry Kegan and Howard Rutman, together with other friends in St. Paul. They called themselves The Jokers and played wherever they could find a piano, including high school dances. Girls gathered around as the boys harmonized pop songs of the day. Bob realized music gave him power to attract and charm people. It was a lesson his friend Kegan picked up on. 'He taught me if you can sing, and / or play, you can get almost anything you need,' says Kegan. 'A meal, a place to stay, a ride, a girlfriend.' Their mothers made sleeveless cardigans for the boys – in red and gray – with the name 'Jokers' stitched in the front. In this getup, the boys performed on a television talent show broadcast on Channel 9 in the Twin Cities. 'We were hugely ambitious and we really wanted to do stuff,' says Howard Rutman. In the summer of 1956 Bob, Rutman, and Kegan paid five dollars to cut a 78 rpm record. Bob played piano as he and his friends harmonized on a medley that included 'Be-Bop-a-Lula' and 'Earth Angel.' It was the first record Bob ever made, but the sound of his voice was already distinctive.

Bob continued to sing with the Jokers until the spring of 1958. In March of that year Kegan went to Florida on vacation with his parents. He was playing with a friend, diving into waves rebounding off a sea wall and riding them out into the ocean, when he missed a wave and landed headfirst in shallow water. He sustained a spinal cord injury that rendered him quadriplegic and confined to a wheelchair for the rest of his life. He continued his singing, however, and his friendship with Bob survived into adult life. For Bob, the fact that a contemporary – a healthy boy who was as ambitious about music as Bob himself was – could have his life frozen by a freak accident remained a sobering lesson. Years later Bob wrote to Kegan that when he reflected on what had happened to his friend, 'I become speechless unto myself.'

The music Bob made with Larry Kegan was limited to summer camp and weekend visits into the Twin Cities. His first Hibbing band began as something of a game with boys he had known since early childhood. Just as Bob's parents had encouraged their sons to take up musical instruments, so had other parents. Bill Marinac learned string bass. Larry Fabbro was interested in the guitar, and another friend, Chuck Nara, played drums. With Bob on piano, they constituted The Shadow Blasters. Bob was the most passionate about music and was soon in charge of the group, getting the boys to play in the style of Little

Richard and his new favorite, Gene Vincent. In 1957 there was a variety show in the high school auditorium. When The Shadow Blasters hit the stage, the boys were wearing pink shirts, dark glasses, and had their hair brushed so it stuck up in mounds. Bob stood at the piano as they made a travesty of two Little Richard numbers. Teachers shook their heads as students laughed. But there was enough spirit for Bob and the boys to be invited to repeat their performance at the Junior College's 'College Capers' review shortly afterward. It was another ragamuffin performance, the end of The Shadow Blasters, but students began to look at Zimbo with new eyes.

As their passion for music grew, Bob and John Bucklen began spending time at a music store on 1st Avenue, run by a man of Finnish descent named Hautala, who, it seemed to the boys, always had the last three inches of a cigar in his mouth. Hautala, who could barely speak English, patiently showed the boys catalogs of guitars from which he could order. Bob, who had recently used his pocket money to buy a cheap electric guitar from Sears Roebuck, keeping the guitar secret from his parents until he made all the payments, became excited about a solid-body Supro electric with a gold sunburst. The guitars were $95 each, but Bob and John Bucklen made a deal to buy two for a reduced price. Late into the evening Bob would strum his new Supro, trying to work out chord changes he had heard on records. Then, after school, he and Bucklen would get together and play the new changes, both plugging into Bob's amplifier. Bob started talking about wanting to become 'a music star.' This was something many of his friends dreamed about too. But Bob was serious. 'He had it calculated all the way,' says Bucklen. 'Each step, how he was gonna do it, and how you get to be a star.'

It soon became apparent that Bob was willing to bend the truth if he thought this would help him become a star. An early example of this came one weekend when Bob and Bucklen visited the Twin Cities, taking turns driving Abe Zimmerman's 1956 Buick. Traveling south, Bob told Bucklen he had black friends in St. Paul. This was strangely impressive to Bucklen, and he was not sure if he believed Bob. His friend was always trying to put him on. They had invented a mind game called Glissendorf whereby they would say crazy things to see how people reacted. 'Say a word,' Bob would say. Whatever answer Bucklen gave, Bob replied: 'Wrong word. I won.'

Another line might be: 'Is it raining out?'

'No.'

'Well, okay then.'

That was Glissendorf. It left the other person wondering if they had missed something. Some people became quite angry about it. The more riled up they became, the funnier the two friends thought it was.

However, this was not a Glissendorf. Bob did know black people in St. Paul. They were the boys in Larry Kegan's doo-wop group. Before introducing Bucklen to this part of his life, Bob said a curious thing that illustrated his willingness to manipulate people and facts to suit his ends. 'When we meet anybody down there,' he said, 'tell them that we're gonna cut a record, and you're my bass player.'

Although a very quiet boy in many ways, there was a definite element of Bob showing off by telling people John Bucklen was *his* bass player. This flashy, one might say fearless, side to his character – a little of which he inherited from his sociable and extroverted mother – became more pronounced as he moved into his later teenage years. After his sixteenth birthday in 1957 Bob convinced his quiet, conservative father to let him get an ostentatious pink Ford convertible. Now Bob could cruise Howard Street on Saturday nights with the other teenagers. Shortly after he acquired the car, Abe, after much persuading by Bob, also helped his son buy a Harley Davidson motorcycle.

Unfortunately, Bob was impetuous and nervous by

disposition, and it was not long before he had an accident with the motorcycle. He collided with a boy who had run out into the road. The child had to go by ambulance to the hospital but, luckily, he recovered. Another time Bob was riding his Harley with LeRoy Hoikkala and other friends when they came to the railroad crossing that separated Hibbing from the adjacent district of Brooklyn. A freight train was going by and they had to wait. Bob sat with his engine running, anxious to be moving. 'He didn't like to wait for anything, or anybody,' says Hoikkala. The minute the caboose passed, Bob shot across the track. He was half way when he saw a second train bearing down on a parallel track. Bob dumped his bike on the strip of ground between the tracks, and lay there as the train rumbled by. 'He almost got killed.' Bob was too proud and aware of his image to show that he was scared by what had happened. 'When the train was gone, he picked the bike up and didn't say a word. He got on and took off.'

LeRoy Hoikkala, John Bucklen, and Bob considered themselves outsiders in Hibbing. They were not very articulate or sporty, and felt disconnected from the mainstream teenage social scene, which revolved around basketball games. 'If you said any of us had a best friend, we kind of did, but we still were loners,' says Hoikkala. 'We did our own thing.'

Echo Star Helstrom, Bob's first serious girlfriend, was another Hibbing teen who did not quite fit in. She was the youngest daughter of Matt and Martha Helstrom, whose respective parents were all from Finland. This made the Helstroms 'Finlanders' in the local argot. They lived in the woods at Maple Hill. Echo Star got her poetic name because she was born so long after her nearest sibling – 'my mother said I was like a little echo' – and because frost made a star pattern on the hospital window the day she was born. She was a strikingly attractive girl with white-blond hair, cast in the role of an outsider from an early age partly because the Helstroms lived in the woods. It was only three miles from town, a pleasant walk in summer, but far enough for Echo to think herself a country person and the girls in Hibbing as 'city girls.' She affected the look of a rebel, wearing a leather jacket and jeans, when most young girls were wearing poodle skirts. As Bob's friend Luke Davich says, 'She just had a wild look about her.' Echo may have looked wild, but she was a warmhearted, sensitive, and upbeat person who did not share the popular enthusiasm for *Rebel Without a Cause* because it was 'depressing' and there was no need to go through life 'being that angry.'

On weekends, Echo would often catch a ride into town with her friend Dee Dee Lockhart. One snowy night in 1957, as Echo and Dee Dee were crossing Howard Street on their way to the L&B Cafe, they saw Bob standing on the corner playing his guitar and singing. Echo thought Bob, whom she vaguely remembered talking to once before, was a 'weirdo.' Bob did not appear to be playing for money as there was no cup for coins and nobody stopped to hear him. For sheer joy, he was singing to himself in the snow. Echo thought it totally bizarre.

The girls settled in a booth and Echo ordered one of her special coke drinks – a mixture of chocolate and orange, or chocolate and cherry flavor, 'just for variety.' Bob came in with John Bucklen. Despite Echo's opinion that Bob was weird, they all started talking and it turned out that Echo was another fan of the late-night radio show *No-Name Jive* and she loved the blues. Sometimes she listened to the radio all night, especially in summer when the signal was stronger and the reception clearer. Echo's love for the blues immediately bound her to the boys. 'My friends didn't understand the intensity of the way we felt about the kind of music we liked,' she says. Bob wanted to play piano, so they went next door to the Moose Lodge. Echo jimmied the lock with her penknife and Bob played boogie-woogie for her. 'He was good!' says Echo. 'He could play the piano like an old blues guy.' They exchanged telephone numbers and agreed to meet the next day. Bob wanted her to come to his house and hear his records.

For a month Echo, Bob, and John Bucklen buddied around together. Echo was used to having boys as friends and assumed Bob and Bucklen were now her *music* friends. Then one night, when they were at Bucklen's house talking about movies, Bob shocked Echo by kissing her. 'I was totally flabbergasted. Because I thought we were just buddies. I had no idea he was interested in me as a girlfriend.' John Bucklen was obliged to make himself scarce while Bob and Echo spent the rest of the evening making out. Bucklen was often bemused by Bob's success with girls. There was Judy Rubin from summer camp, whom Bob saw when he went to St Paul; he had dated fellow student Barb Hewitt for a while; and now he was with Echo, one of the best-looking girls in school. 'I can remember not understanding it. I mean, he was sometimes very successful with girls. He was this little pudgy-faced kid, you know.' Bucklen wanted a woman's point of view, so he asked his sister. 'What do you think that guy has?'

'Well, he's got the prettiest blue eyes,' Ruth Bucklen replied.

It was also true that Bob was exciting company. 'Nothing is boring when you are with Bob,' says Bucklen. When they were not playing music, Bob's legs jerked up and down with nervous energy and he tap-tap-tapped his cigarette in the ashtray. Bob made up fantastic stories and then told them as if they were gospel truth. Once he told Echo about how, when he was walking home from her house, he came upon a snake wrapped around a tree. He told the story with such conviction, making the snake in the tree so vivid, that she believed him for a while. '[Then] I thought, God, he made that up. There's no snakes in trees in Minnesota.' It was one of many examples of tall tales Bob would tell. Echo thought they were silly and unnecessary, but she later reflected that there was no harm in them. Bob was a fantasist, but not in a malicious way, and this was part of his charm.

Bob spent a lot of time with Echo at her home, and he enjoyed playing with her young nephew. Indeed, throughout his life Bob would show an interest in children and a natural ability to get along with them. But Echo noticed, as John Bucklen had, that Bob was less keen on spending time with his younger brother David. As Hibbing High was just two blocks from where Bob lived, Echo often went back there for lunch and she got the impression Bob resented sharing a bedroom with David. 'Sometimes David would come around and want to talk to Bob, and Bob was like, *No not now.* He was irritated 'cause they lived in the same room and I suppose if you spend all your time with somebody you want to get away from them once in a while.'

Before she went to her part-time job at Feldman's, Beatty Zimmerman would leave a lunch for Echo and Bob. After they ate, Bob played boogie-woogie for Echo on the baby grand piano. Bob's grandmother was living with them – sleeping in the third bedroom – and one time she came home unexpectedly. 'Quick, up the stairs!' said Bob. He shut Echo in his bedroom. 'In five minutes I want you to go out on the sun-deck porch,' he said. 'I'm going to tell my grandmother I'm going to the library.' Bob made a great show of leaving the house. 'I'm going to the library now!' he called out. Then he ran around the back to catch Echo, who climbed out of his bedroom window and jumped off the sun-deck roof of the garage into his arms. 'That was really silly,' says Echo. Bob's parents knew full well she came to the house for lunch, and Grandma Stone must have known, too. 'It was totally unnecessary for him to do what he did. It was a game. It was always a game. He likes to play games and make a mystery out of things that don't *need* to be done.'

Bob told Echo she was his 'first love' and gave her his identity bracelet to prove they were going steady. 'We were in love,' says Echo. 'You can be sixteen, seventeen, and still be in love. Not just puppy love.' They were also lovers, which was relatively unusual for teenagers of the time, years before the advent of the contraceptive pill. But, as with most people in Bob's life, Echo did not know the whole story. Twenty years later Bob told her that, although she had been his first love, she had not been his first lover. He said he lost his virginity to one of her friends. 'He was a very naughty boy,' says Echo, wistfully. 'But he was so sweet. He wasn't the football-player, hunky kind of guy. He didn't have a great physique. But to me he was very cute, and I liked his personality. [He was] very magnetic . . . even then.' It seemed to Echo that there was an air of magic about their lives.

As Bob and Echo were falling in love with each other, Bob also pursued his ambitions to be in a real band. His biker friend LeRoy Hoikkala was learning to play drums in the jazz style at the time and another friend, Monte Edwardson, was becoming a good guitar player. Bob suggested they jam together and the trio was soon banging about in the garage behind Bob's house. This was the beginning of Bob's most significant high school band, The Golden Chords. Although Edwardson was the most accomplished musician, Bob decided what songs to play, and how they should play them, even suggesting drum parts. He managed to be in charge without being obnoxious. 'He knew exactly what he wanted,' says Hoikkala. 'He had a lot of confidence.' As Hoikkala says, Bob was always himself; he developed a look of his own, a sound of his own, and adopted phrases – like 'Hey, catch ya later' – that other people might not use. The boys were also impressed with the way Bob could improvise chords on the guitar and piano. It was partly because of his chording that they got the band's name. The 'Golden' part was inspired by LeRoy's gold-colored drum kit; 'Chords' was due to Bob's playing. As he said, 'Hey, I'm a chordy kinda guy.'

Staff at Hibbing High regularly organized what Principal Kenneth Pederson called 'convocations,' a fancy word for having kids put on a show. On February

6, 1958, the auditorium was full for the coronation of the homecoming queen, and a celebration of the school's sporting triumphs. This was the annual Jacket Jamboree. There was a program of entertainment including a magic show, some singing, and a performance by The Golden Chords. Hoikkala rapped out a beat on his sparkling golden drums. Monte Edwardson's electric guitar screamed through his amplifier and, in the middle, bouncing up and down at the piano, Little Richard–style, was Bobby Zimmerman, hair up, feet apart, singing 'Rock and Roll Is Here to Stay' as loud as he could. When Bob broke a pedal off the piano the students howled with laughter. Principal Pederson was appalled. 'He and the others were carrying on in a terrible way, right on the stage, and it got out of hand,' he says. 'I couldn't tolerate it.' He cut Bob's microphone and, when Bob persisted in hollering, he pulled the curtain. It was not so much the noise, it was the way Bob was behaving. 'He got so *crazy*.'

That evening Bob got up on stage again, this time without the band. Echo was in the audience. When she saw Bob, she squirmed down into her seat with embarrassment. It was too terrible to watch him making a fool of himself. Her friend Dee Dee insisted she sit up and listen. To a Little Richard tune, Bob was yelling that he *gotta girl and her name was Echo*. 'Oh my God, he's singing about me!' Again they cut the mike. But Bob was elated. 'What did ya think?' he asked Echo when he met her outside. 'What did ya think?' She thought it was romantic.

A few weeks later The Golden Chords competed in a talent contest that was part of the Chamber of Commerce's Winter Frolics. The show was held at the Memorial Building, an all-purpose civic arena shaped like an aircraft hangar. The Golden Chords came on after a succession of dreary performances including a tap-dancing display. 'The kids were just screaming and hollering. They loved it,' says Hoikkala. 'We got up there and [gave them] some music with feeling. It was something different, something the kids very shortly after that really got into.' The band felt cheated when first prize went to a pantomime artist.

The biggest gig they played was at the National Guard Armory in Hibbing on Saturday, March 1, 1958. This was a hop with a disc jockey spinning hit singles, and The Golden Chords playing at intermission. It was the first time Bob was paid to perform on stage. His name even appeared in a local newspaper advertisement:

Rock & Roll
HOP
FOR TEEN-AGERS
WITH YOUR FAVORITE
100 TOP RECORDS
plus
Intermission Entertainment
by Hibbing's Own

GOLDEN CHORDS
FEATURING:
Monte Edwardson
Leroy Hoikkala
Bobby Zimmerman

'We drew a lot of kids that time. We had a great time playing and the kids really loved it,' says Hoikkala.

Shortly afterward the band appeared on a television show in Duluth, the Chmielewski brothers' 'Polka Hour.' Polka music was very popular in northern Minnesota. It was played in the taverns when the miners got paid. But the television appearance did not lead to anything and Edwardson and Hoikkala wanted to play more in the slick new style of Elvis Presley. Bob was enthusiastic and talented, but he was not a front man for an Elvis-style act. He was not conventionally handsome; he was not a very good singer, in the normal sense; and people laughed at his stage antics. 'It was just one of these things,' says Hoikkala. 'It's not a matter of a formal breakup [because] we didn't have a tight band to begin with. It was messing around.' Edwardson and Hoikkala joined two other boys to form a new band, The Rockets. Bob briefly played with a cousin as The Satin Tones in Duluth, and was invited back to play with The Rockets later on, but he was beginning to realize rock 'n' roll had limitations. 'The thing about rock 'n' roll is that for me anyway it wasn't enough,' he said. ' 'Tutti Frutti' and 'Blue Suede Shoes' were great catch phrases and driving pulse rhythms and you could get high on the energy but they weren't serious or didn't reflect life in a realistic way.'

As Bob became more serious about his music it was clear to him that he needed a stage name. Most of the performers he liked had a name they adopted because it was catchy, and Zimmerman was not that. There has been much speculation over how Bobby Zimmerman became Bob Dylan, and Bob has given several confusing statements, none of which tallies with the version his friends remember. The clearest answer he gave was that he originally wanted to call himself Dillion, after an uncle of that name. In truth, there was no Dillion in the family. However, the name *Dillon* was familiar to Bob. James Dillon was one of the earliest settlers of Hibbing, and a family of that name owned a farm on Dillon Road. One of the best-known football players in Minnesota was Bobby Dillon. A popular television show of the time, *Gunsmoke*, featured a character named Matt Dillon. Any or all of these associations could have brought the name to his attention. Still, Bob chose to spell the name differently.

In the spring of 1958, after the snow had melted and the grass had started to grow up around Echo's home in the woods, Bob drove up in his Ford convertible. Echo met him in the yard. He was excited. 'I've got my name,' he said. 'I know what my name's gonna be now.'

When he told her, Echo asked, 'Do you mean, D-i-l-l-o-n, like Matt Dillon?'

'No, no, no, like this, D-y-l-a-n.' Bob had a book under

his arm and he showed it to Echo. It was a book of poems by the Welsh poet Dylan Thomas.

Dylan Thomas had great notoriety in America when Bob was growing up. The poet undertook a series of successful reading tours in the early 1950s, and died in New York of alcohol poisoning in 1953 at the age of thirty-nine. The fact that he died relatively young, and in strange circumstances, elevated him to the pantheon of tragic idols Bob found attractive, such as James Dean and Hank Williams. Bob also read and enjoyed Dylan Thomas's poetry. Indeed, Bob had surprisingly sophisticated tastes in literature and was very well read. Part of the reason for this may have been that he had an English teacher at Hibbing High who inspired a love and understanding of literature in almost every child he taught. Boniface J. Rolfzen, known as B. J., was a man dedicated to his work. 'I remember him getting me to appreciate Shakespeare,' says John Bucklen. 'He was a good teacher of literature because you could sense that he really enjoyed and knew and loved literature.' When the English class was assigned to write about a favorite author, Bob chose John Steinbeck and developed such an enthusiasm for his novel *The Grapes of Wrath* that he wrote a fifteen-page essay for which he received an A grade. 'John Steinbeck is great,' Bob enthused to Echo, and his interest was such that she was spurred on to read all the Steinbeck books she could find. Echo remembers that Bob frequently had a book under his arm, and the books were often poetry. Beatty said Bob was also constantly *writing* poetry. 'I was afraid he would end up being a poet!' she said. 'In my day, a poet was unemployed.' She and Abe became quite concerned about it, causing tension as Bob grew older.

Partly because of the breakup of The Golden Chords, Bob spent more time in Duluth and the Twin Cities with his friends and cousins in his last years at school. Echo suspected he was seeing girls there. She asked John Bucklen whether this was true, and Bucklen said he thought it was. Echo also suspected Bob was seeing her friend Dee Dee. Bob was becoming blasé about his relationship with Echo. He started going out on his own in the evenings, telling Echo to wait for him at her house. She tired of this and went downtown anyway. 'What are you doing here?' asked Bob, when he saw her.

'I came downtown with my friends.'

Bob put her on the back of his motorcycle and took her home. Echo assumed they were going to spend the evening together. 'He left me there!' she exclaims in disgust. 'And, of course, once I was home my parents wouldn't let me go out again. It was kind of like the beginning of the end.'

Echo confronted Bob in the hallway at Hibbing High, and gave him back his identity bracelet. 'What are you doing?' he asked her, his blue eyes widening with surprise. 'Don't do this here in the hall.' But Echo had decided they were finished. 'It broke my heart,' she says. '[But] somebody doing you dirty like that, you can't trust 'im!' She would remain friendly with Bob, staying in touch into adult life. But she never forgave the infidelity. 'I was very faithful to him and I didn't give up on him until I just couldn't take it anymore.'

John Bucklen believes the breakup was not too upsetting to Bob. 'I could tell she loved him very much. But he didn't feel that way about her. She wanted a permanent relationship. She loved him. It wasn't a forever thing with him.' There was a sad coda to the teen melodrama when Bucklen fell in love with Echo. 'That was unfortunate. The situation was reversed. I mean, we liked each other as friends. To me it was love. To her, it was just friendship.'

It did not damage Bob's friendship with John Bucklen, however. On January 9, 1959, Hibbing High once again had its annual Jacket Jamboree. The Rockets were performing. Bob formed a band for the show with Bucklen on guitar, Bill Marinac on double bass, and three girls singing doo-wop. The name he chose for this unusual group, which performed once, was Elston Gunn and The Rock Boppers. In later life, Bob became notorious in the music business for performing improvisational shows after sketchy rehearsals, or no rehearsals at all. This unusual, almost jazzlike approach helped him remain a fresh and dynamic performer, but it sometimes drove his band members to distraction. He was just as relaxed about rehearsals back in high school. Bucklen recalls that Elston Gunn and his Rock Boppers did not rehearse together even once for their show. Bob was relaxed enough to go out on stage and see what happened.

Three weeks after the high school concert, Bob went to Duluth to see a professional pop concert that lived on in his imagination for years to come as one of the most vivid experiences of his young life. On January 31, Buddy Holly played the National Guard Armory in Duluth together with Link Wray, Ritchie Valens, and the Big Bopper. Bob was right at the front of the stage. For one magical moment, Buddy Holly looked down into the audience and made eye contact with the seventeen-year-old. It was something Bob never forgot, the connection made more special and memorable because, two nights later, Holly was killed in a plane crash.

Five months after this memorable evening, on June 5, 1959, Bob graduated from Hibbing High School and began to think of his own musical career. First he had to endure the graduation party his parents had organized for him, inviting relatives, neighbors, and friends to share the moment. Bob said truculently that he did not want to come. Abe told him he was expected to be there. Grudgingly Bob did attend the party, and stayed longer than Abe and Beatty had hoped, being courteous and charming in his shy way. 'He was always a gentleman at all times,' said Beatty. 'He might have been a little contrary sometimes, but he was always nice to people.' He left the party and came back home in the early hours to find his mother clearing up. There was a surprise present waiting for him. One of Bob's uncles had left a stack of 78 rpm records by Huddie Ledbetter, commonly known as Leadbelly, the folk and blues singer who had spent time in prison for murder before being discovered by musicologists Alan and John Lomax and, as a result, paroled in 1934. His great songs included 'Rock Island Line' – powerful music, with lyrics that said much more than 'Tutti Frutti.' The next day Bob started to work out the meaning of the songs and how they were put together. This was the beginning of his interest in folk music.

In the 1959 Hibbing High School yearbook Bob was pictured with his hair arranged with a suggestion of Little Richard. Beneath the photograph, it was written that Robert Zimmerman's ambition in life was 'to join "Little Richard."' In a way, it was a preposterous thing to write. But the self-confident expression on the face of the boy in the photograph suggested he might be capable of extraordinary deeds and, indeed, he soon did something remarkable.

Shortly after graduation, Bob caught a bus to Fargo, across the border in North Dakota, and got a job working tables at the Red Apple Cafe. It was the only time in his life that he tried to make a living by anything other than music. Bobby Vee was a local musician beginning to make a name for himself with his band The Shadows. After the tragic death of Buddy Holly, Bobby Vee and The Shadows filled in at Holly's next scheduled show. This opportunity launched a career that would lead to hits like 'Take Good Care of My Baby.' Bobby Vee heard about the Red Apple Cafe busboy going about under the pseudonym Elston Gunn and gave him an audition as pianist for The Shadows.

Bob demonstrated his limited piano skills, playing mostly in the key of C, and lied that he had played with Conway Twitty. Bobby Vee decided to try Bob out. He was given a special shirt, so he looked like a member of the band, and they played a couple of small local gigs.

'He was kind of a scruffy little guy, but he was really into it,' says Bobby Vee. 'Loved to rock 'n' roll. He was pretty limited by what he could play. He was pretty hot – in the key of C. He liked to do hand claps, like Gene Vincent . . . He would come up [to the mike] and do that every now and then, and then scurry back to the piano.' They decided not to take Bob on as a member of the band. 'He was just a spacey little guy, you know, just sort of worming his way around.'

Not long afterward Bob returned to Hibbing where he told Bucklen and others that he had played on a new record, 'Suzie Baby,' by Bobby Vee and The Shadows. Some even got the impression Bobby Zimmerman and Bobby Vee were one and the same, which was typical of the way Bob would blur the circumstances of his life in these early years to seem more worldly than he actually was. In a way, it was rather silly behavior, as Echo noted. But in Bob's case it pointed toward an overriding single ambition; by now he knew that he wanted to make his life as a music star.

He never planned a straight career. Bob considered himself to be a musician and music would be his life, whether people liked him or not. His parents saw things differently, of course. It has been claimed that they became so concerned about Bob's wayward ambitions they sent him briefly to a private school in Devon, Pennsylvania, operated by The Devereux Foundation, founded in 1912 by educator Helena T. Devereux to treat young people with emotional, behavioral, and developmental problems. However, if this did happen, it was kept so secret that none of Bob's closest friends found out about it and it seems unlikely they would not have known.*

Abe and Beatty *did* prevail on Bob to at least get a college education before he tried to make his living in

*John Bucklen, Echo Helstrom, and Larry Kegan have no knowledge of it happening.

music. Most of the middle-class families of Hibbing sent their children away to college, if they could, and Bob would have disappointed his parents greatly if he had refused. In any event, he was in no position to refuse, having no income of his own, and no ambition to get a regular job.

At the end of the summer of 1959, Bob enrolled at the University of Minnesota in the Twin Cities. Abe hoped Bob would eventually graduate and join the family business, or get some kind of respectable job. Whatever happened, his mother pleaded with him on one point. 'Don't keep writing poetry, please don't,' she told the boy who became one of America's greatest song lyricists. 'Go to school and do something constructive .... get a degree.'

CHAPTER 2

BOUND FOR GLORY

The Twin Cities of Minneapolis and St. Paul make up the largest urban area in Minnesota, facing each other across the upper reaches of the Mississippi River, a hundred and ninety-one miles south of Hibbing. In the fall of 1959 Bob came 'out of the wilderness,' as he put it, to study at the University of Minnesota, the campus of which is on the east bank of the Mississippi, sandwiched between the Twin Cities.

Bob enrolled in a liberal arts program with music as his major. At first, he lived at a Jewish fraternity house, Sigma Alpha Mu, on University Avenue SE. At least one of Bob's cousins had been a Sammy, as brothers from this fraternity were known, in previous years, and Sigma Alpha Mu was the best of the four Jewish fraternities in and around campus. Membership in the fraternity showed that Bob was from a family with good connections. Abe Zimmerman paid for Bob's rent and board and gave him an allowance so he could enjoy his freshman year without having to work at a job. Bob never fit in with the fraternity, however, having different interests than his fellow Sammies. Indeed, college life in general was anathema to him. He wanted to pass his exams to please his parents, whom he would go home to visit whenever he had a chance. However, Bob's brief sojourn at the University of Minnesota was important principally because of the people he met, and the music he discovered, in the bohemian neighborhood known as Dinkytown that lay adjacent to campus.

The center of Dinkytown was the junction of 4th Street

SE and 14th Avenue SE in downtown Minneapolis. Here was a cluster of stores including Melvin McCosh's radical bookshop, Gray's drugstore, Bridgeman's ice-cream parlor, the Varsity cinema, and the Dirty Grocery. In 1958 the Ten O'Clock Scholar coffeehouse opened on 14th Avenue between 4th and 5th Streets. At the time, places like the Scholar were springing up across the country. An old store, with a regular storefront window, had been cleared to create a long room furnished with wooden stools, tables, and benches. At the back was a coffee bar. Students could hang out all day at the Scholar, nursing cups of coffee or tea, smoking, playing chess, reading, or listening to musician friends who got up to perform on the tiny stage at the front window. Many of the most interesting people on and around campus were to be found at the Scholar. There were attractive, long-haired girls dressed in beatnik black; wild men like 'Red' Nelson, who kept an alligator in his bathtub; hipster poet Dave Morton; and 'Spider' John Koerner and Dave Ray, white boys who played the blues with uncommon ability. Bob was enchanted by the bohemian atmosphere of the neighborhood, and especially by its denizens. He thought of these people – most of whom were slightly older than he was – as being truly extraordinary, likening them to saints. To Bob, Dinkytown seemed a magical place; as he once said, every day there was like Sunday.

When Bob arrived in the Twin Cities to pursue his education he was still on the cusp of his rock 'n' roll phase, still wearing his embroidered Jokers waistcoats and slicking his hair back DA-style. But rock 'n' roll was not fashionable in Dinkytown, and Bob's immersion into the campus subculture changed him. Two years after Jack Kerouac's *On the Road* became a national best-seller, students regularly read beatnik literature, the politics was left-wing radical, and the music that was played and listened to in the Scholar and elsewhere was folk.

American folk music had been recorded as early as the 1880s, and was popular in rural areas until the

Depression, which killed the industry by rendering country people too poor to buy records. Folk music started to recover in the 1940s, and in 1950 The Weavers, a radical singing group featuring Pete Seeger, enjoyed an unexpected folk hit when they recorded a version of Leadbelly's 'Goodnight Irene.' It was the most popular song that year. By the end of the 1950s, partly as an antidote to the anodyne pop music of the time, exemplified by artists like Doris Day, folk music had begun its great popular revival. The payola scandal of 1960, revealing that music labels commonly paid bribes to get pop records played on the radio, was a further unexpected boost for folk music. In contrast to the pop charts, folk music seemed refreshingly untainted.

A sign that there was a major change in the public's musical tastes came in the fall of 1958 when The Kingston Trio, a clean-cut vocal group of three young men, had a number-one hit with the folk standard 'Tom Dooley.' The record shared radio time with bubblegum tunes like 'The Chipmunk Song,' by The Chipmunks, and 'To Know Him Is to Love Him,' by The Teddy Bears. Although The Kingston Trio performed folk songs, their style was too prissy for the tastes of the college students who hung out at the Ten O'Clock Scholar and the like. Students' musical heroes were grittier folk and blues artists like Leadbelly, Pete Seeger, and Woody Guthrie. Another favorite was Odetta, a classically trained African-American vocalist with a formidable stage presence, who sang traditional songs like 'Jack O'Diamonds' and 'Mule Skinner Blues' in an almost operatic contralto. Odetta was one of Bob's important early influences. 'The first thing that turned me on to folk singing was Odetta,' he has said. 'I heard a record of hers in a record store . . . Right then and there, I went out and traded my electric guitar and amplifier for an acoustical guitar.'

Those that followed or considered themselves part of the folk revival placed great importance on an elusive quality in music that might be described as *authenticity.* To be respected in the folk community, musicians had to perform traditional songs in a manner true to the original, while also making the songs distinctively their own. The starting point was to find and learn from the earliest and purest forms of the songs. This involved a degree of musical archaeology. Folk societies, including the Minneapolis Folklore Society, sent away to the Library of Congress for field recordings of hillbilly musicians, convicts, farm workers, and cowboys. Many of the recordings had been made by John Lomax and his son, Alan, the musicologists who had discovered Leadbelly in a Louisiana jail in the early 1930s. Some of the older songs sung by convicts, cowboys, and rural workers were known to academics as Child ballads, songs catalogued by Harvard professor Francis Child that originated in the British Isles and were still sung by descendants of immigrants, particularly in the isolated communities of the Appalachian mountains. These songs had endured through centuries, and across cultural and geographical divides, because they dealt with primal experiences – faith, love, and acts of violence – and because they were written in words both poetic and true. These were the timeworn songs Bob heard when he began frequenting the Scholar in Dinkytown and saw student musicians get up on stage to sing and play acoustic guitar.

Bob had first visited the Scholar on trips into the Twin Cities when he was a high school student in Hibbing. He found a girlfriend there even before he had enrolled in college.

Bonnie Jean Beecher, the second significant girlfriend of Bob's young life, was born a month before Bob in 1941 and raised in Minneapolis by upper-middle-class parents who ran a summer resort. She attended the University of Minnesota High School (U High) and began frequenting the Ten O'Clock Scholar in her senior year. She met Bob there in the spring of 1959, shortly before her eighteenth birthday. He was with a friend, Harvey Abrams, playing guitar and singing a blues song. Bonnie loved blues music. She regularly visited New York, buying records by obscure artists like 'Cat' Iron and Richard 'Rabbit' Brown at Sam Goody's record store in Manhattan. When Bonnie recognized the song Bob was playing, she struck up a conversation with the boys. 'Harvey Abrams made some withering comment to this seventeen-year-old little girl who thought she knew something about folk music,' she recalls. But Bob was pleasant. 'He was not withering. He asked me how I knew [the song].' Bonnie described her trips to New York and told Bob about her record collection. 'I thought he was interesting and attractive and cool and probably knew some real beatniks.' When Bonnie enrolled as a college student at the University of Minnesota in the fall of 1959, to study Theater Arts, she and Bob had two classes together, Astronomy and a Theater History course, and they began a relationship.

Bonnie was a very pretty, elegant girl with long fair hair. She was intelligent, well read, culturally sophisticated, and knew as much about the blues as Bob did. She was the 'actress girl' – inasmuch as she studied acting – that Bob later wrote about in his poem 'My Life in a Stolen Moment,' the girl he fell heavily for but who kneed him in the guts. She was also probably the girl Bob had in mind when he wrote one of his most celebrated love songs, 'Girl from the North Country.' It is true Bob 'fell hard' for Bonnie, as he recorded in the poem, but she was far from being his only girlfriend in the Twin Cities. During his brief time at college, Bob conducted complicated relationships simultaneously, flagrantly, and passionately. Surprisingly, his girlfriends did not seem to mind his philandering ways.

Bob regularly visited his summer-camp girlfriend Judy Rubin at her home in St. Paul. On one trip across town with college friend Bruce Rubenstein, Bob said he was giving Judy 'music lessons.' He also dated Lorna

Sullivan, a friend of Bonnie. Indeed, several of the girls he dated knew one another. One of his most significant girlfriends was Ellen Baker, whose father, Mike, ran the Minneapolis Folklore Society. This relationship was important partly because of the access it gave Bob to music he was then learning about. Bob attended folk music evenings at the Baker home, singing, playing guitar, and listening to Mike Baker's extensive collection of Folkways records.* Ellen's mother, Marjorie, took a maternal interest in Bob. He was invited to home-cooked Jewish meals and was always welcome to stay over if he did not want to go back to the fraternity house, which he tended to avoid. Marjorie fussed about his health, noticing that his teeth were dirty, for instance, and buying a toothbrush for him for when he visited.

Another female companion was Bob's former girlfriend Echo Helstrom, who moved to Minneapolis in the fall of 1959 and got a job with a record distributor, Harold & Lieberman. She and Bob hung out at the Scholar and he asked her over to his fraternity house, telling her to 'dress weird' to impress the Sammies. Bob tried, unsuccessfully, to get her to spend the night. 'We would make out,' says Echo. '[But] I didn't want to get involved with him again.' Echo made it very clear she was finished with Bob when, on December 2, 1959, she married her boyfriend Danny Shivers and moved back to Hibbing to live with him.

Even though Echo had gone home to Hibbing, Bob had plenty of other friends to spend time with. One of his very best friends, Larry Kegan, was a patient at the University of Minnesota Hospital, following his swimming accident, and Bob walked over to the hospital to see his friend almost daily between his classes. Kegan noticed that when Bob visited he usually had a

*Folkways owner Moses Asch produced thousands of recordings of folk artists, including Woody Guthrie, Pete Seeger, and Leadbelly.

poetry book in his hand, sometimes the poems of Dylan Thomas.

Larry Kegan was not able to sit up, but an orderly would transfer him from his bed onto a gurney when Bob came to the hospital. Bob pushed the gurney to a piano in the recreation room and put Kegan in a position where his head lay next to the piano keys. Bob then played the songs they used to sing together, and Kegan attempted to sing along from his prone position. The bond of friendship was strong, and the visits meant a lot to Kegan, yet these visits were not something Bob talked about with others. It was part of his secretive nature to compartmentalize his life and, to his credit, he did not boast to friends about his loyalty to Kegan.

Bob also made new friends in Dinkytown. One of the first musicians he met was John Koerner, known as 'Spider' John because of his rangy physique. An amiable young man from upstate New York, Koerner began playing guitar while studying aeronautics at the University of Minnesota. He dropped out of college after a year and a half of studying, thinking he could make his living as a traveling musician. When he got to California, he had second thoughts and joined the Marine Corps, soon after which he was involved in a car accident. As he recuperated, he read an article in *Playboy* about the new coffeehouse scene and how musicians played folk music in these places. He received an honorable discharge and returned to Minneapolis where he began hanging out at the Scholar and met Dave Ray, a straw-haired boy fixated with the music of Leadbelly. Together with harmonica player Tony Glover, they later formed the celebrated band Koerner, Ray and Glover. Bob and Koerner were part of a group of friends who gathered at the loading dock behind the chemistry building on campus and played music together, passing a bottle of wine between songs. As Koerner says, 'We were all trying to learn together.'

These musicians were part of a convivial network of students who made up an extended bohemian community in Dinkytown. Another member of this community was Tova Hammerman, a flamboyant Jewish beatnik who lived with her boyfriend, Lynn Castner, in an apartment on Hennepin Avenue. Dinkytown musicians often dropped by Hammerman's apartment to talk and play music and Bob was a regular visitor along with everyone else, eating free meals and sometimes sleeping over. Hammerman enjoyed discussing politics at these gatherings, but although Bob listened attentively he did not contribute to discussions. 'He was a sponge. He was taking it all in,' she says. Hammerman also got the impression that Bob was not entirely comfortable in her company 'because I was too Jewish for him.' Bob's apparent reluctance to make friends with people of his own faith was something others would notice during his time in the Twin Cities. It was not that he was ashamed of being Jewish; it seemed more that he did not want to be limited in the eyes of others by being defined simply as Jewish.

When professional musician Rolf Cahn came through the Twin Cities, he stayed with Tova Hammerman and she arranged for him to give a guitar lesson to Bob and Koerner. 'I have only had one guitar lesson in my life,' says Koerner, and 'I think, up until that time, Dylan probably only had one or two.' They took turns going into a room with Cahn for half an hour, watching his fingers as he demonstrated techniques. It was true that Bob was not much of a guitar player, in the technical sense, and he did not have a very musical voice, but he had another quality that impressed Koerner. 'It may not have been confidence, but it's acting like confidence. You know, I'm doing this. Here's my thing. Take it or leave it. [He was] definitely one of the most noticeable people [around] and there were quite a variety of interesting people.'

Along with Koerner, one of the foremost Dinkytown characters was poet and folk musician Dave Morton. He was tall, gaunt, and bearded and seemed much older than Bob, although in fact he was only two years his senior. 'I was the only one with long hair and funny clothes,' says Morton. 'The beats looked like fuckin' Frank Sinatra. They didn't have long hair and a beard. I was just wild.' Morton had been raised listening to folk and blues music, and was proud of the fact that his mother had taken him to a Leadbelly concert in 1948, making him the only member of the Dinkytown clique to have seen Leadbelly before he died the following year. Morton was also the first member of the clique to play folk music at the Scholar.

Budding musicians performed on the little stage in the window of the Scholar, usually while customers continued their conversations. There was a break between sets when performers got a gratis cup of coffee, and maybe something to eat in lieu of payment. Or they slipped out back for a swig of wine (the Scholar was not licensed to serve alcohol). Like most musicians, Morton had a limited repertoire of folk standards including songs like 'Gypsy Davey.' But he was slightly different from the other musicians in that he also wrote his own songs. These were topical songs about humanitarian issues and civil rights. The struggle for desegregation in the South was becoming a bloody business. In February 1960 a bomb exploded in a desegregated school in Arkansas. Two months later ten African Americans were shot in riots in Mississippi. Morton used the melodies of folk standards and then added lyrics of his own, based on events like these, to make a political point. It was a technique Woody Guthrie had used, and one that Bob himself would soon employ.

Although they became friends, Morton was critical of Bob as both a musician and a human being. Bob took little interest in intellectual pursuits and was apathetic about politics, as Tova Hammerman had noticed, despite the fact that Dave Morton and others tried their best to educate him about injustice in America. Morton also agrees with Hammerman that Bob seemed strangely uncomfortable with the fact that he was Jewish. 'He didn't like the Jewish boys [in Dinkytown]. He was pretending not to be Jewish,' says Morton, although living in a Jewish fraternity house was something of a giveaway. 'Is he nice? I don't think so. Is he gracious? I don't think so . . . He's a kind of an introvert in a way, even though he pushes out . . . He was focused and he did what he wanted to do, and he did it pretty good. He wanted to be rich and famous.'

If Bob did not like Jewish boys, it seems the Jewish boys did not like him much either. That winter, the Sammies asked Bob to leave Sigma Alpha Mu. Bob told Bonnie Beecher that his father had refused to pay the rent at the fraternity house and that was why he was kicked out. His relationship with his father had been tense at times. 'His dad was tough . . . very authoritarian,' says Larry Kegan. 'He thought Bob was wasting time with music.' Yet Abe had always been generous and it was not in his character to deny Bob anything. The truth was the Sammies simply did not like Bob. He kept strange hours and did not join in their activities or share their interests, and his introverted nature made him seem aloof. At any rate, Bob was out of the fraternity and there was no going back. He told Bonnie the Sammies had 'disowned' him.

Bob's living arrangements became complicated after he left Sigma Alpha Mu, changing almost weekly. Sometimes he had his own room, such as a garret he rented above Gray's drugstore in Dinkytown. He also slept on the floor of friends' apartments. For a while, he shared a place with Morton and Harvey Abrams on 15th Avenue SE. Bob also shared with another friend, Hugh Brown. Bruce Rubenstein helped Bob move into Brown's place. 'He dropped some pills on the floor. They were rolling around, little round pills, and he made a joke about [it being] dope,' says Rubenstein. 'But, in fact, it was vitamin E that he was taking to get his fingernails stronger.'

Now that he was out in the real world, Bob was frequently short of money, and he became so broke he had to pawn his guitar. Bonnie worried he was not eating properly and sneaked food from her sorority house pantry to wherever Bob was living. It was partly because Bob was not getting enough to eat that he made a strenuous effort to get jobs singing in coffeehouses; it never seems to have occurred to him to try and get a regular job. He earned a modest few dollars by playing on stage at the Ten O'Clock Scholar but lost his spot there when he asked the owner for a pay raise. Bonnie drove Bob around town as he auditioned at new places, at times so desperate for work he offered to perform in exchange for food. Still, it was not easy to find places that would let him play. 'I'm thinking, this guy is actually very good,' says Bonnie. 'Why won't they let him play for sandwiches?' Finally Bob got a regular gig at the Purple Onion, a pizza restaurant in St. Paul, earning five dollars a night, and sleeping on the floor when he had nowhere else to go. He also performed at the Bastille.

The Bob Dylan that appeared on stage in 1960 was very different from the commanding stage performer he would become. He looked much younger than nineteen, and his voice was not the mighty instrument it developed into, but in fact sweet sounding. Yet Bob inhabited the traditional songs that were the mainstay of the Dinkytown scene in a way others did not. Most of his contemporaries affected a nonchalance that tended to seem phony. Bob was not afraid to make mistakes, or to be funny, because there was humor in some of these old songs. When he performed a serious song, he did so with such commitment one forgot he was another white college boy singing the blues. The same innate confidence recognized by Koerner enabled Bob to make his audience suspend disbelief. These were the early signs that Bob had uncommon ability as a performer, and maybe even a special future.

* * *

Dave Whitaker was another important figure during Bob's college life. Whitaker had been a friend of Dave Morton's since they were at U High together. They had also been members of the radical group Unitarian Youth. Whitaker was a tiny man, weighing little more than ninety pounds, highly intelligent, liberal-minded, and well read. He could quote the beat poets as well as Henry Wadsworth Longfellow, and was knowledgeable about politics and social history. 'He was the person that we knew that was an intellectual,' says Bonnie Beecher. 'He read a lot, a lot of weighty things: biographies, historical stuff, political writing. We kind of got our opinions from Morton and Whitaker.'

Considering himself 'a total oddball, a right-brain person in a left-brain world,' Whitaker's first ambition was to become a hobo. 'I remember my mother said, "Oh, you want to be a bohemian? Well, that's all over." But it turned out she was wrong.' He discovered a new bohemian subculture in the literature of Henry Miller and the beat writers and, in the late 1950s, he embarked on an international beat odyssey. He lived on a kibbutz in Israel, met writer William Burroughs in Paris, sampled the skiffle scene in London, and visited Greenwich Village, New York, where he met up-and-coming folk artists like Dave Van Ronk. Whitaker socialized with poets Allen Ginsberg and Lawrence Ferlinghetti in San Francisco, and went drinking with Jack Kerouac. In March 1960, he returned to Minneapolis, met, and made friends with Bob. 'He was like a vessel waiting and wanting to be filled,' says Whitaker. 'I was his first kind of opening to the outside, 'cause I'd been out there. None of these other folks had been out and about, like in San Francisco with the beats. See, my main role with Dylan was telling him about life on the outside, that there was an alternative life out there. That there was a place for him.'

Before the friendship could mature, Bob and Dave Whitaker became rivals for the affections of Gretel

Hoffman, a pretty student with chestnut hair. She was the daughter of radical, intellectual parents and another former student of U High. Gretel developed a love for folk music during her junior year at Bennington College in Vermont. She was studying for a career in modern dance, but changed her mind and came home to Minneapolis. While deciding what to do with her life, she enrolled in a class at the University of Minnesota. Gretel met Bob first, at the Scholar, and they formed a close friendship, despite the fact he was dating Bonnie Beecher at the time.

As Gretel explains, she and Bob spent hours talking idealistically about 'the nature of experience and how people can do evil things to each other. [It was] very adolescent, as I look back on it.' Gretel played guitar and she taught Bob folk songs she had learned at Bennington. Bob made an early attempt to write a song of his own and Gretel became alarmed when she heard the lyrics. 'He wrote a song that he was nineteen now and he was not going to live to be twenty-one. He was, in certain respects, profoundly pessimistic.' Bob, typically uneasy with his Jewishness, relaxed when an Israeli singing group came through town. Gretel, who was a Jew, shared a remarkable evening with Bob. 'It was a very arousing kind of music. It was very lively. We were very excited about this music,' says Gretel. 'In a youthful kind of enthusiasm we just threw our arms around each other and kind of danced up and down . . . just hugging each other.' Although Gretel did not fully realize it at the time, Bob was falling in love with her. Gretel had not thought of their friendship as romantic, partly because Bob – normally so bold with girls – had not made his feelings clear. 'Bob and I were really becoming very close, spending a lot of time together, and I would suspect that our friendship might have turned into something else,' she says. 'I thought he was quite wonderful. I loved to talk to him. I loved to listen to him.'

Then, a couple of months into the friendship, on

March 20, 1960, Gretel met Dave Whitaker at a party. 'I was just simply *bowled* over,' she says. 'I'd never seen anybody so extraordinary.' They promptly eloped to Iowa where they were able to marry without parental consent on May 8. They returned to Dinkytown shortly afterward and rented the first of a series of apartments. Not long after their return, the newly married Mrs. Gretel Whitaker was standing outside the Scholar when Bob came down the road. Gretel called out 'hi!' and was expecting a friendly hello in reply. Instead, Bob almost shouted at her: 'When you get divorced, come and let me know.'

'I remember the *shock*,' she says. 'I can remember standing and watching him go and feeling, *Oh my God!*' From this point on, Bob was cold toward Gretel Whitaker. But there was enough civility for him to visit her husband at their apartment.

There were parties almost every night at the Whitakers' place, with kegs of beer, folk music, and marijuana, a drug Bob was then experiencing for the first time. Dave Whitaker had smoked marijuana on his world travels and had no difficulty obtaining bags of cheap Mexican weed at a time when marijuana was rare on college campuses. Friends who came by the apartment were invited to share the weed, which was full of seeds but powerful nonetheless. Some rolled it into joints while others used pipes. 'We were all stoned,' says Whitaker. 'We used to sit around and smoke and, I guess, we were the first ones – out of thirty, forty thousand students at the University of Minnesota – the first circle of real pot smokers.'

Politics was discussed earnestly at these gatherings, as it was whenever the Dinkytown clique got together. In the wake of the Cuban Revolution, Dave Whitaker was a leading light in the local branch of the Fair Play for Cuba Committee and he and Gretel hosted pro-Castro meetings. Fidel Castro was a romantic hero to many young people on the far left who were disillusioned with Stalinist politics. Whitaker was also involved in a

Trotskyist group, the Socialist Fund. 'This is all happening in my living room and Dylan was there,' he says. To show Bob what they were struggling against, Whitaker took him to see *Operation Abolition*, a propaganda film in support of Senator McCarthy and the House Un-American Activities Committee. 'Their villains were our heroes,' says Whitaker. 'When they'd say, "This communist scum," I'd say, "Fuck you! I'm an American."' Although Bob accompanied Whitaker to the screening of the film, and he listened to Whitaker and Morton talking about radical politics, he remained steadfastly, frustratingly apolitical. As Gretel Whitaker points out, Bob never wrote any pro-Castro songs.

Within his clique of friends, Bob was accepted as Bobby Dylan. People knew his real name and where he was from – there were enough students from the Iron Range to disseminate his true biography – but it did not matter. It must have been a relief to be freed from the social constraints of Hibbing. As he blended into the bohemian subculture of Dinkytown, Bob took less interest in his studies. 'He stopped going [to classes] 'cause it was getting in the way of [his] education,' says Whitaker. The night before he had to take a final music exam, Bob spurned revision and instead went to a party at the Whitakers' apartment where he became blind drunk. The next day he took the exam with a sick hangover, escaping with a C grade. This was typical of his attitude toward his studies.

His calls home were infrequent. One day Whitaker picked up his telephone to find Bob's mother on the line. Using her best telephone voice – 'I remember a very educated accent, like she was an intellectual' – Beatty asked how Bob was getting along. 'She was worried because she hadn't heard from him in a while, and he had left his fraternity and come over to our side . . . I said he was okay, that he was doing good.'

Bob never seemed to have much money, and he did not ever attempt to get a regular job, his only 'work' being the small sets he occasionally performed at places like the Purple Onion and the Bastille. There was little to spend money on, in any case. He had friends who would feed him or put him up for the night. While many people liked him a good deal, and were glad to help him in this way, some of the students on campus looked down on Bob. He was scruffy, rather dirty, and he had an awkward manner with people he did not know well, sometimes hardly saying anything or, conversely, giving the impression of being a braggart. A lot of his awkwardness grew from the fact that he was young, inexperienced, and intrinsically very shy. 'Bob [was] painfully shy, and very nervous,' says Whitaker. 'He used to twitch all the time, [but] he always just had a guitar in his hand, and a great sense of humor. . . . He had a sense that fortune had put her hand on his shoulder, but he didn't really know how, or what, or why.'

Jon Pankake was a university student with a fascination for traditional American music. In 1959 he attended a Pete Seeger concert in Iowa and was inspired to seek out records by The Weavers, the folk group that did so much to popularize the songs of Woody Guthrie. Jon and his friend Paul Nelson also obtained rare copies of Harry Smith's extraordinary six-disc *Anthology of American Folk Music*. Excited and intrigued by the love songs, murder ballads, and religious music on the *Anthology*, the friends founded a mimeographed folk fanzine they called the *Little Sandy Review*.

Pankake's apartment at 1401 6th Street SE became one of the places to hang out in Dinkytown. Bob visited regularly and he and Pankake played music together. 'I was playing the banjo, which he was very curious about,' says Pankake. When Pankake left town for a couple of weeks, leaving his apartment unlocked, Bob came into the apartment and, without permission, took approximately twenty records. These included a rare set of records by

Woody Guthrie's friend and traveling companion Ramblin' Jack Elliott. Jack Elliott, whose given name is Elliot Adnopoz, was the son of a Jewish doctor from Brooklyn. He should have become a doctor, too, but developed what he calls a 'bad attitude towards medicine' and ran away to join a rodeo. Infatuated with the romanticism of the West, he reinvented himself as wandering cowboy singer Ramblin' Jack. He became a disciple of Guthrie, copying him with the accuracy of a natural mimic. By 1960 he had made six Guthriesque folk albums for the British label Topic. Bob was fascinated by the recordings and, when he got the pilfered records home, he insisted Bonnie Beecher listen to them. 'I had to listen to them all,' she says. 'Literally, you are in this room until you've heard them all, and you get it.'

Jon Pankake believes Bob may also have taken his *Anthology of American Folk Music* from the apartment. 'It could well have been one of the records because I don't think there were that many copies of the *Anthology* circulating in Minneapolis.' If he did take it, and Pankake cannot remember for certain, this was Bob's first opportunity to listen to recordings that became one of the foundation stones of his career. References to songs in the seminal collection are scattered throughout his work and, in the 1990s, he began mining the *Anthology* anew, recording two acoustic albums – *Good as I Been to You* and *World Gone Wrong* – that included versions of three songs on the *Anthology*.* His 1997 album, *Time Out of Mind*, was flecked with phrases picked out of the *Anthology*.

*Dylan's 'Love Henry' is a variation of the Child ballad 'Henry Lee,' performed by Dick Justice on the *Anthology*; 'Stack A Lee' is a version of 'Stackalee' as performed by Frank Hutchison on the same (both on *World Gone Wrong*, 1993). On *Good as I Been to You* (1992) Dylan recorded his take on the popular and much-covered 'Frankie & Albert,' included on the *Anthology* as 'Frankie' by Mississippi John Hurt.

The anthology was the work of eccentric ethnomusicologist Harry Smith. Born in 1923 in Portland, Oregon, to a mother who thought she was Czarina of Russia, Smith was a hunchback and an outcast from 'tidy' society, as he called it. Fond of inventing stories about himself, he claimed to be a multiple murderer. In his late twenties, without bothering to seek permission and clearing copyright, he collected old 78 rpm recordings of folk songs, spirituals, blues tunes, and instrumentals that had been made by bluesmen and hillbilly musicians in the 1920s and '30s. He distilled his collection into eighty-four selections divided into three categories: Ballads, Social Music, and, simply, Songs. In 1952 Folkways released these recordings as six long-playing records. They were packaged in hinged two-record sets, each decorated with an etching of a mythological musical instrument Smith called the Celestial Monochord. With the records came a crudely printed handbook in which Smith described each of the recordings with a terse, telegramlike précis of lyrics and subject matter.

The songs sounded as if they had come out of a lost world, sometime around the Civil War perhaps. In fact, several of the artists on the *Anthology* were still alive and would be rediscovered as the folk revival gathered momentum. Many of the songs were Child ballads from Britain that had been passed down through generations. They contained archaic words and strange images that were out of time and place. The cuckoo in the Appalachian standard 'The Coo Coo Bird' is a creature not even native to the United States. Despite anomalies like these, the underlying subject matter was the elementary stuff of life and the songs could be understood easily. Many songs were about love gone wrong. In 'Sugar Baby,' mountain singer 'Dock' Boggs sounded like a man going down to Hell as he grumbled about what to do with his child now his 'sugar baby' had gone. Maybe his sugar baby left him; maybe he killed her. It sounded like Dock was thinking of sending the child the same way. Other songs reported calamitous events – train wrecks, mining disasters, the sinking of the *Titanic*. There were songs that documented changes in the social fabric of America. 'Peg and Awl' described how machine manufacturing had destroyed the handmade shoe industry. Smith's *Anthology* is one of the most remarkable recordings in American music, an enormously important social history and, incidentally, a work of poetry. 'That's where the wealth of folk music was, on that particular record,' Bob has said. '. . . it's all poetry, every single one of those songs.' The language was different from that found in popular song. It was quirky and surprising with words and images taken from the Bible, or born out of real-life experience and the folklore of seemingly foreign lands.

Jon Pankake discovered his record collection had been raided when he returned home from his trip. 'At that time a lot of doors on the streets were unlocked,' he explains. 'I had not lost anything or been the victim of any crime of any kind. So that was a first.' Pankake quickly found out Bob had taken the records. Late at night, accompanied by two friends, he went to confront him. 'He denied everything,' he says. 'I just put him up against the wall and said that I knew he had them for a fact.' He hit Bob and Bob confessed. He returned some of the records immediately and said he would return the rest in the morning.

Looking back on this odd and shabby episode, Pankake does not believe Bob stole the records to sell, although they were worth about a hundred dollars. Bob, in fact, probably did not see it as stealing at all. As Pankake puts it, Bob was 'hungry for the music.' He simply bypassed the usual courtesies of asking permission. It was not the last time he took without asking.

In the summer of 1960 Bob hitchhiked west to Denver,

Colorado. This was a journey of more than nine hundred miles and one of the biggest adventures of his young life. The trip was reminiscent of Jack Kerouac's *On the Road*, in which the hipster hero, Dean Moriarty, often stopped in Denver on his trips back and forth across the country. Bob knew the book and was enchanted by the character of Moriarty. But he traveled to Denver primarily because there was a vibrant music scene there, with several lively clubs including the Satire and the Exodus.

A girl Bob knew suggested he introduce himself to Walt Conley, a singer who was managing and performing at the Satire. Conley's headline act was Dick and Tommy Smothers. The Smothers Brothers performed folk music for a mainstream audience, dressed for the stage in suit and tie. As Conley says, they were from the branch of folk music that was 'trying to get some polish.' In contrast, Bob was from the branch of folk music that was rolling in the dust. Bob played hillbilly ballads and was dressing in worn cotton and denim clothes, looking like a character out of *The Grapes of Wrath* and smelling none too fresh because he was not very punctilious about bathing. However, Conley let him do a short set at the Satire before The Smothers Brothers.

Walt Conley lived in a two-bedroom frame house down the road from the club, sharing it with musicians passing through town. When Bob showed up, Dick Smothers and his wife were sleeping in the spare room and Tommy Smothers was on the couch. 'Bob had no place to stay,' says Conley. 'He asked if he could sleep on the floor and I said yes. I think he slept on the floor one night and then he started jumping around town finding places to stay.' Over at the Exodus, Bob met sixty-four-year-old Jesse Fuller, writer of 'San Francisco Bay Blues.' Fuller was an early musical influence on Bob, coming into his life between Odetta and the full, almost religious revelation of Woody Guthrie, which was yet to come. Fuller was performing in the basement of the Exodus. An original one-man band, he played the guitar and harmonica, working a bass with his foot, while singing the blues. Unfortunately for Fuller, the blues did not have much cachet with mainstream white audiences at the time and he was not doing good business. 'Think of what the blues means today!' exclaims Conley. '[But] in those days they just weren't buying it. They weren't buying Bob Dylan either.'

The Smothers Brothers made it clear that they did not like Bob, the grubby faux hobo, and he soon lost his afternoon set at the Satire. 'Bob starts wandering around Denver seeing what he can do, and trying to sing in certain places, and no one would accept Bob,' says Conley. 'I think of the stature of that man today and think what he was. People *avoided* him.'

Bob had not been in town long when Conley received a telephone call from Sophia St. John, who ran a Western-style saloon in the nearby former Gold Rush town Central City. The town traded on re-creating the look and atmosphere of the Wild West. Tourists could pan for gold. The saloons and hotels looked like something out of a Western, and an actor got paid to stagger up and down Main Street with beer glasses glued to a tray. Sophia St. John's club gloried in the name the Gilded Garter, though it was not a strip club, as Bob later claimed.

'I need a singer up here,' said St. John, when she got Walt on the line. 'I've got a girl called Judy Collins and she's doing well.' Twenty-one-year-old Judy Collins was starting out on her career, and would soon become one of the stars of the folk revival. 'But if you know anybody else, send them up.'

'I've got a guy named Bob Dylan,' replied Conley. 'He's out of work, and he's under foot, and we would like to get him out of town.'

The Gilded Garter was a terrible place for Bob to play. It was impossibly noisy and the tourists were mostly interested in drinking and eating. Bob tried to entertain by playing the piano and singing but he was not a success, and it was not long before he slunk back to Denver and booked into a cheap hotel next to the Exodus.

The Smothers Brothers had left town and Conley was sharing his house with banjo player Dave Hamil. They played music most nights after work, or games of cards. One night they decided to have a quiet evening playing records. As Conley prepared supper, Hamil picked through the albums for something to put on the record player. He discovered several albums were missing, including folk albums and theatrical recordings like *My Fair Lady*. 'Bob Dylan stole them damn albums,' concluded Hamil. Bob knew the house was not locked during the day and he was short of money. Most of the missing records were not to Bob's taste, so Hamil assumed he took them to sell. Conley was not overly bothered by the theft, being an easygoing sort, but Hamil went over to Bob's hotel.

It was around 3:30 A.M. when Conley's telephone rang. 'I've got Dylan and I've found out he's got the albums,' said Hamil. 'He's locked me out of the room and I'm calling the police.'

'You do what you gotta do.'

'I want you to come down here,' said Hamil. 'It's important because you are going to have to identify the records.'

Reluctantly, Conley drove to the hotel. 'There was a police car outside and Dave Hamil was standing there on the pavement and there were two police officers and Dylan.' When Bob realized the police were coming, he had tossed the records out of his third-floor window into the alley at the back of the hotel. The police helped Hamil retrieve the records and then began questioning Bob, who was so upset he was crying. Hamil was pushing for the police to bring charges, but Conley did not want to give evidence in court and Hamil was persuaded to forget about it. Shortly afterward Bob hitchhiked back east. 'I was kicked out of Denver,' he later said. 'I was run out of Denver for robbing a cat's house.' Walt Conley says he felt sorry for Bob, rather than angry, but he would feel some rancor four years later when he met the then famous Bob Dylan in New York and Bob pretended not to remember him at all.

On his way back to college from Denver, Bob stopped at home in Hibbing to see his family and became involved in another curious incident. On August 31, 1960, his former girlfriend, Echo Shivers (née Helstrom), gave birth at Hibbing General Hospital to a baby daughter, Danae. Echo stayed in the hospital two days before going home to her husband, Danny, and Bob came to the hospital, insisting *he* was the father of her child. 'I was laughing,' says Echo. 'It was hilarious, because it's totally untrue.' She says there was no chance Bob was the father. 'After I broke up with him, even though we hung out, I never had sex with him.' Echo believes Bob did not have a malicious motive in saying he was the father of her child; it was another game, if a rather peculiar one. 'He just comes up with these wild ideas.'

Although it was partly a joke, Bob did want children of his own. When he returned to Dinkytown at the end of the summer, and was reunited with Bonnie Beecher, he talked to her earnestly about getting married and starting a family together. 'I was not at all interested in getting married or having children,' says Bonnie. 'He was very interested, mainly, in having children. He wanted to have children really soon.' Yet while Bob was talking to Bonnie about surprising their families by getting engaged, he was also seeing other girls. 'He wasn't faithful,' Bonnie adds. 'I don't think it was even an issue, particularly. Boys didn't have to be faithful.' In fact, Bob was highly promiscuous, a character trait that would remain with him well into adulthood.

The Dinkytown scene was literary almost as much as it was musical. Morton and Whitaker devoured books on a wide range of subjects including radical politics. The books of the beat writers were popular with practically everyone. Bob and most of his friends had read *On the Road*, as well as Allen Ginsberg's *Howl* and Lawrence Ferlinghetti's *Coney Island of the Mind*. Poems like Ferlinghetti's 'I Am Waiting' tapped into their feelings of incipient cultural change.

A fellow student named Harry Weber gave Bob a copy of Woody Guthrie's memoir, *Bound for Glory*, a romanticized account of the Oklahoma-born musician's early life. Weber was a folk musician and he was a little jealous of Bob. 'He was very powerful,' he recalls. 'You'd go to a party and Bob would get a chair and move right into the center of the room and start singing and if you didn't want to listen, you got the hell out of the room, and I resented it.' Weber had a spare hardback copy of *Bound for Glory* and, despite their uneasy relationship, he lent the book to Bob because he knew he would enjoy it. It was an uncut first edition, the pages still joined together because they had not yet been trimmed. Dinkytown legend has it that Bob sat in the Scholar, cutting the pages, until he had finished the book. But it is possible he did not read the whole book until much later. Dave Morton believes the hyperenergetic Bob – '. . . as nervous as a cat . . . energy just flowing' – could not sit still long enough to finish a book. Although he was a reader when he was in Hibbing, he had less time for it in Dinkytown. Yet even if Bob skimmed the first pages of the book, he would have found much of interest.

Bound for Glory began with hoboes riding a boxcar across Minnesota, having jumped the train in Duluth – the town where Bob was born, and the same trains he had watched rattling through Hibbing. The writing was spare, sparkling with vivid phrases. Describing a storm over Minnesota, Guthrie wrote of 'that bright crackling lightning that booms and zooms.' There was much in the book that Bob took for his own. One of the characters in the boomtown scene in chapter two was Big Jim, a name used in Bob's 1974 song 'Lily, Rosemary and the Jack of Hearts.' In another passage, Guthrie made a list,

'. . . stealers, dealers, sidewalk spielers . . .' Bob would echo the line in his 1965 song 'Subterranean Homesick Blues.' Most important, Bob adopted the speech patterns of Woody Guthrie's hobo characters. In the book, the hoboes used double negatives and were forever clipping words short as if there was not time to finish them. For instance, near the start of the book one character said, 'You're too dam low down an' sneakin' to make an honest livin' . . .' Bob started talking like the characters in the book, as if B. J. Rolfzen hadn't taught him nothin' about grammar. The use of hipster expressions, mixed with his magpielike use of unusual words – this was the way Bob would speak from now on. It also became the way he expressed himself in song. 'Don't ask me nothin' about nothin'' from 'Outlaw Blues' (recorded in 1965) and the song title and lyric 'You Ain't Goin' Nowhere' (1967) are typical examples of Bob's deliberately atrocious grammar. It is also noteworthy that in *Bound for Glory* the word 'blowing' was expressed as 'blowin'' as in, of course, 'Blowin' in the Wind.'

It seemed like only a day had passed when Bob came to Dave Whitaker and performed Woody Guthrie's long ballad 'Tom Joad' from start to finish. Bob's fixation with Woody Guthrie had begun. It was Guthrie's music, of course, that was most important, songs that are among the truest writing in American folk music, including 'This Land Is Your Land,' 'Pastures of Plenty,' and 'Deportee.' But Guthrie's colorful memoir helped flesh out a hero Bob could model himself on. When he was drunk, or stoned on Dave Whitaker's marijuana, Bob would put on an old hat and pretend to be Guthrie. It was partly Bob being goofy, but he took the joke a long way. 'If you didn't call him Woody, he wouldn't answer,' says Bonnie Beecher.

At the time, Guthrie was a long-term patient at Greystone Park Hospital in Morris Plains, New Jersey, suffering from the hereditary brain disease Huntington's chorea. Guthrie's mother had died of the disease and he would die of it too. Where he had once been an indomitable little man, at the age of forty-eight Guthrie was a trembling wreck. He was losing his sense of balance. His head lolled forward when he walked. He was no longer able to play a guitar. He could not work a typewriter, or write legibly in longhand. He would have been barely coherent on the telephone, even if he could get to a telephone, but this did not prevent Bob calling the hospital from Dave Whitaker's apartment. 'I was there listening,' says Morton. 'Whitaker ain't got no money to pay for it, but he's calling long distance.'

'I'm coming out there,' said Bob excitedly. It sounded like he was talking to a nurse. 'Tell Woody I'm coming out to see him.'

Before his illness Guthrie played harmonica using a simple wire harmonica rack that he wore around his neck, a contraption that looked like a bent coat hanger. It allowed him to play guitar and harmonica at the same time because he did not have to use his hands to hold the harmonica. Ramblin' Jack Elliott copied the idea, and now Bob did, too. He drew a picture of the rack for Bonnie and she bought one as a gift from Smith's Music Company. Now, whenever Bob came to Bonnie's sorority house, he played guitar and rack harmonica, trying to get a sound like a train engine, like Guthrie had, but instead making a terrible squawking noise. 'Don't do that!' protested Bonnie. She wanted him to play boogie-woogie piano so her girlfriends would be impressed.

But Bob was determined. 'No, I'm gonna master this damned thing,' he said stubbornly, and played on. He started to improve on the harmonica thanks to some friendly advice from Dinkytown musician Tony Glover, who was highly accomplished on the instrument. Glover did not like Bob when they were introduced. 'He seemed kind of like he had a chip on his shoulder,' he says. 'He seemed kind of aloof, sort of arrogant.' But after they played music together, Glover softened his opinion and helped Bob develop his harmonica technique. 'When I first met him, he was playing one of those echo harmonicas. They are the kind of harmonicas like fishermen and so forth play, two harmonicas on top of each other so you get that octave kind of sound, you get that tremulous sort of thing,' says Glover. 'It was kind of a fuller sound, but he couldn't really do what Woody was doing, or Jesse Fuller, or those kind of guys were doing. So I suggested he get a diatonic, which is just a regular single-holed harp. That's when he started to get good on it.'

Bonnie Beecher's sorority sisters took such a dim view of Bob, and her relationship with him, that they actually asked her to leave the sorority house. She moved into a rented apartment and Bob began spending a good deal of time there. In the fall of 1960 Bonnie used her roommate's reel-to-reel Webcor tape machine to record Bob playing and singing in his emerging Guthriesque style. She remembers recording two tapes, one of which eventually circulated among collectors. 'The first two tapings were made before he ever went to New York,' she says. '[The] first set of tapes were horrible quality.' The set was made up of eleven songs, including the antiwar ballad, popular during the American Civil War, 'Johnny I Hardly Knew You,' and four talking songs including Woody Guthrie's 'Talking Columbia,' one of a series of songs he wrote about the hydroelectric operation on the Columbia River. The second set of tapes, which became lost, included folk standards like 'House Carpenter.' Bonnie loved the tapes and listened to them countless times. But Bob had an even higher opinion of the recordings. 'He thought he was terrific,' she says. 'He always had confidence. It's what turned him into the musician he is.' It seemed to Bonnie that Bob's confidence was sometimes out of proportion to his ability, however.

'If the Library of Congress ever comes and asks you for these songs,' Bob told her gravely, 'I want you to sell them for two hundred dollars. I want you to promise me this.'

Bonnie was flabbergasted. 'I thought, what an outrageous ego! To think that the Library of Congress was going to come and ask Bonnie Beecher for Bobby Dylan's tapes!' But Bob made her promise.

'Yes, I give my word,' she agreed, when she stopped laughing.

In the winter of 1960 Bob became ill and contracted a severe cough. Bonnie tried to get him to attend the clinic on campus, but he would not get help and the cough turned to bronchitis, changing Bob's voice. It became rougher, more like the sound he became known for. Although he recovered, she worried he had done permanent damage to his voice. In 1969, when she heard the mellow sound of Bob's voice on the *Nashville Skyline* album, Bonnie was reminded of what he sounded like before the bronchitis. 'That sounded like his voice when he was young.'

Soon after the illness, Odetta came to town. She was then a star of the folk scene in San Francisco and Chicago, where she performed at the prestigious Gate of Horn club. Odetta knew several people in Dinkytown including Gretel Whitaker and Tova Hammerman and Hammerman decided it would be interesting to know whether Odetta thought Bob had a chance of making it professionally as a musician. Bob duly performed for Odetta and the singer pronounced that, yes, indeed it was possible he might make it. 'This was like, wow! Big news in Minneapolis,' laughs Bonnie Beecher, who was mightily relieved the bronchitis voice had not ruined Bob's chances for a career in music.

After the audience with Odetta Bob had to go home to Hibbing to talk to his parents about his future. He decided he should get a haircut and asked Bonnie to give him a trim. When his friends came over, they laughed themselves silly at what they saw. Bob said Bonnie made his hair way too short. 'So he wrote this song, "Bonnie, you cut my hair / and now I can't go nowhere." And it was kind of funny,' says Bonnie. 'But I kept wanting to say, "But you asked me to!" '

Bob caught a Greyhound bus back to Hibbing in mid-December 1960 and told his parents he wanted to leave college and pursue his ambitions to become a music star. He wanted to go to New York where he believed he might be able to make a record. All the major record companies were based in New York and, from talking to people like Dave Whitaker, Bob knew about the vibrant coffeehouse scene in Greenwich Village. Abe and Beatty brought him to a compromise: 'He wanted to be a folksinger, an entertainer. We couldn't see it, but we felt he was entitled to the chance. It's his life after all, and we didn't want to stand in the way,' said Abe Zimmerman. 'So we made an agreement that he could have one year to do as he pleased, and if at the end of that year we were not satisfied with his progress, he'd go back to school.'

Without waiting to spend the holidays with his family, Bob returned to the Twin Cities and went around telling friends he was on his way to New York. He saw Larry Kegan in the hospital, and also visited Howard Rutman. He said they would be hearing about him when he was a star. Neither was convinced. Indeed, Rutman felt Bob was making a mistake in giving up his education. 'I kind of wished he would have stayed at the University of Minnesota for a little longer. I don't know if he gave it a shot. He was just anxious to get going.' Bob said good-bye to John Bucklen and Luke Davich, both of whom were now in the Twin Cities. 'Why don't you come to New York with me?' he asked Bucklen. 'I'm going to see Woody Guthrie.' New York seemed an impossible place, beyond the imagination of most of Bob's friends. 'People couldn't fathom that,' says Davich. 'Everybody has their dreams; I guess his was bigger than most.'

Before setting out on his great journey, Bob hoped to spend the Christmas holidays with Bonnie and her family in Minneapolis. But Bonnie's parents would not allow her to bring him home. 'I remember there being a very big scene between me and my parents,' says Bonnie. 'I almost got to the point of saying, "If he can't come, I'm not coming." Because he really had no place to go for Christmas.' Eventually Bonnie told Bob he could not spend the holiday with them. 'I just remember how upset he was, and how angry I was, and all of my adult life I wished that I had stood my ground.' In the last year of her life, Bonnie's mother apologized for not letting her bring Bob home. 'It was a *big* fight between us,' says Bonnie. 'I always felt that I had really hurt him.'

Snow was falling. Bob found himself alone at the loneliest time of year, in a cold, semidecrepit apartment building near campus. As he later recalled, he just got up one morning and left. 'I'd spent so much time thinking about it I couldn't think about it anymore. Snow or no snow, it was time for me to go,' he said. 'When I arrived in Minneapolis it had seemed like a big city or a big town. When I left it was like some rural outpost you see once from a passing train.'

There may have been another, less romantic reason Bob left town with such haste. Late one night in the middle of the winter two men came into the apartment of Dave and Gretel Whitaker, looking for Bob. 'I was alone, and the house wasn't locked, and I woke up and there were two guys standing over my bed,' says Gretel Whitaker, who was heavily pregnant with her first child. 'That's one of those heart-stopping events you never forget.'

'Where's Dylan?' they demanded.

'He's not here,' replied Gretel. In fact, Bob had not been staying with them for some time. The men said they were going to find him and teach him a lesson. 'They were like thugs. It was very scary.' The men, neither of whom Gretel recognized as being part of the Dinkytown community, then left. It is unclear what they wanted, or whether they found Bob.

Bob packed one suitcase. He picked up his guitar and

walked out onto the highway where he stuck out his thumb for a ride, believing as he later said 'in the mercy of the world.' (Larry Kegan was surprised Bob hitched out of town. 'Usually he would find someone to give him a ride.') The first driver who pulled over looked like the horror-movie actor Bela Lugosi. Bob got into the jalopy and was driven into the whiteness.

The first place Bob stopped was Chicago, Illinois. At the University of Chicago campus he met Kevin Krown, a young folksinger he had befriended in Colorado during the summer. Bob spent the next few weeks scuffling about campus. He played piano for a group of female students in their dormitory, and one girl took him in for a short time.

When Bob left Chicago he backtracked north to Madison, Wisconsin. The University of Wisconsin had a renowned American history department that attracted students from radical families, and partly because of these students there was a thriving folk music scene on campus. The apartment of students Marshall Brickman and Eric Weissberg, on Clymer Place, was where everybody gathered. Brickman and Weissberg later formed the folk group The Tarriers. Later still, Brickman became a noted screenwriter, winning an Oscar for cowriting *Annie Hall* with Woody Allen; Weissberg went on to record the 'Dueling Banjos' theme for *Deliverance*. 'Our flat was the unofficial center of campus folk music. People passing through would inevitably wind up there, playing, singing, exchanging names and numbers, stealing soft drinks from the fridge,' says Brickman. 'I recall a polite, somewhat retiring, thin young fellow named Zimmerman who appeared briefly, though I don't believe he ever stayed the night. He was on his way to New York City and fame.' Dressed curiously in a brown suit and a thin tie, Bob entertained his new friends by playing a primitive blues on the piano. Nobody was very impressed.

While in Madison, staying with a girl named Ann Lauderbach, Bob made an important musical connection when he attended a Pete Seeger concert. Seeger – the tall, distinguished folksinger and radical songwriter, then aged forty – was one of the foremost figures of American folk music. He founded the first urban folk group, The Almanac Singers, and went on to found The Weavers. Both groups performed a repertoire of songs that included work by Woody Guthrie, who was a close friend and former traveling companion. Like Guthrie, Seeger was associated with the struggle for reform in America. He was an important songwriter, the author of such standards as 'If I Had a Hammer,' and a compelling live performer, playing banjo and singing in a schoolmasterly voice of great clarity. To Seeger, words were vitally important; they differentiated folk music from most of the popular music on the radio.

By 1951, due to the McCarthy blacklist, The Weavers were effectively put out of business because of their radical left-wing politics. Seeger used 1952 as a sabbatical year. In 1953 a student wrote and asked him to perform at his college. There was no fee, but the students would take up a collection that would probably pay his bus fare. He accepted the invitation and was soon traveling back and forth across the country appearing at colleges. In retrospect, these small campus concerts helped propagate the folk revival, bringing folk songs to a flowering generation. Joan Baez and Tom Paxton were among those who saw Seeger perform at this time, in California and Oklahoma respectively. In Madison, Wisconsin, Bob was perhaps the most significant young artist Seeger reached. 'I think the most important thing I ever did in my life, bar none, was go from college to college to college to college, from about 1953, singing in schools and summer camps,' says Seeger. 'I sang not only really old folk songs, but I sang songs of Woody Guthrie and Leadbelly and songs out of American history. There's a lot of good music [students] weren't hearing on the radio. It was at one of these concerts around '58 that Joan Baez heard me, and I think I was singing in the University of Wisconsin and Bob was there. I think there was a picket line outside from the American Legion calling me a dangerous communist. [Bob] once told me he was at that concert.'

Seeing Pete Seeger in the flesh and hearing him talk about Woody Guthrie and sing Guthrie's songs, as Seeger invariably did in concert, fired Bob's ambition to meet Guthrie himself. There was no question of going back to the Twin Cities now. In mid-January 1961, Bob met University of Wisconsin student Fred Underhill, who was about to travel to New York with a friend, David Berger. They needed another person to share the driving, and Bob joined them. On January 24, after a long journey, during which Bob irritated Berger by incessantly singing Woody Guthrie songs, they found themselves passing through the New Jersey suburbs heading toward New York City. Suddenly Bob saw the Manhattan skyline. His mind was filled with visions of Broadway, the *Ed Sullivan Show*, and the New York Yankees. He was more than a thousand miles from home, entering the city of his dreams.

CHAPTER 3

City of Dreams

Within two years of Bob's arrival in New York in January 1961, in the midst of a particularly cold winter, his life would be changed beyond all recognition. Events unfolded rapidly from the moment he set foot in the city, as he met many people who became key players in his career and developed quickly as an artist. In the reminiscences of those who knew Bob during this busy, formative time, dates have become confused and an exact chronology of events is sometimes hard to establish. In essence, everything seemed to be – and sometimes was – happening at once. Some of these friends feel a tinge of bitterness toward Bob for using people he met in Greenwich Village and its environs to further his ambitions and then dropping them when they ceased to be of use. This bitterness sometimes seems motivated by an element of jealousy that this unprepossessing youth from Minnesota, just one of the many talented musicians flocking to the city at the time, achieved international and lasting acclaim.

When Bob came to make his fortune in New York he was not quite the lovable innocent that he appeared to be. In his first year in the city he instinctively played upon his baby-faced unworldly looks, and his considerable personal charm, to make friends that would help him in various ways, such as giving him a place to stay or offering him a few dollars' pocket money. He *did* drop some of these friends when his fortunes improved. It is also true that he used people in other ways, mimicking artists he admired, appropriating melodies and song lyrics. Indeed he learned everything he could about music from older, more experienced artists, taking the best of their material and stage craft for himself. He also fabricated stories about his past life, which, in retrospect, makes him seem at times to be dishonest and foolish. There was, in general, a briskness about the way he pursued his ambitions that does not fit with the popular conception of the young Dylan as a romantic, idealistic youth in a shabby corduroy cap and sheepskin jacket, singing his way to fame and fortune.

He did, of course, have a keen awareness of the world; he could not have written the songs he did without such sensitivity. The tumult of ideas inside him seemed to manifest itself during these first months in the city in his physical nervousness, the way he almost ran everywhere, jiggled his feet when he sat down, and fiddled incessantly with his cigarettes. He would occasionally open up to girlfriends. But it was in his songs that he really revealed himself, though it was a while before he started to produce really first-class material of his own. Meanwhile, in everyday life he hid this sensitive side. In conversation with friends, especially male friends, Bob was reluctant to say much about what he was really thinking, often making jokes to deflect questions that probed too deeply. At times this made him seem inscrutable. Perhaps it was the only way he could have protected himself long enough to achieve the extraordinary things he did. It should be remembered that when Bob came to New York he was a fairly naive, pampered middle-class boy who was not yet twenty. Coming from a small Midwestern town, via a provincial university campus, he now was trying to make his way as a performer in the most competitive and sophisticated city in the country. He had to employ every ounce of his cunning, cleverness, and ambition to make his dreams come true.

The primary location for Bob's frenetic first months in New York was Greenwich Village. For decades cheap rents had drawn generations of musicians, artists, and writers to live in the narrow streets around Washington Square, at the southern terminus of Fifth Avenue. In the evenings they frequented the coffeehouses and clubs on Bleecker and MacDougal Streets. Bebop jazz had been the rage in the 1940s and into the '50s; beat writers followed the musicians and, when the beatniks became fashionable, tourists started coming to the coffeehouses looking for them. By 1961, when Bob came to New York, the tourists were discovering that many of the beatniks had departed and beginning to take their place was a generation of earnest young musicians performing folk music. The seriousness and integrity of folk music appealed to those tourists who made a point to come to the Village at this time, partly because it seemed in tune with the feelings for social change in America. John F. Kennedy was newly sworn in as president; there were serious racial problems in the southern states and real fears that the Cold War could escalate into world war. In this social climate, folk music became highly popular.

In many cases, coffeehouse owners exploited the folk music craze and the young musicians like Bob who came to Greenwich Village to perform. The musicians would play for virtually no pay, apart from the paltry tips they collected passing a bread basket at the end of their set, and yet tourists crowded the bars and cafes to hear them. This was a recipe for healthy profits. Once club owners had the customers inside they would charge them as much as possible. A common trick was to turn off the air-conditioning so that patrons became hot and thirsty and ordered more drinks. Coffeehouses could not serve liquor, but customers spent a lot of money on ersatz drinks like rum-flavored cola, despite often exorbitant prices. The owners did not have it all their own way, however. Complicated licensing laws, limiting the types of entertainment that could be staged in coffeehouses, meant owners constantly had to dodge the authorities. 'It was actually when the police began raiding the coffeehouses, because they were presenting unlicensed entertainment, that the publicity brought in enormous crowds,' says Manny Dworman, who ran Cafe Feenjon on Seventh Avenue. He had a red warning light for when the police arrived. 'We were permitted to have string instruments, but no singing and no drumming. So as soon as the light went on, the drummer ran off stage.' The crowds loved the excitement. On weekends the sidewalks around Washington Square were so crowded the police had to stop traffic. Tourists flocked to hear artists like Carolyn Hester, Fred Neil, Phil Ochs, and Tom Paxton who were virtual unknowns at this time, drawn from across the United States with dreams of becoming stars. 'You had to make it in New York first,' says Oscar Brand, a veteran folksinger and radio broadcaster. 'Every place else was the provinces.'

On his first night in Greenwich Village, on or around January 24, 1961, Bob went into the Cafe Wha? on MacDougal Street. It was 'hootenanny' night, open-mike night when almost anybody could get up and perform. 'I been travelin' around the country,' he told the crowd. 'Followin' in Woody Guthrie's footsteps.' *Hootenanny* was a strange word, a union term popularized by Guthrie himself. Before he did anything else, Bob wanted to meet his hero. A couple of days later, before he had a proper place to stay – it seems that Bob slept rough or found a couch to sleep on for the first few nights – he went to the Guthrie family home on 85th Street in the Howard Beach section of the borough of Queens.

Woody Guthrie's children by his second wife, Marjorie, were at home: Arlo was thirteen, Joady was twelve, and Nora eleven. They were being looked after by Anita, a sixteen-year-old from St. Joseph's School who watched them until 7 P.M., when Mrs. Guthrie returned from the dance school she ran in Brooklyn. When the knock came at the door, Arlo was practicing guitar and Joady and Nora were watching Dick Clark's *American Bandstand*. Nora ran home from school for the show each day, but she dragged herself away from the television to answer the door. She immediately recognized the look of the boy at the door. Although Woody Guthrie was descended from Midwestern Anglo stock going back generations, his second wife's family was Russian-Jewish, from Odessa. The boy at the door had the same dark curly hair Nora and her brothers had and his face reminded her of the Jewish boys she knew in and around New York. Only this visitor was scruffier than those boys and, oddly, he was wearing the khaki army-surplus clothes her father wore, with the same pull-on boots he used because laces were too difficult for him. Whoever the boy was, he seemed to have dressed to look like her father. 'He looked as bad as my dad, with Huntington's,' says Nora. 'A very dusty-looking character.'

'I'm looking for Woody Guthrie,' said Bob.

'Oh, he's not home,' replied Nora, and she closed the door.

Nora did not feel she had to explain what she assumed everybody knew. Her father lived full-time in the hospital and had done so for years. (Bob probably did know that himself – after all, he had called the hospital from Minnesota – but he would have had difficulty visiting Guthrie without first meeting the family.) Woody and Marjorie Guthrie had divorced after Woody was diagnosed with Huntington's, a practical measure that meant he would be eligible for free medical care at the Veterans Administration (VA) Hospital in New Jersey on an ongoing basis. Marjorie remarried, and Woody agreed the children should call her new husband 'daddy.' They could call him 'Woody.' This was too much to explain and, anyway, Nora wanted to get back to *American Bandstand*. She was quite cross when Bob knocked again.

'I'm looking for Woody Guthrie. I came all the way from . . .'

'I'm sorry, he's not here and my mother is at work and I can't let a stranger in the house.'

The next time Bob knocked, Nora asked the baby-sitter to answer the door. 'There's a crazy guy out there and he wants to see Woody.' Anita explained to Bob patiently that Mr. Guthrie did not live there and Mrs. Guthrie was not home. If he wanted to leave a message where he could be reached, she would make sure Mrs. Guthrie received it.

'I have no place to stay.'

Arlo was the one who finally let Bob in. 'I thought he was kinda cool,' he says. 'I could tell by his [boots] he wasn't coming by to sell something.' Anita became so nervous about the visitor she lit a cigarette while she still had another one burning, and she called to ask Mrs. Guthrie what to do. Meanwhile, Bob and Arlo played music. Arlo had a harmonica and Bob showed him that by sucking as well as blowing one could make it play in two keys. Within half an hour, with Anita insisting he should come back later, Bob left.

A couple of days later, on Sunday, January 29, Bob succeeded in meeting Woody Guthrie at the home of Bob and Sidsel Gleason, friends of Guthrie who lived in East Orange, New Jersey. Because they lived nearer the hospital than Marjorie did, the Gleasons brought Guthrie to their house on Sundays and friends and family gathered there to see him. When Bob arrived at the Gleason house he found that he had to meet Marjorie before he got to meet Woody himself. Despite the fact that they were divorced, Marjorie remained very much in charge of everything that went on with her ex-husband. She was always pleased to receive people who knew his work, and she found Bob particularly charming, as did most women. 'He was a simple kind of kid. I think my mother responded to the Jewish part of him, too. I think that was endearing to her,' explains Nora.

The Sunday visit to the Gleasons' house was the highlight of Woody Guthrie's week. Sidsel Gleason, known as Sid, was from Montana and she served the hearty Western-style food he loved (though he was never very picky with food after living for a time on ketchup sandwiches during the Great Depression). Old friends came to say hello, including actor Will Geer, Guthrie's manager Harold Leventhal, and Pete Seeger. There were many younger admirers, too. Bob was far from being the first young man to become fixated with Woody Guthrie. Ten years earlier Ramblin' Jack Elliott had been Guthrie's original, and perhaps most dedicated, acolyte. At one time or another John Cohen, Erik Darling, Peter La Farge, Phil Ochs, and other young musicians paid court. Nora sometimes giggled at the youths who gathered around her father as he lay prostrate on the Gleasons' sofa, singing his old songs to him, even smoking the same Camel cigarettes he smoked. Her father basked in the attention. 'He just couldn't believe that his songs were being handed down to [the next] generation,' says Nora. 'He *loved* it when the young guys came over, like a kid in a candy shop, giggling and laughing and twinkling and really showing it, laughing and smiling. So with someone like Bob, who could just play every song my dad ever wrote, it was just delightful.'

Shortly after this visit, Dave and Gretel Whitaker received a postcard in the Twin Cities from Bob in New York, expressing his excitement at having finally met his hero. He wrote: 'I know him and met him and saw him and sang to him. I know Woody – Goddamn.' Within a remarkably short space of time he had achieved one of the main goals he set himself when he came to New York, and the success of making a friendly connection with Woody Guthrie encouraged him in the months that followed. Sometimes, when he was with people, Bob would pull out a card on which Guthrie had written, 'I ain't dead yet.' It was like a talisman to Bob.

He had Guthrie's card in his pocket a couple of days later when he met a new friend in Greenwich Village. Kevin Krown, whom Bob had met before on his travels through Colorado and Illinois, was in New York at the time and introduced Bob to young folksinger Mark

Spoelstra. Bob and Spoelstra met in a cafe in Greenwich Village. A street vendor was frying Italian sausage and onions at the time and the aroma wafted across to the cafe, where they nursed cups of coffee. They were too broke to buy food, although they were both famished. Like Bob, Spoelstra had come east to become a music star. Originally from a Quaker family in California, he had already been in New York a couple of months. In his brief time in the city, he had backed up the veteran folk-blues duo Sonny Terry and Brownie McGhee, and he was performing in the afternoons at so-called basket houses like the Commons and the Cafe Wha? where it was customary to pass a bread basket for tips. It was nothing much, but it was more than Bob knew and Kevin Krown thought Bob could profit by Spoelstra's advice. A friendship was formed and Bob and Mark Spoelstra began tagging around together, scratching for work and, almost as importantly, food to eat. 'We didn't have all that many good meals there, those first few months,' says Spoelstra.

The boys would back each other up on stage, taking turns singing. Their repertoire consisted mostly of Woody Guthrie songs and blues, and their big number was the traditional 'Mule Skinner Blues.' They thought they did it better than anybody. 'Bob loved to perform, and he had a magnetism and a strength up there that would sometimes just make me laugh,' says Spoelstra. As the days and weeks went by, more people came into the Cafe Wha? 'People saw it as a happening thing and this was an exciting place to be. So the girls started coming and the guys started following the girls, you know, and pretty soon the place started to fill up.' This did not mean they made much money. In these initial months the boys lived on tips from customers, the occasional couple of dollars from a club owner, and handouts from friends. It is also probable that Bob's parents sent him a little money from home. He certainly did not try to get a regular day job. His brief stint as a bus boy in Fargo back when he graduated from school would remain

Bob's one and only lifetime experience of regular work.

Bob was a personable, likable character and members of established acts befriended him. The New World Singers, for instance, would sometimes give over the stage to Bob for a brief time during their final set of the evening, introducing him to their audiences, and Bob would perform a solo set. 'We just thought he was the greatest thing,' says band member Happy Traum. 'The audience wasn't so sure, because he was pretty rough and raw . . . But he was very animated. He was very funny.' Bob was grateful for the break and told Traum a little about his past life. But it was not Hibbing – or even Dinkytown – he talked about. Instead he made up stories of his adventures in Gallup, New Mexico, where he claimed to have been a carnival hand and itinerant blues singer. 'We bought into the whole myth,' laughs Traum. 'He was just this street urchin who rode freight trains and hitchhiked his way around the country. He fed right into that romantic myth we all had of the nouveau Woody Guthrie.'

Partly because relatively few performers played harmonica, Bob was occasionally invited, with Mark or on his own, to back other acts. One such artist was Fred Neil, a scrappy ginger-haired fellow from Florida with a deep baritone voice. Unusually, Neil wrote his own songs, and later he became famous for composing 'Everybody's Talkin',' the theme to *Midnight Cowboy*. Neil paid Bob and Spoelstra a couple of bucks to back him on stage. Spoelstra claims Neil also goosed the boys on the backside whenever they met him; while Spoelstra said to knock it off, Bob would just laugh. 'He was open to meeting everybody,' says Spoelstra. 'He was very tolerant of different people.'

This was generally true of Bob's character. Throughout his life he would have several good friends who happened to be homosexual – the most notable being poet Allen Ginsberg – and he never betrayed any prejudice or uneasiness about it. Early on in New York, hanging out almost every night in the downtown bars and clubs of Greenwich Village, Bob and Spoelstra met all sorts of characters. In a 1966 interview, Bob hinted that he was propositioned by homosexuals, and went so far as to claim that when he first came to New York he and a friend operated as hustlers around Times Square. 'We would make one hundred fifty or two hundred fifty a night between us, and hang around in bars. Cats would pick us up and chicks would pick us up.' Spoelstra discounts this as one of Bob's tall tales, and dismisses any suggestion that Bob may have been in any way gay. 'We all had to 'hustle,' that is worry about where we were going to sleep, but I never had to sell my body for it,' he says. '[Bob] never propositioned me and I never saw him do it with any man. That doesn't mean to say we never competed for women. Neither of us stayed lonely for long during that wild half year or so.'

The reality of Bob's first 'wild half year' in New York was that he relied on the charity of kindhearted women. Initially, he spent some time with Guthrie's New Jersey friends, Bob and Sidsel Gleason. Sid worried about the company Bob was keeping in the Village, and gave him pocket money. Bob was evasive about his background and gave the impression that he had been raised in foster homes. Soon he was calling Sid 'Mom' and she thought of him as part of her family. Although she doted upon him, Sid would be just one of several women who helped Bob out in this way over the next few months. He never stayed in one place for very long and got into a habit of taking advantage of the hospitality of people like the Gleasons only sporadically so that he would not outlast his welcome.

It was Bob's apparent vulnerability that endeared him to people like Sid Gleason. But there was also an inner toughness that allowed him to survive well in the city. When Bonnie Beecher came to New York with her theater group in the early spring of 1961, and anxiously sought Bob out, she found him in much better shape than she had expected. Indeed, he was bursting to tell her about his exciting new life. 'One of the things he really wanted me to do was go back and tell [our friends] he really did know Woody Guthrie. That was the big deal,' says Bonnie. To prove he knew Guthrie, Bob took Bonnie to the VA hospital in New Jersey and Bonnie came away with the impression of a special closeness between Bob and Guthrie. As Dylan became successful, stories inevitably grew that Guthrie somehow chose him as his successor. For example, Guthrie has been quoted as saying, 'Pete Seeger's a singer of folk songs, not a folksinger. Jack Elliott is a singer of folk songs. But Bobby Dylan is a folksinger. Oh Christ, he's a folksinger alright.' But Guthrie's manager, Harold Leventhal, discounts this. 'Woody never said anything about anybody visiting him,' says Leventhal. 'At that point he literally never held a conversation. He couldn't.' The truth was that the meetings were much more significant to Bob than they were to Guthrie, who was very sick indeed. He may have laughed and twinkled when Bob sang for him, as Nora puts it, but that did not mean he recognized the boy. 'Bobby was just another visitor,' says Leventhal. 'I don't think Woody thought anything of him.' Pete Seeger agrees with Leventhal. 'Woody just sat on the couch and we weren't quite sure if he recognized anybody or not,' he says. 'He was already too far gone.' If Guthrie had difficulty recognizing a friend of more than twenty years, it is doubtful he would have formed a bond with Bob, whom he knew only briefly and when he was in very poor health.

For the young musician, however, the meetings with Guthrie were momentous. 'He was seeing his guru,' as Leventhal puts it. One Sunday night after visiting Guthrie in New Jersey, Bob sat down and finished 'Song to Woody.' This was his first important composition, a fine tribute to his idol, an acknowledgment of fellow travelers Cisco Houston, Sonny Terry, and Leadbelly, and a way of including himself in that elevated company.

Nora Guthrie believes the song is partly responsible for the public's enduring interest in Guthrie. 'There was always a small circle of people that loved my dad's work – Pete Seeger and Alan Lomax, people like that. But Bob was the first one when the media became mass media.'

The melody of 'Song to Woody' was adapted from a Woody Guthrie song called '1913 Massacre.' This was no ethical lapse; Guthrie himself was known for appropriating melodies. The lyrics were also familiar. One of the most striking and poetic phrases – in the last line of the fourth verse – was an adaptation of 'we come with the dust and we go with the wind' from Guthrie's 'Pastures of Plenty.'

Just as important as Guthrie's melodies and lyrics was the way he sounded when he sang, and in homage Bob copied this, too. Guthrie spoke and sang in the vernacular language of his native Oklahoma, but along with Pete Seeger he prided himself on clear diction. The words to songs were very important to both men. By the time Bob met him, Guthrie's voice was slurred by Huntington's chorea. The sound of his breath preceded his words. Instead of clearly singing, for example, 'I'm ramblin' around,' he would huff, 'hh-I'm ramblin' a-hh-round.' Marjorie Guthrie, who later founded the Huntington's Disease Society and became an authority on the illness, believed Bob, as well as the other young musicians who visited, mistakenly copied these vocal eccentricities as the authentic Guthrie voice. Her daughter Nora says that 'She was convinced that these young guys were picking up these early Huntington's symptoms . . . holding a note and then kind of trailing [off], which was really a lack of control. That became the style [and] the jumping off point for Dylan.'

When Bob was a star, Marjorie Guthrie would go backstage at concerts and tell him that, although she loved him, she could not understand the words. 'You gotta speak clearly,' she would say. 'Woody would never have sung like that.'

* * *

One of the most important folk music venues in Greenwich Village was Gerde's Folk City on West 4th Street, and Bob was eager to perform here. By day the club was a traditional Italian restaurant with red flock wallpaper and a jukebox loaded with Frank Sinatra records. At night owner Mike Porco, who spoke English like Chico Marx, presided over what became known as the best folk club in New York. Major acts were booked in for two weeks straight, at minimum union rates, performing up to three sets a night on the tiny stage. Many talented and up-and-coming discovered artists passed through Gerde's at this time, including The Clancy Brothers, Tom Paxton, and Dave Van Ronk.

Like most Village venues, Monday night at Gerde's was hootenanny or open-mike night. Bob, who spent Monday evenings going from club to club, appeared to be so young that Porco wanted proof of his age the first time he asked to play. Finally the young Dylan got on stage and regaled the Gerde's audience with obscure Woody Guthrie V.D. songs. Tom Paxton and Dave Van Ronk were sitting in the audience drinking beer. Both were imposing young men with more experience than Bob. Paxton had come to the Village from the army and, at first, people thought he was an undercover police officer because of his stature and short hair. Dave Van Ronk was also a large man, a former merchant marine whose beard made him look a good deal older than his twenty-five years. He delivered standards like 'House of the Risin' Sun' in a distinctively gruff voice, and had already recorded an album for Folkways. 'Both Dave and I were impressed [with Bob],' says Paxton. 'And almost from the first day, Bob was what the buzz was about.'

Dave Van Ronk became an important friend and mentor to Bob during his first couple of months in New York, letting him sleep on the sofa at his 15th Street apartment. 'He would stay sometimes two nights consecutively, but rarely more than that. Bob was a very accomplished *schnorer*, a Yiddish term. Somebody who mooches for a living. And a smart *schnorer* never wears out his welcome. He'd stay at our place for a while. Then he'd go over and stay with people in Jersey that he knew.' This peripatetic life did not seem to embarrass Bob. Indeed, he thrived on it and in later life, when he was wealthy and owned several properties, he would often choose to sleep on a friend's couch just because he liked it.

Van Ronk's wife, Terri, worked unofficially as Bob's booking agent for a short time, but it was not easy to find work for Bob. Many club owners were only interested in artists that aspired to the polish of acts like The Kingston Trio. 'Nobody wanted to hire Bobby. He was too raw,' says Van Ronk. Manny Dworman would not even let Bob perform for free at Cafe Feenjon. 'I wasn't crazy about Dylan's music,' he explains. 'To me he looked like some young kid trying to pretend he was a weather-beaten [folk musician].' This sort of reception must have caused Bob concern, but he kept any fear of failure to himself and it was too early to give up and go home – he had been in New York only a month or so.

Bob's relationship with Dave Van Ronk was similar to the one he'd had with Dave Morton and Dave Whitaker in Dinkytown. Here was another slightly older man who was knowledgeable about music, literature, and philosophy, and who filled the role of teacher. Bob learned from him, but he did not want to appear to be learning. 'He was unteachable!' says Van Ronk, who tried to show Bob guitar techniques. 'He had to reinvent the wheel all the time. Any number of people tried to show him finger picking of the guitar, but he just seemed to be impervious. He had to work it out for himself, and he did eventually. He became a reasonably good finger picker. But I can't claim any credit for it. You could almost say he could not acquire anything except by stealing it. That is to say that he would watch, and if you tried to explain to him, he would [affect a lack of interest].'

One reason Bob did not ask advice was that he did not want to look foolish in front of the acerbic Van Ronk or the other friends he was making in the Village. These people were mostly older and more experienced than Bob and he showed wisdom in listening. 'Bobby always had the virtue of knowing when to keep his mouth shut, possibly because he had a tendency to put his foot in it when it flapped open,' says Van Ronk. This restraint dissolved when he was drinking, however, and Bob would tell ridiculously improbable stories about his past life. One of the most extraordinary tales was that he was descended not from eastern European Jews but from Native Americans. Bob claimed that he was, in fact, part Sioux Indian. 'Nobody held it against him,' chuckles Van Ronk. 'Reinventing yourself has always been part of show business. But he sort of got backed into a corner with his own story. I remember he solemnly gave us a demonstration of Indian sign language, which he was obviously making up as he went along.'

When one considers Bob's circumstances it is perhaps understandable that, when he did talk about his background, which was rare enough, he felt compelled to build himself up in front of his new friends. He was, after all, from a relatively insignificant small town in Minnesota, trying to keep his head above water in New York City. He probably did not think his genuine, rather ordinary biography would carry him very far in such a dynamic place. It should also be remembered that he was still only nineteen, with a teenager's mixture of awkwardness and the desire to make a mark in the world.

Despite his awkwardness he continued to enlarge his circle of New York friends, meeting many influential characters at Gerde's Folk City or via people he knew from the club. For instance, in February 1961 Woody Guthrie's closest friend, Cisco Houston, gave a farewell series of performances at Gerde's Folk City. Houston was dying of cancer and had to be helped on stage. The first night was an emotional evening and many old friends came to see him. Marjorie Guthrie was there in the audience with her children and Guthrie family friends Eve and Mac McKenzie, whom she introduced to Bob, telling them he was a singer from New Mexico, the story Bob was then putting about. Bob was huddled in an oversized overcoat, chain-smoking and twitching nervously. Eve McKenzie thought he looked like an undernourished urchin out of a Charles Dickens novel. She offered him a plate of food. 'You don't have to pay for it,' she told him. 'Eat!'

The McKenzies became good friends of Bob and it was through them that he met his first New York girlfriend, Avril, a dancer from California. They lived together briefly in her studio apartment on East 4th Street and sometimes would come to the McKenzies' apartment on East 23rd Street for dinner. One day Avril showed up alone and in some distress. 'He's gone!' she said. 'He just picked himself up and he left.' Bob had apparently made a quick trip back to Minnesota. In his absence, Avril went home to the San Francisco Bay area, which was the end of the relationship. Bob then picked up with a dark-haired girl named Linda, whom he stayed with for a short time. The relationship did not last any longer than with Avril and one day in the spring of 1961 Bob presented himself at the McKenzies' apartment, with his guitar and bag, looking for a place to stay.

'Well, here I am!' he exclaimed.

Bob then stayed with the McKenzie family on and off through the summer of 1961, becoming a member of the family, as he had with the Gleasons. His routine was that he would get up around noon, eat a late breakfast of eggs, coffee, and orange juice, prepared by Eve, who worried he was drinking too much and not eating enough. He would scribble lyrics for songs he was working on, mostly blues-inspired. Then Eve would give him some small change, so that he had money in his pocket, and he would go out to meet Mark Spoelstra. They usually walked down to Greenwich Village together. Although short of stature, Bob walked so briskly Spoelstra almost had to run to keep up. 'You might as well not take the bus if you were walking with Dylan,' he says. 'Just walk with him and you'll beat the bus across town.' Sometimes Spoelstra put his guitar down and asked with irritation, 'What's the hurry, man?' Bob was in a fearful hurry and did everything fast. He even played chess at breakneck speed. He was good, too, beating Spoelstra three times in a matter of minutes.

One of the most important older folk artists Bob met around this time was Ramblin' Jack Elliott, whose recordings he had admired ever since he heard them at Jon Pankake's apartment in Dinkytown. After returning from England by ship over the winter of 1960–61, Elliott went to see Woody Guthrie at the hospital in New Jersey and found Bob sitting by the bed. On the bus ride back into Manhattan, Bob told Elliott he had listened to all his records. Elliott thought him a fascinating and engaging young man, 'barely able to grow a beard at the time – he had a little peach fuzz – he hadn't even started to shave.' Bob then began following Ramblin' Jack around, 'like a puppy dog,' which became tiresome to Elliott, who says he remembers trying to escape him.

When Elliott took a room at the Earle Hotel on Washington Square, Bob took a room a few doors down for a short time. Friends said Bob was copying Ramblin' Jack's performance style, adopting his mannerisms, even the way he held the guitar high up on his chest. But Elliott did not care. 'I went through a period when I was imitating Woody perhaps more than Bob ever imitated me,' he says. 'They thought I was pretending to be Woody. I was just searching for a way to sing and kinda learnin' how, and imitating him. It's very easy for me – I'm a natural mimic. When Bob started doing it to me, I didn't even notice it. I thought that's just the way he was because he was another Woody fan. And I defended him to all those detractors who were very angry about it and very much on my side, supposedly, and would say, "Jack, he's taken the wind right out of your sails! How can you let him get away with that?" Stuff like this, you know, and I thought, well, imitation's the sincerest form of flattery . . . I said, "He's just tryin' to sound like Woody and Cisco." I [said], "This guy, he likes people who have been out there workin', and people who have been traveling around the country and having a hard time. So naturally he is following in the footsteps of Woody and Cisco, singing their style." And that's what I was trying to do, too.'

Another important musical association for Bob in these early months was meeting the Irish folk group The Clancy Brothers. The three brothers – Paddy, Tom, and Liam – played Gerde's Folk City twice in the early months of 1961, invariably with their friend Tommy Makem. Originally from County Tipperary in the Republic of Ireland, the Clancys had become sufficiently successful in America to have their own small record label, Tradition Records, which the elder brother, Paddy, ran from an office on Christopher Street. They had recorded three albums by 1961 and were one of the first folk revival acts signed by Columbia Records, part of the giant Columbia Broadcasting System (CBS).

In their cable-knit sweaters and fisherman's caps, the Clancys looked like a nostalgia act, but they sang fiery songs of the bloody history of Ireland. Paddy Clancy had been a member of the Irish Republican Army and traditional songs like 'Roddy McCorley' commemorated heroes of the Republican cause. The Clancys delivered these songs with white-knuckle passion, but they would also perform heartbreakingly tender songs like 'Eileen Aroon.' Bob was fascinated with the rich language of these traditional Irish songs and moved by the passion of the performances. Although the songs came from a different place and time, the characters reminded him of American folk heroes. The highwayman of 'Brennan on the Moor' was very much like an outlaw of the West. 'One of the things he liked about the songs we sang was that it was *rebellion* music,' says Makem. The supposed romance of outlaw figures later became a motif of Bob's own songwriting.

The younger Clancy brother, Liam, was an exceptionally gifted singer, perhaps the greatest ballad singer Bob had ever heard. Liam – or Willie to family and friends – was also a raconteur, ladies' man, and drinker. Bob began to tag around with the Irishman as he caroused the bars of Greenwich Village, taking Bob into the Lion's Head or the White Horse Tavern, where Bob's namesake, Dylan Thomas, had been a regular customer. There were still people around who claimed to remember the late poet, including a prostitute who said slurrily that he had been a 'lousy man,' which made them laugh. As they hit the bars, the boy from Minnesota and the boy from Tipperary found they had something in common that transcended culture and birth place. They were out of their natural habitat, struggling to make their way in a strange and sometimes hostile city, and this common experience brought them together. 'We were all kind of orphans of the storm,' says Clancy. 'We were artists who didn't know what the artistic mind meant because it was rejected in all the places that we came from, like me coming from a small town in Ireland and Dylan coming from Hibbing. You know, everybody around us was escaping a background of repression and it wasn't that we all took great delight in each other's company. We had a common bond of struggling together for our own particular vision. It was that kind of camaraderie.' It was a camaraderie that endured in Bob's mind. Years later, long after he had lost contact with most old friends from the Village, he was always pleased to see Liam Clancy.

Clancy was one of several friends who began to urge Mike Porco to give Bob a proper paid gig at Gerde's Folk City. Regular Gerde's customers Mel and Lillian Bailey, who had befriended Bob in the same way the Gleasons and McKenzies had, spoke up for the boy. So did Dave Van Ronk and *New York Times* music critic Robert Shelton, who became an important friend. 'Tell me, you would like to work a couple weeks?' Porco eventually asked Bob in late March 1961.

'With who?' asked Bob, knowing he would be supporting a name act.

'With John Lee Hooker.'

'Ooo yeah,' said Bob, excitedly. John Lee Hooker was one of the great blues artists he used to listen to on the radio.

First, though, Bob had to join the American Federation of Musicians. In early April, Porco took Bob to see the local union representative. Because Bob was under twenty-one, the union representative wanted Bob's mother with him to complete the paperwork. According to Porco's recollection, Bob announced to the union man: 'I ain't got no mother.'

'That's all right. Come with your father.'

'I ain't got no father, either.'

The union man whispered to Porco, 'What is he, a bastard?' In the end, Porco – who assumed Bob was a runaway – signed as his guardian. He advanced him the $46 union subscription, gave him some clothes that had belonged to his own children, and money for a haircut. However, Bob had peculiar ideas about his hair. 'The first time I ever got a haircut I got very sick, and since then I've been very superstitious about barbers. I won't let a barber touch my hair,' he told Porco, apparently seriously but it seems suspiciously like one of Bob's fanciful stories made up on the spur of the moment. Bob had a theory about the length of hair. 'The more hair you have outside your head, the less there is cluttering up the inside of your head. Crew cuts are bad. . . . I let my hair grow long so's I can be wise and free to think.' Even though he was probably joking, Bob always did prefer to have his girlfriends trim his hair rather than go to a barber, even after he became rich.

On April 11, 1961, Bob walked on stage at Gerde's Folk City dressed in ill-fitting, borrowed clothes that made him appear somewhat comical. At this point in his career Bob would bumble around on stage, doing bits of business with his harmonica rack and the stool. One of his gags was to leave the strings of his guitar very long and joke that the guitar needed a haircut. The ill-fitting clothes made this stage business seem Chaplinesque, as several people commented. Yet he could also be serious when he sang songs such as 'Song to Woody' and 'House of the Risin' Sun,' in an arrangement cribbed from Dave Van Ronk. Some in the audience, including Oscar Brand, were not particularly impressed. Bob was obviously borrowing ideas from Guthrie, and Brand knew the real Guthrie well enough not to require an imitation. Even so, there was something impressive about the boy. 'He wasn't just singing for a little while until he could become a doctor or a lawyer,' says Brand. 'This is what he did, and this is what he was gonna do, and nothing was gonna stop him, even if he had to sing for pennies.'

Bob was disconcerted that *New York Times* journalist Robert Shelton did not bother to hear his set, being more interested in talking with John Lee Hooker. The blues singer himself was happy to have found a friend in Bob. 'What he was doing was blues, but it was folk-blues,' says Hooker. 'He loved my style and that's why he got with me and we would hang out together all the time.' Hooker was staying at the Broadway Central Hotel, a dive on 5th Street. Bob came up to his room after they had finished playing, bringing his guitar and some wine. Hooker recalls that he had difficulty getting to sleep as Bob and his young friends continued drinking and joking into the early hours. 'We were great friends,' says Hooker. 'A beautiful man.' Bob earned ninety dollars a week for supporting Hooker, which was not much when one remembers they were playing six nights a week. Hooker says Bob was not very interested in money. 'He really wasn't playing with me for money. He was doing it for fun.'

In May, Bob and Mark Spoelstra earned a few dollars performing at the Indian Neck Folk Festival in Branford, Connecticut. It was here that Bob first met art-school student Bobby Neuwirth, who became an important friend a few years later. After the festival, Bob returned to Minnesota, intending to spend some time traveling around the country. It was a chance to actually take some of those exciting road trips he talked about all the time but had, in fact, never undertaken. 'I didn't plan to stay in New York,' he said. 'I left, anyway, in the spring, and didn't plan to come back.' He had much to tell his Dinkytown friends: meetings with Woody Guthrie, performing with John Lee Hooker, and hanging out with Ramblin' Jack and Liam Clancy. He had been in New York only four months, but had enjoyed more success than anyone might have expected. Bonnie Beecher made a recording of Bob at this time, performing songs from his current repertoire. The jokey 'Why'd You Cut My Hair?' was the only original composition, inspired by the too-short haircut Bonnie had given him the previous year. Other songs were traditional numbers like 'Man of Constant Sorrow,' and some Woody Guthrie songs. There was not much originality in this, but Bob was singing with more confidence than ever.

Bob had hoped to stay with Bonnie but in his absence she had become involved with another young man. 'I told him face to face,' she says. 'I remember having a scene with him where he was trying to get it clear whether or not I was going to be his girl or not.'

'Okay, I get it,' said Bob, when she did not say what he wanted. This was the 'kneeing in the guts' Bob later wrote about in 'My Life in a Stolen Moment.' 'I think it had something to do with the reason he left for New York again, and stayed,' says Bonnie. 'I hurt him a lot.' Despite this incident they managed to remain friends for many years to come. 'The relationship lasted quite a long time. We were really close. When we were no longer lovers, or were only occasionally lovers, we would see each other sometimes and then we would be together again for a short while.' In the short term the rejection had the effect of bouncing Bob straight back to New York, before he had a chance to do any more traveling.

Back in Greenwich Village another important folk venue Bob frequented was the Gaslight Club, situated in the basement of a tenement on MacDougal Street. It was diagonally across the street from the Cafe Wha? and a couple of doors down from Israel 'Izzy' Young's music store, the Folklore Center, a hangout for folk musicians. The Gaslight was a claustrophobic, noisy hole with steam pipes that knocked. Its entertainment director was the poet and stand-up comedian Hugh Romney, later famous as Wavy Gravy, Merry Prankster, hippy clown, and Ben & Jerry ice-cream flavor. Wavy Gravy claims the distinction of having introduced Bob to the Gaslight audience, although he offers a disclaimer that not everything he says is reliable because, as he puts it, some of his chromosomes have amnesia. 'I remember when Bob first came down to the Gaslight, I think he was wearing Woody Guthrie's underwear. He had just been to visit Guthrie at the hospital and somehow he had snagged a pair of underwear,' he insists.

Bob first approached Wavy Gravy at the Gaslight some time in the spring of 1961 and asked if he could have a spot on stage on hootenanny night. Gravy agreed to introduce him. 'Here he is, a legend in his own lifetime,' Gravy announced. Then he turned to Bob and asked, sotto voce, 'What's your name, kid?'

Bob and Gravy spent time together during 1961 hanging out at Gravy's tiny apartment over the Gaslight, sitting around an old wood-burning stove, or in a basement across the street where friends kept lighting and sound equipment. 'We'd smoke a little pot and I had a typewriter and Bob would slam away at this old Remington.' Wavy Gravy knew the hippest people in the village, including jazz pianist Thelonius Monk, poet Allen Ginsberg, and comedian Lenny Bruce. He may have introduced Bob to Lenny Bruce. It is also likely he introduced Bob to the recordings of pop-eyed comedian Lord Buckley, who performed in a pith helmet. By the end of the year Buckley's satirical rap 'Black Cross' was included in Bob's evolving repertoire. These times spent with Gravy were sufficiently important to Bob for him to write about them nostalgically in the song 'Bob Dylan's Dream,' recorded in 1963. In the song, he described the times he spent with Gravy in the room with the stove, saying he would give $10,000 to sit there again.

Another character at the Gaslight Bob became friendly with was master of ceremonies and stand-up comic Noel Stookey, known to some as 'Toilet Man' for his impression of a flushing toilet. Although Stookey did not think highly of Bob at first, he was impressed when Bob took a traditional folk song about a fur trapper and rewrote it as a comic song about a club in New Jersey. 'This guy takes years of folk history, and the evolution of the American ballad form, and uses it to reflect something contemporarily,' he says. 'I was flabbergasted.' Stookey then read a story in the *New York Herald Tribune* about a family cruise up the Hudson River to Bear Mountain State Park. The jaunt turned into a brawl when the boat was oversold. 'You know, Bobby, you could write this,' he said, giving Bob the cutting. 'There's real humor about the natural state of human greed here.' Three nights later Bob came back to the Gaslight with one of his best early songs, the comic 'Talking Bear Mountain Picnic Massacre Blues.'

Bob had recently written another good talking blues, 'Talking New York,' which gave a humorous account of his early days in the city, and he came up with several other comic songs during the summer of 1961. Walking uptown with Tom Paxton, Bob improvised a parody on The Almanac Singers' 'Talkin' Union,' which he and Paxton called 'Talkin' Central Park Mugger Blues.' Bob also came up with a satire of the middle classes, 'Here in the Land of the Beautiful People.' With the notable exception of 'Song to Woody,' this was the type of light, satirical material Bob was writing in his early months in New York. Yet, importantly, he was beginning to write with increasing frequency. At the same time he was also learning songs from other artists, songs that became part of his repertoire alongside these talking songs. One of the most significant was 'Baby Let Me Follow You Down,' which he learned from singer Eric Von Schmidt in Cambridge, Massachusetts. Bob performed the song with such care and skill that he made it his own.

By June he had grown sufficiently as a performer to share a week's residency at the Gaslight Club with Dave Van Ronk. In the crowd was Roy Silver, a show business manger who represented the up-and-coming comedian Bill Cosby. 'I met [Bob] in the Village and told him that I would represent him if he would keep quiet and listen to me,' says Silver, who did not realize at first what a significant find he had made. '[Bob was] very young [and] didn't give a lot of himself . . . He was just Bobby.' They signed a five-year 'management agreement,' with Silver taking a twenty percent commission. This was not such a major development as it might seem. Bob saw Silver simply as an agent who might get him more bookings, rather than someone to guide his career, and even with Silver's help bookings were still sparse and poorly paid.

As Bob was working his way up through the New York clubs in the summer of 1961 he met Susan 'Suze' Rotolo, the third significant girlfriend of his young life. A tiny, brown-haired teenager who pronounced her name *Suze-ee*, she was born in November 1943, the youngest daughter of blue-collar Italian-American parents. Her factory-worker father died when she was fourteen, leaving her with her mother, Mary, and elder sister, Carla. The Rotolo women were politically active on the left, and culturally sophisticated. Suze was an artist who read Arthur Rimbaud and Lord Byron, and became involved in Bertolt Brecht theater productions. Carla was secretary to eminent musicologist Alan Lomax. Bob became a regular visitor at the Lomax apartment on West 3rd Street where Alan's daughter Anna – then sixteen – recalls he took particular interest in their copy of the Harry Smith *Anthology of American Folk Music* (which he had probably already discovered for himself in the Twin Cities, but which he was directed to again). 'He used to hang around all the time,' says Anna. 'Alan said to Dylan, "This is what you ought to listen to. You should go and learn all these songs by heart if you want to understand American folk music." '

'Suze was a member of an antinuclear group, SANE, and picketed Woolworth stores because their lunch counters were segregated in the South. On Sundays during the summer she was one of a crowd of people who congregated around the fountain in Washington Square Park to listen to musicians playing folk, blues, and hillbilly music. She also began to attend hootenannies at Gerde's Folk City and elsewhere, first seeing Bob perform with Mark Spoelstra. Suze was initially attracted to Spoelstra, but was won over by Bob's musicianship and engaging stage persona. They began a relationship in July after spending time together at a marathon hootenanny at the Riverside Church on the Upper West Side. Suze was only seventeen, still a high school student, and legally under age if they wanted to sleep together. One day Bob brought her over to meet Spoelstra. 'What do you think?' he whispered, taking Spoelstra aside.

'Why are you asking me?'

'She's really young.'

Spoelstra told Bob he was lucky to have a beautiful young girl so obviously fond of him. It was true that Suze adored Bob, affectionately calling him 'Pig' or 'Raz,' a nickname taken from the initials of his given name. Bob was also besotted. It was not long before he was talking about marriage, just as he had with Bonnie Beecher. As Bob later wrote in his poem '11 Outlined Epitaphs,' Suze was his 'fawn in the forest.' She lived with her mother in an apartment building at One Sheridan Square. Mikki Isaacson, known as the 'folk mother' because she loved to look after the vagabond singers who wandered through the Village, lived in the same building. Bob sometimes spent the night at Isaacson's, sleeping on an inflatable mattress in the lounge. He said he could not sleep until Suze had come down from her mother's apartment to wish him goodnight.

Sometimes Bob and Suze went out as a couple with Dave Van Ronk and his wife, or with bluegrass musician John Herald and his girlfriend, Janet Reynolds, also a friend of Suze. But Herald says he and Bob tended to exclude girlfriends from social occasions, not treating them as equals. 'We were all hard-core chauvinists back then. It was a different world between men and women,' says Herald. 'Even though in our personal relationships we assumed we could do anything we want[ed], the girl-friend would stay at home and maybe cook us a meal.'

Bob and John Herald went to the Apollo Theater in Harlem to see gospel shows. In the summer, they paid a nickel to catch the ferry to Staten Island, then a bus to the beach. Bob was a good and enthusiastic swimmer, and entertained Herald with trick dives. Although they spent a lot of time together, Bob rarely said anything serious about himself. It was usually only when he was performing that he allowed himself to be vulnerable. 'It was hard to talk to him on a personal level, about girlfriends or anything. It would always be a joke,' says Herald. 'But if you didn't need to get personal with him, you just wanted somebody to hang out with and play music with, he was a ball. He just liked to kid around.'

Bob also relaxed by watching movies, just as he had back in Hibbing when he was fixated with James Dean. Now it was foreign films that gripped his imagination. He became particularly enchanted with François Truffaut's film *Shoot the Piano Player*, in which French singer Charles Aznavour played a barroom pianist with a mysterious past. Toward the end of the film the enigmatic Aznavour character is involved in a shoot-out at a snowbound house in the country. This snow scene reminded Bob strongly of his childhood in Minnesota. But the film had more meaning for him than that. The Aznavour character was like Bob in many ways – a shy, unassuming, and diminutive man with enormous talent who lived for music, and for the love of women. Bob saw the movie again and again. 'Everything about that movie I identified with,' he said. When Aznavour came to New York to perform, Bob was in line for a ticket. In later life, when Bob was in a position to make movies of his own, it was *Shoot the Piano Player* he referred to as the sort of movie he was aiming for.

Joan Baez was only six months older than Bob but she was already a major star in America, selling out solo concerts in large theaters across the country. Despite coming on stage barefoot like a simple peasant girl, and singing traditional folk songs in a virginal soprano, Baez was a feisty, egocentric, and clever young woman who had not yet met her equal in life. Her first meeting with Bob was at Gerde's Folk City on a night Bob and Mark Spoelstra were performing. By coincidence, Mark Spoelstra had dated Baez briefly in 1956 when they were teenagers in California. 'Joanie had a way of grabbing men, just like she did to me when I was sixteen. She would grab any man she wanted and just get him. She would just take control of guys. Like her mother once said to me, "Joanie with men, I don't know, she just chews them up and spits them out."' In her well-observed memoir, *And a Voice to Sing With*, Baez described her inauspicious first impressions of Bob, the man she would fall in love with and be associated with for the rest of her life although, in fact, their actual romance was brief. 'He looked like an urban hillbilly, with hair short around the ears and curly on top. Bouncing from foot to foot as he played, he seemed dwarfed by the guitar. His jacket was a rusty leather and two sizes too small. His cheeks were still softened with an undignified amount of baby fat. But his mouth was a killer: soft, sensuous, childish, nervous, and reticent. He spat out the words to his own songs. . . He was absurd, new, and grubby beyond words.'

Despite his grubbiness, Baez felt she wanted to know Bob better. She was more than a little irritated therefore when, the next time they met, not long afterward, Bob showed more interest in her fifteen-year-old sister, Mimi. Joan and Mimi's father, Albert, was born in Mexico and the Baez girls were both dark-skinned with long black hair. Mimi was more slender than Joan and, arguably, slightly more lovely looking. She wore a simple white dress the night she met Bob and looked particularly striking. 'I found [Bob] appealing. He was not really the center of attention that evening, but in fact he was because even then he was charismatic,' says Mimi. Bob flirted with Mimi, although he was dating Suze, and invited her to a party. Joan reminded her little sister she had to be up early the next morning, and had better get home.

The great romance between Bob and Joan Baez was still some way off. So was Bob's recording career, and there were several dead ends before he landed a recording contract. Izzy Young of the Folklore Center took Bob to Folkways Records, but owner Moses 'Moe' Asch was not interested. '[They] kicked him out,' says Young. '[Bob] wasn't dressed the right way or something.' Bob went to Elektra, where he made little impression on company president Jac Holzman. Bob spoke with Manny Soloman at Vanguard Records, the label Baez was with. Solomon did show interest, but there was no deal. Bob and Mark Spoelstra had a tryout recording session as a duo with another label. Spoelstra sang songs including 'Sister Kate' and 'Dry Land Blues' while Bob backed him on harmonica. Bob was despondent as they left the studio. 'I did terribly,' he complained. 'That was really bad.'

'What? You were great.'

'No. I didn't play well at all. It just didn't feel right.' Apparently, he was correct; the session did not lead to anything.

In October 1961, however, the contacts Bob had made and cultivated during his first ten months in New York came together at exactly the right time to influence A&R executive John Hammond to sign Bob to Columbia Records, the biggest record label in America. At the time, Hammond was perhaps the most distinguished record executive in New York. Born into a society family – his father was a banker and his mother a member of the Vanderbilt family – he was educated at Yale and studied music at Julliard. He became a music journalist, theater impresario, and highly successful record company executive famed for discovering Billie Holiday and promoting Benny Goodman. A tall, distinguished gentleman of fifty, invariably dressed in suit and tie, he was signing folk-revival artists to Columbia. He only wanted the best and carefully scouted around Greenwich Village listening to acts and consulting those, like Paddy Clancy, whose advice he respected. He had another adviser closer to home. Much to his displeasure, Hammond's eighteen-year-old son, John Hammond Jr., had embarked on a career as a blues artist. 'He had a problem with me wanting to be a blues singer, or just being any kind of musician, maybe because he knew what an unfair business it was and how it was a tough life,' says Hammond Jr. The relationship between father and son was strained. But when he had a chance, Hammond Jr. would tell his father about the talented young performers he knew in the village, and one of these was Bob.

One of the first folk-revival artists Hammond signed to Columbia was Texan singer Carolyn Hester, another friend of Bob. They met at Gerde's Folk City earlier in the year after she performed Buddy Holly's song 'Lonesome Tears.' Bob had not forgotten his love of Buddy Holly's music and struck up a conversation with Hester, who happened to be a great beauty. In the months that followed, Hester and husband, Richard Fariña, spent some time socially with Bob and Suze. In August 1961 Bob joined Carolyn Hester on stage at Club 47 in Cambridge, Massachusetts. When she decided to use backup musicians on her debut Columbia record she suggested to John Hammond that Bob play harmonica. Hammond independently asked the advice of Paddy Clancy, who agreed he should give Bob a chance. A rehearsal was arranged at an apartment in the village. 'We were all seated around a kitchen table and John was seated next to Bob,' says Hester. 'Bob starts in on the harmonica and John turns and looks at him and couldn't take his eyes off this great character.' When Hammond discovered that Bob wrote his own material, he said he would like to hear him.

Fortuitously, Bob was about to play an important two-week residency at Gerde's Folk City, on a double bill with John Herald's bluegrass group, The Greenbriar Boys. Robert Shelton had already decided to review the show for the *New York Times*, encouraged in part by Bob's booking agent, Roy Silver, who was a friend of his. Many of Bob's supporters were in the audience the opening night and he received such an enthusiastic reception he upstaged the more experienced Greenbriar Boys. Afterward Bob went into the kitchen and gave his first press interview. He laid it on thick for the *Times*, claiming to have learned some of his guitar licks from a blues musician called Wigglefoot whom he had met in New Mexico, and saying he had recorded with Gene Vincent. Shelton wisely passed over this nonsense, writing that Bob was 'vague about his antecedents and birth place, but it matters less where he has been than where he is going, and that would seem to be straight up.' The article was published in the *New York Times* on Friday, September 29, 1961, together with a photograph of Bob looking like Huckleberry Finn, under the headline: BOB DYLAN: A DISTINCTIVE FOLKSONG STYLIST. It was an unprecedented plug for an unknown folksinger in the most influential newspaper in America, the very newspaper Bob's father read.

The next day Bob was at a recording session with Carolyn Hester, passing around the *Times*, as if his friends had not already seen it. However, Bob did not divulge the really exciting news, which was that Mr. Hammond had offered him a record contract with Columbia Records. There was nothing in writing yet, and Bob had not involved Roy Silver; it was just a verbal agreement between Bob and Hammond. 'Dylan thought I was crazy,' Hammond later said. 'He had been turned down by Folkways and every other label there was at the time. But I thought he had something.' Walking along Seventh Avenue after the Carolyn Hester session, Bob passed a record store and stopped to look at the display of new albums by Frank Sinatra and other artists. He could scarcely believe that he, too, would soon have an album in a shop window. 'It was one of the most thrilling moments in my life,' he said. 'I wanted to go in there dressed in the rags like I was and tell the owner, "You don't know me now, but you will." '

A short time later John Cohen, of The New Lost City Ramblers, was walking across West 53rd Street in midtown when he was surprised to meet Bob. 'What are you doing out of the Village?' asked Cohen.

'What are *you* doin'?' replied Bob.

'I'm going to the Museum of Modern Art. Let me take you.' They went in and looked at an exhibition of paintings by Jean Dubuffet. 'This guy's a little bit like you – sophisticated but primitive!' Cohen wisecracked. Bob seemed distracted. 'I've got some stuff to do,' he said after a while, and hurried away. Cohen later realized Bob must have been on his way to the CBS building – known as 'Black Rock' – situated nearby on Sixth Avenue. It is possible he was going to a formal audition before the deal was done.

The Columbia contract was drawn up on October 25,

one month after the Gerde's appearance. It was a five-year contract that gave Bob a small advance against four percent royalties. Columbia would release one album and then decide whether he merited a second. It was not the most advantageous contract from Bob's point of view, but he did not waste time worrying about the small print. 'I was just so happy to be able to record, I didn't even read it,' he later admitted. Bob signed the contract the day he received it in the post and then ran around the Village telling everybody he was going to make a record. Still he was careful not to offend his friends. 'Hey, man, I gotta contract with Columbia!' he told Liam Clancy, adding diplomatically, 'I ain't never going to be as big as you guys, but I gotta contract.'

After signing the Columbia contract Bob began to attract the attention of an imposing businessman from Chicago who was padding around the Village looking for talent he could represent as a personal manager. When he met Bob, Albert B. Grossman was thirty-five, but he could have passed for a man in his mid-forties. Suze Rotolo's first impression of Grossman was that he was 'an old man.' Grossman was a thoughtful, close-mouthed fellow who dressed for business in suit and tie, and kept his prematurely gray hair neatly combed. He had the lumbering, fleshy body of a bear; in fact, people called him 'The Bear' and he thought of himself that way, using the sobriquet for a club he part-owned in Chicago. Facially, he resembled a lugubrious panda bear with his pallid complexion, gray-streaked hair, and black eyebrows arched over tinted spectacles.

Grossman was born in Chicago in 1926 to Russian-Jewish immigrant parents and received an economics degree from Roosevelt University. He worked for the Chicago Housing Authority, leaving – possibly after being dismissed for misconduct – to go into the club business in the late 1950s. In 1957 he opened the Gate of Horn, which became one of the premier folk clubs in the country, and later he operated the Bear. Grossman made a string of enemies as he elbowed his way to success. 'Asses on seats. People buying drinks. Money in the cash register. That's what Albert knew,' says Nick Gravenites, a Chicago musician Grossman managed. 'He didn't know music from dog shit. But he knew the cash register. He knew it real well.' Gravenites claims Grossman started in the club business because he had an interest in a hot dog concession. 'He was trying to figure out a way to get customers into his place so he could sell them hot dogs.' Along the way, he made and lost fortunes. 'He told me he had gone bankrupt twice before he finally hit it big.'

Bob Gibson, one of the regular performers at the Gate of Horn, was the first folk artist Grossman represented as a personal manager. Grossman had ambitious plans for Gibson, pairing him with Bobby (later Hamilton) Camp in the hope of creating a popular folk duo. He then considered putting Gibson and Camp together with a female singer to form a trio. The big idea was to create a popular group like The Kingston Trio but with the added appeal of a woman member. Joan Baez began her professional career at the Gate of Horn and Grossman tried to sign her, but she turned him down. Then Grossman signed Odetta as a client. She was a major star in her own right and was his first step toward success. 'I was working a whole lot. He would book me in different places and these places would then owe him something for my coming,' says Odetta. 'Albert started his business on my back.'

In 1959 Grossman codirected the first Newport Folk Festival, in Newport, Rhode Island, and subsequently became a familiar face on the East Coast folk scene, always looking for a folk act that would reach a mainstream audience and make him rich. If he could not find the right act, he would manufacture it. Grossman's sharp business sense ran contrary to the idealism of the folk revival, with its undercurrent of left-wing politics and its fixation with authenticity. To be a dust bowl poet, like Woody Guthrie, dying in a VA hospital, was glorious, while making a fortune from the music of the working people was anathema. Many performers disliked Grossman. Dave Van Ronk says Grossman derived pleasure from corrupting young artists and points out that one of his favorite books was *The Magic Christian* by Terry Southern, a darkly comic novel the gist of which was everyone had a price. The saintly Pete Seeger, who rarely disparaged anyone, says, 'I pitied the people who had to work with him.'

The less successful Roy Silver accepted office space from Grossman. It was rather like a fly crawling into a spider's web, and it was not long before Silver was working *with* Grossman, giving Grossman access to Bob Dylan. Although it took a while for their relationship to become serious, Grossman would become one of the most important people in Dylan's career.

Grossman advised Bob informally at first, and urged other members of the Greenwich Village folk community to give the young singer a chance. His method was to let others risk their money and he would wait and watch what happened. With Grossman's encouragement, Izzy Young staged Bob's first solo New York concert. Young, a genial folk enthusiast who occasionally promoted artists he liked, not worrying about whether the shows made money, hired a prestigious uptown venue, the Carnegie Chapter Hall, adjacent to Carnegie Hall itself, and set the date for Saturday, November 4. Before the show, he conducted an interview with Bob for the concert program. After stating truthfully that he had been born in Duluth, and that he had attended high school in Hibbing (which he dismissed as 'a nothing little town'), Bob invented a rip-roaring autobiography that took him through New Mexico, Iowa, Kansas, and the Dakotas. He claimed to have raced motorcycles, worked as a farmhand, and sung in carnivals from the age of fourteen. These were some of the most blatant falsehoods he ever told and he chose to forget them in later life.

Bob went on to tell Izzy Young that he did not know what folk music was before he came to New York, and he displayed the scale of his ambition by disparaging performers he had met there. Ramblin' Jack Elliott – one of his mentors – had apparently wasted his chances, he thought. Turning to Joan Baez, Bob said, 'Her voice goes through me,' though he added that Woody Guthrie believed her voice too pretty. Bob claimed to have met Guthrie in California – a state Bob had not yet visited – and said that Guthrie carried a piece of paper on which were written the lyrics of his own composition, 'Song to Woody.'

To get publicity for the concert, Young then sent Bob to WNYC, where his friend Oscar Brand had hosted a live Sunday evening radio show, *Folksong Festival*, since 1945. WNYC was situated in an eyrie on the twenty-fifth floor of the Municipal Building at the windswept southern tip of Manhattan island. Following in the footsteps of Guthrie, Pete Seeger, and many other great performers who had appeared on the show over the years, Bob took the elevator to the top of the building where the wind whistled through gaps under the windows. Brand was doing Young a favor by having Bob on his program, but Bob refused to abide by the conventions of live radio, fidgeting and strumming his guitar as Brand attempted his introduction. 'I was, I will admit, a little flabbergasted,' says Brand. 'He didn't follow any of the rules. While that was terrific for Bob, and made him a great star, for me it was a little daunting.'

Brand began the broadcast shakily. 'Now, November fourth, Saturday, Bob Dylan will be singing at the Carnegie Chapter . . .' He paused, as if willing Bob to keep quiet. But Bob kept playing his guitar in the background. 'And that should be . . . er . . . a very eventful occasion.' Sarcasm did not work, so Brand spoke more quickly: 'Bob was born in Duluth, Minnesota. But, ah Bob, you weren't raised in Duluth, were you?'

'Ah-I was raised in . . . ah . . . Gallup, N-new Mexico . . .' said Bob, catching his breath like Guthrie with Huntington's.

'Did you get many songs there?'

'Got a lot of cowboy songs there. Indian songs . . . Carnival songs. Vaudeville kinda stuff.'

'Where'd you get your carnival songs from?'

'Ah-uh. People in the carnival,' replied Bob, as if answering a stupid question.

'Did you travel with it, or did you watch the carnival?'

'I traveled with the carnival when I was about thirteen years old.'

'For how long?'

'Ah . . . All the way up till I was nineteen.' Bob strummed a chord. 'Every year. Off and on. I joined different carnivals.'

'Well now, I'd like to hear one of the kinds of music that you've been singing. And I know you've been doing *quite* well.' Bob was making a knocking sound now. 'You'll be singing at Carnegie Chapter Hall. Do you wanna pick something out?'

'Well, I'll pick out a carnival song that I learned . . . I wrote there. Wanna hear one of them, hmm?' There was no need to reply. Brand's exasperating guest had already launched into 'Sally Gal.'

It was obvious Bob had made up his biography, but Brand did not hold that against him. Indeed most of Bob's acquaintances forgave a little self-invention; it was, after all, part of show business and did not harm anyone. 'He wrote a poem which was the life that he wanted,' says Brand. 'He cast it for himself. He wrote it for himself, and he acted it himself. . . . That is what made him successful.'

Despite the guest spot on the radio, and Shelton's *Times* review of his appearance at Gerde's Folk City, the Carnegie Chapter Hall was three quarters empty on the night of Bob's performance. Izzy Young's agreement with Bob was that they would share the gate. When only fifty-two people came (Grossman did not attend, perhaps having already guessed it would be a flop), and it was clear Young would lose money, he gave Bob a few dollars out of his own pocket. Bob seemed a little embarrassed about taking charity, but he made no comment on the fact that so few people had come, being mentally strong enough to deal with failure, which was characteristic of him throughout his career. As Young puts it: 'He took it pretty straight.'

Bob also had more important matters on his mind. Two weeks later, just before Thanksgiving 1961, he went into Columbia Studio 'A' in Manhattan to record his eponymous debut album. John Hammond presided over the sessions, which cost an estimated $402. His son, John Jr., was there for moral support, along with Suze, who gave Bob her lipstick holder to fret his guitar when he played the spiritual 'In My Time of Dyin'.' Most of the thirteen tracks on the album were earthy traditional country blues, delivered in lively new arrangements. Jesse Fuller's 'You're No Good' and Blind Lemon Jefferson's 'See that My Grave Is Kept Clean' were among the covers. Bob prefaced 'Baby, Let Me Follow You Down' with a spoken introduction about how Eric Von Schmidt taught him the song after they met in the 'green pastures of Harvard University.' The following track, 'House of the Risin' Sun,' was sung in an arrangement copied directly from Dave Van Ronk, who was not pleased because he wanted to record the song himself. (He also thought Bob had butchered the song, although Bob's recording became definitive.) These were all engaging songs, performed with verve. But the jewel of the album was 'Song to Woody,' which offered a glimpse of a great new songwriter.

There would be four months to wait until the album was released, not an unusually long period of time in the music industry, but an eternity to Bob. In the meantime, he treasured a set of fragile acetate recordings of the tracks he had laid down. Albert Grossman heard these recordings before the album was released and they served to increase his interest.

When Hamilton Camp arrived from Chicago, Grossman told him: 'You wait till you hear this guy.'

'Jeez, I'd love to sing with him,' replied Camp, thinking naively that Grossman might put them together as a duo.

'You're not going to sing with Bobby,' Grossman retorted, putting Camp in his place. 'This guy is going to be huge.'

Bob was attending a party that night at Grossman's Manhattan apartment and Camp was invited. Grossman was not known for entertaining; a previous party of his had consisted of five people, including Grossman. There was nothing to drink and the only food was a handful of potato chips. This party was slightly better and, as promised, Bob was there. 'Hey, kiddo, I hear yer almost as good as I am,' he said to Camp, when they were introduced. The acetates came out and Grossman stood next to Bob, putting the discs onto the turntable as Bob sat rocking himself back and forth. 'Grossman did nothin' but play those acetates. He was focused on this genius,' says Camp. 'Because he *knew*!'

Grossman began telling Bob he could do much more for his career than Roy Silver. He could book him into prestigious clubs like the Hungry Eye in San Francisco and the Blue Angel and Copacabana in New York. (As Bob noted ruefully during a later legal dispute with Grossman, he never did perform at these venues.) At a time when Silver was struggling to book Bob into minor Greenwich Village clubs and getting him occasional out-of-town engagements, Grossman's promises were seductive. Gradually, Grossman undermined Silver in Bob's estimation. 'Albert would do things that today would be looked at askance,' says Silver. 'I could see that I was gonna lose Bobby because Albert was putting the pressure on him.'

Despite the Columbia deal and the patronage of Albert Grossman, Bob was still virtually broke. When he went back to see friends in the Twin Cities in December he slept on a makeshift bed at the end of a hallway at Dave and Gretel Whitaker's apartment. Three days before Christmas, he got together with Bonnie Beecher and friends and sang another series of songs she taped for posterity. Aside from the regular folk standards, and Woody Guthrie songs, Bob entertained with songs from his forthcoming album and an original composition not on the album, 'Hard Times in New York Town.' This well-crafted, sardonic song showed that Bob was not blind to the harshness of New York; he sang about the hard life of poor people in the city while the likes of John D. Rockefeller lived like kings. He sang about the dirt, the overcrowding, and the inequalities. But he ended the song with a challenge to the city: it could try and beat him, but when he left, he vowed, 'I'll be standin' on my feet.' The defiance showed as much as anything that Bob's self-confidence had carried him through his first year in New York. He would not be afraid to go back when this holiday was over.

Bob called Echo Helstrom while he was in the Twin Cities and arranged to meet her in a dime store downtown. He wanted to tell her about his forthcoming record. Echo was already disenchanted with her early marriage. Her teenage dreams of becoming a famous model had come to nothing. Meanwhile Bob had accomplished much of what he said he would do when they had sat in the L&B Cafe in Hibbing talking about the future, which made Echo bitter. 'We had a pact. John [Bucklen], Bob, and I had a pact that whoever got rich and famous were supposed to help the others,' she says. 'He left us on the side of the road like a half-eaten sack of lunch, thank you.' Yet Bob did offer a helping hand, in his way. He asked Echo to move to New York with him.

'What am I going to do in New York?' she asked him plaintively. 'I have a *baby*.' They agreed to part and he went back east without her, but Bob managed to remain friends with Echo, as he did with Bonnie, for years to come.

It would in fact have been rather embarrassing if Echo had wanted to come back to New York with him, because Suze was waiting there. After the new year, in early 1962, they actually began living together in an $80-a-month studio apartment at 161 West 4th Street. Mrs. Mary Rotolo did not approve, worrying that it would lead to an unsuitable marriage. 'I didn't trust him and I didn't like him and I certainly didn't want him living under the same roof as my daughter,' she said. Mrs. Rotolo thought Bob lacked personal hygiene, was not generous with money, and 'his attitude left a lot to be desired.' In short, Bob was not the stuff of a mother's dream. She referred to Bob as 'The Twerp.' Suze's sister, Carla, was also a thorn in his side. Bob became sufficiently irritated with Carla's interjections to call her 'Carla-in-law'.

Part of the problem with Bob was that a small amount of success had gone to his head. Just before his Carnegie Chapter Hall concert, Mark Spoelstra went to Puerto Rico, became ill, and returned to New York to recuperate. 'You really blew it, Mark,' Bob told him. 'You should not have left New York when you did. Because it broke open for me and it would have broken open for you, too.'

'I don't particularly want to be a big star. Look what's happened to you already,' Spoelstra retorted. He felt Bob had contempt for him. Essentially their friendship was over now that Bob's greater ambition had taken him beyond his former partner's more limited horizons and it left Spoelstra bitter.

In the notebook he kept at the Folklore Center, Izzy Young jotted down memorandums of his discussions with Bob. In one of these he noted Bob saying rather pompously: 'I'm sort of disconnecting myself from the folk music scene,' adding that he was weary of playing coffeehouses for tourists who came looking for 'freaks'. Young was taken aback by this. 'It struck me as very strange . . . Why would he say it? [There is] nothing wrong with folk music.'

On a more positive note, Young wrote that Bob had just

written a significant original folk song, 'Ballad of Emmett Till' (later 'The Death of Emmett Till'). This was based on the true story of a fourteen-year-old African-American boy murdered in Mississippi in 1955 for flirting with a white shop girl. 'I like niggers in their place,' said J. W. Milam, one of the two men accused of the killing. 'I know how to work 'em.' There was an outcry when both men were acquitted of murder. The song was perhaps the first original Dylan composition that could be called a protest song – a song speaking out against injustice.

It was because Bob was writing original songs like 'Ballad of Emmett Till' that John Hammond arranged a publishing deal with Duchess Music, Inc. Bob earned a $1,000 advance for signing with the company, which would try to place his songs with other artists looking for material, thereby earning Bob commission. He was very excited about the deal mostly because Duchess suggested they would publish a songbook of his work when he had enough material. Almost immediately, he started writing with new energy and the songs began to pour out of him.

One of these new songs was written to the melody of 'Brennan on the Moor', a song The Clancy Brothers performed. Liam Clancy and Tommy Makem were heading for the subway late one night when Bob ran up and said he wanted to sing his new song to them then and there. It was called 'Rambling, Gambling Willie.'

'Bobby, how many verses are in it?' asked Clancy, who was known to Bob as Willie.

'Only ten, twelve.'

'Why don't you cut it down to about six? The nature of poetry is brevity. You've got fantastic ideas, fantastic poems, but learn to distill them.'

'I can't, man,' said Bob, possessed by the fervor of creation, although this was only a prelude to his greatest fecundity as a songwriter. 'They just keep flowing out of me.'

Bob started to become so frenetic, friends began to wonder whether he was on something. Some of the time he was. Mark Spoelstra recalls Bob talking about using the hallucinatory drug peyote. But this seems to have been little more than an experiment. Marijuana was more to Bob's taste. John Herald was at Bob's West 4th Street apartment when Bob produced a manila envelope with marijuana in it. 'You ever try any of this?' he asked. Herald had never smoked marijuana. Bob motioned him into the toilet cubicle where they solemnly smoked a joint. They were halfway through when they heard somebody coming up the stairs. Bob became paranoid and he threw the joint into the toilet, flushed, and waved the smoke away in case somebody knocked at the door. Nobody came and John fell asleep on the couch, stoned. 'When I woke up, twenty minutes, a half an hour later, [Bob was] playing the guitar and he was sort of singing what sounded to me like gibberish, just sort of stream of consciousness. Every time he heard himself say something, he'd sort of lean over. He had a little pad and he'd write things down. I often wondered, you know, if that's how he wrote, just by a stream of consciousness.'

The fact that Bob was starting to write good, original songs made him unusual in the folk community and news spread. 'It looked like every day this genius from out of nowhere had a new song, and a good one, not a potboiler, a damn good song. Everybody's talking about him,' says Pete Seeger, who met Bob around this time. The astute Pete Seeger noted that Bob had a sardonic sense of humor, and a sly grin, but also an innate seriousness that was deeper in his character than the flip jokiness he used with most of his friends. Seeger also perceived that Bob was much more than a mere Woody Guthrie copyist, as some had defined him. 'He didn't mold himself upon Woody Guthrie. He was *influenced* by him. But he was influenced by a lot of people. He was his own man, always.'

Seeger and former Almanac Singers colleague Agnes 'Sis' Cunningham were launching a mimeographed magazine, *Broadside*, to disseminate topical folk songs.

Bob was invited to a get-together at Cunningham's home in February 1962 to see if he had any songs that might suit. Also present was up-and-coming singer-songwriter Phil Ochs. Born five months apart into Jewish families, Dylan and Ochs had much in common. They had both been obsessed with James Dean in their youth, and became involved in folk music in the coffeehouses of a university town. Both gravitated to New York where they began writing original material. In Ochs's case this was almost exclusively topical material inspired by stories in the daily newspapers. The musicians played for Cunningham and Seeger with such commitment that Seeger was moved to say he thought he was hearing the best new songs of the age all in one afternoon.

The debut issue of *Broadside* included Bob's song 'Talkin' John Birch Paranoid Blues,' a satire on the right-wing John Birch Society and its fixation with communist infiltration. In Bob's song, a society member looked not only under the bed for a Red, but also up his chimney, in the glove compartment of his car, and down his toilet. When he could not find a communist anywhere, he investigated himself. In the last verse, Bob yelped, 'Hope I don't find out anything . . . great God!'

'Let Me Die in My Footsteps' was another excellent new song he wrote at this time, performed for Izzy Young in his shop and later recorded for an album of *Broadside* ballads. It was a reply to the Cold War obsession with building fallout shelters and carrying out air-raid drills. 'Bob had completely captured the zeitgeist,' says Tom Paxton, who felt particularly strongly about the subject because a friend of his was sentenced to thirty days for disobeying an air-raid drill.

With songs like 'The Death of Emmett Till,' 'Talkin' John Birch Paranoid Blues,' and 'Let Me Die in My Footsteps,' Bob was articulating the thoughts of millions of young people. The racial inequalities in the South were scandalous; the paranoia about communist infiltration was risible; and it seemed insane to spend millions of dollars on fallout shelters in expectation of a nuclear holocaust that would make the world uninhabitable. Suze was instrumental in bringing out Bob's social awareness. He had never shown much interest in political or social causes, but she was very active in various antinuclear and civil rights groups, including the Congress for Racial Equality (CORE), and Bob was devoted to her. In February, Bob performed at a benefit concert for CORE. It was one of the very few times in his life that he took an active part in a political event.

Of all the social issues of the day, with the possible exception of the unequal way in which women were treated, discrimination against African-Americans was perhaps the most significant and obvious social inequity in America. Bob himself seemed oblivious to racial differences. 'Bobby, you know, had no color denomination to him at all,' said the singer Victoria Spivey. 'Everybody was people, not color.' Spivey was one of the first female African-American singers to cross over to a mainstream audience, with her song 'Black Snake Blues.' She first met Bob when she performed at Gerde's Folk City in September 1961. Bob ingratiated himself with the fifty- five-year-old by hugging her and telling her she was a 'gorgeous creature.' The following spring Victoria was due to record with 'Big' Joe Williams, who had also come to New York to play at Gerde's. Van Ronk and others assumed Bob's repeated stories about hooking up with Williams as a kid, and riding boxcars with him to Mexico, was part of the fantasy life Bob had constructed for himself, like his claim to be part Sioux Indian. But when Williams arrived in the village, he confirmed the unlikely stories, saying he had known Bob way back in Chicago when Williams was a street singer and Bob accompanied him on spoons. Van Ronk could not help thinking that Bob had got to Williams and persuaded him to go along with his stories, which is almost certainly what did happen. They did get along very well, however. Bob backed Williams on harmonica, having no trouble following his unpredictable guitar work, and the older man referred to Bob affectionately as 'Little Joe.' When Victoria Spivey and Williams went into the studio in early March 1962 to record, Bob played harmonica for them. He had already done some session work – for Carolyn Hester and, curiously, Harry Belafonte (playing on one track for a Belafonte session in New York in the winter of 1961) – and had become accomplished on harp. The unlikely trio of Spivey, Williams, and Dylan cut tracks including 'Sitting on Top of the World' and 'Wichita.' Big Joe was so enthused by Bob's harp work that he was heard to exclaim: 'Play for me, junior!' Bob was completely accepted by these older black artists, as he had been by John Lee Hooker before and would be throughout his career, and the natural way in which he incorporated elements of black music into his work would always be one of his great strengths.

There was, of course, a strong element of black music in the country blues tunes of Bob's debut album, which was finally released in March 1962. 'I thought, wow, this is terrible,' says Arlo Guthrie, who heard the album, titled simply *Bob Dylan*, when he was away at boarding school. 'It was just that nobody sang like that. After a while I loved it, but it took a little [time]. I was listening to guys like Cisco Houston, guys with these beautiful, rich voices . . . they were singers and Bob Dylan wasn't a singer. He was something else.'

The *Village Voice* liked *Bob Dylan* better than Arlo Guthrie did, describing the album as an 'explosive country-blues debut' and praising Bob's unique style. 'It's a collector's item already,' wrote J. R. Goddard. Unfortunately, it was little more than that, selling approximately five thousand copies in the first year. This was poor by the standards of Columbia Records, and in the air-conditioned corridors of 'Black Rock' executives whispered that John Hammond had lost his touch and famously nicknamed Bob Dylan 'Hammond's folly.' But Hammond knew Bob had already assimilated the country blues and Guthriesque songs on his first album into a more mature style of his own. Indeed, a month after his debut was released, Bob was in the studio recording original new songs like 'Rambling, Gambling Willie' and 'The Death of Emmett Till.' Then he made a breakthrough with one of the most famous songs of the postwar era, 'Blowin' in the Wind.'

Bob composed 'Blowin' in the Wind' in a matter of minutes sitting in a cafe across the street from the Gaslight Club. Although he thought 'Blowin' in the Wind' special, he did not understand the full significance of what he had done. 'It was just another song I wrote.' The melody was uncannily similar to the African-American spiritual 'No More Auction Block.' However, borrowing melodies, and even lyrics, was part of the folk tradition and thus perfectly acceptable.* A more pertinent criticism of 'Blowin' in the Wind' concerned the rhetorical lyrics. Many of the most distinguished folk artists in New York were underwhelmed when they first heard the song. There seemed no link between the relentless questions; and, at the end of three verses, none of the questions had been resolved, except to say the answer was blowing in the wind, an image so vague that, arguably, it meant nothing. Pete Seeger did not regard it highly. ' "Blowin' in the Wind" is not my favorite,' he says. 'It's a little easy.' Tom Paxton found it almost impossible to learn. 'I hate the song myself. It's what I call a grocery-list song where one line has absolutely no relevance to the next line.' Dave Van Ronk thought it dumb. Still, within a couple of months of Bob performing 'Blowin' in the Wind' at Gerde's Folk City, Van Ronk noticed to his surprise that musicians hanging around Washington Square Park had invented irreverent

*It is patently untrue that Dylan stole 'Blowin' in the Wind.' This myth arose after musician Lorre Wyatt claimed to have written a song called 'Freedom is Blowing in the Wind.' Wyatt later retracted any claim to the song.

parodies such as, 'The answer, my friend, is blowin' out your end.' As Van Ronk says, 'If the song is strong enough, without even having been recorded, to start garnering parodies, the song is stronger than I realized.'

Roy Silver, meanwhile, knew Bob had created something extraordinary. ' "Blowin' in the Wind" was the key to it all,' he says. 'That song made it all happen.' Despite Silver's enthusiasm, Bob was slipping away from him. Grossman had become much more interested after he learned Bob was capable of writing such unique material, and Bob was talking to Grossman about his career more often than he spoke with Silver. Bob did not succumb to Grossman easily, however. First, he asked Woody Guthrie's friend and manager Harold Leventhal to manage him. Bob liked and respected Leventhal, a trustworthy, serious-minded man, but although Bob made the first move Leventhal could not pin him down to an agreement. 'I would call him and he never responded. I wasn't going to go chasing him.'

In June 1962, Silver decided to sell his contract with Bob to Grossman for a modest cash sum plus ongoing use of space in Grossman's New York office. 'I could see Albert was going to be an asshole about all of this. Albert also had money,' says Silver. 'I had none [so] I sold my contract for approximately ten thousand dollars and that was the end of it. Albert took over.' It was the best deal of Grossman's life. In exchange for $10,000, and space to put a desk, he secured a client who made him a multimillionaire.

The business relationship between Bob and Albert Grossman is a key element in Bob's career. Some believe that without Grossman Bob would never have become an international star. 'Whatever was wrong with Albert, he believed in Bob, he really did,' says Van Ronk. 'He stuck with Bobby. The first album didn't sell and the second album didn't sell very much either, [but] Albert was convinced Bobby would fly and he never let up.' Bob had prodigious talent. Grossman had a ruthless business sense and a worldliness the young man did not yet possess. Together, artist and manager were, as Odetta says, 'a *mighty* combination.'

Bob had cause to be grateful to Grossman, and even at their darkest hour he acknowledged grudgingly that Grossman 'did some good things for me over the years.' But the relationship would end very unhappily. In 1981 – twelve years after they had stopped doing business together – Grossman sued Bob for back royalties. Bob filed eighteen counterclaims, complaining Grossman had exploited and mismanaged him throughout their association. Bob refuted suggestions Grossman had 'discovered' him, pointing out that he had already acquired an agent and a record deal before they met. Bob said he was completely unsophisticated in business at the time. 'I was probably easy to influence,' he said, 'my business knowledge and acumen were nil.' He felt Grossman had taken advantage of this naïveté, and it was not just the money he had lost that rankled with him. He also felt hurt that someone whom he had trusted had betrayed him. The hurt was apparent when Bob gave a sworn deposition in 1981 in support of his counterclaims. By this time he had seen more than $7 million of his earnings siphoned off by Grossman. When asked how long he had known Mr. Grossman, Bob replied carefully: 'Well, I don't think I've ever known the man, Mr. Grossman.' In another statement Bob said, more bluntly, 'Grossman first gained my trust and confidence, and then abused that relationship for his own benefit.'

What ended in acrimony began on August 30, 1962, when Bob and Grossman signed a management agreement. It gave Grossman four years as Bob's exclusive manager, with an option to extend the contract for a further three. The exclusivity worked one way, however; Bob was Grossman's client one hundred percent, but Grossman could represent other acts. Grossman would take a basic twenty percent of Bob's earnings, but he would get an enhanced twenty-*five* percent of gross income from recordings. That extra five percent would be worth a fortune. Bob later claimed he thought he was only agreeing to pay Grossman a flat twenty percent (again, he had not bothered to read the contract, which clearly stated Grossman would receive twenty-five percent of recording income*). Even twenty percent would have been double what theatrical agents were allowed to charge under New York General Business Law. As Bob's attorneys discovered when Bob and Grossman sued each other in the 1980s, Grossman was not even licensed to operate as a theatrical agent in New York. Arguably, the whole thing was illegal.

Almost simultaneously, and very significantly, Grossman created his dream group. After experimenting with Gibson and Camp, he decided to build his Kingston Trio–style crossover act around Cornell graduate Peter Yarrow. Grossman chose the attractive female singer Mary Travers, whose blond hair reached down nearly to her waist. Gaslight emcee Noel Stookey became the third member. Because Peter, Noel and Mary did not sound right, Noel agreed to change his name to Paul, and Peter, Paul and Mary was born. The group had an attractive, hip look combined with a slick sound and Grossman had no difficulty obtaining a lucrative record deal with Warner Brothers. Success was immediate. In June 1962, Peter, Paul and Mary's debut single, 'Lemon Tree,' reached number thirty-five on the *Billboard* chart. In September their cover of The Weavers' 'Hammer Song' got to number ten, and stayed in the top forty for two months. But this was only the beginning. 'Peter, Paul and Mary were ascending like comets,' says Tom Paxton, who had been roommates with Stookey. 'You can't believe success like that.'

In the summer of 1962, Grossman entered into an agreement with song publisher M. Witmark & Sons to introduce songwriters to the company. At the time

*See Source Notes for the relevant extract from the contract.

writers at publishing companies in and around the Brill Building at 1619 Broadway, New York, turned out songs on a production line for singers. This industry was colloquially known as Tin Pan Alley. Although some of the songs were excellent ('Up on the Roof' by Gerry Goffin and Carole King and 'Save the Last Dance for Me' by Doc Pomus and Mort Shuman are distinguished examples), Bob was dismissive of Tin Pan Alley, as many artists were. He lampooned the genre in a 1962 interview, saying the songs were little more than, 'I'm hot for you and you're hot for me – ooka dooka dicka dee.' Bob was a very different type of songwriter than, say, Pomus and Shuman, of course, in that he was not trying to craft top-forty pop hits that appealed to teenagers. In fact, he was the recording artist who virtually killed off the Brill Building companies, because he both wrote and performed his own material and, by example, encouraged a generation of artists to do the same. 'Tin Pan Alley is gone. I put an end to it,' he said in 1985, with perhaps a touch of self-importance. 'People can record their own songs now.' At the start of Bob's career, however, Grossman, and Bob himself to some extent, saw a future in his writing songs for other artists. Grossman was authorized by M. Witmark & Sons to draw on a cash fund of $100,000 to sign songwriters to the company and decided to spend part of this fund moving Bob from Duchess Music to Witmark. Grossman did not tell Bob he had such a fortune to spend, however, giving Bob only $1,000 and instructing him to take this to Duchess and reimburse the money they had advanced him, which was exactly $1,000. Bob did as he was told and was duly released from his Duchess contract. He then signed with M. Witmark & Sons – essentially for nothing – and started coming into the Witmark office on Madison Avenue to record demo versions of his new songs. The hack writers at Witmark insisted the door to Bob's booth be closed when he was recording because they found the high nasal sound of his voice irritating. Little did they know the kid was going to put them out of business.

On July 30, 1962, 'Blowin' in the Wind,' the song that was the foundation stone of Bob's career and a catalyst of the singer-songwriter revolution, was copyrighted to M. Witmark & Sons. The same day, Grossman signed what Bob later called 'a secret deal' with M. Witmark & Sons giving Grossman fifty percent of Witmark's share of the publishing income generated by any songwriter he brought to the company. Now Grossman stood to earn a substantial slice of Bob's publishing fees, over and above the cut he took for managing him. This backhanded deal was one of Bob's primary complaints when he and Grossman were in dispute in the 1980s, although in fairness Grossman was getting an enhanced part of Witmark's share, and not necessarily money Bob himself would have received. Bob claimed indignantly that he had known nothing of Grossman's fifty percent deal with M. Witmark & Sons (Grossman insisted he had told him). Bob also claimed to have had no idea Grossman was given as much as $100,000 to advance to him for signing with M. Witmark & Sons, of which he received one percent. Bob's attorneys asserted that Grossman had 'willfully and maliciously' concealed vital information. The secretiveness was what angered Bob who was, of course, a very secretive person himself.

However, this was not the end of Grossman's machinations. The last part of his plan was, in fact, the cleverest. If Peter, Paul and Mary had a hit with a Bob Dylan–Witmark song, Grossman would earn fourfold. He had his management fee from the two acts, plus his twenty-five percent of Peter, Paul and Mary's recording income from Warner Bros., plus fifty percent of the income Witmark earned from publishing a Dylan song. When Peter, Paul and Mary had a massive hit with 'Blowin' in the Wind,' and top-forty success with two further songs written by Dylan, Grossman became as rich as Croesus.

Suddenly, money had become very important. Mark Spoelstra was at Bob's apartment when Bob and Peter

Yarrow were deep in conversation about their careers. 'Peter was explaining to him in mathematical terms how much money he had to make [so] he would never have to work again – all this stuff about money. Money, money, money,' says Spoelstra. 'Just months ago we had nowhere to sleep and nothing to eat.'

Suze was cooking dinner at the time. 'I'm sitting there kind of out of place and Suze's kind of out of place,' adds Spoelstra, who remembers how nervous Suze seemed. When she brought some soup in, Bob was waving his arms about and the soup spilled over his lap. 'Bob was just furious, and just started berating her as if it was some plan on her part to discredit him in front of Peter,' says Spoelstra. 'I would never, never have thought she did this on purpose . . . But Bob's paranoia, or whatever it was, caused him to just become furious with her and it really upset her. She ran into the bedroom crying.'

The relationship was not going well and Suze had an opportunity to get away. She could go with her mother to Italy to study at the University of Perugia. Bob did not want Suze to go, but on June 8 she boarded a ship for Europe.

Freed from the claustrophobic world of New York, Suze decided her relationship with Bob had become too serious. She was only eighteen, the weather in Italy was sunny and the countryside beautiful, and she was enjoying freedom as well as the attention of boys she met in Italy, particularly Enzo Bartoccioli, with whom she became close and who would later feature significantly in her life. Meanwhile, back in humid, cacophonous New York, Bob wrote letters, telephoned, and became ever more desperate as he sensed Suze's reluctance to talk to him. He once telephoned Dave Van Ronk in the middle of the night, weeping and wailing that he wanted Suze back.

The upset spurred Bob on to make an evolutionary leap in his songwriting, creating two of his best songs about relationships. 'Don't Think Twice, It's All Right' was too ambiguous to be described adequately as simply a love song. It was a yearning for and resenting of the object of his affection. It was hard not to think it had specific reference to Suze, whom Bob had wanted to marry. He gave the object of his love everything, even his heart, but she wanted his soul. It was a waste of his precious time, but she was not to think twice, it was all right. The greatness of the song was in the cleverness of the language. The phrase 'don't think twice, it's all right' could be snarled, sung with resignation, or delivered with an ambiguous mixture of bitterness and regret. Seldom had the contradictory emotions of a thwarted lover been so well expressed and the song transcended the autobiographical origin of Bob's pain. It was a song everybody could understand and empathize with. The second major song composed in the wake of Suze's departure was 'Tomorrow Is a Long Time.' Sick with love, he could not sleep without feeling her heart pounding next to him. He could not speak without betraying his misery. The beauties of nature were nothing to him, and stretching ahead was an 'endless highway' of loneliness.

These songs were far advanced from anything Bob had yet written, and as good as anything he would write. 'He had hit his stride,' says session guitarist Bruce Langhorne, who worked with Bob on his second album that fall. Bob was no longer a Guthrie copyist, or a writer of minor comic and topical songs. He had transmogrified into a great songwriter, bringing profound and poetic language to popular music, and, now that the transformation was complete, he was unstoppable. 'He began writing anywhere and everywhere,' says Mark Spoelstra. 'He'd be in a booth somewhere, in Gerde's Folk City, and everybody else is jabbering and drinking and he's sitting there writing a song on the napkins. And you couldn't interrupt it. He was driven, and obviously enlightened.'

In August 1962, following another trip to Minnesota and back, Bob went downtown to the Supreme Court building in New York and changed his name from Robert

Allen Zimmerman and officially assumed the mantle of Bob Dylan.

An element of serendipity is crucial to most successful careers and Bob's maturity as a songwriter came at an auspicious time. As the twenty-one-year-old Dylan scribbled in his ten-cent notebooks, America entered a period of enormous upheaval and social change.

In the summer of 1962 Martin Luther King Jr. was jailed in Albany, Georgia, as the struggle for civil rights intensified. In September, Soviet missiles were discovered on the communist-controlled island of Cuba, within striking distance of mainland United States. President Kennedy said he would take all necessary steps against Cuban aggression, and Congress empowered him to call up reservists. Soviet leader Nikita Khrushchev warned that an attack on Cuba would trigger nuclear war. Bob was of an age when he could have been drafted for military service – some of his friends were – and the terror was close. Sitting at Wavy Gravy's battered Remington, he wrote 'A Hard Rain's A-Gonna Fall,' a nightmarish vision of the world after a nuclear apocalypse. Bob called it a 'song of desperation . . . a song of terror.' The atomic rain would leave a blasted landscape: trees dripping blood; crooked highways; dead oceans; a woman on fire; a baby surrounded by wolves. The lyrics encapsulated the songwriter's dread. He later said every line was the start of a song he did not think he would have time to write. 'That song kind of roared right out of the typewriter,' says Gravy. 'It roared through him the way paint roared through van Gogh.'

When it was done, Bob snatched the paper out of the machine and hurried over to the Gaslight to perform it. 'A Hard Rain's A-Gonna Fall' was an immediate sensation. When Bob came offstage, Hamilton Camp asked him for the chord changes. 'He showed me and I got the words [and] I started doing it.' As the missile crisis reached its apogee in October, musicians all over the Village were playing the new song, including Richie Havens and Pete Seeger. '"Hard Rain" is almost my favorite,' says Seeger. 'I think it will last longer than almost any others [he has written].'

On October 28, Khrushchev announced that the Soviet missile bases on Cuba would be dismantled. To the profound relief of the people of the Western world, America had won the standoff. Even so, there was still a crackling energy in the air. Bob was the artist who had captured the zeitgeist in song, and he would do so again and again as an extraordinary decade unraveled. 'The truth rang out so loud in his words,' says Arlo Guthrie, 'not just for me, but for an entire generation.'

Bob's photograph was on the cover of the autumn issue of *Sing Out!* magazine, the foremost publication of folk music. He looked like James Dean in the picture, dragging on a cigarette. Despite his displays of ego in recent months, Bob was surprisingly humble in the interview when it came to talking about the new songs he was creating. 'The songs are there. They exist all by themselves just waiting for someone to write them down. I just put them down on paper,' he said. 'If I didn't do it, somebody else would.' This was not false modesty for the purposes of publication. It was the way he talked in private with friends, and it remained his philosophy throughout his career, an unchanging belief that was in many ways a kind of faith. He clearly felt that songs came to him from some other place and, over the years, he would come to believe that the songs were actually given to him by God. 'He felt he wasn't writing songs, he was [just] writing them down,' says Tom Paxton. 'They were there to be captured.'

Shortly before the missile crisis, Dave and Gretel Whitaker came to New York for a visit and met Bob in the Village on the afternoon of September 22. The weather was overcast but Bob wore sunglasses. 'Bobby, why have you got sunglasses on?' asked Gretel.

'So people don't recognize me,' he replied.

Gretel thought he had gone mad. They bought sandwiches and went up to Bob's apartment. As they ate, Bob told his friends he was performing that night at Carnegie Hall. It was the annual *Sing Out!* hootenanny, organized by Pete Seeger. Bob said the show was sold out, but that he could get them passes.

The Whitakers went to the concert, enjoying themselves as they watched the various artists perform. They paid keen attention when Pete Seeger announced a special guest. It was Bob, the same kid they had known scuffling around Dinkytown. Yet he had changed. 'He walked out onto the stage and this roar went up. An absolute roar,' says Gretel. She turned to her husband in astonishment, tears springing to her eyes. The apotheosis of Bob Dylan had begun.

CHAPTER 4

APOTHEOSIS

When Albert Grossman became Bob's manager he initiated a war of attrition against Columbia Records that lasted the full seven years he represented the singersongwriter. Grossman's first complaint was that Columbia was not working hard enough to promote his artist. Partly because of this, he asked his lawyer David Braun to draft a 'disaffirmment' letter to Columbia, stating that their contract was invalid because Bob was under twenty-one when he signed. Grossman wanted to renegotiate. John Hammond was furious his protégé had embarrassed him in this way and called Bob into the office where he prevailed upon him to sign a reaffirmment – now he was of age – meaning he agreed to abide by the original contract. This upset both Grossman and Braun. 'I thought it was a violation of the canons of ethics since Mr. Dylan was represented by an attorney when the disaffirmments were sent in and when the reaffirmments were signed they didn't contact us,' said Braun, who was introduced to Bob at this time. (Before the introduction, Grossman said he was about to meet the 'next Frank Sinatra,' and Braun subsequently became one of Bob's closest advisers.) There was some positive outcome from the skirmish with Columbia, however. 'From that moment on their attitude changed toward Bob and they started promoting his records,' says Braun.

Grossman then decided to get rid of John Hammond. The two men could not have been more different. Hammond was a WASP aesthete, so relaxed during recording sessions that he sat with feet up, reading *The*

New Yorker. Grossman was a Jewish entrepreneur with a shady background, hustling to become a millionaire. But it would not be easy to remove Hammond. He was a legend at Columbia and he was married to the chairman's sister. So Grossman decided to make the producer's life so miserable that he would quit.

Session musicians had been hired by Bob and John Hammond to play on selected tracks on Bob's second album, *The Freewheelin' Bob Dylan*, starting in April 1962 and continuing, in sporadic sessions, into the fall. A drummer, bass player, and guitarist added backup to a cover of the traditional 'Corrina, Corrina.' Grossman now suggested a band back Bob on one of his new songs, 'Mixed Up Confusion.' This was a reasonable suggestion in itself, but Grossman wanted the band to play *Dixieland*-style. Hammond was aghast at this deliberately provocative suggestion, but did make several attempts at the record. None worked and Hammond eventually lost his temper, ordering Grossman's partner, John Court, from the studio. Bob became so frustrated he walked out. Shortly afterward Hammond resigned from the album. 'Grossman hated my father,' says John Hammond Jr. 'Maybe because my father was not into big bucks. And Albert was definitely into big bucks.'

There was a hiatus while Columbia executives found a producer Grossman and Bob would work with. In the interim, on December 14, 1962, a lively take of 'Mixed Up Confusion' was released as Bob's first single. It sounded like a track from Elvis Presley's early Sun sessions, and it flopped.

With problems in the studio, his estranged girlfriend, Suze Rotolo, in Italy, and the Christmas holidays coming, Bob accepted an invitation to get away from it all and fly to England for an appearance in a play for British television. This unlikely idea came about after British director Philip Saville saw Bob performing in Greenwich Village and decided he could fill the role of the anarchist-student in *Madhouse on Castle Street*. As Saville recalls,

Grossman agreed because he was eager for Bob to 'enlarge his repertoire.' Under the terms of their contract, Grossman would earn twenty-five percent of 'any motion picture, or recording of any kind' that Bob agreed to do. Thus it would be to Grossman's benefit if his client forged a second career as an actor. Grossman also told Saville that Bob had an offer of a concert in Germany,* so if the BBC paid his air fare to Britain, plus a fee, Bob would do the play.

It was Bob's first trip outside the United States and he found London – then enlivened by a youthful renaissance in fashion and music – a very exciting place. 'He loved it. He was very fond of London,' says Saville, who took Bob shopping in Carnaby Street and invited him home to stay with his family in the north London district of Hampstead. 'He wanted to hit the road. If it meant [coming] to England, that was part of the road he was on. That was part of the adventure.' Saville found Bob to be a curious but endearing guest. He lived a twenty-four-hour day, sometimes taking meals at three o'clock in the morning. 'His bed times and night times and morning times were all [one] time,' says Saville. At seven one morning, Saville stumbled blearily from his bedroom to find Bob sitting on the stairs singing 'Blowin' in the Wind' for Saville's two Spanish au pairs. Bob also smoked a lot of pot. Once, when he seemed to be missing, Saville found him two streets away from his Ferncroft Avenue house, passed out under a car. 'I think it must have rained and he must have taken shelter under [the] car.' When Bob moved briefly into the grand Mayfair Hotel in Berkeley Square, at the expense of the BBC, he astonished hotel management by playing guitar in the foyer as if he were on a street corner.

Bob spent a fair amount of time in London folk clubs such as the Troubadour, the King and Queen, and the

*This may have just been a gambit on Grossman's part as there is no record of Dylan performing in Germany at this time.

Singers' Club. (The latter was a traditionalist evening at the Pindar of Wakefield public house on Gray's Inn Road.) Bob performed at the Singers' Club on December 22. The senior figures there were Ewan MacColl (writer of 'Dirty Old Town' and 'The First Time Ever I Saw Your Face') and wife Peggy Seeger (half sister to Pete). Both were hidebound traditionalists and they did not give Bob a friendly reception. 'He ummed and awed and looked at his feet and seemed apologetic about being there,' says Peggy Seeger. 'He seemed lost without a microphone, as plenty of U.S.A. performers did in our nonwired clubs. Ewan and I were rather standoffish at that time and perhaps we were not welcoming enough.' Bob made a more friendly connection with folksinger Martin Carthy, from whom he learned the traditional English songs 'Scarborough Fair' and 'Lord Franklin.'

Once Saville got Bob to the television studio, he discovered that the eccentric young folksinger was not a natural actor. He was uncomfortable with learning lines, saying he would rather express himself through song; he was lax about time keeping, invariably arriving late at rehearsals; and he had a habit of wandering off to smoke pot. Eventually, Philip had to hire another actor to deliver Bob's long, anarchic speeches, leaving Bob to play a part that was essentially himself, a character named Bobby who sang songs including 'Blowin' in the Wind.' It is hard to say whether any of this made for good television because the BBC wiped the tapes after transmission of *Madhouse on Castle Street.* Saville, however, recalls the play was well received.

When filming was completed, Bob went to Rome to meet Grossman, who was on tour with Odetta. Mary Travers also joined them. They went to a nightclub where Bob attempted to dance, and took an excursion to look at Roman antiquities. As they were inspecting a relic of the reign of Marcus Aurelius, an Italian woman came up and announced she wanted Bob as her lover, which amused them all. 'I'm sure they didn't know us, [but she] just up and claimed that kid!' says Odetta. 'I'm sure he had, outside of his fan club, a ladies' club that was *huge*.' While Bob was always happy to meet new girlfriends, he seemed preoccupied with his rift with Suze, who had come to Italy the previous summer. While he was in the country, Bob completed an important love song for her, 'Boots of Spanish Leather.' Ironically, though, there was no chance of him meeting Suze because she had just recently returned to New York.

Bob flew back to London and, on January 14, 1963, he took part in a drunken recording session with friends Eric Von Schmidt and Richard Fariña. They were making an album in the basement of Dobell's record shop on Charing Cross Road. Bob turned up with a bag of Guinness bottles. Later that night at the Troubadour club he was so drunk he almost fell off stage. When he met up with Martin Carthy again, Bob told him he had written a new song to the tune of 'Scarborough Fair,' which Martin had taught him before Christmas. It was 'Girl from the North Country,'* which would feature on *The Freewheelin' Bob Dylan* album and become one of the most celebrated songs he ever wrote.

The song 'Girl from the North Country' seems strongly autobiographical. The north country – *where rivers froze – up near the border line* – was presumably Minnesota, and one wondered which girlfriend Bob was singing about. Echo Helstrom was, of course, a north country girl, and Bob later gave Echo the impression 'Girl from the North Country' was her song. But, no doubt thinking that women were flattered by having songs written about them, Bob led another north country girlfriend, Bonnie Beecher, to think the same. Bonnie also recognized the line about a 'coat so warm' as a reference to a coat with a fur collar she'd worn when she was dating Bob. 'It seems to be very important to some people who that song is about,' says Bonnie. 'I actually had a woman physically

*Also known as 'Girl of the North Country.'

attack me one time about whether or not I was claiming to be the girl from the north country.' Later in 1963, when he performed the song on a radio show hosted by Oscar Brand, Bob indicated that the song was about an idealized woman, saying, 'This is dedicated to *all* the north country girls.' It is also hard to imagine that, when he wrote the song, his thoughts were not at least partly on Suze, whom he had been pining for since the previous summer.

While Bob certainly missed Suze, he had not forsworn other dalliances. He was a romantic who loved women; for their part women found him very charming and as a result he became an inveterate womanizer in young adulthood and would remain so throughout most of his life. During Suze's absence, for instance, he had developed a platonic crush on Mavis Staples, a member of the family gospel group The Staple Singers. They first met in 1962, introduced by Robert Shelton. Mavis was a beautiful young African American with one of the great contralto voices in popular music, sounding both spiritual and sexy at once. Bob became so besotted he went to the patriarch of the family, Roebuck 'Pops' Staples, and asked: 'Pops, can I marry Mavis?'

'Don't ask me. Ask Mavis,' replied Pops, not very pleased by the idea. Nor was Mavis, evidently. She did not accept his proposal, although she and Bob remained friends.

Bob was reunited with Suze in New York in January 1963. She soon found herself dragged back into the oppressive relationship she had escaped for more than half a year. Now it was harder to retain her individuality because Bob was becoming famous. 'When I came back from Italy, I was surrounded by these people I didn't even know intruding into my personal life,' she says. 'There were people who were actually angry that I had abandoned him at the "most important time of his life." I was "the woman who deserted him."' Suze was at a club one evening when a singer performed 'Don't Think

Twice, It's All Right' with such vehemence Suze could only conclude it was directed at her.

Despite her fear about being consumed by Bob's celebrity, when Columbia needed a cover photograph for Bob's new album, *The Freewheelin' Bob Dylan*, Suze agreed to pose with him. The image of Suze snuggled into Bob's shoulder as they trudged between snow-covered Greenwich Village brownstones in the fading light of a winter afternoon became one of the most memorable album covers of the 1960s. It also brought decades of unwanted attention. 'Maybe no one would have known what the songs were about if it weren't for the album cover,' she says. 'You see, the story is in the songs. Every song he has ever written about me. It's all there.'

With his best girl posing on his arm for his new album, and brilliant song ideas flowing through him with apparent ease, Bob was now entering the golden part of his early career, and almost each month brought new triumphs. His first important solo concert was staged at the Town Hall in New York on April 12, 1963, promoted by Harold Leventhal. Although the show did not sell out the evening was a major success. Highlights included a rendition of the love song 'Tomorrow Is a Long Time'* and the acerbic antiwar song 'With God on Our Side.' The concert concluded with Bob reading a poem, 'Last Thoughts on Woody Guthrie.' This was a tribute to his hero, but also a symbolic ending to the chapter of his life when Guthrie dominated his thoughts. Bob had never read on stage before, and was noticeably uncomfortable without his guitar. He began diffidently, saying he had been asked to write twenty-five words about what Guthrie meant to him. He found it impossible. So he wrote five pages, which he proceeded to read. The epic ended with an evocation of Guthrie at the Grand Canyon

*Recorded and later included on the 1971 double compilation album *Bob Dylan's Greatest Hits, Vol II.*

at sunset, and the audience exploded with applause. 'He was so charismatic,' says Jane Traum, wife of Bob's Greenwich Village friend Happy Traum. Like many in the audience, Jane felt the concert was a turning point, perhaps the moment when Bob became a star. His confidence, which had been apparent since he was in high school bands, combined now with a mature stage presence and good original songs. Everything came together at the right time and to watch him on stage was suddenly very exciting. As Jane says, still thrilled by the memory decades later, 'Nothing was going to be the same again.'

Television executives became interested in Bob performing on their shows. Earlier in 1963, on a visit to Hibbing to see his family, Bob had gone into his old high school to tell his former teacher B. J. Rolfzen to watch *The Ed Sullivan Show* on May 12. Bob was going to be on the show. But when Rolfzen and most of the rest of Hibbing tuned into CBS-TV on the night, Bob was nowhere to be seen. During rehearsals he had been asked not to perform the satirical 'Talkin' John Birch Paranoid Blues' because the lyrics stated John Birch Society members sympathized with the politics of Adolf Hitler. CBS feared a lawsuit. Rather than change his set list, Bob withdrew from the show. The press coverage made him appear principled and made *The Ed Sullivan Show* seem foolish. Bob later alluded to the incident in concert. 'This is called "Talkin' John Birch Blues,"' he told his audience at Carnegie Hall on October 26, pausing for applause. 'And there ain't nothin' wrong with this song.'

Three hundred copies of *The Freewheelin' Bob Dylan* had already been shipped to stores when the *Ed Sullivan Show* controversy broke. Columbia recalled the records and resequenced the album, possibly deciding to take this action even before the program aired because they were already becoming concerned about potential slander. Four songs, including 'Talkin' John Birch Paranoid Blues,' were replaced with recordings made under the direction of Bob's new producer, Tom Wilson, a thirty-two-year-old jazz specialist. Although Bob seems to have been irritated initially by the need to change the album, and even complained to CBS Vice President Clive Davis, the changes had to be made and they were in fact to his ultimate benefit because he substituted better songs. These included two of his best new compositions: 'Girl from the North Country' and what is probably the best antiwar song he ever wrote, 'Masters of War.'

The liner notes for *The Freewheelin' Bob Dylan*, written by journalist friend Nat Hentoff, indicated that 'Masters of War' – which was written over the winter of 1962–63 – was inspired by the Cold War arms buildup. Yet like many of Bob's best songs, 'Masters of War' transcended the time in which it was written. It would have great meaning during the looming Vietnam War and it still rang true nearly three decades later during the Gulf War in 1991. Part of the appeal was the hardness and anger in the lyric. In the last verse, Bob wrote that he hoped the warmongers would die, and soon; he would stand over their grave until he was satisfied they were dead. This fierce language was one of the characteristics of Bob's mature style, and a quality that set him apart from the idealists of the folk revival. When Judy Collins recorded a version of 'Masters of War,' dropping the aggressive last lines, Bob thought she missed the point. But no one song – even one as powerful as 'Masters of War' – could define Dylan's songwriting. He was interested in writing songs that came out of social concerns, but he was also interested in love songs and comic songs. To categorize Bob as having become simply a 'protest singer,' as journalists increasingly did, was to sell him short.

As happened with so many of the major songs Bob wrote as a young man, he stood accused of using another musician's melody for 'Masters of War.' Veteran folksinger Jean Ritchie recognized that Bob had appropriated the tune from her arrangement of 'Fair Nottamun

Town,' a traditional song sung in her family for generations. 'He might not have realized when he wrote the song. He might have just thought he made it up,' says Ritchie. 'A lot of times people do that . . . I don't think he was out to try and rob anybody.' Jean wanted an acknowledgment on the song credit that the arrangement was hers. Instead, Bob's lawyers paid Jean $5,000 to settle and agree not to make any more claims. As far as the world was concerned the song was now wholly his.

Before the *The Freewheelin' Bob Dylan* was released Bob flew to California, in mid-May 1963, to appear at the Monterey Folk Festival, with Joan Baez joining him on stage for 'With God on Our Side.' Baez was at the pinnacle of her career, having appeared on the cover of *Time* the previous November. After the festival, she and Bob traveled down the coast to her house outside the picturesque town of Carmel. It was the start of one of the most celebrated love affairs of the decade. 'Joan was wild about him,' says her sister, Mimi. 'And, in her usual fashion, [she] gave a hundred percent attention to the thing that charmed her the most.' Bob was in Carmel when *Freewheelin*' was released at the end of May. Then he flew home to Suze. It was not long before rumors of the affair with Baez reached her. In fact, Bob and Suze were together in New York when their friend Geno Foreman asked Bob with supreme tactlessness, 'Are you still fucking Joan?' Suze had also probably heard stories about Bob asking Mavis Staples to marry him. It all helped to destabilize their relationship and fray Suze's nerves.

The Freewheelin' Bob Dylan was Bob's first great album, and it included five classic songs. The opening track, 'Blowin' in the Wind,' would have ensured the album's place in music history on its own. Years later when he was in dispute with Albert Grossman, Bob gave this as the primary reason the album was a success: 'Although I didn't know it at the time, the second album was destined to become a great success because it was to include "Blowin' in the Wind."' But there was much more to *Freewheelin'* than one song. 'Blowin' in the Wind' was followed by the lovely 'Girl from the North Country' and followed in turn by the ferocious 'Masters of War.' The first side ended with another masterpiece, 'A Hard Rain's A-Gonna Fall.' The first track of the second side was the great 'Don't Think Twice, It's All Right.' All five songs became mainstays of Bob's repertoire. The rest of the album was filler of a very high standard, including the blues 'Down the Highway,' which described Bob's longing for Suze during their separation, and the delightful 'I Shall Be Free.' In the latter, President Kennedy called Bob on the telephone and asked what it would take to make the country grow. In reply, Bob suggested a list of fantasy women – Brigitte Bardot, Anita Ekberg, and Sophia Loren – groaning comically: 'Country'll grow!' Lightweight material balanced the big songs and helped make *The Freewheelin' Bob Dylan* an album one could listen to time and again without becoming emotionally exhausted. Although it received mixed reviews upon release, it would stand the test of time as one of the masterworks of his career. Bob's pride in the material is borne out by the fact that he has performed songs from the album throughout his career.

'Blowin' in the Wind' and some of the other songs on *The Freewheelin' Bob Dylan* would forever be associated with the struggle for reform in America, but Bob had no firsthand experience of segregation, the fundamental issue of the day, never having visited the South. This was not lost on friends in the folk community. The Student Non-Violent Coordinating Committee (SNCC, pronounced 'Snick') was organizing voter registration rallies in the South to enfranchise African Americans. There was to be a rally in Greenwood, Mississippi, in July. Theodore Bikel, The Freedom Singers, and Pete Seeger were scheduled to perform. Bikel suggested to Albert Grossman that Bob should join them. 'It looks different and feels different when you're in the midst of it,' Bikel told Grossman. 'I think Bob should go.'

'He can't afford to,' replied Grossman. 'The fare's too high.'

'I'll tell you what,' suggested Bikel, writing a check. 'Here, buy him the ticket. Don't tell him where it came from. Tell him it's time to go down and experience the South.'

Dylan and Bikel traveled together on an evening flight from New York, changing planes in Atlanta. As they flew on to Jackson, Mississippi, Bob scribbled lyrics on the backs of envelopes. They were met in Jackson by two civil rights workers and driven to Greenwood where they slept in the loft of a church. In the morning, they lay flat in the car as they were driven the last three miles to the rally. 'If the cops saw a car with mixed blacks and whites, that telegraphed civil rights workers,' says Bikel. 'They'd pull you over on any pretext, or none, and put you in jail.'

The rally was in a farmyard on the edge of a cotton patch. The hootenanny was due to start at 10 A.M., but it was so hot they postponed until dusk. Three hundred or so people assembled by sundown, mostly African-American farmworkers. They were watched by policemen in a patrol car and groups of white men on the other side of the highway. Dylan and Bikel met up with Pete Seeger and The Freedom Singers, who had traveled separately. 'What I remember is the black man who gave a speech,' says Seeger. 'He had a fierce grin, as though he knew they were winning, and the Ku Klux Klan didn't know what the heck to do with it. He knew some of us are gonna get killed, but they are not going to be able to kill all of us.' Bob sang 'Only a Pawn in Their Game,' his song about the killing of Medgar Evers, Mississippi field secretary for the National Association for the Advancement of Colored People. Evers had been shot dead in Jackson a month earlier. Byron De La Beckwith, a local member of the Klan, was indicted for the crime.

Bob sang that the killer was a pawn in a game of ignorance, prejudice, and hatred. He leaned forward as he sang the words, never smiling for cameras that were on hand to record the event for television and newspapers. This was serious and it demanded a serious demeanor. As Seeger says, 'One of Bob's most important things is refusing to smile for cameramen.' As darkness closed in Bikel, Dylan, and Seeger joined hands with The Freedom Singers and sang 'We Shall Overcome.' Bob rarely took a public stance on a political issue, and it was a powerful event; in private, Bob put his money where his mouth was by making a donation to SNCC.

Peter Yarrow had no doubt he was hearing poetry the first time Albert Grossman played him 'Blowin' in the Wind.' He did not share others' misgivings that the song was simply rhetorical. 'It is precisely because Bobby was a poet that he invited people to participate in the definition of what his message truly was,' he says. 'And like a true poet, I think he stepped back from prescribing an interpretation.' Peter, Paul and Mary recorded a sweetly melodic version of the song, sung in perfect three-part harmony. Unfortunately, they made a mistake with the lyric. 'Mary to this day, even though I pointed it out to her, still sings "How many years must a mountain exist,"' says Noel Paul Stookey. '[It is] "How many years can a mountain exist."' Despite this, the single sold a phenomenal three hundred thousand copies in its first week of release. On July 13, 1963, it reached number two in the *Billboard* chart, with sales exceeding one million. Peter Yarrow told Bob he might make $5,000 from the publishing rights. Bob was almost speechless; it seemed like a fortune.

Bob was to receive visceral evidence of the power of the song within days when he and Peter, Paul and Mary performed at the Newport Folk Festival, which was held each summer in Freebody Park outside the harbor town of Newport, Rhode Island. Surrounded by the palatial summer mansions of society families including the Vanderbilts and Astors – with millionaires' yachts anchored offshore – Newport was an incongruous venue for folk music. Indeed, the setting underscored the gulf between the proletarian roots of this music and the privileged lives of most of the performers and the majority of the audience. Thirty-seven thousand people visited the Newport Folk Festival over the long weekend of July 26–28, and it seemed at times as if the crowd was focused only on Bob. Peter, Paul and Mary helped build him up for the crowd. 'This song was written by the most important folk artist in America today,' Peter Yarrow announced, when the group took the stage to sing 'Blowin' in the Wind.' Bob came on after them to a rapturous reception, and then the other stars of the festival joined him for an emotional rendition of 'We Shall Overcome.'

Backstage, Bob wore movie-star sunglasses and cracked a bullwhip he had received as a gift from Joan Baez. The whip added to the frisson surrounding the couple, a semisecret affair made more exciting because Suze was also at the festival. Baez headlined the evening concert on Sunday. Before performing 'Don't Think Twice, It's All Right,' she told the audience it was a song about a relationship that had lasted too long. Suze walked out of the arena, apparently close to tears. Dylan and Baez sang 'With God on Our Side' as a duet. The song, set to a folk tune also used by Dominic Behan, had become *their* song. 'That was a big, big breakout festival for Bob,' remembers Tom Paxton. 'The buzz just kept growing exponentially and it was like a coronation of Bob and Joan. They were King and Queen of the festival.'

Baez was planning a summer tour and invited Bob along as her guest. This seems to have caused Suze enormous distress. The circumstances have never become entirely clear, but some time after the Newport festival, and possibly after she learned Bob was going to tour with Baez, Suze apparently tried to take her own life at Bob's West 4th Street apartment by letting the gas run. 'I got a call from Bobby telling me to come and help and she came [and] stayed with me,' says her sister Carla Rotolo, who believes the incident may have been a bid for attention. Suze did not move back in with Bob afterward, but lived instead with Carla on the Lower East Side of Manhattan. '[Bob] left a lot of damage behind him,' says Carla. 'Bobby at that time was a very fucked-up person.' By which she means that his drive for success had become all-important, and he did not seem to care what happened to those who fell by the wayside. It is impossible to know what he felt deep down about what happened with Suze, because he did not talk about it, but considering his sensitive nature he must have been very upset. The tour with Baez, however, would continue.

Beyond the distress it caused to Suze, many in the folk community thought that Dylan and Baez's relationship had a cynical side. They seemed to be using each other to enhance their respective careers: it did Baez good to introduce a major new talent to audiences, and Bob profited by the exposure. 'Everybody used everybody else,' says Oscar Brand. 'His drive to success [was] such that he [may] have done a lot of things – that I would find appalling . . . I always thought he went out with Joan [because] she was doing his songs.' This was the gossip going around the folk community when the tour began in New Jersey on August 3, 1963. By the time Dylan and Baez reached Lenox, Massachusetts, later in the month, a routine had been established. Baez sang 'Blowin' in the Wind,' which got a big reception. Then she asked the audience casually: 'Would you like to meet the author of that song?' People yelled out that they certainly would and then Bob came out to huge applause. Albert Grossman had actually negotiated a larger fee per appearance for Dylan than Baez received, even though she was purportedly the star. Baez had always taken a relaxed attitude to money. 'The minute anyone would discuss money with her she would just black out,' says Nancy Carlen, Baez's close friend and producer. 'She was an entertainer who never went looking for [success]. It came looking for her, [and] the value she put on it is the value [of] somebody who has had things come easily.' However contrived these shows were, and whatever the feeling in sections of the folk community that Bob was using Baez, and vice versa, the couple came across as natural and charming to concert-goers like Eve Baer. She saw the show in Lenox and found herself smitten with what appeared to be this 'humble, shy guy.'

Some of the concerts were in huge venues, like the Forest Hills tennis stadium in Queens, New York. Here Baez introduced Bob to an audience of approximately fifteen thousand, nearly the population of Hibbing. 'There's a boy wandering around New York City and his name is Bob Dylan,' she said. 'It just so happens that Bob Dylan is here with me tonight.' It was gratifying to Baez to introduce a genius to the world and Baez's friends and family felt that she played a key role in boosting Bob's career, the insinuation being that he never gave her sufficient credit (in fact, he gave her almost none). 'Those shows are underestimated in historical accounts of his career,' says Mimi. '[Joan] really went all-out to promote him.' Perhaps Bob became irritated by the slightly patronizing nature of Baez's relationship with him. In her memoir, *And a Voice to Sing With*, Baez wrote, perhaps condescendingly, about 'dragging my little vagabond out onto the stage' as a 'grand experiment.' Baez was doing a fellow artist a favor but she was also clearly besotted with Bob's energy, humor, and quirky intelligence.

Baez's help was only part of the story of Bob's success. By the summer of 1963 Bob was beginning to stand on his own. *The Freewheelin' Bob Dylan* was selling ten thousand copies per week. Many artists wanted to perform and record versions of his songs. Some were good, but when Hamilton Camp treated Bob to a rendition of 'Girl from the North Country' Bob put his hands over his ears to show his displeasure. 'He couldn't stand it,' says Camp. However, every cover helped promote the songwriter, partly because fellow artists would often thank Bob warmly in concert. Peter, Paul and Mary in particular rarely missed an opportunity to talk about Bob from the stage; it seems likely that their mutual manager Albert Grossman would have encouraged them in this, although Noel Paul Stookey insists it was all quite natural. Peter, Paul and Mary also had much to thank Bob for because some of their biggest successes were with covers of his songs. In September, the group had another major hit with a cover of the Dylan song 'Don't Think Twice, It's All Right.'

As the manager of both Bob Dylan and Peter, Paul and Mary, Albert Grossman was becoming rich. When the big money started coming in, he indulged himself with luxurious living. One of his first major purchases was a Rolls-Royce Silver Dawn, which Bob and Barry Feinstein (a photographer friend of Grossman, and husband of Mary Travers) drove from Denver to New York. One night they raced a freight train across the Nebraska plains at seventy miles per hour, road and rails running parallel for more than a hundred miles. There was a three-quarters moon in the sky, and in the headlights of the Rolls the corn shone like aluminum. Sometimes they would pull ahead of the train, and other times the train would lead, exchanging horn blasts as they flew across the land.

Grossman bought a large stone house on a secluded property in the Catskill Mountains hamlet of Bearsville, a little more than a hundred miles north of New York City. He installed a professional car wash for the Rolls and had a room above the barn converted into an apartment for Bob, who became a regular visitor. The quiet of Bearsville appealed to Bob; the mountain air was clean and nobody bothered him. The neighboring town of Woodstock had been a haven for creative people since 1902 when followers of British philosopher John Ruskin, a leading figure in the Arts and Crafts Movement, assisted in the growth of a burgeoning artistic community in the area. Over the decades, local people became used to well-known and eccentric characters moving into town.

Baez came to join Bob in Bearsville in the summer of 1963. They went swimming in Grossman's pool, ran movies on his home projector, and rode Bob's Triumph motorcycle through the backwoods. Part of each day was given over to writing: lyrics, liner notes, or stream-of-consciousness poetry. Bob would sometimes be stirred in the middle of the night to waken, light a cigarette, and start typing. Words came easily at this time in his career; there were more songs than he had albums to put them on. There was no reason to think it would ever be different, although in later years he would find the process of writing far more difficult.

Sometimes Dylan and Baez drove into Woodstock and had coffee at the Cafe Espresso on Tinker Street, owned by Frenchman Bernard Paturel and his wife, Mary Lou. The couple sat at the open fireplace, sometimes singing or drawing pictures. Bob liked to play chess, which he had played with increasing skill ever since his days in Dinkytown where it was a favorite pastime at the Ten O'Clock Scholar and elsewhere. By this time he was a formidable opponent whom few could beat. When Grossman's house became busy with guests, and Bob wanted quiet, the Paturels invited him to stay in a room above the cafe. The White Room was thirty feet by twenty with a high, beamed ceiling and a view over Tinker Street. It was a perfect place to write. As the Paturels observed, Bob used different methods to create songs. He went through a phase when he spread photographs, postcards, and other pictures across the floor and walked around them, looking for ideas. 'He was like an abstract painter composing a picture,' says Bernard Paturel. Occasionally he came downstairs in the late afternoon with a new song. Mary Lou remembers: '[He] would be all excited and ask us if we'd care to hear it.' Bob bought a secondhand upright piano for the family so he could play for them. He also loved playing with the Paturel children, laughing with delight when baby Gerard spat eggs over his face because the boy was tired of Bob teasing him.

Although Bob was writing songs that became anthems of the civil rights movement, Joan Baez noted that he rarely took part in rallies or demonstrations, as she frequently did. He was as uninterested in party politics as he had been in Dinkytown. Although he had sympathy for the great social issues of the day, his mind was preoccupied with the tradition of folk music, the blues, French symbolist prose poems, and biblical stories. A song like 'When the Ship Comes In,' which he wrote on the road with Baez in mid-August 1963, was seen at the time as a metaphor for the struggle for social change, a song that came directly out of the times. Yet the lyric was most obviously made up of fable and scripture, and also contained a good deal of childlike invention – 'fishes will laugh' – and exuberant imagination. It is for these reasons that the song would endure, sounding fresh long after the social concerns of 1963 passed into history.

One of the few overtly political appearances Bob made was at the March on Washington. On August 28, 1963, Bob sang with Baez at the Lincoln Memorial in front of two hundred thousand people. They were feet away from Martin Luther King Jr. as he delivered his keynote 'I Have a Dream' speech. (As King spoke, Wavy Gravy leaned over to Bob and whispered, 'I hope he's over quick. Mahalia Jackson's on next.') To the marchers, and the millions who watched on television, Bob appeared as one of the leaders of the struggle for social justice. Yet it was hard to tell whether he cared one way or another about such matters. Friends like the politically committed Pete Karman assumed Bob was political. 'He *seemed* to be [political],' says Karman. 'He was associating with a lot of these New York radicals.' Bob scandalized Baez by telling her he wrote 'Masters of War' simply because he thought it would sell. He was probably being deliberately provocative, knowing exactly what to say to irritate Baez, but at the same time he did not write the song simply because it chimed with antiwar sentiments then in vogue. It is noteworthy that he rarely included direct references to current events in even his most socially aware songs, like 'Masters of War,' because he must have known that the names of specific politicians, and mentioning specific political events, would date the material (a fate that befell fellow songwriter Phil Ochs). Without these references, the songs would remain relevant as the years went by.

When they were in New York, Dylan and Baez hid from the world at the Earle Hotel on Washington Square, the same place Bob had stayed when he was following Ramblin' Jack Elliott around. Baez attempted a transformation of her scruffy boyfriend, buying Bob a smart jacket, crisp white shirt, and lavender-colored cuff links. She later described this as the best time in their relationship. When her concert tour took her to California in the fall of 1963, the pair also spent time together at Baez's house in Carmel Valley. This was also a very happy interlude. She bought a piano so Bob would be able to work at the house. Although he was beginning to make very good money from his songwriting and concert performances, it seems to have amused Baez to treat him as if he were a penniless kid just blown in from Minnesota. Bob did not mind. At this stage in his career he let Albert Grossman take care of all his financial affairs, being content just to draw petty cash when he needed it. If Baez wanted to help him out further, that was fine, too. He played the piano she bought him and set up his typewriter in her kitchen, at a window overlooking the mountains. Each morning he went straight to the typewriter and worked at it through the day. 'He would stand all day in the kitchen pecking away,' says Nancy Carlen. 'He'd drink black coffee all the morning and then, at lunchtime, he would switch to rot-gut red [wine]. And he would drink rot-gut red the rest of the day.'

During his stay in Carmel, Bob worked on pieces of extended Rimbaud-like verse, later published in a book he titled *Tarantula*. He also wrote at least one important song at this time. 'The Lonesome Death of Hattie Carroll' was a compelling account of a recent court case. Drunken landowner William Zantzinger, aged twenty-four, struck fifty-one-year-old hotel maid Hattie Carroll across the head and shoulders with his cane during a charity ball, apparently after shouting abuse because she was not serving him quickly enough. Hattie Carroll, a mother of eleven children, collapsed and later died in the hospital of a suspected brain hemorrhage. The incident at the dinner was related in the first verse of the song. Bob cautioned that the time to weep had not yet come. In the middle verses he described the disparity between the privileged life of Zantzinger and Hattie Carroll's life of servitude. The final verse revealed Zantzinger had been given a mere six-month sentence (for manslaughter, not murder as originally charged). Bob wrote, 'Now's the time for your tears.' He told the story with the economy of a news reporter and the imagery of a poet, without needing to state the underlying fact that William Devereux Zantzinger was white and Hattie Carroll black. Bob knew the power of subtlety. The extraordinary thing was that 'The Lonesome Death of Hattie Carroll' was not a story of the days of slavery, or of life on a southern plantation. The crime happened that very year, in the state of Maryland, not far from Washington, D.C. William Devereux Zantzinger has continued to live in Maryland, embittered by the song. 'It's actually had no effect upon my life,' he says of the song that has made his name infamous. Naturally he is vitriolic in his scorn for Bob. 'He's a no-account son of a bitch,' he rages, claiming that the song is inaccurate. 'He's just like a scum of a bag [*sic*] of the earth . . . I should've sued him and put him in jail.' Yet while he says the song is a 'total lie,'

Zantzinger has never attempted to prevent Bob performing it.

After returning from California, Bob gave a sold-out solo concert at Carnegie Hall on October 26, 1963, demonstrating his new star status and grossing over $8,000 for a night's work. Abe and Beatty Zimmerman came in from Hibbing for the concert, Beatty fussing with Suze about Bob's scruffy appearance. Beatty was hurt that Bob persisted in obfuscating his background with stories of being an orphan. A few days before the Carnegie Hall concert Bob had spoken with a *Newsweek* reporter to whom he said, foolishly, 'I don't know my parents. They don't know me. I've lost contact with them for years.' Bob knew mystery enhanced his image as an artist and it was in his nature to enjoy making up stories and having fun with people, as he had been doing all his life. But now he was about to be found out and it proved embarrassing when the *Newsweek* reporter discovered that, far from being an orphan, Bob's proud parents were in New York for the Carnegie Hall show. The journalist also contacted Bob's teenaged brother, David, who said Bob had been home to Hibbing as recently as three months ago. In one of the very few times David Zimmerman would ever be quoted on the subject of his famous brother, he gave *Newsweek* some insight into Bob's character. 'We were kind of close,' said David, who was seventeen at the time. 'We're both kind of ambitious. When we set out to do something, we usually get it done. He set out to become what he is.' He added a hint that even he did not fully understand Bob's inscrutable ways: 'Bobby is hard to understand.'

The November 4 edition of *Newsweek* duly carried an article that mocked Bob's image and affectations of speech – a subheading read 'Dig it, Man' – and revealed that, far from being the Huckleberry Finn of folk music, his Hibbing background was conventional and middle class. He was portrayed as a vain young man who had manipulated the truth to help his career. Bob virtually screamed with anger when he saw the article, claiming that Grossman should never have authorized the interview and that family should not talk to journalists. (His anger must have been fierce because his family rarely spoke to reporters after this, other than to make the occasional circumspect comment.) Bob sulked afterward, wondering what lasting damage the article would do to his reputation, and perhaps regretting his harsh words.

The memory of the article was soon wiped from everybody's mind, however. On November 22, President John F. Kennedy was assassinated in Dallas. Bob watched the coverage on television. The murder depressed him, but surprisingly he found he could empathize with the alleged killer, Lee Harvey Oswald. Nobody might ever have known Bob's unorthodox feelings on the subject if he had not then been invited to a fund-raising dinner on December 13 in New York for the Emergency Civil Liberties Committee (ECLC). The committee had decided to give Bob their prestigious Tom Paine award. Named after the eighteenth-century English philosopher and political radical, this was an honor given to a public figure that struck out for social justice. The previous year it had gone to philosopher Bertrand Russell. Bob was uneasy about giving an acceptance speech and drank too much during the cocktail reception and dinner at the Hotel American. After accepting the award – a framed picture of Tom Paine – he gave a speech that seemed to be made up of the first thoughts that popped into his head.

He began by insulting the old-school radicals in the audience with what might have been a misdirected attempt at humor, saying he wished he was addressing people with 'hair on their head.' This extraordinary remark was greeted with guffaws. Bob went on to say that it was not a world for old people. He wanted 'youngness' and told the audience they should not be running things, but relaxing 'in the time you have to relax.' There was more laughter. 'It is not an old people's world. It has nothing to do with old people,' he continued. 'Old people, when their hair grows out, *they* should go out.' After a few confusing comments about Cuba and race relations, Bob turned to the recent Kennedy assassination. 'I got to admit that the man who shot President Kennedy, Lee Oswald, I don't know exactly where . . . what he thought he was doing, but I got to admit honestly that I, too . . . I saw some of myself in him.' This remark caused an uproar. 'I don't think it would have gone . . . I don't think it could go that far,' he bumbled on. 'But I got to stand up and say I saw things that he felt in me.' Beset with boos and hissing, Bob then left the stage.

In a subsequent interview with Nat Hentoff, a friend who was then at *The New Yorker*, Bob said he simply felt for a man caught up in violent times; he did not condone the assassination. 'I saw a lot of myself in Oswald, I said, and I saw in him a lot of the times we're all living in. [And] they looked at me like I was an animal. They actually thought I was saying it was a good thing Kennedy had been killed. That's how far out they are.' It is perhaps the single most important aspect of Bob's talent that he is able to empathize with almost anybody – good or bad – and express that individual's experience in song. While he is arguably a genius at this, he is far less articulate when called upon to talk extemporaneously. Self-conscious on stage without his guitar, he would always remain uncomfortable with public speaking and the results were invariably curiously fascinating. It was life looked at sideways. If anything, this goes to prove that an artist can have enormous natural ability in one discipline and yet be rather ordinary in other ways. This was certainly true of Dylan who, in everyday life, had elements of being awkward, withdrawn, manipulative, spiteful, egocentric, and chauvinistic. Yet with a guitar in his hand he was transformed into a much greater person.

The third Bob Dylan album, *The Times They Are*

A-Changin', was released in January 1964, expressing more eloquently some of the ideas he shared with the audience at the ECLC dinner. The title of the album was proffered as a popular slogan and the cover design – block lettering on white – made it look like a poster. The title song, 'The Times They Are A-Changin',' was a rallying call to youth as America raced through momentous changes. Parents were asked to step aside if they were unable to lend a hand and, adapting a phrase from the Sermon on the Mount, Bob reminded his youthful listeners that *they* would inherit the earth. 'With God on Our Side,' 'Only a Pawn in Their Game,' and 'The Lonesome Death of Hattie Carroll' also expressed dissatisfaction with society. Yet the album was not only a work of protest. 'One Too Many Mornings' was a love song, and 'Restless Farewell' an apology for past misdemeanors, conscious or not. The liner notes – a piece of free verse entitled '4 outlined epitaphs' – added yet another dimension. Still smarting about the *Newsweek* exposé, Bob stated that his background in Hibbing was neither rich nor poor. It was just a dusty memory, like the ghost town of North Hibbing. He wanted people to accept him for his work, not to judge him by his past, or by the stories he had told about that past. The *Newsweek* experience had taught him a lesson. In the future Dylan would be so close-mouthed about his personal life that it would become almost impossible for the press to find out anything significant about him.

As Bob became more famous he built a team of people to look after him and ensure his privacy. One of the key figures in this personal retinue was Victor Maymudes who, in the spring of 1964, became Bob's first road manager. A tall man six years Bob's senior with stern, saturnine features, Maymudes appeared intimidating but was in fact a good-natured and gentle fellow. He met Bob in New York in 1962, via mutual friend Ramblin' Jack Elliott. Maymudes's duties at the start of their association included being chauffeur, bag carrier, bodyguard, and paid companion. One of his qualifications was that he was a match for Bob at chess, pool, and the Chinese game of Go – all of which they played obsessively and all of which Bob was good at. His intelligence lent itself to games of all kinds, and he was happy to spend hours playing in near silence.

Dylan and Maymudes's life on the road began on February 3, 1964, when they set out on a cross-country trip reminiscent of the novel *On the Road*. Two friends accompanied them, with all expenses paid by Bob's new production company, Ashes & Sand. Pete Karman was put forward by Suze because she knew the boys were headed for California, the home of her rival, Joan Baez. Despite the fact that she had moved out of Bob's apartment, Suze was still seeing Bob when he was in New York. Still, when he was away on the road, she could do little about him seeing other women. 'Suze suggested I join the trip to keep an eye on him, not as a spy, but as a chaperone,' says Karman. 'She was very jealous of Baez.' The second companion on the trip was Paul Clayton (also known as Pablo), a musicologist and songwriter. The melody for 'Don't Think Twice, It's All Right' was derived from one of his tunes. He did not bear a grudge against Bob for that; instead friends believed Clayton harbored unrequited homosexual love for Bob. Clayton was a drug abuser, with a predilection for amphetamines. Part of his luggage was a suitcase that opened out to display an array of pills. 'It was an apothecary shop,' jokes Karman.

The four men – Dylan, Clayton, Karman, and Maymudes – clambered into a powder blue Ford station wagon that was Bob's first touring vehicle and set out to drive to California, where Bob would give a concert on February 22, 1964. There would be a couple of other concerts en route, but the main purpose of the trip was to see something of America, and maybe write some songs. As Maymudes drove, Bob sometimes crawled into the space behind the seats and hunched over a notepad. Other times he used a portable typewriter. In this way he came up with the song 'Chimes of Freedom.'

They zigzagged across the country, stopping frequently. In North Carolina they called unannounced upon aged poet Carl Sandburg. It was a disappointing encounter because Sandburg had never heard of Bob. They swung down through South Carolina, Georgia, and Louisiana to New Orleans where Mardi Gras was being celebrated. Nobody had booked a hotel so the four men had to share one room. There was some grumbling when Karman brought a hooker back. 'There was a good deal of drugs and booze and it was Mardi Gras, so!' says Karman, who did not see the problem.

As Maymudes drove them west from New Orleans, Bob started writing 'Mr. Tambourine Man.' This celebrated song was partly inspired by the wild scenes they had witnessed at Mardi Gras, and partly by Bob's friendship with Bruce Langhorne, the guitarist who played on sessions for *The Freewheelin' Bob Dylan*. Langhorne had a big Turkish tambourine – Bob described it as being 'big as a wagon wheel' – which he carried with him. 'I had it in a big case, like a cymbal case,' says Langhorne. 'I used to sometimes just pull it out and play it, in Washington Square Park, or in a joint, or something, and it always generated a lot of energy – people dancing and banging along.' Langhorne was Mr. Tambourine Man in the flesh. But there were other influences on the song. Bob himself has cited the Federico Fellini movie *La Strada*, and the phrase 'jingle jangle' – 'In the jingle jangle morning I'll come followin' you' – occurs in a Lord Buckley recording. Bob has contradicted the popular assumption that drugs were a major influence on the song. 'Drugs never played a part in that song,' he has said, adding that drugs were never that important to him. 'I could take 'em or leave 'em, never hung me up.' This seems a bit disingenuous because drugs were certainly prevalent during the road trip. The four young men smoked a lot of grass, and Clayton was high on pills. In fact, the one facet of the trip that was properly organized was the drugs.

Whenever they rolled into town, there would be a parcel of marijuana waiting at the local post office. Karman says they were stoned during the whole trip.

Mostly songs came to Bob perfectly formed, as he has stated time and again, and he simply had to write them down. Sometimes, though, he worked hard over a longer period of time – hours, days, even weeks – sweating over rhymes. 'Mr. Tambourine Man' had a particularly long and difficult gestation. Bob began writing it on the road trip, but it was weeks before he finished and, consequently, many people remember him working on it when he was with them.

They drove on, via Dallas, to Colorado and Bob revisited Central City where he had worked briefly in the summer of 1960 at the Gilded Garter. He was unable to show club owner Sophia St. John that he had made good because the Garter was closed for the winter. He gave a concert in Denver, only remembering the engagement at the last minute. 'It was all very ad hoc and [so] badly organized,' says Karman. 'We practically missed the concert.' The car radio was on as they left town and Bob heard the new smash hit 'I Want to Hold Your Hand' by The Beatles. The British group had arrived in America the previous week, causing hysteria at Kennedy Airport, and were introduced to the American public on *The Ed Sullivan Show*. Bob was startled by the way The Beatles had reinvented rock 'n' roll, rejuvenating the music he had listened to as a teenager.

They crossed the Rockies in a snowstorm. After gambling in Reno, Nevada, they made it over the Sierra Nevada Mountains and into California. Maymudes headed straight for San Francisco, the destination of Dean Moriarty and Sal Paradise in *On the Road*. In the novel, Kerouac wrote of San Francisco as 'the great buzzing and vibrating hum of what is really America's most exciting city.' In many ways Bob was the spiritual heir to the beat poets. He knew their work, he had a similar sensibility, and he was excited to meet them. 'I think it was in the back of everybody's mind that this was sort of an *On the Road* redux,' says Karman.

Bob had already met Allen Ginsberg, author of the momentous poem 'Howl' and the inspiration for Carlo Marx in *On the Road*. They had been introduced in New York by Al Aronowitz, a journalist who suddenly became ubiquitous at this stage in Bob's career. Aronowitz met Bob after being assigned to write an article for the *Saturday Evening Post*. Bewitched by Bob's charisma, he became a member of the Greek chorus that fawned over and flattered Bob. 'I loved him. Victor loved him. We all loved him. We all adored him,' says Aronowitz. 'We all thought he was God. In fact, I got so crazy I thought he was the new Messiah.' The journalist introduced Bob to Ginsberg in the winter of 1963. Ginsberg was wary of Bob's charisma at first, saying, 'I thought he was just a folksinger, and I was also afraid I might become his slave or something, his mascot.' After Ginsberg attended Bob's concert in Princeton, New Jersey, in November 1963, however, he became enamored with the younger man. Although it is true that beat writing influenced Bob's songwriting, Bob arguably had a greater influence on Ginsberg, who tried to become a recording artist in emulation of him. 'I think Allen Ginsberg's poetry suffered from his deciding early on that he wanted to be a rock star, like Bob Dylan,' says fellow beat poet Lawrence Ferlinghetti. 'Ginsberg realized from the beginning that the unaccompanied voice stood very little chance if you were on the stage following a rock group, or any other kind of musical group.'

Ferlinghetti did not doubt Bob was a fine poet. 'His early songs are really long surrealist poems,' he says. 'I thought that it was too bad he became a successful folksinger. He could have developed as a very interesting writer.' Bob met Ferlinghetti and talked about writing a book for his small San Francisco publishing company, City Lights Books, since it would make sense to be published alongside the other beat writers. But Bob also had an eye on the commercial value of his writing and eventually signed with Macmillan to write *Tarantula*.

Bob invited Ferlinghetti to his concert at the Berkeley Community Theater on Saturday, February 22. Joan Baez was going to appear on stage with him as his guest. Bob held the capacity audience captivated, including influential *San Francisco Chronicle* critic Ralph J. Gleason, later a cofounder of *Rolling Stone* magazine. A few months earlier, Gleason had seen Dylan and Baez together at Monterey and dismissed him as 'another New York Jew imitating Woody Guthrie.' He was now a believer, expressing his faith with the gushing language of a convert. He wrote that the audience heard Bob sing his songs of 'vision and warning,' heard him confront hypocrisy and celebrate his 'belief in life' through poetry. 'And it was none the less poetry for being delivered in a nasal voice by a slim youth with uncombed hair wearing a chamois jacket, blue jeans and boots.' Gleason wrote that Bob was a genius and offered an apology for not recognizing this earlier. 'When I first heard Bob Dylan at Monterey I did not like him. I was deaf. He is truly a great artist and to judge him by the standards of others is a total mistake.' Now he was charmed and moved by Bob's duets with Baez. 'Together they were magnificent Saturday night and Dylan alone is one of the great warning voices of our time.' Gleason met Bob and drove him around San Francisco, smoking pot during the tour. Suddenly it occurred to Gleason that he might have a wreck, while stoned, and kill the genius, and he quit using marijuana immediately.

Now that Bob was reunited with Baez, Pete Karman, who had been Suze's eyes and ears during the trip across the country, had to leave the entourage. 'I had had it,' he says. 'I wasn't getting along too well with Dylan.' His place was taken by Bobby Neuwirth, the boyish former art student from Ohio whom Bob had met at the 1961 Indian Neck Folk Festival. Neuwirth had pretensions as a painter, singer, and filmmaker, but his main talents were his wit and an ability to make friends with important people. Over the next few years he would become one of Bob's closest associates. His loyalty has endured through the years ('I think Bob Dylan is a true artist and the greatest, most influential songwriter of my time,' he says). At first Neuwirth's role as Bob's faithful gofer earned him the not altogether flattering nickname 'Tacos-to-Go.' As they grew closer, their friendship took on an aspect of cruelty. Neuwirth encouraged Bob in the psychological games he enjoyed, an advanced form of Glissendorf that verged on the sadistic now that Bob had the added power of celebrity. 'Neuwirth was the master of head games,' says Al Aronowitz. 'He was nasty as hell.'

Bob continued south after the Berkeley show, traveling with Clayton, Neuwirth, and Maymudes in the Ford, Baez following in her silver Jaguar. They stopped at her house in Carmel and then drove on to Los Angeles, where Bob was scheduled to give a few concerts. He had also been invited to a string of Hollywood parties and was asked to make a guest appearance on Steve Allen's television show on February 25. This was not altogether successful.

'Our exchange was undoubtedly one of the more difficult interviews of my fifty-odd years of doing that sort of thing,' says Steve Allen. 'It was easy to see [that] Mr. Dylan was indeed uncomfortable working on television.' After a desultory exchange during which Bob swiveled on his stool nervously, Allen asked Bob for an explanation of 'The Lonesome Death of Hattie Carroll.' Bob said it would take longer to explain than sing, so he got up and did just that. The Allen show experience was representative of Bob's discomfort with the medium and he would seldom appear on live television in following years, even though chatting with talk show hosts is a standard way to promote an album. Occasionally he would come on and sing a song, but he became one of very few major stars who would not sit down and talk with the hosts. The reason seems to have been his shyness. 'He was terrible at small talk, and he still is,' says summer-camp friend Howard Rutman who, by coincidence, became production assistant on *The Steve Allen Show*. 'He's terrible in an interview. He just doesn't know what to say, and he's *bashful.*' Bob once asked Rutman to write him gags so he would have material to fall back on at times like this. 'I looked at him, and I said, "Bob, what are you, nuts? They want to hear you sing, man. They don't want to hear you tell jokes."'

Four days after the Steve Allen show, on February 29, Bob played the Santa Monica Civic Auditorium. 'Here was something new,' says Maria Muldaur, an Italian-American singer Bob was acquainted with from New York. 'No more little basket house. No more Gerde's Folk City. No more little funky concerts in the basement of [a] church. Here is the Santa Monica Civic Auditorium which, I'm sure, held a couple of thousand people, filled to the rafters.' The songs were very different from the routine Muldaur remembered from Bob's early days in Greenwich Village. 'These were chilling songs,' she says. 'This wasn't about no stinkin' Bear Mountain picnic.' A great roar went up after the performance and Bob dashed for the dressing room where Maymudes, Muldaur, and Neuwirth were waiting for him. 'Man, was that okay?' he asked. As Bob changed his clothes, fans pounded at the door, some pretending to be relatives so they could get in. 'Every time we tried to peek out to see if it had died down, it was worse,' says Muldaur. 'Dylan was walking back and forth like a caged animal.' He even considered climbing out through the bathroom window. Eventually Maymudes and Neuwirth forged a way through the crowd, with Bob and Muldaur following behind. 'I felt like my ribs were gonna be crushed,' she says. 'When Elvis did a show in New York, people would press at him and rip his clothes off. It was like that.' They got to the station wagon, edged onto the road, and then headed for Hollywood, stopping to eject girls who had stowed themselves under a tarpaulin in the back of the car. Fans also followed in cars. To lose them, Maymudes crawled to stop lights, turning quickly when the light changed to red. Elated by the show, the friends tuned the radio to Wolfman Jack and beat out a rhythm on the dashboard. They were going to a party at the Hollywood Hills home of Benny Shapiro, a colleague of Albert Grossman.

'Talk about a swell pad!' exclaims Muldaur. 'Here we are, the scruffy little folk musicians from the village, and here we are in [this] gorgeous house with white carpets and sliding glass doors and a pool. We'd never seen houses like this.' The guests were slightly older, dressed for a cocktail party, and they appeared impossibly sophisticated. Yet, somehow, Bob changed the dynamic of the party when he entered the room. 'A line was forming of people to talk to Bob,' says Muldaur. 'These beautiful women in gorgeous cashmere outfits, young women, were all saying "I'll follow you anywhere, Bob." ' She stepped back to observe what was going on. 'I realized, the Big Star Trip Has Now Officially Begun.'

The months since the Newport Festival, the previous summer, had been miserable for Suze. Bob was conducting a flagrant affair with Joan Baez and yet expecting to continue a relationship with her, too, seeing her whenever his touring engagements and recording dates brought him to New York. When he was in the city, he and Suze attended parties together and went about as a couple, but the relationship was so damaged by Bob's infidelities and the pressure of his fame that it was clear it would not last much longer. Suze had not moved back into Bob's New York apartment after her apparent suicide attempt the previous summer, but lived instead with her sister Carla – with whom she did not get along very well – in a depressingly cramped railroad flat on Avenue B in the Lower East Side. The kitchen doubled as entranceway and was lit by a single, bare bulb. There were two cubicle-like bedrooms but no doors so there was no privacy when Bob came to visit. An already difficult situation took a desperate turn when, at some stage during this period, Suze became pregnant with Bob's child. According to Carla, Suze had the pregnancy terminated. 'At that time abortions were illegal,' says Carla, who nursed her sister afterward. 'There were some bad things between them.'

The abortion precipitated the final, wretched breakup of the relationship. Late one evening in March 1964 Carla Rotolo came home from work to find Suze and Bob arguing in the kitchen. 'They split up, finally split up, and he didn't want to go,' says Carla. The scene became hysterical, with Bob and Suze screaming at each other into the early hours of the morning. With no doors on the rooms, Carla was forced to listen. 'It was getting so bad that I had to become involved.'

'Come on, Bobby, leave,' she told him. 'You can talk another time.'

Bob refused to leave. Carla pushed him. He pushed back. Soon they were practically fighting. 'I remember it as being a terrible, terrible experience,' says Carla. Friends were called and finally Bob was forcibly removed.

Upset by the breakup, and angry with Carla, Bob wrote 'Ballad in Plain D,' one of his most directly autobiographical songs, with some of his most nakedly emotional lyrics. He wrote about two sisters. He loved the younger, whose skin was like bronze. The relationship ended in a fight in a room with a bare bulb, the older sister – whom Bob described as a *parasite* – screaming at him to leave. When Carla heard the song, she had no doubt she was meant to be the parasite. 'It was about the breakup, sure. It was about that night.' Carla resented the term, pointing out that she worked to pay the rent, and she rejects the inference that she had been interfering in Bob and Suze's business. 'I got dragged into something that, frankly, by then, I didn't give a fuck about,' she says. 'Because [Suze] was going to choose whoever she liked, [but] I couldn't keep sitting in my no-door room with screaming and yelling going on.' Carla was left with a very negative view of Bob, considering him selfish, manipulative, and emotionally immature. She also felt maligned by 'Ballad in Plain D,' a song she first heard when it appeared on Bob's next album, *Another Side of Bob Dylan*. He did not warn Carla he was about to record it, much less ask permission.

It seems Bob ultimately came to reproach himself for the song. He hinted as much in the liner notes to the 1985 *Biograph* box set. 'I don't write confessional songs,' he said. 'Well, actually I did write one once and it wasn't very good – it was a mistake to record it and I regret it . . . back there somewhere on maybe my third or fourth album.' This cryptic statement was as far as he ever went toward a public apology to Carla or Suze. Around the time *Biograph* was released, Bob telephoned Carla to reminisce and, in his own awkward way, to try and make peace. It was too late; by this time his life as a superstar was so far removed from his old friends that it was like talking to a stranger. 'He certainly must have felt terrible about things he did to people in his past,' says Carla, who also became estranged from Suze partly because of the messy breakup with Bob. Looking back on her relationship with Bob, Suze is guarded in her comments. For her, the songs contain the truth of what happened. 'If you listen to all the songs, they couldn't be more clear,' she says. 'Anything about our relationship, and about our life together, is very clearly in the songs.' The memory is a complicated one. 'It's all good,' she says. 'It's all bad.' Unlike his breakups with Bonnie Beecher and Echo Helstrom, Bob was unable to maintain a friendship with Suze.

However bad his personal life, Bob was fortunate in that he always had his music and concerts to distract himself after a crisis. After the breakup with Suze, Bob was kept busy on a tour of New England in April, traveling with Victor Maymudes and a group of friends including musician John Sebastian, later of The Lovin' Spoonful. 'It was a very, very moving experience,' says Sebastian, who watched the performances in colleges and other small venues. 'Just this guy with one guitar and a spotlight. It was totally riveting. I found myself in tears several nights.'

Bob, Maymudes, and Grossman then flew to London where, on May 17, Bob gave an important performance at the Royal Festival Hall. Bob was doing the sound check when a call came from the stage door to say a John *Beeklin* was there to see him. 'Bucklen!' said a voice in the background. The minute Bob saw his school friend, he ran to embrace him. Bucklen was serving with the United States Air Force, and was on a three-day pass from his base in East Anglia. It was the first time they had seen each other since the winter of 1960 when Bob had set out for New York. 'He had changed quite a bit,' says Bucklen. 'He had lost a lot of weight.' But much more significant than the change in Bob's physical appearance was the magnitude of fame he had achieved, as Bucklen now witnessed at firsthand.

The Royal Festival Hall was filled to capacity for the show, and the audience listened with the attention one might expect at a classical recital. Bob received a telegram from John Lennon at intermission. In the five months since Bob first heard The Beatles' 'I Want to Hold Your Hand,' the group had achieved a phenomenal four number-one hits in the United States. The Beatles started paying attention to Bob after hearing *The Freewheelin' Bob Dylan*. 'We just played it, just wore it out,' George Harrison has said. 'The content of the song lyrics and just the attitude – it was just incredibly original and wonderful.' The Beatles had not yet met Bob, but Lennon found time to send a telegram saying they wished they could be at the Festival Hall. Unfortunately, they had a filming commitment. 'Oh man! That's pretty neat,' exclaimed Bucklen. Bob also seemed pleased, but not impressed. He admired The Beatles in many ways, but 'I Want to Hold Your Hand' did not have the weight of 'Don't Think Twice, It's All Right.'

During the second half of the concert, Bucklen struggled to reconcile the fact that the man on stage was Bobby Zimmerman. 'I couldn't relate to the image Bob was presenting, and [to] him as a person,' he says. 'One of the songs was 'With God on Our Side' and after every verse people cheered. What the hell? This is *Bob*. I remember this guy sitting next me, a big guy, he started to weep.' After the show, Albert Grossman had to rescue his artist from a crush of fans. 'Bob, I could tell, was enjoying it,' says Bucklen, who got into a black cab with Dylan, Grossman, and three girls. They spent the evening visiting parties, meeting old friends like folksinger Martin Carthy, and getting stoned. 'Here. This is good stuff. You want some?' asked Bob, offering John Bucklen a joint. It was the first time Bucklen had ever smoked marijuana.

Bob has avoided talking in detail about his use of drugs, saying in one interview that he could take drugs or leave them. There is overwhelming evidence that he frequently smoked marijuana. There is evidence that he experimented with other drugs as well. Record producer Paul Rothchild claimed he introduced Bob to the hallucinogenic drug LSD in April 1964. It was in Bob's character to experiment, and he was acquainted with heavy drug users, including heroin addicts like Howard Alk, an actor turned filmmaker friend of Grossman from Chicago who became part of the entourage. 'I never got hooked on any drug,' said Bob when pressed by a *Rolling Stone* interviewer in 1984 to talk about the subject. However, he added: '[But] who knows what people stick in your drinks, or what kinda cigarettes you're smokin'?'

Waiting for a cab, Bob asked Bucklen a curious question. 'What do you think of me now?' he said. 'How do I look to you?'

'Well, you look kind of strung out and seem a little

In the North Country

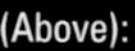

(Above):
Bob Dylan's parents, Abe and Beatty Zimmerman, married in 1934 and made their home in Duluth, Minnesota, before moving further north to the mining town of Hibbing. Abe and Beatty are seen here with one of Abe's nieces.
Courtesy Jack Zimmerman

(Left):
Before he became known to the world as Bob Dylan, Bobby Zimmerman was a Hibbing teenager in love with rock 'n' roll. In this 1959 high school yearbook photograph, his hair is arranged with a suggestion of Little Richard's pompadour.
Hibbing High School yearbook

(Left):
Women are an integral part of the story of Bob Dylan's life. His first significant girlfriend was fellow Hibbing High School student Echo Helstrom.
Hibbing High School yearbook

(Left):
The Zimmerman family home at 2425 7th Avenue, Hibbing, where Bob spent most of his childhood. Bob's bedroom was to the rear of the house. **Howard Sounes**

(Below):
The mining town of Hibbing, Minnesota, was the quintessential small town where everybody knew each other. This photograph – taken *circa* 1948 – shows Howard Street, one of the two main streets in town, where Bob spent much of his youth. His ba mitzvah party was held in the Androy Hotel to the left. The L&B Café was on the opposite side of the road.
MS2.9/HB2/p15, Minnesota Historical Society

Bound for Glory

(Right):
In the fall of 1959, Bob enrolled as a student at the University of Minnesota in Minneapolis. He dated several girls, the most important of whom was fellow student Bonnie Beecher (a.k.a. Jahanara Romney). A beautiful young woman, Bonnie was probably the inspiration for Bob's song, "Girl from the North Country." However, Bob also gave Echo Helstrom the impression the song was about her. Aivars Perlsbach/courtesy Jahanara Romney

(Below):
After arriving in New York City in January 1961, Bob spent the first few months scuffling around the coffee houses and small clubs of Greenwich Village, performing whenever and wherever he could. Here is a rare photograph of a baby-faced Bob on stage (center) at The Gaslight club with friends Ralph Rinzler (left) and John Herald (right) of the bluegrass group, The Greenbriar Boys. John Cohen

(Left):
Harold Leventhal was the manager of Bob's hero, Woody Guthrie. Harold also promoted Bob's first major New York concert, at the Town Hall on 12 April 1963. Harold is seen here in a recent photograph holding the original advertisement for that historic concert. Howard Sounes

(Left):
Bob met Suze Rotolo in the summer of 1961, and she became the most important girlfriend of his early years in New York. Bob wrote numerous songs about Suze including "Boots of Spanish Leather." She was photographed with Bob for the cover of his second album, *The Freewheelin' Bob Dylan*. The song "Ballad in Plain D" was about their unhappy break-up in 1964.
Joe Alper/Courtesy the Alper Family Collection

(Below):
In July 1963, Bob and fellow artists – including the distinguished folk singer Pete Seeger (left) – traveled to Greenwood, Mississippi, to perform at a rally to encourage African-Americans to register to vote.
Danny Lyon/Magnum Photos

The most famous love affair of Bob's life was with singer Joan Baez. Although the romance was brief, and Bob treated her rather badly, the relationship caught the public imagination. Here Bob and Joan pose together at Newark Airport, New Jersey, in 1964. Joan did not know Bob was also dating another young woman, Sara Lownds, who soon became his first wife. © Daniel Kramer

(Above):
In July 1965, Bob caused uproar among folk music traditionalists at the annual Newport Folk Festival in Newport, Rhode Island, by performing with an amplified rock 'n' roll band. Here Bob and his band conduct an afternoon sound check. At the Hammond organ, wearing dark glasses, is Al Kooper, who played organ on "Like a Rolling Stone." On the left, playing lead guitar, is another close friend, Mike Bloomfield. © David Gahr

(Left):
Bob confers with his manager, Albert Grossman, before a concert at Forest Hills tennis stadium, New York, in August 1965. Some believe that Bob would not have become an international star without Grossman's support. Bob was grateful to Grossman at first, but their relationship ended acrimoniously in the 1980s with a bitter legal dispute.
© Daniel Kramer

Full Power

(Facing page):
By 1965, Bob had revolutionized popular music by combining poetic lyrics with amplified rock 'n' roll – showing artists everywhere that pop music could express profound ideas. Bob is seen here in the studio at the time of the *Highway 61 Revisited* album. As photographer Daniel Kramer recalls, Bob was writing the lyrics for "Positively 4th Street." © Daniel Kramer

(Above left):
In 1965–6 Bob toured the world with The Hawks, a bar band from Toronto, Canada, later acclaimed as The Band. Bob is seen here on stage with lead guitarist Robbie Robertson. Audiences who were used to Bob performing with acoustic guitar in the folk style were not best pleased with his new amplified band sound. "Everywhere we went they booed us," says Robertson. "It was a very interesting process to pull into a town, set up, play. People come in. They boo you. You pack up. You go on to the next town. You play. The people boo you. And then you just go on. You go all the way around the world with people just booing you every night." © Larry Keenan

(Below left):
During his 1965 tour with The Hawks, Bob visited Lawrence Ferlinghetti's book store, City Lights, in San Francisco, and posed in an alley behind the store with Robbie Robertson (far left) and beat poets Michael McClure (second from left) and Allen Ginsberg (right). Bob's original intention was to use one of the pictures from this session on the cover of his next album, *Blonde on Blonde*. © Larry Keenan

(Above):
Albert Grossman bought a country estate at Bearsville, near Woodstock in upstate New York, and Bob came here to relax. One of his recreations was to ride motorcycles through the backwoods. On Friday 29 July 1966 Bob suffered a motorcycle accident that closed the first part of his extraordinary career. © John Launois/Colorific!

(Right):
This is the likely scene of Bob Dylan's fabled accident. Striebel Road is a steep country lane directly outside the entrance to the Grossman property in Bearsville. Although his injuries were relatively minor, Bob retired from public life after the incident.
Howard Sounes

thinner.' Bob just stared at his old friend. 'Yeah, well, what do you think of me?' asked Bucklen.

'Well, you look a little strung out and a little thinner,' replied Bob, apparently displeased, and his mood deteriorated during the rest of the evening and culminated in a scene at the Mayfair Hotel when they returned there with a couple of girls. Bob got into a belligerent argument with the management because he wanted to take his girl to his room. 'They wouldn't let him do it, and he really got irate,' recalls Bucklen. 'I said, "Hey, Bob, let's just go someplace else." And he turned [and said], "Mind your own damn business . . . Let me take care of this. It's no concern of yours." I said, "Okay, fine." I just turned around and walked out . . . That was the last thing he said to me.' The friends were to meet once again, twenty- five years later, backstage at a concert in Madison, Wisconsin, in 1989. Bucklen had contacted Bob's tour company to ask to get tickets so he could bring his children to the show and maybe introduce them to his old friend, and Bob sent word that they would be welcome. Almost the first thing he said to Bucklen was to apologize for talking harshly to him at the Mayfair a quarter of a century before. He said he had been under a lot of pressure. The fact that Bob had held this in his mind for so many years offers a glimpse of his sensitive nature. As other friends would note during his career, if Bob had behaved in an insensitive way he would invariably reproach himself for it for a long time afterward.

After the London concert, Bob traveled through Europe on vacation. He flew with Victor Maymudes and a friend, Ben Carruthers, to France where they met singer Hugues Aufray. Bob was excited to be in the land of Rimbaud and was eager to imbibe the culture. He made Aufray laugh by eating Camembert with a spoon, and they drank good wines. Bob spent a romantic evening with the chanteuse Nico, and met the expatriate writer Mason Hoffenberg, coauthor of *Candy*. They rented a Volkswagen and drove to Germany to see the Berlin Wall. A few days later Bob concluded his European vacation by visiting Greece. In a village outside Athens he wrote some of the songs that would appear on his fourth album, *Another Side of Bob Dylan*, working on notepaper from the Mayfair Hotel. 'Mama, You Been on My Mind' was one of the songs. Although it would not appear on this album,* it was one of the finest love songs he ever wrote. The ravishing opening line described how a chance image – the 'color of the sun cut flat' on the crossroads where he was standing – could cause memories of an old love to flood back, perhaps indicating the private regrets he felt over the way he had treated Suze. In real life, he had made a terrible mess of the relationship, but in song he could express himself with delicacy and maturity.

Another Side of Bob Dylan was recorded in one remarkable six-hour session – between 7.30 P.M. on the evening of June 9, and 1:30 the following morning – just after Bob returned to New York from Europe. Columbia wanted the record for a forthcoming sales conference and Bob was happy to work fast to oblige them. A group of friends came into Studio 'A' to support him, including Ramblin' Jack Elliott and Al Aronowitz. The visitors brought bottles of Beaujolais, and several children scampered around. The relaxed atmosphere affected the recordings with Bob chuckling on takes of 'All I Really Want to Do' and 'I Don't Believe You,' belying the sadness at the root of both songs. And he was not fazed when a four-year-old burst into the studio when he was recording. 'I'm gonna rub you out,' Bob admonished the kid, with good humor. 'I'll track you down and turn you into dust.' The visitors were more of a problem for producer Tom Wilson. He tried to confine the children to the control room, which he had to share with Bob's friends who were making suggestions in support of Bob. When

*Recorded in 1964, 'Mama, You Been on My Mind' eventually appeared in 1991 on the three-CD compilation of outtakes and previously unreleased material, *The Bootleg Series Volumes 1–3*.

Wilson pointedly ignored them, Aronowitz traced a square in the air behind his head.

The songs had been written over a long period of time. Bob began working on 'It Ain't Me, Babe' in Italy. 'Chimes of Freedom' came from the road trip to California. Other songs were written at Cafe Espresso, and in Greece. The dominant theme was relationships, and many of the songs – including 'To Ramona' and 'Ballad in Plain D' – seemed to have specific reference to Suze. Although there was a tinge of resentment and melodrama to 'Ballad in Plain D,' it featured a memorable description of Suze as 'The could-be dream-lover of my lifetime.' The song was performed with care, in contrast to the sloppiness of some of the recordings that evening. The two comic talking songs – 'Motorpsycho Nightmare' and 'I Shall Be Free No. 10' – were less engaging than similar songs on *The Freewheelin' Bob Dylan*, and overall this was a slightly weaker album than that and *The Times They Are A-Changin'*. 'My Back Pages' was strong, expressing the fact that Bob had outgrown the certainties of youth. Unfortunately, the song was recorded in the early hours of the morning, by which time Bob sounded tired, and this lessened the impact of the record as a whole.

There was nothing on the album that could be considered a protest song and the album title, *Another Side of Bob Dylan*, seemed a turning away from the past, although the truth was that Bob had never seen himself simply as a protest singer. He wrote all types of songs. He blamed Tom Wilson for the title, which played into the hands of those critics who wanted to seize upon an apparent rejection of what they thought he had been doing. 'I begged and pleaded with him not to do it,' Bob said in 1985. 'I knew I was going to have to take a lot of heat for a title like that and it was my feeling that it wasn't a good idea coming after *The Times They Are A-Changin'* . . . It seemed like a negation of the past which in no way was true.' Once again, Bob composed lengthy poetic liner notes for the album – 'Some Other Kinds of Songs' – that included references to his private life. Apart from thanking the Paturels for the use of their spare room in Woodstock, he could not hide his bitterness regarding the breakup with Suze. He wrote 'i used t'hate enzo' and went on to describe how he became so jealous of Enzo Bartoccioli – the young man Suze had met in Italy in 1962 and subsequently married – that he fantasized about murdering him. Again, here was a real insight into Bob's truest feelings. Only the deepest hurt and jealousy could have engendered such violent thoughts, although one might consider that Suze had more reason to be angry for the way he had behaved toward her.

Critical reaction to the album was mixed, and the Newport Folk Festival that summer was not quite the triumph it had been the previous year. Artists like Phil Ochs, who had hitched their careers to the wagon of protest, received the most enthusiastic reception. Bob's new songs about relationships seemed self-indulgent to some, although he also premiered 'Mr. Tambourine Man' to acclaim. After the festival, the editor of *Sing Out!* published an open letter to Bob that was critical not only of his introspective new songs but also of the apparent changes in him as a man now that he was a star. 'I saw at Newport how you had somehow lost contact with people,' wrote editor Irwin Silber, adding that Bob now traveled with an entourage of drinking buddies, and his songs were tinged with maudlin and cruelty, which was true enough. Despite the mixed reception to his new work, the festival was personally important for Bob because he finally met country artist Johnny Cash, whom he had been corresponding with and whose music he had long admired. Bob and Johnny were so happy to become acquainted that, together with Joan Baez and June Carter Cash, they jumped up and down on the bed in Cash's motel room, 'like kids,' as Cash described it.

A few days after the festival, Bob flew to California

and, in the last days of July and the beginning of August, he had a brief romantic interlude with his old girlfriend Bonnie Beecher. 'I drove him to the airport and ended up getting on the plane and spending a week in Hawaii with him,' she recalls. Bob gave a concert in Waikiki, after which he said good-bye to Bonnie and flew east to stay at Albert Grossman's house in Bearsville with Joan Baez, sister Mimi, and Mimi's new husband, Richard Farinã, recently divorced from Carolyn Hester. Mimi was no easier to handle than Suze's sister. When she decided Bob was not treating Baez with sufficient respect, Mimi grabbed Bob's hair and yanked his head back. It was becoming clear to Mimi – partly because Bob flirted with almost every woman he met – that Bob was not as much in love with Joan as she was with him. Joan seemed blind to this, and was as besotted as ever, but their romance had already passed its brief peak period and it would not be long before it ended altogether.

It was during Bob's stay in Bearsville that a meeting was arranged between Bob and The Beatles. The group was in New York in the summer of 1964 at the end of a second U.S. visit, about to give a fund-raising concert at the Paramount Theater. The Beatles knew journalist Al Aronowitz, who had been assigned to write about them for the *Saturday Evening Post*. In the process, he became besotted with the group, just as he had with Bob. John Lennon asked Aronowitz to contact Bob and arrange a meeting at their hotel. So Bob came down from Bearsville and he and his entourage were duly ushered into The Beatles' suite at the Hotel Delmonico, where they were protected from fans by a phalanx of police. The Beatles had just finished dinner with their manager, Brian Epstein, when Bob came in. Aronowitz made the introductions, bursting his shirt buttons with pride. It was one of the greatest moments of his life, and a meeting of considerable importance. The subsequent influence the musicians had on one another had an important effect on popular music as Bob integrated a Beatles-like use of rock 'n' roll into his music and The Beatles began to write lyrics that had the depth and seriousness of Dylan songs.

The American visitors suggested they all smoke a joint. The Beatles were drinkers rather than drug takers (Scotch and coke being their favorite tipple), and although it has been reported in books about the era that they had never smoked marijuana before, Harrison and Lennon at least had smoked pot.* The point was that none of The Beatles had ever smoked high-quality marijuana. Bob was surprised; he had assumed the middle eight in 'I Want to Hold Your Hand' was 'I get high! I get high!' John Lennon explained the lyric was 'I can't *hide*.' Bob clumsily rolled the first joint, spilling marijuana. Because there were police directly outside the door, they adjourned to an interior room before lighting up. Bob handed the first joint to Lennon who told Ringo Starr to try it, joking that Starr was his taster. The drummer started smoking as if it were a cigarette, not passing it to the others, so Aronowitz suggested that Victor Maymudes roll another joint. It was not long before everybody was mightily stoned. McCartney decided he had discovered the meaning of life and searched for a pencil so he could write it down. Starr giggled. Brian Epstein said he felt he was on the ceiling.

In the bleary light of the next day McCartney looked at his pencil-written notes to discover the meaning of life boiled down to one sentence: 'There are seven levels.'

During the next few days Bob and The Beatles saw more of one another, at the hotel and around New York. The bond of friendship was formed most strongly between Dylan and Lennon and Harrison. When The Beatles played the Paramount Theater on September 20, Bob went along to watch his new friends in action. It was pandemonium, with the teenybopper audience

*Interviews the surviving Beatles gave for *The Beatles Anthology*, published in 2000, and other sources have made it clear that members of the group smoked pot before meeting Dylan.

screaming so loudly as to render the group virtually inaudible. The diminutive Bob stood on a chair in the wings to get a better view. He remarked with satisfaction that the show was the opposite of his concerts, where audiences listened to every word in silence, applauding at the end. 'He was proud of that,' says Aronowitz.

Part of the reason for Bob's increasing coolness toward Joan Baez was that he was spending a lot of time with another girlfriend, model Sara Lownds, whom Baez knew nothing about at this stage. Sara Lownds would soon take over as the main woman in his life and ultimately become Bob's first wife, mother of his children and inspiration for some of his greatest songs.

Despite her almost aristocratic manner, Sara came from humble beginnings. In fact, she had a very difficult upbringing and, in later life, it seemed there was a lot about her past that she wished to forget, which, together with her refusal ever to give interviews, has resulted in much of her life story remaining mysterious until now. She was born Shirley Marlin Noznisky in Wilmington, Delaware. Although her year of birth has been given as 1940, she was in fact born a year earlier, on October 28, 1939. Her father, Isaac, was a Belorussian Jewish immigrant who settled in Wilmington shortly before the First World War and ran a scrap-metal business on Claymont Street. He never learned to read or write English. Shirley's mother, Bessie, ran a dry-goods store at the junction of 8th and Lombard Streets, the latter the street on which Shirley was born. She had one brother, Julius, sixteen years her senior. When Shirley was nine, her mother suffered a stroke, after which her great aunt Esther helped look after her. In November 1956, when Shirley was completing high school, her father was shot dead by a man with a grudge. Shirley's widowed mother died five years later, leaving her alone in the world.

Shirley was a beautiful young woman, with pale skin

and dark hair. But it was her eyes that were most remarkable. They were sad eyes, perhaps expressing the pain of her early life. She attended the University of Delaware briefly before moving to New York City, around 1960, where she worked as a bunny girl at the Playboy Club. She became a fashion model, represented by the Ford agency, and met her first husband, photographer Hans Lownds. Hans was a German Jew, born in 1914 as Heinz Ludwig Lowenstein; he fled to America in the 1930s and changed his name to Henry Louis Lownds (Hans was a nickname). He became a successful photographer of men's fashion, known for using beautiful young women in his pictures. Despite the fact Hans was twenty-five years older than Shirley, she became his third wife in late 1960 or early 1961. 'My father was the one who changed Sara's name,' says Peter Lownds, who discovered he had a new stepmom – only five years his senior – when he came home from Yale and Sara answered the door. 'My father said, "I can't be married to a woman named Shirley." [So] he had her change her name to Sara.'

Sara and Hans lived in a large five-story house on 60th Street in Manhattan, between Second and Third Avenues. Sara continued with her modeling career – appearing in *Harper's Bazaar* as 'lovely, luscious Sara Lownds' – and then became pregnant. Her daughter Maria was born October 21, 1961. Within a year of the birth, the marriage began to fail. Sara started going out on her own, driving around town in an MG sports car Hans had given her, and gravitated to the youthful scene in Greenwich Village. According to Peter Lownds, this is where she met Bob. 'Bob was the reason [she left Hans],' says Lownds. 'He was famous and she was very beautiful.' Hans and Sara separated – soon to divorce* – and

*This and other aspects of Bob's early relationship with Sara seem to be echoed in the lyrics of the 1974 song 'Tangled Up in Blue,' especially the second verse.

Sara went to work as a secretary for the film production division of Time-Life. Sara was in the neighborhood coffee shop in midtown Manhattan when she struck up a friendship with waitress Sally Anne Buehler, who happened to be dating Albert Grossman. Sally invited Sara up to Bearsville and this became another link with Bob. When Sally and Albert Grossman married, on November 12, 1964, Bob and Sara were among the guests at their wedding.

Shortly after the Grossmans' wedding, Bob gave up his apartment on West 4th Street, which was really too small for two people, and he and Sara lived together for a short while at Grossman's apartment in Manhattan, while Albert and Sally went on their honeymoon in Europe. Soon after this Bob took an apartment of his own at the Hotel Chelsea on West 23rd Street. Built as an apartment building in 1884, the Chelsea was favored by artists, musicians, and writers because suites could be rented cheaply on flexible leases and the management was relaxed about the eccentricities of guests. Willem de Kooning painted there. Aaron Copland composed on a piano wheeled up by management. Arthur C. Clarke wrote *2001*, and the beats regularly partied and wrote there too. The Chelsea was bohemian, but for the most part safe enough for children to stay in. This was important because when Bob moved into room 211 – a modest one-bedroom suite overlooking the street – he did so with Sara and three-year-old Maria, the nucleus of a family that became very important to him.

Hans Lownds threatened to go through the courts to get sole custody of Maria. He did not want his daughter raised by Bob, whom he referred to disdainfully as 'Zimmerman.' However, Hans's attorney told him that he would have little chance of winning and, after receiving this advice, he decided to have no further contact with Maria. Although he lived until 1995, Hans never saw her again, and for all intents and purposes Bob became Maria's father.

When he was at the Chelsea, Bob lived a remarkably quiet life with Sara. He had a piano in his room, and he composed songs, but few people knew he was there. 'He was very shy, very quiet,' says Stanley Bard, who ran the Chelsea. When he craved excitement, Bob went out drinking at the Kettle of Fish in the Village. Sara usually would not be with him on these occasions. Instead, his companion would invariably be Bobby Neuwirth, although other acolytes included Al Aronowitz and singer David Cohen. Bob held court in the upstairs bar, testing friends with mind games. Essentially he and Neuwirth would pick on weaknesses, goading a reaction. When John Herald walked in one evening, Bob and Neuwirth sniggered, 'Here comes the Armenian secret service guy.' This was simply a play on the fact that Herald was of Armenian extraction, but if he had taken offense Herald knew he would have suffered the full force of their sarcasm. He was able to laugh about it and was therefore welcome to join their table. Others were not so lucky. 'I've seen them make people cry,' he says. Bonnie Beecher, for one, was terrified of Neuwirth and hid behind Bob when Neuwirth was in the room. 'I am extremely shy and, for me, being in a room with Neuwirth was like being in hell. Because he was always parrying to me and I would go blank. I would just be helpless,' she admits. 'I would leave a room just shaking, and on the verge of tears.'

On his trips away from the Chelsea, and the companionship of Sara, Bob was drawn into circles of New York society where wealth and fame were revered, where sarcasm was celebrated and exclusivity considered good – the antithesis of the values of the folk revival. Neuwirth was his guide in this superficial underworld. One of the subterranean characters they became friendly with at this time was model Edie Sedgwick, a mentally unstable peroxide blonde whose society family put her in an institution in 1962. By 1964 she was one of the most celebrated figures in New York, famous for living extravagantly. Shortly before Christmas 1964, a Cadillac limousine crunched to a halt in the snow outside the Kettle of Fish. Edie had come to pay court. Together with Neuwirth, Edie and Bob went to look at the lights outside a church on Houston Street. Edie later went on to have an affair with Neuwirth. Although a peripheral figure in the story of Bob's career, Edie is widely believed to be at least partly the inspiration for some of Bob's later songs including 'Just Like a Woman.'

After the Christmas break, Bob recorded *Bringing It All Back Home*, one of the most important records of his career, the album that integrated what he had learned from the success of British bands like The Beatles with his own, more poetic lyrics. Rock 'n' roll, a form of music that had begun in America most popularly in the 1950s with artists like Chuck Berry, Elvis Presley, and Little Richard, had dwindled away into formulaic top-forty pop in its native country. The Beatles, however, who had grown up with a love of early American rock 'n' roll, had come from Liverpool to prove in the space of one year that this form of music could still be exciting and hugely popular. 'America should put statues up to The Beatles. They helped give this country's pride back to it,' said Bob, who recognized the importance of the group in bringing new life to a musical genre he had grown up with but had abandoned for folk music because it did not seem to offer him enough. It was not just The Beatles that were pointing the way forward. In the summer of 1964, another British group, The Animals, had a hit with an R&B cover of 'The House of the Risin' Sun,' a song they learned from Bob's debut album. By combining the powerful lyrics of this traditional song with swirling rhythm and blues music, The Animals created something slightly different again – a pop song that had the seriousness of traditional music.

Bob himself took the process one crucial step further by combining his self-written, poetic lyrics with rhythm and blues music. By doing so he created folk-rock, although the phrase is misleading. He had stopped dealing in folk songs long ago. Beginning with *The Freewheelin' Bob Dylan,* his songs were essentially poems set to music; the music just happened to be the acoustic sound of folk. With *Bringing It All Back Home* – the album title was a reference to the fact that this was American music British groups had borrowed – Bob recorded his songs with rock 'n' roll backing, demonstrating to musicians everywhere that they could also express their deepest feelings in rock 'n' roll songs. This was the simple but nonetheless revolutionary idea that emancipated artists from The Beatles through Bruce Springsteen and beyond, allowing them to write pop songs that aspired to the intellectual level of art. In making this transformation, folk music's brightest star exchanged his acoustic guitar for a newfangled solid-body electric guitar, a sacrilegious symbol to many folk revivalists. 'He had a lot of balls to do that,' says Kenny Rankin, who played on Bob's January 1965 electric sessions. '[It was] quite a thing for Dylan just to pick up an electric guitar.'

Despite the momentous nature of what was afoot, there was little sense of nervousness when the musicians assembled in New York on January 13, 1965, for the *Bringing It All Back Home* sessions. Back in high school, Bob had shown a disinclination to rehearse with his bands. As a solo performer he could please himself. Now that he was working with a full, electrically amplified band of professional musicians, he led whither his fancy took him, and the musicians had to follow as best they could. There were no rehearsals, much less a discussion about what he wanted to achieve. 'None of the songs that I played on were [even] counted off,' says guitarist Kenny Rankin. 'He just started strummin' and we jumped in after about two or four bars.' The resulting music was a joyous fusion of freeform verse and good-time rock 'n' roll. 'There's no overdubbing. There's no patching up. There's no splicing,' says Rankin. 'What you heard is what we did.'

The songs included the rollicking 'Maggie's Farm,' a comic protest, the name supposedly inspired by Maggiore's Farm, near Kingston, New York, which Bob passed each time he traveled to Woodstock; and the machine-gun rat-a-tat-tat of 'Subterranean Homesick Blues,' set to a Chuck Berry riff.* The lyrics of 'Subterranean Homesick Blues' consisted of snippets of images, jokes, and flashing aphorisms that became catch-phrases. Best known perhaps is the line about not needing a weatherman to know which the way the wind blows; this reference provided a name for the anarchist-terrorist group the Weathermen, formed in 1969. 'Love Minus Zero / No Limit' features the wonderful simile 'she's true, like ice, like fire.' Although in writing this may look like a cliché, it sounded quite beautiful when sung. Indeed, it is a feature of Bob's work that, by his vocal phrasing, he can lift a seemingly simple couplet to the heights of lyricism. His spoof on the founding of America, 'Bob Dylan's 115th Dream,' was begun with such alacrity that he left the band behind. 'I was ridin' on the Mayflower,' he started singing, and then broke down in hoots of laughter because the musicians were just watching him. 'We didn't know where to cut the groove. So he went "I was ridin' on the Mayflower . . ." and we all should have come in on "ridin'", but everyone sat there,' says Bruce Langhorne. 'Wait a minute, fellas,' said Tom Wilson, laughing heartily. 'Okay, take two.' The tape was still running and they plunged back in. This was the recording – complete with false start – that was used on the album.

As a conciliatory gesture to his established folk listeners, the four long songs on the second side of the

*Just as local Woodstock lore has it that Maggiore's Farm in Kingston was Maggie's Farm, some locals believe the pump that does not work (because the vandals took the handle) noted in 'Subterranean Homesick Blues' was inspired by a water pump in Annandale-on-Hudson, which, at one time, was missing a handle.

album were acoustic: 'Mr. Tambourine Man,' 'Gates of Eden,' 'It's All Over Now, Baby Blue,' and 'It's Alright, Ma (I'm Only Bleeding).' Delivered at a furious pace, this last song was a grim masterpiece. From the opening image of darkness at noon, the song seethed in anger. It was also loaded with some of the most memorable images Bob ever created: flesh-colored Christ figures glow in the dark; money did not talk, it swore; even the United States President had to stand naked. Here was a song that would never date, partly because Bob was shrewd enough not to mention the current U.S. president by name. As a result successive generations would, in their mind, associate the song with the president of the day, and the song never had more power than when Bob performed it in 1974 during Richard Nixon's Watergate crisis. 'I've written some songs that I look at, and they just give me a sense of awe,' Bob said in 1997. 'Stuff like, "It's Alright Ma," just the alliteration in that blows me away.' It was also amazing that he had recorded this remarkable album in just three days.

The cover for this most important album was a minor work of art in itself. It featured a carefully composed and technically innovative photograph by Daniel Kramer that recalled a style of portraiture popular during the Renaissance. Bob posed in a well-appointed room around which were placed objects that had symbolic meaning and constituted visual jokes. Perhaps like Flemish painter Jan van Eyck's celebrated 1434 portrait, *The Marriage of Giovanni Arnolfini*, the subject was balanced by the presence of a beautiful, enigmatic woman. The impression was playful and sophisticated. 'I wanted to do something that would really be special because I was so impressed by what [Bob] was doing,' says Kramer, who also photographed the recording sessions. He devised an adapter for his camera that allowed him to take a picture of Bob while objects on the periphery blurred, as if moving. 'I wanted Bob to be the nucleus, the center, and the universe of music turning around him.' The blurred objects would form a circle, as if Bob were at the hub of a revolving LP. Bob liked the idea and one snowy night he drove Kramer to Grossman's house in Bearsville. The next morning they set up the scene in the living room. Sally Grossman put on a red pants suit and reclined on her chaise longue, smoking a cigarette. Bob perched at the other end of the chaise longue, wearing a white shirt with blue pinstripes and a black jacket. Artifacts that told a story about Bob's life and music were arranged on the seat, floor, and mantelpiece. These included albums by Lord Buckley and Eric Von Schmidt, his own *Another Side of Bob Dylan*, a copy of *Time* magazine, and a fallout shelter sign. Bob held Sally's Persian cat on his knee. The final visual joke was the lavender-colored cuff link peeping from his left sleeve. It was onc of the pair given to him by Joan Baez.

When *Bringing It All Back Home* was released in March 1965 it became his most successful album yet, reaching the sixth position in the charts. Some folk purists were disdainful, but many reviewers recognized Bob's achievement and Bob was inundated with requests for interviews. He gave a press conference in New York to mark its release but said precisely nothing about the record and, instead, used the opportunity to poke fun at the reporters. Asked if he had a rock 'n' roll band in high school, Bob replied: 'I had a banana band in high school.' Questioned about his romance with Joan Baez, he said she was his fortune teller. Asked who could save the world, Bob immediately nominated his sidekick Al Aronowitz. Although his answers were stupendously silly, Bob was playing a shrewd game. By refusing to abide by the conventions of press interviews, and by avoiding talking about his songs in a serious way, he made himself more intriguing to the press and his public. In any case, after the *Newsweek* debacle, he was not going to be drawn into talking about his personal life.

Bringing It All Back Home proved even more popular in Britain where it reached the number-one position on a wave of publicity generated by Bob's spring concert tour of the United Kingdom, which started in April. Here, too, he was not exactly forthcoming in his interview comments. Asked by *Melody Maker* what 'Subterranean Homesick Blues' was about he replied: 'It's just a little story, really. It's not about anything.' Indeed, how could he possibly give a serious answer to such a question when the song was an almost indefinable amalgam of surreal images and jokes? Bob's arrival in Britain was made more exciting because he was accompanied by Joan Baez who, as far as the press and public were concerned, was his partner (nobody knew about Sara yet). But behind the scenes the relationship between Dylan and Baez was falling apart. Baez had come to Britain with Bob partly because she thought he was going to introduce her to his enthusiastic English audiences, returning the favor she had done for him in America, where she was more popular. It was a reasonable expectation; they had been touring the United States together as recently as the month before, and Bob had actually invited her to come with him to England. But once they arrived, Bob did not seem to want her around. Possibly he realized that he was so popular in Britain he did not need to share a stage with anybody. Whatever was going through his mind, he did not ask Joan to sing with him on stage and she was reduced to practicing her ear-splitting soprano in hotel rooms and backstage as she tagged along behind him. These embarrassing scenes would be captured on camera for posterity because, along with Bob's entourage of Albert and Sally Grossman, Bobby Neuwirth (employed as road manager, and also filling the role of court jester), and producer Tom Wilson, Bob was accompanied by a film crew. This last was headed by D. A. Pennebaker, a filmmaker friend of Sara Lownds from Time-Life. Pennebaker had struck a deal with Grossman to make a cinema verité documentary of Bob's British tour, to be called *Dont Look Back*, without an apostrophe. ('It was my attempt [to] simplify the language,' explains

Pennebaker.) In return for a modest investment, and granting Pennebaker almost unlimited access, Bob and Grossman would receive a share of profits, which were not actually expected to be substantial. '[Bob] had no idea anything was going to come of it,' says Pennebaker. 'It was just a home movie for him, and hardly even that.' Assisting Pennebaker was Grossman's friend Howard Alk, and Howard's wife, Jones.

One of the first sequences in the film was a press conference at Heathrow airport. Bob held a large lightbulb and parried reporters' inane questions with nonsense answers. Asked what his 'real message' was, he said: 'Keep a good head and always carry a lightbulb!' Journalists were to be toyed with or ignored, as he explained in one interview during the tour: 'They ask the wrong questions, like, What did you have for breakfast, What's your favorite color, stuff like that. Newspaper reporters, man, they're just hung-up writers . . . They got all these preconceived ideas about me, so I just play up to them.'

To make a statement that Bob was a star, Grossman had booked Bob into the Savoy, one of the grandest hotels in London. After journalists had been invited to the hotel to be further bamboozled by Bob, celebrities came to pay respects, including all four Beatles and members of The Rolling Stones. The Beatles had sense enough not to be caught by 'The Eye' – Bob's apt name for Pennebaker and his shoulder-held camera – but others were less astute. Pennebaker captured Grossman haggling for appearance money and bullying hotel staff. 'You're one of the dumbest assholes and most stupid persons I've ever spoken to in my life,' he ranted at a hotel employee in Sheffield. 'If we were someplace else I'd punch you in your goddamn nose.' In other scenes, Neuwirth sniggered, Baez looked miserable, and Donovan and Animals keyboard player Alan Price were ridiculous. Drunken guests trashed part of Bob's art deco suite at the Savoy by throwing glass shelves out the window. 'Who threw that glass in the street?' Bob demanded with righteous anger. 'Who did it? Now, you better tell me, now if somebody doesn't tell me who did it, you all gonna get outa here and never come back.' Tom Paxton stayed off camera. 'It was a disgusting party,' he says. 'Some of the people in Bob's coterie were really being *awful* to the hotel employees who had no recourse but to try to do their job. It was an ugly scene.'

The chief prankster was Bobby Neuwirth. He laughed whenever Bob laughed, and aided Bob in the humiliation of Baez who, strangely, was a friend of Neuwirth's. When Baez floated around in a translucent blouse, Neuwirth picked up on Bob's apparent lack of interest. (When they were on camera at least, Bob hardly looked at Baez, he did not talk to her much, and he showed no signs of wanting to be with her.) Neuwirth referred to the translucent blouse cattily as 'one of those see-through blouses that you don't even wanna.' Laughing with what seemed false bravado, Baez announced she was sleepy and was going to *fag out*. 'Let me tell you sister, you fagged out a long time ago,' Neuwirth sneered. 'You fagged out before you even thought you were faggin' out.' Off camera, Baez was in tears. 'There was such a deep affection involved in getting [Bob] on the stage and being with him and presenting him,' says sister Mimi. 'It was a stepping stone for him and my sense of it was that he stepped and walked away. So that's always been uncomfortable. And [Joan] never wanted to see it that way, because her heart was so involved in it. But it's what her younger sister saw.' Pennebaker felt Bob was going through a period of transition. When Bob toured with Baez in America in March, they had been a team. Now he was done with team spirit. 'He was trying to get out from under being her partner, or her companion in song.'

Bob did not ask Baez to join him on stage at any point during the tour of the United Kingdom. In fact, they would not sing together in public again until the mid-1970s. When Bob went to Sintra, Portugal, for a brief break in the British tour, Baez was not invited to come along. Instead, Sara flew in from America to be with him. Baez still did not know of Sara's existence. During a recent stay at Grossman's house she had even worn one of Sara's nightdresses without realizing to whom it belonged. When Bob returned to London and was confined to his hotel suite with a brief illness, Baez visited to see how he was and Sara answered the door. This was how Baez finally found out about the woman Bob had been seeing behind her back for so many months. It was the end of Baez's affair with Dylan, and she promptly removed herself from the entourage to attend to her own career (she was giving solo concerts in the U.K. at the same time). Although upset, Baez was a strong personality and she took the rejection in her stride, managing to remain friends with Bob, even managing to laugh about it. As friend Nancy Carlen says, 'The ability to laugh at things is one of her strong points.' There would also be times in years to come when the romance with Bob would be resumed.

Ever the Don Juan, Bob tried to seduce singer Marianne Faithfull while he was in London, ordering her out of his suite when she refused him. He also spent some time hanging out with sixteen-year-old pop singer Dana Gillespie whom he had met at a party in London and saw when Sara was not around. 'I guess he was juggling women, like most musicians,' says Gillespie, philosophically. She carried his guitar and, when Bob had time off, lounged about in Bob's hotel suite. One time, Bob borrowed Gillespie's pants, bedecked with pink and orange roses. 'I was stuck in my underwear because he had taken my trousers. He could fit into mine, but I couldn't fit into his. I had to sit in the hotel waiting for him to come back. He said, "I'll only be a few hours." It was about fifteen hours [before] he came back.'

Often Bob was called away from Gillespie to shoot sequences for Pennebaker's movie. The memorable opening sequence of *Dont Look Back*, in which Bob flipped over cards on which were written lyrics from 'Subterranean Homesick Blues,' was filmed by Pennebaker in an alley beside the Savoy. This snatch of film was one of the forerunners of the pop music video and it was Bob's idea. 'He wondered if it was a good idea for a movie and I thought it was a terrific idea,' says Pennebaker. 'We started off in the garden back of the Savoy and we got interrupted by a bobby, who threw us out, so we then went to the alleyway. I think we did one take each place. Then that was it. Put it away and nobody knew what to do with it afterwards. It wasn't till I was editing the film that I thought maybe I should begin [the film] with that.'

Bob came across well in *Dont Look Back* – human, humorous, and bristling with energy. Although he lost his temper on occasion, and did not treat Baez well, he was for the most part tolerant of fans, journalists, and visitors. Even when he discovered, to his considerable anger, that one of his guests had thrown glass out of the window of the Savoy, he soon regained his composure and actually ended up shaking hands with the culprit. 'I just didn't want that glass to hurt anybody,' he explained, reasonably. Pennebaker agrees. 'I thought he was never really mean,' he says. 'He didn't grind his foot down.'

A striking example of Bob's wrath did make it into the film when he berated a correspondent from *Time* magazine. The confrontation happened before the first of two important concerts at the imposing and elegant Royal Albert Hall on May 9–10. Bob was in a bad mood during sound check. 'He was a little pissed at Neuwirth because of his harps. He felt maybe his harps weren't cleaned out,' says Pennebaker. 'I think he was nervous about the concert. It was a big concert and he knew a lot of people were going to be there. The Beatles were going to be there and a lot of people like that.' After sound check, Bob and his entourage went upstairs to have lunch. Journalists were invited to join them, including Horace Freeland Judson, the London-based arts and science correspondent for *Time*, who had been waiting for an opportunity to talk to Bob.

Irritated by the events of the morning, and concerned about the upcoming show, Bob launched into a verbal attack on *Time*, becoming so agitated that he questioned the very worth of Judson's existence. 'You're going to die,' Bob told the journalist. 'So am I. I mean, we're just gonna be gone. The world's gonna go on without us. All right now, you do your job in the face of that and how seriously you take yourself, you decide for yourself.' It may be that Bob was nursing hostility toward news magazine journalists in general, stemming from the *Newsweek* exposé of 1963. Pennebaker does not think Bob planned the tirade, and points out that Bob backed off toward the end as if not wanting to be too cruel. However, Judson believes the confrontation was contrived to make an entertaining sequence for the film. 'The conversation was flat. Suddenly, however, Dylan leapt to his feet and started berating me,' he says. 'He said, for example, something like, 'You'll never understand it; it happens so fast it'll go right past you,' and more of the same. I was startled, yes, but kept on trying to ask sensible, interesting questions; the attack persisted. I shrugged and left. The whole episode was entirely unprovoked . . . That evening, I went to the concert. My opinion then and now was that the music was unpleasant, the lyrics inflated, and Dylan a self-indulgent whining show-off.'

As far as virtually everybody else was concerned, however, Bob gave a tremendous performance at the Royal Albert Hall. The Beatles and Rolling Stones were in the audience, and everyone clearly hung on Bob's every word. It was an intense, almost mesmeric performance, one man holding a vast audience enthralled. 'I feel like I've been through some kind of thing, man,' said Bob as he left the theater with Grossman and Neuwirth. 'I mean, something was special about that.' At the age of twenty-four, Bob had now achieved great artistic and commercial success on both sides of the Atlantic. He was certainly near his peak, but still not quite there. Following his return home to the United States in early June, he would take another huge leap forward both as a songwriter and live performer, pushing himself until he reached the apogee of his success and the limit of his physical and mental health.

CHAPTER 5

FULL POWER

In the first week of June 1965, when Bob flew home from England, the so-called Dylan sound was sweeping America. The Byrds, a Los Angeles group featuring Roger McGuinn and David Crosby, reached number one on the Billboard chart on June 5 with a cover of 'Mr. Tambourine Man' that was the quintessence of folk-rock. By cutting verses and adding a jingly-jangly guitar introduction that echoed the lyric, the ballad was transformed into a surprising pop hit. 'The time signature, changed from 2/4 to 4/4, is the most important difference,' says McGuinn. 'It rocks!' The success of 'Mr. Tambourine Man' led The Byrds, and other acts, to release a series of Dylan covers that dominated the charts throughout the summer. The Byrds and Cher both had top-forty hits with 'All I Really Want to Do.' The Turtles went to number eight with 'It Ain't Me, Babe.' Even pastiches of the Dylan sound – like 'Eve of Destruction' – were major hits. These songs, and new work by The Beatles and The Rolling Stones, were inspired by the fusion of poetic lyrics and rhythm and blues on *Bringing It All Back Home*, which had been an enormous influence on fellow artists and which had brought Bob his biggest commercial success to date.

During his British tour, Bob had visited John and Cynthia Lennon at their substantial home in Kenwood, outside London. On his return to the United States, he bought a similarly imposing property for himself and Sara, who was expecting their first child. They decided to live in the Arts and Crafts Movement colony of

Byrdcliffe, a mile from both the center of Woodstock and Albert Grossman's Bearsville estate. Bob and Sara chose a sprawling eleven-room Arts and Crafts mansion named Hi Lo Ha on Camelot Road. The property was snuggled in thick woodland with a mountain stream filling a natural swimming hole, with space for basketball games and a large heated garage, part of which Bob used as a private pool hall. Hi Lo Ha was purchased in July – a bargain at under $12,000 – in the name of Davasee Enterprises, Inc., a 'blind' company created by lawyers so Bob's name would not appear during the transaction. The house was transferred into his name three months later. The mansion was the first substantial purchase of Bob's career, the first time he had done anything to enjoy the wealth that his success was bringing. Yet he would be unable to spend much time at the house in the foreseeable future. Grossman's desire for his client to continue working as hard as possible while there was money to be made (neither, of course, knew how long his career would last), as well as Bob's own ambition, meant he would be in the studio and on the road for most of 1965 and into 1966. He would see Sara only when he returned home to Byrdcliffe for breaks and when she occasionally joined him on the road.

While the purchase of Hi Lo Ha was being made, Bob worked in New York on perhaps his most famous song, 'Like a Rolling Stone.' The word he used most often when talking about the song was 'vomit.' The outpouring of contempt came to him like a 'long piece of vomit,' he said, created as a Kerouac-style typescript that was 'very vomitific in its structure.' He also described it, in his characteristically Delphic way, as '. . . a rhythm thing on paper all about my steady hatred directed at some point that was honest. In the end it wasn't hatred, it was telling someone something they didn't know, telling them they were lucky. Revenge, that's a better word.' In simple terms, it was a very angry song, born out of a well of rage that made up such an important part of Bob's unusual character. Indeed, 'Like a Rolling Stone' might be interpreted as misogynistic. The target was clearly female and several people, including Joan Baez, have been suggested as the specific inspiration. It is more likely that the song was aimed generally at those he perceived as being 'phony.' The song's abiding success is due in no small part to the empathetic feelings of revenge it inspires in listeners. There is some irony in the fact that one of the most famous songs of the folk-rock era – an era associated primarily with ideals of peace and harmony – is one of vengeance.

'Like a Rolling Stone' was recorded in New York during a summer rainstorm on June 16, 1965. Bob arrived at the Columbia studio with young Chicago blues musician Mike Bloomfield, who would play lead guitar on the track. A prodigiously talented musician, Bloomfield had excellent rapport with Bob, who was not always the easiest of artists to work with because he did not like to rehearse and did not talk about what he was doing. 'Michael knew that Dylan just wanted to come in and start playing and he wanted everybody, as if by magic, to fall in right behind him and [play] a tune they never heard before,' says mutual friend Nick Gravenites. '[Michael] could identify immediately what Bob was playing, what style it was, what chord it was.' Fledgling musician Al Kooper, only twenty-one, had been invited to the session by Tom Wilson. He had the chutzpah to inveigle himself behind the Hammond organ, even though he did not play the instrument. Paul Griffin, who had actually been hired to play organ on the session, moved to piano. Joseph Mack played bass and Bobby Gregg was on drums. The song kicked off with the pistol crack of Gregg's snare and rolled for almost six minutes, like a river in full spate. Bob celebrated the downfall of his subject in four venomous verses, culminating in crescendos of sound and emotion at the bridge. 'How does it feel,' he sang with mounting glee.

During playback, Bob asked Tom Wilson to bring

Kooper's organ part up in the mix. 'Hey man, that cat's not an organ player,' Wilson told him.

'Hey, now don't tell me who's an organ player and who's not,' replied Bob, who was beginning to tire of Wilson. Bob was dressed in a dark jacket and had his shirt buttoned to the neck. Standing at attention in the control room while the others slouched, he had the commanding presence of a general, and now that he was a genuine star he possessed real authority. He did not necessarily abuse his power in the studio, but he made sure people did exactly what he wanted. If they did not abide by his wishes, they were out, as Wilson would discover. 'Just turn the organ up,' he ordered.

'Like a Rolling Stone' was released as a single on July 20. Although twice as long as most singles of the day, at five minutes and fifty-nine seconds, making it ill-suited for radio, it steadily climbed the charts and, importantly, had enormous influence on fellow musicians. 'I knew that I was listening to the toughest voice that I had ever heard,' says Bruce Springsteen, then a teenager in Freehold, New Jersey. John Lennon and Paul McCartney heard the record on a day when they met to write Beatles songs. 'It seemed to go on and on forever. It was just beautiful,' says McCartney. '[Bob] showed all of us that it was possible to go a little further.'

Four days after 'Like a Rolling Stone' was released Bob was at the Newport Folk Festival. A usually predictable and fairly sedate annual event, it was turned on its head in 1965 by Bob's decision to perform his new amplified music. He did not come to Newport with that in mind. It just happened that way.

On the afternoon of Saturday, July 24, he performed 'All I Really Want to Do' as a solo artist, playing acoustic guitar as he always had. That same afternoon Paul Butterfield's electric blues band – featuring Bob's friend Mike Bloomfield – performed as part of the Bluesville Workshop. Alan Lomax, who had a purist's disdain for middle-class white boys playing the blues, sneered at the

Butterfield band during his introduction. Albert Grossman, who was thinking of managing the band, was outraged and confronted Lomax and soon they were fighting. 'They were rolling in the dirt,' says Sally Grossman, with amusement. 'It was the clash of the elite and the common.' Bob then made what was seen at the time as a momentous decision. He would perform his new songs with a fully amplified band – seemingly, just to show Lomax and others that this sort of music could not be suppressed. Although he had already recorded an album partly made up of rock 'n' roll tunes, to bring this music to the main Newport stage was an outrage to traditionalists who considered rock 'n' roll tainted by commercialism. 'Dylan just got a hair up his ass: *Well, fuck them if they think they can keep electricity out of here, I'll do it,*' explains Jonathan Taplin, roadie and later road manager for Grossman's acts. 'On a whim he said he wanted to play electric.'

Bloomfield put the band together, conducting auditions late into the night at a nearby mansion belonging to a friend of Grossman named George Wein. Al Kooper happened to be at the festival and was delighted to reprise his organ part. Bloomfield's friend Barry Goldberg was chosen to play piano. 'It wasn't so much a rehearsal as it was seeing who could play this kind of stuff, who was capable. They were looking for people who could play the changes,' says eyewitness Nick Gravenites. 'Jerome Arnold, the bass player, he just auditioned.' The final member of the band would be Paul Butterfield's drummer, Sam Lay.

Bob came to the sound check the next day, July 25, dressed in the fashionable style of London's Carnaby Street: tight black trousers, pointed boots, impenetrably black shades, and a shirt decorated with polka dots the size of drink coasters. Bob's clothing was extraordinarily ostentatious, considering that in previous years he wore the washed-out cotton uniform of the folk revival. At the sound check, Bob played a few bars of each song he was thinking of performing while Peter Yarrow struggled to balance the sound. 'Peter had no time to get anything set up,' says Jonathan Taplin. 'It was completely chaotic.' The band was so under-rehearsed that Jerome Arnold wrote the chord changes out and taped them to his bass for the show.

Pete Seeger introduced the evening concert as being about the serious issues in the world. These issues included the ongoing civil rights struggle and the burgeoning conflict in Vietnam, where U.S. airborne troops had recently gone on the offensive against the North Vietnamese. Most of the performers were folk traditionalists who exemplified liberal values and the audience, most of whom did not know about Dylan's sound check with a full band, expected him to give an acoustic performance of socially aware songs. Nothing could have been more shocking than what happened next. Bob came on stage wearing a black leather jacket, and led his band of hipsters into an uproarious version of 'Maggie's Farm.' Mike Bloomfield hunched over his electric guitar, playing myriad notes that fused into feedback. The sound mix was off. The band could not hear clearly, and partway through 'Maggie's Farm' the beat turned around. This was beyond folk-rock. It was blazing white noise at what seemed like incredible volume.

People began booing. The hecklers included friends of Bob, like Mark Spoelstra. 'All you could hear was Al Kooper and the guitar and the bass and this kind of agonizing sort of a scream of a voice, but you had *no idea* what he was saying,' says Spoelstra. No one was more shocked than Pete Seeger. 'I was absolutely screaming mad,' he says. 'You couldn't understand a goddamn word of what they were singing.' Seeger went to the sound board and demanded the sound be adjusted. But the board was guarded by Bob's supporters – including Grossman and Bobby Neuwirth – and they refused. 'Goddamnit!' cursed Seeger, who rarely lost his temper. 'If I had an ax, I'd cut the cable.' The apocryphal story is that Seeger and / or Alan Lomax actually did attempt to cut the power with an ax. Axes were available – Seeger had used one as a prop during a performance of work songs – but both men are adamant they did not attempt to cut the power. 'I would never do a thing like that. That's ridiculous,' says Lomax. Seeger says, 'I did not have an ax, and I did not cut the cable. [I] said, *if* I had an ax I'd cut the cable.' However, the story has gathered such momentum that Seeger admits even his wife does not believe him.

After 'Maggie's Farm,' Bob and the band roared through 'Like a Rolling Stone' before concluding with an early version of 'It Takes a Lot to Laugh, It Takes a Train to Cry,' then known as 'Phantom Engineer.' Those of the audience who were grumbling and jeering as Bob came offstage were upset for different reasons. Some were simply affronted that Bob had performed with an electric group at a folk festival. 'It was the antithesis of what the festival was supposed to be doing,' says Oscar Brand. 'The electric guitar represented capitalism . . . the people who were selling out.' Others were annoyed because the sound quality was so bad. Another section of the audience felt shortchanged when Dylan – the big star of the night – left the stage after performing only three songs. He did not inform the audience that his band had not learned any more. 'For all his talent, he's really not a great communicator,' says Noel Paul Stookey. 'So when he leaves the stage with no word, people are left to their own resources. What on earth are we supposed to think?'

Peter Yarrow came on stage to calm the audience. 'He will do another tune if you call him back,' he announced. 'Would you like Bobby to sing another song?'

Backstage Bob appeared dazed by the experience, sitting on the stairs, staring at his boots. 'He was visibly shaken,' says Theodore Bikel. Meanwhile Seeger was going about the backstage area, raging that he felt like smashing Bob's guitar.

'Bobby, can you do another song please?' asked Yarrow from the stage.

After a while Bob summoned his wits. He strapped on a guitar, borrowed from Johnny Cash, and climbed back up the steps to the stage. As he emerged into the lights, and the crowd could see the acoustic guitar, they cheered victory. Bob asked if anybody in the audience had an E harmonica. Harmonicas clattered on stage. 'Thank you very much,' he said, with a small laugh that caused the audience to laugh with him. It was the sort of ingratiating routine he had used back in the Village. He fitted a harmonica into his rack and played 'Mr. Tambourine Man.'

Throughout the communal dinner for the artists that night, in one of the nearby mansion homes, the elders of the folk establishment sat on one side of the room and the younger performers sat on the other. There was so much tension between the traditionalists who were angry at Bob and the younger musicians who were his friends, that Richard Fariña tapped his plate with a spoon as if there was going to be a prison riot.

After dinner The Chambers Brothers performed as a dance band. Bob was sitting in a corner, legs crossed, fidgeting nervously. Almost everybody who saw him during the evening has a different account of his behavior and apparent feelings after the show. Some say he was cocky, giving the impression he did not care that people had booed; others say he seemed shaken by the reaction of the crowd and depressed in the aftermath of the show. The truth is that he probably went through a gamut of emotions, and did not want his hurt to show. The clearest insight into his private turmoil came when Fariña suggested to Maria Muldaur that she go over and ask Bob to dance. It would take his mind off things.

'Bob, Dick seems to think I should come over and ask you to dance,' said Maria doubtfully, putting her hand on Bob's shoulder. She had never known him to dance before. 'Do you feel like dancing?'

Bob looked up at her, still twitching with energy. 'I'd dance with you, Maria,' he replied. 'But my hands are on fire.'

After the festival Bob went back into the studio to finish recording songs for what became the album *Highway 61 Revisited*. Tom Wilson had produced the outstanding lead track, 'Like a Rolling Stone.' But he was out of favor now, and was replaced with Bob Johnston.

Johnston would work with Bob for almost five years, during which time they recorded some of the most important albums of Bob's career. A forthright Texan who had done most of his production work in Nashville, Tennessee, Johnston had written songs for Elvis Presley films and produced Patti Page's comeback hit, 'Hush, Hush, Sweet Charlotte.' From the start, he showed almost slavish respect and devotion to Bob. 'I'm awed by him . . . I always was,' he says. In fact, Johnston would come to see Bob as superhuman. It was partly the way he behaved in the studio. Johnston felt Bob was looking through him when they spoke. Sometimes Johnston walked toward Bob and, when he got to where he thought he was standing, found that Bob had mysteriously shifted to the other side of the room. Bob rarely spoke to Johnston. The only clue he offered when he was about to sing was that his foot would start tapping, apparently in time with a metronome in his head. Johnston ran tape continuously so as not to miss anything. 'I truly believe that in a couple of hundred years they'll find out he was a prophet,' he says, adding without irony: 'I think he is the only prophet we've had since Jesus.'

Even so, Johnston was not all peace and love. He was an irascible opponent of studio executives – 'Those fucking no-talent people, tapping their foot out of time, whistling out of tune' – and kept engineers on a tight rein. When he took over as Bob's producer, he removed the clocks from the studio, to 'get everybody up off their ass.' This suited Bob because it meant he could record as he liked and how he liked; he never had to wait for engineers and musicians to get in place, or for the tape to start running. When he walked in the studio, everybody was ready. Here again was the power of his celebrity, but it was also a mark of the respect he commanded among the people he worked with. Many, like Johnston, thought he was no less than a genius and they were happy to oblige him in any way possible.

The bulk of *Highway 61 Revisited* was recorded in four sessions between July 29 and August 4. Using a group of session men – including Al Kooper and Mike Bloomfield – Bob created music that, at times, was like the slightly off-kilter white noise of Newport, with jackhammer drums and squibs of guitar. His voice was huge, sighing with ecstasy like Ray Charles on many of the numbers, and sounding completely assured throughout the sessions. The music fitted the vocal perfectly. Despite its roughness, it was soulful, powerful rhythm and blues music, not the effete rock 'n' roll of the pop charts. A strong feeling of the blues came through particularly strongly on 'From a Buick 6' and 'It Takes a Lot to Laugh, It Takes a Train to Cry' even though the lyrics were far from being classic blues motifs. The lyrics were surreal, and often very silly. Humor was in the music, too. Kooper wore a police-siren whistle on a chain around his neck during the sessions. 'I used it as a gag,' he explains. 'If anybody started using drugs anywhere, I'd walk into the opposite corner of the room and just go *whoooooooooo*.' Bob fixed this toy in his harmonica rack and blew so hard that Johnston thought the top of his head was coming off. 'God almighty!' exclaimed the producer. This was the siren sound that began the title number, 'Highway 61 Revisited.'

Bob played the stately piano chords that introduced the inscrutable 'Ballad of a Thin Man.' He could not help but laugh as he sung his greatest Dadaist lyric (Joan Baez has described Bob's deliberately absurd song lyrics as being like Dada art). It was filled with geeks, midgets, and freaks, and the mocking refrain challenged the mysterious Mister Jones to define what was happening. Bob was asked many times over the years who Mister Jones was, as if it were about a specific person. Typically, he never gave a straight answer, and surely the truth is that Mister Jones was not a single individual. The anonymous surname just contrasted nicely with the outlandish images in the song. Mr. Smith might have been just as effective. There was a lot of laughter among the musicians during the playback of the song. As Al Kooper reports, 'There was a silly edge on it at that point.' But 'Ballad of a Thin Man' would stand the test of time, becoming a mainstay of Bob's concert appearances for decades to come.

Apart from the raucous title track, the songs on the second side of the album were more lyrical. 'Queen Jane Approximately' and 'Just Like Tom Thumb's Blues' were exquisite, regretful ballads, while 'Desolation Row' was a surrealistic poem of epic length. Bob recorded two further tracks intended as singles: 'Can You Please Crawl Out Your Window?' – which was put to one side and rerecorded later in the year – and 'Positively 4th Street,' which was close in sound and meaning to 'Like a Rolling Stone.' Recorded just days after his cataclysmic performance at Newport, 'Positively 4th Street' was an indignant put-down of former friends from the folk community, friends he used to know around West 4th Street in New York. He described them as insincere opportunists who talked about him behind his back, being frustrated by their own failure. The song title implied they were *fourth* rate, not second or even third rate. Bob sang that when they wished him good luck they would rather see him 'paralyzed.' He knew better than most, through his friendship with Larry Kegan, what a vicious comment this was. It was the hardest language he could employ.

'Like a Rolling Stone' peaked at number two on the *Billboard* chart on August 14 and stayed at that position two weeks. It was the high-water mark in Bob's career as a singles artist. The follow-up, 'Positively 4th Street,' stalled at number seven. Bob never had a number-one single on the *Billboard* chart. In fact, he achieved only four top-ten singles in the 1960s, and none in subsequent decades. His singles were too spiky for mainstream audiences, who preferred his songs as more accessible covers. This was demonstrated by the fact that artists like The Byrds and Peter, Paul and Mary had bigger hits with Dylan songs than did Bob himself. Even imitations proved more successful. The bathetic pastiche 'Eve of Destruction,' by Barry McGuire, reached number one shortly after 'Like a Rolling Stone' had stalled at number two.

Bob was enjoying what was for him a high level of commercial success. This was a mixed blessing, however, as he was also being harshly criticized in the folk music community for having sold out. In particular, he was lambasted in the pages of *Sing Out!* magazine. Yet Bob decided that his future lay in amplified music, and began making plans for a tour. At a meeting with Albert Grossman in New York, Bob said he wanted to put together a rock 'n' roll band for a series of high-profile concerts. Grossman agreed, but suggested a compromise whereby only half the show would be electric; Bob would play acoustic on his own for the other half. This would put Bob under huge pressure. Effectively, he had to give two concerts in one, a strange format that he would use into 1966, and which became exhausting.

Al Kooper was available to play organ, but Mike Bloomfield turned Bob down because he wanted to concentrate on working with The Paul Butterfield Blues Band. John Sebastian was rehearsing a prototype of The Lovin' Spoonful in a hotel on Long Island. 'You wanna come out on the road as a bass player?' Bob asked him over the telephone. But Sebastian turned him down, too, wanting to continue with his own project. 'I do remember thinking to myself, *I must be out of my mind*,' he says now. Bob eventually chose Harvey Brooks, a musician employed on *Highway 61 Revisited.* He still needed a drummer and lead guitarist.

It was Grossman's secretary, Mary Martin, who suggested Bob consider using members of a bar band that had been backing rockabilly singer Ronnie Hawkins, a gruff showman who greeted audiences by leering, 'It's Saturday night. Let's get drunk.' Hawkins was an American based in Toronto, where he played nightclubs. It was here that he'd trained a first-class backing group called The Hawks. 'After three or four years of playing every day and practicing five days a week they got really, really good and became strong,' he says. 'Everybody started noticing them.' Led by drummer / vocalist Levon Helm, a farmer's son from Turkey Scratch, Arkansas, The Hawks ventured out on their own in late 1963, playing clubs and doing session work. Bob may have seen members of the band when they played on John Hammond Jr.'s album *So Many Roads*, although The Hawks do not remember Dylan being at the sessions. As Hammond recalls the occasion, Bob came into the studio and heard lead guitarist Robbie Robertson. 'Oh, God, listen to that!' he exclaimed as Robertson played a lick. Son of a Mohawk mother and a Jewish father, Robertson had worked with Hawkins from the age of fifteen. By twenty-two, he was a guitar virtuoso.

Levon and The Hawks were playing Tony Mart's nightclub in Somers Point, New Jersey, alongside a revue of go-go girls on 'limbo nite.' Bob reached Helm by telephone and asked if The Hawks would play two shows with him. The first would be at the Forest Hills tennis stadium in New York and the second at The Hollywood Bowl in Los Angeles. Not being familiar with Bob's music, Helm asked who else would be on the bill at these enormous venues, places where artists like Frank Sinatra would perform. 'Just us,' said Bob, casually. Levon and The Hawks was a five-piece band, but only Helm and Robertson were hired initially, augmenting Al Kooper and Harvey Brooks.

It became apparent during rehearsals that Bob had little experience playing with a band. 'He said, "Oh no I played with . . ." like, he had a couple of names, strange names – Bobby Vee,' says Robertson. 'But you could tell that he just didn't know very much about that.' Bob's lack of experience did not seem to worry him at all. He approached the show with quiet determination, even though he guessed correctly that the audience response would not be entirely good because of the controversial electric part of the show. The 'Dylan's gone electric' debate seemed irrational to Robbie Robertson, who was raised on rock 'n' roll with no experience of the emphasis folk musicians and folk music fans placed on authenticity. 'It seemed kind of a funny statement to me at the time, that somebody's *gone electric*,' says Robertson. 'It was like, Jeez, somebody's bought a television.'

It was unseasonably cold and blustery on the evening of August 28, 1965, when Bob and his band performed at Forest Hills. The audience of more than fourteen thousand applauded Bob's opening, forty-five-minute acoustic set and booed the second half when the band joined him on stage. They booed as if they thought booing was what was expected. The final song of the night was 'Like a Rolling Stone.' As Al Kooper has noted, the audience sang along with the verses and booed when it was over. Confronted with clear evidence that his audience did not like what he was doing, Bob might have been excused for changing direction. He headed out to California with his band for the Hollywood Bowl show, however, apparently never thinking he might have made an error of judgment.

Arriving in Los Angeles with time to spare, Bob ensconced himself at the Hollywood Sunset Hotel and relaxed with friends including Kooper and Neuwirth. When Bob was interrupted by a business call during lunch, he crammed an egg sandwich into the mouthpiece. Then he poured a glass of milk into the mouthpiece, telling the caller: 'Thanks for having lunch with us.'

'Eve of Destruction' was playing on the radio all across the country at the time. P. F. Sloan, the song's author, had been a writer of surf songs, for Dunhill Records, until he discovered Bob's music. The experience changed his life. 'I had heard my mystical rabbi speaking,' he says. Believing his purpose was to 'touch the mainstream' with Bob's metaphysical message, he started writing songs that sounded like Dylan, but singularly lacked originality, style, or wit. Consequently, Sloan became a figure of fun in Bob's court.

'Get P. F. Sloan,' Bob demanded. 'Let's have P. F. Sloan up here.'

Sloan was duly summoned to the Hollywood Sunset Hotel where Bob played him acetates of *Highway 61 Revisited*. Sloan rolled about on the floor laughing when he heard 'Ballad of a Thin Man.' Bob laughed too. He slapped his knees as if it was the biggest joke in the world. Then he said, seriously, 'I gotta big problem here. Columbia Records doesn't have any idea what this song is about. They think it's communistic.' Before Sloan had time to digest this shocking piece of information, David Crosby of The Byrds entered the suite and he and Bob went into the bedroom, leaving Sloan on his own. What happened next seems to have been an elaborate stunt arranged by Bob to cause the already excitable Sloan to freak out. 'Two women come in from the bedroom half-naked – topless – sit down like book ends on the couch, and they don't say a word, just sit there,' says Sloan. 'In from the window, from the outside, comes a man, flying in from a rope wearing a Zorro outfit, with a black hat and black mask, wearing black silk pajamas.' The man dressed as Zorro sat between the topless girls and stared at Sloan. 'I can only imagine that Bob had set this up, but I don't know. And he's in the other room with David Crosby. About fifteen, twenty minutes go by. The girls get up. Nobody says a word.' Zorro and the girls exited via the front door, leaving Sloan again on his own. 'David Crosby comes out of the bedroom and shakes hands with me and Bob continues to play me the rest of the album.'

After antics like this the actual show at the Hollywood Bowl, on September 3, was relatively uneventful. A more tolerant West Coast audience gave Bob and his band an enthusiastic reception. He even performed an encore.

Following the Los Angeles trip Bob resolved to hire The Hawks as a complete band to travel with him on a full U.S. tour, so he flew to Canada to hear the rest of the group. Aside from Levon Helm and Robbie Robertson, there were three more Hawks to meet, all Canadian multi-instrumentalists with strong characters. Rick Danko, who played bass and fiddle and had a quavering singing voice, was a sweet-natured former butcher. Richard Manuel, who played piano, drums, and was also a talented vocalist, was a melancholic with a drinking problem. Garth Hudson's ponderous manner made him seem older than his years. A classically trained musician, he played the organ like he was in church, his eyes rolling in ecstasy as he swept elements of Bach into rock 'n' roll. He was also accomplished on saxophone and accordion. 'We'd taken a couple of weeks off, which we hadn't done for years, just while Levon and Robbie went to play with Bob at Forest Hills. So by the time that Bob came to see us up in Toronto our voices were gone,' says Danko, meaning the musicians needed to warm up again before they sounded their best. 'We had run out of noises, you know. So he basically heard us playing instrumentals. But he hired us on the spot.'

Bob had an old Lockheed Lodestar he used for touring. It was one of a pair leased by Grossman; the other was used by Peter, Paul and Mary. The Lockheed had an intermittent air-conditioning system and was very slow, taking what seemed like a whole day to cross the country. The Hawks called the plane 'The Volkswagen of the Sky.' It would be home for the rest of the year. Bob sent the plane to Canada to pick them up, and met them in Texas for the start of the tour, leaving Sara at home in Byrdcliffe. A bookish, quiet person, Sara would travel only rarely with Bob, partly because the music industry did not interest her much (which Bob found refreshing) and partly because she had Maria – and later other children – to look after.

Bob's first tour with The Hawks – one of the most important of his career, and one of the few truly historic tours in popular music – began in Austin, Texas, on September 24, 1965, and wound its way across America and then on around the world until the following summer. The audience was enthusiastic on opening night, but it soon became clear that most nights they were going to receive catcalls and boos during the electric portion of the show. 'Everywhere we went they booed us,' says Robertson. 'It was a very interesting process to pull into a town, set up, play. People come in. They boo you. You pack up. You go on to the next town. You play. The people boo you. And then you just go on. You go all the way around the world with people just booing you every night.'

The booing affected the musicians differently, depending on their personalities. Robertson was confident they were good, no matter what the audiences did. 'We would listen to these tapes sometimes after the show, just to see what they were booing at, and . . . we thought, God, it's not that bad. It's not terrible. And nobody else sounds this way. It's got something. That was the only thing that enabled us to go on.' Danko, Hudson, and Manuel were phlegmatic. In their time as a bar band, people had thrown bottles at them. This was not *that* bad. 'After the first two or three concerts where they booed, they didn't seem to be throwing anything dangerous and they didn't threaten us out in the hall, or in the alley, so we kept doing it,' says Hudson, dryly.

Levon Helm, however, was a more emotional person and he became very upset. 'You're used to people going, "Yeah! Bravo!"' he says. 'And instead of that it's just, Booo! The worst! Get out! Go! Leave! You know. It's a hell of a sound. At the time it cut me all the way to the bone. I just . . . I couldn't take it. I really couldn't. And didn't after a certain time.' Helm quit the tour at the end of November and went to work as a deckhand on oil rigs in the Gulf of Mexico. He departed with respect for Bob, however, who had ignored those who advised him to drop The Hawks and go back to performing solo, acoustic shows. 'He probably had to deal with mountains of bullshit,' as Helm puts it. Bob did not seem to care what audiences did. 'By God, he didn't change his mind or direction one iota,' says Helm, paying a tribute to Bob's single-mindedness, which was one of his defining characteristics. It may have made him difficult to deal with on a personal level, especially for the women in his life when they discovered he was focused on music to the exclusion of almost everything else, but it made him a great artist. From a musician's point of view, it also made him a great bandleader. Bob always knew exactly what he wanted and he followed that vision until he was tired of it; in this respect, playing music with Bob was fun. Still, musicians had to be ready to put up with the reaction of audiences who had not yet caught on to what Dylan was trying to do. This would be a feature of Bob's music throughout his career. 'Bob is a funny guy like that. He don't care, you know,' says Helm. 'And I like Bob's policy: if you bought the ticket, you should be allowed to boo. If you don't like it, voice your opinion. But, goddamnit, it's a hard one to take.'

During a break in the tour, on November 22, 1965, Bob married Sara Lownds. It was a secret ceremony under an oak tree outside a judge's office on Long Island. The only guests were Albert Grossman and a maid of honor for Sara. No one else attended the wedding, not Sally Grossman, not even Bob's parents. This must have upset Abe and Beatty a great deal. As neither they nor Bob ever spoke about it, it is hard to know for certain why they did not attend. Bob's almost paranoid insistence on keeping his personal life private must have been a large factor in his having the quietest wedding he could. Even after he was married, Bob was reluctant to admit it. A few days later Ramblin' Jack Elliott wandered into the Kettle of Fish on MacDougal Street and found Bob and Sara at a table.

'Congratulations, Bob!' exclaimed Elliott.

'What for?' asked Bob, suspiciously.

'I heard you got married.'

'I didn't get married,' replied Bob.

'Well, I'll be darned! I swear I heard that you got married,' said Elliott, his face clouding over. 'I heard from *two* people that you got married.'

'No, I didn't get married,' Bob assured him. 'If I got married, you'd be the first person I'd tell.'

The wedding was a brief interlude in a very busy year. That winter Bob went back into the studio with The Hawks (with Bobby Gregg temporarily replacing Levon Helm on drums). They rerecorded 'Can You Please Crawl Out Your Window?' as a swaggering single. The lyric was slight, utilizing the opening phrase from 'Positively 4th Street,' but the band swung like a wrecking ball. Bob proudly played the song to Phil Ochs as they were riding together in a limousine. When Ochs's reaction was less than enthusiastic, Bob told the driver to stop. 'Get out, Ochs,' he said. 'You're not a folksinger.' Going for the jugular, he added: 'You're just a journalist.' Although this was vicious, Ochs admired Bob so much that he forgave him and the two men continued an uneasy friendship up until Ochs's suicide in 1976. Indeed, most of Bob's friends were prepared to put up with a lot of abuse from Bob because they considered him special. It would take decades of sharp comments, coldness, and ultimately simply ignoring people before Bob managed to dispense with nearly all his old friends.

Bob and The Hawks also attempted to record an early version of what became 'Visions of Johanna.' But Bob was not satisfied and he began to think of making his next album with different musicians. Bob Johnston had been urging him to move to the Columbia studio in Nashville, Tennessee, where Johnston lived. 'Dylan's answer, naturally, was "hmmmm," ' says Johnston, making a thoughtful sound. 'You know, he never said, "Yeah, let's go!" Just "hmmmm." He always was thinking about things. [Then] Grossman came up to me and said, "If you ever mention Nashville to Dylan again, you're gone." I said, "What do you mean?" He said, "You heard me. We got a thing going here." '

In the meantime, more concerts were scheduled. Because Bobby Gregg had studio commitments, he was replaced with Sandy Konikoff, a drummer Ronnie Hawkins had been training to replace Helm. Hawkins was not pleased to be losing yet another musician to Bob Dylan ('He threatened to break my legs,' says Konikoff of Hawkins, laughing). The tour was to be overwhelming for the unworldly young man whose previous experience of the big time was playing clubs with Hawkins. Suddenly Konikoff was playing his drums in large theaters and meeting famous and intimidating people. Everywhere Bob went, celebrities flocked to see him: people like Baez, Marlon Brando, and Allen Ginsberg. It was a sophisticated, fast-paced life with a lot of drugs and extremely intelligent people battling wits and for more ordinary people this could be intimidating. 'It was very, very intense,' says Konikoff. 'All these giants.'

When Bob arrived in the San Francisco Bay area on December 2, to play the Berkeley Community Theater, he asked Ginsberg to invite poets and writers to the concert. Ginsberg invited *One Flew Over the Cuckoo's Nest* author Ken Kesey, beat poet and playwright Michael McClure, and Zen poet Gary Snyder. The writers came with various partners and friends, including photographer Larry Keenan. At the time, members of the Hell's Angels were hanging out with the beat poets and a formidable contingent of Angels also came, including Sonny Barger, Freewheelin' Frank, and Terry the Tramp. The beats, their friends, and the Angels filled the two front rows. In their midst was the dainty figure of Baez.

The show could hardly have been more bizarre. Despite her recent humiliating experience in London, Baez trilled along with Bob from her seat during the acoustic half. Ginsberg screamed the line 'Two-wheeled gypsy queen' in unison with Bob during 'Gates of Eden.' Things turned weirder still when the curtains parted for the second part of the show to reveal not only Bob and The Hawks on stage, but two giant teddy bears. The bears were propped up as sentries on the amplifiers. During the maelstrom of sound that followed, one disgruntled fan threw a boot. The solitary boot landed on the stage, joining Bob and the teddy bears as a piece of absurdist art. As Baez later said, Bob had become 'The Dada King.' The beat poets were enchanted. McClure still talks with wonder about the stage presence of Dylan, as he interacted with Robertson: 'The dance that Bob did with Robbie was an extraordinary thing. . . It was right on the edge of being something you would think of as being homoerotic, but it wasn't at all. It was a very, very handsome and very daring thing, that went with his daring use of electric music.'

Backstage, Terry the Tramp and Freewheelin' Frank shared a joint with McClure, to the consternation of Bob, who was concerned they might get busted. He stayed with tea, laced with honey. 'I just figured he was taking huge amounts of speed,' says McClure. Bob was too exhausted to talk much so the poets chatted with the Angels – who were apparently charming – and to Baez. 'She was very concerned that Allen and I take care of Bob,' says McClure. Baez had been shouting from her seat with enthusiasm during the show, but she was troubled that Bob had smiled only three times during his performance. She was still completely in love with him, and worried about him. In a letter to McClure, written after the show, she wrote that she hoped God would watch over and protect Bob, as he was more vulnerable than most people.

After the show, Bob attended a party in Berkeley. Everybody had been relaxing, sitting around on the floor. 'When Dylan walked in, everybody stood up,' says Larry Keenan. 'They kind of queued up for him.' Ginsberg made the introductions and Bob, still jiggling with energy, received his admirers with a limp handshake. One guest tried to play the new Rolling Stones album for him. 'Okay, cool, man,' said Bob, dismissing the record after a few bars. When Ken Kesey was introduced, the conversation turned to the Hell's Angels, with whom Kesey was friendly. Bob complained that the Angels had broken the arm of a friend of his. He bent one arm into a weird angle to demonstrate. Several Angels were in the room and Kesey seemed relieved when the meeting was concluded. Next in line was the photographer Keenan, who told Bob he liked the teddy bears on stage. 'Bear vomit, bear vomit . . .' muttered Bob in reply. There was going to be a gathering of poets at Lawrence Ferlinghetti's City Lights bookstore in San Francisco's North Beach on Sunday, with Keenan taking pictures. He wanted to photograph Bob, too. Bob said he would come. He thought a picture of himself with the poets would be good for the cover of his new album.

At noon that Sunday a motley collection of poets and hangers-on assembled outside City Lights on Columbus Avenue to be photographed for what was billed as the Last Gathering of the Beat Poets. Journalist Leland Meyerzove arrived by ambulance and lay down in the gutter. Ginsberg was accompanied by two boyfriends. Ferlinghetti – dressed in an Arabic cloak and carrying an umbrella (though it was not raining) – turned in a false fire alarm. When the fire truck swung around the corner, siren wailing, the morose poets perked up. 'The firemen jumped out, [but] they said there was nothing going on so they left,' says Ferlinghetti, chuckling about the prank. When Bob arrived with Robbie Robertson and, unusually, Sara Dylan, who had just joined Bob for a few days, pandemonium broke out. 'Hey, Bob, come over here. Pose with us,' yelled the poets. Bob and his entourage swept past, into the store, and down to the basement. 'Dylan in his infinite wisdom did not want to make it a Dylan scene. He wanted to make it a beat scene,' says Keenan, who was ushered into the basement before the door was locked. 'He liked the beats. So while we are in the basement [people] start crashing and banging and they are yelling for Dylan.' They then escaped via a back door into the alley, where Bob posed for photographs with Ferlinghetti, Ginsberg, and McClure. On the far end of the group was a rather self-conscious Robertson, who did not want to be there, and no doubt wondered what the other guys in the band would say. 'I don't think he thought of himself as a poet and he thought he didn't belong,' says McClure.

After ten minutes they adjourned for drinks at the Vesuvio saloon. High on the excitement of the event, the poets ostentatiously ordered cocktails. 'I'll have tea,' said Bob. When they heard what he was ordering, the poets promptly canceled their cocktails and said they would have tea too. It was a small incident that demonstrated the power of Bob's celebrity, even among those who themselves enjoyed a degree of fame.

After concerts in the Bay area Bob invited Ginsberg and McClure to accompany him to Southern California. They traveled in Allen's Volkswagen camper van, driven by his lover, poet Peter Orlovsky. The Hawks traveled in the Volkswagen of the Sky. 'One of the things he was really concerned about was he wanted to know how the audience responded to his performance, not what people told him, but he really wanted to know what people were saying,' says McClure. Bob gave Ginsberg money to buy a tape recorder, so Ginsberg volunteered to go out into the audience and tape fans' comments. Bob was pleased when Ginsberg brought him evidence that some, at least, liked what he was doing. A little encouragement of this sort was a welcome change from the often hostile press coverage the shows were receiving.

There was a frightening experience before the San Jose concert when Bob and the poets were walking through the backstage area to the green room. Many fans had hidden backstage and suddenly they emerged from side doors, from under tarpaulins, and even out of trash bins. 'There was so many of them, and they appeared in such an astonishing way, that it was alarming and Bob started to run,' says McClure.

Everything seemed strange and dreamlike now. Fans emerged from garbage cans. Teddy bears on stage. In Los Angeles and San Francisco, Bob gave absurd answers to journalists' questions. 'What is the most important thing in your life these days?' asked a reporter at the Beverly Hills Hotel.

'Well, I've got a monkey wrench collection and I'm very interested in that.'

In Los Angeles, The Hawks stayed in a large house they called the Castle. It looked like a set from a Robin Hood movie. Beautiful girls and famous actors came through looking for Bob. Bob himself had plans to make things even stranger. 'He wanted to rent an elephant from a zoo,' recalls Sandy Konikoff. This was to be for the first part of the concert, when he played acoustic. 'He would just say to the elephant: 'Give me a C harp,' and the elephant [would] reach out to the stool with his trunk and hand [it to] him,' adds Konikoff. 'I tell you, man, I thought that was just incredible.'

During a break in touring, in January 1966, Bob entered into an important new agreement with Albert Grossman. They created a publishing company, Dwarf Music, into which Bob would lodge new songs. Bob later claimed he did not understand that he and Grossman were becoming partners in Dwarf. He thought Dwarf Music was his own company outright. In fact, the agreement meant Grossman would have a fifty percent claim on every song Bob wrote for the next ten years. This was clear in the contract, which Bob signed months later when the paperwork was ready. Once again he did not read the contract however. 'I signed the papers based upon Grossman's word that it was okay to do so. Grossman told me that I could rely on him, and I did rely on him, to read documents, to explain them to me, and to tell me if it was all right to sign them,' Bob said. 'We followed that procedure throughout our relationship.' Bob only started reading contracts after he ended his association with Grossman, which was of course a little late. This time, at least, Bob had some excuse for being distracted. Sara was due to give birth to their first child the week the contract was negotiated. A son, Jesse Byron Dylan, was born in New York on January 6.

While he was in New York, Bob visited the Factory studio of artist Andy Warhol. They had mutual friends, including filmmaker Barbara Rubin (the woman massaging Bob's head on the back cover of *Bringing It All Back Home*) and model Edie Sedgwick. Bob agreed to come in for a 'screen test' for one of Warhol's underground films. 'Andy always played the fan,' says Gerard Malanga. 'So he was Bob Dylan's fan for that day at the Factory – "Oh, Bob Dylan's coming to the Factory! Oh!"' After the screen test, Warhol showed Bob a series of portraits of Elvis Presley, known as the *Double Elvis* pictures. They were silk screens of Elvis from one of his movies, slinging a gun cowboy-style. One image was overlaid onto another and printed almost life-size. Warhol was usually reluctant to give artwork away, but he wanted to impress Bob, who enjoyed playing the game of seeing what he could get out of the artist. 'They were kind of dancing around each other in a funny way, a solicitous kind of dance,' says Malanga. 'Who was going to get what out of whom.' Bob won the game, leaving the studio with one of the Elvis silk screens. He and Neuwirth tied it to the roof of Bob's station wagon and drove it up to Woodstock.

Although it seemed to the people at the Factory that

Bob had wanted Warhol to give him the silk screen, and he was quick enough to take it when offered, once Bob got the artwork home he made it clear that he loathed it. He showed his disdain for the picture, according to accounts of various visitors to Hi Lo Ha, and to rumors that reached Warhol, by hanging it upside down and putting it in a cupboard. Eventually he showed it to Sally and Albert Grossman.

'I don't want this,' he told them. 'Why did he give it to me?'

Bob said he and Sara wanted something 'practical' for the house, so he made a deal. The Grossmans gave him a sofa. He gave them the silk screen. Warhol was mortified when he found out. But the joke was on Bob. In 1988 Sally Grossman sold the picture at auction for $720,000.

Touring resumed in February 1966 with Bob scheduled to give concerts across North America and then on around the world until mid-summer. Between shows he found time to record his new album, *Blonde on Blonde*, the album for which he originally intended to use the photograph of the beat poets.* Unsatisfied with tracks recorded with The Hawks in New York, Bob agreed with Bob Johnston's suggestion that the album should be recorded in Nashville, and now that Bob had made his mind up there was nothing Grossman could do about it.

Bob wanted to record *Blonde on Blonde* live, with the musicians all together in one room as if they were on stage. The Columbia 'A' studio on Music Row in Nashville was divided into sound booths, so Johnston's first job was to get rid of the booths. 'I sent in the janitor with a saw and [a] sledgehammer and I had him tear up everything in the fucking studio and carry it out and burn

*According to Larry Keenan, Bob changed his mind after problems with photographers at the City Lights photo-opportunity over copyright. A Jerry Schatzberg photograph was used instead.

it.' Robbie Robertson and Al Kooper were the only musicians invited from New York. The other musicians were well-known Nashville session men, led by Charlie McCoy. 'He wanted someone who was not strictly from the old country school, [who] was kind of into R&B and into rock 'n' roll,' says McCoy, who grew up listening to the blues on the radio, as Bob had, and was noted as a fine guitarist and exceptional harmonica player. 'Then we assembled a rhythm section for him.' Kenny Buttrey played drums; Hargus 'Pig' Robbins played piano; Wayne Moss played guitar; and Henry Strzelecki was on bass. These musicians had made countless famous recordings – including major hits by Roy Orbison and Elvis Presley – and were in such demand they often fitted several sessions into one day. Most unusually, they were booked to work solidly with Bob until *Blonde on Blonde* was finished. In the process they clocked approximately forty hours of studio time. 'That was unheard-of down here, because everyone was so budget conscious,' says McCoy.

Bob arrived in Nashville in mid-February 1966 with scraps of songs. He spent the daytime in his room at the Ramada Inn working up ideas as Kooper sat at the piano playing chords 'like a human cassette machine.' When they went into the studio, it seemed to Robertson at least that the session men were circumspect of a young artist whose work they did not know well. 'Everybody was a little standoffish. They were [doing] their sweet southern country boy thing with Bob, but they were very, very . . . distant otherwise,' says Robertson. 'I wasn't sure why we were there.'

Bob and his friends looked strange in Nashville. Al Kooper was tricked out like a Carnaby Street character and got into trouble with local youths as soon as he ventured downtown. Luckily, Elvis Presley's bodyguard Lamar Fike was on hand for protection. Bob was something else again. By this time he had a thicket of hair so bushy and tangled it might have made a nest for a bird. 'To go over and whisper something in his ear, it was like sticking your face in a bush,' says Kenny Buttrey. Although most guitarists grew their fingernails long, Bob's fingernails were unusually long, and also dirty. Bob did not smell too good, either. 'There was a certain air about him,' as Wayne Moss remembers.

The musicians were called for the session around two in the afternoon. Bob showed up four hours late and still he had not finished writing the lyrics for the song he wanted to record. The musicians left the studio so he could work. They hung out in offices downstairs, playing cards and sending out for food. Some gathered around a Ouija board and tried to divine whether these curious recording sessions would come to anything. Hours passed. In the middle of the night, when the musicians were fighting to stay awake, they were called back into the studio because Bob had a song ready: 'Sad-Eyed Lady of the Lowlands.'*

After only the sketchiest rundown by Bob, the red recording light came on and they attempted a take. It was a slow, bluesy love song in which Bob used a series of arresting images to describe a woman. She had 'flesh like silk' and a 'face like glass.' He intoned the similes like a man in a trance. Three minutes into the number, Bob showed no sign of winding up the song. The musicians were used to playing tunes that lasted on average two minutes and twenty seconds, which was the optimum length for radio. But each time 'Sad-Eyed Lady of the Lowlands' neared a place where it might have ended, and the musicians instinctively worked to a climax of sound, Bob let it drop down and started another verse. 'I was playing one-handed, looking at my watch,' says Kenny Buttrey. 'And it kept on and kept on . . . We'd never heard anything like this before.' The musicians fought off tiredness, trying to stay focused. After more

*There is conflicting evidence about the sequence in which the *Blonde on Blonde* songs were recorded. See Source Notes for further information.

than eleven minutes, Bob signaled that the song was finished. It was the longest popular song recorded up to that time, at eleven minutes and twenty-three seconds, five times the length of pop songs of the day. It would take up the whole fourth side of *Blonde on Blonde*, which, also unusually, would be a double album. 'That was the introduction to Bob Dylan,' says Charlie McCoy, who went home exhausted. 'That's something you don't forget.'

Joan Baez has been suggested as the inspiration for 'Sad-Eyed Lady of the Lowlands.' Baez's friend, Nancy Carlen, believes the reference to Cannery Row in the last verse relates to a cafe in California that Baez and Bob frequented. The song is not about Baez, however, but rather a paean to Sara Dylan. It is no coincidence that metal is used twice as a metaphor in the lyric – Sara grew up the daughter of a scrap-metal dealer. It was Sara who had a former husband who worked in magazines, as per verse five – magazine photographer Hans Lownds. Most obviously it was Sara who had the sad eyes. Three months into his marriage, Bob was celebrating his wife with a truly monumental love song. Here was evidence of a deep-seated romantic nature, although it was something Bob did everything he could to cover up in everyday life, and which he wrapped in metaphor in the song. The imagery was so deft, and his marriage was so low-profile – many of the musicians who worked on the record did not even know Bob was married – that it is little wonder few realized who the song was about at the time.

'I Want You,' to which Wayne Moss gave a delicate Chet Atkins–style guitar introduction, was a song of yearning desire. 'Just Like a Woman' and 'Leopard-Skin Pill-Box Hat' seemed to have specific references to Edie Sedgwick. It has been suggested that something of her pathos inspired the former song, and some of her exuberance is evidenced in the latter; she also wore leopard skin. 'Stuck Inside of Mobile with the Memphis Blues

Again' unfolded like a movie. Bob chuckled as he composed these remarkable lyrics, working with pencil on Ramada Inn notepaper. He would usually run the song down once for the musicians, but never, as Buttrey recalls, 'completely from top to bottom.' Then they would play whatever way seemed most natural. Often songs were recorded in one or two takes. The musicians had no realistic idea of the length of the songs, or in what direction they would run, because Bob would ad-lib during the recordings. 'You had to be on your toes,' says bassist Henry Strzelecki. '[But] we could count on his timing.'

Bob never talked much to the musicians, but late one evening he asked them: 'What do you guys do here?' Moss and the others muttered something about playing golf. 'That's not what I mean. What do you *do* here?' They realized he was asking what they did to get high. They said they occasionally had a beer. Bob said he had a new song, the lyric of which included the refrain 'everybody must get stoned.' He said, 'I'm not going to do this with a bunch of straight people. We'll send out for something.'

Studio custodian Ed Gazzar was sent to the nearby Ireland's bar with an order for Leprechaun cocktails – potent, green-colored concoctions that came in a shot glass. 'Except when the guy came back with 'em for us they were not in shot glasses, they were in large milk-shake cartons,' says Moss. It was extremely unusual to drink at a recording session at the time, but all the rules were being broken. 'It takes a very small amount of that to really knock you on your butt,' says Moss. 'We had a huge amount.' Marijuana joints were passed around. Pig Robbins and Henry Strzelecki accepted. 'I got pretty wiped out because I'm not a grasser and it was pretty strong stuff,' recalls Strzelecki. Although some of the musicians remained completely straight, including Charlie McCoy, Robbins says he and others were 'all fucked up.'

Bob said he wanted a sound like a marching band, but not too slick. McCoy put in a call to Wayne 'Doc' Butler, who put his tenor trombone in the back of his Ford and drove straight to the studio. McCoy played trumpet. The other musicians decided to swap instruments to give the track the raggedy-march feel Bob was looking for. Moss told Strzelecki that he wanted to play bass. 'Shit I don't care,' said Strzelecki, handing him his guitar. He played Kooper's organ. He could not work the pedals with his feet so he lay down on the floor and pushed them with his hands, creating a comical *dom, dom, dom, d-d-d-dom* sound. Kooper shook a tambourine. Buttrey dismantled his drum kit and set up the bass in two hard-back chairs facing each other. When everybody was ready, around midnight, Buttrey counted the band off by whomping the side of his bass with a timpani mallet. He played a splashy high hat with his right hand and his snare with his left 'so that I couldn't get too fancy with it.' Doc Butler played a woozy blast of tailgate trombone – 'I hadn't even got warmed up.' And Bob began to sing the lyric that included the repeated line: 'Everybody must get stoned.'

Although he was on the floor, Strzelecki had his head up by a microphone and was braying with laughter. 'I was so stoned, I was laughing through the whole track, man.' Soon everybody was laughing, including Bob, who stumbled over the lyrics as he watched the musicians go crazy. 'We were having a marvelous time,' says Moss. After four and a half minutes, everybody put down their instruments and went into the control room to hear the playback. They were slapping one another on the back and saying what a great song this was going to turn out to be when it was finished. Buttrey put his arm around Bob. 'Hey, Bob, what's the name of this song we're working on?' he asked, facetiously. They had heard 'everybody must get stoned' so many times it seemed obvious this would be the title.

' "Rainy Day Women #12 & 35," ' replied Bob, without

a flicker of smile. Furthermore, it had not been a rehearsal. The song was finished. It was released as a single one month later and rose to number two in the charts.

The lyrics on *Blonde on Blonde* are among the best Bob would ever write – poetry as Professor Christopher Ricks has said, that is 'variously extraordinary and insinuatingly true.' The music was perfectly suited to the words. Bob said this music was the closest he ever got to 'that thin, that wild mercury sound' that he heard in his head. 'I Want You' and 'Temporary Like Achilles' were gloriously sexual. The exuberance of 'Obviously Five Believers' was infectious: Bob groaned as he signed off the last verse; Robertson ripped off a guitar solo; McCoy wailed on the harmonica. They rode the song like a boxcar to the end of the line. 'Visions of Johanna' was a cornucopia of richly packed imagery. The line 'In this room the heat pipes just cough' was perfectly evocative of early mornings in old city hotels, like the Chelsea, where he had lived with Sara. 'Pledging My Time' sounded like being up too late. 'Nobody has ever captured the sound of 3 A.M. better than that album,' says Al Kooper. 'Nobody, not even Sinatra, gets it as good.'

Echo Helstrom thought the album title, *Blonde on Blonde*, might be a reference to her white hair and white skin. Others point to Edie Sedgwick's bleached beauty. The truth is that Bob came up with the album name in the same way he came up with the quirky song titles. 'The titles were gotten at a mixing session,' says Kooper. 'When they were mixing it, we were sitting around, and Bob Johnston came in and said, "What do you want to call this?" And [Bob] just like said them out one at a time, right then and there. Free association and silliness, I'm sure, played a big role.'

Blonde on Blonde reached number nine in the U.S. charts and its success helped change Nashville's music scene. Non-country acts flocked to the city to try and emulate Dylan's sound, and the session musicians he worked with were sought after, becoming minor stars in their own right because for the first time in the history of Nashville their names were listed on a record sleeve. 'One of the things I would like to thank Dylan for, publicly, is putting names on albums,' says Wayne Moss. 'That didn't happen before he got here.' It was a nice gesture on Bob's part, but it did not cost him anything and he did not pay the musicians any more money for their excellent work. As Kenny Buttrey notes with some bitterness, Dylan's office did not even send them complimentary copies of the album when it came out.

Bob kept his distance from the musicians, as he did from most people. He made more albums with these Nashville players in the years to come, but he never spent any time with them socially; he did not keep in contact with them between sessions and he rarely talked to them when he was in the studio. The music they made together, though, stands for these players as some of the best fun they ever had in the studio. The music was also important to the commercial life of the city. Eventually, Nashville would rival New York and Los Angeles as the music capital of America, partially because Dylan made it legitimate for non-country acts to record there. 'When [Bob] came down to Nashville, he broke it wide open,' says Bob Johnston. 'He sank Tin Pan Alley with his "Subterranean Homesick Blues" and "Like a Rolling Stone." But he changed everything. He changed country music. He made it popular.'

Between recording dates and mixing sessions for *Blonde on Blonde*, Bob was on the road with The Hawks. In Ottawa, Ontario, Canada, they played an ice rink so cold they had to keep their coats on. They froze on a night flight from Montreal to New York when the heater in the Lockheed failed. Even when the heater was working, the flights were frequently uncomfortable. 'We had a couple of major scares in that plane,' says Sandy Konikoff. 'Sometimes when we were asleep the pilots would bust our balls and go into dives.'

Bob's lack of experience playing with an amplified band caused some problems. He frequently wanted the volume louder than the P.A. system could handle. He would get too close to the mike when he was singing and, worst of all, he was not always in step with the band. This could be particularly frustrating to a perfectionist like Garth Hudson, and there were tense moments between Bob and members of The Hawks.

After a show in Denver, on March 13, Bob and Robertson decided to travel to Los Angeles on a commercial flight, giving the rest of the band a ten-day vacation. 'You be captain of the plane,' Bob told Rick Danko, who proceeded to order the pilot to fly the Lockheed to Taos, New Mexico, where Danko ate peyote for a week and a half. Hedonism was part of life on the road for The Hawks, as much as it was for Bob. Hudson was fairly straight. But Robertson liked to let his hair down; Manuel was a fearsome drinker; Helm, who later rejoined the group, developed a heroin habit; and Danko experimented with just about everything. It was after taking LSD that Danko informed Bob that he had ambitions to do more than just back up a front man. 'One thing I didn't want to be was a Bob Dylan sideman for the rest of my life,' he says. 'When I took my first acid trip, you know, I had a good talk with Bob. Like a fool, I explained we had our own row to hoe.' Although Bob worked more closely with The Hawks than with almost any other musicians in his career, all the same he kept some distance from them, channeling his comments via Robbie Robertson.

Sara Dylan joined Bob for part of the spring tour, but the musicians saw little of her; as with most everyone in the music industry, they were shut off from this part of Bob's life. Bob and Sara were so fastidious about maintaining their privacy that the marriage became more like a secret life. Remarkably, Bob and Sara were never photographed together in public during the early years of their marriage, and very little was written about them in the press. When they were out, they walked slightly apart; Bob did not speak about his family in interviews; and Sara never spoke to journalists at all. Sometimes they went to extremes to maintain privacy. On March 26, Bob and Sara were together at a show in Vancouver, Canada. Two disc jockeys had been invited backstage and Bob was concerned about them seeing Sara. 'Sara,' he said, opening the door to a walk-in closet. 'When they arrive, I want you to get in here.' Sara looked questioningly at her husband, but stepped forward to do as he asked.

Sandy Konikoff left the tour at the end of March 1966. 'I was scared by the mystery of the thing and the odd people that were hanging out sort of intimidated [me] to a certain extent, and all the psychedelics, the drugs, and so on,' he admits. 'There were so many elements that made me feel sort of uncomfortable.' He was replaced with Mickey Jones, an experienced drummer who had been touring with Johnny Rivers. After playing Hawaii on April 9, Bob and The Hawks, with Jones in the band, flew to Australia.

It was while they were in Australia that 'Rainy Day Women #12 & 35' reached number two in America. It was also named in the influential Gavin Report – sent out to more than a thousand U.S. radio stations – as a 'drug song.' In certain parts of the United States this was enough to have a song banned from play lists. Drug imagery in songs, and the use of drugs by artists like Dylan, was becoming an issue with the media, and Bob was asked repeatedly about his position. In a 1966 interview with *Playboy*, he said: 'I wouldn't advise anybody to use drugs – certainly not the hard drugs; drugs are medicine. But opium and hash and pot – now, those things aren't drugs; they just bend your mind a little. I think everybody's mind should be bent once in a while.' He told Robert Shelton: 'It takes a lot of medicine to keep up this pace . . . It's very hard, man. A concert tour like this has almost killed me.' In a 1969 interview with *Rolling Stone*, Bob was asked whether taking drugs influenced his songs. 'No,' he replied, 'not the writing of them, but it did keep me up there to pump 'em out.'

The drug used most openly on the tour was hash. In Australia, Mickey Jones saw a big brick of hash being scored with a knife by a member of the touring party so that it could be divided up. There is also little doubt that Dylan was using pills to keep him going, in one way or another, as well as hallucinogens. The openness with which hash was used attracted the attention of the police, who carried out a dawn raid at the Sheraton Hotel in Melbourne. 'About five or six policemen rolled me out onto the floor [and] started going through my stuff,' says Jones. 'The big question was, "Were you at the pot party last night?"' The drummer was clean, but he says a member of the road crew was deported.

Bob and The Hawks departed Australia on April 26, 1966, en route to Sweden, changing planes in Sydney and London. Only Garth Hudson was able to sleep during the exhausting thirty-six-hour journey. Swedish newsmen were assembled on the tarmac at Stockholm when they arrived. A fellow passenger yelled to the press pack: 'Here come the animals!' and the reporters and photographers pushed close trying to get to Bob, who kicked at their shins. 'I almost did it myself until I thought, what's this going to look like on the news?' says Rick Danko. 'I tried to get his attention to not do that.'

Bob reluctantly agreed to give a press conference, with Robertson beside him. Robertson had become so close to Bob that The Hawks called him Barnacle Man. 'He was stuck to Bob,' says Jones. 'It was like Robbie was there if Bob went to take a leak.' Asked by the Swedish journalists what he thought about protest songs, Bob spluttered, 'Um . . . er . . . God . . . No, I'm not going to sit here and do that. I've been up all night. I've taken some pills and I've eaten bad food . . .' Soon he was on a roll, however, grinning as he gently mocked the journalists. Asked about his new hit, 'Rainy Day Women #12 & 35,' he described it as having to do with 'cripples and Orientals and the world in which they live . . . It's a sort of Mexican kind of thing, very protest, very, very protest and [one] of the pro-testiest of all things I've protested against in the protest years.' But in these madcap press conferences – and he gave them all over the world – there were moments of clarity. Asked what he would call his style of music, Bob replied directly: 'Well, I've never heard anybody that plays and sings like me.'

While in Sweden, staying in a hotel outside Stockholm, Bob had an important meeting with Albert Grossman's attorney, David Braun. Braun was touring the continent with Artie Mogull, of M. Witmark & Sons, selling sublicenses in Bob's song catalogue to foreign publishing companies. This had not been wholly successful. Braun later admitted that possibly the most important of these foreign deals – with B. Feldman and Company in Britain – had not been the most advantageous deal possible, because neither he nor Grossman were experienced in such matters. 'Had we known a little more about foreign publishing, we could have done better,' he said. 'We gave the copyrights away for a long time when we didn't have to.'

The Dwarf Music contract Bob and Grossman had verbally agreed upon at the start of the year had been drawn up – with the contract backdated to January 1 – and Braun had the documents with him for Bob to sign. These were the key documents that would make Bob and Grossman partners in the publishing of all his new songs for ten years to come – the agreement Bob later claimed to have misunderstood. Bob and Braun started talking about the paperwork, and Braun was about to explain everything to him when Grossman interrupted them. 'He came in, racing into the room, while I was explaining them to Bob and terminated the discussion,' Braun said. 'He indicated there was no need for me to explain [the documents] fully to Bob, that Bob knew what they were about.' This later became another of Bob's complaints against Grossman: not only had Bob been misled into thinking Dwarf Music was solely his company, as he claimed, but Grossman had stopped their attorney explaining the deal. Braun says he persevered in trying to explain the paperwork, but it was to no avail. 'Mr. Grossman was determined that the conversation not continue.' Under these rather odd circumstances, Bob signed the Dwarf agreement, one of the worst business blunders of his career. This seems to have been due to simple inexperience. Bob was certainly intelligent enough to understand contracts, but he did not want to bother himself and he believed he could rely on others. When he had time later to sit back and think about his business affairs, he realized that deals struck in his name had not always been in his best interests and he started to take a firmer grip on his finances.

Filmmaker D. A. Pennebaker had been hired to help Bob make a color tour documentary for American television. He joined the tour in Stockholm to start work. Bob was to direct, naively thinking he could create an experimental film between touring commitments, but he needed help. '[Bob] said, "You gotta help me now. I helped you with your film, you're gonna help me with mine." It was never going to be my film,' says Pennebaker. 'I was just supposed to be the cameraman.' Once again, Howard and Jones Alk assisted.

Bob had little interest in filming his stage performances, or in having his offstage life documented as in *Dont Look Back*. Instead, he wanted to improvise scenes in the style of an art film. The most revealing sequence in what became known as *Eat the Document* – the title meant 'a nondocumentary,' according to Pennebaker – had Bob and John Lennon swapping witticisms as they were driven through London in a limousine. Lennon later said he was 'very high and stoned,' but he looked healthier than Bob, who appeared painfully thin and very pale. For a while, the banter was charming, like a scene from a Beatles movie. Lennon snapped off smart comments and Bob giggled. 'Do you suffer from sore eyes, groovy forehead, or curly hair?' Lennon asked, in his comedic voice. 'Take Zimdon.' When the car passes a couple kissing in the street, Bob directed the camera to them. 'Oh! Oh! Get those two lovers over there,' he said, brightly. But his words became increasingly slurred and muddled. Toward the end of the segment, he begged chauffeur Tom Keylock to hurry to the hotel because he said he was about to vomit.

The tour moved on to Denmark where the film crew trailed Bob to Kronborg Castle, the setting of Shakespeare's *Hamlet*. Bob was interested to learn all he could about the fabled Prince of Denmark. The day Bob toured the castle, news came through from California that Richard Fariña had been killed in a road accident. He was a passenger on a motorcycle that skidded over an embankment and into a fence. The Farinã tragedy was one of a series of deaths of people close to Bob, all within a short period of time. Geno Foreman was an activist friend from Greenwich Village who had developed a drug problem. He approached Bob during the European tour and asked for money. Bob told him to go away in such an aggressive manner that people with Bob were embarrassed. Foreman died shortly afterward of an overdose. Bob's road trip companion of 1964, Paul 'Pablo' Clayton, died in April 1966 after years of drug abuse. 'He couldn't take it,' says Liam Clancy. 'He got into a bathtub and pulled an electric heater in after himself.' Peter La Farge, another old friend from Greenwich Village, died in the shower stall next to Liam Clancy's apartment around this time after slitting his wrists.

Many more people from Bob's circle of friends would die prematurely in the years to come. A high proportion of the deaths were drug-related, or suicides. Clancy saw a link between the suicides of ambitious songwriters like Clayton and La Farge and the phenomenon of Bob's success. It is hard to say how these deaths affected Bob, because he said little or nothing about most of them. He rarely attended funerals; and, as the 1960s progressed and drug abuse claimed so many lives, he must have become used to the fatalities. Liam Clancy blames many of these deaths on what he calls 'frustrated dreams and visions.' He explains: 'Dylan had taken off as a star into the firmament. He was one of us and, suddenly, there he was. [He] was what every one of us probably hoped to be, and [we] realized now that the lightning had struck. It couldn't strike twice.' When Clancy asked Bob in the 1990s whether he felt any responsibility for the tragic deaths of so many old friends who had been in his shadow, Bob replied: 'Man, how can I be responsible? . . . These people had to do what they did. If I were to dwell on that, become obsessed with it, I wouldn't get on with my life. I wouldn't create anything. I wouldn't write anything.' Here was Bob's toughness, but he seemed to be using it to protect his sensitive nature.

A somber feeling descended as the tour moved on to Ireland. There was slow hand clapping and booing when the band came on stage at the Adelphi in Dublin. Vincent Doyle probably expressed what many fans felt when he wrote in the music paper *Melody Maker* that 'It was unbelievable to see a hip, swinging Dylan trying to look and sound like Mick Jagger and to realize after the first few minutes that it wasn't a take-off.'

In London, Bob met up again with Dana Gillespie, and received The Beatles at the Mayfair Hotel. Bob Johnston flew in from America to assist in the recording of British concerts, and sat up most of one night while Bob rapped to The Beatles. Johnston believes the experience changed the group forever. 'All four of The Beatles were in his hotel room and he talked to them all night long. They never even talked,' he says. 'When [they] came out the next morning they were John Lennon and George

Harrison and Paul McCartney. They weren't The Beatles [any more].' As McCartney has said, 'Dylan was influencing us quite heavily at that point.'

It was during the British leg of the world tour that the most famous bootleg of Bob's career – and possibly the most famous bootleg in all of popular music – was recorded. The so-called Royal Albert Hall bootleg was actually made at Manchester's Free Trade Hall, a hundred and eighty-five miles north of the capital, on May 17. Bob appeared on stage looking surprisingly small and frail, dressed in a buttoned-up houndstooth suit. But his voice roared as he poured himself into the songs. The Hawks were with him all the way, breathing in music and exhaling music, and it was beautifully sharp, surprisingly sophisticated music. 'Baby, Let Me Follow You Down' swung like jazz. Still, the audience slow-clapped sulkily.

Bob spoke between songs, slurring his words as if wasted. 'This is, um . . . this is cawlled, "Yessss . . ." ' he drawled the introduction to 'Leopard-Skin Pill-Box Hat.' The crowd laughed. He tried again: 'This is . . . er . . . this is called, "Yes I See You Got Yer Brand-New Leopard-Skin Pill-Box Haaat." ' But he enunciated perfectly when the band kicked in. Much of his stage act was showmanship, worthy of vaudeville. Before the next number he mumbled a stream of nonsense words. The moment the audience shut up to hear what he was actually saying, he deadpanned: '. . . if you only just wouldn't clap so *hard*.' He had used the same trick the night before in Sheffield. The gag got a cheer and Mickey Jones had his cue to strike the first note of 'One Too Many Mornings.'

Bob took Richard Manuel's seat at the piano to play the toysoldier march of 'Ballad of a Thin Man.' Garth Hudson spun arpeggios of sound on the organ.

There was a lull before the next song.

'JUDAS!'

The taunt was loud, from the back of the hall. People applauded the heckler, Keele University student Keith

Butler. He was upset that Bob had taken songs like 'One Too Many Mornings' from acoustic albums and performed them now in a radically different style.

'I don't believe you,' retorted Bob, strumming the opening chords of 'Like a Rolling Stone.' Then he became angry, retorting with vehemence: 'You're a LIAR!' Bob turned to The Hawks. As they began the song, he exhorted them to 'play fuckin' loud.' The music swelled toward the bridge. Bob squirmed one skinny leg up against the other, shuddering with ecstasy, as he keened: 'How does it *feel*?' Again: 'How does it feeeeeeel?' Jones used his heavy right foot to punish the bass drum and Hudson's organ shimmered. Keith Butler stomped out of the theater, pausing to tell Pennebaker's film unit that 'pop groups could produce better rubbish than that. It was a bloody disgrace, it was. He wants *shooting*.'

After concerts in Scotland, Bob and The Hawks flew to Paris, where they performed at L'Olympia on May 24 in front of an enormous Stars and Stripes. This upset members of the French audience partly because of America's controversial involvement in the former French colony of Vietnam. Bob seemed oblivious to the politics, as usual, even though his world tour coincided with a huge escalation in the conflict in Vietnam. After large-scale U.S.A.F. bombing of North Vietnam, thousands of U.S. combat troops were sent to bolster the campaign, many of them drafted. A large protest movement was gathering momentum. On September 25, 1965, just after the start of Bob's U.S. tour, an antiwar concert was staged at Carnegie Hall in New York featuring many of Bob's friends, including Joan Baez, who urged young men to resist the draft. Bob was invited to participate at this and similar events, but was notable only by his absence. 'Everybody came except Bob Dylan,' says Izzy Young, who emceed at Carnegie Hall. '[Bob] wasn't particularly active at all.'

There was also an uproar at the Paris concert when Bob seemed incapable of tuning his guitar during the acoustic part of the show. 'He was tuning it and tuning it for a long, long time and I remember saying to Albert Grossman, "Tell him to give me the guitar and I'll tune it for him real quickly. People are getting hostile out there," ' says Robbie Robertson, who was in the wings. 'It seemed like it was turning into a game. That's why the people got upset. They thought he was just messing with their head.' The crowd seemed relieved when The Hawks came on stage and played actual music. It was one of the few times the band was cheered and Bob's acoustic set was booed.

The day of the Paris performance was also Bob's birthday. Having transformed popular music and written some of the greatest songs of the century he was, amazingly, only twenty-five years old.

Despite the fact that the Manchester show became known as the Royal Albert Hall concert, the actual Albert Hall dates were two days after the Paris show, on May 26 and 27. There was a spacey feeling to the London shows, with slurred introductions and remarkable acoustic performances that sounded as if Bob was singing to himself. The vastness and grandeur of the ninety-five-year-old theater – opened by Queen Victoria and named after her Prince Consort – was hugely impressive to The Hawks, who had been playing a club in New Jersey just a few months earlier. Soon they would be transformed into The Band, one of the most celebrated groups of the era, filling great theaters on their own. This was just one of the remarkable repercussions of the extraordinary world tour that was now concluded. 'We went from a bar band to the Albert Hall because of Bob,' says Garth Hudson. 'Any exaggeration would be an understatement when it comes to the help we got from Bob Dylan.'

Bob returned home from Britain exhausted. His once cherubic face was pinched; his eyes were dark; his skin was paper white; and his long pale fingers were stained with nicotine. His speaking voice was slurred with weariness, words stretched out, sentences not completed. Substances he had been taking to endure the tour had reduced him to a shadow. As Pennebaker says: 'He was very wasted.' Yet if Albert Grossman had his way, Bob would get back on the road in August for a sixty-four date American tour. He would be on the road interminably, until every last ticket dollar had been sucked up, or until his heart gave out and, like Hank Williams, he slumped back for the rest that never ends. All this time Bob had been doing as he was told by Grossman, but now he was starting to feel the pressure of the workload that had been put on his shoulders, and he became noticeably irritable.

Even Bob's brief summer break was crowded with tasks. *Eat the Document*, which ABC-TV wanted to screen, was miles of nonsensical footage with a sound track that did not synchronize. Bob wanted Pennebaker to edit the film. Pennebaker had little enthusiasm for what was essentially Bob's home movie, but he and Bobby Neuwirth made a rough cut. Bob thought it too much like *Dont Look Back*, and decided to recut it himself, using equipment Pennebaker sent up to Hi Lo Ha, and employing Howard Alk as his assistant. Dylan and Alk worked night and day on the film, but though he clearly wanted to be a film director when he assumed control of *Eat the Document*, and he would try his hand at directing in years to come with other projects, Bob was no filmmaker. 'It's not something you learn parking cars in a garage. You gotta know some of the rules,' says Pennebaker. 'And he didn't know any of the rules.' Bob hacked up the original footage to make a rough cut, which ABC-TV would ultimately reject because it was believed it would be incomprehensible to a mainstream audience, indeed to almost any audience. In the process, Bob destroyed valuable original film, including concert recordings. Pennebaker asked Bob's office if he could make a duplicate, so that raw footage would at least be preserved for posterity, but he was met with indifference. He was in dispute with Grossman at the time, over money owed for *Dont Look Back*. As Pennebaker says: 'It got to be a little nasty.'

There were other pressures. Macmillan was about to publish the long-promised book, *Tarantula*, which it turned out was not the Dylan novel many had been expecting. The book was comprised of short segments of unpunctuated free-form verse. Familiar phrases from song lyrics appeared, together with a cast of famous names. Sometimes the imagery was startling, and parts were funny, but it was the least commercial book imaginable – a hundred and thirty-seven pages of liner notes for a Dylan album that did not exist. Macmillan had printed *Tarantula* button badges and *Tarantula* shopping bags as part of a major promotional campaign. When Bob saw the galley proofs he had second thoughts about the whole project and told Macmillan he wanted to make changes. They gave him two weeks.

As if the film, the book, and the upcoming tour were not enough to think about, Grossman was attempting to renegotiate Bob's contract with Columbia, and Columbia in turn wanted a new record from Bob. It was all too much.

On the morning of Friday July 29, 1966, Bob and Sara were leaving the Grossmans' Bearsville house. Bob had retrieved an old motorcycle from the garage and wanted to ride it to a repair shop. Sara followed him in a car. As they pulled out of the drive, Sally Grossman was in the hall talking by telephone to Albert, who was at his office in Manhattan. She was still speaking with Albert a short time later when Sara's car reappeared in the drive. 'Hold on,' she told Albert, as she saw Bob emerge from the car. Apparently, he was hurt. 'He was kind of moaning and groaning.'

Bob came up to the house and 'sort of lay down on the porch.' When Sally came closer, Sara told her excitedly, 'Keep away from him!' Sally gathered that Bob had 'slipped off the bike' – which was nowhere to be seen – and hurt himself. Yet he was not cut or obviously roughed up. The only evidence he was hurt was his moans of pain. Sally went back to the telephone to tell Albert what was happening.

What exactly happened to Dylan after he rode out of the Grossmans' property that morning has remained extraordinarily mysterious. Despite the fact that it seems to have been a fairly minor fall off a motorbike – and Bob, with his poor eyesight, was known for his haphazard road skills – the incident seethes with intrigue. There are contradictory accounts of where exactly the accident happened, and even whether there was an 'accident' at all. This is because the timing was very convenient for Bob; the accident gave Dylan an excuse to get out of the numerous business commitments then threatening to overwhelm him.

There certainly was an accident, or rather an *incident*. But it was not as serious as was reported at the time. Sally Grossman, who has never previously discussed the matter publicly and is a key witness to part of the events of that day, believes it occurred on Glasco Turnpike, the country road that led from Bearsville to Bob's house in Byrdcliffe. A close friend of Bob, who wishes to remain anonymous, says the accident happened on Striebel Road, which runs directly outside the Grossman property. The source says Bob later admitted to him that when he came out of the Grossmans' drive, onto the steep and slippery Striebel Road, he simply lost his balance and, rather feebly, fell off his bike. The bike then fell on top of him. In a quite different version of what happened, former Woodstock constable Charlie Wolven recollects Bob being involved in an accident several miles away, on Zena Road, near the hamlet of Saugerties, at a sharply twisting S-shaped bend. Although Wolven says he was called to do traffic duty after an accident here, and he thinks the accident involved Bob, he did not see Bob and there is no police report of Bob being involved in an accident on Zena Road. It seems very unlikely that this was the fabled accident. Apart from anything else, it would be almost impossible for Bob to ride to Zena Road and have Sara bring him back to Bearsville in the short time Sally was on the telephone with Albert. 'I know it wasn't that long a time, because I was standing in my hallway talking to Albert when they pulled out, and still talking to him [when] they came back.' Considering all the evidence, it seems almost certain that the accident happened very close to the Grossman property, probably on Striebel Road or a little farther on, perhaps at Glasco Turnpike.

Subsequent press reports stated that Bob was rendered unconscious, broke his neck, and was almost killed. Yet by Sally's account, there were no obvious injuries and Bob was conscious. Furthermore, if Bob was that badly injured common sense has it he would have been rushed to the nearest general hospital, only fifteen minutes away in Kingston. But Sally confirms that no ambulance was called. Neither were there any police. Most important, Bob's doctor, Ed Thaler, now reveals that Sara did not take Bob to the hospital. She drove Bob directly from the Grossman property to Dr. Thaler's house-cum-surgery in Middletown, fully fifty miles away. This was a grueling one-hour drive by country roads, not a journey for a man in dire need of medical help.

As Bob lay in Dr. Thaler's surgery, radio stations across the country flashed dramatic news that Bob Dylan – an artist at the height of his fame and creative powers – had been in a motorcycle wreck. The *New York Times* reported that Bob's injuries were so serious he was forced to cancel a concert in New Haven scheduled for the following Saturday. In this way the first part of a remarkable career drew to a close.

CHAPTER 6

COUNTRY WAYS

Life had moved fast since Bob arrived in New York from Minnesota in 1961. Following the motorcycle accident of 1966 there was a period of slowing down and reassessment. In many ways the accident was a blessing. 'I was pretty wound up before that accident happened,' he later said. 'I probably would have died if I had kept on going the way I had been.'

The true extent of Bob's injuries is still unclear. By Bob's own account, he suffered several broken vertebrae in the accident. Friends saw him wearing a neck brace for a while and say he received ultrasound treatment. He complained of back pain, and took up swimming again partly as therapy. So there is evidence that he had suffered some injury and lasting effects. At the same time, however, he did not require intensive medical treatment.

Bob chose to stay with Dr. Ed Thaler in Middletown for six weeks following the accident. This was despite the fact that he had a comfortable home of his own in Woodstock, and a wife and child waiting for him. Dr. Thaler denies the suggestion that Bob used this time to wean himself off drugs. 'He did not come here regarding any situation involving detoxification.' Dr. Thaler's wife Selma says Bob used their house rather as a refuge, a place where he could have sanctuary from the press. 'He had some kind of anonymity here. As it turns out the people next door had a teenaged daughter who recognized him, [but] nobody bothered him and they certainly would have in [Woodstock] . . . maybe we being ten years older than Bob [was] reminiscent of his childhood,' says Selma Thaler. 'The house was peaceful [and] he felt comfortable here. His friends were able to visit him. Nobody stalked anybody . . . He could be alone. I don't know whether he was writing or thinking or what he was doing, but it was away from [his] ordinary daily life – and I think that provided some peace of mind.'

In the summer of 1966, after an exhausting tour of her own, Odetta visited Dr. Thaler for personal reasons, stating, 'I needed a dose of my Thalers.' She discovered Bob was living in a spare room on the third floor. 'Eddie and Selma had the [room] made so it was like his apartment,' she says. When Odetta sat down with Bob to talk, he was well enough to complain about artists recording cover versions of his songs with mistakes in the lyrics. 'He was well on his way to being whole again.'

The convalescence coincided with the expiration of Bob's contract with Columbia Records. Bob considered switching to M.G.M., for a reputed $1 million advance, and actually signed a contract at one point. But M.G.M. executives had second thoughts and were slow to countersign. *Tarantula* was another problem. Bob now realized he had embarked on the book for the wrong reasons. As he said, he had agreed to write a book simply because a publisher had offered to publish him. He did not, however, really have a book to write. 'I just put down all these words and sent them off to my publishers and they'd send back the galleys, and I'd be so embarrassed at the nonsense I'd written I'd change the whole thing.' Publication was postponed for the foreseeable future.

After fully recuperating, Bob settled down to a relatively quiet domestic life at Hi Lo Ha. A few friends visited, including Allen Ginsberg, who brought a parcel of books. D. A. Pennebaker found Bob engaged in editing *Eat the Document*. 'He didn't seem in peril particularly,' says Pennebaker. 'The accident was, to some extent, a period when he was resting up from whatever traumas he was enduring.' Partly for security, Bob and Sara acquired two huge dogs that lived in a large kennel at the entrance to their property. Their first pet was a giant poodle named Hamlet. The second was an aggressive Saint Bernard they called Buster. Next to the dogs' kennel on the drive was a sign that warned PRIVATE PROPERTY. NO TRESPASSING.

In addition to editing *Eat the Document*, Bob decided to shoot additional scenes that he thought might be used in that film or for another project he had vaguely in mind, and he invited friends to come to Woodstock to act with him. Rick Danko and Richard Manuel arrived in February 1967. Since Bob's accident, The Hawks had been a road band without a road to go on, kicking their heels at the Hotel Chelsea. They were still on the payroll and Bob did not know quite what to do with them. Snow was thick on the ground when Danko and Manuel got to Woodstock, giving the town the look of the penultimate scenes of Bob's favorite film, *Shoot the Piano Player*. Streams were frozen like glass, and roofs were covered in sparkling white blankets of snow. Danko and Manuel got up at five each morning to work with Bob in the first hours of daylight. 'That was really my first exposure to Woodstock,' says Danko, 'in the wintertime, shooting the snow.' The other Hawks drifted upstate, lodging initially at the Woodstock Motel. Eccentric performer Tiny Tim became part of the gang. Bob had an idea about working with 'Mr. Tim,' as he laconically called him, on what Pennebaker describes as 'a circus film.' Tim was also involved in a Peter Yarrow film called *You Are What You Eat*. 'Everybody thought you could make money in films after *Dont Look Back*,' says Pennebaker. 'But it seemed very unorganized and casual and off the wall.'

When the light faded each day, Danko and Manuel met friends in a local restaurant. The restaurateur had a house to rent near the hamlet of West Saugerties. 'She wanted $275 a month. It was in the middle of a hundred acres, a lot of privacy. The way she explained it, it was beautiful,' says Danko. The house was a large split-level building, painted the color of a strawberry milk shake. Danko decided it would be better than living in a motel. 'So Garth, Richard, and myself moved into Big Pink,' he says, using the name they would give to the property. Robbie Robertson rented a separate place with his girlfriend Dominique. Levon Helm was still estranged from the group, presently drifting around the south.

After years on the road, The Hawks were accustomed to a nocturnal lifestyle of working at night and going to bed at dawn. Bob quickly readjusted to a more conventional life. He and Sara, now expecting their second child, were woken early each day by one-year-old Jesse. After breakfast, Bob walked five-year-old Maria to the school bus stop on Upper Byrdcliffe Road. Around noon he got into one of his cars – he now had a baby blue Mustang as well as the Ford station wagon – and drove to Big Pink. Robertson also made his way to Big Pink at the same time. 'Bob and Robbie, they would come by every day, five to seven days a week for seven or eight months,' says Danko. '[Bob] would show up like clockwork around noon.' Bob made a pot of coffee and clattered on a typewriter, extra loud if The Hawks were still in bed. 'It amazed me, his writing ability,' says Garth Hudson. 'How he could come in, sit down at the typewriter, and write a song . . . Also what was amazing was that almost every one of those songs was funny.'

Between February and the fall of 1967, Bob composed more than thirty songs, which he and The Hawks recorded, together with numerous cover songs, on a two-track reel-to-reel system Hudson had put together. Most songs were recorded in the basement of Big Pink with the poodle Hamlet sprawled across the floor. It was a relaxed and happy time for Bob, a period of friendship and sharing with The Hawks, and the musical collaboration at Big Pink proved fruitful and enjoyable for all concerned.

As spring turned to summer, they left the windows of Big Pink open to get a breeze through. The mellow, country atmosphere seemed to influence the music they created. It was a very different sound from the ruckus Bob and The Hawks made on stage in 1965–66, and altogether distinct from the late-night city sound of studio albums like *Blonde on Blonde*. It was closer to the rural old-timey music of the Harry Smith *Anthology of American Folk Music*, and influenced by the diverse musical tastes of Bob and the individual Hawks. Bob introduced Robertson to traditional folk music. 'I didn't care that much for what he was turning me on to,' says Robertson. '[But] when he sang those songs I liked them a lot. And I couldn't tell which were the songs that he wrote, and which were the songs somebody else wrote. For instance, when we were in the basement, and he would sing all these songs, I didn't know whether he wrote "Royal Canal" or whether it was an old folk song.* And [it] was an extraordinary education to be connected to all of this great music. A lot of it came from the British Isles and from the mountains of America and down those mountains and into the cities.' In return, Robertson broadened Bob's knowledge of rock 'n' roll. 'I would play him records. I would turn him on to things.' Danko's family had played country music in rural Ontario. Manuel was a fine boogie-woogie pianist and possessed a pop sensibility. Hudson was steeped in Anglican church music, horn playing, and the avant-garde compositions of Aleksandr Scriabin. Everybody had favorite musicians and recordings – knowledge that informed the music they made together – and for the first time in their careers they had months to simply sit around and jam. Out of this convivial mix came singular compositions like 'Lo and Behold!' 'I Shall Be Released,' and 'Crash on the Levee (Down in the Flood).' Bob wrote the lyrics, but the music was created largely through improvisation with the Hawks. Bob shared songwriting credits on two major

*'The Royal Canal' was written by Irish playwright Brendan Behan for his play *The Quare Fellow*, first produced in 1954.

songs. He collaborated with Manuel on 'Tears of Rage' and with Danko on 'This Wheel's on Fire.' When Ian and Sylvia became the first of many artists to record a cover version of 'This Wheel's on Fire,' Danko began to receive substantial royalties. He referred to the royalties as 'checks from God.'

These songs became known as 'The Basement Tapes,' though not all were recorded in the basement at Big Pink. Some were recorded at Hi Lo Ha – in the so-called Red Room – and others at the Ohayo Mountain home of Clarence Schmidt, the Man of the Mountain. Clarence Schmidt was an eccentric retired mason who dressed in overalls and had a long beard matted with creosote, paint, and tar. This was the sticky concoction he used to construct a large junkyard folly, decorated with oddments of wood, metal, and plastic, car fenders and broken-down kitchen appliances. Schmidt glued fragments of mirror, religious figures, and plastic flowers to the folly, and incorporated shrines to favorite musicians. Bob and The Hawks became friendly with Schmidt and made some recordings in the old man's house, near the folly. Something of the strangeness of the setting permeated the music. The musicians have forgotten what songs exactly were recorded at the Schmidt house, but Garth Hudson thinks 'Apple Suckling Tree' sounds like it may have been recorded there. Surreal numbers that sound like they should have been recorded there include: 'You Gotta Quit Kickin' My Dog Around,' during which The Hawks barked like dogs and quacked like ducks; and 'See You Later, Allen Ginsberg,' set to the tune of 'See You Later, Alligator.' There was a lot of silliness. The Hawks sang harmonies in Elmer Fudd voices. Bob burbled obscenities on 'Next Time on the Highway.' Robertson and Manuel sometimes played drums, making sounds like children bashing saucepans. On 'The Spanish Song,' Bob and The Hawks wailed like a drunken mariachi band. They also covered such unlikely numbers as 'Coming Round the Mountain' and 'Flight of the Bumblebee.' At times the sessions sounded, as Robertson has said, like 'reefer run amok.' The sessions also sounded like friends having a great time together, enjoying easy companionship and musical freedom.

Although the sessions were loose and friendly, Bob was in charge. He called out in which key he wanted the songs played and told Garth Hudson which songs to tape. After the sessions, Bob would call Hudson on the telephone and ask for recordings of songs he wanted to work on further. Part of the purpose of recording the songs was to use them as demos that Dwarf Music could send to other artists looking for material. In this way, some of the weird and wonderful songs created in Woodstock filtered through to the public via the radio. Manfred Mann had a top-ten hit with one of the most Dada-esque of the 'basement' songs, 'Quinn the Eskimo (The Mighty Quinn).' The Byrds charted with 'You Ain't Goin' Nowhere.' And Peter, Paul and Mary had a hit with 'Too Much of Nothing,' making a mistake in the lyric, just as they had with 'Blowin' in the Wind' years before. This time the group invented a character named Marion. 'I do think we did not take care of business on "Too Much of Nothing,"' admits Noel Paul Stookey, who wondered if the mistake was part of Bob's disenchantment with the group. 'We just became *other hacks* that were doing his tunes.'

Pop versions of the 'basement' songs kept Bob's name in the public consciousness during his seclusion. The fact that he was obviously working, but not appearing in public, added to his mystique. Many people already considered Bob a genius. Now he became that even more intriguing phenomenon, a reclusive genius. The release of D. A. Pennebaker's documentary *Dont Look Back* in May 1967 also reminded the public of his work. The film was panned in middle America, but was a success in California and New York. Indeed, its release was an excuse for journalists to heap praise upon Dylan for his past achievement. *New York Times* critic Richard Goldstein wondered whether one film could sum up 'the man who defined his generation' and went on to compare Bob with William Shakespeare. It was only five years since 'Blowin' in the Wind,' and two since 'Like a Rolling Stone' had been a hit. But already the intelligentsia was elevating Bob to legendary status. *Bob Dylan's Greatest Hits* was released in March. Although the compilation contained only one track not available on a previous album – 'Positively 4th Street' – it reached number ten in the album charts, proving Bob's popular appeal. It went on to become the biggest-selling single album of his career, selling three million units in the United States.*

This sort of success enhanced Bob's reputation and reminded Columbia Records of Bob's value. On July 1, 1967, Bob signed a new five-year contract with Columbia, after Vice President Clive Davis offered him a very generous deal to stay with the company. Under the terms of his 1961 contract Bob had received a miserly four percent royalty on albums. Under the terms of the new contract, Columbia guaranteed Bob an advance of $200,000, payable over three years; a twenty percent royalty on new albums; an enhanced five percent royalty on his back catalogue; and an unusually high level of control over his material. For example, Columbia was not allowed to reedit master recordings after Bob had approved them. Davis figured it was worth treating Bob well, partly because Bob gave Columbia kudos; other acts – often more profitable acts – wanted to record with Columbia simply because Bob was a Columbia artist. Bob agreed to record four new LPs over a five-year period, the first album to be delivered within six months.

* * *

**Bob Dylan's Greatest Hits Vol II* (1971) is RIAA certified as Bob Dylan's best-selling album with five million sales. It has sold 2.5 million *units*, but the number is doubled because it is a two-disc set.

While Bob was secluded in Woodstock during the summer of 1967 – the so-called summer of love – The Beatles released *Sgt. Pepper's Lonely Hearts Club Band*. Hallucinogenic drugs, technological gimmickry, and intellectual pretension were suddenly the order of the day and bands from London to San Francisco tried to take it all one step further. The Rolling Stones made *Their Satanic Majesties Request*. Jefferson Airplane recorded *Surrealistic Pillow*, with its pop hit 'White Rabbit.' Bob was removed from the pop world, and he was one of the few who considered *Sgt. Pepper* less than a masterpiece. It was, he said, 'a very indulgent album . . . though the songs on it were real good. I didn't think all that production was necessary.' In the peace of Woodstock he stayed relatively drug free, raising a family, playing music with his friends that had a vibrant, natural sound, and spending part of each day reading the Bible and the Hank Williams songbook. These were the influences behind *John Wesley Harding*, his first studio album since the accident and his first album for Columbia under their recently renegotiated contract. 'Every artist in the world was in the studio trying to make the biggest-sounding record they possibly could,' recalls producer Bob Johnston. 'So what does he do? He comes to Nashville and tells me he wants to record with a bass, drum, and guitar.'

With tried and trusted session musicians Kenny Buttrey on drums, Charlie McCoy on bass, and, for the first time, Pete Drake on steel guitar, Bob recorded *John Wesley Harding* in three curt sessions in the fall of 1967. 'Kenny and I were amazed at the change from *Blonde on Blonde* to *John Wesley Harding*,' says McCoy. 'The recording was different. Of course, he sounded different. He looked different . . . When he first came for *Blonde on Blonde* it was the wild fright wig. The next time he came back his hair was a lot shorter. His voice sounded different . . . We just flew through that stuff.' The three *John Wesley Harding* sessions totaled nine hours, a fraction of the time The Beatles were then taking to record a single track (*Sgt. Pepper* was recorded over five months). 'We went in and knocked 'em out like demos,' says Buttrey. 'It seemed to be the rougher the better. He would hear a mistake and laugh a little bit to himself as if [to say], *Great, man, that's just great. Just what I'm looking for.*' Under the terms of Bob's new contract, half the cost of hiring musicians was deducted from royalties so it was in his interest to use a small band and work fast.

Unlike *Blonde on Blonde,* all the lyrics to Bob's new songs were complete when he arrived in Nashville so he was ready to start immediately. As Charlie McCoy puts it, 'He knew everything.' These were radically different lyrics from both the songs on *Blonde on Blonde* and the words he and The Hawks had recently been singing in Woodstock. They were terse parables. Most unusually, none of the songs on *John Wesley Harding* had a chorus. The album title, and title track, alluded to the life of Texas outlaw John Wesley Hardin (whose name Bob accidentally misspelled). Another song was about Saint Augustine. Gunman and saint, though seemingly disparate, in the landscape of Bob's imagination became identical outcasts from society, dealing in truth and lies, life and death. These themes and the use of archaic phrases and allusions to scripture gave the album a biblical flavor. This was a record out of time, a fact illustrated by a meeting Bob had with Noel Paul Stookey. The Peter, Paul and Mary singer – intoxicated with flower power – drove to Woodstock in the fall of 1967 to ask Bob about the meaning of life. Bob listened to a stream of rather absurd questions that were then common currency. 'I'm talking about how I'm really blown away by The Beatles. I love what they're saying about love, and I'm wondering if he senses what's happening in their music . . . what does he feel life's all about?' says Stookey. When Stookey paused for breath, Bob asked: 'Do you ever read the Bible?' While it is true that Bob had drawn on the Bible for imagery from the start of his career, his comment to Stookey, and the nature of the songs on *John Wesley Harding*, were clear indications that he was approaching a religious state of mind. His journey toward faith in God was a long one, but these new songs showed that he had seriously begun that journey.

'All Along the Watchtower' had echoes of Isaiah and Revelation. When Jimi Hendrix had a hit with a searing cover six months later, he invoked the howl of the apocalypse with even more zeal. References to the Bible also featured prominently in 'The Ballad of Frankie Lee and Judas Priest' and 'Dear Landlord.' The latter would be seen by some as a message to Albert Grossman, the landlord of Bob's career, though Sally insists, 'None of us thought about it that way.'

There was also a lighter side to the album. The country pastiche 'I'll Be Your Baby Tonight' was a delightful love song. 'Down Along the Cove,' with its reference to 'my little bundle of joy,' might be a song dedicated to a baby. It is perhaps not a coincidence that three months before it was recorded – on July 11, 1967 – Bob had become a father for the second time when Sara gave birth to a daughter, Anna Lea.

Another, more sobering influence on *John Wesley Harding* was the fact that near the time of recording, on October 3, Woody Guthrie died. At fifty-five, Guthrie had finally succumbed to Huntington's chorea. 'Late in the afternoon I got this call from [Bob] wanting to know what's happening,' says Guthrie's manager Harold Leventhal. '[He] asked me if I'm planning a memorial concert, and to be sure to let him know.' Bob was as good as his word and made his first public appearance since the summer of 1966 at the tribute to Woody Guthrie held at Carnegie Hall on January 20, 1968. Bob shared the bill with artists including Judy Collins, Ramblin' Jack Elliott, and Arlo Guthrie, now a folk artist in his own right. Bob came on stage with The Hawks, dressed in western-style suits and cowboy boots. Levon Helm, back behind the drums, noticed that although Grossman was at the show he and Bob were not speaking to each other. Indeed, ever since Bob's accident and decision to stop touring their relationship had been strained. Bob and the Hawks performed three songs rarely heard outside of Woody's own recordings, injecting fire into 'I Ain't Got No Home.' Bob howled the refrain as if truly dispossessed. The fire he put into the lyric made one's hair stand on end and showed that, despite the fact he had been secluded most of the time in his idyllic country home, anger and passion still thrived within him.

There were two shows at Carnegie Hall – a matinee and an evening show – and a party afterward at the Dakota, which Bob attended. Even though he was obviously physically well again, and even willing to socialize with old friends, Bob had no intention of returning to touring for the foreseeable future. 'I won't be giving any concerts for a while,' he said. 'I'm not compelled to do it now. I went around the world a couple of times. But I didn't have anything else to do then.' By this he meant that he now had a family to care for. Bob's elusiveness had the effect of sharpening the public's appetite for his music and *John Wesley Harding* sold at a faster clip than had any of his previous albums.

When Bob walked Maria to the bus stop on Upper Byrdcliffe Road each morning he sometimes met neighbor Bruce Dorfman and his daughter, Lisa. As the little girls became friendly, the men fell into conversation. Dorfman lived in a small house in front of Bob's property. He was an artist who worked each day in an adjacent studio. After a while Bob showed up at the studio with Buster, snarling and barking in an alarming fashion. 'Just came to pay a neighbor a visit,' he would tell Dorfman, turning to admonish the dog. 'Shut up, goddamnit!'

Dorfman was painting life-size pictures of what he called his 'fantasy women,' and Bob took a keen interest in the work. As they chatted Bob realized that Dorfman was not interested in his celebrity, knowing little about popular music. The artist reacted to him with refreshing normality. So when Sara bought Bob a box of oil paints for his twenty-seventh birthday, Bob asked Dorfman how to use them. The artist set up an easel in the corner of his studio and asked Bob what he wanted to paint. Bob produced an art book with a reproduction of *Girl with Flute*, by Jan Vermeer. He did not want to copy the painting but simply to do something in that style. 'Sure this is where you want to start?' asked Dorfman, surprised by the audacity of Bob's ambition. 'Talk about immaculate painting!' But he humored him, demonstrating the basics of how to use oil paint. 'He was very, very attentive, really wonderfully attentive and absorbing it all very carefully.' Naturally, Bob could not paint like Vermeer. The next day he came with a book of Claude Monet reproductions. He had a series of these art books. 'Same deal. An hour, a mess.' The third day Bob had a book of Vincent van Gogh's paintings, and he had some success using a landscape as a starting point. After skipping a day, Bob appeared with a Marc Chagall book. 'This is the one that worked,' recalls Dorfman. 'It was perfect, because you had all these multilayered images – things flying, things walking, clocks flying, rabbits with green faces. It was all there. Chagall was it. He made the connection.' Bob began making a canvas that was clearly inspired by Chagall's style, but the images were from 'All Along the Watchtower.' Technically, the painting was so-so, but he was enjoying himself.

The neighbors were soon painting together in the studio almost every day, forming a close friendship revealed now for the first time (Bob has never spoken about it and Dorfman has finally chosen to set down an accurate record). The country lifestyle had mellowed Bob enough for him to be able to form a natural, everyday connection with a neighbor; indeed it was like therapy to him after the recent, frenetic years in New York and on the road. Dorfman was a good-humored, calm, and engaging companion of his own age – Dorfman was four years his senior – who was teaching Bob something he found interesting. The fact that Dorfman was not at all interested in show business was probably also attractive to Bob, as was the fact that Dorfman was discreet. Consequently, Bob relaxed and became uncharacteristically open and talkative.

The friends would talk about 'everything on earth,' as Dorfman says, but Bob particularly enjoyed talking about his children, which was a subject they had in common. 'He was a doting parent,' says Dorfman. 'He loved to talk about his kids . . . Best thing in the world.' Bob came to trust Dorfman so much that he asked him to write a reference, in the spring of 1968, when Bob was going through the process of adopting Maria as his own child. In a reciprocal gesture, Bob wrote a letter to the Guggenheim Foundation recommending his neighbor for a grant (which was not successful, possibly because Bob's letter was more an exercise in dry humor than a compelling commendation).

There was a lot of playfulness in the friendship, and the two laughed together a lot of the time. Dorfman was experimenting with the idea of remote-controlled mobiles, hanging models from the ceiling of the studio. Talking it over with Bob, they decided the world needed a giant flying art object that could materialize over cities, changing shape and color. 'There were drawings made,' says the artist. 'The concept was mine. The additions, some of them, were Bob's . . . The idea would be that somehow you could get this thing to appear suddenly somewhere and get people to stop what they were doing.' Dorfman knew a financier who might fund the project. Bob said he would get celebrity backing. 'He was going to talk to Muhammad Ali and The Beatles, and between us we are somehow going to make this,' laughs Dorfman.

They also shared ideas and experiences. Dorfman taught Bob about art. Bob gave his neighbor a musical instrument as a gift (a type of Middle Eastern string instrument known as an oud) and gave and lent books. After years when he'd had little time for books, Bob was reading voraciously. Hi Lo Ha was becoming a veritable library, as Beatty Zimmerman noted when she visited. Bob lent Dorfman a copy of Isaac Bashevis Singer's wise and witty folk story *Gimpel the Fool*, which was a favorite. Bashevis Singer wrote about the existence of God, moral choices, and inexplicable mystery – all subjects close to Bob's heart. Bob was also reading William Blake and gave Dorfman a handsome edition of *Songs of Innocence and Experience* as a Christmas gift.

Bob was not normally extravagant with money, but now he could afford anything he wanted. His children had wonderful toys. There was expensive film editing equipment at the house and a pool table in the garage. Although Bobby Neuwirth and Victor Maymudes had temporarily left the entourage, other friends would come by to play games with Bob. 'If he starts playing Go, we play Go,' says Al Aronowitz, who came up to the house regularly at this time. 'If he wants to play pool, we would play pool.' Dorfman was shocked by their sycophancy, noticing that Bob's friends allowed him to win when they played basketball in the yard. Other signs of wealth included a Cadillac limousine, a model designed to be driven by a chauffeur. It had a glass screen divider and the most sophisticated in-car sound system available, with speakers built into the doors and a control panel in Bob's armrest. Bernard Paturel, the former owner of Cafe Espresso, became Bob's chauffeur. Bob's wealth meant he also could make impulsive and peculiar purchases. When he needed a vehicle to haul equipment, he bought a Grumman truck. 'Not something you would normally park near a house,' says Dorfman. '[But] there it was!' For a while, the truck was Bob's favorite toy. When Bob needed a suit in order to attend a function with Sara, he and Dorfman set out on a shopping expedition. Instead of being driven in the Cadillac, or taking the Mustang, they went in the truck. Bob could afford the finest clothing from the smartest stores in Manhattan. Yet they went to Sears Roebuck in nearby Kingston. Bob picked a green poplin suit off a clearance rack. Dorfman wondered what Sara would think; despite her humble background, she deported herself like Jackie Onassis. Bob bought the suit anyway, together with a big bag of white chocolate, which he munched contentedly on the ride home.

Bob was at Hi Lo Ha on the afternoon of June 5, 1968, when he received a telephone call from Minnesota. When the conversation was over, he turned to Bernard Paturel and asked if he would get the Cadillac. Bob packed a small suitcase, fetched his guitar, and then Paturel drove him to New York, putting him on a flight to Minnesota. Bob did not tell Paturel why he was going to Minnesota. It was a couple of days later, when Bob returned, that Paturel discovered what had happened. 'I found out that he'd gone there because his father had died. He never told me. I don't think he told anybody, except perhaps Sara.' The afternoon Bob received the call, Abe Zimmerman had collapsed at home and died of a heart attack. He was fifty-six. The fact that Bob could receive such momentous news and not tell Paturel, who was with him at the house at the time and then on the long drive to New York, reveals much about Bob's self-contained personality. Even at a moment of such deep personal stress he was as impassive as stone. One might think he did not care. In fact, he was deeply shocked and upset, but he did not want to show his feelings. Part of his distress was that he regretted not being close to his father in recent years. His parents did not attend his wedding. They had to find out about the motorcycle accident through journalists. Bob rarely visited Hibbing, and his brother and parents rarely came to Woodstock. Despite the distance between Bob and his family, Abe and Beatty were very proud of their eldest son, and Bob was on good terms with brother David, whose high school graduation he had attended in 1964. (David then took a degree, married, and began working in the music industry in the Twin Cities.) Beatty decorated their basement recreation room with Bob's album covers and posters. Abe had followed Bob's career in the trade magazines. In recent years there had been a slight thawing of relations between father and son, but now it was too late to be truly reconciled. 'Bob felt terrible,' says his friend Larry Kegan.

Something of his emotion became apparent at the funeral. Although it is not customary to have visitations at Jewish funerals, Abe's open casket was displayed at the Dougherty Funeral Home in Hibbing so his many friends and neighbors could pay their respects. After the funeral service at the synagogue in town, the funeral cortege made the long drive to Duluth where Abe's casket was buried in the Jewish cemetery. Bob broke down, one of the rare times in his life that he showed such emotion in public. He later confessed to Harold Leventhal that he had never known his father. Harold urged Bob to get back in touch with his Jewish faith, which he did over the next few years, reading widely on the subject and visiting Israel. The death also brought Bob closer to his mother. Beatty came to Woodstock after the funeral and stayed at Hi Lo Ha for some time. Bob remained close to his mother for the rest of her life, especially as his own children grew up and became attached to their grandmother.

Soon after he returned to Woodstock, Bob sat down at home with his musician friends John Cohen and Happy Traum to do a major interview for *Sing Out!* He talked about a range of subjects, including *Eat the Document*, which ABC-TV had rejected. But there was no mention of the death of his father. Neither was there conversation about family life. It was only when Maria came in from school and complained her shoes were pinching that something of Bob's ordinary life was revealed ('How was school? You learn anything? Well that's good. "My shoes hurt right here." Well, we'll see what we can do about it.') The rest of the time he glided through the questions, keeping himself to himself. Bob made a picture for the cover of the edition of the magazine in which the interview appeared, working with Bruce Dorfman in the studio to paint a man with a guitar sitting in a room, with another figure looking in through the window. He did not tell Dorfman what the picture was for. 'I was really surprised when I saw the thing on *Sing Out!* magazine. I was almost annoyed . . . he should have said something.'

A month later, at the end of July, Sara checked into a New York City hospital to give birth to their third child. While Bob waited, he spent some time with poet Michael McClure. They were at the Village Gate club when Dizzy Gillespie walked in. Bob casually introduced Gillespie to McClure, to the poet's delight. There was still time to kill, so they visited the Guggenheim Museum to look at an exhibition of paintings by Marc Chagall and Odilon Redon. 'Bob wouldn't look at the Redons,' says McClure. 'He had eyes for nothing but the Chagall. Chagall was the meaningful world to him.' Bob would continue to paint in the style of Chagall for some time – although it should be remembered that Bob's paintings were not very accomplished – and something of Chagall's dreamlike quality would permeate his songwriting in later years.

Bob had recently established an office near Gramercy Park in New York to handle publishing and other business. His chief employee was Naomi Saltzman, who formerly worked for Trio Concerts, a company operated by Albert Grossman and others principally to promote concerts by Peter, Paul and Mary. Saltzman took care of Bob's bookkeeping, maintained his press clippings, and assumed responsibility for the administration of some of his song publishing. She and her husband Ben became close to Bob and Sara, and it was Naomi Saltzman who drove Bob to and from the hospital when Sara was pregnant. Sara gave birth to a son on July 30, 1968. They decided to name the boy Samuel Abram, the middle name in honor of Bob's late father. Saltzman was driving Bob to the hospital to see his new son when Bob announced to her that he wanted to change the name of his publishing company, Dwarf Music, to celebrate the birth. Saltzman informed Bob that he was not free to change the name as he wished, because Grossman owned half of Dwarf Music, and they had a ten-year contract. This apparently came as a shock. 'He couldn't believe it,' says Saltzman. 'He told me I was making it up.' She assured Bob she was not, and would find the paperwork to prove it. By this time Bob was angry. He said she better find it. Although Bob had signed the Dwarf Music papers back in 1966 – when David Braun brought the documents to Sweden – he had never read them and only now did he comprehend what he had agreed to. Shortly after the discussion in the car Bob called a meeting at Saltzman's house with attorney Braun and accountant Marshall M. Gelfand. The meeting was the beginning of a long battle to extricate himself and his songs from Grossman's control. However, the people he chose to advise him in this matter were perhaps not the most obvious choices. Braun was Bob's attorney, but he also represented Grossman. Bob later admitted: 'I went to the only lawyer that I knew.' Gelfand had also worked for Grossman. This should not have surprised Bob; it was Grossman who introduced them when Bob needed someone to prepare his tax returns. Yet Bob did not fully understand Gelfand's connections until years later. For a man of such intelligence, Bob was proving himself to be remarkably naive in business.

Bob saw less and less of Grossman as his disquiet over their business relationship increased. Even though they were neighbors, Grossman was rarely seen at Hi Lo Ha. Bob and Sara entertained other friends, however. Despite his reputation as a recluse, Bob was at times sociable enough to host dinner parties, particularly at Thanksgiving. Those invited included Jane and Happy

Traum, who had also made their home in Woodstock, the Dorfmans, and members of The Hawks. Bruce Dorfman found the one Thanksgiving dinner he went to at the Dylans' house to be an awkward experience. 'There were all these people who were waiting on him,' he says. 'If he burped somebody would say Amen. It was ridiculous.'

Bob was painting in Dorfman's studio on Thanksgiving 1968 when Pattie and George Harrison's car came up the road toward his property. Bob put down his brushes and asked Dorfman excitedly, 'Aren't ya comin'?'

'Well, Bob, I've got work to do. You go ahead.' It seemed to Dorfman, as Bob left, that his friend was irritated by his lack of interest in such a distinguished visitor.

Thanksgiving dinner that year was enlivened by the outrageous antics of author Mason Hoffenberg. At one point he drunkenly said, 'I want all the boys over on this side, and all the girls over on this side. The first couple to get all their clothes off and screw wins.' Bob and George Harrison wrote a song together, 'I'd Have You Anytime.' They played some music and posed for photographs. Then the Harrisons went on their way. A couple of days went by without Bob coming to the studio. Eventually Sara rang Dorfman to say Bob felt he had been rude when he had left abruptly to meet the Harrisons. She said he was having a terrible time with himself, and did not know how to apologize. Dorfman said he should forget about it. Then Bob called. 'You gonna be around?' he asked, awkwardly, like a small boy getting back together with a friend. He showed up at the studio shortly afterward, muttering that it 'wasn't such a hot visit after all.' To Dorfman this episode showed that behind his facade Bob was a very sensitive man indeed, and that he would reproach himself for a long time if he acted in a way that caused hurt. 'If he did something that wasn't altogether thoughtful, he would feel terrible.'

* * *

Despite the failure of *Eat the Document*, Bob had not lost his enthusiasm for film. In the late 1960s he was asked to write songs for film sound tracks. Otto Preminger wanted Bob to work with him on the melodrama *Tell Me That You Love Me, Junie Moon*, and arranged a screening at his Manhattan town house. The film was abominable, but Bob told Preminger he would like to view it again that evening, with Sara. He wanted Preminger's butler to serve them dinner and would prefer the director not to be present. Preminger protested that this was his home; he could not be expected to vacate it so that Bob could entertain his wife. Still, he reluctantly agreed. Bob later admitted he had absolutely no intention of watching the film again. He wanted to show Sara the house because it had some interesting features they might incorporate in their own home. Pete Seeger accepted the commission instead.

More significantly, Bob was asked to contribute a song to *Midnight Cowboy*. He wrote 'Lay, Lady, Lay' but did not deliver it in time and director John Schlesinger instead used Fred Neil's song 'Everybody's Talkin'.' However, 'Lay, Lady, Lay' became the standout track on Bob's next album, *Nashville Skyline*, which was recorded in Nashville in February 1969.

The distinctive sound of 'Lay, Lady, Lay' was created partly by chance after drummer Kenny Buttrey asked Bob what he heard in his head for the drum part. 'Bongos,' Bob replied, with a faraway look in his eye. Buttrey asked producer Bob Johnston, and received the equally strange suggestion that he play cow bell. Determined to prove how nonsensical the suggestions were, Buttrey found a beat-up cow bell and pair of bongos that looked like a souvenir from Tijuana, the skin attached with thumbtacks. (He had to run a cigarette lighter under the skin to tighten it and get a tone.) The young Kris Kristofferson was working as a janitor at the studio and Buttrey asked Kristofferson to hold the bongos and cow bell next to his drum kit during the take. Without having worked out any drum part, the drummer got the signal they were going to record and he improvised a distinctive *tick-tock* introduction on bongo and cow bell that blended perfectly with the shimmer of organ and Pete Drake's steel guitar. Bob stepped up to the microphone and delivered the seductive lyric in one take. 'Lay, Lady, Lay' sounded unlike anything Bob had yet recorded. His voice was ultrasmooth, like a crooner's. The words were guileless, little more than *la la la*. If Bob had his way, the song would have been buried. But Clive Davis realized Bob had recorded a classic, and insisted it should be a single. 'I begged and pleaded with him not to,' said Bob, who never felt close to the song or thought it was representative of his work as a whole. Davis prevailed and the song became a major hit, reaching number seven and staying in the top forty for eleven weeks in the summer of 1969. By stepping outside himself, Bob had achieved his final pop hit of the decade.

Johnny Cash was at the same studio in Nashville working on his own album. On the spur of the moment, the friends decided to record together. 'I had microphones set up and stools and tapes, and everything,' says Johnston. 'They looked at each other . . . got their guitars and started playing.' They recorded approximately eighteen songs, mostly playing acoustic on their own, but also using members of Cash's band. Bob Johnston called out requests. 'After about two hours Dylan said, "That's all of it,"' says Johnston. Only one song was officially released, a ragged version of 'Girl from the North Country,' which became the opening track for *Nashville Skyline*. Aside from this and 'Lay, Lady, Lay' there were two other songs of note on the album: 'I Threw it All Away' and 'Tonight I'll Be Staying Here With You.' The other six tracks were short, insubstantial pieces, including an instrumental and the vacuous 'Peggy Day.' Critics naturally commented on the shallowness of some of the lyrics when the album was released, in April 1969, and much was made of the apparent transformation of the radical artist into a country act. The fact that Bob's two previous albums had also been recorded in Nashville, with the same core musicians, was overlooked. Also, although *Nashville Skyline* sounded like broad country and western to New York critics, and the album title emphasized that impression, it did not play that way in the South. 'By Nashville standards, I wouldn't call that a country record,' says Charlie McCoy. 'But it wasn't pop or R&B or anything like that. It had a folk feel to it.' The debate was of little consequence to the public. The album was a hit, reaching number three in America and number one in Britain. Many of the songs have endured the test of time. 'I Threw it All Away' became a powerful concert song in 1976, and Bob performed 'Country Pie' with great verve in 2000.

The new songs on *Nashville Skyline* were published by a company Bob established independently of Albert Grossman as part of his efforts to disengage himself from Grossman's control. As David Braun explained in the 1980s legal battle between Dylan and Grossman, Big Sky Music was created as a 'kind of a palliative' to appease Bob at a time when he was becoming disillusioned with his manager. Under the terms of the agreement, new songs would be lodged with Big Sky Music, rather than Dwarf Music, and Bob's office would be in charge of administration. However, Grossman still shared profits on Big Sky songs in the same 50/50 proportion as Dwarf Music songs. In essence, the deal gave Bob the paperwork while his manager received royalties as normal. As Braun commented later, 'It didn't work for very long.' Bob would never really be satisfied until Grossman was out of his life altogether but that would take several years; in the meantime Bob formed other publishing companies that gave him more and more independence.

Encouraged by the commercial success of the slight *Nashville Skyline*, Bob returned to Nashville two months later in late April 1969 with an armful of songbooks. 'He said, "What do you think about doing an album of other people's songs?"' recalls Bob Johnston, who told Bob that if he could not do it, nobody could. The sessions lasted longer than anyone expected. *Self Portrait* would be a compilation of songs recorded in both Nashville and New York, utilizing dozens of musicians over eleven months, and Bob would not be done with the record until the spring of 1970. Bob's core group of Nashville sidemen played on the early sessions, augmented by musicians including Fred Carter Jr. and Charlie Daniels. These sessions yielded such covers as 'Let It Be Me' and 'I Forgot More Than You'll Ever Know,' pop tunes that seemed to have no relevance to Bob's previous work. Bob, though, had appreciation for almost any well-made song. 'You could tell he really liked them,' says Daniels, who does not remember any sort of hint that the sessions were meant as a 'joke,' as Bob later claimed. 'I think it was something he wanted to do for a long time.' There was also an original song, 'Living the Blues,' but it was so glib it did not sound like a Dylan song at all.

During the course of the eleven months it took to complete *Self Portrait* several songs were overdubbed with syrupy string arrangements, horns, and backing vocals. It was partly these ornamentations – unprecedented for a Dylan record – that shocked critics when the record was eventually released in June 1970. The critics were primarily dumbfounded that the greatest songwriter of modern times was recording corny covers. But Bob may have had a hidden agenda. By this stage, he and Grossman were on such bad terms that Grossman did not even attend recording sessions. 'It was just as well,' Bob said. 'His presence made me uncomfortable.' Bob knew Grossman would get a half share in new songs registered to Big Sky. By recording songs written by other artists, songs such as 'I Forgot More Than You'll Ever Know,' Bob denied Grossman publishing income.

There was another factor. Several of the songs were associated with one of Bob's musical heroes, Elvis

Presley, including 'Blue Moon' and 'Can't Help Falling in Love.' Many of the musicians called upon to play for *Self Portrait* were veterans of Presley sessions. Bob Moore played bass on virtually every Presley recording for more than ten years. Delores Edgin and Millie Kirkham sang backup for Presley. Working with Bob was very different, however. 'He was kind of unwashed,' says Edgin. 'Very eccentric and kind of earthy.' By having these people around, Bob was given a flavor of a musical tradition he loved.

Dylan and Presley had mutual respect for each other's work. Presley performed Bob's song 'Tomorrow Is a Long Time' at an RCA session in 1966. Bob had always admired Presley's Sun recordings. Bob Johnston knew both artists and, when Bob wrote a song they thought might work for Presley (Johnston does not recall exactly when this happened, but within this period of time), he tried to arrange a meeting between the artists. 'I tried to get them to record together. I think Dylan would have done it in a second,' he says. But Presley's manager, Colonel Tom Parker, blocked it for reasons unknown.

An attempted collaboration between Bob and another hero, Jerry Lee Lewis, also failed. When Lewis was in Nashville recording, and Bob was in town working on his own album, Johnston took Bob to meet the tempestuous rock 'n' roller in the studio. 'Jerry Lee, this is Bob Dylan,' said Bob Johnston, making the introductions.

'So?'

'Man, maybe we could do something together some time?' suggested Bob, politely.

'No!' exclaimed Jerry Lee, and pounded his piano with fury as Bob and Johnston made their retreat.

Of all the music stars based in the South, Bob's warmest relationship was with Johnny Cash. It was a mark of his affection for Cash that Bob overcame his deep dislike of television to appear on the debut of Cash's ABC television show, recorded live at Nashville's Ryman Auditorium – home of the Grand Ole Opry – on May 1,

1969. '[Bob] was very nervous about that,' says musical director Bill Walker. 'He was very nervous [because] it was live.' It was also true that major stars looked down on television at the time. 'It was considered almost uncool.'

Bob spent some time before the show with fellow guest artist, Cajun fiddle player Doug Kershaw. The so-called Ragin' Cajun wore an Edwardian-style velvet suit on stage. Bob tried on one of the velvet suits, apparently considering wearing it for the show, but ultimately chose to wear a simple dark jacket that made his face look very pale. He was, in fact, terrified. The studio audience consisted of adoring Cash fans, and there was no way Bob could rectify any possible mistakes because the show had to be wrapped that night. In addition, the Ryman was a small theater, oppressively claustrophobic with all the television equipment, crew, and musicians. It added to the pressure. 'I think he originally thought he wanted to do it. But that was the first live performance Dylan had done [since the Guthrie tribute],' says Kenny Buttrey, who played drums in the backing group. 'He was more or less a recluse.' When the red light came on, Bob turned and looked pleadingly at his band. 'I've never seen anybody that scared,' adds Buttrey. 'He was like a kid at a talent show who was so frightened he was getting ready to run off stage to mommy.' They played three songs, with Cash joining Bob for 'Girl from the North Country.' Although Bob was very uncomfortable, the show was deemed a big success for Cash and became a long-running favorite. It also helped promote the sales of *Nashville Skyline*.

The fact that Bob made his home in Woodstock was widely reported in the press and, as his reputation as a recluse became fixed in the public imagination, fans sought him out. Fortunately, local people proved to be very protective. Without being asked by Bob and Sara not to say where they lived, they did not give out the address. However, the more persistent fans had little trouble discovering that Bob lived in a big wooden house a short walk from the center of Woodstock, and they began hiking over to Hi Lo Ha. This became a nuisance and then a serious problem. Fans climbed trees to see into the property. One day Bob found a family of hippies swimming in his pool. Kids ran up to the house in the middle of the night screaming, as if on a dare. When Bob was driving, he found himself followed by fans in cars. When he met fans face-to-face, Bob was polite but firm. 'He always wanted to [make] people understand that he had a private life and this was not a concert hall – it was where he lived, not worked,' says Bernard Paturel, who was helping out around the house at the time.

When Bob received a neighborly call warning him that a fan was coming toward Hi Lo Ha, he tried to head them off. Sometimes he asked Bruce Dorfman to come with him. 'We'd just walk the road until we were face to face with whoever it was who was coming up the road,' says Dorfman. Usually it was Bob who carried out the confrontation. 'He would just walk up to the person and say, "You know, you really oughtn't to be doing this. What do you think you're doing?" Something like that, which would be so disarming the person would be embarrassed.' Sometimes fans were not so easily deterred, getting onto the property, even inside the house. One time Bob called Dorfman to come over urgently. Together they walked through the many rooms of Hi Lo Ha. Eventually they reached Bob and Sara's bedroom. There in the bed – apparently having just had sex – were a couple of hippies.

'What are you doing?' asked Bob, with remarkable calm.

'We're leaving,' they replied, getting into their clothes.

Local police chief Bill Waterous was called to Hi Lo Ha to find 'another nut' sitting in Bob's living room. He was reading poetry. Perhaps surprisingly, Bob saw the funny side. 'He was kind of chuckling,' says Waterous.

Some of these incidents were threatening. One young man came to the house three times within a month. 'The first time he tried to break into the house,' says former Woodstock constable Charlie Wolven. Bob did not want to press charges and Wolven warned the man about trespassing. Shortly afterward the same man got inside the house. 'I don't think Bob was too much on locking doors,' says Wolven. Again, Bob did not want to press charges. Wolven took the intruder to Route 28 and showed him the way to New York. On the third occasion, Bob and Sara woke to find the man watching them. 'That time he did sign a complaint because we did arrest him,' says Wolven. 'He didn't threaten Dylan, but he was in the bedroom.' After the intruder was charged with trespass, his attorney surrendered two rifles to police. 'They sent [the intruder] for a mental exam,' says Wolven. 'The next thing I know he was away in a mental hospital.' These frightening incidents were not reported in the press. Members of the Woodstock constabulary liked Bob, and wanted to protect his privacy. At the same time Bob took measures to protect himself. He acquired a rifle and kept it near the front door. According to Dorfman, Bob referred to the weapon as 'the great equalizer.'

It was partly because of intruders that Bob and his family left Hi Lo Ha. In May 1969 they moved to a twelve-room Arts and Crafts mansion on the other side of town, high up on Ohayo Mountain Road. The Walter Weyl house was on thirty-nine acres of private land, set back from the road on a dais of lawn with views to the Hudson River. There was a swimming pool, which Bob had enlarged. He had a basketball court built and, just like in the song 'Lay, Lady, Lay,' a 'big brass bed' was installed in the master bedroom. The house was purchased in the name of his blind property company, Davasee Enterprises, Inc.

In an attempt to ensure privacy on Ohayo Mountain Road, Bob bought an additional eighty-three acres of surrounding woodland, giving him a considerable spread of land. He wanted to buy the cottage at the end of his drive as a gatehouse. But the owner, Danielle Beeh – who kept a menagerie of pets including a donkey that would get into Bob's kitchen looking for food – declined to sell. One evening Bob and Sara were talking with Beeh, standing on her terrace, when she noticed one of their children nonchalantly urinating over her garden. 'They were looking at the land and saying, "Oh, it's nice," and then suddenly the [child] goes pee pee right through his pants – made a little jet – and nobody said a word. Dylan went right on as if nothing had happened,' says Beeh, who was greatly amused by the incident. 'It was very bizarre.' Despite this incident, the Dylan children were not badly raised. Bob and Sara were actually rather strict parents who succeeded in bringing up remarkably well-adjusted children, especially when one considers the peculiar pressures caused by Bob's fame.

In the cocoon of Woodstock The Hawks were transformed from Bob's backing band into a major recording group in its own right. For years they had been known as the band that played with Bob Dylan. Now signed to a management deal with Albert Grossman, and a recording contract with Capitol Records, they became The Band. The songs they wrote were published by Dwarf Music, which meant Bob owned a share in their catalogue. This proved one of his better business deals, earning money for years to come.

The Band's debut album, *Music from Big Pink*, grew out of their work with Bob. Dylan was the author of one of its outstanding tracks, 'I Shall Be Released,' which was created at the Big Pink sessions. It was one of the most famous songs he ever wrote, yet The Band released their version years before Bob put it on an album of his own. Bob cowrote two of the album's other outstanding tracks, 'Tears of Rage' and 'This Wheel's on Fire.' The cover of the album featured a painting by Bob that was clearly influenced by Chagall. He also offered to play on the album. This last offer was politely declined. Levon Helm for one felt they should not lean too heavily on their famous friend. 'We didn't want to just ride his shirttail all the time.' Despite Bob's influence, *Music from Big Pink* avoided being derivative and the personalities of the members of The Band were very evident. Robbie Robertson wrote four of the non-Dylan songs, including 'The Weight,' which was destined to become a classic. (When 'The Weight' was used for a Diet Coke commercial in 1994, Bob earned in excess of $500,000, which he shared with members of The Band.) The musicianship was superb, the songs were heartfelt, and the voices of all the musicians created a multilayered sound that was highly original. In the age of psychedelia, *Music from Big Pink* was refreshingly unpretentious and highly praised by critics. It might have sold more strongly if The Band had toured, but Rick Danko broke his neck in a car accident, putting him out of operation for a while. 'I had to recuperate, and I wouldn't let Grossman tell anybody that I'd had an accident. So [we] weren't available,' he says. The fact that The Band did not tour had a positive effect in the long run, creating a mystique around the group. 'You know, if people can't have what they want, that's when they really want it . . . there's something to be said about mystery. That's why Bob was a good influence,' says Danko.

The Band's reputation was further enhanced by interest in the now legendary Basement Tapes. Jann Wenner, publisher of the increasingly influential *Rolling Stone* magazine, reviewed the tapes on the front page of the June 22, 1968, issue under the headline DYLAN'S BASEMENT TAPE SHOULD BE RELEASED. There was no official Columbia release at the time, but a bootleg double album, *Great White Wonder*, soon went into production. This record was made up of acoustic songs recorded years earlier in Dinkytown, and some of the songs recorded in Woodstock with The Band. Copies of the tapes Garth

Hudson had made had been given to various friends and also to Bob's office to be sent out on acetate discs to artists looking to cover the songs. Somewhere along the line illegal copies were made and passed to bootleggers who manufactured pirate albums. It was not long before *Great White Wonder* was being sold openly in stores like the Psychedelic Supermarket in Hollywood. The original bootleggers were a couple of California hippies who spoke to *Rolling Stone* in 1969. 'Bob Dylan is a heavy talent,' said one of the men, identified only as Patrick, 'and he's got all those songs nobody's ever heard. We thought we'd take it upon ourselves to make this music available.' Official recognition of the public's hunger for the music came a few years later when, in 1975, Columbia released a selection of tracks recorded at Big Pink (with some overdubs) as *The Basement Tapes*. That it took so many years for the recordings to be officially released may, once again, have had something to do with the feud between Dylan and Grossman. *The Basement Tapes* songs were among the last Dylan compositions Grossman had a fifty percent claim to and, by delaying release, Bob deprived his manager of income. The complete Basement Tapes – the so-called *Genuine Basement Tapes* – is an astonishing bootleg of one hundred and sixty-one tracks of Dylan and The Band. There is enough material to fill a box set edition. It remains one of the secret masterpieces of Bob's career, available complete only on the black market.

One of the unique aspects of Bob's career is that he is the most pirated recording artist in America* (despite being far from one of its best-selling artists on the legitimate market). His most ardent fans have such an appetite for his work that there is demand for recordings of studio outtakes, rehearsals, and virtually every concert performance he has ever given. *Great White Wonder* was the

*According to a statement by a senior RIAA executive in a 1998 court case involving Dylan (see chapter 10).

first significant Bob Dylan bootleg in America. Not only was it reviewed in *Rolling Stone*, it was played on the radio. Tony Glover was working at a radio station at the time and, to his consternation, he realized that part of the record included selections from his own tapes of Bob in Dinkytown before Bob became famous. 'It was the first bootleg I had ever seen,' he says. 'There was the stuff with The Band and all that. Then there's these acoustic songs and the titles are familiar . . . I had a pause button on my machine, and I clicked it out of pause when he was ready to play, so it starts with a kind of *keeeooow*. I recognized that [sound] and I said, "That's my fucking tape. What the hell happened?" ' Glover discovered that a dub-copy of his tape – labeled 'Dylan / Minneapolis' – had been stolen from the home of his Dinkytown friend Paul Nelson.

Great White Wonder precipitated an avalanche of illegal Dylan recordings, which Bob and his lawyers could do little to stop, even though they launched numerous lawsuits over the years. The nature of bootlegging made it almost impossible to pin down who was responsible, and even if one illegal recording was removed from the market the recordings would invariably appear on another record under a different name. The trade infuriated Bob, who denounced bootlegging as 'outrageous' in a 1985 interview, adding that with exploitation of this kind it was no wonder artists like himself felt so paranoid about their work.

During the summer of 1969, Bob and Sara vacationed on Fire Island, New York, renting an oceanfront house at Bayberry Dunes near the Davis Park ferry landing. Neighbors included musicologist David Amram who jammed with Bob most days. Paul Simon visited and played music with Bob, and Bob's mother came to stay. Bob enjoyed the seaside so much he later bought a house not far away in East Hampton, Long Island, spending several summers in the area with Sara and their children. 'He would ride his bicycle, and he came over to our house a couple of times,' says Tom Paxton, who lived in East Hampton. 'One of the things I remember about that – he was over at my house and he had a Clancy Brothers album and he said, "Let's listen to that. I haven't heard them in a long time."' These were the happy family holidays Bob later wrote about in his 1975 song 'Sara.'

Bob returned to Hibbing for his ten-year high school reunion in August 1969. 'I bullshitted with him a little bit, [but] I think everybody was happy [for him],' says former school friend Luke Davich. Echo Helstrom stood in line to talk to Bob and handed him her reunion booklet to sign. 'He turned around and told Sara, "It's Echo." And I said hello, and that was it because people were jostling to get near him,' she recalls. 'I heard somebody tried to pick a fight with him afterward.' Bob took Sara to see his boyhood home at 2425 7th Avenue. Beatty had sold the house in December and moved to Minneapolis. The new owners were a young couple, Angel and Terry Marolt, who had bought some of Beatty's old furniture. Consequently, the house looked almost the same as when Bob was a child. He also found time to get together with old Minnesota friends to form a band, The Chart Busters, that played for fun at a couple of parties in St. Cloud, Minnesota. Each member had a pseudonym; Bob's was Jack Smith.

By the late 1960s Albert Grossman represented many of the most fashionable acts in music. Aside from Dylan, he managed The Band, Electric Flag, and Janis Joplin. Some of his clients lived in Woodstock; others were frequent visitors. Woodstock was an easy bus ride from New York and hippies started flooding into town, gathering on the village green, playing guitars and drums into the night, drawn by the proximity of their heroes. The actual stars were elusive, of course, and none more so than Bob. Even when he came into town with Sara – giving her a ride to Victor Basil's hairdressing salon, for instance – he would stay in the car until she was ready to go home again.

There was concern in the town when a group of businessmen, trading under the name Woodstock Ventures, Inc., decided to stage a music festival that capitalized on Woodstock's notoriety. There had been a craze for festivals since the success of the 1967 Monterey Pop Festival, not least because festivals were an opportunity to make huge profits. The rush to cash in on the craze had resulted in poorly organized, hastily arranged events. Woodstock residents had read alarming reports of violence, drug abuse, and vandalism at recent festivals in California and Colorado. Consequently, the Woodstock Music and Arts Fair – commonly known as the Woodstock Festival ('three days of peace and love') – was pushed out to the town of Wallkill, and then farther away to Max Yasgur's dairy farm near Bethel. Yasgur's farm was sixty miles from Woodstock, but the event was still known as the Woodstock Festival. The event was so far away from Woodstock itself that local police chief Bill Waterous admits he did not know exactly where Bethel was. Yet he still had to deal with thousands of hippies who came through Woodstock because of the name association. There was a sharp increase in drug trading in the town, from marijuana to heroin. 'Everybody talks about Haight-Ashbury, and we used to say, *What the hell are they talking about? It's worse here*,' says Waterous. 'The place was so wild after a while, we had to get narcotics people in.'

One day when they were painting, Bruce Dorfman asked Bob what part he was going to play in the festival.

'*I'm* not going,' he said.

'They're all going to be waiting on line for you. They expect you to go.'

Bob replied that people's expectations and realities were not always the same thing.

Normal life was becoming impossible and Bob was

more than a little resentful. He had been driven out of Byrdcliffe by fans. Now there were incidents at Ohayo Mountain Road, including a break-in. 'That Woodstock Festival . . . was the sum total of all this bullshit,' he complained. 'And it seemed to have something to do with *me*, this Woodstock Nation, and everything it represented. So we couldn't *breathe*. I couldn't get any space for myself and my family.' His image as a figurehead of hippiedom was not one that accorded with Bob's actual lifestyle, or even with his cultural perspective. Although he could be wild and even anarchic in his music, by this stage in his personal life Bob was a quiet, law-abiding family man. He was in some ways rather conventional: he was polite and nicely spoken, expecting his children to be the same; he was faithful to Sara, as far as one could tell; and he was not involved in any type of scandalous or outrageous rock star behavior. There were no drug busts at the Dylan house or riotous parties. He was a good neighbor and on excellent terms with the local police. His old friend Wavy Gravy, who had become an iconic hippy figure (he was master of ceremonies at the Woodstock Festival), says that he never perceived Bob as part of the world of beads, tie-dyed T-shirts, and incense sticks. 'Bob, in my opinion, was a conduit for the divine. That's what [the hippies] were reacting to,' comments Wavy Gravy. 'The Bobster, I don't think he was ever [a hippy], never maintained he was that and always turned away from that.'

There was another good reason for Bob not to perform at Woodstock: he had a better offer. Two young Englishmen, Ray Foulk and his brother Ron, wanted to stage a festival on the Isle of Wight, off the south coast of England. Unlike the Woodstock Festival, which had a plethora of big-name acts, none of whom were well paid, the Foulk brothers planned to build their festival around a big star who would receive the lion's share of appearance money. Grossman's associate, Bert Block, of I.T.A., dealt with the booking (relations between Bob and

Grossman were so bad by then that they could not deal with each other directly). Bob would headline for $50,000 plus expenses. Bob wanted to perform with The Band, who were then touring the United States. He made a guest appearance with them in Edwardsville, Illinois, on July 14. 'He was beginning to get itchy,' says Jonathan Taplin, The Band's road manager. The fee for The Band was an additional $20,000. It was further stipulated that one other Grossman-managed act would be on the bill, and so Richie Havens was hired for a fee of $8,000. By making the Foulk brothers take all three acts, Grossman earned nearly $16,000 in commission. This was the last big deal Grossman made with Bob before their seven-year management contract expired on August 19, 1969. Ray Foulk agreed to pay Bob's production company, Ashes & Sand, $50,000 in return for Bob's assurance that this would be his exclusive festival appearance for the summer. The $50,000 would have to be paid in full before Bob left the United States. If gross profits exceeded a certain figure, Bob would receive additional money.* Bob's advisers hired Lord Goodman, one of the most eminent solicitors in London, to ensure that the money was paid promptly.

As a result, despite speculation that Bob would make a dramatic last-minute appearance at the Woodstock Festival, he never had the slightest intention of appearing. In fact, on August 15, the first day of the Woodstock Festival – which would draw a phenomenal three hundred thousand people to Yasgur's farm – Bob and his family boarded the ocean liner *Queen Elizabeth 2*, intending to sail to England. Unfortunately, Jesse Dylan hit his head on a doorknob and they had to leave the ship minutes before it departed. When they had established that the boy was not seriously hurt, Bob and Sara caught a flight to London. Al Aronowitz carried their luggage.

When they reached the Isle of Wight, the Dylans were

*The festival did not make sufficient profits to pay a bonus.

accommodated in a sixteenth-century manor house at Forelands Farm, Bembridge. They were provided with a housekeeper and a chauffeur-driven Humber Super Snipe. An adjacent barn was used for rehearsals with The Band. Bob was nervous about what was – despite the Guthrie tribute, the Johnny Cash show, and his one guest appearance with The Band – his big comeback appearance after years of not touring. It was proving to be a much larger event than he had originally expected, with a weekend attendance of a hundred and fifty thousand people. There were rumors Bob would be on stage for up to three hours and might hold a 'super session' with members of The Beatles and Rolling Stones. The Beatles rumor was fueled by the fact that George and Pattie Harrison were houseguests at Forelands Farm. Bob knew he could not live up to the hype, and complained to Bert Block about the press coverage. Block passed the complaints on to Ray Foulk, who tried to calm everyone down. Meanwhile, his brother fed stories to the press to publicize the event. Tempers began to wear thin. In the days preceding the show, Ray Foulk tried to give Bob and Sara a holiday. One of the diversions was a chauffeured drive to Osborne House, former residence of Queen Victoria. As they were getting ready to leave, housekeeper Judy Lewis suggested Bob might prefer to drive himself in her little Triumph Herald. 'That's a great idea,' said Bob, taking the keys from her. Then he noticed promotional stickers all over the car reading 'Help Bob Dylan Sink the Isle of Wight.' Bob started to peel them off, and then lost his temper. 'What is this shit?' he said, and stomped away.

A couple of days before the concert a Daimler limousine pulled up at Forelands with The Beatles' road manager, Mal Evans, who jumped out and marked out a cross on the lawn. A helicopter then descended, carrying Ringo Starr, John Lennon, and Yoko Ono. The Beatles played Bob acetates of their new album, *Abbey Road.* George Harrison complained that he had been allowed only two of his own compositions on the record. In the evening, Bob jammed with members of The Beatles and The Band. It was a night that would live in the memory of those present. Dylan, Harrison, and Lennon sang duets on Beatles songs, but played mostly old rock 'n' roll numbers.

The concert itself, on Sunday, August 31, turned out to be anticlimactic. The show ran late because of a problem with the press and VIP area. 'All manner of people suddenly started to arrive about tea time – six o'clock – and the press [enclosure] was getting fuller and fuller to the point whereby it was just sort of ridiculous,' says Ray Foulk. Apart from members of the national and international press, organizers had to find space for celebrities such as Jane Fonda. The Band did not start their set until after 9 P.M. Bob came on stage at 11 P.M. One couple took his appearance as their cue to strip and make love. '*Freaky*, baby!' exclaimed an onlooker.

Dressed in a white suit and wearing an orange shirt with cuff links – quite different to the crushed velvet, flared trousers, and beads favored by concertgoers – Bob looked 'very grown-up and adult-like,' as Ray Foulk says. Bob's clothes and sound were evocative of Hank Williams at the Grand Ole Opry rather than of the psychedelic sixties. Bob sang in the mellow voice of *Nashville Skyline* and The Band sounded loose and country, even on 'Like a Rolling Stone.' The performance was the antithesis of the screaming brilliance of his last British appearance, another performance out of its time. 'I felt it was slightly low-key,' says Ray Foulk. 'Dylan was always going to [be] unpredictable . . . the way that he just changes his material, changes the tunes, changes the delivery and so on is something he has always done. That is his entitlement and is maybe something that distinguishes him from other artists because he didn't much care about whether people liked it or not. He just does what he wants to do.' Bob fulfilled his contract exactly, playing one hour. He would not perform again in public for two years.

* * *

Sara Dylan had been noticeably pregnant during the Isle of Wight festival and, when they returned to America, she and Bob made a decision to find a new home in which to raise their large and growing family. Woodstock had been a secure refuge for several years, and Bob had worked fruitfully at his music during their seclusion in the country. In many ways, the years he and Sara spent in Woodstock were the happiest and most stable they would know. They had dealt successfully with the pressures of Bob's fame, and they were content together as a couple. But the crazy events of the late 1960s changed the town for the worse and this impinged on their lives to the extent that they no longer felt comfortable or safe in Woodstock. Indeed, society in general seemed to be in a parlous state at the close of the 1960s. Richard Nixon was president. Young Americans were still being killed in Vietnam. The terror of the Cold War gripped the entire world. Brian Jones was among those princes of pop culture whose hedonistic lives had ended in squalid, pointless death. In California, the maniacal Charles Manson was arrested for ordering the killing of actress Sharon Tate and others. Manson claimed to have received his orders to kill from messages discovered in the songs of The Beatles. In many ways the so-called decade of peace and love had yielded a disappointing dividend.

With the birth of another child imminent, Bob and Sara decided to relocate to what they hoped would be the relative sanity of New York City. In the fall Bob bought a town house in Greenwich Village. On December 9, 1969, Sara gave birth in New York to a son, whom they named Jakob Luke. Including Maria, she and Bob now had five children. Their family was complete, and a new era in their lives was about to begin.

CHAPTER 7

ON THE ROAD AGAIN

Because Bob had fond memories of Greenwich Village, and maybe because he wished to reclaim something of his youth, when he moved back to New York he bought a house in the heart of the Village at 94 MacDougal Street. This was a handsome and spacious home, the only double town house in a terrace of four-story buildings. Yet it was not ideal for a famous man who relished privacy. The lower part was divided into apartments, with sitting tenants, and almost anybody could reach the back of the house because there was a communal garden and residents were not allowed to erect barriers. The front door opened directly onto MacDougal Street, so Bob had to face the public each time he stepped outside. He would soon rue the day he bought such a place.

The move from Woodstock was both a symbolic and a literal break with Albert Grossman. In April 1970, following the expiration of their management contract, Bob's New York office took over administration of the publishing company Dwarf Music in addition to Big Sky Music. Grossman still received income from his share in the songs, but Bob's staff controlled the books. Three months later Dylan and Grossman signed what became known as the 'July 1970 Agreement.' Under the terms, Bob was not allowed to sell any part of his Dwarf catalogue without Grossman's approval, but the ten-year publishing partnership signed in 1966 was modified to expire three years earlier, in 1973. Grossman would retain a fifty percent publishing interest in songs registered to Big Sky Music until October 1971, and Bob would have to register all new songs in Big Sky until that date. 'I was willing to enter into the July 1970 Agreement because I thought that I would finally be rid of Grossman,' Bob later explained. But he came to regret a clause that seemed to absolve Grossman of any wrongdoing during their association. Furthermore, Grossman continued to take at least fifty cents on every dollar that came to Bob.* This rankled with the songwriter, and ultimately led to legal action. In the meantime, Bob could not bring himself to speak with Grossman, or keep anything that reminded him of his former manager. Bob had a valuable medieval lectern, which Grossman had given to him as a gift, and which he used to hold a Bible. He now sent the lectern to the Bear, a restaurant in Bearsville owned by Grossman, asking Bernard Paturel to deliver the lectern to Grossman at his nearby house. Bob could easily have had the lectern delivered directly to Grossman's door, but he did not want even that much contact.

As David Braun recalls, it was probably before the July 1970 Agreement that Bob asked him to make a choice: he could continue working for Grossman, or he could work for the singer-songwriter. Braun chose Bob, to Grossman's great displeasure. 'I don't think I was at the *door* when it was all over the streets that I had fucked Albert Grossman, the man who gave me Bob Dylan,' Braun later recalled. Braun then became a key member of Bob's advisory team, along with Naomi Saltzman and accountants Marshall M. Gelfand and Marty Feldman. In the future, Bob would manage himself with the help of these advisers. He never had another manager, in the sense that Grossman had been his manager. 'Maybe it's an aversion,' says Nick Gravenites, whose band Electric Flag was managed by Grossman. 'He's so scarred by that

*Fifty percent share in Dylan's publishing, and commissions from preexisting contracts.

relationship that just the mere thought of having a manager probably sends chills up and down his spine.'

Grossman diverted his energy into promoting Janis Joplin, who unfortunately died of a heroin overdose in October 1970. Grossman received another blow that fall when Peter Yarrow was given a three-month jail sentence for indecency with a fourteen-year-old girl. The scandal effectively put Peter, Paul and Mary out of business for the time being. Grossman would have limited success with other acts in the future, but without Peter, Paul and Mary, Bob Dylan, or Janis Joplin, his days as the most powerful manager in the music business were over. In a way, he had brought his downfall upon himself. 'You shouldn't be bigger than the people you represent,' says Woody Guthrie's former manager Harold Leventhal. 'If you are bigger than them, then you are stealing from them.'

When Bob went back to work in March 1970, following the move from Woodstock, he recorded at the Columbia studios in New York, working on songs for the *Self Portrait* album and its follow-up, *New Morning*. Although Bob had made some of his greatest albums in Nashville, including *Blonde on Blonde* and *John Wesley Harding*, he had decided to break with the city. He gave no explanation, and the suddenness of the decision surprised his Nashville sidemen. 'You would think that if one had had some great, great success somewhere in his career that maybe [he would] venture back there to try to catch a little bit of it again,' says Charlie McCoy. 'I don't think Dylan's ever considered coming back.' Drummer Kenny Buttrey felt personally hurt at the way he and his friends were discarded. 'No thank-you note . . . No phone calls through the years, no complimentary albums; we had to buy our own,' says Buttrey. 'That's what's sad.'

As Bob had already begun the *Self Portrait* album in Nashville there was a period of transition in which he recorded basic tracks in New York, singing and playing guitar, and the tapes were sent to Nashville to be overdubbed with backing music. These songs included covers such as Paul Simon's 'The Boxer' and the instrumental 'All the Tired Horses,' a riff for overdubbed female vocals and strings. The basic tracks were so rough that arranger Bill Walker had to remove most of Bob's guitar playing. This was difficult because he sang close to the microphone, with his guitar high on his chest. 'Bob wasn't Segovia,' says Walker, meaning his guitar playing was at times fairly rudimentary. 'We had to get rid of a lot of the things that he played.' Although most of these songs were insubstantial, there *were* strong songs recorded for *Self Portrait*. The best tracks included a fine cover of Paul Clayton's 'Gotta Travel On.' 'It Hurts Me Too' was an attractive song, in which Bob sang of his concern for a lover, or maybe a child. Two months after finishing *Self Portrait*, Bob went back into the Columbia studio in New York to record more covers, including such unlikely material as 'Spanish Is the Loving Tongue' and 'Mr. Bojangles,' popularized by Sammy Davis Jr. Although the songs seemed incongruous choices, he sang them with feeling and no hint of irony.

On May 1, 1970, George Harrison joined the sessions, playing along with Bob, Charlie Daniels on bass, and drummer Russ Kunkel. 'It was a day I'll never forget,' says Daniels. 'It wasn't Bob Dylan and George Harrison. It was four guys in the studio making music.' The musicians called out songs for Bob to sing. 'Anything you threw at [Bob], he could sing . . . It was such a nice thing, such a great day, hour after hour.' The tracks did not officially appear on an album, at least not with a credit for Harrison because he did not have a U.S. work permit, but copies of the tapes soon passed into the hands of bootleggers. 'I could never figure out how Dylan's stuff was so easily bootlegged,' says Daniels, who hand-delivered master tapes to Bob's office at the end of each session. 'Still it would get bootlegged!'

When Harrison left town, Bob turned his mind to new songs. Many of the lyrics were expressions of a contented family man. 'If Not for You' was a love song to Sara and later became a hit for Olivia Newton-John. 'One More Weekend' and 'The Man in Me' were imbued with a sense of serenity. Bob's voice almost cracked with emotion on 'Sign on the Window,' in which he sang joyfully about raising a family. The musicians were introduced to Sara during the sessions, and were struck by the couple's happiness. 'When you were around him and Sara and the kids you envied what a great family feel this guy had,' says guitarist Ron Cornelius.

Even so, love was not the only subject on Bob's mind. As Cornelius says, '[Bob] was like a different person every day.' The song 'Went to See the Gypsy' was about meeting Elvis Presley, as the session musicians understood it, although it remains unclear when and where Dylan and Presley actually met. (Dylan himself has never spoken about it.) At least three songs, including 'New Morning,' were written for a stage play by Archibald MacLeish, but they were not delivered on time. 'Day of the Locusts' was written in direct response to Bob receiving an honorary Doctor of Music degree from Princeton University. He received the degree, as former Princeton president Robert F. Goheen says, because his songs 'eloquently expressed antiwar sentiments that many of us felt.' (Two months earlier, President Nixon ordered troops into neutral Cambodia to attack Viet Cong bases.) Bob drove to Princeton on June 8, 1970, with Sara and friend David Crosby. He was very nervous, missing the black-tie dinner the night before commencement, and arriving on campus the next day looking 'noticeably ill at ease,' according to Goheen, who made the presentation. He feared Bob might try to escape altogether. However, they got the singer to the podium. During the ceremony a swarm of locusts settled on old trees on the front campus, making a loud droning sound. It was this sound that inspired Bob to write the song. The man next to him in the song, whose 'head was exploding,' was Crosby, who says they had been smoking 'some killer weed.'

Bob told his session musicians he had written the song 'Three Angels' after watching a church being decorated for Christmas. The lyric described a tableau of New York characters – a 'concrete world full of souls' – walking past the church and taking no account of the decorative angels hanging there, blowing on celestial horns. 'When the album came out, some guy wrote this big long thing about Dylan's insight into mankind and "this concrete world full of souls" and I thought, You poor fool,' says Charlie Daniels. 'Here you are trying to categorize this man's music and you have no idea what it is [about]. It's about three decorative angels hanging on a church.'

Bob had complete freedom to do what he liked at the sessions; with the ability to experiment, without interference from Columbia or management, he made surprising decisions. He worked up a jazz arrangement for 'If Dogs Run Free,' which was later released on the *New Morning* album. The drummer played with brushes and vocalist Maeretha Stewart scat sung the backing vocals in jazz style as Bob crooned the lyric. 'It was very unusual,' she says. 'It was really a fun thing.' The result was charming, with Al Kooper playing cocktail lounge piano and Ron Cornelius riffing jazz chords on the guitar.

Meanwhile, *Self Portrait* was released to caustic reviews in June 1970. Critics could not believe that the great poet-singer had released a double album largely made up of cover songs, with a few inconsequential live recordings and instrumentals. To hear Bob Dylan warble 'The Boxer' and 'Blue Moon' seemed absurd. The instrumental 'All the Tired Horses' did sound like a 'joke,' as Bob later claimed the album had been intended. If so, it was a joke that fell flat. Greil Marcus began his coruscating review for *Rolling Stone* by asking, famously, 'What is this shit?' It was the first time a Dylan album had been the cause for mockery in sections of the media where he had previously enjoyed adulation, and it was clear to Al

Kooper at least that Bob was upset by the reaction. Although he was not one to say much about his feelings, Bob showed his concern by taking radical action. The month *Self Portrait* was released to scathing reviews, he went back into the studio to make an album from the new songs he had been working on, hoping that this would undo some of the damage suffered to his reputation.

Bob Johnston was no longer Dylan's producer. The singer offered no explanation, but it seems a rift developed when Johnston went to Europe with a Leonard Cohen tour. 'I took off and figured he would call. I don't really know what happened,' says Johnston. 'I think it was just I wasn't around, or he wanted a change.' Johnston had produced two records with Leonard Cohen, using Ron Cornelius and Charlie Daniels in the band, and Cornelius believes there was rivalry between Dylan and Cohen. Both were Jewish poet-songwriters competing for a similar audience, both signed to Columbia. The rivalry manifested itself that summer when Bob attended a Cohen concert at Forest Hills. It had rained heavily and Cohen was morose, convinced the open-air show had not gone well. When told Bob was there to see him, Cohen apparently asked: 'So?' Bob came backstage and they had a stilted conversation. 'It was like two cats with their hair up,' says Cornelius. 'It was like "What's going on?" The answer would be like, "Everybody's gotta be somewhere." "Oh yeah, well where are you?"' Cornelius sensed that Bob wanted his producer and musicians to choose which artist they wanted to work with. Like David Braun, they could not serve two masters. 'We would have had to quit Leonard to go with Bob,' says Cornelius. He and Charlie Daniels talked about it and decided that they wanted to tour with Cohen. It is probably no coincidence that neither of the musicians, nor Bob Johnston, ever worked with Dylan again (although Bob briefly consulted Johnston over an album, in 1978). Bob had become used to the fact that almost anybody he wanted would come into the studio to play with him – even a former Beatle like George Harrison – and this naturally gave him a sense of self-importance. When Cornelius, Daniels, and Johnston chose to work with somebody else, his pride precluded him from asking them back. Of course, there were countless musicians eager to take their place.

Al Kooper stepped in as producer, bringing in members of his own band to complete *New Morning*, giving the album a lightness that fit the upbeat lyrics and title. *New Morning* was released in the fall of 1970, shortly before the long-delayed official publication of Bob's book, *Tarantula*. Ralph J. Gleason wrote an appreciation of the new album in *Rolling Stone* under the headline WE'VE GOT DYLAN BACK AGAIN! 'God, it's beautiful,' he wrote, saying he had played it a dozen times and could not find a poor track. To less devoted fans, *New Morning* sounded a little self-satisfied. Coming after other soft albums like *Nashville Skyline* and *Self Portrait* it seemed to confirm that Bob had sold out to commercialism. This harked back to the misconception during the folk era that Bob was at heart a radical, a protest singer, a 'spokesman of his generation.' That was a media term, and he had long since outgrown it – if it had ever been true. As we have seen, by the time Bob reached maturity he was quite different from his popular image: he was a family man with conservative values, a man who had little interest in politics or social movements. As an artist, he felt entitled to make any sort of music he wished – folk, rock 'n' roll, country, or even jazz. The notion that he should adhere to an image created in the press, or a style of music one group of fans liked, was ridiculous to him, and he certainly did not see himself as a spokesman for his generation. 'I wasn't going to fall for that, for being any kind of a leader,' he told journalist Anthony Scaduto, who was then writing the first biography of Dylan. 'The magazines fed that pap – that Dylan, The Stones, The Beatles, we were all leaders . . . I didn't want any part of that.'

However, Bob's most ardent fans did want him as a

leader. One particularly obsessive fan, twenty-five-year-old dropout A. J. Weberman, became so upset about Bob's apparent lack of interest in radicalism that he formed a protest organization, the Dylan Liberation Front, and began to lead demonstrations outside Dylan's house on MacDougal Street. 'FREE BOB DYLAN!' chanted the demonstrators, during a demonstration in January 1971. 'Free Bob Dylan from himself!' The members of the D.L.F. were upset about a variety of things in addition to Bob's apparent apathy toward political issues. But mostly they enjoyed making a spectacle of themselves. As reported in *Rolling Stone*, a demonstrator climbed onto a windowsill and peered inside. 'They've got furniture inside!' he announced, as if this was something extraordinary. There was such a commotion that Bob came around from the back of the house and stood on the other side of the road, glaring at the demonstrators. They did not see him for a while. Then Weberman noticed him. 'Bob, we've come to talk to you.'

'And I wanna talk to *you* . . . What'd ya bring these people around to bother my children for, huh?'

He led Weberman away from the other demonstrators to a recording studio on West Houston. Despite his anger, Bob sat down to hear what Weberman had to say. He already had an idea of what to expect; Weberman had plagued him since the previous summer, first coming to the house on his own, then stealing his garbage, and now whipping up demonstrations.

An overweight, unkempt young man with wispy hair and spectacles, Weberman supported himself partly by selling 'bookleg' copies of *Tarantula* on the street. 'He was revolting even to look at,' says Paul Colby, a friend of Bob who ran the Bitter End club on Bleecker Street. 'He was that kind of a person – if you saw him on the subway you'd change seats.' Born Alan Jules Weberman in Brooklyn in 1945, he became obsessed with Bob's music when he was at Michigan State University in the early sixties. Listening to the albums while stoned on marijuana or LSD he made what seemed to him a major discovery. 'I realized it was poetry and required interpretation,' he explains. 'I developed the Dylanological Method, which is looking at each word in the context in which it appears and looking for words that have a similar theme that cluster around it (concordance). I started to devote a lot of time to just sitting around interpreting Dylan's poetry.' Weberman also devoted time to drugs. He was arrested for selling marijuana while he was at college and spent time in jail in 1964. He would collect several criminal convictions over the years, including one for felonious assault on a police officer. It was while he was out on bail for the drug offense that Weberman concocted a set of theories about Bob, notably that he was a heroin user. There were clues to it in his songs, according to Weberman, especially on *John Wesley Harding*. When Bob sang about his little 'bundle of joy' on 'Down Along the Cove' he did not mean his daughter Anna. According to Weberman, he meant his fix. Weberman placed an advertisement in the *East Village Other* appealing for a specimen of Dylan's urine so he could prove this theory. In the meantime, he began coming by the Dylan house on MacDougal Street. On a Sunday morning in August 1970, Weberman barged past Sara Dylan into the entranceway. From there, a flight of stairs led up to another door that opened onto the Dylans' open-plan living room. Bob opened the door at the top of the stairs and shouted to Weberman to tell him what he wanted.

'It's about your poetry,' he said, feebly.

'Oh, how nice!' retorted Bob with monumental sarcasm, and shut the door.

As he was leaving the building, Weberman noticed the household garbage that was kept near the entrance. 'So there's something that was inside that's outside now.' He grabbed a bag of garbage and hauled it over to his apartment on the Bowery, where he started rooting through the contents. The first item he pulled out was a soiled diaper. Unwrapping parcels of newspaper, he found excrement from Bob and Sara's new dog, Sasha; empty tin cans; and stale coffee grounds and numerous other aromatic delights. There was such a stink he had to open his street door to get some fresh air. He found discarded music papers, the beginnings of a letter from Bob to Johnny Cash, a postcard from Beatty Zimmerman on vacation in Florida. There were track lists for *Self Portrait*. But there were no syringes, which is what he was really looking for. Still, by going through Dylan's garbage, Weberman decided he had invented a science. He called his science *garbology* and used the items in the trash as the basis of newspaper articles and, ultimately, a book, *My Life in Garbology*, that gave him fleeting notoriety. As he admits: 'I was publicity hungry.' Bob responded by putting extra dog shit in his garbage.

When Dylan and Weberman sat down together to talk on the step of the recording studio in January 1971, Bob asked whether it was true that Weberman was spreading gossip that he was a junkie. 'Well, man, are you?' asked Weberman, who claims Bob then rolled up his sleeves to demonstrate his arms were clear of track marks. This was not enough to convince Weberman, who figured Bob was probably snorting heroin. For his part, Bob did his best to calm Weberman down and they parted company on fairly good terms.

Weberman then wrote an article based on their meeting and a week later he managed to get Bob on the telephone to talk about it. Weberman taped the conversation, which was then transcribed and reported in *Rolling Stone* in March 1971. As they spoke, Weberman revealed more of his bizarre theories, one of which was that Dylan had written 'Dear Landlord' about Albert Grossman, Weberman himself, or both of them.

Bob replied witheringly: 'It wasn't written for anybody, it was an abstract song, it certainly wasn't written for you.'

'*It wasn't*?' asked Weberman in great surprise.

'It sure as hell wasn't, no. I was not even aware of you at the time.'

Weberman said his article would include a reference to a phrase from *New Morning*, 'Don't expose me.'

'I never said "Don't expose me" in *New Morning*, what's that?'

'Backwards, backwards,' replied Weberman, excitedly. 'You play a part of it backwards.'

'And it says, "Don't expose me"?'

'Yeah.'

'Oh fuck, man. *Jesus!*'

Weberman suggested that in another part of *New Morning* – again when played backwards – Bob sang 'Mars invades us.'

'Hooh! Hooh!'

Bob told Weberman that he might write a song about *him*.

'Well, I could use the publicity.'

'Yeah, well, that's one reason why I wouldn't do it, but I got a good song if I ever want to do one.'

'What's it called?'

'It's called "Pig".'

'I'm a pig eh?'

'Yeah.'

'Ah, bullshit, I'm a pig, man.'

Realizing he had Weberman on the defensive, Bob taunted him. 'You go through garbage like a pig,' he said. 'You're a pig mentality.' He said people walked on the other side of the street when he 'came down oinking.' In fact, he might get badges made. They would have Weberman's face and the word 'PIG.'

On May 23, 1971, the day before Bob's thirtieth birthday, Weberman gathered another mob outside 94 MacDougal Street. He stood on a garbage can to address them. 'Dylan's sold out!' he shouted through a megaphone. His followers chanted 'Pigs!' Then Weberman unveiled his pièce de résistance – a birthday cake decorated with candles in the shape of hypodermic needles.

Bob and Sara were not home when Weberman staged his tasteless birthday demonstration. They were on vacation in Israel, but even here they could not find peace. Bob encountered reporters at Lod Airport, and was surprised they knew he was coming. Then the local office of CBS put an advertisement in the *Jerusalem Post* wishing him a happy birthday, and asking him to get in touch. When Bob went to the beach for a swim, he was confronted by *Jerusalem Post* reporter Catherine Rosenheimer. Bob told her he had no intention of contacting the CBS office. 'I doubt if they'd really like to see me,' he said, adding, 'My next record won't be released through them in any case.' He visited the Wailing Wall on his birthday and a photograph of this event – which seemed to show that Bob was rediscovering his Jewish heritage – was flashed around the world. *Time* reported Bob was considering changing his name back to Zimmerman, and that he was sympathetic with the Zionist group the Jewish Defense League. Bob dismissed questions about this as 'pure journalese.' Yet he *was* rediscovering Judaism. While in Israel, he investigated the possibility of taking his family to live on a kibbutz. His renewed interest in his religion had started with the death of his father in 1968. Woody Guthrie's former manager Harold Leventhal had lent him books about Israel and generally 'helped him to maintain his Jewishness.' According to Bruce Dorfman, Bob returned from Israel mesmerized. 'He was going to become a Hasid. This was really serious.' Dorfman saw Bob as someone looking for 'an anchor' in life and Judaism seemed at the time to be an answer.

In the wake of a series of natural disasters and a bloody civil war, the newly created state of Bangladesh in 1971 was facing a humanitarian disaster. Indian musician Ravi Shankar brought the plight of the people of Bangladesh to the attention of George Harrison in the hope that he could do something to help. Riding high on the success of a number-one album and single, the former Beatle promptly staged two huge benefit concerts at Madison Square Garden on August 1, one in the afternoon and the second in the evening. The concerts would be recorded for a live album and concert film, profits going to UNICEF. It would also provide a stage for Bob's first concert appearance since the Isle of Wight festival in 1969.

Harrison announced his special guest: 'Like to bring on a friend of us all – Mr. Bob Dylan!' Bob trotted out onto the stage dressed in denim, with an acoustic Martin guitar over his shoulder and harmonica rack around his neck. He looked very much like the folksinger of old, and he received a huge reception not least because he had appeared on stage in America at only three events since 1966. He was backed on electric guitar by Harrison and on bass by Leon Russell, who had recently recorded with Bob, including the song 'Watching the River Flow.' Ringo Starr played tambourine. Bob sang five songs at both the afternoon and evening concerts, and greatly enjoyed the thrill of performing after such a long layoff. 'Just Like a Woman' was particularly powerful, with Bob slowing down the song and singing the chorus in harmony with Harrison and Russell. The fact that it was the first time Bob had ever sung on stage with a former Beatle added to the frisson. 'The impact he had on the audience was incredible,' says Jim Horn, who led the horn section for the concert.

One of Weberman's main complaints about Bob was that he had apparently forsaken humanitarian causes in recent years. So when Bob played the Bangladesh benefit for free, Weberman announced that he would not bother Bob anymore. He found he could not stop himself, however. 'I should have left him alone,' he says. 'But I was a publicity addict.' He went back to the house with a journalist to look through the rubbish. Sara came out and started berating Weberman, who slunk away. He claims he was walking along Elizabeth Street when Bob came up and attacked him. Although slightly built, Bob proved more than a match for the chubby Dylanologist. 'He overpowered me,' says Weberman. 'He was choking me.' He claims Bob knocked his head against the pavement – presumably trying to knock some sense into him – until passersby intervened. Weberman suffered no serious injury. Indeed, he came to see even this humiliating episode as a triumph. 'Not too many people have that opportunity – to have Dylan on top of them,' he says. 'Maybe his wife.'

Weberman was not the only cause of trouble at MacDougal Street. Bob's neighbors were upset when he erected a stucco wall to section off his part of the back garden for privacy. This contravened the common agreement by which tenants managed the estate. Even though Bob had donated a small area of land for a communal basketball court as a gesture of goodwill to his neighbors, some of them decided to take matters into their own hands. When Bob was out of town, they came with sledgehammers and knocked the wall down. 'It was a very unpleasant thing that happened,' says Gloria Naftali, who lived next door to Bob. She liked the Dylans, and did not approve of what her fellow neighbors had done. But she also felt that the house was not suitable for a person of such notoriety. 'When you are a superstar among people who are not . . . life becomes very difficult.'

Between Weberman and the neighbors, life in New York City had become almost as unbearable for Bob as life upstate. He still owned the Ohayo Mountain Road house in Woodstock, but rarely visited. He also had a beach house on Long Island for summer holidays. He now bought a ranch house in Arizona as a getaway, and in addition he rented a family home in Malibu, California.

* * *

In the fall of 1971 Bob recorded a topical single, 'George Jackson,' about the killing of an inmate in San Quentin prison. He also played on some sessions for Allen Ginsberg. The Ginsberg collaboration arose after Ginsberg had invited Bob and mutual friend David Amram to his apartment in the East Village. The moment Dylan and Amram came through the door, Ginsberg thrust a guitar into Bob's hand. He simultaneously pushed the button on a tape recorder, demanding Bob accompany him on a song he had written.

'Bob, the key of G!' he shouted.

Bob told Ginsberg to turn off the tape recorder immediately. He was not about to be bushwhacked into recording a song. But he was sufficiently amused by Ginsberg's 'fabulous chutzpah,' as Amram describes it, to join the poet and musician friends – also including Ed Sanders and Happy Traum – for a series of informal recording sessions at the Record Plant in New York. Two Ginsberg albums were eventually compiled from these sessions. Bob also joined Ginsberg for a musical performance on New York public television. 'Allen wanted to expand,' explains Sanders. 'He wanted to do music.' Although Bob liked Ginsberg, and was interested in the beats, it seemed to Amram at least that Ginsberg was chasing after Bob. 'Allen Ginsberg was fascinated with Dylan and kind of followed Dylan and was enamored of Dylan's work, and Dylan's celebrity, and Dylan was nice enough to allow Allen to be, in a sense, his disciple,' says Amram. '[Dylan] was nice to Allen, but it was really Allen who initiated and sought out Dylan.'

Shortly after this collaboration, Happy Traum went into the studio with Bob to record on their own. 'He had very cryptically said to me, "You know, you ought to learn how to play the bass,"' recalls Traum. 'So I borrowed a bass, an electric bass, and learned a little bit about it. This was maybe a year or two before this recording session. I don't know if it was premeditated or just a coincidence.' Dylan and Traum spent a day in New York playing songs written in Woodstock when Bob was hanging out with The Band, songs including 'I Shall Be Released' and 'You Ain't Goin' Nowhere,' with Traum playing electric bass and banjo and singing harmony. These were important compositions that had been covered by other artists – notably The Band and Peter, Paul and Mary – but not included on any Dylan album. 'They were very popular songs of his that he wanted to put his own stamp on,' says Traum. They ran through the songs with the informality of two friends sitting around a kitchen table, giving the recordings a fresh feeling. Bob changed lyrics during the session, extensively in the case of 'You Ain't Goin' Nowhere.' The song now had an introduction that alluded to the Cary Grant movie *Gunga Din* and also made reference to Bob's friend Roger McGuinn of The Byrds. (As Traum points out, *McGuinn* is a name that rhymes with *Gunga Din*.) The newly recorded tracks were added to *Bob Dylan's Greatest Hits Vol II.* Released in the fall of 1971, this double album became the best-selling record of Bob's career, certified in 1997 by the RIAA as 'Multi-Platinum' with five million sales in the United States.

Bob was in New York sporadically during 1972, playing as a sideman on an album for singer Doug Sahm – an old friend from the sixties – and attending concerts by artists ranging from Elvis Presley to The Grateful Dead, meeting The Dead's leader Jerry Garcia backstage at a show in New Jersey. The men subsequently became good friends. Often Bob attended concerts on his own, taking a regular seat in the stands. Indeed, despite his great fame, and the attentions of obsessives like A. J. Weberman, he seemed determined to live as normal a life as possible. It would be wrong to say he resisted fame; he could, after all, have stopped recording if he wanted to slip out of the public eye altogether. But when not working in the studio or on tour, Bob retreated from show business, rarely giving interviews and making few personal appearances. The problem was, of course, that fans would not let him be a normal person. For example, in July 1972, Bob and Sara attended the Mariposa Festival on Toronto Center Island in Canada. Bob attempted to disguise himself with the look of a hippy so he could mingle with the crowd and enjoy the music in a normal way. He had grown a drooping mustache, wore ragged jeans, wrapped a red handkerchief around his head as a bandana, and wore a large white hat. This fairly thin disguise worked for a few hours, and then he was recognized. Word spread rapidly through the crowd and soon many people were pushing to try and see him. 'Everybody was running over to [where he was],' says John Cohen, who was performing with The New Lost City Ramblers. 'Somebody discovered him towards the end of the day and it was like a queen bee with thousands of people around him. He would take two steps to the left and thousands of people would take two steps to the left. It was scary.' Little by little, Bob worked his way over to the performers' area, and the first person he met was Cohen. 'We gave each other a big hug, because that was very tense. We were talking about it. He said, "You don't want to be part of this." He was right. Suddenly all the press guys came running after him.' The crowd and press were convinced that Bob was about to give a surprise performance and the atmosphere became almost hysterical. The police eventually had to take Bob and Sara off the island.

Since he was a boy Bob had wanted to be a film star. He had experimented with the ill-fated *Eat the Document*, but now he was given the opportunity to appear in a major Hollywood production. The project was the Western *Pat Garrett & Billy the Kid*, directed by Sam Peckinpah. The story was based on a true tragedy of the West. William H. Bonney – aka Billy the Kid – was a hired gun who roamed New Mexico in the 1880s. Fellow outlaw Pat Garrett traveled with him until he was made a sheriff and ordered to hunt down his friend, whom he ultimately killed. In the Peckinpah movie, Kris Kristofferson played the Kid and James Coburn played Pat Garrett. Bob, who admired Peckinpah's *The Wild Bunch*, signed up to create the music and play a supporting character, Alias, a friend of the Kid. Filming began in Durango, Mexico, on November 13, 1972, and Bob and Sara moved there with their children. It was not to be a happy experience.

At the age of forty-eight, Peckinpah was a paranoid drunk constantly fighting with his studio, M.G.M., and prone to outlandish displays of temper. As author David Weddle reports in his biography, *If They Move . . . Kill 'Em!*, Dylan and Kristofferson were in the screening room watching dailies when Peckinpah urinated all over the screen because the picture was out of focus. 'I remember Bob turning and looking at me with the most perfect reaction, you know: what the hell have we gotten ourselves into?' says Kristofferson. Peckinpah would come on the set late, having steadied himself with vodka. He drank through the day, staggering off to his trailer in the late afternoon. Sometimes he blacked out. Other times he threw knives and fired live rounds at his reflection in the mirror. The weather turned bad, and cast and crew were struck down with influenza. By mid-December the film was nine days behind schedule. They had to shoot through the Thanksgiving, Christmas, and New Year holidays. Peckinpah hosted uproarious parties to make up for the inconvenience, and cast and crew dined on the turkeys Bob had pursued on horseback during one of his few scenes. Sensitive Sara Dylan was miserable in Mexico surrounded by drunken, rowdy men. When she asked Bob what they were doing there, he did not know how to answer. In early January, the Dylans had a break and visited their friends George and Pattie Harrison in England, but Bob soon had to return to Mexico for more filming and to record the sound track.

Work on the sound track began in Mexico City and was

completed in California in February 1973. Bob gathered together an eclectic group of musicians including Booker T. Jones, of Booker T. and the M.G.s, Roger McGuinn, and another old friend, Bruce Langhorne. They assembled in a studio in Burbank in front of a giant screen on which a rough cut of the movie was projected. Bob scored the film in his own singular way. 'I thought that Bobby didn't know anything about film scoring,' says Langhorne, who worked on film scores for a living at this stage in his career. He knew that it was customary to pay close attention to the cuts, matching tempo to action. But Bob did none of this. 'I realized afterwards that it really wasn't about them doing the best film score,' he adds. 'It was about capturing the feeling of the film.' Bob succeeded in this. The incidental music he created was highly evocative of the Wild West, although he wrote only two new songs, one of them the magnificent 'Knockin' on Heaven's Door.'

Peckinpah's first edit of *Pat Garrett & Billy the Kid* was considered a masterpiece by some, including, most notably, Martin Scorsese. But M.G.M. wanted the film to be shorter and Peckinpah lost control of the movie. The version put on general release in July 1973 was a mess of desultory, unconvincing scenes. Bob's part had been slight to begin with. Now it was so insubstantial as to be irrelevant. Kristofferson talked expansively about Bob's unique screen presence, comparing him to Charlie Chaplin, but it could also be argued that Bob looked merely self-conscious on-screen. The fact that he had third billing was absurd considering he said almost nothing. Yet Bob had received a lesson in filmmaking on a grand scale, and came away enthusiastic about making a film of his own. He also had a hit in 'Knockin' on Heaven's Door.' The song went to number twelve in the U.S. charts in September 1973 and transcended the film in later years when it became a staple of his live concerts and was covered by numerous artists, including Eric Clapton and Guns N' Roses.

* * *

Entrepreneur David Geffen established Asylum Records in 1970 when he was only twenty-seven. After enjoying early success with The Eagles and Joni Mitchell, Geffen sold Asylum for $7 million in 1972 and took control of a merged Elektra / Asylum a year later. He then set about wooing Bob away from Columbia.

Geffen began his campaign by befriending Robbie Robertson, knowing the guitarist had Bob's confidence. He was then introduced to Bob and began spending time with him in California, where Bob was living part of the year. They came to a loose agreement whereby Bob would not re-sign with Columbia when his current contract expired, but would make one studio album for Asylum, backed by The Band. If it went well, there might be other albums. Geffen would promote the first album by staging a comeback concert tour for Bob and The Band for which Bob would receive most of the profits. A spin-off live album would also be recorded. Bob thought Columbia undervalued him at the time, and he remained disgruntled about the way Albert Grossman had earned such a large percentage from previous Columbia deals, so he signed with Geffen, who seemed more like a friend than a businessman. To publish the new songs, Bob's lawyers created Ram's Horn Music, the first music company Dylan owned entirely on his own.

The studio album, *Planet Waves*, was recorded quickly in Los Angeles in November 1973. 'We all loved the way Bob wanted to really sing [the songs] only once a day, one rendition a day. So we'd often get the song on the second take. I think there may have been some first takes there,' says Garth Hudson. 'Best way to do 'em.' The songs included 'Forever Young,' which Bob said he had written thinking of one of his sons, but not wanting to be overly sentimental. Jakob Dylan, then approaching his fourth birthday, came to think the song was about him. The phrase 'forever young' is quite common of course, and was certainly not coined by Dylan. John Keats used it in the third verse of his well-known Romantic poem 'Ode on a Grecian Urn' ('For ever panting, and for ever young'). Part of Bob's cleverness as a songwriter, however, was that he could take a commonplace phrase and give it extra meaning by its context and by the way he phrased it. On the page, the lyrics of 'Forever Young' do not seem very striking, being somewhat bland, but the number had great emotional power in performance and became one his most popular concert songs.

Of the other songs on the album, 'Wedding Song' seemed to relate to Bob's own life, to the wife who had saved his life and given him 'babies one, two, three' (although in fact Sara gave him four). 'I hate myself for lovin' you' were the opening words of 'Dirge,' a song that spoke of a love affair in terms of shame. Bob played piano on the recording, setting up a feeling of doom with elemental chords. His voice had lost its country mellowness and regained the uncompromising truth-tone of old. Although not a popular or very well known song, 'Dirge' was a signpost to the future.

The subsequent Dylan–Band tour – Tour '74, as it was called – was the first major stadium tour of the rock era. Dylan and The Band played forty shows, in the biggest theaters and sports stadiums across the country, over six weeks. They traveled between concerts in a private jet, Starship 1. David Geffen promoted the tour in association with impresario Bill Graham, who handled logistics. The artists made the major decisions about the musical format of the shows, the staging, and the length of the tour, and also received most of the profits. This was an innovation, as was the extravagant level of hype for the tour. 'This event is the biggest thing of its kind in the history of show business,' David Geffen bragged to the press. Ticket prices were high for 1974, at an average of $8. Part of the hype created by the promoters was that more than seven percent of the U.S. population applied for tickets. The truth was that some shows sold faster than others, and tickets could be had even at the last minute. However, all 658,000 tickets were eventually sold, generating a gross of approximately $5 million.

The tour began in Chicago on January 3, 1974. Bob opened with a rewritten song from the early 1960s, 'Hero Blues,' almost yelling that he had 'one foot on the highway, and one foot in the grave.' Despite weeks of rehearsals, this was one song he had neglected to tell The Band he was going to sing. The music was startlingly fast and furious, very different from the soulful music Bob had made with The Band in Woodstock, and different too from the music on *Planet Waves*; it was closer to the sound they had made during their 1965–66 world tour. 'Whenever we would do something in the studio it was like one group of musicians and when we went and played live it was like a different group of musicians,' says Robbie Robertson. 'When we played live the music got very dynamic and violent and explosive. And when we played in the studio it wasn't like that at all . . . Even on the first tour in '66 that we did, it was the same kind of thing: when we started playing the songs, they would all go in this very aggressive, bombastic attitude. When we got together to do the Tour '74 thing, the same thing happened again. We just automatically reverted to a certain attitude towards the songs . . . it's fast and aggressive and hard and tough.' In 1966, audiences had howled abuse at Bob and The Hawks. The same musicians created almost the same sound for Tour '74 and yet they were received like heroes. 'Everybody cheered and acted like, *Oh, I loved it all along*,' scoffs Robertson. 'There was something kind of hypocritical in it.'

Bob's voice was huge and indignant during the acoustic part of the concert, attacking cant and hypocrisy with strident performances of 'It's Alright Ma (I'm Only Bleeding).' In the white heat of the Watergate scandal, the crowd roared when Bob sang that even the president had to stand naked. Thousands held aloft matches and cigarette lighters in a spontaneous gesture of solidarity. It was the first time this had ever happened at a concert. 'We knew we were in the presence of greatness,' says Barry Feinstein, who photographed the sea of flickering flames for the cover of the subsequent live album, titled *Before the Flood*. By the time Tour '74 concluded, in Los Angeles in mid-February, Bob and The Band had earned a fortune. Not only had the tour sold out, but *Planet Waves* had become the first Dylan album to reach number one. This was despite the fact that Columbia released a rival album, which executives called simply *Dylan*, comprised of outtakes from the *Self Portrait–New Morning* sessions. Some of the money from Tour '74 was invested in complex tax shelters and, unfortunately, disappeared when investments failed (much to the disgust of down-to-earth Levon Helm, who had opposed the investments in the first place). They also squandered money on high living.

Tour '74 presented Bob as a rock star on a grand scale. Although he enjoyed the money, it had not been a satisfying experience. He was much more interested in experimentation. During a lunch with Arlo Guthrie, Harold Leventhal, and Pete Seeger in Malibu he became enthused about the idea of touring China. Following Richard Nixon's historic trip to China, a few selected Westerners were making visits and Leventhal and Seeger had been among the first. 'He wanted to know what was happening with China. "What's it like? Can I go there? Could you get me to go there? Could you arrange it?"' says Leventhal. 'He was all excited. He even said to me, "[Why] don't you manage me?"' Leventhal reminded Bob he had said the same thing several times before. Evidently, he was still not truly serious about it because he did not hire Leventhal and neither did he tour China.

Long-term sales of *Planet Waves* were good, but not spectacular. Bob thought it should have done better considering the number of people who had seen him and The Band on tour. He became sufficiently disenchanted with Asylum to re-sign with Columbia on August 1, 1974. 'Bob Dylan has made a decision to bet on his past,' said Geffen, bitterly. The dalliance with Asylum had made Columbia appreciate Bob more, and he was able to negotiate a better deal. As Geffen said: 'He should thank me.' The breakup was not a happy one, though Dylan and Geffen eventually renewed their friendship.

Bob and Sara sold their Woodstock house in 1973, retaining a hundred acres of undeveloped land on Ohayo Mountain. They still owned the town house in New York, a ranch house in Arizona, and the beach house in the Hamptons, but from now on their main residence would be in California.

Bob bought a modest property on the Point Dume peninsula, ten miles north of Malibu Beach and a short walk from secluded Zuma Beach. Neighbors included film people – notably novelist and screenwriter John Fante – but it was not a high-powered showbusiness community. Point Dume was a place where one could live quietly, with good public schools nearby for the children. Bob would eventually own eight adjoining parcels of land, together with several houses, outbuildings, and private roads, giving him a compound of more than twelve acres overlooking the Pacific. But they started with one house on a single plot of land, and Sara said it needed an extra bedroom. They called in architect David C. Towbin, who specialized in designing homes for celebrities. Bob and Sara moved their family to a nearby rented property while Towbin did the remodeling. Bob came by the site one day and discovered to his amazement that apart from one wall the house had vanished. He asked the workmen where the house was. They said they had knocked it down to make way for the new bedroom. Bob decided that as long as they were going to knock down the house, they might as well create something really spectacular.

In discussions with Towbin, Bob discounted having his new house built in any particular style, as was popular in communities like Beverly Hills where faux English Tudor mansions were thrown up next to fake French chateaus and re-creations of antebellum plantation houses. If he wanted an English-style house, Bob said he would go live in England; neither did he want a Mexican house, or any other style of house. 'I want my own fantasy,' he informed the architect. Over the next three years Bob and Sara worked with Towbin to create the most extraordinary and extravagant fantasy mansion. Just one wall of the original property was left standing – to satisfy building ordinances that, technically, this was a remodeling – and around this wall an outlandish wood-frame fairy-tale palace was constructed. When complete, there would be approximately twenty rooms including a vaulted Great Room, a huge kitchen with a slate floor, and a large bedroom wing, each bedroom with customized en suite bathroom. Bob and Sara had a separate master bedroom suite on the second floor, with a private patio that gave them a view of the ocean. Surprisingly, for a relatively thrifty man, Bob spared no expense. He told Towbin he wanted the Great Room big enough to 'ride a horse through,' and added to the costs by frequently changing his mind about the details. The massive stone fireplace in the Great Room was torn out and resited so many times in different positions that a fireplace footing was built around the entire perimeter. Bob phoned Towbin from Minnesota to say he had bought back one of the first cars he ever owned. He wanted to suspend it from the ceiling.

'With or without the engine?' asked Towbin.

Hippy artisans were hired to handcraft fixtures and fittings, including the intricate glasswork, wood carvings, and tiles for the bathrooms and kitchen. Eventually fifty-six artisans were living in teepees and gypsy caravans on the premises, payrolled for more than two years. A kiln was built so that tiles could be manufactured on site. The five Dylan children were asked to design tiles for their personal bathrooms. Jakob's room was decorated with a mural of a seagull in flight. A large slate mural in the shape of a whale was built into the entrance galleria. Every door in the house was handmade, and no two were alike. The swimming pool was designed to look like a natural water feature, with huge artificial mushrooms growing out of it. There was a bridge over the pool, the bridge supports carved in the shape of women's legs. Although everything in the house was brand-new, Bob wanted the house to look old. So the beautiful wood- and plaster work had to be deliberately scuffed and distressed. Contractor Frank Neisner became so frustrated that he quit the project twice, and had to be talked into coming back to finish the job. At first, Bob wanted an observatory of glass on top of the house. This changed to a Russian-style onion dome made of copper. There were stairs up to the dome and a view down the coast to Santa Monica pier. Bob said the dome helped him recognize his house when he came home.

'That [house] was kind of Sara's folly. Bob went along with it, but it just got out of control in terms of the cost of building it,' says Jonathan Taplin. 'I think from Bob's point of view it was like, *When is this gonna end? When are these people gonna get out of my house?*' Towbin agrees that the building of the house was a source of friction. Bob and Sara had seemed blissfully happy until they came to California (Bernard Paturel says he never heard them argue in Woodstock). Now they were bickering. To help, Towbin gave Bob and Sara different parts of the project to oversee. At times he felt like a diplomat as much as an architect. Yet, he says, Bob also enjoyed looking over the plans and devising new ideas for the house.

Another threat to Bob and Sara's relationship came in the spring of 1974 when Bob attended an art class at a studio in Carnegie Hall, New York. The class was conducted by Norman Raeben, a seventy-three-year-old painter who had a commanding presence and acerbic tongue. 'You see this vase?' he asked Bob one day. He whipped the vase away. 'Draw it!' As Bob started to draw he realized he had looked at the vase but not really seen it. This was an important lesson in art and also a perspective that he might apply to life in general.

Norman Raeben did not know who Bob was when they first met. 'Raeben thought he had no money and thought he was a poor kid. Bob was taking this stuff very seriously and working at it and Raeben liked him quite a lot,' says mutual friend Jacques Levy. Raeben became concerned that his scruffy student might not have a place to stay, and said Bob could sleep in the studio in return for cleaning up. The misunderstanding endeared Bob to the old man. 'Bob really likes the idea that people don't really know who he is, or don't respond to him in that starry-eyed, awestruck way,' says Levy. Indeed, Bob became infatuated with the painter, later describing him as 'more powerful than any magician.' The infatuation seemed to cause problems with his marriage. 'I went home after that and my wife never did understand me ever since that day,' he said. 'That's when our marriage started breaking up. She never knew what I was talking about, what I was thinking about. And I couldn't possibly explain it.'

While he was in New York, Bob appeared at a benefit concert, on May 9, at the Felt Forum. Phil Ochs had organized the show to benefit the victims of oppression in Chile, where political dissidents were being tortured and murdered following a military coup led by Augusto Pinochet. The 'Friends of Chile' concert was chaotic, with performances going over time and the evening dragging on interminably. By the time Bob was due to perform he seemed the worse for drink, swigging from a bottle on stage. In fact, many of the performers had turned to drink as they waited around backstage. 'I remember Phil and everybody else [getting] kind of sloppy,' says Arlo Guthrie.

Bob was actually drinking quite heavily. He was also

smoking cigarettes again after having quit for a while – another small sign that something was amiss. His life with Sara had been stable and harmonious for years. Perhaps the happiest period of his life had been between 1966 and 1974, when he was raising a family, not touring, and making music when and how he liked. It seems that he had also managed to remain faithful, which had not previously been in his nature. There was a change following his return to the road with The Band for Tour '74. Bob was experimenting again with his old ways and temptations. It did not help that Sara had no time for the rock 'n' roll lifestyle. 'She despised it,' says Jonathan Taplin. 'People who just wanted to talk about music, it was boring to her.'

Bob also had easy access to women on the road, and Sara was not there to stop him. 'I think he clearly probably succumbed to temptation from time to time,' adds Taplin. In July 1974 there were press reports that Bob's marriage was breaking up. He would be linked with a number of women, including twenty-four-year-old Ellen Bernstein, a Columbia Records executive. Author Clinton Heylin has reported that Bob met Bernstein when Tour '74 swung through California in February, and that she became his girlfriend for a short time. Actress Ruth Tyrangiel claims she also began an affair with Bob in February, during Tour '74, and that this was the beginning of a nineteen-year relationship. Her story was revealed in a palimony suit she brought at Los Angeles Superior Court in 1995. She allegedly became 'nurse, confidante, companion, homemaker, housekeeper, cook, social companion [and] advisor' to Bob. She says he told her he would divorce Sara and make her his wife. Although Tyrangiel's palimony case was ultimately dismissed in court, in 1995, when she failed to prove her allegations, there was some evidence that she knew Bob, and members of Bob's entourage at the time have little doubt that he was beginning to pursue relationships outside his marriage. This behavior was becoming an intolerable strain on Sara Dylan, and so they separated.

Bob spent much of the summer of 1974 in Minnesota, without his wife. He had recently bought an eighty-acre arable farm northeast of Minneapolis, on the banks of the Crow River. He leased the land to local farmers to grow crops, and converted an old farmhouse on the property into a family home and an adjacent barn into an art studio. Bob's brother David came to live full-time on the property with his wife and three children, building his own house just to the side of Bob's. The fact that Bob invited his brother to share the farm with him demonstrated some level of closeness between them, but their relationship was limited by the fact that Bob inevitably spent most of the year away from Minnesota. The brothers also had very different personalities. David was much more straightforward and outgoing than Bob, who, in his private life, seemed at times to be positively introverted. Also, although they were both involved in the music industry, David confined himself to working in the Twin Cities. He had no ambitions to get involved in the music scenes in New York or Los Angeles where Bob was most active and so their paths did not often cross. Their mother, who had remarried since Abe's death, becoming Mrs. Beatty Rutman (she married Joe Rutman, an uncle of Bob's friend Howard Rutman), was living in Minneapolis at the time and she became a frequent visitor to the farm, especially when all eight grandchildren were there. It was an idyllic place for the children. There was pony riding, swimming, and trips into the Twin Cities to see films. In the winter, everybody went ice-skating. The farm was a secure family base, a happy place Bob would return to for holidays each winter and summer for years to come. Sara rarely visited, however, and it became increasingly obvious that there was a serious rift between her and Bob.

It was during his first summer on the farm that Bob wrote the songs for *Blood on the Tracks,* the first album since *John Wesley Harding* that rivaled the glories of his past. The general impression was that the songs addressed failed relationships, maybe his own failing marriage to Sara, but in fact they reflected many facets of love. The ideas of art teacher Norman Raeben strongly influenced the way in which the songs were constructed, as Bob later explained in liner notes for the 1985 *Biograph* box set. Just as a painting can portray different parts of a story simultaneously, he said he wrote the songs on *Blood on the Tracks* so that past, present, and future were evoked at once. This was particularly true of 'Tangled Up in Blue,' where the meeting of the lovers, their relationship, and the narrator's reflection on the relationship were all jumbled together. 'Simple Twist of Fate' was similarly constructed. The romantic opening line in which lovers sat in a park 'as the evening sky grew dark' turned into a song of regret as the listener realized the lovers were lost to each other. These songs were rich in metaphor, studded with interesting similes: time moved fast, like a plane in 'You're a Big Girl Now'; in the same song, Bob wrote of soured love turning 'like a corkscrew to my heart.' The monumental 'Idiot Wind' was a rage against failure, pulsing with apocalyptic allusions. The line about inheriting a million dollars from a woman's estate – he could not help being 'lucky' – is one of the best examples of black humor in Bob's songbook. 'Lily, Rosemary and the Jack of Hearts' was a complex love story wrapped in Wild West metaphor. 'Buckets of Rain' was sung like a nursery rhyme. 'You're Gonna Make Me Lonesome When You Go' was apparently inspired by girlfriend Ellen Bernstein, who spent time at the farm that summer. It has been claimed by Clinton Heylin that the mention in the lyric of a specific place name – Ashtabula – is a reference to her hometown in Ohio. Despite the romance of the song, Bob tired of his relationship with Bernstein before the year was out.

Bob began recording these new songs at Columbia's studio in New York in September 1974, but with limited success. He worked initially with Eric Weissberg and his band. Weissberg had recorded 'Dueling Banjos,' the instrumental hit from the film *Deliverance*, and his bright, dynamic sound came through most clearly on 'Meet Me in the Morning.' This song was a blues, rather than being made in the painterly style of 'Tangled Up in Blue,' but it contained images just as striking. Bob sang of the sun 'sinkin' like a ship' and his voice brimmed with emotion as he wailed that this was just like his heart when he kissed his lover's lips. As he experimented in the studio, Bob used the tune from 'Meet Me in the Morning' for another song, 'Call Letter Blues.' The music was almost identical, but in the latter song Bob sang bitterly of children crying for their mother, and having to tell them their mother had gone on a trip. He also alluded to the male character in song perhaps taking comfort with prostitutes. This raw song did not make it onto the album and, although the music recorded with Weissberg's band had a strong and distinctive sound, Bob changed musicians for the rest of the New York sessions. He had finished *Blood on the Tracks* by the end of September and Columbia began to prepare for its release. However, Bob came away not entirely satisfied with the way the LP sounded.

He went home to the farm in December and, over the Christmas holidays, which Bob always celebrated even though he was born into the Jewish faith, he played a test pressing of *Blood on the Tracks* for his brother David. Bob said the album was ready for release, with album jackets already printed, but he was still unhappy about approximately half the tracks he had recorded in New York, particularly the song 'Idiot Wind,' which contained lyrics that might easily be construed as being about his marriage to Sara. David suggested they go into a local studio and rerecord the worrisome songs.

David worked in the Twin Cities where he made jingles for television and radio advertisements, and also produced recording artists. He called together musicians who regularly worked for him, including bass player Billy Peterson and drummer Bill Berg, for a session at Sound 80 Studios in Minneapolis with engineer Paul Martinson. Bob was very reserved at first, and David acted as the go-between for anything Bob wanted to tell the musicians. The first song they worked on was 'Idiot Wind.' Bob rewrote the lyrics, working with a pencil at his music stand and then tucking a piece of paper into the strings of his guitar so he could refer to the new words while he played. He blurred the edges of the song in the rewriting, making it less autobiographical. (Bob would later deny that *Blood on the Tracks* was at all autobiographical, but even his son Jakob says the songs are 'my parents talking.') Bob was pleased with the new 'Idiot Wind.' He told engineer Martinson quietly: 'You have a nice way of picking things up here.' It was the most he had said to anybody, apart from his brother, since he had entered the studio. They recorded one more track that day, 'You're a Big Girl Now.' Then Bob and David took a rough mix home with them to the farm.

Bob and David returned to the studio three days later, bringing Bob's children. There was a family atmosphere at the start of the session, but the mood darkened when Bob sang his extraordinary songs of broken love. 'It was a little down,' says Billy Peterson. 'The sentiment was a little heavy.' Bob rerecorded three more songs, starting with 'Tangled Up in Blue.' Next he worked on 'Lily, Rosemary and the Jack of Hearts.' This now had a quick tempo and a slight country shuffle. It also featured some additional guitar players, giving the song a different sound as compared to the other tracks. Bob overdubbed the organ. (There were few other overdubs on *Blood on the Tracks* and, apart from cleaning up technical imperfections on 'Idiot Wind,' rough mixes were used for the album.) At the very last minute he decided to recut 'If You See Her, Say Hello.' He wanted to do the song with a mandolin accompaniment from local musician Peter Ostroushko. They struggled through several takes before

Bob stopped and told Ostroushko that he wanted a different sound. Not knowing the terminology, he conveyed his meaning in metaphor. 'There's a kind of sound that I'm looking for on this instrument,' he said. 'It's like birds' wings flapping in the air.' Then he took the mandolin and, with surprising skill, tremeloed the notes.

Blood on the Tracks was released three weeks later, in January 1975, to virtually universal acclaim and went to number one. Despite the fact that Bob had recorded the album with different combinations of musicians in two studios over several months, there was nothing jarring about the album. Indeed, the different string parts added to the richness of the sound. The lyrics were among the best Bob ever wrote. For many listeners, *Blood on the Tracks* became the great Dylan album. For his part, Bob said he did not understand how people could enjoy such pain.

There was time to relax after the album was finished, and for Bob to enjoy the first truly major artistic and commercial success he had had in years. He went to see old friend Dana Gillespie perform in New York; and attended various parties including one for The Faces in California, meeting guitarist Ron Wood, who became a close friend. While he was in California, Bob performed at a benefit concert Bill Graham had organized in San Francisco to raise money for schools. Although they had been separated for a while, Sara Dylan unexpectedly accompanied him to the show. They had decided to try for a reconciliation, although it was clear to musicians at the San Francisco event that there was still tension between the couple, and one can only presume that Sara was not very happy with some of the songs on *Blood on the Tracks* as they seemed to be so specifically about her marriage. However, as she has never talked about any aspect of her life with Bob, and has been remarkably discreet in her conversation with others, this is difficult to know for sure.

The reconciliation did not last long, and a couple of

months later Bob went to France alone to stay with painter David Oppenheim, who had created the artwork for the back cover of *Blood on the Tracks*. It was a vacation to celebrate Bob's thirty-fourth birthday, and although Sara was supposed to join him for a time, and he called her frequently, she did not come to France. Bob was 'completely despairing, isolated, lost . . .' according to Oppenheim who says they went on a bacchanalian revel to cheer up. 'We screwed women, we drank, we ate,' he says. 'Pathetic and superb at the same time.' On Bob's birthday they attended a gypsy festival, meeting the self-proclaimed King of the Gypsies. The experience inspired a new song, 'One More Cup of Coffee.' Bob also began to think of another song, which showed how much he missed his wife. It was to be called 'Sara.'

Bob was back in New York during the humid summer of 1975, spending most evenings at the Other End restaurant on Bleecker Street. He drank Mouton Cadet wine while chatting with the club owner, Paul Colby, and socializing with old friends Ramblin' Jack Elliott and Bobby Neuwirth. They were among the artists performing next door at the Bitter End. Colby, who ran both establishments, reserved a booth for Bob so he could watch the shows, and Bob was soon making guest appearances on stage. In this way, he met younger musicians, including Mick Ronson, formerly a guitarist in David Bowie's band, and Rob Stoner (son of photographer Arthur Rothstein), who led a rockabilly group and sometimes played bass for Ramblin' Jack. As Bob returned to the club night after night, a convivial and exciting musical scene developed that amounted to a Greenwich Village renaissance.

Walking through SoHo one day that summer, Bob bumped into theater director and lyricist Jacques Levy, who cowrote songs with Roger McGuinn, including 'Chestnut Mare.' The two had met before and Bob accepted an invitation to go up to Levy's loft apartment. 'You know, I'd like to write some songs with you,' Bob told him. He sat at the piano and began playing tunes he had been working on over the summer. 'One More Cup of Coffee' was finished, and he had nearly completed 'Sara,' which was very much an autobiographical love song to his wife. In the song, Bob described Sara as the love of his life and stated that he had written 'Sad-Eyed Lady of the Lowlands' for her. 'People had always thought it was Joan Baez,' says Levy, who was surprised by the directness. 'He had never really been so open about stuff, without disguising it. He was a little hesitant to do that. And when he sang this thing, I just thought it was wonderful. I encouraged him to continue.' Bob had snatches of ideas for other songs, including a strange tune he called 'Isis.' Levy sat with Bob on the piano stool and began collaborating on the song, stitching Bob's ideas into a narrative that became a mystical love song with Wild West imagery and a smattering of sly humor. When it was finished, Levy typed up the words and they went to the Other End. It was almost closing time, but a few of Bob's friends were still there. Bob asked, 'Would you like to hear a new song?' He then took out the lyric of 'Isis' and declaimed it as a poem. 'Everyone sat there, glued,' recalls Levy.

The reception to 'Isis' was so enthusiastic Bob suggested he and Levy collaborate further, in what became the first sustained period of cowriting in his career. One idea Bob had was to write a song about former middleweight boxer Rubin 'Hurricane' Carter, serving a life sentence in New Jersey for a triple murder he claimed he had not committed.

Rubin Carter had been in and out of detention centers and prisons from an early age, a victim of racism but also of his violent temper and propensity to commit impetuous crimes, including purse snatching. Carter became a successful boxer in the early 1960s, and a devout Muslim. In 1964 he was quoted in the *Saturday*

Evening Post apparently calling for white policemen to be murdered. Carter claimed his comments were taken out of context, but he was widely condemned, and his critics included fellow African-American fighter 'Sugar' Ray Robinson. Carter believed the *Post* furor was partly responsible for policemen framing him with murder after three people were gunned down on June 17, 1966, in a bar in Paterson, New Jersey. Two African Americans were seen leaving the scene and Carter and a friend, John Artis, were identified as the culprits. The main prosecution evidence came from Alfred Bello and Arthur Dexter Bradley, small-time crooks attempting a burglary near the scene of the shooting. Carter believed Bello and Bradley falsely identified him and Artis in exchange for avoiding prosecution. In 1967 Carter was given a life sentence for the murders. He considered himself the victim of a racist court and corrupt, white policemen who were determined to put him away for his 'cop-hating, cracker-hating' rhetoric.

The case was resurrected in September 1974 when Bello and Bradley admitted to lying under oath. Carter wrote a powerful memoir, which he called *The Sixteenth Round*, and many were convinced of his innocence, including Madison Avenue advertising executive George Lois. It was Lois who organized the Hurricane Trust Fund to raise money for a retrial. Copies of *The Sixteenth Round* were sent to celebrities including Bob, who was so moved by the book that he visited Carter in prison. They liked each other and Bob offered to write a song about the case. 'Hurricane' was brilliantly dramatic, owing in part to Levy's theatrical sensibility, opening the number like a movie with pistol shots ringing out in the night. It was also an excellent piece of journalism, condensing a complex case – involving several characters and conflicting testimony – into eight minutes. If the song had a fault, it was that Carter did not seem a fully rounded character. There was no reference to his antagonistic rhetoric, criminal history, or violent temper.

The repeated refrain that he could have been 'champion of the world' was slightly misleading considering he lost seven of his last fifteen fights. However, Bob did succeed in emphasizing the essential truth that Carter was in prison for a crime he had not committed.

The lively scene at the Other End, where Bob spent most evenings, meant it was hard to concentrate on songwriting in New York. So Bob invited Levy to stay with him at his beach house just off Lily Pond Lane in Long Island – the place Bob wrote about in the song 'Sara.' It was a big empty house, cooled by pleasant ocean breezes. There was no sign of Sara or their children, and there was no housekeeper to look after them. Bob and Levy wheeled a shopping cart around the local supermarket, 'like the Odd Couple,' as Levy says. The collaboration continued to work remarkably well, with Levy's sense of theater complementing Bob's more abstract approach to songwriting. The men were also attracted to the same sorts of themes, such as outlaw figures adrift in society. Thus they wrote the elegiac song 'Joey,' based on the life of New York Mafia figure Joey Gallo, whom Levy had known. Many of the other songs conjured up exotic locations, and came out of a mutual interest in literature: 'Black Diamond Bay' grew from their love of the stories of Joseph Conrad. At the end of the song it was revealed that the narrator had been watching the story on the evening news. 'There is a certain Brechtian notion about that,' explains Levy. 'Instead of being inside the story, as you think you are all along, all of a sudden you step out and look at it as an observer.' Other songs were equally exotic, though resulting from more prosaic influences. 'Mozambique' started as a game to see how many *-ique* rhymes they could find. 'Romance in Durango,' with its opening line about chili peppers, was prompted by a postcard from Mexico showing chili peppers drying on a roof; the words 'Hot Chili Peppers in the Sun' were written on the front. The subject matter came from Bob's experiences making *Pat Garrett & Billy the Kid.* 'It [became] a kind of cowboy story,' says Levy. 'A guy on the run and a girl . . . like an old Western.'

Although it was just seven months since he had completed *Blood on the Tracks*, Bob found that he had a complete set of strong new songs that he wanted to put on record and so he telephoned Columbia to say he was coming to the New York studio. He did not have a band to work with, but there were numerous musicians hanging out at Paul Colby's place that he could use. Bob also picked up a musician on the street. He was driving along 13th Street in New York when he saw a tall gypsy-like woman carrying a violin case. Her hair fell three feet down her back. 'Can you play that thing?' he asked, stopping the car. She said she sure could.

Scarlet Rivera was a shy young woman, a fiddle player from the Midwest then working in a New York Salsa band. After spending a day and night making music with Bob, she was invited to Columbia's Studio 'E' in midtown to begin work on a new album, which Bob would name *Desire*. Rivera's violin helped define the sound of the record, even though she had never been in a recording studio in her life. The scene that confronted her at Studio 'E' was near chaos. A couple of dozen musicians had been called for the sessions starting on July 14, so many musicians that an adjoining studio became a green room. There was a large buffet, and some drinking and pot smoking. The musicians ranged from Village folkie Erik Frandsen to superstar Eric Clapton. Also present were members of Dave Mason's band and all ten members of British R&B band Kokomo, summoned across town after playing a gig in Central Park. There were numerous false starts, misunderstandings, and some losses of temper that first afternoon. Only one song, 'Romance in Durango,' was eventually completed to Bob's satisfaction.

'Okay guys. That's the end,' said producer Don De Vito. 'Bobby's lost his voice.'

'What fucking voice?' growled Kokomo guitarist Jim Mullen.

There were at least three sessions like this before Bob sent the cattle call of musicians home and settled down to record the bulk of *Desire* with a small band comprised of Scarlet Rivera, Rob Stoner on bass, and Stoner's drummer Howie Wyeth, a relative of the artist Andrew Wyeth. Sheena Seidenberg added percussion and Emmylou Harris sang backing vocals. Together, they completed the album in two days, whistling through the songs in the style with which Bob was most comfortable.

Sara Dylan arrived unexpectedly on the night of the second session, July 31. 'She came to New York, I guess, to see if there would be some kind of a getting back together. I guess that was in her mind. I know it was in his mind,' says Levy, who had not seen Sara the whole summer (she had been on vacation in Mexico). Bob went back into the studio with his band and picked up a guitar. He sang 'Sara' to his wife as she watched from the other side of the glass. The song began by recalling holidays on the beach when the children were small, and mentioned the long-ago holiday in Portugal when they were first together. He asked her forgiveness for his recent transgressions, and sang at the end: 'Don't ever leave me, don't ever go.'

'It was extraordinary. You could have heard a pin drop,' says Levy. 'She was absolutely stunned by it. And I think it was a turning point . . . It did work. The two of them really did get back together.' This remarkable first take of 'Sara' became the last track on *Desire*.

Bob flew his new band to Chicago in mid-September for a televised tribute to his former producer John Hammond. They performed with the scantiest backstage rehearsal, but managed to follow Bob through three long songs, including 'Hurricane' and 'Simple Twist of Fate.' The show seemed to be Bob's way of testing the musicians to see if they could cope with his off-the-cuff performance style. Rob Stoner stood slightly behind Bob so he could watch the back of Bob's left hand for the chord changes, and see the tapping of his boot heel for the beat. 'You can anticipate when the chord is going to change by watching the [hand] muscles relax,' says Stoner, who assumed the role of bandleader. 'Then you can see which way the hand shifts, seeing what chord it is going to go to.' This was a method that many of Bob's bandleaders would use, watching his hands and feet closely and then signaling the changes to the other musicians.

For years Bob had been talking to friends about a touring revue show, maybe traveling by train, playing small towns. It was a carnival-type ideal, recalling his early fantasy life in the Dakotas. That fall, following the Hammond tribute, he made the decision to do just this. He would use a core group of musicians led by Stoner – like a 'pit band in a vaudeville show,' as Stoner puts it – and invite guest artists to join them. Bobby Neuwirth was one of the first signed up, 'as payback for all the service he'd given to Dylan,' according to Stoner. He was certainly not a star attraction. One evening at the Other End, Ramblin' Jack Elliott was also invited. 'Bobby and I were talkin' about playin',' said Dylan, handing Elliott a glass of wine. 'We're going to go on tour, with a bus, and play little gigs.' (He pronounced this as *leetle geegs.*) 'Could you dig it?'

'Count me in,' said Elliott.

Jacques Levy would stage the show. Bob's summer-camp friend, Louis Kemp, who had made a fortune in the fish-farming business, would oversee logistics. Bob invited Roger McGuinn to be another of the guest stars, and he gladly accepted. He also asked Joan Baez and she agreed, too, despite the unhappy way they had parted in 1965. She never quite got over her love for Bob, and had recently written a remarkable song, 'Diamonds and Rust,' in which she wistfully recalled their affair, comparing Bob's blue eyes to the blue of robins' eggs. Many thought it was the best song she had ever written.

In the fall of 1975, what became known as The Rolling Thunder Revue began to take shape as more and more artists were invited to tour. The Revue grew organically, with friends passing the word on to musicians they knew. For instance, Bobby Neuwirth was staying with abstract painter Larry Poons at his loft on Broadway. Guitarist Mick Ronson was also staying there, as was Henry 'T-Bone' Burnett, a tall Texan guitarist with very prominent eyes. One night after a few drinks at the Other End, everybody adjourned to the loft for a jam session. Before playing, the musicians shot baskets at one end of the loft, and Larry Poons showed Bob the enormous abstract paintings he was working on. He created pictures by flinging paint at a canvas and then cropping the canvas. Poons asked Bob where he thought the crop should go. 'He knew straight off,' says Poons. 'Then he called it, "The Pumpkin Painting." Because it had pumpkin colors in it, like orange and black.' The name stuck. There was a glorious jam session in Poons's loft that night, with Bob alternating between guitar and grand piano as he played the new songs from *Desire*. 'That was one of the most memorable nights of my life,' says T-Bone Burnett. 'Bob put a stack of typewritten pages on the piano and started singing "Joey," "Romance in Durango," "One More Cup of Coffee" – all those songs.' There seemed to be a magical quality about Bob. 'That was the first time I noticed – I don't know whether he time-travels or shape-shifts or what you would call it,' adds Burnett, laughing. 'But you would look at him one moment and he would be like a fifteen-year-old kid and you would look at him the next moment and he would look like an eighty-year-old man, and at the time he was in his mid-thirties.'

T-Bone Burnett and another young guitarist at the session, Steven Soles, joined the pit band. 'That was kind of how The Rolling Thunder Revue was born,' says Soles. 'It was born out of that night.' The band was completed with the addition of Luther Rix on percussion and teenager David Mansfield on violin, slide guitar, and mandolin. Mansfield began playing with Neuwirth at the

Bitter End after his girlfriend brought him to the club. 'It was kind of a scene down there,' he says, 'kind of a one-ring circus with a sort of drug and tequila haze over the whole thing.' Allen Ginsberg was invited to recite poetry. Actress and singer Ronee Blakley – who had recently starred in the Robert Altman movie *Nashville* – canceled a tour of her own to join the Revue. She also sang backup vocals on a new version of 'Hurricane,' which had to be rerecorded because of a legal problem with the lyrics. George Lois took a tape of the song to Rubin Carter in prison, telling him it would be released as a single. 'He lost his mind! It was beautiful,' says Lois. 'There was tears in his eyes. He was crying.'

Everybody booked into the Gramercy Park Hotel, which was near Bob's publishing office, as Levy conducted rehearsals. To the surprise of many of the musicians, Bob had decided to make a movie of the tour. At his own expense, he hired two professional crews – 'A' and 'B' – under the supervision of Howard Alk and Mel Howard. It became clear that Bob envisaged the film, which he would call *Renaldo & Clara*, as much more than a concert documentary. It would be a work of art in the style of European auteurs, with Bob and his friends acting out dramatic scenes. Bob hired the young playwright Sam Shepard to write a script. 'We don't have to make any connections,' Bob told him when they met, which made no sense to Shepard or anybody else and was a foretaste of the chaos that was to come. Shepard just nodded his head as if he understood. Meeting Dylan was such a powerful experience, and one inevitably had so many preconceptions about the man, it was hard to stop and say, *Wait a minute, what are you talking about?* Bob then asked if Shepard had ever seen *Shoot the Piano Player*.

'Is that the kind of movie you want to make?'

'Something like that,' he said, as enigmatic as ever.

The playwright soon discovered that his scriptwriting services were, in fact, completely superfluous. 'We never actually wrote a script,' says Shepard, who decided instead to write a book about the tour, eventually published as the *Rolling Thunder Logbook*. 'In a way it's a failed book because it was an attempt to at least make something useful out of that time where I felt I just kind of [came] along for the ride.'

There was an Alice in Wonderland atmosphere even before the Revue set out on tour. Allen Ginsberg was screaming for attention, anxious to get as much of his poetry on film as possible. Scarlet Rivera was so nervous she was virtually unable to talk, and absorbed herself by painting patterns on her face with stage makeup. Roger McGuinn walked around with a slightly crazed expression, and an attaché case that contained a state-of-the-art mobile telephone. The press was represented by *Rolling Stone* journalist Larry Sloman, a man so seedy in appearance that Joan Baez nicknamed him Ratso after the character Ratso Rizzo in *Midnight Cowboy*.

On October 23, the cockeyed troupe, attended by film cameras and hangers-on, packed Gerde's Folk City, where Bob and so many of his contemporaries had performed at the start of their careers in the early 1960s. Gerde's owner Mike Porco, who had taken Bob to join the musicians' union back in 1961, was celebrating his sixty-first birthday, and he was delighted to welcome Bob back to the club for a night of music and revelry.

Years before, when he was Bob's traveling companion and gofer, Bobby Neuwirth was known as 'Tacos-to-Go.' Now he appeared on stage at Gerde's, wearing a Zorro mask and Bob's gray fedora hat, as 'The Masked Tortilla.' This was the character he adopted for *Renaldo & Clara*. After he read a poem at Gerde's for the benefit of the cameras, Neuwirth surrendered the fedora and microphone to a pallid, unhealthy-looking Phil Ochs. Bloated by alcoholism, Ochs was a tragic figure, banned from the nearby Bitter End because of his drunkenness. Ochs had been one of the first people Bob had talked to about The Rolling Thunder Revue, and he desperately wanted to join the troupe. Unfortunately, it was inconceivable; part of the time he believed himself a character called John Train, and as such he was paranoid, aggressive, and suicidal. 'He was in a psychotic tailspin,' says friend Dave Van Ronk. Ochs's performance at Gerde's was sad for many to watch. Wearing Bob's fedora, he sang directly to Dylan and, when Dylan got up from his chair at one point, Ochs called out plaintively as if worried that he might leave the room. Bob replied that he was only going to the bar.

The Rolling Thunder Revue opened a week later, on October 30, 1975, in the historic town of Plymouth, Massachusetts. Plymouth's War Memorial Auditorium was a little theater, in accordance with Bob's stated aim to keep the tour intimate. It was so small that few name artists ever played the town, so there was high excitement in Plymouth when local radio announced a revue featuring Bob Dylan and Joan Baez, with sophisticated supporting characters including beat poet Allen Ginsberg and movie star Ronee Blakley. 'It was like the circus came to town,' says Blakley.

There was a party atmosphere from the start of the tour, with a good deal of heavy drinking. (At an uproarious gathering later in the tour, at Gordon Lightfoot's house, Neuwirth threw his jacket onto an open fire.) There was also heavy use of cocaine, a drug most musicians then considered a 'recreational energy source,' as Stoner puts it. 'You were suspicious of anybody who didn't do drugs back then.' Ramblin' Jack Elliott says he was warned not to buy cocaine from dealers. 'They were afraid if I had coke in my pocket I might be busted. It would be embarrassing for them and me.' Instead, artists could get cocaine from someone who traveled with the tour. 'So right before the show every night I'd go see that guy, and go [*makes huge sniffing sound*] "Thank you!" And I'd go on stage . . . It was good coke.'

Use of cocaine was partly responsible for the extraordinarily energetic show that opened in Plymouth;

several of the musicians who crowded the stage seemed wired. Even so, there was clearly an undeniable passion for the music. 'I've been seeing Bob perform since 1966,' says Ratso Sloman. 'I've never seen him as good as he was during the Rolling Thunder tour, night in, night out. He was just amazing, phenomenal energy, and incredible passion. They tried to go out and do something unique and they succeeded. It was just amazing music every night – the most incredible conviction and spirit.'

There was an old-fashioned, almost vaudevillian feel about the way the show was staged. A yellow stage curtain, stenciled with circus-type lettering, rolled up to reveal gypsy-like musicians standing on a funky carpet, and they were playing instruments that were incongruous in the age of disco music – including mandolin, violins, and big, old acoustic guitars. (Mick Ronson tried to get Bob to play electric guitar with a foot pedal attachment that would have given him a more contemporary sound, asking Bob's roadie to hook up the gadget. Bob asked suspiciously: 'Yeah, but will it make me sound like Buddy Guy?') The staging was very effective. 'I was able to make this stuff very theatrical in the sense that the audience was taken on a ride,' says Levy. 'For the beginning of the evening I would have the whole band come on and each of the guys would do a number. We'd go through a chunk of the program like that before we got to the next segment and during that time, in between songs, I would turn everything shadowy blueish. Some people would go off and others would come on and, at one point, I just had Bob come on without any introduction. At first the crowd didn't think it was him, because the big star usually comes on last. He had a hat on and he would be in the shadows, standing there with the band, and they would start up a song and, little by little, lights would come up and it would be him playing along on somebody else's song. The crowd would go crazy.'

Bob appeared wearing his fedora, with flowers in the

hat, and some nights his face was painted white. One night he wore a transparent plastic mask. His clothing was faded blue jeans, a white shirt, and black vest. His performances made for riveting theater, his eyes fixed on the middle distance as he poured out his songs. 'On the third or fourth song, Bob pulled out a harmonica, played one note, and the audience made a sound that was louder than anything I had ever heard, except maybe a jet taking off,' says T-Bone Burnett. *Desire* had not yet been released, but the new songs from the record were delivered with such energy that the crowd took them up with enthusiasm and responded with thunderous applause. 'There wasn't a moment of question mark on the audience's face,' says Scarlet Rivera. One of the unexpected highlights of the concerts was the strange song 'Isis,' which Bob performed at a blazingly fast pace, most unusually without his guitar. His left hand twitched nervously by his side as he burned through the song. Then he threw his hands to his face and played his harmonica like a demon. On December 4 Bob told the audience in Montreal, Quebec, that 'Isis' was a song 'about marriage.' At the end of the penultimate verse there was an exchange between narrator and lover, who asked if he was going to stay with her. Bob delivered the answer with a gleeful 'YES!' and the audience joined in. Here was the same cathartic energy unlocked by the refrain in 'Like a Rolling Stone,' but without the negativity. This Montreal performance was recorded, later featured in *Renaldo & Clara* and included in the *Biograph* box set. 'That particular track embodies the . . . great free, rollicking wild Rolling Thunder Revue thing, with Mick Ronson rockin' out and two drummers wailing,' says Stoner, who screamed the last verse with Bob. 'It was like Coltrane.'

Although the show ran very long – up to four hours some nights – Bob was usually on stage less than an hour, and his contributions were carefully timed for maximum dramatic effect. Consequently, he usually concluded

Act I with 'Isis,' leaving the audience wanting more. At the start of Act II, Dylan and Baez often sang Johnny Ace's love song 'Never Let Me Go,' one of the first songs Baez learned as a child. They began behind the curtain, the audience *thinking* they were hearing Dylan and Baez singing together, though realizing that this had not happened since the mid-sixties. Then the curtain was rolled up to reveal that it was indeed Dylan and Baez together. Apart from the nostalgic impact, there was also an obvious sexual chemistry between them, and this became one of the central themes of the film *Renaldo & Clara*. Sara Dylan was with the tour, fragile-thin and looking older than her thirty-six years, but she seemed remarkably cool about Baez's presence. Indeed, according to Baez, they even became friendly.

Filming was constant, recording every aspect of the tour, but Bob was most concerned with the improvised scenes. These could be quite bizarre, and did not follow the conventions of filmmaking, partly because no one individual was directing. (When Ronee Blakley asked Bob in exasperation who was directing 'this goddamn movie,' she says Dylan and Neuwirth pointed at each other.) Before the Plymouth show, Scarlet Rivera was invited to drive with Bob and a film crew to an abandoned farmhouse to shoot a scene. Typically there was no script for the scene and no direction from Bob or anybody else about what Rivera should do. They simply talked to each other. 'I think it had to do with destiny,' she says, 'having met some time in some other place. Two spirits meeting again . . . it just evolved.'

The Revue rolled through autumnal New England, with frequent stops along the way to film more improvised scenes, including a visit to Jack Kerouac's grave in Lowell, Massachusetts, where Bob told Allen Ginsberg that he wanted to be buried in an unmarked grave.

The excitement of the tour attracted big-name guest stars, such as Joni Mitchell, who flew in from California to play songs from her new album, *The Hissing of*

Summer Lawns. Another star who paid a visit, but did not perform with the Revue, was Bruce Springsteen. 'Who's this guy, *Springfield*?' Bob asked Rob Stoner, before a show in New Haven, Connecticut. It was almost inconceivable that Bob did not know the shy, pock-marked young Springsteen, who recently was signed to Columbia by John Hammond, and was being hyped as 'the new Dylan.' With a massive promotional campaign, his *Born to Run* album had already gone gold and would eventually sell more than six million copies in the United States – far more than any Dylan album ever would. (*Blood on the Tracks* and *Desire* were the two best-selling studio albums of Bob's career, yet it was not until the 1990s that they reached multiplatinum status*; their combined sales still do not approach those of *Born to Run.*) It was well known that Springsteen's career was being boosted with seemingly endless amounts of Columbia money. 'Big Red,' as Columbia was called within the industry, never promoted Bob in that way. He came from an earlier era when artists were left to their own devices. 'I didn't know if [Bob] was joking or not. How could he have *not* known who the guy was?' asks Rob Stoner. The meeting between Dylan and Springsteen was perfectly amicable and the only reason Springsteen did not perform with the Revue was that he wanted to use his E Street Band, and Bob wanted guests to use the house band. In years to come they would actually become fairly close friends.

Although there was a convivial, almost family atmosphere about the tour, with friends joining the company as they rolled along, Bob set himself apart from most of the musicians and crew. He traveled in his own deluxe motor home. Musicians and guest stars followed in a cramped tour bus, taking turns resting on the six tiny cots

*In 1994 the RIAA certified *Blood on the Tracks* as having reached two million sales in the United States. *Desire* reached the same level of sales in 1999.

available. Although the musicians saw Bob every night on stage, he rarely spoke to anybody outside his coterie of favorites and remained for the most part a figure of mystery to the others.

'Isn't Bob wonderful?' Ronee Blakley asked Mick Ronson one day.

'I don't know,' he replied. 'He's never spoken to me.'

Despite the fact that Sara was with the tour for much of the time, there was plenty of gossip about who Bob was sleeping with. Many assumed he was involved in a relationship with Scarlet Rivera. She refuses to confirm or deny it. Sexy Ronee Blakley was also linked with Bob. 'Oh I loved him, right away, just loved him,' she says. 'He was exactly what I thought he would be like. Funny and mysterious and shy and dear and vulnerable.' But she denies a sexual relationship. 'I was not lovers with Bob. I was friends with Bob . . . I was blamed for the breakup of his marriage. But it's not true.'

Ruth Tyrangiel, the actress who later launched a palimony suit against Bob, was also on the tour. She played 'the girlfriend' in a scene opposite singer Ronnie Hawkins, who played 'Bob Dylan' in *Renaldo & Clara*. Hawkins tempted the girl to come on tour with him, apologizing that he did not have time to 'court or romance' a young lady of 'your caliber.' Beethoven's sweetly romantic 'Moonlight Sonata' played in the background, contrasting sharply with Hawkins's blatantly lustful intentions. 'Ronnie Hawkins would pretend to have an affair with one of Dylan's old mistresses, replicating his impression of Dylan's relationship with her,' explains associate producer Mel Howard, who also says Bob's old girlfriends were 'coming out of the woodwork' during the tour. 'Some of them traveled with Bob; it was quite an open thing.'

Sara Dylan had agreed to join the tour partly because she was going to be one of the principal actors in the movie, playing roles such as a prostitute and the woman called Clara. Despite the fact that she was obliged to play a whore, it seems that Bob intended the film to be in part a tribute to his wife. (The name of Bob's production company – Lombard Street Films, Inc. – was taken from the street in Wilmington, Delaware, where she was born.) Bob played the part of Renaldo, Clara's roving lover. In the scenes they had together, Bob and Sara held and caressed each other in a surprisingly intimate way considering how much they valued their privacy. At one point in the film, Joan Baez interrupted them. Sara (as Clara) asked Baez coolly if she had the correct room. In another scene, Renaldo and Clara held each other tightly as 'Sad-Eyed Lady of the Lowlands' played. In yet another scene, Baez asked Bob: 'What would've happened if we ever got married, Bob?'

'I married the woman I love,' said Bob, looking slightly uncomfortable. It was one of the most direct comments he ever made about his relationship with Sara.

After five weeks of concerts, filming, and playacting, the first leg of The Rolling Thunder Revue culminated in a benefit concert at Madison Square Garden on December 8, 1975. The Night of the Hurricane was intended to raise money for Rubin Carter's legal battle. Muhammad Ali spoke to Carter on the telephone from the stage. The excitement and confusion was such that by the end of the concert many, including Bob, erroneously believed Carter had been acquitted.

After a Christmas break, a second benefit concert for Carter was staged at the Astrodome in Houston, Texas, on January 25, 1976. Despite the fact that both *Blood on the Tracks* and *Desire* had hit number one in recent months, Night of the Hurricane II was a flop that foreshadowed a difficult second leg of The Rolling Thunder Revue. Stevie Wonder was added to the bill at the Astrodome to help the draw, but ticket sales were still very poor; on the night of the event the acoustics were dreadful, and it did relatively little for the cause Bob was championing. The combined gross of this benefit and the one in New York was more than $600,000, but after costs only a sixth went to the Carter fund.

Two months after the Houston show there was better news, however, when the New Jersey Supreme Court ordered that Carter be given a retrial and then freed him on bail. For a short time there was jubilation among his supporters. However, Carter would be convicted once again at his second trial in December and he was returned to prison where he remained until 1985, when the conviction was finally overturned. 'He got framed worse than the first time,' says campaigner George Lois. 'I was embarrassed, not for myself, because I know what I did was right, but for Bobby and Muhammad who worked so hard. Most people said, *Son of a bitch. After all that, the guy's guilty!*'

After a spring break of almost three months – during which time Bob worked with Eric Clapton on Clapton's new album, *No Reason to Cry*, sleeping in a tent of bed sheets in the garden of the Shangri-La studio in California – The Rolling Thunder Revue reconvened in April 1976 in Clearwater, Florida. The venue for rehearsals was the Belleview Biltmore, a big resort hotel that was popular with retired people. When the musicians arrived to begin work, they found the atmosphere was very different from that of the first leg of the tour. Bob had finished filming *Renaldo & Clara*, so the film people were gone from the entourage. So was Sam Shepard. Ramblin' Jack Elliott had been rather cruelly dropped from the show, though he went to see Bob personally in California during the spring break to ask to stay on. 'I was anxious to know and willing to go out again. [Bob] was embarrassed by this question, because they weren't planning to take me. He said, "I don't have anything to do with who gets to go, but I heard a rumor that Joan Baez is going and Kinky Friedman."* Indeed,

*A comedic Jewish country and western artist who later became well known as a novelist.

Kinky Friedman was my replacement, and they never called me.' Stars who had been invited back began demanding better billing and more pay. Joan Baez in particular wanted more money. Bob seemed removed from all the politics, spending his time instead with various girlfriends in a bungalow in the grounds of the hotel. There was no sign of Sara for the time being.

During rehearsals in the Starlight Ballroom, Bob and the musicians learned that drunken, crazed Phil Ochs had hanged himself at his sister Sonny's house in Queens, New York. He had been thirty-five. One of his final disappointments had been the fact that he was not asked to join the tour. Bob and Phil Ochs had always had an uneasy relationship, and had disagreed in the past. Bob was clearly upset by the news that Ochs had killed himself. Still, he did not attend the funeral or even respond when asked to take part in a tribute concert held on May 28. 'If Dylan really cared about Phil he would have had the courtesy to pick up the telephone or write a letter,' says Sonny, who was left feeling very bitter about Dylan, perhaps with some justification.

Meanwhile, Bob began the second leg of The Rolling Thunder Revue. After giving warm-up concerts in nearby resort towns, a show was staged at the Belleview Biltmore in Clearwater on April 17 for an NBC television special. During the show, a row of torpid bodies sat behind Bob on a platform raised above the stage. It was partly because of this lifeless audience that Bob hated the film and refused to allow it to be screened. As a consequence, he would have to make a replacement concert film for NBC before the end of the tour. Unfortunately, the subsequent tour of the southern United States lacked joie de vivre. There was less enthusiasm for Bob in the South than there had been in the northeast of the country and at least three shows were canceled due to poor ticket sales. 'It was meant to be done once and when they tried to milk two out of it, it really wasn't happening,' says Rob Stoner.

It was also clear that Bob's marriage was in its terminal stages. Although his relationship with Sara had seemed strained and maybe unorthodox during the first leg of the tour, there had been an undeniable aura of romance around the couple. On the second leg, Bob had flagrant affairs with various exotic women including Stephanie Buffington, who joined the entourage to teach Bob how to tightrope walk. When Sara descended upon the tour for a brief visit, she sent groupies scampering for cover. One day Joan Baez walked past Bob's dressing room and saw Sara sitting upright in a chair, with Bob kneeling before her in what looked like a distraught state. The marriage was unraveling fast and Bob and Sara had several bitter public arguments. One of the worst scenes was in New Orleans on May 3. Sara left the tour shortly afterward and Bob channeled his frustration into nightly performances of 'Idiot Wind.' The band could not help but be inspired by Bob's towering rage. 'Bob was filling it with such black energy and venom,' says David Mansfield. Bob also looked different on stage. The fedora with its cheerful spray of flowers was gone. Instead his head was wrapped in a bandana as though he was injured.

Bob decided that he would make the replacement concert film for NBC on May 23 at an open-air sports stadium in Fort Collins, Colorado. The weather was inclement and Sara unexpectedly turned up with the children and Bob's mother, grimly determined to celebrate Bob's thirty-fifth birthday the next day. Beset by personal problems, forced to perform for the cameras in bitterly cold and wet conditions, Bob gave a brilliant performance, later released as the *Hard Rain* television special and live album. 'Bob was in a pretty awful state of mind, and on top of it all, the physical conditions of the concert were grueling. Because it wasn't just raining, it was also freezing,' says Mansfield, who was so cold he had to play wearing gloves. Instruments were out of tune because of the damp and musicians were getting electric shocks. The sound was also ragged because Bob insisted on playing lead guitar. 'That was the other thing that was a new development during that tour. Bob, for the first time, started playing electric lead guitar. And at that time he really couldn't play it very well at all,' adds Mansfield. 'Sometimes he might be in another key for a couple of notes.' One high point in Fort Collins was when Dylan and Baez harmonized on a thrilling 'I Pity the Poor Immigrant,' propelled by Howie Wyeth on piano. They shared a microphone and, on the final notes of the refrain, their mouths came so close it seemed they would kiss. Bob widened his mouth further at the last moment, getting closer still as he rang the last nuance from the phrase. Then Baez broke away into a sexy dance, grinning broadly as she shook her maracas. 'Idiot Wind' was a howl of anger, twisting into regret, as Sara and the children stood just off stage. The performance was grimly fascinating for those who saw it live, as well as for those who saw it later on film; it was like watching a house burn down.

After one more show on May 25 in Salt Lake City, where Bob played an unprecedented live version of the epic 'Lily, Rosemary and the Jack of Hearts' (writing the first line of each verse on his cuff so he'd remember the words), the tour was over. The musicians now had to return to normal life, where they did their own laundry, paid their own bills, and did not have to dial nine to get an outside line. Bob seemed as disoriented as everybody else. Despite the fact that the second leg of the tour had been a less than pleasant experience, he told Baez that he wanted it to go on indefinitely. Teachers and nannies would be hired so everybody could bring their children. They would become true gypsy troubadours. This was clearly a fantasy, and a reflection of the fact that he did not want to get back to his day-to-day life because he had so many problems to sort out with Sara. It was easier to be on the road.

* * *

Bob did not go back on the road in 1976, but he gave one more major live performance, at a concert celebrating The Band.

The Band's fortunes had declined since the early seventies. Their records were increasingly less successful and the group was riven with problems, including the fact that Richard Manuel was a floundering alcoholic and Levon Helm and Robbie Robertson by this time barely spoke to each other. A grandiose farewell concert was staged, with a fabulous lineup of guest artists ranging from Ronnie Hawkins through major stars like Eric Clapton, Joni Mitchell, and Van Morrison to Bob himself. Warner Bros. backed the project with $1.5 million on the condition Bob would participate in a film of the show, directed by Martin Scorsese, and allow his guest appearance to be featured as part of a triple live album. *The Last Waltz* was staged on Thanksgiving Day 1976 at the Winterland Theater in San Francisco, the set decorated with props from a production of *La Traviata*.

Like The Rolling Thunder Revue, *The Last Waltz* was fueled by cocaine. 'It was ankle deep,' says Michael McClure, who read poetry as part of the concert. 'When I look at that film, I get a coke high.' Backstage there was a cocaine room, painted white and decorated with noses cut out of Groucho Marx masks. A tape played sniffing noises. Neil Young came out to sing 'Helpless' with a white lump hanging from his nose. The producers had to hire a Hollywood optical company to have the lump removed from the film.

Minutes before he was due on stage Bob informed the producers he did not want to be filmed. In fact, he wanted all seven cameras turned *away* from the stage. He made his decision partly because he had his own film coming out. Martin Scorsese nearly had heart failure. Without Bob, there would be no movie. A succession of people went into Bob's dressing room to plead with him. He was closeted with David Braun, Howard Alk, and Louis Kemp. It was Alk who was most insistent that Bob should not jeopardize the exclusivity of *Renaldo & Clara* by appearing in another movie. The delegates begged Bob to reconsider, if not for the sake of the movie then for the sake of The Band. Bob finally conceded that they could film two out of the four songs he planned to perform. He would have people on stage to make sure his wishes were seen to.

'Louis [Kemp] was put up there next to me and Marty [Scorsese] and Bill Graham, right up [on] stage, to kind of monitor when they could film and when they couldn't,' says Jonathan Taplin, executive producer of *The Last Waltz*. Bob said they could not film his opening number. Consequently, in the movie Bob was not seen coming on stage. They started filming from 'Forever Young.' Then, on a whim, Bob reprised the first song, 'Baby, Let Me Follow You Down.' According to Taplin, Louis Kemp froze 'like a deer in the headlights,' not knowing what to do. 'He started to turn to me and said, "Turn off the cameras! Turn off the cameras!" Bill Graham just grabbed him by the jacket and said, "Shut the fuck up and get out of here." Marty was saying, "Fellas, keep shooting! Keep shooting!"' Out of this chaos came one of the best music documentaries ever made.

At the end of the concert Bob returned to Point Dume, California, where his fantasy mansion was almost finished. He would have to try and make sense of the *Renaldo & Clara* film project, which he had put to one side during the past year, and he and Sara would now have to decide whether they had any future together as a couple.

CHAPTER 8

FAITH

The $2.5million remodeling of Bob and Sara's fantasy home at Point Dume in California had caused some of the problems in their marriage. Each time Bob returned from a trip, he altered the design of the house and they fell to bickering over details. The mansion eventually became so extraordinary it attracted the interest of the press. Photographs of the property began appearing in magazines, as photographers hired helicopters to fly overhead. Fans who saw the pictures came to the house, as they had come in search of Dylan in Woodstock and in New York City. One deranged fan sprayed black paint over the windows, and Bob had to hire security guards for protection. There were also problems with neighbors, just as there had been in New York. In September 1976, the Dylans were sued by the people next door, Stanley and Maria Primmer, over use of an access road. This case rumbled on until 1978, and the Dylans had to give statements and deal with lawyers. It was a petty aggravation, but it nonetheless added to the pressures they were under.

Following the 1976 tour and The Band's *Last Waltz*, the Dylans' marriage took another turn for the worse. Bob became 'continuously quarrelsome,' according to Sara. He sometimes looked at her in a menacing way and ordered her from the house. 'I was in such fear of him that I locked doors to protect myself from his violent outbursts and temper tantrums.' She also claimed the children were disturbed by Bob's 'bizarre lifestyle.' Part of this lifestyle was his womanizing. Sara claimed that she came down to breakfast on February 13, 1977, to find

Bob at the table with the children and a woman named Malka whom Bob had apparently moved into a house on the estate. Sara believed he wanted Malka in the mansion. There was an argument and Bob allegedly hit Sara, injuring her jaw. She claims he then told her to leave.

Sara moved to a hotel and set about finding a lawyer. At the time, the most famous divorce lawyer in California was Marvin M. Mitchelson, who made his name by representing Lee Marvin's girlfriend in her ground-breaking palimony lawsuit. (It was Mitchelson who coined the term 'palimony.') As Mitchelson recalls, Sara was recommended to him by mogul David Geffen. 'I want to send someone over to you. I'd like you to take good care of her,' Geffen apparently told Mitchelson. 'Her name is Sara Dylan.' Mitchelson did not immediately realize to whom Geffen was referring. He quips: 'About $60 million later I knew every song he ever wrote.'

Mitchelson says Sara came to him in a 'feisty' mood. 'She loved Bob Dylan – no question about it – but he chose to spend his time elsewhere and took up new relationships, and that all became part of the case.' The fact that Sara had endured years of marital problems before deciding to take this step was, in Mitchelson's experience, sadly typical. 'These things don't happen on the spur of the moment. They build up.' Sara dragged up grievances from the past, including the allegation that Bob had not been present at the birth of their first three children. She then filed for divorce at Los Angeles Superior Court on March 1, claiming permanent custody of their five children; exclusive use of the Point Dume mansion; child support; alimony; and a division of Bob's fortune. Her counsel applied for a restraining order against Bob because Sara claimed to be frightened of him. Superior Court Commissioner John R. Alexander granted Sara temporary custody of the children. Because they were minors – aged between six and fifteen – the judge further ordered, on March 8, that the case be sealed. At the time, Bob was working with Howard Alk on the editing of *Renaldo & Clara*. Alk lived on the Point Dume estate, in a guest house separated from the main residence by a chain-link fence. There was an editing suite in the garage and, after weeks when Bob had shown only passing interest in the project, he came here most days to edit the film with a view to a cinematic release in 1978. ('I realized he was getting serious when he put his glasses on,' Alk joked.) Because Bob was working on the film, he was allowed to continue living at Point Dume and another house was rented for Sara and the children down the coast at Malibu Colony.

Under California law, Sara was entitled to half the 'community property' acquired during marriage. This included houses and land in five states, cash, and music rights. 'Those musical rights were enormous,' says Mitchelson. 'That was the real value.' The years of Bob's marriage had been the most creative and successful period in his career, spanning the albums *Blonde on Blonde* through *Desire*, and including all his major hit singles. Mitchelson compiled a list of the songs Bob wrote and recorded between 1965 and 1977. 'It went on for pages and pages,' he says. 'I became sort of a fan [because] I realized how good he was.' Music rights boosted Bob's notional wealth to approximately $60 million. Because Bob wanted to keep the Point Dume mansion, real estate was traded against cash and Sara's share rose to $36 million. If Bob ever sold his music catalogue, Sara would be entitled to a further payout. All the time he retained ownership, she would share in the royalties. 'They keep coming in, year after year after year,' says Mitchelson. 'We're talking about millions.'

Sara needed help with the children and was introduced to Faridi McFree, a pixielike woman of Middle Eastern descent with a passion for New Age ideas. McFree meditated under a copper pyramid and had invented a concept called Art Healing, which amounted to expressing oneself by drawing pictures. Sara had a penchant for New Age ideas herself and she hired McFree to help mind the children, and to do Art Healing with them. McFree would spend half of each week in the carriage house on Sara's rented property and the two women naturally talked about Bob. 'She just said that Bob was too much of a womanizer and she couldn't take it anymore,' says McFree. 'This evidently happened all through their marriage.'

The relationship between McFree and Sara soon soured, however, partly because McFree felt Sara treated her like a maid. Before they parted company, Sara asked McFree to look after the house while she took the children on a vacation to Hawaii. McFree agreed and she was at the house on her own when, on June 30, news broke that the Dylan divorce had been settled. McFree found Bob's number in Sara's address book and called him at Point Dume, even though they barely knew each other.

'Are you okay?' she asked.

'No, I'm not,' replied Bob. 'I need somebody to talk to. What are you doing tonight?'

McFree drove to Point Dume that evening. She found Bob standing in the driveway, looking like a crazy person. They entered the mansion, walking past the huge slate mural of a whale, and went on into the Great Room with its stone fireplace, bare concrete floor, and a sofa the children had worn out by bouncing up and down on it like a trampoline. Bob lit the fire and opened a bottle of wine. Outside, the trees were rustling and the waves were breaking down on the beach. 'It got all romantic,' says McFree. 'And before you know [it], I didn't go home.' McFree says she and Bob fell in love that night and that he asked her to move in. He also put her on salary; she became a postproduction assistant on *Renaldo & Clara*. McFree had to face Sara when she went back to pick up her things from Malibu Colony. 'She hardly looked at me,' says McFree. 'She thought I had betrayed her, just like so many women.'

During the divorce, Bob's mood alternated between depression and forced jolliness. He and Allen Ginsberg added raucous backing vocals to a Leonard Cohen song, called 'Don't Go Home With Your Hard-on,' at a session produced by Phil Spector. Bob hung out in Hollywood with friends, including sometime girlfriend and actress Sally Kirkland, and, uncharacteristically, he posed for press photographers. It seemed he wanted Sara to see him having a good time. McFree noted that Bob had numerous girlfriends, and apparently unlimited opportunities for sex. A maid suggested they have a threesome. Friends came on to Bob in front of her. 'This is how women were with him. It was just disgusting.' McFree also noticed that although Bob was very private he sometimes liked to have fun with his celebrity. One day he stopped to give a girl hitchhiker a lift, making sure the girl recognized him. Bob told McFree that although he was comfortable with his fame, it had been a problem in his marriage. 'He told me [Sara] didn't know how to handle it, but he did,' says McFree. 'I believe him, too, because he was easy with it.'

There were also periods of deep unhappiness. McFree claims Bob told her that he had, at one stage, considered suicide. However, this seems very out of character for such a strong-minded individual; Bob's negative emotions were more often angry than despairing. During 1977 Bob went to visit Steven Soles, who had formed the Alpha Band with fellow Rolling Thunder alumni T-Bone Burnett and David Mansfield, and he performed a set of new songs for them that expressed his anger at the breakup of his marriage. 'They were all very, very tough dark, dark, dark songs. None of those saw the light of day. I never heard them again . . . They got discarded because I think they were too strong,' says Soles. 'They were the continuation of the Bob and Sara Tale . . . more on the angry side of that conflict.' One song, title 'I'm Cold,' sent a shiver down Soles's spine. 'It was dark . . . scathing and tough and venomous,' he says. '[A song] that would bring a chill to your bones. That's what it did to me. T-Bone and I, when he left, our mouths were just wide open. We couldn't even believe what we'd heard.'

Meanwhile, the divorce had been settled quickly but the custody battle dragged on. Bob's relationship with McFree made things more complex because Sara did not want a woman she thought had betrayed her to be involved with her children. Bob's lawyers advised him to stop seeing McFree, but he did not want to. Neither did he want to refuse point-blank, so he hid his girlfriend when his lawyers came to Point Dume to talk to him, and he sneaked her up to Minnesota for a family holiday without telling them. As Samuel's ninth birthday fell during this time, McFree helped organize a party to cheer up the sensitive boy. She also played tennis with the children and painted with them in Bob's art studio, while Bob used the vacation to write new songs. McFree was in bed at the farm on August 16, 1977, when Bob gave her the news that Elvis Presley had died. McFree said she never cared for Presley's music. 'That's all I had to say – he didn't talk to me for a week.' Bob retreated into a period of mourning. 'I had a breakdown!' he later said. 'If it wasn't for Elvis and Hank Williams, I couldn't be doing what I do today.'

By the time they returned to California, Bob decided he wanted permanent custody of his children. His decision was partly caused by Sara taking them to Hawaii. He worried Sara would make her home there, and his lawyers complained that Sara had taken the children out of California without prior agreement. Bob wanted them returned immediately. He had the children home by October and they had fun together over Halloween, trick or treating with Allen Ginsberg in the L.A. suburb of Pacific Palisades, a short drive from Point Dume. 'Allen and Bob wore these masks [so] no one could tell who they were,' says McFree. 'They were free to be who they really were – crazy clowns.' The custody battle was fought with increasing bitterness through the fall. On advice from his lawyers, Bob wore a business suit – borrowed from the wardrobe department of a film studio – for court appearances. But he did not shave or cut his long fingernails, and so he looked rather strange. In court, Sara's lawyers named McFree as the children's surrogate mother and accused her of being unfit to care for them. Bob hired a psychiatrist to provide contrary evidence that he did have a home fit for children. The psychiatrist interviewed McFree, who told him about her New Age beliefs. This, she says, led people to think she was 'a lunatic.' Despite her unusual beliefs, the psychiatrist agreed with Bob that he would be the best parent to look after the children. This obviously partisan evidence did not impress the judge when it was presented in court. 'They just went in there to get a quick opinion and thought that would help them with the court,' says Mitchelson. 'The judge became somewhat angry and [said], "I determine what's in the best interests, and not some doctor."'

As the hearing continued, Bob had the children with him at Point Dume and he remained reluctant to share custody with Sara. Bob and his lawyer met with Mitchelson in a parking lot in Malibu to try and solve the problem. The meeting turned into a brawl when McFree became enraged and attacked Mitchelson. 'He was talking to Bob and he was just such a belligerent, arrogant human being that I lost control,' says McFree. 'I grabbed him by the throat.'

Mitchelson then obtained a court order demanding Bob return the children to Sara, and sent process servers to Point Dume to give Bob the papers. The security guards would not let them in, however. So Mitchelson gave Sara what turned out to be some ill-judged advice. 'I had to tell Sara: Look, they are not going to give you the kids. Go out with a couple of [the] detectives. Go to the school. Try to do this nicely. And just show them the court order and pick the kids up from the school.' This led to one of the most unpleasant episodes in the custody battle.

Until now, the Dylan children had been raised in a relatively normal way. Apart from the eldest child, Maria, who attended boarding school in Vermont, they were educated at public schools, using the regular school bus and bringing friends home to play. They used the distinctive surname Dylan, and yet there had been no need for special security. Their protection were the rules of simple good sense that Bob and Sara had instilled from an early age. If Dad, as the children called their father in a straightforward way, was approached by fans or press, the kids crossed the road and blended with the crowd. No member of the family – other than Bob – ever spoke to the press or posed for photographs. Consequently, despite the fact that Dad was one of the most famous entertainers in the world, virtually no photographs of the children, or articles about them, appeared in newspapers. When they were written about, their names and ages were invariably incorrect, something that caused amusement within the family. In marked contrast to the children of other celebrities, the Dylan children did not become victims of reflected fame. As Bob once said: 'Marriage was a failure. Husband and wife was a failure, but father and mother wasn't a failure.'

What happened at Point Dume school was therefore shocking to the children; suddenly their mother was chasing them. When Sara was confronted by teachers, demanding to know what authority she had to take the children, an ugly scene ensued. 'Unfortunately, a melee took place because the teachers there were, of course, influenced to some degree by the fact they were dealing with a celebrity like Bob Dylan and were very protective,' says Mitchelson. 'They didn't wanna cooperate and we had a legitimate court order.' In an undignified skirmish, teacher Rex Burke was allegedly struck in the chest. Police were called and Sara was fined $125 for disrupting the school. 'I can honestly say that day is the most sensitive part of my life,' says Jakob Dylan. 'I remember it more vividly than almost any other day. I've never really discussed it with anybody. If I talked about it, I'd probably end up with a therapist within a half hour.'

Despite the incident at the school, Sara was eventually awarded custody. She moved from Malibu Colony into Beverly Hills, and enrolled the children at Beverly Hills High. During the holidays they spent time with their father on the farm in Minnesota or at his mansion at Point Dume, but only under the condition that Faridi McFree not have anything to do with them. Bob signed an agreement to that effect and let McFree drop out of his life. 'I wasn't a part of it anymore,' she says. 'He just wanted to have [the divorce] behind him and everything that was associated with it, including me.'

Renaldo & Clara premiered in Los Angeles and New York City on Wednesday, January 25, 1978. Bob made himself available in order to promote the film and explain what he had intended to do. 'It's about the essence of man being alienated from himself and how, in order to free himself, to be reborn, he has to go outside himself,' he told *Playboy*. The reviews were terrible. Many critics seemed to be grasping for an excuse to show that the legendary Bob Dylan was not infallible after all. But there was also some truth to many of the negative reviews. Pauline Kael wrote in *The New Yorker* that Bob was 'overpoweringly present' in the film and the viewer was 'invited to stare' at the legend, 'yet he is never in direct contact with us.' Parading one's ex-lover and ex-wife before the public as a thinly veiled fiction was a tease, and the film was unsatisfying because the improvisational scenes were neither an honest depiction of Bob's personal life nor convincing drama. The faults were magnified because the film ran to a tiresome length of almost four hours. It was virtually impossible to watch at one sitting, despite exciting concert footage, and was quickly withdrawn from an already limited cinema release. The failure crushed Bob's ambitions to direct further films and seriously depleted his bank account, having spent $1.25 million of his own money on the movie. 'I've got a few debts to pay off,' he told the *Los Angeles Times* candidly. 'I had a couple of bad years. I put a lot of money into the movie, built a big house . . . and there's the divorce. It costs a lot to get divorced in California.'

To recoup his losses, Bob signed with Jerry Weintraub's Management III – the company behind mainstream entertainers like Neil Diamond – and embarked on a lucrative world tour. Starting in Japan and continuing through the Far East, Europe, and the United States, he would play one hundred and fourteen shows to almost two million people in 1978, grossing in excess of $20 million. 'He agreed, more or less, [to] sell his soul,' says Patrick Stansfield, an associate of Neil Diamond, who became production supervisor for the tour. With the help of tried and trusted bass player Rob Stoner, Bob assembled an eight-piece band in the style of Neil Diamond's stage shows. Two of the most musically sophisticated members of The Rolling Thunder Revue – David Mansfield and Steven Soles – were asked back, but the 1978 tour was to be the antithesis of the informal carnival of 1975–76. Billy Cross, who had worked in the stage show *Hair*, was flown in from Denmark to play slick lead guitar. The drummer was big-hitting Englishman Ian Wallace, formerly of the rock band King Crimson. On percussion was Motown veteran Bobbye Hall, whom Bob paid $2,500 a week to compensate her for session work she would miss. He also paid handsomely for Steve Douglas, who played saxophone on many of Phil Spector's records. Alan Pasqua, a member of the modern jazz group Tony Williams' Lifetime, played keyboards. There would be three backing singers: Debi Dye-Gibson and Jo Ann Harris had sung together for years in stage shows including *Hair*; Helena Springs was a strikingly attractive girl out of high school. There were grumbles within the band that Springs was chosen more for her looks than any musical ability. 'As a singer, she was a hell of a dancer,' says Debi Dye-Gibson. In the style of Neil Diamond's stage show, the musicians would have to wear costumes. These were designed – in primarily black or white fabrics – by Hollywood costumer 'Spoony' Bill Whitten, and they were garish. 'We looked like hookers,' grumbles Dye-Gibson. 'I felt stupid singing "Blowin' in the Wind" with [my] boobs hanging out.' The men felt equally self-conscious in their rather ostentatious outfits, which they referred to as *uniforms*. 'The band looked like a large aggregation of pimps,' laughs Billy Cross.

The 1978 tour was, essentially, a greatest-hits show. Bob received a telegram from the Japanese promoters stipulating which songs they expected him to perform. He sent guitar technician Joel Bernstein to a bookstore to buy a copy of his collected lyrics, *Writings and Drawings*. 'He started flipping through it [and] playing things out of it that he hadn't played in years.' The band rehearsed at an old factory at 2219 Main Street, Santa Monica, which Bob named Rundown Studios (that part of Santa Monica was then rather seedy). Apart from rehearsal space, there were offices for his touring company, and beds so that he could sleep over. He would often hang out at Rundown after work, drinking and talking with the musicians. As Cross recalls, Bob bemoaned the state of his private life: '[Bob] said, "You know, [this] lawyer's calling me and this other lawyer's calling me, and they wanna take my money and they wanna take this and I said, 'Hey, wait a minute! You can't do that to me – I'm Bob Dylan!' " ' The audacity of this remark – as if Bob believed he was too important to be affected by the routine procedure of divorce – took Billy Cross's breath away. Then, to his credit, Bob realized what a foolish thing he had said and laughed about it. 'You realize, of course, why shouldn't he think like that?' says Cross. 'He's certainly paid the price for having been Bob Dylan, God only knows.'

During rehearsals, Bob and Stoner worked up elaborate

big-band arrangements of Bob's most famous songs, presenting them as show tunes in incongruous idioms. 'Don't Think Twice, It's All Right' became a reggae number. 'All Along the Watchtower' became a frenzied tribute to Jimi Hendrix, with David Mansfield imitating the guitar break on violin. 'It's Alright Ma (I'm Only Bleeding),' which Bob customarily performed solo with an acoustic guitar, now played as heavy rock. There were some new songs, like 'Is Your Love in Vain?' The backing singers rehearsed the lyric 'Can you cook and sew, make flowers grow' so many times that they began parodying it: 'Can you cook and fuck and drive a truck?' The band thought this most amusing, but Bob who rarely used the word 'fuck' and also took his songs very seriously did not laugh.

It would be a luxurious tour, the musicians staying in the best hotels, and Bob traveled with the band at all times. In 1974, instructions had been sent out that nobody was to talk to Bob, and he was a remote figure during most of The Rolling Thunder Revue. Now he was willing to be part of a gang, even when band members kidded him about his failed movie, calling it *Renaldo & Bozo*. They flew to Tokyo on February 16, in a leased BAC-111 jet. It had two suites, a bedroom for Bob, and a fully stocked bar. The arrival of Dylan in Japan was a huge event. 'It was like The Beatles are coming,' says Joel Bernstein. However, the sell-out audiences were puzzled by the new song arrangements. Sometimes Bob would be a minute or two into a number before it became clear which song he was performing. As the tour progressed, the band gave far better performances, but it was the Tokyo concerts that were recorded for a double live album, called *Bob Dylan at Budokan*. Part of the problem at first was the tense relationships between the musicians and singers. Debi Dye-Gibson came off stage in tears because the backing vocals were so inept. She told Bob that Helena Springs was incapable of singing in harmony. Bob replied that he liked her 'street' sound.

It soon became apparent that Bob was having an affair with Springs, who seemed delighted with the situation. 'She was stoked,' says Billy Cross. 'That was perfect.' By March, when the tour reached Australia, Bob and his new girlfriend were writing songs together. This was something he had done with women in the past (Levon Helm's girlfriend, Joanna Bull, wrote songs with Bob in 1965, each composing alternate lines), but Bob had never treated the results with much seriousness. He even went to the trouble of copyrighting the songs he wrote with Springs, including 'If I Don't Be There by Morning.' But the special attention she was receiving caused friction within the band.

Soon after the band found out about Bob and Springs, another of Bob's girlfriends joined the entourage. Mary Alice Artes was a large woman, not classically beautiful but with a strong personality. Almost everybody liked her except, as it seemed to the band, Helena Springs. 'There were terrible scenes,' says Billy Cross. 'I think [Bob] was lucky to escape without getting his eye blacked . . . Mary being larger than he was.' In New Zealand, Bob reportedly became involved with yet another woman, a Maori named Ra Aranga. It was not lost on the band that all these girlfriends were black. 'Bob is really into black culture. He likes black women. He likes black music. He likes black style,' says Cross. 'When he asked for musical attitudes, they would always be black.' When Bobbye Hall was invited to Bob's suite for dinner she was surprised to find a banquet of soul food. 'He ate soul food after every show. We used to go up to his room and there was the whole big spread [of] soul food laid out. It was very strange to me . . . He seems to be infatuated by going out with black women . . . he was infatuated by that whole black thing, [even] eating the food.' Perhaps there was also an element of Bob searching for company at a difficult time in his life. Divorced from his wife, and separated from his children by the fact he was on the road for a whole year, he took comfort in the strong personalities and clearly defined culture of his African-American, Christian girlfriends.

The first leg of the world tour ended on April 1 in Sydney, Australia. Although he had worked hard to make the tour a success, Rob Stoner had become very unpopular with colleagues in the band. 'Rob wanted to be the boss,' says Steven Soles. Stoner was fired in Sydney and replaced with Jerry Scheff, who had played bass for Elvis Presley. Debi Dye-Gibson also left the tour, partly because she was pregnant and also because she could not get along with Helena Springs. She was replaced with Carolyn Dennis, who later assumed particular importance in Bob's life. Carolyn Yvonne Dennis – also known as Carol or Carole Dennis – was born in Missouri in 1954. Her mother was Madelyn Quebec, who sang with Ray Charles as a member of thc Raelettes. Carolyn had grown up in a strong tradition of gospel music to become a fine singer in her own right. She was a large woman with a powerful but angelic voice and a very pretty face. She was on tour with Burt Bacharach when she received a call about working with Bob. 'I have [to] say – as embarrassing as it might be – I didn't know who he was, because my young life had been so reclusive and so sheltered,' says Carolyn. 'So I called and I asked, "Who is Bob Dylan?"'

Bob had three months before he had to go back on the road. In the meantime, he wanted to record a new album, to be called *Street-Legal*, the first album that would be delivered under a recently renegotiated contract with Columbia. Bob consulted his former Columbia producer Bob Johnston about booking into the Record Plant, but they could not get convenient dates, so Bob decided to record at his rehearsal studio in Santa Monica without Johnston or any name producer. He worked in a large upstairs room formerly used as a gun factory. Acoustically, the room was terrible, with a linoleum floor and polystyrene ceiling tiles. To muffle Ian Wallace's battery of drums, Bob's assistant, Arthur Rosato, suspended a parachute above the kit. Power leads were fed out through windows to a mobile recording unit in the street. With regular breaks for coffee and pastries next door at the Napoleon cafe, the album was finished in less than a week. Bob enjoyed working at a brisk clip, and was not overly concerned about sound quality. He told Billy Cross that a recording was merely the performance of a song that day. He was not looking for perfection.

The songs had for the most part been written the previous summer on the farm, when Bob was with Faridi McFree, and were registered to a newly created publishing company, Special Rider Music. The songs were concerned primarily with the travails of love. However, autobiographical references were disguised with dense imagery including references to tarot cards in 'Changing of the Guards,' and astrology in 'No Time to Think.' Bob's interest in this sort of mystical mumbo-jumbo seems to have been a hangover from his relationship with McFree and was perhaps indicative of Bob searching for something to give meaning to his life. He seemed less self-assured than in the past and a lack of focus weakened the impact of many of the songs on *Street-Legal*. There are, however, some lively numbers. 'New Pony' was a lustful blues that some of the band members thought of as being inspired by Bob's relationship with Helena Springs. 'Señor (Tales of Yankee Power)' can be seen as a signpost to Bob's conversion to Christianity. In the song, he beseeched the 'Señor' – an enigmatic, Messiah-like figure – for direction, sounding frightened by the place he found himself in. While the song contains powerful images, and interesting biblical references, as does so much of his work, 'Señor' also sounded contrived to some ears, incorporating in its imagery some of the showy exoticism of *Desire* and a tinge of the specious nonsense of tarot. 'Baby, Stop Crying' was a fine love song. Perhaps the best song on the album was 'Where Are

You Tonight? (Journey Through Dark Heat),' in which Bob seemed to accept the failure of his marriage and appeared to give vent to feelings of regret and maybe his wish to return to a time when he and Sara were happy. Beginning with the patter of Bobbye Hall's tomtoms, the song was a sinuous drag through a broken love affair. The first line described the classic lonesome image of a 'long-distance train rolling through the rain.' The song built to a climax of longing and despair that segued into a guitar break from Billy Cross that sounded like the weeping of tears.

Unfortunately, *Street-Legal* sounded like it had been recorded under wet cardboard, and Bob was not pleased with the result. 'After the recording, they fired all of us,' says keyboard player Alan Pasqua, who remembers word coming to him via one of Bob's gofers. 'The whole band got fired . . . I guess he didn't like the record.' But Bob needed his band to complete the world tour, so they were all quickly hired back again. Bob's misgivings about *Street-Legal* were borne out, however, when it was released to mixed reviews in the summer of 1978. Greil Marcus wrote in *Rolling Stone* that Bob sounded 'utterly fake.'

The album proved more successful in the United Kingdom, where Bob opened the European leg of his tour in June with six sold-out shows at London's eighteen-thousand-seat Earls Court arena. The concerts drew celebrities and even royalty – Princess Margaret attended – and were acclaimed in the press. After a stilted beginning in the Far East, the band was in top form. 'Earls Court, I think, was one of the best shows he's ever done,' says promoter Harvey Goldsmith. 'It was fantastic.'

While he was in London Bob went to see a show by rockabilly star Robert Gordon, a cult figure for followers of Britain's new punk movement, and met there his estranged bandleader Rob Stoner and also Sid Vicious of The Sex Pistols. Stoner played with Gordon before The Rolling Thunder Revue and was now back with him again. He had a civil reunion with Bob backstage, and then Sid Vicious lurched up to Bob with a knife, threatening to stab him for reasons he did not explain clearly because he was so stoned. Luckily, Vicious was hustled away before he could injure anybody.

Although the punk and new wave bands despised most established music stars – and Sid Vicious clearly had something against Bob – Dylan commanded respect from most young musicians then coming to prominence. 'His lyrics were great,' says Sex Pistols guitarist Steve Jones. 'You kind of like him 'cause he was kind of rebellious, when he did that thing when he was acoustic and went electric and everybody hated him.' Bob also made friendly connections around this time with The Clash and new wave artists like Elvis Costello and Graham Parker.

After the London concerts there were shows in the Netherlands and Germany. Bob and his band traveled in a private train carriage from Berlin to Nuremberg, where they performed on July 1 at Zeppelinfeld, an arena built for Adolf Hitler's rallies. Patrick Stansfield arranged it so that Bob would not have to perform on the *Führersteig* – the dais Hitler stood upon. 'I think all of us were sort of moved and excited to play there, and especially when Dylan did a wonderful version of "Masters of War," ' says David Mansfield.

An even more impressive concert was staged two weeks later, on July 15, when Bob returned to Britain and played a huge open-air show at the Blackbushe aerodrome south of London. Three square miles of the disused airfield were fenced in to accommodate an audience of approximately one hundred and sixty-seven thousand people, making the Picnic at Blackbushe one of the biggest one-day paying concerts ever staged. The large support bill included Eric Clapton and Graham Parker and The Rumour, one of the new wave bands to whom Bob had taken a liking. 'I really love that song of yours,' he told Parker when they met backstage. As

Graham waited nervously to discover which song he was referring to, Bob seemed to lose his train of thought. 'That song . . . um . . . erm . . . errmmmm . . . ahh . . . ooh, man.' Parker grinned fixedly while he waited. 'It seemed to go on and on, this sort of pause, where he was trying to think of the title, and sweat was starting to bead out of my head,' he says. 'My lip . . . went up above my teeth and I became so nervous it dried out and stuck there.'

'"Don't Ask Me Questions!"' Bob finally exclaimed, remembering the title.

At that moment a photographer took a picture of them for the newspapers. 'It looks like I'm having a great time,' says Parker. 'But I was really sweating bullets.'

Bob came on stage at Blackbushe wearing a top hat, just as the light was fading. 'The kids had grabbed whatever was flammable and had been lighting bonfires in the audience, 'cause it had been getting colder as the sun set, and there were some dozens of bonfires burning in this three- or four-square-mile compound,' says Patrick Stansfield. 'The black smoke would rise up and sort of a pall hung over.' It was a dramatic setting for a memorable show that was perhaps the highlight of the entire world tour.

By the time the U.S. leg of the tour started in September, Bob and the band had been on the road for the best part of eight months and much of the verve had gone. 'That American tour was a tough tour,' says Ian Wallace. 'I think we were playing like six nights a week . . . and those were three-hour shows and, even though we had our own plane and everything, that's pretty demanding.' Tensions within the band became pronounced. 'You know, a band is a lot like a family,' says Wallace. 'And things started to get out of hand at one point. There was all kinds of rumors flying around, who was doing this to [whom], you know. When you are on the road, little things take on big proportions.'

Most of the intrigue surrounded Bob, naturally, who had by now begun a relationship with his new backing singer Carolyn Dennis. 'I never got involved with anything like that, but eventually [it] seemed to be that the girls who were singing always had something going on with [Bob],' says Jo Ann Harris. A fierce rivalry developed between Helena Springs and Carolyn Dennis, and Harris was literally caught in the middle when Bob asked her to stand between his girlfriends on stage. 'Carolyn and Helena almost had it out on stage one night, with me in the middle,' she says. 'Bob said, "Jo Ann, you stand in the middle tonight." I said, "No, I always stand on the end. You know that's my spot." He goes, "No, you stand in the middle." I went, "Oh no! I'm not going to get my hair ripped out, am I?" '

There was a case of influenza sweeping through the band, being passed from musician to musician, as they all lived and worked in such close proximity. Ian Wallace felt so ill he had to have a bucket beside him on stage. Whereas the Far East and European tours had been lavish, costs were cut in America. On the eve of Thanksgiving the band was in a Howard Johnson's in Norman, Oklahoma, with just the local bowling alley for entertainment. Bob began to speed the songs up as he lost enthusiasm for the tour. 'The tempos kept getting faster and faster and faster and words kept getting more and more and more slurred,' says Stansfield. Reviewers made invidious comparisons with Las Vegas–type entertainment. Bob defended his band to journalists, but glared at his musicians on stage and called meetings to tell them the shows were becoming too formulaic. 'It wasn't as street-sounding and spontaneous as he would like,' says Harris. Bob wanted the girls to sing louder. 'You know, we were *screaming*.' Bobbye Hall was amazed that such a shy man could get so tough. 'When he spoke to us, he was not the poet.'

Yet on the last night of the tour, in Miami, Florida, on December 16, 1978, Bob joined the band for drinks in the hotel and talked about keeping the show on the road into the following year. He seemed reluctant to get back to his normal life and its problems, just as he had at the end of The Rolling Thunder Revue, and had been calling Weintraub to book more concerts. In many ways he seemed an unhappy and lonely figure. 'We sat up until the early hours of the morning talking, and he was telling me about all the plans he'd got for '79, what we were going to do, and everything,' says Wallace. That was the last he or the other musicians saw of Bob, however. Over the Christmas break, Bob changed his mind and fired the whole band, having decided to take a radical new direction in both his life and his music.

The 1978 world tour had consisted of a year of frenetic and hedonistic activity, a diversion from Dylan's failed marriage and wrecked home life. But in its final stages it was as unsatisfying as Tour '74 had been four years earlier. Bob was earning a fortune on the road, but he took little pleasure in playing formulaic greatest-hits shows to football stadium–sized crowds. At a time when he was feeling low, needing someone or some thing to lift him up, he found himself surrounded by Christians, particularly Christian women. His girlfriend Carolyn Dennis came from a Midwestern gospel background. Mary Alice Artes had recently been 'saved.' A third girlfriend, Helena Springs, had suggested Bob pray when he was experiencing doubt and confusion. Some of the men in the 1978 band, as well as other musician friends, had become Christians in the recent past. Indeed, there was something of a vogue for Christianity in the music business at the time, perhaps partly as a reaction to the excess of the 1960s and early 1970s and the fact that many musicians' lives had been blighted by drug abuse, alcoholism, and other problems in the aftermath of that self-indulgent era. 'Beginning in 1976, something happened all across the world,' says T-Bone Burnett, who was a convert, as were colleagues David Mansfield and Steven Soles. 'It happened to Bono and Edge and Larry

Mullens [of U2] in Ireland. It happened to Michael Hutchence [of INXS] in Australia, and it happened here in Los Angeles: there was a spiritual movement.'

There were signs during the latter stages of the 1978 tour that Bob had become caught up in this enthusiasm for Jesus Christ. Bob met his old college friend Dave Whitaker after a concert in Oakland, California, in mid-November, and spoke to Dave's eleven-year-old son, Ubi. 'Would you send me a guitar?' asked the kid. The next day a truck pulled up with a gift from Dylan – a brand-new Fender Stratocaster decorated with quotations from the Book of Paul. A few days later Bob played a show in San Diego. He picked up a cross that a fan had thrown on stage and started wearing it. Shortly after this incident Bob felt what he later described as 'this *vision and feeling*,' which he believed to be the presence of Jesus Christ in the room. Billy Cross was sitting next to Bob on the bus when he looked over and noticed that Bob seemed to be writing a spiritual song – 'Slow Train Coming' – the lyrics of which were only partly formed at this time but which described a resurgence of faith in God. The band played the song at a sound check in Nashville on December 2.

The catalyst to Bob's extraordinary full-blown conversion to Christianity seems to have been his relationship with sometime girlfriend Mary Alice Artes, although his relationship with Carolyn Dennis also focused his mind on the subject. Artes was linked with the Vineyard Fellowship, a small but growing evangelical church in the San Fernando Valley of Los Angeles. The Fellowship was founded in 1974 by Kenn Gulliksen, a singing pastor with a Lutheran background. 'I did an album of my own and had a number-one song in the Christian world,' he says. 'It sounded like The Carpenters, it was so boring.' Popular music was used to enliven services at the Fellowship, with people encouraged to get up and play songs. Several well-known musicians were associated with the Vineyard Fellowship, including a member of The Eagles. Church meetings were informal and Pastor Kenn often dressed in shorts. Because the Fellowship did not have a dedicated church building, they would lease buildings or meet on the beach. Ideologically, the Vineyard Fellowship was Bible-based, taking a fairly strong line on drugs, excessive drinking, and adultery.

Pastor Kenn says Mary Alice Artes approached him one Sunday in January 1979 after a service in a rented church building in Reseda and said she wanted somebody to speak with her boyfriend at home. Two of Pastor Kenn's colleagues, Paul Emond and Larry Myers, duly went with Artes to an apartment in the West Los Angeles suburb of Brentwood. It was here that they met Bob. According to Pastor Kenn, who received a report back, Bob told them his life was empty. The pastors replied that God was the 'only ultimate success' and Bob indicated that he wanted what Pastor Kenn calls a 'lifestyle relationship' with God. 'He was apparently ready to ask for God's forgiveness for sin,' says Pastor Kenn. Larry Myers spoke to Bob about Jesus Christ, and talked about the Bible, from Genesis through to the Revelation of St. John the Divine. 'Sometime in the next few days, privately and on his own, Bob accepted Christ and believed that Jesus Christ is indeed the Messiah,' says Myers.

Bob later said that Mary Alice Artes was instrumental in his conversion. But she resists suggestions that any one person was responsible. 'I cannot lead anyone to the Lord . . . I could only say that God did what he had to do,' she says. 'I think that too many people wanna be glorifying themselves in a situation that really should not have any glory at all.'

Bob and Mary Alice enrolled in the Vineyard Fellowship's School of Discipleship, attending Bible class most weekday mornings for more than three months at the beginning of 1979. At first Bob thought there was no way that he could devote so much time to the project; he felt he had to get back on the road. Soon, though, he found himself awake at 7 A.M., compelled to get up and drive to the real estate office in Reseda where Bible classes were held. 'I couldn't believe I was there,' he said.

Assistant Pastor Bill Dwyer, who taught a class on the Sermon on the Mount, recalls Bob as being withdrawn in Bible class and also when he made rare appearances at church. 'He probably needs to be,' says Pastor Bill. 'The few times he would [come] into church people would glom onto him: *Oh, it's Bob Dylan!*' Indeed, Pastor Bill, who had all Bob's albums, had to restrain himself from doing the same.

It was during this late winter/spring period of 1979 that Mary Alice Artes was baptized in a swimming pool at Pastor Bill's house. 'This was total immersion. Because baptism is a symbol of burial, burying guilt, and then pulling the new man out of the water,' says Pastor Kenn. Bob attended the baptism and, not long afterward, Bob was himself baptized, probably in the ocean, which was where the Fellowship normally conducted baptisms. By being immersed in water, Bob became, in common parlance, a born-again Christian, though he would later shrink from the term, claiming he had never used it. Yet he was clearly quoted in a 1980 interview with trusted *Los Angeles Times* journalist Robert Hilburn saying: 'I truly had a born-again experience, if you want to call it that. It's an overused term, but it's something people can relate to.'

An element of religiosity had always existed in Bob's work, and it was particularly strong on the album *John Wesley Harding*. Religion had in fact been with him since childhood when his father instilled a strict moral code in his eldest son and sent him to study with a rabbi for his bar mitzvah. As a songwriter, Bob had always felt himself to be a channel for inspiration. At the start of his career, he told *Sing Out!* that words just came to him: 'The songs are there. They exist all by themselves just waiting for someone to write them down.' In this sense, he had a powerful everyday connection with a mysterious source of information and, over the years, he came to think that the songs arose from God. It was a small step, apparently, from this to flinging himself headfirst into orthodox religion. Yet Bob of course was born and raised in the Jewish faith, and it is fundamentally wrong to most Jews to think of Jesus Christ as the Messiah. 'For a person to be a "completed Jew" is very offensive to them,' admits Pastor Kenn. 'They think that is an oxymoron, where as I see it, Christians see it, and Jewish Christians see it as the [truth].' Indeed, Bob's embracing of Christianity caused consternation, and some offense, among his Jewish friends and family. 'I think it was for publicity, that's what I think. Because he is Jewish-minded, plenty Jewish-minded. He was brought up that way. He was bar mitzvahed,' says Bob's aunt, Ethel Crystal.

Bob's conversion to Christianity also caused considerable upset to his own children, who had been raised in the Jewish faith. Suddenly, packs of journalists were following their father to the Vineyard Fellowship in the hope of getting pictures of him going to a Christian church, and then staking out his home. The children saw this commotion when they visited their father. It was embarrassing and one of the few times when his celebrity was a problem in their lives.

Faith inspired Bob to write new songs. They were so overtly religious that, at first, he considered giving them to Carolyn Dennis to record. Then he decided to record them himself at the Muscle Shoals Sound Studios in Sheffield, Alabama, with R&B producer Jerry Wexler, who was well known for his work with Ray Charles and Aretha Franklin. Wexler was initially surprised by the religious content of the songs, and bemused when Bob attempted to evangelize him. 'You're dealing with a sixty-two-year-old confirmed Jewish atheist,' he told

Bob. 'Let's just make an album.' Wexler had recently produced the *Communiqué* album for the British band Dire Straits and suggested that the band's leader, Mark Knopfler, should work with them on what would become the album *Slow Train Coming*. Knopfler was a talented guitarist and, as a songwriter, heavily influenced by Bob. He describes himself as 'having been a huge fan of Bob's since I was eleven.' Indeed, he sometimes sounded almost like a parody of Bob, who was aware of the influence. 'Mark does me better than anybody,' he told Wexler. In addition, they would use Dire Straits drummer Pick Withers. Wexler also suggested Tim Drummond play bass, and Drummond became Bob's new bandleader. Wexler's coproducer, Barry Beckett, would play keyboards. Carolyn Dennis, Helena Springs, and Regina Havis would sing backing vocals; Carolyn and Helena managed to bury their differences so that they could work together. This ensemble of musicians and singers created a pleasing musical combination and, for a change, Bob would be working in a first-class studio with a great producer. '[Bob] said that he wanted to make a professional record,' says Knopfler. 'That he'd been making like home recordings.'

Excellent rhythm playing on the title track, 'Slow Train Coming,' made the song chug forward just as the lyrics suggested, the sound enhanced by Knopfler's stinging guitar breaks. Bob delivered here arguably the best lyric on the record, words vivid with alliterative phrases and clever images, and he sounded completely committed to his new faith as he sang. His singing was also impassioned on 'When He Returns,' which spoke directly of his relationship with Jesus Christ. In the lyric to 'I Believe in You,' Bob sang about walking alone 'a thousand miles from home.' It was a stock image of popular music that was associated with the wandering troubadour life of musicians like Woody Guthrie, but Bob twisted the image by saying he was not alone anymore because he had belief in God. 'Gotta Serve Somebody' was another strong song that would become a surprising hit single, but 'When You Gonna Wake Up?' was hectoring in its tone and provided a foretaste of Bob's next and much less successful Christian album, *Saved*. 'Man Gave Names to All the Animals' is essentially a children's song, a novelty included on the album partly because backing singer Regina Havis's three-year-old son liked it. All in all, Pastor Kenn was delighted by what he heard, considering Bob's new songs the modern equivalent of Charles Wesley hymns. 'It was a magnificent demonstration, I think, of what he genuinely went through. It was born of the spirit in his heart. I think he became really Jewish for the first time in his life by recognizing Jesus as the Messiah.'

Bob worked closely with Columbia Records art director Tony Lane on the presentation of the record. Columbia executives held long discussions about how overt the Christian message should be. 'There were great worries that they were going to lose their Bob Dylan core audience,' says Lane, who recalls Bob talking about himself in the third person as he went through options for the cover design, typography, and liner notes. They eventually settled on a cover drawing of a railroad worker swinging an ax that in its shape also suggested a cross.

Although some reviewers sniffed at Bob's expressions of faith, Jann Wenner wrote in *Rolling Stone* that the album might be Bob's greatest. 'Faith is the message,' he began the review. 'Faith is the point. Faith is the key to understanding this record.' It was Bob who insisted 'Gotta Serve Somebody' should be the single, against the advice of Wexler. Bob turned out to be right; the song became a top-forty hit – his last chart single of the seventies* – and its success did much to propel sales of the album. *Slow Train Coming* proved remarkably

*As of 2000, 'Gotta Serve Somebody' remains the last Bob Dylan single to have reached the *Billboard* top forty. It peaked at number 24 in the United States on October 6, 1979.

successful, reaching number three in the charts, certified gold at the end of 1979 and platinum a year later, making it one of his best-selling studio albums.

Bob then put together a road band featuring the rhythm section of Tim Drummond and Jim Keltner, the leading session drummer in America. Keltner had known Bob since 1971 but had resisted previous invitations to tour because he did not like traveling. He made a good living doing session work for artists such as John Lennon, but that lifestyle had fueled a drug habit that, by 1979, had almost killed him. 'I was in very poor shape, physically and spiritually,' says Keltner. 'I fell into a really bad scene.' Keltner believes he was saved from an early death by the support of close friends, including Bob, and says the experience of touring with Bob was like a religious epiphany, and it changed his life. The other musicians in the road band were Fred Tackett on lead guitar; 'Spooner' Oldham (who cowrote several classic songs, including 'I'm Your Puppet') on the B-3 organ; Terry Young played gospel piano; and Terry's wife, Monalisa, sang backup vocals with Helena Springs and Regina Havis. After an appearance on the *Saturday Night Live* television show in New York, Bob and the band flew to San Francisco in November 1979 for a remarkable two-week residency at the Fox Warfield, an old Vaudeville-type theater.

Before the shows Bob prayed with his musicians. 'No one had any objections to forming a circle before each gig and just hold hands and somebody would say a prayer. It would be a minute or less, usually,' says Spooner Oldham. 'It was just "Praise the Lord!" You know, "Thank you, Jesus, for keeping us safe and well." . . . I guess it was a prayer said for a good show.' Often prayers were led by Larry Myers, on secondment from the Vineyard Fellowship. Sometimes Monalisa Young led the prayers, asking that 'the light of love be mirrored in us.' One night they prayed for Bob simply because he had a sore throat and afterward, almost miraculously, he got up on stage and sang like nothing was wrong. 'Thank you, Jesus!' exclaimed the girls.

The first Fox Warfield show opened with singer Regina Havis delivering a religious monologue. She was then joined by Helena Springs, and Monalisa and Terry Young. They sang six gospel songs in harmony as Terry Young played piano. The sound of the piano was, as Jim Keltner says, like 'diamonds sparkling off the stage.' At the end of the gospel song 'This Train,' the lights dipped and then came up again to reveal Bob on stage with the full band. Dressed in a black leather jacket and white T-shirt, he looked like a rock 'n' roller. But when he stepped to the microphone he sang 'Gotta Serve Somebody,' the first of seventeen new songs, every one of which celebrated his newfound belief in Jesus Christ. Even those who knew about his new album hardly expected the entire show to be made up of such material. 'The crowds didn't know what to make of it,' says Keltner. 'They were out there wanting to see a Bob Dylan show and a bunch of them were smoking pot – as they always have at rock concerts – so the air was heavy with pot and there was a lot of screaming and yelling after the first few numbers that were all songs about God, with lyrics that they didn't recognize. They started yelling and screaming, a bunch of them, for him to play some rock 'n' roll. They were very profane, and yelling out really loud, and standing up and waving their arms to get his attention. I'm watching all of this from my position, and I'm sure Bob was, too. Then on a few occasions . . . somebody [would] stand up [and] they would say, "Bob, we love you!" and "We love your new music." And there would be like verbal fighting within the audience . . . It was something to watch.' Bob seemed oblivious to the hecklers, just as he had been in 1965–66 when he was booed almost every night. He was transfixed by the extraordinary music. The singers were wailing. Terry Young's delicate piano contrasted with Oldham's B-3 organ, which seemed to extrude a gas of sound. Bob howled through his harmonica. 'There were times, musically, when Bob would elevate just completely off the ground . . . would just go to another world,' says Keltner. When they reached the second number of the evening, 'I Believe in You,' Keltner found himself weeping. He cried virtually every night during the rest of the Fox Warfield residency, which is something he had almost never done before. 'He's always had a lyric that will get you right to the bone,' he says. 'But in this case it was tremendous.'

The controversy caused by Bob's spiritual concerts exceeded even the wildest days of his first electric tour. Electricity had annoyed folk purists, but religion bothered everybody. 'I went out on tour and played no song that I had ever played before live,' said Bob. 'I thought that was a pretty amazing thing to do. I don't know any other artist who has done that.' He was right, but most critics ridiculed him. The *San Francisco Examiner* carried a front-page headline stating, BORN AGAIN DYLAN BOMBS. In the *San Francisco Chronicle*, BOB DYLAN'S GOD-AWFUL GOSPEL was the headline of Joel Selvin's review. The following week the letter page included the briefest of notes signed by four readers. It read: 'Editor – is Selvin deaf?' There were demonstrations outside the theater for and against Bob's new identity and music. 'What I found to be really amazing was the amount of people who mistrusted Bob,' says Keltner. 'There were so many Christian people that mistrusted him, saying, *This is not for real. He's a phony.* [And] people in the Jewish community mistrusted him. They were offended, or mistrusted whether he was for real with it. Bob [was] offending everyone. And at the same time I know, from being out there with him, and talking with certain people, that a lot of people's lives were changed forever. In the Christian world, they say "saved". I know for a fact that happened to a lot of people.'

One night Bob received a note from Maria Muldaur, who was then living in Marin County. Muldaur, who had a pop hit in 1974 with 'Midnight at the Oasis', had turned to religion after realizing how degraded her life had become since her youth in Greenwich Village. Pot smoking had progressed to cocaine use. Free love turned out to be not so free after all. 'It just all seemed not so pretty any more, not such a cool lifestyle.' When Muldaur saw the negative reviews of Bob's shows, she sent him a note offering moral support and explaining how she too had been 'zapped by the Holy Spirit.' Bob came out to see Muldaur on his day off. When she asked questions about Jesus Christ, he reminded her that all the answers were to be found in the Bible. This was a little disappointing to Muldaur, who found the Bible almost impossibly difficult to read. 'I was hoping he was going to turn me on to a book that was an easier version.' Bob seemed specifically preoccupied with the Revelation of St. John the Divine, which prophesied a cataclysmic battle between good and evil at Armageddon. The theory that Armageddon was an actual place – Meggido in the Middle East – and that international political affairs indicated that the battle was imminent, found an outspoken proponent in author Hal Lindsay, who wrote about it in detail in his 1970 book, *The Late Great Planet Earth*. Bob had read Lindsay's book and told Muldaur that dramatic events would soon unfold. When Iraq and Iran went to war the following year, and Soviet troops invaded Afghanistan, Muldaur figured Bob had red-hot information.

After the Fox Warfield shows, Bob played a series of concerts at the Santa Monica Civic Auditorium to benefit World Vision, a Christian relief organization. Again, he performed only spiritual songs, interspersing them with sermons about biblical figures, ranging from Moses to Satan. The audience was packed with Vineyard Fellowship members who ate it up. 'It was the first concert I'd been to,' says Pastor Kenn. 'I had goose bumps. I was so astonished at the power . . . how awesome and brilliant it was.' He adds: 'To me, it was like Jesus on the hillside telling people the truth.'

The next stop was Tempe, Arizona, where Bob played two shows to secular college audiences who treated his spiritual material with robust skepticism. They hollered for rock 'n' roll and mocked the backing singers, using 'filthy mouth stuff,' as Bob said. (A curious aspect of his conversion was that he began using quaint expressions like this.) The second show almost disintegrated as Bob stopped to admonish the kids, who he thought should know better, considering they were 'higher learnin' people.' He told them angrily that if they wanted rock 'n' roll they should go and see the rock group Kiss, noted for painting their faces and poking their tongues out. They could 'rock 'n' roll all the way down to the pit!' After the show he typed a letter to Muldaur, saying the rudeness of youth was another sure sign that what he called the 'End Times' were nigh. It seemed that faith had temporarily displaced one of Bob's most endearing characteristics – his sense of humor.

Helena Springs left the tour after an argument with Bob during the winter of 1979–80, although she would remain an employee of Bob's Music Touring Co, Inc., for some time. She told members of the band that she wanted to pursue a solo career, but it seems that her personal relationship with Bob had come to an end. She was replaced in the touring band with another of Bob's girlfriends, Carolyn Dennis.

Most of the songs on *Slow Train Coming* had an element of Christian compassion. In concert, however, Bob was performing new songs, such as 'Saved' and 'Are You Ready?,' that were much more judgmental and reflected his eschatological belief that the end was nigh and non-believers would burn in hell. In February 1980, Bob and his road band returned to Muscle Shoals Sound in Alabama to record these fire and brimstone songs as the album *Saved*. The eponymous title song was the highlight of the record, an exhilarating number despite its lyrics being particularly indigestible to nonbelievers. Ironically, Tim Drummond, the only irreligious member of the band, was given a cowriting credit for providing Bob with the bass line. Other songs were lifted only by the occasional interesting phrase or by the skill of the musicians in playing their parts. The song 'Pressing On' began with particular promise, but degenerated into a soulless thud. Indeed, many of the songs floundered when they should have rocked, and most of the lyrics amounted to little more than religious clichés. An artist celebrated for his rigorous intelligence and non-conformity, Bob was now setting Christian dogma to music.

A week after he finished work on *Saved*, Bob performed at the Grammy Awards ceremony in Los Angeles. He was nominated in the crudely described category of Best Male Rock Vocal Performance for 'Gotta Serve Somebody,' the single from his current album. Bob and his band appeared on stage in tuxedos, bringing the celebrity-studded audience to its feet. They were swinging and clapping with the beat even before he uttered a word. 'What are they standing up for?' he shouted to Tim Drummond in bemusement. He delivered a tremendous version of 'Gotta Serve Somebody' with what seemed like ad-libbed changes to the lyrics. Bob won the Grammy, the first of his career, although 'Gotta Serve Somebody' did not rank with his best work. 'I didn't expect this,' he said in his acceptance speech, 'and I wanna thank the Lord for it.' After the show he attended a party thrown by Warner Bros. at Chasen's restaurant in Hollywood, and was confronted by Harold Leventhal, a plain-speaking Jew who had known Bob long enough to tell him what was on his mind. 'I helped him once before when he wanted to visit Israel. I lent him books,' says Leventhal. 'So I felt a sense of betrayal.'

'This is ridiculous, what you are doing here,' said Leventhal. 'What have you got this cross dangling around you for?'

Bob was taken aback, and suggested they have lunch together to talk about it. Sure enough, he called Leventhal the next day to arrange the lunch, but Leventhal was not available.

Bob had a similar experience when he met his summer-camp friend Howard Rutman on a trip back to Minnesota. Bob's mother, without saying who she was, telephoned the dental surgery Rutman ran at the time, asking the secretary if her son, whom she referred to as Bobby Zimmerman, could come in immediately and have his teeth cleaned. 'And then I just got a tap on my shoulder and looked around and there he was,' says Rutman. 'Evidently [he] was in the parking lot waiting to come in.'

As he was working on Bob's teeth, Rutman noticed Bob was wearing a heavy gold cross. It was encrusted with rhinestones. 'Bob, what's up with this?'

'Howard, I'm looking for the one truth.'

'Bob, you're Jewish,' said Rutman.

Rutman then invited Bob to his house for lunch, and the singer duly arrived with one of his Christian girlfriends. 'My ex and myself were there and we had a lunch for him and we talked and everything and then [Bob's girlfriend] was talking to my ex about Christianity and all that kind of stuff. And my ex is major-league Jewish,' says Rutman. 'We kept kosher, the whole thing. So they were going back and forth about Justification and all that. You know, they look in the New Testament for Justification for why Jews should be like Christians and all that kind of stuff. And all Bob could do was just sit there with his hands to his head, thinking *Why did I bring her? Oh my God, why?*' Rutman was utterly bemused by his friend's change of faith. 'He's a Jew, you know, [a] Jewish guy. And his soul, too. He's *really* Jewish . . . He was, I don't know, kinda leaning towards the woman he was going with . . . She was a born-again and he was stuck on her.'

Some believed Bob's espousal of Christianity was motivated by commercial considerations. Keith Richards of The Rolling Stones, for example, referred to Bob as the 'prophet of profit.' Ronnie Hawkins also mocked Bob's Christianity when, on April 20, 1980, Bob's tour reached Toronto and they spent some time together. 'After this [record] sells a few, you are gonna be an atheist and sell to all them cats who don't believe nothing,' Hawkins told him, with a gruff laugh. Bob was not amused. 'He didn't laugh. He just looked at me. But I knew what he was doing. And he knew I knew what he was doing – he was selling records. That's his business.'

Hawkins's cynical perspective on Bob's faith seems to be unfair. All the indications are that he genuinely believed in what he was singing and, ultimately, he suffered for making his faith so public. Though *Slow Train Coming* was a commercial success, Bob's Christian conversion had a detrimental effect on his long-term career. In recent years nearly all his studio albums had reached the top ten. But *Saved* reached only number twenty-four – his lowest charting album since 1964 – and its failure signaled a precipitous downturn in his fortunes. Not only did *Saved* sell badly but Bob was starting to have difficulty selling out theaters when he was on tour.

Those who did come to the concerts were treated to the extraordinary spectacle of Dylan sermonizing like a television evangelist. 'You don't hear much about God these days. Well, we're gonna talk about Him all night,' he told an audience in Hartford, Connecticut, on May 7, 1980. A few nights later, in Akron, Ohio, Bob was pleased by a relatively friendly response from the crowd. He acknowledged this by saying he was used to the devil 'working all kinds of mischief' in audiences. Satan did his work in the box office – the final show on the tour was canceled due to lack of ticket sales – and Bob suffered more misfortune in the following months as his life, both professionally and personally, was beset with adversity and, ultimately, tragedy.

* * *

After a summer break, there were signs that Bob was passing through the unattractive, judgmental phase of his newfound faith into a more moderate state of mind. This was expressed in a new song, called 'Every Grain of Sand,' that stands among his best work. The lyric seemed to spring from a line of scripture, the Gospel according to Matthew (10:30): 'The very hairs of your head are all numbered.' But instead of regurgitating Christian dogma, Bob here described his relationship with God with humility, admitting that temptation was never far away. As he later observed, the song was also reminiscent of the poetry of John Keats.

Bob telephoned singer Jennifer Warnes to say he had a new song he thought she might like to record with him. Warnes was a Christian who would have two big hits in the 1980s ('Up Where We Belong' and '[I've Had] The Time of My Life'). She was dating Leonard Cohen when Bob's conversion became public. 'Leonard used to wander around the house, wringing his hands saying, 'I don't get it. I just don't get this. Why would he go for Jesus at a late time like this? . . . I don't get the Jesus part.' Leonard felt a certain kind of brotherhood with Bob because he was a Mr. Zimmerman and Leonard is so Jewish,' she says. 'I think it seriously rocked his world to see Bob go [Christian].' Warnes accepted Bob's invitation to come down to Rundown Studios to hear the new song.

Sitting at the piano, Bob sang 'Every Grain of Sand' once before turning to Warnes and saying, 'Okay, let's try it.'

'What do you mean, *let's try it*?' asked Warnes, who assumed she would be taking a tape home to learn the song before they sang it together. Bob wanted them to record it there and then, though, which they did, while his dog barked in the background. This remarkable take was later released on the box set *The Bootleg Series, Volumes 1–3*.

The lyrics of 'Every Grain of Sand' were one sign that Bob's faith was starting to mellow. There was further evidence of this when he opened his fall tour with a second two-week residency at the Fox Warfield in San Francisco, lightening the set list by including songs that predated his Christian conversion. The songs he chose – including 'Señor' and 'Blowin' in the Wind' – had lyrics open to a Christian interpretation. (The vague lyrics of the latter were particularly suitable in this respect.) But at least he was giving the audience more of what he thought they wanted to hear. This did not mean he got better reviews, however; the San Francisco press mocked him as before.

Mike Bloomfield joined the band as a guest star one night at the Warfield, playing lead guitar on 'Like a Rolling Stone' and a remarkable new song, 'The Groom's Still Waiting at the Altar,' that could be enjoyed by a secular audience. Bob was very fond of his old friend and invited Bloomfield to join the band. 'Give me two weeks. I'll get my shit together and I'll meet you out there on the road,' Bloomfield told him. Sadly, he did not manage to get himself fit for the tour and died of a drug overdose three months later.

Another old friend, John Lennon, died on December 8, 1980, gunned down outside his New York home by a deranged fan. Bob became convinced that there would be a wave of similar assassinations. 'When John Lennon got shot he was really scared that they were going to go out and kill all sixties rock stars,' says musician friend Ted Perlman, who met Bob around this time via his wife, who was a close friend to Carolyn Dennis. 'He thought they were going to take out him and Mick Jagger.' Advance men were sent to check concert halls. Around this time, Bob surprised bass player Tim Drummond with a gift-wrapped parcel. 'I thought, Bob Dylan's given me a present!' says Drummond. 'Maybe a box full of diamonds?' It was a bullet-proof vest.

The killing of Lennon was particularly alarming to Bob because, as The Beatles had, he attracted fanatical fans. Some were clearly unbalanced, such as the man who had repeatedly broken into Hi Lo Ha in the late 1960s. At the time of the Lennon shooting, Bob was suffering from the attentions of yet another obsessive, a woman named Carmel Hubbell who, most alarmingly, also used the surname *Dylan*. Hubbell wrote to Bob in May 1979, claiming they had met in Kalamazoo, Michigan, earlier in the year. She implied they had had an affair and she had come to California to continue the relationship. When Bob did not reply to her letters, she telephoned his Music Touring Company, located on Main Street in Santa Monica. Bob refused her calls. In the fall of 1980, when Bob was performing in the northwest, Hubbell began to hang around the theaters and hotels. In the flesh, she turned out to be a small woman with brown hair, aged twenty-eight, usually wearing a white golf hat and carrying a knapsack. Then, during the first half of 1981, Hubbell began loitering around 2219 Main Street, trying to talk to Bob, members of his band, and other staff. Bob hired a security man, Don Williams, to live on the premises. Williams had a full-time job dealing with Hubbell, whose behavior became increasingly threatening and then frightening as the year wore on, fueling Bob's paranoia that he might be assassinated. It would be several weeks before the problem was resolved, and in the meantime Bob went about his work as best he could.

Bob worked on the songs that would eventually make up his next album, *Shot of Love*, over an unusually long period of time. 'Every Grain of Sand' was first recorded back in the fall of 1980. The final sessions took place in May 1981. During that time, Bob had worked through many powerful new songs, though he grew tired of some of the best of them before the album was finished.

As Bob explained to the producer he eventually chose for the album, recording was not his forte. 'I've made a lot of records, but record making isn't [my] area of expertise,' he said. 'I always approach it with some discomfort.' *Shot of Love* became more of a project than an album per se, a project of such richness that outtakes became highlights of the box-set editions *Biograph* and *The Bootleg Series, Volumes 1–3*, released in 1985 and 1991 respectively. His core band for these sessions consisted of Tim Drummond and Jim Keltner, with Fred Tackett on guitar. Other musicians included guitarist Steve Ripley and Benmont Tench from Tom Petty's band, The Heartbreakers, and Jim Keltner's guitarist friend Danny Kortchmar.

Regina McCrary, Carolyn Dennis, and Carolyn's mother, Madelyn Quebec, together with another former Raelette, Clydie King, made a quartet of backing singers. Clydie King was a good deal older than Bob, but still sexy looking. She became romantically involved with Bob, just as Carolyn Dennis and Helena Springs had before her (his relationship with Carolyn had lapsed into a platonic friendship for the time being). For a while, Bob was infatuated with Clydie King. 'I get chills when I hear her just breathe, something about the texture of her voice so deep and so soulful, so tough and sensitive at the same time,' he said in 1985, in an interview for the liner notes of *Biograph*.

The songs Bob and his musicians worked on at the early sessions included 'You Changed My Life,' which was a more secular 'Covenant Woman.' Following a vacation in the Caribbean island of St. Vincent, where he had taken up sailing, Bob composed 'Caribbean Wind.' He said it came to him when he was considering living with someone for the wrong reasons. The lyrics did not quite work but it was a powerful song nonetheless. The same could be said of the enigmatic 'Angelina,' which began with a disarming phrase about it being Bob's nature to take chances, but the song got lost in a labyrinth of images. 'The Groom's Still Waiting at the Altar' was a more focused love song, spiked with apocalyptic references of cities on fire and the coming of a new age. Sadly, none of these songs made it onto *Shot of Love*. Bob was working through the songs before he had a producer he felt comfortable with to help him make a recording. In

March 1981 he tried working with Jimmy Iovine at Studio 55, the former Decca studio in Hollywood, but it did not go well, as Tim Drummond recalls: 'We're in the studio, and they come up to me and they said, "What are we going to do today?" I said, "Why are you asking *me*?" ' When Bob came in, assistants nervously asked him the same question. 'I'm gonna do "White Christmas," ' Bob told them, 'because Bing Crosby did it here. Go get me the sheet music.' Assistants went scurrying for the music, but Bob did not really intend to record the song; he just did not like being asked questions. The sessions were quickly abandoned.

David Geffen then suggested Bob call Chuck Plotkin, an easygoing former A&R executive who was then working closely with Bruce Springsteen. 'Do you know my work?' asked Bob, when he got Plotkin on the telephone later in March.

'Yeah,' replied Plotkin. A Dylan fan of long standing, he restrained himself from gushing that he knew Bob's songs by heart and felt they captured the essence of human experience in all its 'blooming, buzzing amazingness . . . so it resonates the reality of your own [life, and] you sing the things over and over and over like prayers.' Instead, he said he knew the work quite well and liked it.

'Would you consider helping me make a record?'

Plotkin relaxed. 'He was just complete[ly] disarming. I stopped feeling uncomfortable. I stopped feeling frightened,' he recalls. Plotkin came to Rundown to hear Bob play his new songs with his band, which he was doing virtually every day. Plotkin found a nearly blind sixty-three-year-old conducting Bob in a rendition of the song 'Shot of Love.' When they got to the end of a line, the man would shout 'STOP!' and Bob would obediently comply. The conductor was Robert 'Bumps' Blackwell, producer of Little Richard's greatest hits. The take of 'Shot of Love' that became the lead track on *Shot of Love* was the one Blackwell conducted, and Bob thought he had done a terrific job. But Blackwell was not going to continue work on the album, partly because of ill health but also because Bob had been told by advisers that Blackwell was not contemporary enough. As a consequence Bob agreed to come into Plotkin's Hollywood studio, Clover, in April 1981.

On the first day of recording, when Plotkin and the musicians were ready to begin work and were waiting for Bob to arrive, Plotkin received a telephone call. It was Bob asking whether he was supposed to be at the studio that day.

'Yeah, but don't worry about it,' said Plotkin, patiently. He could wait. 'Where are you?' he asked.

Bob replied that he was in Minnesota. Plotkin managed to stay calm, telling Bob he would be ready to start work when he got back to Los Angeles. However, there was so much grumbling from the assembled musicians about their time being wasted that Plotkin gave them a speech. 'One thing I know is that none of us can do what he does,' he told the band. 'He's gonna get whatever slack he needs because, you know, he could [decide] not to do this and that would be terrible. That would terrible for us, and it would be terrible for everybody else in the world, because we wouldn't get this music.' Plotkin would be reminded of his words in the days to come when Bob was regularly late for sessions, by two hours on one occasion because he had taken the wrong exit off the freeway and gotten lost in East L.A. The fact that he had been driving around Los Angeles for more than fifteen years did not matter; Bob supposedly had his mind on higher things. 'He got lost because he is actually present where he is. He is not just simply following some map. He doesn't want to be following some map back to the same spots day after day,' says Plotkin. 'He just takes a new route that he's never taken and ends up someplace that he's never ended up . . . The guy's a songwriter. He has to keep that alive . . . And it's *Dylan.* It's not some ubiquitous pop-tune hack,' says Plotkin. 'He doesn't have to be a regular guy. Can you sit down and talk to him about a football game, you know, have a beer and watch a football game? Sure. Does he give a damn [about] a lot of the same things that everybody else seems to give a damn about? From time to time, in certain ways, up to a certain point. Is he a regular guy? No. Why would you want him to be?'

Plotkin discovered that there were numerous other challenges in making a Dylan album. Bob liked to record live, of course. Yet unlike almost any other musician who worked this way – including Bruce Springsteen with his E Street Band – Bob did not wear headphones. This meant there had to be monitors in the studio so that he could hear what he was playing. This caused feedback problems. Bob also worked ridiculous hours. They first cut 'Heart of Mine' at 4 A.M. 'Two of the guys had left and one of the other guys was asleep,' says Plotkin. 'Who knows what we were doing there at four o'clock in the morning?' Bob would play songs only two or three times before he tired of them and, once he was satisfied with his vocal, he considered a song finished, whether Plotkin had a good recording or not. This would leave the producer with the problem of remixing the recording to correct the overall sound, but Bob did not like his basic tracks altered too much; he wanted a natural sound. In addition, he was very reluctant to do overdubs. When Bob moved to the piano and, without warning, began playing 'Every Grain of Sand,' Plotkin realized there was no microphone for the vocal. Knowing this might be the only chance of recording this very important song, Plotkin ran over and held a microphone next to Bob's mouth while he sang. It was the only take, and it went on the album.

Bob's eccentric habits were also a challenge for the musicians, and even for his friend Jim Keltner who over the years played on more Dylan albums than any other session musician. Bob played guitar *against* the drums, as if trying to drag the song away from the beat, and he scowled at Keltner as if challenging him. 'Bob has always, even up to quite recently, been acutely aware of the [guitar] and drum rub,' says Keltner. 'Bob was trying to create a tension.' Again, this gave a rough edge to the music, which Bob liked.

Other songs of note on the album included 'In the Summertime,' which was a fine and tender song that might be either about a woman or about Bob's relationship with Jesus. 'Lenny Bruce' was an homage to the late comedian, which Bob wrote the night before the session. 'Trouble' was noisy, but weak. 'Dead Man, Dead Man' and 'Watered-Down Love' were inconsequential, but free of the dogma present on his previous two albums. However, 'Property of Jesus' was just as preachy as anything on *Saved*.

Shot of Love was essentially complete when Ringo Starr came into the studio on May 15. Bob told Plotkin that Ringo wanted to play on something, and Plotkin seized this more or less social visit as an opportunity to rerecord 'Heart of Mine,' the song they had first cut at four in the morning and which was, consequently, slow and drowsy. Bob was hours late for the 'Ringo session'; by the time he arrived there was a party atmosphere in the studio as Starr jammed with Ronnie Wood and others. Bob slipped in and sang the loose take of 'Heart of Mine' that was later released as a single. 'The Groom's Still Waiting at the Altar' became the B-side after Plotkin subtly sped up the tempo. It was added to later pressings of the album as a bonus track.

It was at the mixing stage that Plotkin had his most frustrating experience with Bob. He had worked night and day to get the best-sounding record he could, mixing the songs so that they were clear. But that was not what Bob wanted. 'Let me just tell you something about the mixes that you are doing, Charlie,' he said. 'You're cleaning this stuff up too much. We're sounding a bit like The Doobie Brothers.' Plotkin reminded Bob that *Slow Train Coming* was a well-made record. 'I didn't like making that record,' he replied, even though it had been so successful for him. As a result, *Shot of Love* was essentially assembled from rough mixes. It sounded terrific to some ears, very fresh and alive, but it was not necessarily the sort of sound that would appeal to the general public who, by the late 1970s, as technology continued to improve, had become accustomed to high technical standards and a smooth sound.

The final problem with the album was that many of the best songs Bob had written and recorded in recent months, including 'Angelina' and 'Caribbean Wind,' did not make it onto the final pressing. This was partly because there were too many long songs to fit them all on, but it was also because Chuck Plotkin was trying to create a cohesive piece of work. 'An album is a program of music. It's not just simply the best ten songs that you wrote during that period of time. It has to add up to something,' he says. Yet Plotkin admits he fought with Bob, but failed to get songs like 'Angelina' on the record. Bob's decision to keep these songs off the album, for reasons he did not make clear, prevented *Shot of Love* from being the excellent album it almost was.

In June 1981, on or around the first day of the month, Bob was rehearsing at Rundown, in preparation for a major tour, when the obsessive fan Carmel Hubbell walked in through a loading door. One of the first people to approach her was the office manager, Barbara Moldt. Hubbell threatened: 'Don't get near me, bitch – you'll be sorry.' Hubbell was hustled from the building by Bob's staff while Moldt telephoned the police. Ten days later, Bob's office staff found notes stuck to the windows of the building and cars parked outside, including one that referred to 'death devices.' The police treated these notes as death threats and had little doubt as to who had written them. That same night Hubbell showed up at Point Dume, where she had been making a nuisance of herself for weeks.

Hubbell was one of several such fans who regularly trespassed on the property. Howard Alk and his second wife, Jones, who lived on the estate, kept an eye open for intruders, but there were so many that Bob also employed a full-time security team. Robert Kirby, head of security, kept a log of the people who came to the main gate. One man would frequently drive up and challenge the guards to a fight; the fellow claimed to have been a friend of Bob since he gave the singer a sack of potatoes. Hubbell, however, was the most persistent offender. By Kirby's count, she trespassed nineteen times between May 20 and June 17, 1981. She posted notices on the fence and left envelopes containing letters, birthday cards, and a key to her room at the Malibu Driftwood Motel on Pacific Coast Highway. Notes were addressed to her 'Sweetheart' or 'Dear Dreamboat.' One was signed 'Covenant Woman.' The messages were sometimes aggressive, sometimes suggestive. 'How about another hot date, Dylan?' read a note left from June 1. When Kirby stopped Hubbell on June 9 she screamed death threats at him. On June 11, Howard Alk restrained Hubbell while the security man called the police. She was back four days later, leaving a test tube filled with nuts as a gift for Bob. Three days after this incident, Hubbell confronted Joan Alk at a local market warning her to 'watch out!' Hubbell continued to trespass over the next few weeks, and her notes became more sinister. One read, 'lives are forfeit.' Another, 'Ms X = Ms Manson.'

In the early hours of Sunday, June 21, Helena Springs received a telephone call at home. 'There's threats being made on Bob's life and everyone involved with him,' said the caller. 'So leave your house for a few days 'cause there's someone watching you.'

'Who are you?' asked Springs, who was still on the payroll of Bob's touring company, though she and Bob were no longer dating.

'My name is Carmel!'

Springs asked who was watching her.

'The KKK and the Nazis . . . There's a chain reaction because Chapman is going on trial Monday and Manson is being released from prison.' (Mark David Chapman was due in court in New York on Monday, June 22, at the start of his trial for the murder of John Lennon; Charles Manson was securely imprisoned for the 1969 Tate-LaBianca murder spree, though periodically he came up for parole.)

'Are you serious? Are you sure someone is trying to kill me?' asked Springs.

'Yes, someone has already been killed in the Warfield Theater.'

'Someone in the band?'

'No, one that was a follower!'

Asked again who she was, the caller replied: 'I'm Carmel Dylan!'

Springs took the call seriously. She moved to a friend's house and filed a complaint with the County of Los Angeles Sheriff's Department.

Bob was out of town at the time, having decided to tour extensively in Europe and America to support his new album. He warmed up with a few shows in the Midwest. Shortly before the first concert, at the Poplar Creek Music Theater in Poplar Creek, Illinois, staff at the venue received a call from a woman claiming to work for promoter Jerry Weintraub. She said her name was Carmel and that the concert was canceled. The local police also received a call. This time the caller said Bob was about to be kidnapped by his road manager, Patrick Stansfield.

Carmel Hubbell then leased an unfurnished apartment in a house next to the Point Dume estate for $36 a day. She gave her name as Dylan, and immediately got into trouble with the landlord for causing a disturbance and damaging the premises. The landlord began legal action to evict her. Los Angeles Superior Court then granted a petition, brought by Bob's lawyers, prohibiting Hubbell from harassing Bob and his staff. She was also ordered to stop using the surname Dylan.

While Hubbell was handled by the courts, a legal problem of a different kind arose, one that would ultimately be much more troublesome. In recent years Bob's former manager, Albert Grossman, had decided he was being shortchanged on his share of royalties from Dwarf Music and Big Sky Music. Bob heard via his accountant that Grossman was intending to sue him. So he telephoned Grossman to ask why. Grossman said Bob should read their contracts and said he had not been paid 'what I deserve.' Bob retorted: 'You have been paid enough.' In recent years, he had been paying Grossman approximately $250,000 per annum.

Lawyers representing Grossman and two of his companies – Albert B. Grossman Management, Inc. and Grossman-Glotzer Management Corp. – filed a lawsuit in the state of New York on May 18, 1981, claiming Bob owed at least $51,000 in back royalties and commissions from songs registered to companies in which Grossman still had an interest. He wanted the money, plus $400,000 punitive damages. Bob later counterclaimed on eighteen different points, alleging that Grossman had mismanaged him; appropriated $15,000 from one of his bank accounts to fund two of Grossman's other companies, Callee and Albet Music Corps; and overcharged him with commissions to the tune of at least $7.1 million. Thus began a mammoth legal battle that would drag on for years, bringing up grievances dating back to the very beginning of their association, a battle fueled by bitter enmity, stubbornness, and seemingly bottomless pockets to pay for lawyers. The case file – Albert B. Grossman et al. vs. Bob Dylan – became one of the largest in the state of New York.

Bob flew his band to Europe in mid-June 1981. Three years earlier, Bob had sold out major arenas across the continent and received rave reviews. Nowhere was he more popular than in England. In 1978 Bob and his band had played six nights at the huge Earls Court arena in London, receiving a rapturous reception. DYLAN LAST NIGHT – THE GREATEST CONCERT I HAVE EVER SEEN, was the headline for Ray Connolly's glowing review in the London *Daily Mail*. But in 1981 there were large areas of empty seats as Bob staged six more concerts at Earls Court. Audiences were put off by the publicity about his Christian conversion, and by the fact that spiritual songs still made up a good proportion of each show. Bob's mantle as arguably the greatest figure in popular music was also threatened by Bruce Springsteen, whose recent U.K. tour had been a triumph. Critics compared Bob's concerts unfavorably with those high-energy Springsteen shows. This was slightly unfair as Bob's London concerts were, in fact, long, impassioned performances with a fair smattering of greatest hits. But the references to Jesus, and the gospel singers, were off-putting to many fans who were not accustomed to this type of material.

The final date of the European tour was a major open-air concert, on July 25, in the French city of Avignon. Just as Bob took the stage there was an explosion and the power went out. A Dutch fan had climbed a power pylon and crossed two high-voltage lines at a transformer cage. The crowd turned to see a silhouetted rag doll-like figure doing cartwheels in the air until it hit the ground. Patrick Stansfield ran to the scene. 'He sat up,' says Stansfield. 'In English, he said: "I'm okay. *I'm okay.* I'm okay." And then he fell down and died. Fuck!'

Bob stayed on stage while one of his road crew, Roland Grivelle, walked up and down between the seating blocks calling out in French through a bullhorn that Bob would play once the power came back. Bob stayed on stage throughout, and finally began the show. But the concert was dogged with tragedy; a second fan died that evening when she fell three stories from a seating area.

Dylan returned from this difficult tour for the U.S. release of *Shot of Love* in August. The album fared even worse than had *Saved*, reaching only number thirty-three on the charts. The singles from the album did not chart at all. The failure was a major disappointment and a surprise to Bob who had tried hard to incorporate his faith into a well-made, contemporary-sounding album that could be enjoyed by a secular audience. The public were not buying it, however, and this seems to be part of the reason he decided not to release another album for two years.

A couple of months after the release of *Shot of Love*, Bob flew to New York to give a deposition in the Grossman lawsuit. Interviewed by a team of lawyers representing Grossman, at their Park Avenue office, Bob was unfailingly polite, invariably addressing his interrogators as 'sir,' even when they were being provocative. He described why he thought the Dwarf Music contract was fundamentally unfair. He did not know any other performer signed to such a deal, and maintained that he had never been made aware of what he was agreeing to. Sometimes speaking of himself in the third person as 'Bob Dylan, the writer,' he displayed a good memory regarding his career, but only a basic grasp of business, freely admitting he hardly ever read contracts. He refrained from using harsh language about Grossman personally, talking instead about his feeling that 'something sneaky was going on.' Asked whether he thought Grossman had a reputation as a truthful man, Bob replied, 'I don't know, sir.' In conclusion, talking about the hundreds of thousands of dollars he had paid Grossman each year under their agreements, Bob said: 'It's a lot of money, huh?' Bob intuitively felt that his former manager had earned enough, and he did not want to pay him another cent. He was not concerned with what the contracts said; it was a matter of what was *fair*.

Ten days after giving the deposition, on October 16, 1981, Bob began a U.S. tour with a concert in Milwaukee, Wisconsin. He was on the road until November, the concerts becoming increasingly secular as he traveled across the country. Part of the credit for this change may be due to Al Kooper, who had joined the band and encouraged Bob to play songs they had recorded in the sixties. 'I think that tour was the crossroads. I think that's when he sort of came back,' says Kooper. 'He was drinking coffee, smoking cigarettes. He was ready to rock again.'

Larry Kegan was another familiar face on the tour. Kegan was a good singer and Bob got him up on stage in Merrillville, Indiana, on October 19 to sing an encore of 'No Money Down.' Bob produced a saxophone – an instrument he had never been known to play in public – and barped into it a few times, bluffing that he could play, while Larry Kegan sang. The segment with Kegan went so well that the friends repeated their performance the next night at the Boston Orpheum Theater, Kegan coming on stage both nights in his wheelchair. 'Bob inspired me my whole life and taught me the real meaning of keep on keeping on, no matter what,' says Kegan. 'I owe him a lot, and every moment with him was always exciting.' Traveling in the winter exhausted Kegan, however, and after the Boston show he was taken by ambulance to the hospital. He had contracted pneumonia and had to be left behind to recover as the tour continued. It was depressing for Kegan and Bob felt partly responsible. It would be years before he agreed to take his friend on tour again.

Although these were good concerts, the negative publicity of the previous spiritual tours and the last two devotional albums put people off, as had happened in London. 'They had been turned off by the Christian thing and they were expecting more of that, so they didn't turn out for the shows,' says Bob's assistant Arthur Rosato. 'They had wrong expectations that it was just going to be proselytizing all night and it wasn't that at all.' Poor ticket sales cut the tour short and added to the weight of evidence that Bob was out of touch with his audience. He had always been fairly phlegmatic about his being contrary to the tastes of fans, but now he was making an effort to please them by adding well-known songs to the shows and they were still showing a lack of interest. The only logical decision was for Bob to stop and reassess just what he was doing in his career.

Bob's feelings that his career was going off the rails were compounded when his close friend Howard Alk met a tragic and very sad death. Alk had traveled with the recent tour as one of Bob's retinue of friends. He and Bob had been close since the mid-sixties when they had worked together on *Dont Look Back* and *Eat the Document*. In recent years they had worked together on *Renaldo & Clara*, and lived as neighbors on Bob's Point Dume estate. Bob was sufficiently fond of Alk to sing 'Happy Birthday' to him from the stage in Bethlehem, Pennsylvania, on October 25, when the filmmaker turned fifty-one. During the tour, Alk shot footage for another improvised film, along the lines of *Renaldo & Clara* but on a smaller scale. Bob acted in scenes, along with Al Kooper and crewman Roland Grivelle. There was talk about editing this footage into a movie, but Bob failed to commit. 'Bob was waffling about the project,' says Arthur Rosato. 'Because it wasn't a *real* project – we were going to make it up as [we went] along – and Howard was trying to get more commitment out of Bob as to really what he was doing . . . I think he was feeling that Bob was sort of putting the project to sleep.'

The halfhearted film project was one of several problems that came to a head for Alk at the end of 1981. He had separated from his second wife, moved out of the house on the Point Dume estate, and was sleeping on a cot at Rundown Studios. He stayed there over the Christmas / New Year holidays as the rest of the staff went home to their families. 'He had a bedroom, a converted little work space,' says Rosato. 'It definitely wasn't where you want to be at that stage of your life.' At some time over the holiday, Alk injected himself with heroin. He was found dead of an overdose on January 3, 1982. Following an autopsy, the coroner recorded a verdict of accidental death. But Alk's first wife, Jones, who spoke to him shortly before he died, had no doubts about what had happened. 'He said he was going to kill himself,' she says. There is no way she could tell whether he meant it, but she is confident he did not die by accident. 'Howard was an experienced drug user,' she says. 'It is possible that, by mistake, he killed himself. Sometimes junkies do. But I think that [he] killed himself [deliberately].'

Howard Alk's death was the last in a series of calamities that had befallen Bob over the past five years. First there was the divorce from Sara, and the wretched custody battle over their children. Bob's Christian conversion had upset his family and friends and led to some of the worst reviews and most disappointing record sales of his career. The macabre deaths in Avignon cast a shadow. He had lost friends (albeit distant ones) in Michael Bloomfield and John Lennon. Carmel Hubbell caused more unhappiness, and made him fear for his own safety. He was facing years of expensive, time-consuming, and unhappy legal argument over his dispute with Albert Grossman. But it was the death of Alk that stopped Bob in his tracks. 'That's kind of when Bob decided to stop touring for a while,' says Rosato. 'He told me he wasn't going to go out [on tour] until '84 . . . He was upset, and he talked a little bit. He wanted to know if I was going to be okay . . . But he shut down the studio then and there.' Having reached the age of forty, Bob Dylan's brilliant career had begun to falter and it would be a long time before he regained his assurance and the acclaim of the public.

CHAPTER 9

GLIMPSES

The early years of Bob Dylan's career were filled with remarkable achievements as he wrote songs with fecundity, recorded extraordinary albums, and regularly gave brilliant concerts. He had continued to produce outstanding work throughout the 1970s, if less consistently. From 1982 to 1992, as he moved into middle age, Bob seemed at times to have lost touch with his talent and also with his audience. Yet even this difficult period provided glimpses of his genius.

In the year after Howard Alk's death, Bob made only two public appearances. On March 15, 1982, he was inducted into the Songwriters Hall of Fame. The ceremony took place at the Hilton Hotel in New York in front of songwriting luminaries such as Harold Arlen and Sammy Cahn. The occasion made Bob highly nervous and Oscar Brand noticed him swallowing pills. Brand had little doubt what they were. 'One was to make him high, and the other was to take him down a little bit. He was trying to find a place where he could be happy.' Bob's anxiety also manifested itself when he greeted Brand with a hug and a kiss on the cheek, which was very out of character. In his acceptance speech, Bob said he was particularly honored, considering he could not read or write music. Comedian Tony Randall then made a joke about finding him a teacher. Most people laughed, but Bob was clearly stung by the remark, a sign of how easily he could be hurt.

His second and final public appearance of the year was a ramshackle duet with Joan Baez, on June 6, at a nuclear disarmament rally in Pasadena, California. Although there had been long gaps in their relationship, they occasionally resumed their romance and he fled to Baez's home around this time after running into trouble with one of his girlfriends.

Although Bob never had another manager who controlled his career like Albert Grossman had, in 1982 he hired the management services of Elliot Roberts, a protégé of David Geffen. Meanwhile, Grossman pursued his lawsuit for back royalties. Bob retaliated by stopping quarterly payments from the companies in which Grossman had an interest, Dwarf Music and Big Sky Music. Bob's lawyers had even more to deal with when a man filed a personal injury suit claiming he had been attacked by one of the guard dogs at Dylan's Point Dume estate.

In the midst of this turmoil, the most significant personal event of 1982 was the bar mitzvah of Bob's second son, Samuel. The ceremony was conducted at a temple in Los Angeles and attended by Sara Dylan, close friends, and music business associates. After the ceremony, David Geffen introduced Bob to his escort, Carole Childs, a petite, red-haired A&R executive at Geffen Records. As Childs recalls, she took to Bob immediately. Raised as a Jew in Great Neck, Long Island, she was a thirty-eight-year-old self-proclaimed pantheist whose conversation was sprinkled with quotations from the Christian handbook *The Daily Word*, occasional expletives, and shrieks of laughter. She was the type of slightly eccentric woman Bob had always found attractive, and he invited her to his home. Childs soon found herself very much in love. 'I'm this little Jewish girl from Great Neck that always thought a cute guy with curly hair who was skinny [and] had a motorcycle was the grooviest thing on earth . . . he just happened to be Bob Dylan,' she says. Their relationship lasted ten years. During this time, Childs traveled extensively with Bob and also suggested musicians and producers he might work with.

Still, she never deluded herself into thinking she was of vital importance to Bob's well-being; he was such a self-contained man it seemed he did not really need anybody. His music, which was by far the most important thing in his life, was something he created alone. 'He would [write songs] if he were with a canary,' says Childs. 'He writes those songs alone. He is his own man. He stands proud in his shoes. He don't need nobody to do nothin' [for him]. He's that gifted and that talented.'

During Bob's sabbatical, the music industry went through major changes that would have repercussions for his career when he went back to work. Compact discs were introduced in 1982, an innovation that would eventually alter the means by which music was both recorded and marketed. More significant in the short term was the advent of music videos. MTV had more than sixteen million subscribers within two years of its launch in 1981. When Bob resumed his career in 1983, to make the album *Infidels*, he had to take into account these notable changes. As a result, he produced a record that had a contemporary sound and made pop videos to promote it.

Since they worked together on *Slow Train Coming*, Mark Knopfler's band, Dire Straits, had become one of the premier acts of the MTV-CD age. To get a bright, modern sound Bob asked Knopfler to coproduce and play on his new album, along with Dire Straits keyboardist Alan Clark. Although Knopfler was an accomplished guitarist, Bob also hired Mick Taylor, formerly of The Rolling Stones, to play guitar. Jamaican rhythm artists Sly Dunbar and Robbie Shakespeare played drums and bass.

Bob came to the sessions with a number of strong songs. 'Lord Protect My Child' had something of the sentiment of 'Forever Young,' but seemed more specifically about Bob's own sons, now in their adolescence. Bob delivered the song with a quiet intensity that characterized his mood during the sessions. 'Foot of Pride' was a biblical stomp that showed Bob had not abandoned his eschatological views. 'Blind Willie McTell' was simply one of the greatest songs he had ever written. Born sometime around 1901, 'Blind' Willie McTell was a blues singer and twelve-string guitarist who lived most of his life in Atlanta, Georgia, making recordings that had the easy sound of an artist utterly assured of his music. Although not a name familiar to mainstream audiences, the blues player was legendary among musicians. In lamenting the passing of McTell, who died in semi-obscurity in 1959, Bob conjured up a vivid dreamscape of the South: magnolia flowers in bloom, plantations, and ghostly slave ships. The narrator stepped back from the tableau in the last verse – a Brechtian shift in perspective, as in the last verse of 'Black Diamond Bay' – and stared out of a hotel window, contemplating the fact that nobody could sing the blues as well as Blind Willie McTell. The modesty of these lyrics – though 'Blind Willie McTell' illustrated clearly that Bob himself was a mighty blues singer – added to the power of the song, completing a great tribute to the heritage of African-American music.

'Jokerman' was a collage of images reminiscent of *Blonde on Blonde* and, together with 'I and I,' had a subtle reggae feel. 'We can slip it in so quietly that you wouldn't realize that's what we're doing,' says Sly Dunbar, who was impressed by how easy it was to work with Bob. 'He would just come into the studio with his 'armonica and his guitar, and he start to play the song, and we just fall into the groove. He would take different takes of a song in different keys and he would change words on the fly.' The track 'Jokerman' was finished before Dunbar realized they were recording. 'He look at us and say, "That's the take." . . . We couldn't believe how smooth it went.' 'Sweetheart Like You' was a pretty love song, with a lyric – about a woman's place being in the home – that clashed with modern sensibilities.

Political correctness, as ever, was unimportant to Bob, who was in many ways an old-fashioned chauvinist and gave the impression he believed that women should not work. He told *Rolling Stone* in 1987 that he hated to see female artists perform, 'because they whore themselves. Especially the ones that don't wear anything.' Several of the other songs likewise had a reactionary element. 'Union Sundown' was a diatribe about how American industry had been undercut by emerging foreign economies. Bob made gloomy prognostications for the future of mankind in 'License to Kill,' singing that the moon landings were man's first step toward doom. 'Neighborhood Bully' seemed to support Israel in its battles with its Arab neighbors. This song, and the photograph of Bob in Jerusalem on the inside sleeve of *Infidels*, appeared to confirm press reports that he had taken up with a fundamentalist Hasidic group. In the fall of 1983, Bob's seventeen-year-old son Jesse had a belated bar mitzvah in Jerusalem – Jakob and Samuel had already been bar mitzvahed in California – and Bob was photographed wearing a yarmulke at the Wailing Wall, adding to speculation that he had returned to Judaism. 'As far as we're concerned, he was a confused Jew,' Rabbi Kasriel Kastel told *Christianity Today*. 'We feel he's coming back.' In fact, Jesse was on vacation in Israel with his grandmother, Beatty, when they discovered a bar mitzvah could be conducted quickly and easily at the Wailing Wall and Bob simply flew in to play his part. He still believed Jesus Christ was the Messiah, and kept a broadly Christian outlook, although he had not maintained regular contact with the Vineyard Fellowship since the early flush of his conversion.

The recording sessions were progressing well when Mark Knopfler had to fly to Germany for a brief tour with Dire Straits. He offered to come back and finish *Infidels* after the tour. Although Bob had committed himself to taking more time with this record than with virtually any previous album, he felt he had been in the studio long enough. He told Knopfler his new contract with Columbia meant he had to put out a record almost every year. 'He was in a hurry to [get] it out there, and I was in no hurry at all . . . he went in [with] another engineer instead of Neil Dorfsman,' says Knopfler. Bob and his engineer rearranged, remixed, and overdubbed tracks, until the resulting album was perhaps less impressive than it might have been had he waited for Knopfler to return. Most startling was the fact that when Bob sequenced the album he did not include the best songs and, for some reason, chose to leave out 'Blind Willie McTell.' Larry 'Ratso' Sloman, the journalist from The Rolling Thunder Revue, who had become a friend, was aghast when Bob played him the album in the studio. 'Where's "Blind Willie McTell"?' asked Ratso.

'Didn't make it.'

'WHAT? How can you not put one of the greatest songs you ever wrote [on] the album?'

'Oh, Ratso, it's okay,' said Bob, adding that he had made dozens of records. One more did not matter much. But the fact that Bob overlooked one of his greatest songs is a decision so eccentric it is almost impossible to fathom. When pressed for an explanation, he said simply that he did not think he had 'recorded it right.'

Now that the album was complete, the long lead track 'Jokerman' was chosen as a single and Columbia asked Bob to make a pop video to promote it. Considering his long-standing interest in filmmaking, Bob seemed to be an artist who would take naturally to this new medium. After all, he had directed movies and acted. The remarkable scene opening the documentary *Dont Look Back*, where he flipped over cards printed with the lyrics of 'Subterranean Homesick Blues,' was seen by many as a prototype of the music video. Yet when it came to making a video for 'Jokerman,' Bob was uncomfortable about acting and disdainful of the medium in general. 'I know they're thought of as an art form, but I don't think they are,' he said. 'They're on and they're over too fast.'

For his first venture into video, Bob hired Ratso and George Lois as producer and director for the 'Jokerman' video. Lois had the innovative idea of intercutting close-ups of Bob with images from the history of art, including *The Musicians' Hell* by Hieronymus Bosch, and overlaying the lyrics so that they could be read on-screen. The difficult part was getting Bob to mime for the cameras. 'His dubbing was way off,' says Lois. 'I'd say, "Bob you've got to work harder. You've gotta dub the motherfucker. You gotta put your words to your own work. It's gotta match. If it doesn't match, you look like a schmuck."' Although the 'Jokerman' single failed to chart, the video was widely praised. Everybody seemed to like it, in fact, except Bob. 'When I saw the videos [*sic*], all I saw was a shot of me from my mouth to my forehead on the screen,' he told *Rolling Stone*. 'I figure, "Isn't that somethin'? I'm paying for that?"' Lois was taken aback when he read the interview: 'It was ungracious.'

In the fall of 1983, around the time *Infidels* was released, Bob experimented by working with young musicians raised on the music of bands like The Clash that had emerged from the British punk movement of the late 1970s. It was music that his sons loved and, despite his age, and his association with the sixties, Bob also found the music exciting. 'I think Bob has always listened to other stuff. He is not one of those guys who lives in a time warp,' says drummer Charlie Quintana, one of a handful of young L.A. musicians invited to Point Dume to jam with Bob. Others included bass player Tony Marisco and guitarist J. J. Holiday. They drove to Point Dume in an old Volkswagen bug for the first session, not knowing quite what to expect. Some of the musicians were so young they did not fully realize who Dylan was.

The Point Dume estate had become even more extraordinary since Bob and Sara had divorced. In an attempt to obtain more privacy, Bob had planted fast-growing conifers around the perimeter. A military-style sentry box was built at the gate, with security men on duty.

Once past the gate, there were several abandoned vehicles – vintage cars, vans, even an old ambulance rotting in a weed patch. There was a stack of rusting powerboats – testament to Bob's brief enthusiasm for boating – and a gaily-painted gypsy caravan left over from the hippy artisans who had helped build the mansion. Bob had introduced chickens and pheasants to the property. Together with horses and several fearsome dogs, the clucking, squawking fowl gave the estate a farmlike atmosphere. Adjacent to the wood-frame mansion, with its copper dome and towering stone chimney stacks, was a private garden reserved for Bob's use and the enormous, polymorphous swimming pool. The rest of the twelve-acre property was mostly overgrown with thick hedges and trees that hid garages and sundry outbuildings. The musicians were directed to drive the Volkswagen down a track to a guest house and to set up in a room overlooking the ocean.

After lunch, Bob came down from the big house wearing a raincoat, rubber boots, and swinging a stick. 'To me, he looked like he had just got off the fishing boat,' says J. J. Holiday. Bob had a monstrous dog with him. 'What's the name of that dog?' they asked. Bob said it was called Baby, which made them laugh. He said they could practice until six o'clock, but then they had to stop. Apparently he had neighbor problems. Sure enough, when they forgot the time and played past six, the neighbor called the police and a squad car pulled up outside.

The musicians played with Bob regularly at Point Dume over the winter of 1983–84, gaining a remarkable insight into his creative method. They played anything they felt like, as Bob made idiosyncratic suggestions. One day he asked them to play like an old blues musician crossed with a striptease show. Bob's sometime girlfriend Clydie King came by occasionally to sing duets on old doo-wop songs. Bob also sang lyrics the musicians had never heard before. They asked for the titles of these songs, eager to learn Bob's material, because he had suggested at one stage that they might do a South American tour. 'I remember him saying, "Well, this won't be like a Bob Dylan tour. This will be more like just a band playing gigs,"' says Holiday. 'So we [were] doing not necessarily a bunch of Bob Dylan songs. We were doing all kinds of stuff. We did "We Three", [by] The Ink Spots, [and] "My Guy."' When they asked Bob what the names of some of the other songs were, he would answer vaguely. But if they played the song twice, the lyric would often be different and the musicians began to understand Bob was making up songs as he went along. 'I would play a riff just off [the top of] my head and he would start singing and then that would be a song!' says Holiday. 'He was just going with it completely.'

After playing at Point Dume for several months, Bob decided to take the young musicians with him to New York in March 1984 to appear on *Late Night with David Letterman*. Bob had agreed to perform on the popular talk show to promote *Infidels* so long as he was not required to talk to the host. The nervous musicians asked Bob what they should wear and what songs he wanted to play. Bob said they should 'look cute and punky,' and remained vague as to the set list. On the show, Letterman introduced Bob as his very special guest and held up a copy of *Infidels* for the camera. It was, he said, 'a fine piece of work.' Almost any other artist would have launched straight into one of the new songs from the album they were publicizing, but Bob began with the old Sonny Boy Williamson blues 'Don't Start Me to Talkin'.' Quintana says they did not even rehearse it. Indeed, Bob seemed determined to be as contrary as possible. He stepped so far off his mark that he was almost out of camera shot. When he performed the third song, 'Jokerman,' he turned his back on the cameras and rummaged for a harmonica for what seemed like several minutes. 'You'd think he would go to a great deal of trouble to get it together for a major TV appearance like that,' says Holiday. 'But he didn't care what happened.

That's what's great about him. We just went out on the Letterman show and jammed.' It was one of the most engaging television appearances of his career, but it did little to help sales of *Infidels*, which reached only number twenty in the U.S. album charts despite favorable reviews.

Bob did go back on the road in 1984, but not to South America with the band he put together for the Letterman show. Instead, he signed with Bill Graham to do a lucrative stadium tour of Europe. In terms of the size of the venues, it would be one of the largest tours he ever undertook. To fill massive spaces like Wembley Stadium in London and the Parc de Sceaux in Paris, Bob needed a big sound and he asked Mick Taylor to assemble an experienced rock 'n' roll band. 'Basically, we put a band together that was quite simple and straightforward,' says Taylor. 'It was just bass, guitar, drums, and keyboards. Me and him played guitar.' Ian McLagan, formerly of The Faces, was hired to play Hammond organ. The drummer was Colin Allen, an old friend of Taylor. Bass player Greg Sutton was the only American in the band.

The tour opened at the Roman amphitheater in Verona, Italy, on May 28 and traveled through Europe until July, playing to audiences of up to one hundred thousand people. The first show was a ragged performance on an inauspiciously wet evening. The band was under-rehearsed and, according to McLagan, they had only a vague idea of the set list. Taylor noticed that Bob was apprehensive before going on stage. But as the tour progressed he gained in confidence and wanted to play longer sets. 'When we [were] rehearsing for the tour, I remember Bob saying: "I'd like you guys to play a couple of songs on your own,"' says Taylor. 'But after about two or three gigs we couldn't get him off stage, and he ended up doing like a twenty-five-minute solo spot in the middle of the show, just on acoustic guitar.'

Bill Graham booked support acts, headed by Carlos Santana and augmented with artists such as Joan Baez. She thought she would get equal billing with Bob, and would sing with him on stage like the old days. She managed to get Bob to sing 'Blowin' in the Wind' as a shaky duet at the St. Pauli Stadion, Hamburg, and they did two songs together at the Olympia Stadion, Munich, but Baez was not invited on stage with Bob again after that. Indeed, Bob seemed uncomfortable with her. Her name did not appear next to his in promotional material, as she had expected, and after a few days she found herself singing at the bottom of the bill to half-empty stadiums in the rain. Feeling demoralized, she quit the tour. Bob called her into his dressing room to say goodbye. He was sprawled on a sofa, looking tired, but not too tired to flirt.

'Wow, you got great legs,' he said, running a hand up her skirt. 'Where'd you get them muscles?'

Baez brushed the flirtation aside and kissed him goodbye. The tour had been a miserable experience for her, with Bob letting her down much as he had in England in 1965. Looking at their relationship over the past twenty or so years, Bob had behaved so badly that one wonders whether he ever cared for Baez at all.

The tour concluded for Bob four weeks later with shows in Britain and Ireland, by which time he was a commanding presence on stage in a black frock coat. The shows sold out, proving that, despite a lukewarm reception in 1981, he could still be a big draw. 'When he came back and we did the Dylan-Santana show, [he] rose to the top,' says promoter Harvey Goldsmith. He also showed he was not afraid to experiment, even in front of such huge audiences, and introduced a reworked acoustic version of 'Tangled Up in Blue.' Bob had never been entirely happy with the *Blood on the Tracks* version, and now made extensive changes to the imagery as well as a change in the tense. Few major artists would have had the nerve to alter one of their most popular songs, but arguably he improved 'Tangled Up in Blue,' and it became the highlight of the 1984 live album *Real Live*.

The European tour had catered to a broad audience, with its mainstream rock sound and a set list of well-known songs. *Infidels* had also been one of the most accessible albums of his career. His next album carried forward this popularizing approach, engineered to sound as modern and commercial as possible. The basic tracks for what became *Empire Burlesque* were recorded in New York and Los Angeles between July 1984 and March 1985. A host of musicians played on it, including old friends Al Kooper, Jim Keltner, Ted Perlman, and Ronnie Wood. The new songs did not contain explicit biblical references or an obvious religious message. Instead, Bob turned to film culture for the imagery on at least three of the record's tracks. 'Tight Connection to My Heart (Has Anybody Seen My Love)' drew on Humphrey Bogart's dialogue in *Sirocco* (where Bogart says: 'I've got to move fast – I can't with you around my neck') along with lines from *The Maltese Falcon*. Other cinematic references included the mention of actor Peter O'Toole in 'Clean Cut Kid' and lines from Bogart and Clint Eastwood movies in 'Seeing the Real You at Last.'

Bob had already recorded most of the songs when he hired engineer/producer Arthur Baker to work on the album. A twenty-eight-year-old Bostonian, Baker had achieved great success in recent months remixing songs by Cyndi Lauper and Bruce Springsteen – 'Girls Just Want to Have Fun' and 'Dancing in the Dark' – into dance hits. Baker was summoned to Bob's New York hotel suite to find the door open. He walked into a living room littered with food trays, three or four cassette players, and piles of cassettes. 'It looked like he hadn't had any-one clean the room for a while,' recalls Baker. 'Then he walked in the room and I was definitely fazed by him because I had grown up as a real Dylan fan.' Bob did not explicitly say he wanted his album to sound like a dance record and Baker rather liked Bob's natural approach to recording. Even so, he felt sure he had been hired to make *Empire Burlesque* sound 'a little bit more contemporary.'

With Baker in the studio, Bob recorded two new tracks. The first was a retake of the apocalyptic 'When the Night Comes Falling from the Sky.' Bob had previously recorded a version for the album with members of Bruce Springsteen's E Street Band. The song pulsed with life and he had delivered an excellent, snarling vocal. Bob thought it sounded too much like a Springsteen record however, so Baker duly produced a new version with an echoing drum sound. The other new song was 'Dark Eyes,' which Bob wrote to conclude the album, performing alone with acoustic guitar. 'I finally figured out that the tenth song needed to be acoustic, so I just wrote it,' he said. 'I wrote it because none of the other songs fit that spot, that certain place.' Although not a great song, the last verse delivered the most interesting image on the album as Bob sang about 'a million faces' at his feet (presumably meaning the impression he got of an audience when on stage), but that all he saw were dark eyes.

There was a long period of reworking the tracks, and Bob agreed to overdub vocals, something he also did for *Infidels* but which he generally disliked doing. He sang with various backing singers including Carolyn Dennis, Peggi Blu (wife of Ted Perlman), and 'Queen' Esther Marrow. The girls would bring their children to the studio and each evening Bob had soul food sent over from Sylvia's Restaurant in Harlem. Bob's teenage son Jesse was hanging out at the sessions, giving a family atmosphere to the evenings. Bob was relaxed, singing the Madonna song 'Like a Virgin' for a joke and asking Baker if they could get a sound like her albums.

Baker spent a month remixing *Empire Burlesque* in the spring of 1985, overdubbing the type of electronic effects that were then the height of fashion in the music business. Jim Keltner was shocked that his backbeat on 'Trust Yourself' was replaced with a clap from a drum machine. 'I was very, very disappointed,' he says.

The mixing process seemed interminable to Bob. 'We mixed the whole of *Blonde on Blonde* in two days,' he grumbled one day. Baker reminded him that that was four-track recording; he was working with forty-eight tracks. Bob became so bored he went out to see a movie.

At the end of the day, Bob was pleased enough with *Empire Burlesque* to ask Baker to produce his next album (although it ultimately did not happen). But *Empire Burlesque* was not a record that found much favor with critics or public. 'Some of the songs sort of stand up and some of them don't. Some of it I would have done differently,' says Baker. 'But they were good songs. Songs like "Emotionally Yours," "I Remember You," and "When the Night Comes Falling" – all those were covered by other artists.'

Again Columbia wanted Bob to make a video to promote a single from the album, and this time he chose to work with Paul Schrader, screenwriter of *Taxi Driver* and director of *Mishima*. Bob had known Schrader since the 1970s and had talked with him previously about developing what Bob described as 'these films lying around in [my] head.' At a party in 1978 Bob had pitched a movie about two Spanish aristocrats in love with the same woman. About twenty minutes into the pitch Bob fell into a musical cadence. 'It was sort of dom-de-dom-de-dom. In fact, he was humming it,' says Schrader, who had to tell Bob that his idea was not a movie but a song. 'He was a little disappointed. He sort of made a gruff noise [and] went out the door.' Bob now wanted Schrader to make a video for 'Tight Connection to My Heart (Has Anybody Seen My Love),' the lead track to *Empire Burlesque*. He considered it one of the most visual songs he had ever written. They decided to shoot it in Tokyo with the *Mishima* crew.

When they arrived in Japan, Schrader realized the

project was misconceived. 'None of this is a happy memory for me, because I truly fucked this up,' he says. He did not know or understand the medium of music video. Even worse, it became clear that Bob did not really want to make the film, even though it had been his idea. 'He was trying to find a way so that he could do the video and not actually appear in the video, which is certainly not a good sign.' Schrader apologized for accepting the commission. 'If you ever hear I'm doing another music video, take me out in the back yard and hose me down,' he told Bob. Since they were halfway through filming, they completed the video and the experience was not entirely negative, from Schrader's point of view. 'It was always pleasant to be with him because you are in the presence of somebody you not only respect enormously, but is fucking brilliant.' From Bob's point of view, it was a colossal waste of time and the video was terrible, as they both feared, with Bob self-consciously acting out a literal interpretation of the lyric. He made two further videos, with other directors, to promote singles from *Empire Burlesque* ('When the Night Comes Falling from the Sky' and 'Emotionally Yours'). But it was all to no avail. Nothing could excite interest in what remains one of the least engaging albums of his career. Schrader got the impression that Bob was not overly concerned about the poor sales because Columbia was committed to supporting him. 'Columbia carries him . . . they would never, ever drop Bob Dylan,' says Schrader. 'He could have an indeterminate number of flops, one after another, and the label would never drop him. [He] was one of the two or three sacrosanct, protected artists on that label. He had gone through times when albums just did not sell, you know, and yet they stood by him.'

In the winter of 1984, while Bob was planning *Empire Burlesque*, Irish singer Bob Geldof had cajoled a number of his fellow pop stars into recording a British charity single, to raise money for the humanitarian disaster in Ethiopia. The success of the project spawned an American charity single, 'We Are the World,' recorded in January 1985 while Bob was making *Empire Burlesque.* He found time to take part, along with such great artists as Ray Charles and Stevie Wonder. Although he appeared thoroughly glum during the recording – almost scowling at photographers – Bob was, in fact, privately enthused about the project. 'I just did something that's going to be a big hit,' he told friends Ted Perlman and Peggi Blu. 'It'll be number one!' Sure enough, the record was number one for four weeks in the spring of 1985.

Bob Geldof then got together with Bill Graham and Harvey Goldsmith to stage twin charity concerts – at Wembley Stadium in London and JFK Stadium in Philadelphia – on Saturday, July 13, 1985. Live Aid was the biggest charity concert ever, rivaling the Woodstock Festival as the greatest popular music concert of modern times. The fact that Dylan was chosen to headline the Philadelphia show, the last act before a host of artists crowded the stage for a finale singalong to 'We Are the World,' was testament to his enduring legend. It was also a result of Bill Graham's involvement. 'Bill worshiped Bob and respected Bob as a poet,' says Patrick Stansfield, one of Graham's senior assistants in Philadelphia. 'He had the power to decide [who went on], in the face of the TV gods.' The original plan was for Bob to sing 'Blowin' in the Wind' with the re-formed Peter, Paul and Mary. They rehearsed together, but Bob backed out at the last minute. 'Mary was like a woman scorned,' says Noel Paul Stookey. 'She was really hurt.' Instead, Bob chose to perform with Keith Richards and Ronnie Wood. He spent the long, humid afternoon of July 13 hanging out with the Stones in his trailer, along with girlfriend Carole Childs. Arthur Baker visited backstage and says he is sure, due to the heat for one thing, that Bob and the Stones had a few drinks.

Late at night, at the climax of the show, Jack Nicholson came on stage and said: 'Some artists' work speaks for itself. Some artists' work speaks for its generation. It's my deep personal pleasure to present to you one of America's great voices of freedom. IT CAN ONLY BE ONE MAN,' he said, becoming suddenly very excited. 'The transcendent BOB DYLAN!' It was a terrific buildup and Bob walked out to a roar from the stadium crowd, with a billion people watching on television. Microphones had been set up at the lip of the stage, in front of the curtain, behind which Graham's crew was setting the stage for the finale. Bob looked good, in a white jacket and black pants, and seemed sober. The same could not be said of the Stones, who lurched on stage with acoustic guitars, looking like they had just been thrown out of a pub. Bob started with 'Ballad of Hollis Brown.' There were shrieks of feedback because Bob and the Stones were performing in front of the speakers and the sound was feeding back into the gigantic PA system. This was an elementary mistake in staging and it is surprising Bob even agreed to perform under such unprofessional conditions. Most acts on the bill worked on the main stage in the routine way, but because of pressure to get the stage changed in time for the finale, and because Bob did not need space for a full band, he had been cajoled into performing like this. The conditions tested his nerve and sweat glistened on his face as he dragged 'Ballad of Hollis Brown' to its conclusion. Then, before the next song, he said, 'I'd just like to say I hope that some of the money that's raised for the people in Africa, maybe they could just take a little bit of it – maybe one or two million maybe – and use it, say, to pay the . . . er . . . pay the mortgages on some of the farms . . . the farmers here owe to the banks.' There was some cheering from the Philadelphia crowd. But Bob Geldof, watching on television in London, was aghast. He thought Bob displayed a 'complete lack of understanding of the issues raised by Live Aid.' Bob struggled through 'When the Ship Comes In' before concluding with 'Blowin' in the Wind.' He broke a string and had to borrow Ronnie Wood's guitar. It was a merciful moment when Lionel Richie came on stage for 'We Are the World.' As he came off, Bob passed Arthur Baker. 'The first thing he said to me [was]: "Do you think they understood what I was saying?"'

Bob's comments at the concert seemed injudicious; American farmers may have been suffering hard times, but people in Africa were starving to death. Yet his words led indirectly to another major charity event; shortly after Live Aid, Willie Nelson was inspired to organize the Farm Aid benefit concert to help debt-ridden American farmers. Bob naturally agreed to appear at the show, held in an open-air sports arena in Champaign, Illinois, on September 22. He would be backed by Tom Petty and The Heartbreakers. Like Mark Knopfler, Petty was a singer-songwriter from a younger generation who had been greatly influenced by Bob. For Farm Aid, Bob also called upon the services of a quartet of African-American backing singers: Peggi Blu, Queen Esther Marrow, sometime girlfriend Carolyn Dennis, and her mother Madelyn Quebec. Despite adverse weather, the performance was a triumph. Bob breathed life into songs from *Empire Burlesque* and made even the timeworn 'Maggie's Farm' sound fresh.

Although Bob's affinity with farmers might seem unexpected, he had of course grown up in a small town in the Midwest and he still spent part of each year on his own farm in Minnesota. The Midwest was a region he felt close to and enjoyed visiting. That year he had turned up unexpectedly in an old station wagon outside his childhood home at 2425 7th Avenue, Hibbing. 'Ma, that looks like Bob Dylan in that car,' said teenager Pat Marolt, home from Hibbing High for lunch. Angel Marolt, who had bought the old Zimmerman home from Beatty after Abe had died, walked outside.

'Can I help you?' she asked.

'Well, I was just going to Duluth where my father's buried [and] I just thought I'd come and see the house,' said Bob. He was very bashful, looking down when he talked. But he accepted Angel Marolt's invitation to come inside. Bob talked about how his father had spent a whole winter putting up the pine paneling in the basement. Then he looked at his bedroom and said how small it seemed. In the kitchen, he found plates his mother had left behind. His nostalgia for his home, and the town where he had grown up, was obviously very strong.

In the fall of 1985 Columbia released *Biograph*, a five-record box-set compilation of fifty-three Dylan songs, eighteen of which were previously unreleased tracks. It was the first time a living popular music star had been given such a major retrospective. The compilation came with two booklets based on interviews with Bob, conducted by former *Rolling Stone* journalist Cameron Crowe, in which Bob revealed much about his work and philosophy, saying he felt like a troubadour from the Dark Ages, singing for his supper. He also conceded that he sometimes got by on fifty percent of his talent, maybe less. *Biograph* cost very little to produce, because the music was already recorded, and it retailed at $30. Even at this price it sold well, unexpectedly going gold and then platinum with sales in the United States of more than a quarter of a million units.* This generated $7.5 million in gross sales and showed record executives that maturing music listeners were now affluent enough to pay twice for music they already had, as long as it was packaged nicely and some bonus tracks were included. The success of *Biograph*, therefore, led to a spate of box sets from other artists.

To celebrate the launch of *Biograph*, Columbia hosted a party for Bob at the Whitney Museum in New York on November 13. The party was attended by old friends

*Because *Biograph* is a multidisc set, the RIAA counts each disc separately. Thus even though *Biograph* unit sales reached only 250,000, it was classified as a million-selling platinum record.

including Harold Leventhal, who had overcome his anger over Bob's Christian conversion and gave Columbia a Woody Guthrie drawing to present to Bob, and celebrities such as David Bowie and Yoko Ono. Carole Childs, who had been dating Bob for three years by now, was his date for the evening, but she had only to open *Biograph* to see that she was not the only woman in his life. One of the two booklets that came with the set was liberally illustrated with photographs of Bob with Clydie King, including a picture next to the gypsy caravan at his Point Dume home. Childs knew about the relationship and claims it did not bother her. 'Clydie was on the road with Bob for years,' she says. 'Show me a fidelious [*sic*] guy and I'll show you a liar.'

The fact that Bob was dating both Childs and King did not stop him picking up another woman at the party. Susan Ross was a blond, thirty-three-year-old former road manager. Invited to the Whitney by a friend, she turned up in a five-dollar thrift-shop dress of blue lace. Almost every other woman was wearing chic black, making her feel out of place until she found herself standing next to Bob and he made it clear he was interested in her. He asked what she thought of the party, and asked for her telephone number. Ross claims Bob came to her hotel three days later. 'We hung out and talked for about four hours, just necking.' They did not see each other for the next few months, because Bob was abroad, but they spoke by telephone and when Bob returned to the United States they began seeing each other. Ross says she became pregnant with Bob's child and, although she says the pregnancy was terminated, it was the start of a long but often difficult relationship. Ross says Bob was a 'raging alcoholic' when they met, was reluctant to make any commitment to her, and was even wary of buying her gifts.

Ross also knew Bob was seeing other women. Indeed, he had an abundance of girlfriends. Some of his female admirers were distinguished in their own right. Elizabeth

Taylor was smitten with Bob. She made her feelings clear when they met backstage at a tribute concert to Martin Luther King Jr. in Washington, D.C., in January 1986. 'We were sitting in the green room and I had Liz Taylor on one side of me and Bob on the other side and Elizabeth saw Bob and just hit on him,' says Ted Perlman. 'She got all giddy over him. Bob was wearing this flannel shirt outside his dirty jeans and he's got work boots on. He's got dirt under his fingernails. His hair hasn't been washed for three days . . . He's skinny and he's grungy and his personal hygiene – he has no hygiene. That's just the way he is . . . But women don't care. He has a kind of power over them.'

Despite his labyrinthine love life, Carole Childs maintains that Bob is, at heart, a 'wonderful family guy. Wonderful, basic Midwestern family guy [with] tremendous principles. All straight-ahead, good, aware-thinking principles.' These principles were about to be tested to the limit. Apparently not content with the company of Childs, King, and Ross – and whomever else he could pick up – Bob had recently resumed his relationship with backing singer Carolyn Dennis.

Bob had dated Carolyn Dennis on and off since she started working for him during the 1978 world tour, when she took over from Debi Dye-Gibson. Carolyn then married a drummer and had a family. The marriage did not last long, and she began dating Bob again. Maria Muldaur was friendly with Bob, Carolyn, and several of the other backing singers who worked with him over the years. 'I think he [dated] some of these black girls because they didn't idolize him. They were real down to earth and they didn't worship him,' she explains. '[They are] strong women who would just say, *cut off your bullshit.*' Bob's music was not popular in the African-American community and black people rarely came to his shows. While women from his own, white middle-class background often saw him as an overawing presence, he was just another guy to African-American women and this was refreshing to him. 'These girls all tell me that they had no idea who he was,' says Muldaur. 'But then, of course, they get on the tour with him and they see what a big deal he was and I do believe, despite everybody's pure Christian intentions, there was a lot of jockeying for position to see who would end up being Bob's girl.'

At the age of thirty-one, Carolyn Dennis became pregnant with Bob's child. She gave birth to a daughter at the Humana Hospital West Hills in Canoga Park, California, on January 31, 1986. The child was named Desiree Gabrielle Dennis-Dylan, with the name of the father listed on the birth certificate as Robert Dylan. The birth was one of the most closely guarded secrets of Bob's career. Not even close friends and members of Bob's family knew at first, and the full facts have not been revealed until now.

Three days after Desiree's birth, Bob flew to New Zealand to begin a major tour with Tom Petty and The Heartbreakers. A film made from two of the shows in Sydney, Australia, was later shown on HBO in America and released on video as *Hard to Handle*. During a rare press conference in Sydney, Bob seemed bored until he was asked about the importance of women in his life. 'I couldn't live without them,' he replied, with a wolfish grin. An actress, Amelia Caruana, later claimed to have been Bob's lover during this tour.

After Australia, Bob traveled to Japan. He was there when he received the sad news that The Band's keyboardist and vocalist, Richard Manuel, had died. The Band had reformed in 1983, but without Robbie Robertson, who did not want to go back on the road. They were soon reduced to playing club dates. Manuel was particularly sensitive to the loss of status and was drinking very heavily and using cocaine. On March 3, 1986, The Band performed two sets at the Cheek to Cheek

Lounge in Winter Park, Florida. In the early hours of the following morning Manuel used his belt to hang himself from a shower-curtain rod in the bathroom of his room at the Quality Inn Motel. He was forty-two.

The far east tour had given Bob time to think about the situation with Carolyn Dennis, and the fact that he was a father again seventeen years after the birth of Jakob. Bob made a momentous decision. Although he was insistent that the existence of a sixth Dylan child should remain secret – seemingly because of his distaste for people knowing anything about his personal life, but also to protect the child – he would do everything to make sure Desiree had a stable family life. The first step was to marry her mother. The wedding of Bob and Carolyn Dennis took place in Los Angeles on June 4, 1986. The certificate was filed with the Los Angeles County Registrar as a 'confidential marriage.' There was not even a hint in the press. 'We were [all] sworn to secrecy never to mention it,' says Ted Perlman.

Bob did not see fit to tell Carole Childs he was married, and they continued to date. Apparently those basic Midwestern principles did not preclude deception, and she chose not to be bothered by the situation. 'I didn't know he was married to [Carolyn]. But I knew she was a friend of his,' says Childs. 'You might say, *You're a very stupid girl, Carole . . . What kind of girl are you to stick around, and he sees other girls?*' When she heard rumors that Bob was married, she decided not to believe them because Bob himself never spoke about it. 'And it didn't make any difference, 'cause it had nothing to do with me. I can only deal with me.'

Far from ending his relationship with Childs, Bob helped provide her with a $500,000 Beverly Hills home. The property was registered to the Oak Pass Trust, an entity created by Bob's accountant Marshall M. Gelfand. Although Gelfand was 'the trustee,' the property remained in the ownership of 'the settlor' of the trust, who was Bob. It was a legal device that allowed him to own real estate anonymously. '[Bob's] a wonderfully generous guy,' says Childs. 'I lived there for many years.' But she now concedes that the fact Bob was secretly married to another woman while they were a couple is far from being a minor matter. 'I don't know why [Carolyn is] a secret,' she says. 'The whole thing is so, so strange. I wish Bob hadn't been so important. 'Cause he's such a cute guy. Maybe if he wasn't so important, life would have been easier.'

Carolyn Dennis declines to talk about her relationship with Bob. 'Mr. Dylan is a very private person,' she says, 'which is why the world has such a hard time trying to find out anything about his life.'

Two days after the secret wedding, Bob performed with Tom Petty and The Heartbreakers at an Amnesty International benefit in Los Angeles. He seemed particularly happy on stage, grinning widely as he romped through a joyful cover of the Joe Morris song 'Shake a Hand.' Perhaps married life was agreeing with him. Three days later, Carolyn was on stage with him in San Diego as a member of his group of backing singers, The Queens of Rhythm, a name devised by Bob. From June 9, 1986, Bob toured the United States with Tom Petty and The Heartbreakers and The Queens of Rhythm. Carolyn was on stage with him each night, often looking across at Bob as she sang harmony with her mother Madelyn Quebec, who was now, of course, Bob's mother-in-law.

Tom Petty and The Heartbreakers opened the show; then the girls came out, dressed in sparkly stage costumes, vamping a prelude to Bob. When he came on stage, he was also wearing unusually ostentatious clothing. Around the time of his marriage to Carolyn, Bob began to appear in leather pants and singlets, leather gloves with the fingers cut off, and garish multicolored T-shirts. For the first time in his career, he also wore jewelry – jeweled rings and dangly earrings. His hair was

Woodstock

After his motorcycle accident, Bob lived in seclusion near Woodstock, New York. Albert Grossman lived nearby in Bearsville with his wife, Sally, who was a friend of Bob's wife, Sara. This photograph – taken by Daniel Kramer before the accident, for the cover of *Bringing It All Back Home* – was taken in the living room of the Grossman house. The photograph is loaded with visual jokes and references to Bob's life. He is wearing the jacket and cufflinks given to him by former lover Joan Baez. Albums by artists who influenced Bob's work are scattered around the room – including recordings by Robert Johnson, Eric Von Schmidt and Lord Buckley. The woman lounging on a chaise-longue is Sally Grossman. The cat was the Grossmans' pet,

Above):
3ob and his first wife, Sara, aised a family of five children in he Woodstock area. Sara had a laughter from a previous narriage and she and Bob had our more children together: esse, Anna, Samuel and Jakob. Here Bob and Sara and one of he younger children are photographed in Woodstock.
© Elliott Landy/Redferns

Above right):
3ob and Sara had two homes in he Woodstock area. The first was this Arts and Crafts Movement mansion, Hi Lo Ha, situated in the wooded area of 3yrdcliffe. **Howard Sounes**

(Below):
Partly because he was plagued by fans at their Byrdcliffe house Bob moved his family to this more secluded mansion on Oha Mountain Road, on the other sic of Woodstock. The Dylans lived here around the time of the *Nashville Skyline* album with its hit single, "Lay, Lady, Lay." Whe Bob sold the house, the new owners found a big brass bed in the master bedroom. **Howard Soune**

Right):
'he sign at the entrance to 3ob's first Woodstock mansion, warning unwanted visitors about trespass. **Howard Sounes**

On the Road Again

(Above):
The Hawks became The Band during the years of Bob's Woodstock seclusion. In 1974, Bob and The Band teamed up again for a high-profile tour of the United States, reprising the raucous music they made in 1965–6, but this time playing to ecstatic audiences and rave reviews. Here Bob is seen with Robbie Robertson and Levon Helm on stage at Madison Square Garden, New York.
© Daniel Kramer

(Left):
Driven out of Woodstock, and New York City, by obsessive fans, Bob bought several adjoining parcels of land on the Point Dume peninsula, north of Los Angeles, California, and spent $2.5 million building what he called his "fantasy" house. Differences of opinion between Bob and Sara over the house caused problems in their marriage. **Associated Press**

(Above):
The Rolling Thunder Revue of 1975–6 was linked with a campaign to win a re-trial for former prize fighter Rubin "Hurricane" Carter, in jail for triple murder. Here members of the Revue visit Carter. Clockwise from bottom they include: **multi-instrumentalist David Mansfield** (checked shirt); **percussionist Luther Rix** (against wall/ moustache); **"Ramblin'" Jack Elliott** (cowboy hat/ hand on Rubin Carter's shoulder); **bass player Rob Stoner** (black jacket/behind Carter); **Peter Orlovsky, friend of Allen Ginsberg** (glasses/ behind Stoner); **Carter campaigner George Lois** (balding/ open neck shirt); **Joan Baez; guitarist Steven Soles** (moustache); **drummer Howie Wyeth** (floppy cap); **guitarist Henry "T-Bone" Burnett** (left of Wyeth); **Bobby Neuwirth** (hand to face); **Roger McGuinn** (long hair/black jacket/sitting); **Allen Ginsberg** (glasses); **Sally Grossman** (far right); **Mick Ronson** (hand on hip); **Ronee Blakley** (in front of McGuinn); **and violinist Scarlet Rivera** (center front).
Ken Regan/London Features International

(Left):
Bob is seen here with Greenwich Village club owner and friend Paul Colby backstage before the first show on The Rolling Thunder Revue – in Plymouth, Massachusetts, 30 October 1975. **Courtesy Paul Colby**

(Left):
When Bob and Sara Dylan divorced in 1977, Sara hired Faridi McFree to help look after the children. McFree began an affair with Bob, to Sara's disgust. "She thought I had betrayed her," says Faridi, "just like so many women."
Courtesy Faridi McFree

(Right):
In 1978 Bob toured the world to replenish his bank accounts following his expensive divorce from Sara Dylan. During the tour he became involved with several women, including backing singer Helena Springs, seen here backstage during the tour.
Courtesy Debi Dye-Gibson

(Right):
The open-air *Picnic at Blackbushe* concert in England on 15 July 1978 was attended by one hundred and sixty-seven thousand people – one of the largest single-day paying concerts ever.
© Stephen Morley/Redferns

(Below):
After The Woodstock Festival, the twin Live Aid concerts in London and Philadelphia on 13 July 1985 was the greatest popular music event ever staged. It was an acknowledgement of Bob's enormous influence on popular music – rather than his relatively modest record sales – that he was the last act on stage at Philadelphia before the sing-a-long finale. Joined by Rolling Stones Ronnie Wood and Keith Richards, Bob's performance was, unfortunately, a shambles.
Anthony Suau/Black Star/Colorific!

Secret life

(Above right):
Because of comments Bob made on stage at Live Aid, Willie Nelson and others staged Farm Aid at Champaign, Illinois, on 22 September 1985, in aid of impoverished U.S. farmers. Bob's performance with Tom Petty and The Heartbreakers was very powerful. One of the four backing vocalists, Carolyn Dennis, later became Bob's second wife. © Ben Weaver/London Features International

(Right):
On 4 June 1986 Bob secretly married backing singer Carolyn Dennis. She had given birth to his sixth child earlier in the year, an event they also kept secret. Carolyn is seen here on stage with Bob and Tom Petty's band in Hartford, Connecticut, on 11 July 1986. Carolyn is the second backing singer from the left, looking towards Bob. John Hume

(Below):
Bob and his new wife, Carolyn Dylan, went to extraordinary lengths to keep news of their marriage from the press. Although Bob owned a huge property at Point Dume, California, and many other properties across the country, they set up home together here in this unassuming bungalow in the Los Angeles suburb of Tarzana. Howard Sounes

Glimpses

(Above):
In October 1992, Sony Music celebrated Bob's career with a Thirtieth Anniversary Celebration Concert at Madison Square Garden, New York. Joining him on stage were many friends including George Harrison, Roger McGuinn, Johnny Cash, G.E. Smith, Tom Petty and The Clancy Brothers.

(Left):
In 1997, Bob released the remarkable *Time Out of Mind* album. The record was a major artistic and commercial success, selling more than a million copies and winning three Grammy Awards. Bob is seen here with producer, Daniel Lanois, accepting the awards at Radio City Music Hall, New York, in February 1998.

A lifetime of fame has aged Bob Dylan beyond his years. Seen here in Germany in May 2000, he is a gaunt and austere figure. One of the true giants of contemporary culture, the hundred or so concert appearances he gives each year have come to assume a special significance. John Hume

(Below):
Bob Dylan began his career playing in coffee houses. Forty years on he has returned to his roots by building his own coffee shop – the 18th Street Coffee House in Santa Monica, California. Typically, he has kept his involvement in the coffee shop secret. Howard Sounes

(Below right):
Bob Dylan's mother, Beatty, is seen here with her brother Vernon Stone in Las Vegas. Bob was very close to his mother, and her death in January 2000 was a cause of great sadness. When Bob resumed touring a few weeks later, he wore black and there was a new somberness to his performances.
Courtesy Lewis Stone

tricked up into a bouffant. He liked it to lay down in the back and stand up in the front, and he would ask the girls to fix it in place with hairspray before the show. With Bob, Petty's band, and the singers, there were ten people on stage. This lineup switched around during the show. Members of the band exited, and Bob sang with the girls. Bob's mother-in-law was particularly skillful at improvising duets with Bob, who rarely sang anything the same way twice and thus was a challenging partner.

The backing singers were very important to Bob, not just because of his relationship with Carolyn but because he enjoyed experimenting with different vocal arrangements. Part of Carolyn's role in Bob's life was to help hire experienced singers for The Queens of Rhythm, the lineup of which changed frequently. One of these recruits was Louise Bethune, who had sung with The Shirelles and The Crystals, and who joined the U.S. and world tour of 1986–87. She recalls that Bob would often summon all the girls to his room in the middle of the night to practice harmonies, deriving huge pleasure from these informal sessions. Bethune says the only way to work with him on stage was to watch him intently and be 'in his mouth' because he was so unpredictable. Also, although there was no longer such an explicit religious element in his albums, and it was reported in the press that Bob had returned to Judaism, Bethune reveals that Bob prayed with his Christian backing singers every night. 'There wasn't a show without a prayer going forth.'

Carolyn, her mother, and some of the other regular backing singers formed a close circle of support around Bob, who felt comfortable with these strong-minded, no-nonsense African-American women and perhaps even protected by them. For a while he seems to have regained some of the happiness he had had with Sara and their children. He still kept in regular, close contact with those children, but this new family was very important as well.

Not only was he married to Carolyn, and touring with

her, but they also worked together when Bob went into the studio to make his next album, *Knocked Out Loaded.* Sessions were held in London and Los Angeles during breaks in touring in 1985 and 1986. T-Bone Burnett, Al Kooper, and Tom Petty and The Heartbreakers were among the musicians. The songs included two covers, two minor original compositions, and three cowritten songs. With the notable exception of *Desire*, Bob had rarely collaborated on lyrics before. Words had come to him with such ease that he did not need help. By the late 1980s, however, he found it increasingly hard to write. 'He said that the words stopped coming,' says Ted Perlman. 'Suddenly, it just wasn't there anymore, like the well ran dry.'

Tom Petty cowrote 'Got My Mind Made Up,' one of the most forgettable songs of Bob's career. 'Under Your Spell' arose from a surprising collaboration with pop lyricist Carole Bayer Sager, an old friend of Carole Childs. 'Although it was really exciting, it was probably one of the least collaborative experiences I had with anybody,' says Bayer Sager, who wrote in a notepad while Bob strummed guitar. 'It was kind of like going back to grade school when you are given a test and you put your hand over your work so nobody would copy it.' It was only when she received an advance copy of the song that Bayer Sager found out which of her ideas Bob had used. Aside from the title 'Under Your Spell,' virtually none of the lyrics were hers. Yet Bob said he would never have written the song without her.

The most significant collaboration was 'Brownsville Girl,' which took up most of the second side of *Knocked Out Loaded.* This epic was cowritten with Sam Shepard, who had worked with Bob on *Renaldo & Clara* and subsequently became well known as a playwright and actor. The song came about almost by accident. 'We tossed around a bunch of ideas, none of which really got anywhere, and then we just sort of [started] telling stories to each other,' he recalls. 'One of the stories that he began was actually the first line of that song. He says, "One day

I was standing in line for this Gregory Peck film." And I said, "Why don't we just use that . . . as we're not getting anywhere?" ' From Bob's recollection of his experience of seeing *The Gunfighter*, they built an epic song of the West, with a shifting perspective. Shepard was impressed by the way Bob came up with the images. 'He has a suprising mind,' he says. 'You are going down a dark alley and, all of a sudden, you see the sunlight . . . It's not the usual track of thought.' There were many verses, with unusually long lines. 'I think the most surprising thing is his phrasing,' he adds. 'I'd say, "But how the hell are you going to fit this into the melody?" He said, "Don't worry about it. It'll work." And inevitably it did. The way he squashes phrasing and stretches it out is quite remarkable.'

Bob recorded a masterful rendition of the song for *Knocked Out Loaded*, using the exuberant call and response talents of his wife – who had recently taken to calling herself Carole rather than Carolyn – and other backing singers. Nothing else on the album approached the quality of 'Brownsville Girl.' In fact, the other tracks seemed almost thrown together. 'If the records I'm making only sell a certain amount anyway, then why should I take so long putting them together?' asked Bob, in an interview. It was a self-fulfilling prophecy. *Knocked Out Loaded* was Bob's lowest-charting album since his Columbia debut in 1961. Few would have noticed that slipped in among the very lengthy 'special thanks to' notes on the inner sleeve was the name of Bob's new daughter.

Bob had always been interested in films. He had made films, acted in *Pat Garrett & Billy the Kid*, and turned to movies for song ideas when inspiration ran dry. It was therefore not altogether surprising when he now accepted an invitation to act in the mainstream motion picture *Hearts of Fire*, directed by Richard Marquand, best known for making the thriller *Jagged Edge*. There was a good chance it would be a box-office success, and Bob apparently received $1 million for his role.

Bob played the part of legendary music star Billy Parker, faded from glory and living on a chicken farm. The parallels with Bob's actual life were obvious. Parker took up with would-be singer Molly McGuire, played by a twenty-five-year-old pop singer turned actress named simply Fiona. Parker and McGuire went to England for a rock 'n' roll revival show and met young rock star James Colt, played by Rupert Everett. McGuire had an affair with Colt and Parker went home to the U.S., leaving the girl to discover that the rock star life was not all she'd hoped. The movie was made in England and Canada in the fall of 1986. At a London press conference, Richard Marquand said *Hearts of Fire* would address 'stardom and whether you can handle stardom.'

Toward the end of filming, Bob agreed to an interview with the BBC arts program *Omnibus*, during which he also explored the nature of stardom. In the interview he commented that when artists embark on their careers they often say they want fame and money. In his experience, he said, it was money they wanted most. Fame could be a curse. He offered the analogy of walking past an inn and looking through the window to see ordinary people behaving normally, being 'very real with each other.' Yet when somebody like himself walked into that inn and tried to join in, everything changed. As he explained: 'When you walk into the room, it's over. You won't see them being real anymore.' This story revealed a lot about Bob's own contradictory attitude to success: he relished the opportunity to record and perform, but the notoriety he had achieved rendered a normal personal life almost impossible. He had been unusually revealing in his comments to the BBC and, as Bob predicted during the interview, this little documentary would be a good deal more interesting than the feature film he was then making.

* * *

As Bob progressed into middle age, he was becoming increasingly eccentric. He dressed in a strange way, often sleeping in his clothes, and took to wandering the streets on his own. He enjoyed exploring deprived city districts, especially ethnic areas where he was not necessarily recognized. He also wandered about more affluent Los Angeles suburbs near where he lived. One day, Ted Perlman returned to his town house in the San Fernando Valley and found what looked like a bum sitting on the curb. Perlman was just about to send the vagrant on his way. Then he recognized Bob. 'I wanted to stop by and see you and Peggi.'

'How long have you been here?' asked Perlman.

'About an hour and a half. I've been walking around the neighborhood,' replied Bob, who then came inside and ate a meal cooked by Peggi Blu. She was like a sister to Carolyn Dennis, and was one of the few people who knew about the secret marriage.

Bob told the Perlmans that he had been invited to sing at a George Gershwin tribute concert in New York. He had been thinking of performing the Gershwin song 'Swanee,' but then found the song 'Soon.' It was a beautiful song, but not material one would expect Bob to perform. After dinner, Bob and Perlman worked on an arrangement whereby Bob would deliver the song in a more conventional style. 'Do I sound stupid?' he asked, as he practiced. The Perlmans assured him that he did not and Bob duly surprised the audience at the Gershwin gala on March 11, 1987, appearing in a tuxedo and singing 'Soon' with great care. 'He actually was singing, not doing his Bob voice,' says Ted Perlman.

Two months after the Gershwin tribute Bob moved to the other end of the musical spectrum, thrashing through rock 'n' roll songs with former Sex Pistol Steve Jones. The project was *Down in the Groove*, another album of cover songs and minor original compositions. Why Bob chose to contact Steve Jones remains a mystery to everybody, including Jones himself, who had never met or even spoken to Bob before. 'He called me up and said can I put a band together to do some sessions in the studio? I said, *Yeah*. Paul Simonon was in town at the time, from The Clash. So was the guitar player I was working with [and] a drummer from Pat Benatar's band.' They met at Sunset Sound in Hollywood. 'It was a strange, fucking surreal day.' Bob had a long list of songs and, without preamble, began working through them. The band had to keep up as best they could, but were unable to get a very satisfactory take on anything because Bob would move so rapidly on to the next number. 'It was like that all night, basically just fucking about,' says Jones. The only track to make the album was 'Sally Sue Brown.'

While the material Bob recorded for *Down in the Groove* seemed slight, the album had a cohesive and natural sound, and some of the songs worked well on the modest level in which they were intended. Bob delivered a fine rendition of the standard 'Shenandoah,' and invested the songs 'Ninety Miles an Hour (Down a Dead End Street)' and 'Rank Strangers to Me' – a song Bob knew from the venerable bluegrass group The Stanley Brothers – with the chill authority of age. At forty-six, his voice was beginning to resonate in a way that suited this material and, in this respect, *Down in the Groove* was a prelude to his later career when he turned increasingly to songs about alienation, aging, and death.

Two of the songs on *Down in the Groove* – 'Silvio' and the less successful 'Ugliest Girl in the World' – were cowritten with Robert Hunter, lyricist for The Grateful Dead. Bob first met The Dead in 1972, becoming close to leader Jerry Garcia, and appeared with them as a guest on stage in 1986. He also turned up unexpectedly at a show of theirs in Oakland, accompanied by Wavy Gravy, his friend from Greenwich Village days. By coincidence, Gravy had married Bob's college girlfriend Bonnie Beecher. She became known as Jahanara Romney

(Romney being Gravy's true surname and Jahanara being a name Bonnie chose for herself. When he heard they had married, Bob told Gravy: 'Better men than you have tried that.'). Bob and Gravy wandered through the Oakland Coliseum unnoticed. 'It was really great until he put his sunglasses on,' says Gravy. 'Then everybody went, "Wo!" We had to get security to snatch him out of the crowd.'

The Grateful Dead loved Bob's music. 'He's been inspirational to us all along,' says founding member Bob Weir. 'The guy, as far as I'm concerned, is a living oracle.' So the band was delighted when Bob agreed to do a short stadium tour with The Dead in the summer of 1987. But things did not turn out as well as they had hoped.

Bob came to rehearsals in San Rafael, California, without a guitar so Bob Weir got a selection of guitars for Bob to try. One was a modulus guitar made, as a test, in a color Weir calls 'Pepto-Bismol pink.' Bob could not decide whether he liked this guitar or a standard Fender Stratocaster.

'You had any luck there deciding on a guitar?' asked Weir.

'Well, the Fender plays really well . . . But the modulus,' said Bob, picking up the outrageously pink guitar. 'It's really the right color, isn't it?'

The Dead rehearsed what seemed like a couple of hundred songs through June 1987, excited to be working with Bob. Yet when the tour began at the Sullivan Stadium in Foxboro, Massachusetts, on July 4, there was something wrong. 'It's as if we had never practiced,' says Weir. '[Bob] came up with a set list [that] didn't have much to do with what we had rehearsed.' Bob played in the wrong key and seemed to forget his own lyrics. The official reason was that he was not feeling well because of back pain. It was true he had suffered back pain ever since his motorcycle accident of 1966, but there were also mutterings that he was drinking too much.

The consensus within The Grateful Dead was that the least bad show had been Giants Stadium, New Jersey, on

July 12. So when it came to putting together a live album of the tour, which would be called simply *Dylan & The Dead*, it was this show The Dead wanted to use. Bob vetoed the chosen tracks, however, partly because he did not want to use songs that had appeared on previous live albums. Instead, a motley selection of songs was chosen from three inferior concerts. Jerry Garcia went to Point Dume to talk about the mixing of the album and was amazed to find Bob listening to a tape on a cheap boom box. Based on the sound, he told Garcia his voice was mixed too high. 'What am I going to do, pop him one?' Garcia asked colleagues in exasperation. As a result, Bob's voice was mixed so far down on the record that the lyrics were drowned in the music, emphasizing the impression that he was mumbling.

Bob's relationship with The Grateful Dead took its most bizarre turn a couple of years later. On February 12, 1989, he showed up at a Dead concert in Inglewood, California, coming on stage for the second part of the show. Bob insisted he play only Grateful Dead songs. Unfortunately, he did not know the words and he made a mess of five of their songs before the band forced him to sing his own. As The Dead came off stage, one band member asked angrily, 'What the fuck is he doing here?'

Bob had a wonderful time in any case. The next day he called The Grateful Dead office and said he wanted to join the band. He made it clear that he was serious. So the band took a vote. 'I was in for that, but one of our members didn't particularly care for him,' says Weir. 'I think we would have [taken him], if it hadn'tve been for that one guy. We would have picked him up as a sort of temporary band member.' For Bob even to consider joining an established act like The Grateful Dead shows that the pressures of trying to maintain a successful career as a solo artist had become almost too much for him. His desire to join a band like The Dead was surely motivated by a desire to escape his problems and be supported by others for a while. Of course, this was practically impossible; Bob was so famous and such a powerful musical presence that he would alter any band he joined out of all recognition – The Grateful Dead, for instance, would simply have become his backing group. The strange episode revealed Bob to be an artist who had lost his way and was not thinking clearly.

Away from the concert stage, Bob continued to battle with his former manager, Albert Grossman. Bob had suffered a limited defeat in 1985 when a judge dismissed some of his eighteen counterclaims. However, there were still numerous allegations on both sides and Bob seemed willing to fund his lawyers indefinitely. In this respect, the singer had an advantage over Grossman. By this stage in their lives, Bob had the much larger fortune. Grossman's legal bill was increasing at a rate of approximately $176 an hour. They had been locked in dispute for five years and still had not had a full court hearing. Bob's method was to 'stonewall,' as Sally Grossman put it. She says the case was a source of stress for her husband, but she insists he kept a sense of humor about it.

On January 25, 1986, Grossman flew to London on business. During the flight, in the early hours of the following morning, he suffered a heart attack and died. He was fifty-nine. Bob did not attend the funeral, and the legal battle continued with Grossman's estate. Lawyers acting for Sally complained bitterly of the 'procrastination, obstructionism, and dilatory tactics' that had caused the case to drag on for years and blamed 'the obdurate Mr. Dylan' and his advisers.

Finally, in November 1987, almost two years after Albert had been buried on his property at Bearsville, Bob paid Sally approximately $2 million to settle. Grossman had been right all along, but Bob was the ultimate winner. He now had sole ownership of virtually all his song publishing, a catalogue that, if it ever was sold, would be worth tens, and maybe hundreds, of millions of dollars.

A few months before the settlement, Bob had embarked on another leg of his tour with Tom Petty and The Heartbreakers, performing in Israel and in Europe. The Heartbreakers flourished during the period they worked with Bob. 'We've learned you don't have to worry about playing everything exactly right,' said guitarist Mike Campbell. 'Sometimes it's better to wing it and hope that the magic happens.' However, the so-called Temples in Flames tour was not the best of their collaborations. It opened in Tel Aviv – Bob's first concert in Israel – but failed to excite a crowd that expected a greatest-hits show. Bob was unapologetic about mixing less well known songs into the concert. 'You don't want to just get up there and start guessing with the people what they want,' he said. 'For one thing, no one agrees on that. The songs a few people want to hear may not mean anything to a whole lot of others, and you can't let the audience start controlling the show.'

Bob's womanizing caused an unhappy incident during the tour that led to road manager Gary Shafner leaving the staff. During the tour, Shafner had to fly home to California to attend to some private business. While he was away, Bob apparently became involved in a relationship with Shafner's girlfriend, Brita Lee, even though Bob's wife Carolyn was on the tour as one of the backing singers. The embarrassment and unhappiness resulted in Shafner's departure. People close to Bob talk about this incident as one of the worst things Bob ever did to an employee. Shafner was devoted to Bob, yet Bob repaid him in the cruelest way. Shafner will not criticize his former boss, however, saying diplomatically: 'It was a privilege to be there for the years I was there . . . As an artist, I respect the guy.' But it was the end of their friendship, and Shafner never spoke to Brita Lee again.

The tour reached London in time for the world premiere of *Hearts of Fire*, held at the Odeon Marble Arch on Friday, October 9, 1987. Bob was booked into his regular London haunt, the Mayfair Hotel, in nearby Berkeley Square, and he did not have a show that night. Yet he was conspicuously absent at the premiere. The reason soon became obvious to those who had the misfortune to watch the film. The songs Bob had provided for *Hearts of Fire* were certainly minor; Bob's acting was adequate, hinting at the charisma he exuded on stage; Fiona and Rupert Everett were rotten, but that was hardly their fault. The main problem was that the script was pitiful, and the film lacked any style or tension. *Hearts of Fire* closed after a few weeks and was never given a cinematic release in the United States.

Bob looked thin, tanned, and healthy in *Hearts of Fire*. But on stage he was starting to look overweight and pasty, and although his concerts varied in quality, with an occasional very strong performance, at times he seemed to have lost interest in what he was doing. Harvey Goldsmith was so disappointed by a show at London's Wembley Arena in October that he got up from his seat and went home early. Later that night he received a call from Bob's security man, Jim Callaghan, asking him to come to the Mayfair Hotel to see Bob. Despite his poor eyesight, and the fact that there were at least ten thousand people in the audience, Bob had noticed Goldsmith leaving. 'I saw you get up and I saw you leave. Didn't you like it?' he asked, when the promoter arrived at the hotel.

'No, I hated it,' replied Goldsmith. He reminded Bob that Britain was his biggest audience outside the United States, and he had to deliver high-quality shows. 'What you played today was just crap.' Bob did not seem to be offended or angered by the criticism. 'He was amused,' says Goldsmith. 'He took it in his stride and we went down to the bar and had a drink.'

Ironically, as his artistic successes declined, Bob found himself bedecked with an increasing number of honors.

After returning to New York, on January 20, 1988, he was inducted into the Rock and Roll Hall of Fame at a lavish $10,000-a-table ceremony at the Waldorf-Astoria. Bruce Springsteen gave the induction speech, saying he would not be where he was if it had not been for the inspiration of Bob's music. 'There isn't a soul in this room who does not owe you their thanks.'

There was something absurd and bogus about such bourgeois, self-congratulatory events. A $10,000-a-table black-tie dinner at the Waldorf-Astoria was the antithesis of the music Bob performed, as well as the music that had influenced him. Arlo Guthrie pointed this out that very evening when he accepted a posthumous honor for his father. In his speech, Arlo said that he did not know where Woody Guthrie would be if he were still alive. 'But I can guarantee you he wouldn't be here,' he affirmed.

Bob must have recognized the truth in Arlo's words, and realized how empty such events were. Yet he seemed happy enough to attend and he rarely missed an opportunity to accept other awards in the years to come. (Almost exactly two years later he would be made Commandeur des Arts et des Lettres by the French government.) Possibly, these honors made him feel better about himself at a time when his career seemed to be in serious trouble.

When Bob's career was reaching its nadir he was unexpectedly lifted up with a big success, thanks to his friend George Harrison. When the former Beatle needed to borrow a studio in the Los Angeles area to record an extra song for a European twelve-inch single to promote his new album, *Cloud Nine*, he asked Bob for help. Harrison and his producer, Jeff Lynne, formerly of the Electric Light Orchestra, wanted to use Bob's home studio at Point Dume. Bob said to come on over. Lynne was also producing a comeback album for Roy Orbison at the time, so Orbison came as well, as did Tom Petty. Bob did not turn away so many famous visitors, but he grumbled about having to feed them all.

The five musicians sat around together playing music and, taking inspiration from a label on a box behind Bob's garage door, they soon came up with a song called 'Handle with Care.' It had a clever lyric about middle age and a strong melody and they shared the vocals, out of which Orbison's voice soared. Harrison coined a name for the de facto group. They were the Traveling Wilburys, each member having a jokey moniker. Bob became Lucky Wilbury.

'Handle with Care' was too good to throw away on a promotional single. The Wilburys decided to use it instead as the foundation of an album, with Jim Keltner drafted in as a 'sidebury' on drums. *Traveling Wilburys Volume 1* was recorded in April and May 1988, over ten days at the Los Angeles home of Dave Stewart of the Eurythmics. Much of the work was done in the kitchen, with Keltner rapping dowel sticks on the fridge to get the *rickety-tick* sound on the song 'Rattled.' Most of the songs were lightweight fare, though Bob's playful wit was particularly evident on 'Dirty World.' The music was lifted greatly by Orbison's operatic vocals, especially on 'Not Alone Anymore.' The album was a major commercial success when it was released in the fall of 1988, reaching number three in the U.S. album charts, and selling more copies than any Dylan album of the decade. Its success stood in marked contrast to his recent studio album, *Down in the Groove*, which did even worse business than had *Knocked Out Loaded*. It was a pleasant change to be part of a successful project, but the popularity of the Wilburys album also highlighted the relative failure of Bob's solo career, which continued its downward trend.

Years of poor album sales, and the negative publicity of his Christian conversion, had considerably reduced Bob's stature as a solo artist. He was no longer able to fill major stadiums without the support of a name band, such as Santana, The Heartbreakers, or The Grateful Dead. During the latter stages of his recent European tour with The Heartbreakers, he came to realize he was hiding behind bands and his backing singers. 'I had [the singers] up there so I wouldn't feel so bad,' he said. He was on stage in Locarno, Switzerland, when it struck him most strongly that he had lost touch with what he was doing as a performer. As he later recalled, a single phrase came to him as if from nowhere: *I'm determined to stand whether God will deliver me or not.* The audience came to see him, not the band or singers, and he had to perform his songs to the best of his ability. It was an epiphany. 'Everything just exploded. It exploded *every* which way.'

After his return from Europe, Bob stopped working with Petty and his band; he dispensed with the services of his backing singers – including his wife – and in the summer of 1988 he began to rebuild his stage show by playing with a small band in small theaters, hoping to find the thread of his career again. There was also a financial necessity to make this process work. Bob had great wealth on paper because he owned his music publishing, but the song catalogue provided a relatively modest income for a man with so many demands on him. With each new album selling fewer copies than the last, touring was an important source of cash. To keep costs down initially, and to force himself to take charge of his shows, Bob worked with the smallest band possible, a trio led by G. E. Smith, best known for leading the house band on *Saturday Night Live.* On bass was Kenny Aaronson, who wore his hair in a quiff. Aaronson's fellow New Yorker Christopher Parker played drums. The first concert was at the Pavilion in Concord, California, on June 7, 1988. It was the start of what Bob referred to casually as the Never-Ending Tour. The phrase came to have almost literal meaning as he toured relentlessly during the remaining dozen years of the century, and on into the next. The constant touring seems to indicate that he desired to escape permanently from normal life; by this time, however, his music and his fame had taken over his life to such an extent that he really had no 'normal' life to run from. Life on the road became the norm.

This first leg of the Never-Ending Tour was conducted with great verve. Bob drew the songs from all stages of his career and mixed them with eclectic covers ranging from the Irish ballad 'Eileen Aroon' to Chuck Berry's 'Nadine.' The use of a small, versatile band allowed Bob to experiment. Over the years of the Never-Ending Tour, audiences came to relish the fact that Bob did not perform a standard greatest-hits show, like so many other artists who had come to prominence in the 1960s. The way in which he reinterpreted his songs, and introduced new songs, rarities, and stillborn creations, enhanced his appeal to fans. Backing Bob on stage required concentration and an ability to learn fast. A touch of telepathy was also helpful; Bob rarely said what he wanted to do and, if pressed for guidance, he would talk metaphorically. 'I remember just thinking to myself, *what's he talking about?*' says band member Kenny Aaronson.

There was a short break in early August so Bob could attend the wedding of his daughter Maria, aged twenty-six, to musician Peter Himmelman, an orthodox Jew from Minneapolis. Bob was back on the road with a show in Portland, Oregon, on August 18 and toured until mid-October.

In his return to his musical roots, Bob rehired Victor Maymudes as road manager, more than twenty years after Maymudes last held the job. He took over from the unhappy Gary Shafner. Maymudes knew Bob's quirks better than anybody, but Bob was much more eccentric now than he had been in his youth, having become extremely secretive and withdrawn. After the exhibitionism of the show – as Bob himself said, he sometimes felt little better than a pimp on stage – he hid himself away from people. His wife and child were sometimes on the road with him, but Carolyn and Desiree were never seen with Bob in public. This was Bob's peculiar life on the road as he worked to rebuild his stage show.

As Bob struggled to get his career back on track, and when it seemed he might never make another first-class album, he came up with *Oh Mercy* – a return to form that would rival *Infidels* as his best album of the decade. He chose to make the record with Canadian musician-producer Daniel Lanois, who made his name producing the Neville Brothers' album *Yellow Moon*. Lanois had an innovative approach to music making, setting up a mobile studio wherever it was convenient to the artist. For the Neville Brothers, this was in a New Orleans apartment. The control board was in the same room as the musicians, without a screen between them, and Lanois sat in with the musicians during the sessions, smearing sounds together to give the music a rich, languid quality. Bob had visited the sessions when he was on tour in Louisiana in 1988, partly because the Nevilles were covering two of his own songs, and he asked Lanois to make a record for him using the same methods.

Initial sessions for *Oh Mercy* were held at the apartment studio, but the only album track that resulted was 'Where Teardrops Fall.' Lanois then changed musicians, calling in *Yellow Moon* players Tony Hall on bass, Brian Stoltz on guitar, and 'Mean' Willie Green III on drums to get what he calls 'that Louisiana swamp sound.' Lanois rented a five-story house at 1305 Soniat Street in uptown New Orleans, setting up the soundboard in a large ground-floor room, with the musicians arranged in a horseshoe configuration around him. The first track they cut was 'Political World.' The musicians had been working up an arrangement for an hour when Bob walked in. 'So what is this supposed to be?' he asked. When they told him, he picked up a guitar and said: 'That's not how it goes, this is how it goes.' It was the take that made the album. 'Most of the Time,' one of the best songs on the album, is about relationships but was so subtle the term 'love song' did not do it justice. It was a song 'from the Tree of Life,' as Bob once said of the songs of Hank Williams. The atmospheric 'Man in the Long Black Coat' was written quickly in the studio, but is among the most intriguing songs on the album. As has been noted by author Clinton Heylin, it could be interpreted as a development of the traditional folk song 'House Carpenter,' which Bob had performed in his youth, written from the point of view of the carpenter whose wife had left him for a sinister stranger.

When it came to choosing tracks for the album Bob held back strong songs including 'Dignity,' 'God Knows,' and 'Series of Dreams.' He had reached a stage when he did not know when words would come to him again, and he was more cautious than he had once been about using up his good ideas on one record. This conservative approach frustrated Bob's producer. ' "Series of Dreams" was a fantastic, turbulent track that I felt should be on the record,' recalls Lanois. '[But] he had the last word.' *Oh Mercy* was seen as a return to form when it was released later in the year, and sold better than recent albums.

On the Never-Ending Tour, and while making *Oh Mercy*, Bob lived his personal life like a fugitive. In one of the most extraordinary aspects of his secret second marriage, he established a home with Carolyn Dennis in the undistinguished San Fernando Valley suburb of Tarzana – a place where nobody would expect to find them. The property at 5430 Shirley Avenue was a large modern bungalow with high iron fencing around the perimeter. It was a short walk from a McDonald's restaurant and very near the roar of the Ventura Freeway. The purchase of the house, on April 14, 1989, was as covert as every other aspect of Bob's marriage to Carolyn. Neither of their names appeared in the paperwork. Instead, the property was bought by Fifth Floor Realty, a blind corporation operated by Bob's accountant, Marshall M. Gelfand, out of an office in Century City. The neighbors in Tarzana never discovered that one of the legendary figures of popular music was living in the yellow bungalow down the road.

The lengths Bob felt he had to go to in order to ensure his privacy seemed to have a detrimental effect on his mood. When he began a European tour in May 1989, Bob tried to hide himself from people. While on stage, he sometimes wore a baseball cap with a sweatshirt hood drawn up so that his face was almost invisible. He was furtive and unhappy off stage. 'He was a different kind of Bob, sort of sneaking around, sneaking up the back stairways of places,' says Kenny Aaronson.

Aaronson left the band after a show in London on May 8 to return home for an emergency skin-cancer operation. In the interim, Bob hired thirty-three-year-old Tony Garnier, who had played bass with Robert Gordon and Asleep at the Wheel. When Aaronson asked to rejoin the band in July, after his operation, Bob said he did not want to make changes. 'Elliot [Roberts] and Bob both said to me, "You know, we really love you. We love your playing. You're a great guy. As soon as you get your health back, you can have your job back." So much for that,' says Aaronson. Meanwhile, Tony Garnier became Bob's new bandleader.

In the fall, Bob made another change when he parted company with de facto manager Elliot Roberts. The apocryphal story that went around the music industry was that Bob telephoned Roberts's office one day and, when he was put on hold longer than an artist of his status might expect, he decided to give Roberts's job to the next person who came on the line. This happened to be Roberts's assistant, Jeff Kramer. Whether this is accurate or not, Kramer did take over from Roberts, and began handling Bob's concert bookings from an office in Beverly Hills. Meanwhile, Jeff Rosen had recently become administrator and general manager of Bob's publishing concerns in the New York office.

Bob became a grandfather on November 7, 1989, when Maria Himmelman gave birth to a son, Isaac. A couple of months earlier Bob had appeared with son-in-law Peter and actor friend Harry Dean Stanton on the annual Jewish Chabad telethon in Los Angeles, playing flute, recorder, and mouth organ. All three men wore yarmulkes, and gave a spirited rendition of 'Hava Negeilah.' The Chabad appearance demonstrated the importance Bob placed on his roots, both culturally and musically. He was feeling particularly sentimental as the decade ended with the world being turned upside down as the Berlin Wall fell and revolutions swept through eastern Europe. Finding himself in Greenwich Village around this time, Bob called at the apartment of his old friend Dave Van Ronk. 'He was in the neighborhood and, on impulse, he rang the bell,' says Van Ronk. 'You know, he really hadn't changed all that much. He was as nervous as ever.' They talked about songwriting. Bob complained that young performers did not know traditional music. He added, gloomily: 'The Devil is the Lord of this world.'

In the spring of the following year, 1990, Bob recorded a second Traveling Wilburys record – jokingly called *Volume 3* – with George Harrison, Jeff Lynne, and Tom Petty. The fifth Wilbury, Roy Orbison, had died the previous December at the age of fifty-two. Without Orbison and his mellifluous voice, which contrasted so well with the others, the songs sounded mediocre. 'It was Roy's presence [that] made them rise to the occasion,' says Jim Keltner, who again played drums. 'The second album was really deflated . . . it was just sad and the enthusiasm wasn't there. So the writing suffered.' The record did not sell anything like the numbers of the first and, although the Wilburys had considered touring, the band was finished.

At almost the same time Bob was working on his own

album, *Under the Red Sky*, with producer brothers David and Don Was, who had been recommended by Carole Childs. Bob began with 'God Knows,' one of the songs left over from *Oh Mercy*. The Was brothers recorded an exciting new version, and then assembled a distinguished cast of session musicians including Al Kooper, David Lindley, and Stevie Ray Vaughan, with guest appearances by George Harrison and Elton John, to make an album. It was what Kooper calls a 'hood album.' Bob showed up each day in one of his hooded sweatshirts and he kept the hood up during the sessions. As he hardly said anything at recording sessions anyway, it became even harder to communicate with the man. 'You know, there was a weariness about him that actually made me feel so much more for him,' says David Was, who perceived the pathos in Bob's situation. 'There were times when he looked absolutely beleaguered, doing this stuff. It occurred to me that it was a continuous burden having to be "Bob Dylan" after all these years.' Yet Bob could hardly stop being Bob Dylan; having tried and failed to hide behind other bands, he knew he had to work his way out of the slump he was in on his own.

The songs on *Under the Red Sky* appeared to be simple, but the album as a whole was not as weak as some would have it. The opening track, 'Wiggle Wiggle,' certainly had little to recommend it, apart from an audaciously silly title. 'T.V. Talkin' Song' and 'Under the Red Sky' were minor, even if one accepted the theory that the latter was a fable about Hibbing, but 'Unbelievable,' 'Handy Dandy,' and 'Cat's in the Well' were good songs, delivered with power. 'God Knows' was better still, shuddering with the conviction of Bob's enduring belief in the End Times. He warned that God's judgment would not come by water, but a fire next time. It was a vivid image from 2 Peter (3:4–7), used in numerous folk and gospel songs.

Under the Red Sky received bad reviews and sold so poorly that Bob would not make another studio album of new songs for seven years. Yet, as was often the case, he could take songs that sounded insipid on record and give them new life in concert. When he was in the mood to perform, Bob found meaning and enjoyment in even the seemingly throw away songs on *Under the Red Sky*. It was also true that at this stage in his career Bob was capable of giving simply terrible shows that ended, like train wrecks, in a tangle of discordant sounds, leaving audience members struggling to remember why they were applauding.

On June 6, 1990, Bob was in Toronto to play the O'Keefe Center. He called Ronnie Hawkins on stage to join him in a rendition of 'One More Night,' a song from the *Nashville Skyline* album. 'He kicked the song off in the wrong key,' says Hawkins, laughing. 'I knew then that we had a monkey act. So the guitar player is showing him what key to go to. But meanwhile Bob is too loud to hear him.'

Afterward Hawkins went back to Bob's dressing room. 'He had about a hundred and fifty yes-men in his room,' he says. 'If he had reached for a cigarette, so many lighters would have come out that it would turn the sprinkler system on.'

'What d'ya think, Hawk?' asked Bob.

'Well, Bob, let me tell you something, kid,' said Hawkins, who had nothing to lose by telling the truth. A hush descended over the room. 'In my long career, Bob, I have had guitar players in my band that are as bad as you are.' Bob's hangers-on tensed as they waited to hear what would come next. 'But you're the only one of them making a living.' When Bob laughed, the yes-men laughed with him.

Ronnie Hawkins says he was surprised that, at the age of forty-nine, Bob was still disporting himself after the show. 'He was having a little bit too much fun at the O'Keefe Center. Too hard for him. He's too old to be drinking and doing all that shit now. That's strictly for under thirties,' he comments. 'And if you don't die before you're thirty, you quit. And he [was] still having a little bit too much fun. But he [didn't] do it all the time, I'm sure. He couldn't. He wouldn't be alive.'

Bob received a salutary lesson in the ravages of alcohol six days later when he was traveling through Wisconsin. He asked his bus driver to pull over by the Mississippi River, just outside the town of La Crosse, so he could get some air before the show. Bob was standing by the river when a small, emaciated man with long matted hair approached and shouted, 'Hey, Bob Dylan!' It was Bob's college mentor, Dave Whitaker, reduced to a scarecrow by years of alcoholism. Bob made a gesture with his hands and his security people let Whitaker through. They hugged and spent a couple of hours talking. Although Whitaker's life was tragic – at times he had lived in near-poverty in San Francisco, abusing drink and drugs and estranged from members of his family – he did not think fame and wealth had brought Bob much joy. 'I don't know how many friends he really has,' says Whitaker who, like other old friends, saw Bob as a lonely man. 'He's a very isolated kind of person.'

Loneliness was at the heart of Bob's life now; he was deriving little companionship from his marriage to Carolyn. Having dispensed with using backing singers, there was little reason for her to drag around the world after him, hiding in tour buses and sneaking between hotels. So she stayed at home with their daughter in the Tarzana house. Due to his touring and recording commitments Bob rarely visited, and Carolyn eventually decided she could put up with this situation no longer. On August 7, 1990, she filed for a dissolution of their four-year marriage.

It is hard to know what Bob thought about the fact that his second marriage was ending after so short a time, as he hardly spoke a word about it to even his closest friends. It must have caused him disappointment and pain, however. In the meantime, as his lawyers did the paperwork, he simply carried on touring.

In October 1990, Bob played a show at the West Point military academy in upstate New York, treating the cadets to 'Masters of War.' G. E. Smith left the band a few nights later, apparently disenchanted with touring with Bob, although he declines to say exactly why he left. Part of the reason may have been that during their time together Bob had not asked Smith to record with him in the studio, despite the fact that Smith was one of the best guitarists Bob ever worked with. Smith was replaced with the relatively inexperienced John Jackson. Bob also replaced drummer Christopher Parker, rehiring Ian Wallace instead, the drummer from his 1978 band.

Wallace found many changes from the grand world tour of 1978. They were playing mostly small theaters now, with grueling overnight road trips by bus. There was no private airplane. When they booked into hotels, it was no longer deluxe accommodations. 'Bob had this penchant for staying out of town in little motels,' says Wallace. 'We were stuck in some really out of the way places.' Bob had a singular set of criteria for motels. They had to accept dogs, because he liked to travel with his mastiffs; and the windows had to open, because he did not like air-conditioning. Other than that Bob seemed unconcerned where he was, primarily because he rarely left his room and had the luxury of staff to bring him whatever he needed.

The main concern was to book Bob into hotels where he would not be accosted by the obsessive fans who followed him wherever he went. Bob's staff had a list of people who had posed a threat to Bob's security over recent years. It ran to more than five hundred names. Indeed, Bob's music had always seemed to excite the mentally unstable. In perhaps the most bizarre case of fanaticism, Richard Dickinson of Hobart, Australia, became so fed up in 1987 with his mother complaining about him playing the *Desire* album in the middle of the night that he trampled her to death to the accompaniment of 'One More Cup of Coffee.' (He was found not guilty of murder on grounds of insanity and jailed for an indefinite period.) Two women followed Bob around America in the late 1980s, posing as his wife. One had adopted the name Sara Dylan and stood at the front at concerts, tossing pennies on the stage. Band members became used to seeing a mad face peering up at them. Although the audiences were smaller than they had once been, many of the same people came back night after night. Most fans were perfectly sane, of course, but there were many who could not resist trying to make contact with Dylan off stage, and would follow his tour buses along the freeways and search out his hotels. To these devoted fans, Bob was a mesmerizing presence, his every gesture and utterance a source of fascination. 'The audience was incredible. Absolute worship,' says Kenny Aaronson. 'It's like a cult.'

At times Bob seemed to behave almost as outlandishly as those people who followed him around. Most of the time his odd behavior was apparent only to members of his entourage and to those who came to the shows. But on February 20, 1991, millions saw Bob behaving strangely on national television. He was receiving the latest in a string of honors, a Lifetime Achievement Award, presented at the Grammy Awards at Radio City Music Hall, in New York. Before the presentation Bob sang 'Masters of War,' a controversial choice at a time of patriotic support for U.S. troops fighting in the Gulf War. He did not look well on stage and he sounded awful. His band had the impression he was suffering with the flu, but it looked like he was drunk. 'I know people were wondering what the hell was going on because he mumbled his way through it and nobody knew what he was singing,' says Ian Wallace. 'It was very strange.' After being given his award by Jack Nicholson, Bob gave a remarkable off-the-cuff speech about the advice his father had once given him: it was possible to become so 'defiled' in this world, he said, that a parent might abandon his own child. It seemed to many watching that Bob was talking about himself, meaning that his father would have been shocked by the state he was in if he could have been there to see him. This, at least, shows that Bob had some self-knowledge of the trouble he was in.

Whenever it seemed Bob's career was in terminal decline, as was apparently the case at this time, his reputation had always been saved by an unexpected triumph. Just such a thing happened in March 1991 when Sony Music – the company that bought Columbia Records in 1987 – released a box set of fifty-eight previously unreleased studio recordings, demos, and live performances that spanned the first thirty years of Bob's career. Entitled *The Bootleg Series, Volumes 1–3*, the set reminded the music business and audiences that Bob could not be dismissed as a relic of the past. Many of these songs were masterpieces, confirming Bob's assertion, when *Biograph* was released in 1985, that he had masses of unreleased material in the vault. 'If it was worth my while, I could put together a ten-record set of unreleased songs,' he said.

Some of the most exciting finds were from the glory years of the mid-1960s – songs like 'Mama, You Been on My Mind' and 'I'll Keep It with Mine.' But there was also great work from the very recent past, including 'Angelina,' 'Lord Protect My Child,' 'Foot of Pride,' 'Blind Willie McTell,' and, most recently, the whirling 'Series of Dreams.' Bob had rejected these songs when he was putting together *Shot of Love*, *Infidels*, and *Oh Mercy*. Yet the songs were superb, far better than many of the tracks on the albums as released. Most of these songs were familiar to Bob's friends, and to those fans who collected bootleg recordings, but to the critics and general public here was a revelation like the opening of a pharaoh's tomb. The box set would not sell in huge numbers, but as Eric Weisbard wrote in *Sing Out!*, the answer to the perennial question about what was Dylan's best album since *Blood on the Tracks* was that his best latter-day releases were compilations like *Biograph* and *The Bootleg Series, Volumes 1–3*. Here was genuinely brilliant music.

A few months after the release, in May 1991, Bob turned fifty and found he had to face the emotional and financial cost of a second failed marriage. In June, the house at Tarzana was transferred to Carolyn Dennis's name, one of the first steps in the process. Bob was drinking heavily, downing brandy and other types of liquor as if it were water. He also became grumpy and unreasonable with his band. 'He was going through a pretty rough time himself with one thing and another,' says Ian Wallace. 'He'd stop in the middle of songs, kind of put his hands on his hips and look at everybody in disgust.' They toured Europe in the summer and then South America before coming back to the United States. Traveling through the Midwest on his tour bus, Bob talked to *Los Angeles Times* journalist Robert Hilburn. He dismissed the idea of himself as a legend, as he had before, and admitted to some confusion as to what his position and purpose were anymore, saying it was hard to know why people came to his concerts, 'what they are looking for or listening for.' Although these were not new sentiments, the way he spoke seemed to indicate a weariness that was new to his character.

Meanwhile, he changed his road band again the following spring by hiring an additional string player, William 'Bucky' Baxter, who had been with Steve Earle's band. Baxter added country-style pedal-steel guitar and accordion to Bob's band, softening the sound. 'It sounded too much to me like a garage band when I joined,' he says. Baxter soon found that playing in Dylan's band was not a fun experience. 'Most of the time it's pretty serious. It's challenging, and it's interesting. But I don't look back on it as having [had] a lot of fun. It's intense, and he's intense, so it's not your normal rock 'n' roll band.'

As well as hiring Baxter, Bob added a second drummer, Charlie Quintana, who had played with Bob on *Late Night with David Letterman* in 1984. The existing drummer, Ian Wallace, arrived at a rehearsal in Los Angeles to find two drum kits set up, which naturally upset him. 'I wasn't too happy,' he says. As in the past, though, Bob had become remote from his road musicians and Wallace felt unable to sit down and talk to Bob about his concerns now that he was apparently being squeezed out. 'He just wasn't approachable for me at that time,' says Wallace. 'I didn't feel I could talk to him.' Indeed, none of the musicians had many opportunities to speak to Bob. He traveled in his own bus, stayed apart in hotels, and often the first time they saw him during the day was when they walked on stage together. When the show was in progress, he would often scowl at them as if he thought everything was terrible. Afterward he went directly with Victor Maymudes to his tour bus and disappeared into the night.

It was in the midst of this unhappy period, on October 16, 1992, that Bob was honored by Sony with the Thirtieth Anniversary Celebration concert at Madison Square Garden in New York. This huge and prestigious show was very different from the regular gigs he was then playing with his band on the road and was a tribute to his importance as a songwriter, and musical innovator, rather than a reflection of his current commercial status. In fact, he had never known such lean times as a recording artist. The double CD and video spin-off of the event – featuring star names such as Eric Clapton and George Harrison – sold well in the first few months and then sales fell sharply. Artists who were featured on the CD received a percentage of royalties and were surprised to see how modest these were. 'Some of the statements I got didn't read very well,' says Liam Clancy. 'You know, Denmark: two copies.'

Around this time, Bob's marriage to Carolyn Dennis finally ended. Although not nearly as expensive as his 1977 divorce from Sara Dylan, Bob is understood to have paid Carolyn a multimillion-dollar settlement. He did not have enough cash on hand, evidently, because a trust deed was created for Carolyn using part of the Point Dume estate as a surety until Bob paid the full settlement (he had done the same thing during his divorce from Sara). Under community property law, Carolyn would be entitled additionally to a half share in all the new songs Bob had registered during their marriage, a share of future royalties and performance rights income, and child support. Carolyn also had the Tarzana house, which was valued at $661,300 in 1994. In an effort to hide the divorce from the press, court records listed Bob as R. Zimmerman and, after an application by lawyers, a judge issued an order to seal the file.

Bob plunged back into relentless touring. By the end of 1992, he would have played one hundred and five concerts, the second busiest year of his career as a performer. (Tellingly, the busiest previous year had been 1978, following his first divorce.) He felt compelled to work in this way partly because he was bereft of inspiration for studio albums; because he did not know what else to do with himself; and also to raise money to pay for another expensive divorce. The fact that the divorce was from a woman Bob had never been able – due to his innate secretiveness and desperate desire for privacy – to acknowledge publicly as his wife was sad indeed. Now in his early fifties, Bob was more lonely and isolated than ever before, a melancholy figure facing an uncertain future.

CHAPTER 10

NOT DARK YET

The Carolyn Dennis divorce would immerse Bob in considerable expense for years to come. This was just a fraction of the costs he bore as the head of a large and growing family of two ex-wives, numerous girlfriends, six children, and an increasing number of grandchildren.

Sara Dylan continued to live in Beverly Hills, supported by her multimillion-dollar divorce settlement and share in Bob's royalties. She dated a number of men after her divorce, including Bob's friend David Blue (who died in 1982 of a heart attack while jogging in New York), but she chose not to marry again. Despite press reports in the 1980s that Bob and Sara were reconciled, and even considering remarrying, they were never really close after the divorce. Sara lived alone after the children grew up, suffering from ill health and becoming something of a recluse. She had little contact with the showbusiness community and cut a forlorn figure when she did go out.

Although Sara and Bob were not close, they had made sure to provide amply for the children. The rich trust funds they established meant that the children would never have to work unless they wanted to. Thus assured of financial security for life, most of the Dylan siblings settled down at a young age, married, and started families of their own.

Maria Dylan had always been set slightly apart from the rest of the family because she was older, but also because she had a different natural father. She never saw Hans Lownds, speaking with him only once by telephone when she was at boarding school. Yet there was also distance between Maria and her adoptive father. 'Bob wasn't the greatest father to her,' says Peter Lownds, half brother to Maria. 'I think that she felt an outsider, that she got different treatment . . . being the oldest and being a half sister has not been easy for her.' After qualifying as a lawyer, Maria was the first sibling to marry. Following their first child, Isaac, in 1989, she and husband Peter Himmelman had three more children between 1991 and 1996. Maria became a copyright lawyer who fought on behalf of songwriters, but most of her time was taken up with caring for her children at home in Santa Monica where she lived as an orthodox Jew.

Like Maria, Desiree Dennis-Dylan was slightly set apart from the core of the family. In her case this was because she was so much younger and came from an African-American, Christian background. However, Bob told his other children about her and it was understood she would eventually share in his fortune.

The eldest Dylan son, Jesse, attended New York University but he did not graduate. An outgoing, slightly overweight young man, he made pop videos and television commercials for the Los Angeles production company Straw Dogs, which later merged with Paradise Music & Entertainment, Inc. Jesse became a major investor, along with celebrities including Leonardo Di Caprio and Matt Damon, and was appointed chairman and C.E.O. The corporation grew quickly and reported sales of $8.1 million in 1999, giving Jesse the unexpected status of a successful businessman. In his personal life, Jesse married girlfriend Susan Traylor. Their first child, William, was born in 1995 and they live comfortably in the Hollywood Hills.

Anna was a shy young woman who spent many years in further education, eventually finishing college in 1999 when she was thirty-two. She was a painter by avocation, and had lived with her mother before moving to a condominium in Santa Monica. She married, but kept the surname Dylan. Her younger brothers, Samuel and Jakob, were like twins in appearance – both tall and skinny with curly brown hair and distinctive eyes that were blue like Bob's and doleful like Sara's. Samuel was quiet and sensitive like Anna, with a slightly fey manner. After graduating college, he experimented with photography before going to work with brother Jesse at Straw Dogs. In 1995 Samuel married Stacy Hochheiser, who had grown up in Woodstock. They had a son, Jonah, two years later.

Bob introduced all his children to music, filling the house at Point Dume with instruments they might play, and often taking them on tour with him as they got older. As a consequence of such nurturing, the children grew up to share Bob's love and knowledge of American roots music, as well as picking up a love of more contemporary artists such as Elvis Costello, The Clash, and X. Some of the siblings were moved to try and write songs of their own, inspired by their father's belief that anybody could do anything if they really put their mind to it. Most of the children realized at an early age, however, that there was an apparently God-given element to their father's talent, and that it was almost impossible to compete with him. They contented themselves instead with more modest occupations.

The youngest child, Jakob, was slightly different, however; he had his father's itch to succeed in the public eye. Jakob briefly attended art school in New York before dropping out to form a band, The Wallflowers, which was signed to Virgin Records. Bob had a natural, parental concern about Jakob entering a business he knew to be fickle and cutthroat. 'My initial thought was that I just didn't want to see [Jakob] get roughed up,' he said. He did not even like to see Jesse and Samuel working behind the scenes in show business. But it was the business they had grown up with, and Bob would never tell them *not* to do something. As it turned out, The Wallflowers's eponymous debut album flopped upon its release in 1992 with sales of only forty thousand units. Meanwhile, Jakob married his childhood girlfriend, Nicole Paige

Denny, in a ceremony at Sara Dylan's house in 1992, with Bob attending as he would attend the weddings of all his children. Jakob's first child, Levi, was born two years later. He had a second son, James, in 1998, and a third son in 2000, and the family lived near Jesse's house in the Hollywood Hills. Aside from his musical career, which inevitably involved some self-promotion, Jakob shared his siblings' desire for an anonymous, family-oriented personal life. 'The world's as big as the block you live on, and I like to keep it small,' he says. 'I have the same friends I've had since I was eleven years old.'

It is to Bob and Sara's credit that their children grew up unspoiled by wealth and celebrity. Yet the children were obviously affected by the fact that their father was a superstar, with all the craziness celebrity attracted, and by the breakup of their parents' marriage. By marrying young and building stable home lives of their own they were surely reacting to these factors. Also, although the children talk of their Dad as being an exceptional father – being extremely wise, very supportive, and nonjudgmental about their choices in life – and although they always had regular contact with him, Bob was not perfect. No parent is without faults, but even to his own family Bob seemed to be a driven, introverted, and insular man consumed with a monomania for his music. They loved him and were proud of his achievements, but he was undeniably difficult.

Outside his immediate family, Bob had never been known for his largesse. Ruth Tyrangiel, who claims to have had a nineteen-year relationship with Bob, apparently received only two gifts in all that time – a silver rose and a mandarin orange. Susan Ross never got the ring she says Bob promised her, nor the New York apartment she asked for, although this was admittedly a much more ambitious request. However, Bob was generous with some particularly close girlfriends who had been like wives to him.

It has been reported widely in the press that Bob married backing singer Clydie King in the 1980s and that she may have had a child with him. This seems to be untrue, inasmuch as no documentary evidence – no marriage certificate, no birth certificates of a King-Dylan child, or any divorce papers – has been found. Furthermore, sources close to Bob indicate it is not true. (King, who has suffered from ill health in recent years, declines to speak about Bob.) However, friends of Bob say that, after he and Clydie King broke up, he helped her buy a house in Los Angeles. In general, Bob has taken care to conceal such acts of kindness, especially where it might reveal details of his tangled personal life. A classic case was Carole Childs and the house she lived in courtesy of Bob's Oak Pass Trust. While Childs was living in the Beverly Hills house, Carolyn Dennis was set up in another home courtesy of Bob half an hour's drive away in Tarzana. Childs says she did not know about Carolyn and, in all probability, Carolyn did not know about Childs. Bob himself flitted about, never spending more than a few nights in one place, so it was practically impossible to say whom he was living with at any one time. This was representative of the peculiar, secretive way in which he conducted his life. Then there were women like Ross and Tyrangiel who claim to have lived with Bob during roughly the same period of time he was involved with Childs and Dennis. These claims are hard to substantiate, but there is evidence they had some relationship with Bob. 'There is a lot of intrigue,' admits Childs with a laugh. 'He has been a stand-up guy with me. [So] it wouldn't matter to me what he did. That might seem childish and that might seem foolish. But it's fine.'

In January 1993, Childs accompanied Bob to Washington, D.C., for the presidential inauguration of Bill Clinton. Bob performed 'Chimes of Freedom' at the Lincoln Memorial. It was an opaque rendition, but seemed to please the First Family nevertheless. That evening he performed at the Absolutely Unofficial Blue Jeans Bash, a party in honor of the president at the National Building Museum. The Band was on the bill, reformed without Robbie Robertson and sadly missing the late Richard Manuel, and for old times' sake Bob played with the remaining three members.

Shortly after the inauguration, Bob ended his ten-year relationship with Carole Childs. He did not say anything had changed, and Childs continued to live in the Beverly Hills house, but Bob did not visit anymore. He was simply gone from her life, 'just *poof!* like smoke,' as she puts it. 'There is no explanation for that. There's nothing.' Childs denies this has been hurtful, saying, 'I think we ran our course.' But it seems an extraordinary way to behave. Asked who took her place in Bob's affections, she says with a touch of sarcasm: 'I have no idea. He has some *dawgs*, some nice *dawgs*. They are excellent dawgs, you know – mastiffs.' She adds, 'It's probable maybe he doesn't have somebody.'

Musicians found themselves dismissed in a similarly cold, nonconfrontational way. Bob went back on the road in the spring of 1993 with a European tour that began in Dublin, Ireland. Ian Wallace's drums were shipped across for rehearsals. Two days before Wallace was due to fly to Dublin, he received a call from Bob's office saying Bob wanted to make a change in the band. Winston Watson – who had already replaced Charlie Quintana as the second drummer in the band – would be the sole drummer from now on. 'I think I'm the only person he has fired twice,' says Wallace, who had also been dismissed at the end of the 1978 world tour. 'I don't hold any grudges or anything, [but] the way that it was done was a little upsetting.'

Following Wallace's departure, there were two European tours in 1993, together with lucrative festival appearances where Bob could earn $250,000 for a short set. In August, he embarked on a two-month U.S. tour with Santana. By teaming up with another headline act,

Bob could play arena shows where he and his co-headliner demanded up to ninety percent of net ticket sales. If the shows sold out, they made substantial profits. It was no coincidence that Bob overcame his dislike of interviews in the press before the tour; he wanted the tickets to sell. Although he was certainly rich by any standard, most of Bob's wealth was tied up in copyrights, trust funds, and property and he needed cash from tours like this to pay for his staff, maintain his family and properties, and meet his divorce payments.

During the 1990s Bob seemed more money-oriented than before, but he would also do things that made next to no money. During a break in touring in May 1993, for instance, he recorded his old song 'Ballad of Hollis Brown' with Pete Seeger's half brother Mike for the latter's album *Third Annual Farewell Reunion*. 'That recording [was] the first take and had all that great intensity of feeling that is so characteristic of Bob's singing of trad' songs,' says Mike Seeger, who had known Bob since the early sixties. 'He makes you feel the words and make the pictures.'

When Bob wrote 'Ballad of Hollis Brown' in 1962, the words had flooded through him. In recent years, however, inspiration had virtually dried up. Tired of forcing himself to write, and disillusioned with the time-consuming modern recording process, Bob returned to the source of his musical life. In 1992 and 1993 he recorded two albums of what he called 'the music that's true for me.' These were mostly traditional songs, the building blocks of American music. He recorded them in the most minimal way possible – at his home studio at Point Dume, accompanying himself on acoustic guitar and harmonica.

The first of these albums, released in November 1992, was *Good As I Been to You*. He sounded genuinely sorrowful on the old song 'Hard Times,' his voice quavering as he strained for the high notes. This and many of the other songs he was covering had formed part of Bob's musical education as a young man. 'Tomorrow Night' was recorded by Elvis Presley in Memphis as part of the Sun sessions before he was shot through the cannon of fame. Bob loved it then and sang a moving new version that benefited from the fact that his voice sounded rough and cracked; this deepened the sense of melancholy in the lyrics. Bob knew 'You're Gonna Quit Me' from his earliest days in Greenwich Village where the tune was often performed by Reverend Gary Davis. Bob sang as if the lyrics were as vivid to him now as they were then, carefully phrasing every word. The album concluded with the children's song 'Froggie Went A-Courtin',' sung as if lulling one of his own children to sleep. The novelty tune provided Bob with a neat ending: 'if you want any more / you can sing it yourself.'

The second album, released in the fall of 1993, was the emphatically entitled *World Gone Wrong*. Bob wrote in the quirky liner notes that these were songs for 'the New Dark Ages.' 'Blood in My Eyes' was a song performed by the prewar group The Mississippi Sheiks. The song was a fixed stare of lust that might turn to violence; menace and, again, melancholy pervaded this album. Bob had performed 'Delia' back in Dinkytown when his career was only a glimmering hope. He was trying a little too hard then. Now when he sang 'all the friends I ever had are gone' his ruined voice and life's experience made it real. Bob knew 'Stack A Lee' from the rendition by Frank Hutchison on the *Anthology of American Folk Music*. Hutchison was a miner in the hills of West Virginia in the early years of the twentieth century. He recorded until the Depression, and died in obscurity around the end of the Second World War. As Harry Smith explained in the *Anthology* booklet, writing in his customary uppercase lettering, 'Stack A Lee' was about a petty crime that had led to a squalid murder: 'THEFT OF STETSON HAT CAUSES DEADLY DISPUTE.' Nothing could be further removed from 1993 rock-star Malibu heaven, yet in this new recording Bob sounded as though he could have been back in the mining town of Ethel, West Virginia. Indeed, he was by now as much a part of the folklore of American music as Frank Hutchison.

Good As I Been to You and *World Gone Wrong* sold very few copies. To the casual observer, the records may have added to the general impression of an artist in decline. They were fine records nevertheless, and important reference works for the great comeback album that was brewing in Bob's imagination.

During this time Bob continued to tour relentlessly, making regular excursions to play shows in Europe, South America, Asia, and Australasia. In May 1994 he performed as the headline act at the Great Music Experience, an elaborate festival at the Todaiji Temple in Nara, Japan. Bob played on stage with a rock 'n' roll band assembled for the show, plus the Tokyo Philharmonic Orchestra, a partially successful experiment that was hindered by the way the stage was set for the television cameras. 'It was just a mess because the drums are way in the back. The artists were way up front, a huge amount of space in-between,' says drummer Jim Keltner. He says it was a 'terrible nightmare' as a drummer, but Bob was paid a handsome fee and probably felt differently about the show.

In addition to lucrative stage appearances of this sort, Bob also began to exploit his song catalogue as never before, licensing use of his songs for various commercial projects, including films. The sound track to *Forrest Gump*, which was the outstanding box-office hit of 1994, featured two Dylan songs, earning large amounts of money for years to come as the soundtrack album and video also proved popular.

There was also a philanthropic side to Bob, although typically he tried to keep it secret. On April 12, 1994, Bob played a show in Rockford, Illinois, and happened to pick up a copy of the *Rockford Register Star*. The newspaper reported that the Page Park School, a local school for mentally and physically disabled young people, needed $20,000 to build a playground. There was a photograph of some of the students with an old basketball hoop, which was the only piece of outdoor equipment they had. Bob wrote a personal check for $20,000, asking only that he not be identified as the patron. 'He wanted the donation to be anonymous, [but] word got out of course,' says principal, Nancy Adamany.

The school donation came a few days before Jakob and Paige Dylan had their first child, Levi. Bob was on stage in Fort Wayne, Indiana, at the time of the birth and sang 'I'll Be Your Baby Tonight.' Although his touring commitments kept him away from home for large parts of the year, Bob was a doting grandparent who made a point of seeing his children and grandchildren whenever he returned to California – where they all lived – and keeping in touch by telephone at other times. His mother, Beatty, was also in close touch with the younger members of the family, seeing them when they visited Minnesota, where she lived during the summer (she had a house in Arizona for the winter), and when she came to California for visits.

A summer tour took Bob away from his family to Europe, but he returned to America in August 1994 to be one of the headline acts at Woodstock '94. This was a huge festival held in Saugerties, New York, to capitalize on the twenty-fifth anniversary of the 1969 Woodstock Festival. Bob snubbed the original festival when he was the undisputed leader of the prevailing popular culture, preferring to headline at the Isle of Wight. Yet here he was in late middle age lured by a reported fee of $600,000. He arrived to see hundreds of thousands of seminaked youths writhing in mud to the flamboyant antics of the Red Hot Chili Peppers. It was bands like this that the young fans came primarily to see, and it was this band in particular Bob had to follow on the bill. For once, he seems to have almost lost his nerve.

Bob insisted his two tour buses drive right up to the back of the North Stage so that he could just walk out onto the stage. This blocked two precious loading docks, causing considerable problems for the crew. He then stayed in his bus for an unusually long time. 'We were behind. Everything was waiting. Everything was ready and Bob wouldn't come out of the bus,' says Patrick Stansfield, one of the stage managers. Stansfield had worked with Bob on major concert events since 1974 and it was the first time he had ever sensed that Bob was unsure of himself. 'I think he didn't know how he was going to be received . . . It was the only time I had any flash or inkling that there was an unsteadiness of purpose.' Eventually Bob emerged from his bus wearing a black western-style stage suit with white piping. He caught sight of Mitch Fennell, another old friend, and followed Fennell out onto the stage.

The moment Bob came into the lights, before he had even sung a line, the audience went berserk. 'The kids were ready for him,' says Stansfield. 'What he didn't know was that they loved [him] and they wanted him there. I don't know why. I didn't think they had it in them, the little weasels in the mud.' It was the affirmation Bob needed and he gave a tremendous show. 'A thrilling set, a blistering fuckin' set,' says Stansfield. Indeed, Bob's reception at Woodstock '94 was one of the first strong indications that his music had transcended its time and was being embraced by the children of the people who had first heard him in the sixties and early seventies.

A few months later, in November 1994, Bob took part in another youth-oriented event when he played two shows in New York for the MTV *Unplugged* series. The producers took care to present Bob as an iconic figure; he wore dark glasses and a polka-dot shirt, as he had at the time of *Highway 61 Revisited*. Backing him was his regular road band plus Brendan O'Brien on a noticeably plugged-in Hammond organ. During rehearsals, Bob was characteristically vague about what songs he wanted to play during the actual show. 'We rehearsed at Sony studios for a couple of days and I swear to God we didn't play any of those songs,' says drummer Winston Watson. 'We played a lot [of] country blues, songs I had never heard before, real quiet, gentle . . . not really a rock 'n' roll trip at all.'

Bob finally decided he wanted to play old folk songs for the MTV special, which was being recorded for CD and video release, but Sony executives said this would not be right for the audience. 'The record company said, "You can't do that, it's too obscure," ' said Bob. 'At one time I would have argued, but there's no point. Okay, so what's not obscure? They said, "Knockin' on Heaven's Door." ' As a result he put on a show comprised mostly of greatest hits. The freshest song he performed was 'Dignity,' written in the *Oh Mercy* period. It provided a hard-rocking number, especially with Watson on drums, and Bob seemed to relish the lyric. He also found interest in 'John Brown,' an antiwar ballad from the start of his career. The MTV project was not as commercially successful as the phenomenal *Eric Clapton Unplugged* of 1992, which went to number one and spawned a hit single in the acoustic arrangement of 'Layla,' but *Bob Dylan MTV Unplugged* reached twenty-three in the album charts, becoming his most successful album in years in terms of sales.

While he toured, Bob sometimes sketched with pencil, charcoal, and pen in order to relax. In 1994 Random House published a book of drawings made between 1989 and 1992, titled *Drawn Blank*. In the introduction Bob talked about drawing as a way to wind down and also to 'vaguely get at something other than the world we know.' The drawings depicted the world of a traveling entertainer: diners, highways, train tracks, and the restaurants, swimming pools, and bedrooms of hotels. The few portraits included drawings of members of his road crew. Sometimes there were drawings of voluptuous, naked African-American women. But mostly Bob seemed to be alone in empty rooms. He often drew the view from his balcony, a view of empty streets, parking lots, and bleak city skylines. Here was his life pictured, and it seemed lonely and disconnected.

Bob's main source of companionship when he toured was road manager Victor Maymudes, who went everywhere with him. They had known each other since the early 1960s, and Maymudes was the only member of Bob's traveling company of musicians, technicians, managers, and stage crew – up to sixty people – who could be called a friend. There were barriers, literal and metaphorical, to ensure Bob did not see anybody he did not specifically ask for. There might be ten thousand people out front at a show, and sixty production personnel hurrying hither and thither, but backstage Bob was solitary as a castaway, sitting, smoking, strumming his guitar, and reading books. Carole Childs, who could not abide Maymudes in most respects, calling him a 'haughty son of a bitch' and worse, concedes that Bob needed somebody who could ensure his privacy in this way and says Maymudes was excellent at this.

If Bob did not have somebody to stop people getting to him, he would be swamped not just with fans but with the numerous friends and fellow celebrities who came to concerts to see him. Wherever Bob traveled in the world – but particularly when he was in New York, Los Angeles, and London – friends asked for complimentary tickets and passes to get backstage. If they got backstage, it did not mean they could easily get in to see Bob. Even people who had known Bob for decades found it impossible at times to get close enough to speak to him. For example, Bonnie Beecher had seen Bob practically every time he came to the San Francisco Bay area, where she lived with Wavy Gravy. 'We stayed friends for a really long time,' she says. 'We would always find each other.'

Then one time she tried to see Bob at a show and he walked past her as if she did not exist. Bonnie tried to get his attention, but was blocked by security men. 'I thought, I'm never doing that again . . . It's just too humiliating.' Maymudes tried to make Bonnie feel better by saying Bob had walked past George Harrison in the same way. Without his spectacles, which he refused to wear on stage for simple vanity, Bob was blind as a bat. But the singer could hardly have mistaken Bonnie's voice plaintively calling his name. She remembered the support she had given him when he was starting out in Dinkytown; how she had sneaked him food from her sorority house; and agreed not to sell her home tapes to the Library of Congress for less than $200. Did all this count for nothing?

Ramblin' Jack Elliott had a similar experience backstage at a show in Berkeley in May 1995. 'We could not get close enough to even say hi,' he says. Shortly afterward his record producer, Roy Rogers, wrote to Bob's office to ask if Bob would sing on Ramblin' Jack's new album, *Friends of Mine*. 'About two months later when no response was heard, Roy called up Bob's manager again and said, "Did you get our letter?" And he said, "Yes, Bob has your letter." Like the ball's in Bob's court now. That was the answer.' Elliott says he is hurt by 'the whole kind of mafiosi politics way [Bob] does business with his friends.' Numerous old friends tell similar stories. Some who had known Bob for thirty years and more found they could not even get complimentary concert tickets. Increasingly, Bob's contact with people was limited to a handful of trusted employees, girlfriends, and family members.

Bob toured in this fashion throughout 1995. There were two sojourns in Europe and two extended U.S. tours in-between. In total, he played ninety-nine shows. While some performers work harder – B. B. King appears on stage almost every night – one hundred or so shows a year is an unusually high number for an artist of Bob's stature. It also meant he earned a lot of money. In an average year, a hundred shows might gross around $35 million, of which Bob would personally earn approximately $15 million after expenses and taxes.

He also raised money through the judicious management of his music catalogue. In the spring of 1995 Bob changed his affiliation from the American Society of Composers, Authors and Publishers (ASCAP) – the organization that collected his performance rights income – to the rival Society of European Stage Authors and Composers (SESAC). He received an unprecedented advance of at least $2 million from SESAC just to make the switch. Bob also sanctioned an official CD-ROM, *Bob Dylan: Highway 61 Interactive*. On February 2, 1996, he gave a private show in Phoenix, Arizona, for employees and guests of the finance company Nomura Securities International, Inc. Company president Ethan Penner reportedly paid Bob $300,000.

At times it seemed Bob would do almost anything for money, and there was disquiet among fans when he allowed 'The Times They Are A-Changin'' to be used in an advertisement for the Bank of Montreal. There was even more concern when the song was used in a television commercial for accountancy giant Coopers & Lybrand. Company spokesman Brian Carty said, 'When the song was written, it was about social justice and the change of institutions. It's still an important song, but it's about different things today.' The decision to endorse an accountancy company was perhaps not that surprising when one remembered that Bob was close to his own accountants at Gelfand, Rennert & Feldman and that this company is a division of PricewaterhouseCoopers. After so many years of neglecting his money, Bob was now a shrewd businessman.

As Bob took more of an interest in his financial well-being, he also began to take care of his health. Although associated with drug use in the public consciousness, his main vices had in fact been heavy smoking and drinking. He drank more than was healthy at different periods in his career and had been drinking particularly heavily in recent years, to the extent that his health declined and some members of his immediate circle feared he was in danger of becoming an alcoholic. Few people were able to talk to him directly about his bad habits. But he did listen to the advice of his children and, partly due to their concern, Bob stopped drinking in the mid-1990s. This was a turning point; he began to look and sound better on stage, and performed with more vigor and focus. The change was apparent to many in the summer of 1995 when he supported The Grateful Dead. 'He opened for us [three] times in '95 and he was brilliant. Just wonderful,' says a senior Dead source. 'Why couldn't [he] have done that in '87?'

Part of Bob's affection for The Grateful Dead was his friendship with the band's avuncular leader, Jerry Garcia, so it was distressing to him when Garcia died of a heart attack on August 9, 1995, while in a drug rehabilitation center. He was fifty-three. Bob was shocked by the loss of a friend who was close to him in age and had been through many of the same experiences. He made the effort to attend Garcia's funeral – something he had not done for other departed friends – and released a eulogy via his publicist. It read in part: 'There's no way to measure his greatness or magnitude as a person or as a player. . . . To me he wasn't only a musician and a friend, he was more like a big brother.' Although this statement was no doubt heartfelt, it was perhaps motivated by the emotion of the moment rather than the fairly small amount of time the two had spent together over the years.

A month after Garcia's death, in September 1995, Bob performed at the opening of the Rock and Roll Hall of Fame in Cleveland, Ohio, duetting with Bruce Springsteen on 'Forever Young.' Asked by reporters what he thought about the curious idea that there was now a museum dedicated to rock 'n' roll, Bob said nothing surprised him anymore. Two months later he appeared at a tribute to Frank Sinatra on the latter's eightieth birthday. He sang 'Restless Farewell' to the old man and posed with him for photographs. Fellow guest and comedian Don Rickles caused much hilarity by haranguing Bob in jest: 'You know what your problem is? You gotta stop mumbling when you sing.'

The following year a group of Bob's admirers promoted the idea that Bob should receive Sweden's Nobel Prize for Literature. A formal nomination was made by Professor Gordon Ball, of the Virginia Military Institute, who said sagaciously, 'The point is that he's continued to evolve. That's one of the signs of a great artist, as is his independence of mind.' British academic Professor Christopher Ricks thought the nomination appropriate. 'If the question is does anybody use words better than he does, then the answer in my opinion is no.' Ricks was one of several leading academics who rated Bob highly as a poet. Britain's Poet Laureate, Andrew Motion, considered Bob 'one of the great artists of the century' and said 'Visions of Johanna' was the best song lyric ever written. Bob did not win the Nobel Prize but honors were being laid before him with increasing frequency, and the idea that he might one day receive the world's most prestigious literary prize did not seem impossible. Indeed, in 2000 he was honored in Sweden with the respected Polar Music Prize. His fellow recipient was the violinist Isaac Stern, and the presentation was made by the King of Sweden.

At a time when Bob was being lauded more for his past achievements than for his current work, he made *Time Out of Mind*, his first album of new songs in seven years, and the record that marked his resurgence as an artist. It was a work of bleak harshness, concerned with aging and lost love but shot through with dry wit. The foundation stones for this work were the two albums of traditional songs he had recorded in 1992–93, as well as the songs from the *Anthology of American Folk Music*, music that interested Bob as much as it ever did when he was young. By meditating on these old songs, Bob found he was inspired to write new work. Words came gradually at first, often at night. If there was a storm Bob would stay up late and work as the heavens crackled and rain splashed around his hotel. A maxim replayed in his head: 'Work while the day lasts, because the night of death cometh when no man can work.' He was sure it was from the Bible, but could not find the reference. Maybe he had invented it subconsciously. By late 1996 he was writing prolifically. During a stay in Ireland with Ronnie Wood he was coming up with songs every day, tearing up cigarette packets to scribble lyrics.

Bob met *Oh Mercy* producer Daniel Lanois in a New York hotel over the winter of 1996–97 and read the lyrics to him as if they were poems. 'The words were hard, were deep, were desperate, were strong, and they came from having lived a number of lives, which I believe Bob has,' said Lanois. 'So that's the record I wanted to make.' Lanois decided that he wanted to frame these new, multi-layered songs with a rich, but subtle musical accompaniment. To achieve this, they decided to use many musicians. First there was Bob's road band, one of the few times he would record with his road musicians. They also called in Jim Keltner, one of four drummers who played on the record. Cindy Cashdollar from Asleep at the Wheel played slide and steel guitar. Blues guitarist 'Duke' Robillard was on Bob's list, as was Bob Britt, a guitarist he met in a club in Nashville. Bob wanted keyboard players Jim Dickinson and Augie Meyers, whom he had known since the early sixties when Meyers played with Doug Sahm in the Sir Douglas Quintet. Bob had a fondness for the sound of Meyers's 1963 English-built Vox organ and super reverb amp. 'I'd like you to play on my next album,' said Bob, calling Meyers in Texas. 'I want you to bring your *magic Vox*.'

Dylan and Lanois decided to record at Criteria Studios in Miami, Florida, starting in mid-January 1997. Bob took an apartment in Miami Beach. The musicians were accommodated separately in hotels in South Beach. Criteria was an old studio in a shabby neighborhood of Miami. The sessions were held in a large room with a high ceiling. Bob positioned himself on a stool next to the drums with a Steinway grand piano facing him, for when he wanted to move to a keyboard. Next to the piano, facing Bob, was Augie Meyers. The other musicians were arranged on either side to form a large circle of up to a dozen people. Everybody played together live, as Bob worked through different arrangements of what he modestly told Meyers were 'sketches' of songs. Bob approached the sessions with more seriousness than he had on perhaps any previous record. He would arrive at the studio around lunchtime, slipping in through a back door. 'He comes in the room, you don't know he comes in,' says Meyers. 'And when he leaves, you don't know he's left.' They would work through the afternoons, stopping for something to eat around dusk, and then continue until midnight or later. '[Bob] looked very tired when he'd leave at night,' says Duke Robillard. 'But he seemed in good health.'

Lanois made it clear to the musicians that he wanted a blend of sounds, a 'moosh,' as guitarist Bucky Baxter calls it. It was not to be a record where there would be standout solo performance. This caused some minor conflicts with the musicians. Duke Robillard for one felt Bob wanted him at the sessions to play blues guitar, but says Lanois told him he did not want to hear a note of blues guitar. Similarly when Lanois asked Cindy Cashdollar to play a part in a different style, Bob told him to let her do what she was doing.

Bob tried different versions of each new song, changing both music and lyrics radically as he moved between guitar and piano, transposing keys in his head.

'I can't sing that,' he said one day when they were

working on the song 'Cold Irons Bound.' Resting on an instrument case, he redrafted the lyrics. By the time the song was finished it had transmuted into a fast rockabilly number, a charnel cart clattering to hell. Bob's vocal had the menace of nightmare. He sang about wading through mist, 'almost like I don't exist.'

'Love Sick' was a stalking blues with a world-weary lyric that would become the single from the album and, in time, a very popular concert song. 'Dirt Road Blues' was constructed around a cassette tape of an earlier, abandoned session, and had something of the sound of the early Elvis Presley Sun sessions that Bob had admired since he was a teenager.

The *Time Out of Mind* songs contained phrases that Bob had picked magpielike from songs on the Harry Smith *Anthology*, as well as records by Fats Domino and Jimmie Rodgers, the 'singing brakeman' who died in 1933. For example, 'Standing in the Doorway' borrowed from the traditional song 'Moonshiner' with its lyric 'Let me eat when I'm hungry, let me drink when I'm dry.' Phrases like this are part of the common currency of American language, of course, but Dylan was making use of stock phrases more than ever before. '[The] lyrics are composed almost entirely of figures of speech,' says poet and friend Michael McClure, who noticed the development. 'In the earlier works that I know – say *Blonde on Blonde* – there are no figures of speech, except just to connect the multilayered, multidimensional imagery.'

Bob found a way to incorporate religiosity into these new songs without preaching. 'Tryin' to Get to Heaven' was as much a song of faith as anything he wrote during his Christian conversion. Bob still had broadly Christian beliefs, but he was now able to express these views without being sanctimonious. Again, the lyrics of this song had phrases borrowed from previous songs. The line 'I've been all around the world, boys' echoed 'Worried Blues,' an old Frank Hutchison song ('I've traveled this world / Boys . . .').

There was no braggadocio in the songs of relationships; Bob sounded too weary for crowing. ' 'Til I Fell in Love With You' was resigned, helpless, weary beyond words. 'Not Dark Yet' sounded like the interior monologue of a man about to die. The words escaped in small, sighing breaths. Bob sang that he was born and would die here, but it was against his will. He turned the phrase so it made one shudder. (Cindy Cashdollar, for one, felt goose bumps rising on her skin.) At times his burden was more than he could bear. It was not dark yet, 'but it's getting there.'

Bleak though the songs were, Bob did not seem depressed to his fellow musicians. One meal break he cracked up laughing when Augie Meyers showed him a trick with a lemon and a Kleenex, making the lemon into a 'bar critter' that rolled about comically. When Meyers played a lick from 'Like a Rolling Stone' Bob made eye contact immediately. 'I smiled at him and he smiled back,' says Meyers. 'He said, "That's been done before." '

When it came to recording 'Make You Feel My Love,' Bob wanted Meyers to play piano while he played guitar. When Meyers discovered that Bob had written the song at the piano, he persuaded him to play it that way. 'Just close your eyes and sing it,' he urged, believing this was the only way Bob would get the sound that was in his head. Bob was reluctant, not thinking himself a very good pianist. 'Bob, you're a great piano player.'

'You think so?'

'Well, sure. I don't see why you've even got me here.'

It was true. He might not play in a conventional way, but he played with tremendous feeling. They performed the song the way Meyers suggested, with Bob playing piano and Meyers accompanying him on organ, and the first take went on the album.

'Highlands,' the long song that concluded *Time Out of Mind*, was a talking song set to a hypnotic guitar riff inspired by a Charley Patton record, with a lyric that was philosophical and playful in the style of a shaggy-dog story. As with many past albums, Bob liked to conclude with a song that had an element of hopefulness, even humor. In 'Highlands,' the humor was most evident in the delightful exchange between the narrator and a Boston waitress who bullies him into drawing a picture for her. They get into a conversation in which he thinks she is accusing him of not having read female authors. He retorts indignantly that she is wrong; he had read Erica Jong (Bob laughed when he said the name of the feminist author and had to dub in the line again later). When the waitress went away, the narrator escapes into the street. There is a shift in perspective so it seems the narrator is floating over the world, like a figure from one of Bob's beloved Chagall paintings, looking down at young people enjoying themselves in a park, wishing he could change places with them. Suddenly the listener is given insight into what it might be like to be Bob Dylan, to have had acclaim and great wealth and yet find oneself getting old and having regrets for things that can never be changed. There was no way to turn back the clock. Dylan is doomed, like everybody else. He murmurs that he is lost; he must have taken some wrong turns. Confusion and regret were strongly expressed in the song and would probably resonate with many listeners whose lives had not turned out the way they had hoped. In the songs on *Time Out of Mind*, and in this song in particular, Bob was communicating with his audience as he had in his prime, with words poetic and true that flew like magic birds from his mouth into the mind of the listener. When the album was released later in the year it would be greeted as a triumph that ranked alongside the best work of his career.

Shortly before Bob began work on *Time Out of Mind*, in the fall of 1996, he had again changed drummers in his road band. Winston Watson, who had drummed for him for four years, was replaced with David Kemper, who had formerly played with Jerry Garcia's band. Bob simply wanted a change; he liked to switch things around so that the band sounded fresh, and Watson took the news well. He knew that nobody stayed in the band forever. He had been fortunate to tour with Bob at a time when the singer had hauled himself out of his slump. 'He really got serious again,' says Watson. 'It was always a treat to glimpse the back of the master's head, and watch him do something special every night.' Over the approximately five hundred shows he played with Dylan, Watson estimates they performed more than three hundred different songs

After a tour of Japan in the spring of 1997, guitarist John Jackson also left the band and was replaced with multi-instrumentalist Larry Campbell. The newly configured band played across North America throughout April 1997. Bob sang 'Desolation Row' in New Brunswick, Canada, as a tribute to Allen Ginsberg, who died of cancer on April 5, aged seventy.

There was a show in Evansville, Indiana, on May 1, then two in the southern states before Bob went into the studio to record an overdub for a tribute album to one of the long-dead fathers of hillbilly music, yodeling brakeman Jimmie Rodgers. Bob had been working on the project for his own Egyptian Records label, a subsidiary of Sony Music that had been established for specialist projects. The simple, truthful songs of Jimmie Rodgers had been an enduring inspiration to Bob, and had also affected fellow artists like Steve Earle, Alison Krauss, and Willie Nelson, who all contributed fine cover versions to *The Songs of Jimmie Rodgers – A Tribute*. The record had been gestating since 1994 and would not be released until the late summer of 1997, when it would pass largely unnoticed. Yet it was a first-rate album and an important rejuvenation of the work of a largely forgotten pioneer. Bob's slightly tired overdub on 'My Blue Eyed Jane' would be the last recording he made for some time.

On May 21 Bob performed three songs at the Beverly Hilton Hotel, Beverly Hills, at a show in aid of the Simon Wiesenthal Center. He then took a short break before a scheduled tour with Van Morrison, all the while continuing to tinker with the sequencing of *Time Out of Mind*. He stayed at home during his break so he could see his family.

Saturday, May 24, was Bob's fifty-sixth birthday and, as Bob was in California, daughter Maria Himmelman gave him a small birthday party at her home in Santa Monica with the children gathered around their grandfather. Maria noticed Bob was looking unwell at the party. In fact, he had been suffering chest pains, but a doctor assured him it was nothing serious. Maria did not agree and persuaded Bob to talk on the telephone with a doctor at the University of California at Los Angeles. When Bob described his symptoms, it became apparent to this doctor that Bob had been misdiagnosed. He was admitted to St. John's Hospital in Santa Monica the next day.

Bob underwent tests, including a blood test and chest X rays. The doctors said he was not about to have a heart attack; he had pericarditis, an inflammation of the sac around the heart, preventing the heart from expanding and filling correctly. A potentially serious condition, it made breathing difficult. The condition was caused by a fungal infection, histoplasmosis. *Histoplasma capsulatum* is a fungus that grows in soil enriched with bird droppings in certain parts of the Midwestern and southeastern states, and along the Ohio and Mississippi River valleys. When the ground is disturbed, fungus spores float into the air and can be inhaled. Bob had taken a motorcycle ride through a swampy area in the South while on tour. A storm had blown up – which might have disturbed the fungus – and he had to ride through a foggy area to get back to his bus. He was convinced this was when he had breathed in the spores. If he had been properly diagnosed initially, the illness would not have been serious. As it was, Maria was credited with saving his life.

News that Bob was ill with what his publicist, Elliot Mintz, admitted was a 'potentially fatal infection' made the front page of *USA Today* on Thursday, May 29, and the news went out around the world. The forthcoming tour was canceled, although the band was kept on salary. Meanwhile, Bob lay in the hospital suffering from excruciating pain.

Doctors brought the illness under control through drug therapy and released Bob at the beginning of June 1997. 'I'm just glad to be feeling better,' he said in a statement, adding with a flourish of characteristic idiosyncrasy: 'I really thought I'd be seeing Elvis soon.' He recuperated at home, so exhausted he was unable to get out of bed. He was resting when he received a get-well letter from former band drummer Winston Watson. 'He [later] told me something that made me misty, that he hadn't gotten many letters from people he worked with. In fact, none,' says Watson. 'He said I was the first person that wrote him.' After a lifetime in the music business, after years of screening out old friends, and peremptorily sacking band members, Bob was discovering how few true friends he had.

As medication brought his symptoms under control, Bob began to venture outside the house. He spent some time at a little coffeehouse in Santa Monica, a place with mismatching chairs and a jukebox stocked with old records. Coffeehouses were fashionable again, just as they had been in the 1950s when Bob was starting his career, and this particular establishment was owned by the singer.

The curious story of Bob's coffeehouse goes back to 1995 and an incident involving his tour manager, Victor Maymudes. In late summer of 1995, on about August 17, Maymudes was detained by police following the alleged rape of a seventeen-year-old girl whom he had allegedly met on tour in the Pacific northwest and invited home to Los Angeles. David Braun and Marshall M. Gelfand posted bail of $50,000. Maymudes was not charged, or even questioned about the alleged incident. He says he simply sat in the lobby while bail was posted and has no knowledge of what the complaint was really about. When Bob found out, however, it was decided Maymudes would no longer accompany him on tour.

Maymudes's job went to Mark Rutledge. Although Maymudes did not travel with the tours anymore, he remained on salary and began to acquire and develop investment property for Bob. This property included two parcels of real estate in Baja California Sur, Mexico; a house in Santa Monica; and, in 1996, a business complex in Santa Monica that became known as the Broadway building. Like several of Bob's property interests, the Broadway building was purchased by the Oak Pass Trust.

Situated a mile and a half inland, away from the bustle of Santa Monica's shopping district and beach, the Broadway building was a large multipurpose complex reflecting Bob's singular needs, hobbies, and tastes. A retail space at the front was turned into a coffeehouse very much like the establishments Bob had frequented in his youth. There were exposed wood beams, Naugahyde booths, and mismatched chairs. Unlike other celebrity restaurants where the name of the famous owner is advertised far and wide, in a bid to attract customers, the fact that Bob Dylan owned the 18th Street Coffee House was a secret. To the casual visitor, it was just another Santa Monica hangout. But if one knew what to look for, there were clues. Over the serving counter was a painting, rendered in Bob's distinctive amateur style, of an African-American woman. The jukebox was a valuable antique Wurlitzer loaded with favorite 45s from Bob's youth, including 'Sh-Boom' by The Chords and 'Maybelline' by Chuck Berry. There was a glass panel behind the serving counter allowing a person to see who was in the coffee shop before they ventured into the public area. When the coast was clear, Bob would often sit at a table, sometimes meeting his children for lunch. Behind the coffeehouse was warehouse space that had been converted into a private gymnasium for Bob, complete with full-size boxing ring (in recent years he had taken an interest in boxing and liked to work out in gyms). Above this gymnasium was a complex of offices that Bob also owned, some rented out and one for Bob's own use. Paradoxically, for a Jew who had famously become Christian, Bob leased the adjacent meeting hall for use as a synagogue.

Victor Maymudes hired his twenty-four-year-old daughter, Aerie, to manage the coffeeshop. Unfortunately, it did not go well. Bob's accountants noted that the shop had a net loss of $92,992 in the first nine months, and there were concerns about the way Aerie was running the business. When Bob had recovered enough from his illness to leave home, he decided to sort out the situation himself. So on July 8, 1997, he arranged to meet Maymudes and his daughter in the gymnasium behind the coffeeshop.

Many people who have experienced a brush with death are subdued by the experience, and adopt a more relaxed attitude to life afterward. In Bob's case, he seems to have emerged from his recuperation as feisty as ever. According to a declaration Maymudes later made in a legal action that arose out of the incident, he and his daughter met Bob as arranged. Then Bob told Aerie angrily: 'You're outta here!'

'Why? Tell me why,' asked the girl.

'I don't have to. You're outta here.'

Aerie was so upset Maymudes felt he had to take her home. After an exchange of words with Bob, he left the building and did not come back. It was effectively the end of Maymudes's thirty-five-year relationship with Bob.

Although Carole Childs was no longer dating Bob, she kept in touch and says she jumped in the air with joy when she heard Maymudes was gone from the entourage.

When they were together, she had asked Bob numerous times to get rid of Maymudes. 'I don't know why Bob keeps people around like that,' she says. 'I'm kind of glad [that] Bob doesn't have to pay him any more good, hard-earned money.'

In 1998 Maymudes retained a lawyer and filed a lawsuit against Bob and his touring company – East-West Touring Company – for breach of employment contract and recovery of retirement benefits. He also made a claim on the property in Mexico. In essence, Maymudes said Bob had unfairly sacked him. Bob's lawyers said Maymudes had quit.

As part of their defense, lawyers representing Bob, and his senior employee, Jeff Rosen, revealed a lot about how the spokesman of his generation guarded his privacy, wealth, and position in society as he approached sixty. Part of Maymudes's case concerned the work he did for Bob as a sort of property manager. Mario Testani, a senior accountant working for Bob, said in a declaration that Maymudes had not been a property manager. He said Maymudes actually knew little of Bob's property interests and revealed that Bob owned approximately seventeen properties scattered across the United States and abroad. Each property was looked after by a manager when necessary. For example, Bob owned property in New Mexico looked after by his bus driver, Tom Masters. A portfolio of seventeen substantial properties would, of course, be worth many millions of dollars. The Point Dume estate alone was valued for tax purposes at approximately $6 million, and would sell for a great deal more on the open market. If the other sixteen properties were worth only an average of a million dollars each – and in reality many, like the Minnesota farm, were worth more – Bob's property portfolio would be worth well over $20 million. Maymudes's lawyers wanted Bob to give a videotaped deposition in the case. As part of an effort to stop this happening, Jeff Rosen argued in a declaration that such a deposition might fall into the wrong hands. As background, presumably to impress the court with the magnitude of Bob's fame and achievement, he revealed the extent of Bob's success over the past thirty-seven years. Worldwide record sales were approximately fifty-six million. Twenty albums had been certified gold by the RIAA – with U.S. sales over five hundred thousand – and seven had been certified platinum, with sales over a million. Rosen diligently listed the numerous awards Bob had received, starting with the honorary degree from Princeton University in 1970 and working up to the recent Nobel Prize nomination. He said Bob took extreme care not to be photographed or filmed without being able to control the material. Bob had an agreement with Sony Music that they could not even release so much as an advertisement with his name and photograph without express permission. 'Mr. Dylan has always taken extraordinary steps to protect his image and likeness from any unauthorized exploitation,' said Rosen. 'This has included making his image extremely controlled and thereby creating more value to that image.' Bob had exploited the 'value' of his image by licensing its use on videos, posters, T-shirts, and other merchandise to Sony Signatures for 'substantial sums.' Consequently, there were stalls at concerts selling everything from Bob Dylan clocks, wristwatches, and coffee mugs to, appropriately enough, a $40 'Highway 61' leather wallet.

During the case, RIAA official Frank Creighton gave evidence that the worldwide industry in bootlegging was worth $5 billion each year, and he backed up Jeff Rosen in his assertion that Bob was the single most pirated artist in America if not the world. 'I am of the opinion that Mr. Dylan is probably the most bootlegged artist in the history of the music industry,' said Creighton in a declaration. To further illustrate this point, Rosen had sent an employee shopping in New York for Dylan bootleg material. Shopping in just three stores, the person purchased sixty-four illegal recordings costing in excess of $2,500. It was not just outtakes of recording sessions and concert tapes that were pirated; Bob's answering machine messages were on sale. In the past Bob's office had deposited tapes of new copyrighted songs with the United States Copyright Office. Yet a tape had been stolen even from this facility, apparently the only time such a theft had occurred. Following this incident, Rosen took special security measures with copyrighted material and demo tapes. 'The location of all such material is kept secret, doors and elevators require several key accesses, are fully alarmed, and the most valuable material is maintained in vaults,' he said. Only two people had access to these vaults. The point in all this was that a unique, videotaped deposition would certainly find its way onto the black market.

Thus here was a portrait of Bob Dylan in late middle age: after years when he had fumbled his business affairs, he was a hugely wealthy man who had learned to fiercely protect his copyrights, capitalize on his image, and had become so paranoid about security his archives were locked in secret vaults.

After a massive amount of paperwork and much time-consuming legal argument, Bob's lawyers eventually settled the case in Maymudes's favor in 1998 by paying him $75,000.

After three months of illness and recuperation, and following the conflict with Victor Maymudes, Bob returned to touring on August 3, 1997, with a show in Lincoln, New Hampshire. As he worked his way across the United States and Europe, his face appeared puffed out and he sweated profusely, dark patches soaking his stage suits. 'I'm still taking medication three times a day. Sometimes it makes me a little light-headed and dizzy,' he told *USA Today*. 'And I need to sleep a lot, [but] I guess I'll make it through.'

A month later Bob played for Pope John Paul II at the

World Eucharistic Congress in Bologna, Italy. It seemed incongruous to see a wandering Jew singing 'Knockin' on Heaven's Door' for an aging pontiff, who appeared to be falling asleep during the performance. Bob enjoyed the show, but was unnerved by having to stop after two numbers, doff his Stetson, and climb the dais to greet His Holiness. Bob had no idea what to say; the Pope seemed much more in control, treating the audience of two hundred thousand people to a sermon based in part on Bob's lyrics. 'You say the answer is blowing in the wind, my friend,' he said. 'So it is: but it is not the wind that blows things away. It is the wind that is the breath and life of the Holy Spirit, the voice that calls and says, "Come!"' Bob could not have said it better himself.

Bob was in Europe when *Time Out of Mind* was released in America on September 30, 1997. By using rough mixes, Daniel Lanois had managed to retain the natural sound of the extraordinary Miami sessions. 'It was just like being right there all over again,' says Cindy Cashdollar. Friends were surprised by the personal nature of the lyrics; Jacques Levy says, 'You can get a sense of [the] genuineness of his emotional life.' The songs, as Bob said, had to do with 'the dread realities of life rather than the bright and rosy idealism popular today.' This made it a challenging album; Greil Marcus, writing in *Mojo*, found it 'shocking in its bitterness, in its refusal of comfort or kindness.' Yet there was much to appreciate. Elvis Costello hailed *Time Out of Mind* as the best record Bob had ever made. While there was a touch of hyperbole in this, critics generally agreed that the album was a major achievement and its release signaled a revival of interest in Bob's career. Suddenly, he was fashionable again. Moreover, he was feted as a grand figure of American culture. In October he appeared on the cover of *Newsweek*, twenty-three years since he had last had the honor. Back in 1974, when he first appeared on the cover, Bob was thirty-two, barnstorming across America with The Band. In 1997 he appeared as an owlish older man, in a portrait by Richard Avedon, under the headline, DYLAN LIVES. It was as if he had been resurrected. 'It is a spooky record, because I *feel* spooky,' he told *Newsweek*. 'I don't feel in tune with anything.'

The revival was also newsworthy because it coincided with the phenomenal success of Jakob Dylan and his band The Wallflowers. After their 1992 debut album failed, Jakob moved to Interscope Records and teamed up with his father's old sideman turned producer T-Bone Burnett, who made clean, fresh-sounding recordings of Jakob's catchy melodies, using session musicians and distinguished guest artists to enhance the band's sound. The album, *Bringing Down the Horse*, was lifted by the success of a single, 'One Headlight,' and went on to astonish everybody by selling in excess of four million copies. This is twice as many as *Blood on the Tracks* sold in more than twenty years. 'As far as Jakob is concerned, I can't imagine having larger footsteps to follow in,' says Burnett. 'But Jakob's character is clearly defined and he handles [success] with grace, which also says a lot about Bob as a father.' He adds that the Dylan family connection had virtually nothing to do with the success of *Bringing Down the Horse*. 'I don't think [Jakob] sold a single record because he is Bob's son. I think he sold a lot of records because "One Headlight" is a very good song. I wonder how many Wallflowers fans even know who Bob Dylan is.' Jakob was given the cover of *Rolling Stone* in June 1997. Reluctant to talk about his father, he ventured so far as to say: 'I get asked all the time, "What was your dad like as a parent?" And I say, "I'm twenty-seven years old; I'm not a crackhead; I don't go on afternoon talk shows and spill." I mean, you can probably figure it out for yourself that he did a decent job.' He added: 'My family might be labeled "dysfunctional" like anybody else's family could be. But nobody ever beat me. Being hurt, molested, those are real problems growing up. I didn't have any of that. I just had my family – whatever it was.' As The Wallflowers toured in support of the album, they invariably crossed paths with Bob on his Never-Ending Tour. On November 14 father and son were booked for a corporate show in San Jose, California. The Wallflowers opened and Bob took top billing.

For a brief time it seemed possible, as the media speculated, that Jakob would rival the success of his father. Jakob, naturally enough, was acutely aware of the gulf between the success of one album and the extraordinary body of work Dad had created over a lifetime. 'He's in an exceptional position, and always has been. I don't think anybody could follow that, and nor should they attempt to.' After the early flush of success, Jakob struggled for four years to release a follow-up album, *Breach*, released in 2000 to good reviews but moderate sales.

Bob was surprised to find that, although *Time Out of Mind* had only just been released, his audiences quickly learned to like its songs. 'Love Sick' was greeted with almost the same enthusiasm at shows as were classic songs of the past. Bob was thus encouraged to include more songs from the album in his concerts, and to perform with more energy and joy than he had shown in years.

He paused for forty-eight hours to receive the prestigious Kennedy Center medal at a ceremony in Washington, D.C., on December 7 presided over by President Bill Clinton. The right-wing press mocked the baby-boomer president for bestowing an establishment honor on the figurehead of his generation, a figurehead associated with hedonism and rebellion. As it turned out, Bob appeared for the gala dressed smartly in a tuxedo and accompanied by his mother.

Bob had been offered the Kennedy medal before, but had turned it down. His decision to accept now seemed to correlate with feelings associated with aging. 'I think he did it because of his children,' says Bob's aunt, Ethel

Crystal, one of a contingent of Minnesota relatives invited to Washington to share the occasion. 'He wanted his children to know that he got it.' At the head of the family delegation was eighty-two-year-old Beatty. She sat near Bob at the ceremony and the similarity between them was striking: strong, alert faces, a slightly proud look, and heads crowned with a frizz of hair. Hers was snow white, and Bob's was now salt and pepper gray. Bruce Springsteen sang 'The Times They Are A-Changin'.' President Clinton said Bob probably had more impact on his generation than any other creative artist. The Minnesota relatives had a great time and were delighted to meet the President and First Lady – 'a very charming young man,' according to Aunt Ethel, 'and his wife is a doll' – and to rub shoulders with fellow honorees Lauren Bacall and Charlton Heston. Bob slipped away early, excusing himself by saying he had a show in New York. 'He's very unassuming, and he's very quiet,' says Aunt Ethel. 'As he has been all his life.'

The fortieth annual Grammy Awards were held two months later at Radio City Music Hall in New York, on February 25, 1998. Bob was nominated in three categories for *Time Out of Mind*: Best Contemporary Folk Album; Best Male Rock Vocal Performance for 'Cold Irons Bound'; and Album of the Year.

At the ceremony, Bob gave an effective performance of 'Love Sick.' Behind him were actors, fashionably dressed in black, hired to dance to the music. Out of this crowd burst a young man with 'SOY BOMB' written across his naked chest who began gyrating frantically to Bob's left. Bob looked at him askance, stepping aside when security came to drag the intruder away. He was twenty-six-year-old actor Michael Portnoy, trying to get publicity. According to him, 'SOY BOMB' meant 'kind of this dense, transformational, diverse, organic, explosive life.' In other words, nothing.

The evening was a triumph nonetheless. *Time Out of Mind* won all three categories in which it was nominated, including the prestigious Album of the Year. In his acceptance speech, Bob thanked his musicians, including Jim Keltner and Augie Meyers, 'just every old buddy,' and he recalled having seen Buddy Holly at the Duluth National Guard Armory when he was a teenager. 'I was three feet away from him and he *looked* at me, and I have some kind of feeling that he was – I don't know how or why – but I know he was with us all the time when we were making this record, in some kind of way.' Bob's past and future were neatly represented on the night: the recently reissued *Anthology of American Folk Music* was given two Grammys and The Wallflowers also won an award.

The attention the Grammy Awards brought to *Time Out of Mind* helped sales exceed a million copies in America. It was Bob's most successful studio album since *Slow Train Coming*.

As Bob was beginning to enjoy success again, something of his past came back to haunt him. Actress Ruth Tyrangiel had brought a palimony case against Bob at Los Angeles Superior Court in 1995, and the case dragged on until 1997 when it was dismissed and she was ordered to pay legal costs. Her case was picked up by the press, however, and made headlines in June.

Susan Ross also appeared prominently in the newspapers, talking about a memoir she was writing. She said that the book, *Wait Till Your Father Gets Home*, would include revelations about her alleged twelve-year affair with Bob. She gave an interview to the London *Daily Mail*, which quoted her as saying Bob had made her pregnant, but at times he had also been impotent from drink. Her motivation to speak seems to be that she was hurt that Bob had never publicly acknowledged their relationship, and had failed to make a commitment to her. 'I didn't betray him any more than he betrayed me in the past. It was just I did mine in one fell swoop,' she says, adding of the interviews she gave: 'I suppose [it] was a very big deal because he's never forgiven anybody who has gone to the press with him.' Ross now claims that aspects of the intense press coverage were inaccurate, disowning comments she reportedly made about Bob's alleged impotence. 'That's totally ridiculous,' she says. 'We wouldn't be together fifteen [*sic*] years if there wasn't a tremendous intimacy and closeness.' She does maintain, however, that she became pregnant by Bob in 1986, a pregnancy she says she terminated, and she also asserts that Bob had been married a total of three times, fathering several other children. Based on Ross's comments, the London *Sunday Mirror* reported in March 1998 that Bob had a 'thing about Carols,' linking him with not only Carole Childs, but also with Carolyn Hester and Carole Bayer Sager and claiming he had been married to Clydie King. Hester and Bayer Sager both flatly deny any relationship with Bob and, while he has had a very active love life, there is no evidence he has married more than twice – to Sara Lownds and Carolyn Dennis – or fathered more than five children, plus adopting a sixth. Whatever the truth of Ross's relationship with Bob – and much of it is unsubstantiated – she hurt herself in going to the press. She was not paid for the articles, her book was not published, and, by her own admission, Bob did not talk to her for two years afterward.

The success of *Time Out of Mind* spurred Bob on to play one hundred and three shows in 1998. After the Grammy Awards, he went to Miami for two concerts and then traveled to South America where he interspersed his own shows between guest appearances with The Rolling Stones. The Stones had recently recorded 'Like a Rolling Stone' and Bob performed the song on stage in an unlikely duet with Mick Jagger who, despite being only two years younger than Bob, pranced about like a teenager. Bob stood impassively, like a patient grandfather. The contrast between the two was so absurd that

Bob cracked his stony expression and laughed aloud.

Returning to North America, Bob shared a bill with Van Morrison and Joni Mitchell, and toured Europe and Australasia before the year was out. The new songs from *Time Out of Mind* were well received by audiences all over the world, and were proving successful for other artists, too. Billy Joel and Garth Brooks both recorded 'Make You Feel My Love,' the latter taking it to number one in the country charts. At this time of regained popularity, *Time* magazine featured Bob on its cover, naming him as one of the hundred most influential artists and entertainers of the century. The editors of another very popular publication, *People*, included Bob in a special edition, 'The Most Intriguing People of the Century.' He had also received another award, the Dorothy and Lillian Gish prize for achievement in the arts. Talking about this plethora of honors, Bob said it was always nice to be appreciated, adding dryly, 'especially while you are still alive.'

In 1999 Bob teamed up with Paul Simon for a summer tour of the United States, performing in arenas and large outdoor venues. The two singer-songwriters had known each other since the late sixties, and although they were not particularly close friends the combination of two such major artists – who would perform part of the concerts together on stage – drew big crowds willing to pay dearly to share a unique experience. Ticket prices were set high, reaching $123 for the best seats at Madison Square Garden in New York.

Bucky Baxter was dropped from the band before the start of the Dylan-Simon tour. Playing with Bob had been a mixed experience. The fans, in particular, were strange. 'I always felt people weren't listening to what I was doing,' he says. There was something odd about the way the same faces would be in the crowd night after night. 'What kind of person would want to go see the same shit over and over again? I think most of them were pretty crazy . . . kooky, you know.' Bob replaced Baxter with Charlie Sexton, a guitar prodigy from Austin, Texas, who had a pop career in the mid-1980s.

The Dylan-Simon tour crisscrossed the United States between June and October 1999. On Saturday, July 3, in the middle of a heat wave, the band gave an outdoor show in Duluth, at the Bayfront Festival Park, a piece of parkland jutting into Lake Superior. It was a major event, only the second time in his career that Bob had played the town of his birth, and it serves as an example of the income generated by such a tour. Tickets for the Duluth concert were $40 and the open admission capacity crowd was twenty-five thousand. In theory, the show could have generated a gross of $1 million. But Duluth was a small town and there was a threat of rain on the day so only about twenty thousand people came. After the promoter, the opening act, and Paul Simon were paid, East-West Touring would receive approximately $340,000. Bob had to pay his band, production staff, touring costs, and tax out of that sum before he took a profit as sole shareholder of East-West. He was left with a net profit of about $200,000 for one night's work.

Before the Duluth show Bob welcomed Sam Shepard and his wife, the actress Jessica Lange, into his customized Prevost tour bus, its panels painted with a swirling abstract mural in black and off-white. The bus looked austere from the outside, with impenetrable black windows and expanses of shiny chrome, but was homey inside with folksy handcrafted wood fittings, leaded glass panels, and a breakfast nook and bar. 'He's a gypsy at heart, you know, and loves it. I think he'd rather live in his bus than anything else,' says Shepard, laughing.

Paul Simon played first, giving a polished but unexciting performance. Bob joined him on stage for three songs. Seeing the two near-contemporaries side by side, one was impressed by Bob's abundant personal charisma in direct contrast to Paul Simon, whose music was affecting but whose stage presence was minimal.

The stage was struck and then set for Bob's show, with two burning braziers positioned on either side, smoke drifting back as a freshening northeasterly wind rolled banks of fog in from the lake. Dressed in black, Bob began his set at dusk with acoustic songs. There was a change of gear on the fifth number, 'Tangled Up in Blue.' The band kicked in hard at the end of the first verse and people got up from their deck chairs at the back of the park and started swaying to the music. Younger people at the front bounced up and down with exuberance. There was loud applause at the end of the number. Bob then swapped his acoustic for a Fender Stratocaster and blazed through 'All Along the Watchtower.'

Bob did not say anything to the crowd the first time he played in Duluth – just the previous October – other than to introduce the band. Now he spoke in staccato bursts, accompanied by self-conscious gestures. 'You know, I was born right up on that hill over there,' he said, nodding to the north of town. There in the gloaming, on the other side of the 35 freeway – an extension of Highway 61 – was the outline of St. Mary's Hospital where he was born. Above the hospital on the steep incline of 3rd Avenue was the woodframe duplex he had lived in as a small boy, before the family moved to Hibbing. House lights glinted faintly.

'I'm glad to see it's still there,' he said, although he was not able to see the actual house, or make out the hospital clearly. Presumably he meant the neighborhood itself.

Then came one of those curious moments that added to Bob's reputation as an eccentric. This serious man, who came on stage fifty minutes ago with a severe expression, made a joke so childish he might have learned it from one of his grandchildren. 'You know, my first girlfriend came from there. She was so *conceited*,' he said, emphasizing the word giddily as if he had just discovered it. 'I called her Mimi [*mee-mee*].'

Bob stepped back, laughing. David Kemper smote the drums and the band rolled into 'Stuck Inside of Mobile with the Memphis Blues Again.' Between verses, Bob lifted his head and regarded the audience with pride and amusement. 'He's an extraordinary writer but he's also one of the most amazing live performers I've ever seen,' says Sam Shepard, who sat at the side of the stage with his wife and children. 'When you see his *nature* on stage, his true rhythmic soul, it just blows you away.' He adds: 'He's like a little Banty rooster with his tail up.' Bob twisted his body into contortions as he howled the pin-sharp words of 'Highway 61 Revisited.' White stage lights flashed. Fireflies glowed green as they danced between the gantries. Smoke from the braziers drifted back from the stage. Fog rolled in. Sailboats rocked on the choppy water, their rigging jiggling against metal masts. Bob dragged out the last line of the song – 'Highway sixteeeeee . . . one' – dropping the last syllable like a bomb, his lips curling over large, horselike teeth. Twisting down into a crouch, he traded guitar licks with his band, making eye contact with fans who urged him on, arms aloft, heads nodding vigorously. Two more songs and then encores. 'Like a Rolling Stone' sucked words out of the crowd: 'How does it *feel*?' One wondered at the store of malevolence they drew upon. The band changed to acoustic instruments for 'Blowin' in the Wind,' which Bob delivered with more feeling than anyone might expect of an artist who had been singing the song for almost forty years. Then they changed back to electric instruments and rocked out with a cover of Buddy Holly's 'Not Fade Away.' As Bob said at the Grammy Awards, he saw Holly play the nearby Duluth Armory when he was a kid. It was thrilling and incongruous to see the fifty-eight-year-old, careworn Dylan singing a pop song from his youth in three-part harmony with his guitar players. Larry Campbell and Charlie Sexton looked young enough to be contemplating a love bigger than a Cadillac. But Bob obviously felt it too. His eyes sparkled. He grinned, bending his left leg and twisting his body into a crouch, holding up the neck of the Fender and making pantomime looks of surprise. They reached a crescendo of sound, propelled along by the swing of the drums. Jessica Lange leaned forward in her chair clapping with delight. A fake ending, a switchback – *kerpow* – white lights flashed and Bob handed his guitar to a roadie. He fluffed his hair and bowed low as the final sonic boom echoed across the dark lake. Fireworks shot into the sky. At the other end of the park a Ferris wheel revolved – electric yellow – and carnival music played.

After a short break in the tour, during which Bob had a cameo in the *Dharma & Greg* television sit-com, he was back on the road in October co-headlining with former Grateful Dead member Phil Lesh. Ironically, according to Bob Weir, it was Lesh who had vetoed Bob joining The Dead back in 1989.

Bob and Phil Lesh were on the road in November when Bob's old friend Doug Sahm died of a heart attack. He was fifty-eight, the same age as Bob. A month later Rick Danko died at his home near Woodstock. In recent years Danko had struggled with health problems and had become grossly overweight. The fortunes of The Band members had dwindled considerably since Robbie Robertson's decision to retire from touring. Richard Manuel had killed himself, and then Levon Helm decided to work on his own. That left just Danko and Garth Hudson, whom Danko called affectionately 'H.B', for 'honey boy,' because he sweetened the sound of whatever music they played. The two friends toured in Danko's mobile home, often traveling long distances to play clubs. Despite the dichotomy between this modest life and the enormous success The Band enjoyed in the 1970s, Danko and Hudson remained good-humored. Danko had returned home from a short tour when he died of a heart attack on December 10, the day after his fifty-sixth birthday.

Bob was off the road in January 2000 when his mother took ill. Beatty was at her winter home in Scottsdale, Arizona, and returned to St. Paul, Minnesota, to see her doctor. She went into the hospital for an exploratory operation that confirmed she had cancer. The family flew in to be with her. She died in the hospital on Tuesday, January 25, aged eighty-four. The funeral was held the next day in the Jewish cemetery in Duluth, where Beatty was buried next to Abe. Here Bob and his brother David stood again, as they had in 1968, in the cemetery on the outskirts of town with the wind whipping in from the lake.

Apart from being the matriarch of the family, and a link to the past, Beatty was a source of unconditional love and support to her siblings, two sons, nine grandchildren, and numerous great-grandchildren. She even maintained a friendship with Sara Dylan. As brother Lewis says: 'She loved everybody, and everybody loved her.' Consequently her death was keenly felt. Bob had been particularly close to his mother, although the number of times they met each year was limited by his touring commitments. 'He was a fabulous son. [So] he must feel good about that. He gave it all he had. He was always available to her,' says Carole Childs, who spoke to him after Beatty died. Even at a time like this, Bob kept his feelings to himself. 'You know, he doesn't talk a lot [so] you can only know he would be very sad.' In the last year of her life Beatty gave a few rare, guarded comments to the *Duluth News Tribune*, talking lovingly of her famous son. 'For a man that is labeled a celebrity, he is not,' she said. 'He's a wonderful human being, a normal, good person.'

Six weeks later Bob was back on the road. Without a big-name act to tour with, he played mostly small theaters. He started on March 10 with two warm-up shows at the tiny Sun Theater in Anaheim, California.

The next night he was at a college gymnasium in San Luis Obispo. Bob appeared on stage as a man in mourning, wearing a Bible-black western-style suit and silk tie. He had lost weight. His face was sunken and very pale. The shows began with a set of somber acoustic songs that looked far and wide across the landscape of American music, and included The Stanley Brothers song 'I Am the Man, Thomas.' There was a thoughtful reading of 'It's Alright Ma (I'm Only Bleeding),' each syllable perfectly shaped and delivered. 'Things Have Changed' was a new song – written for the Michael Douglas film *Wonder Boys* – that sounded like an exercise in misanthropy. Bob sang that he used to care, but things had changed. He let the phrase trail off like the words of a dying man. He was an austere figure, bone-thin, but his blue eyes blazed as he warned, 'If the Bible is right, the world will explode.' The lights turned through shades of the spectrum, making the backdrop curtain seem to glow. Other times it was graphite-black, with white light flat on the musicians so that they appeared as cut-out gunslingers accompanying their marshal.

'You're the man, Bob!' somebody shouted.

He traveled inland across the wintry San Joaquin Valley, the land in which Woody Guthrie had ridden boxcars during the Depression, past fields of clipped fruit trees and nodding oil derricks, through Lost Hills and Wasco. Rusted pickup trucks cruised the highway, dogs swaying for balance on the back. Coming into Bakersfield there was a billboard for a Hispanic radio station, RADIO LOBO, with the face of a wolf with yellow eyes.

Bob played the Bakersfield hockey arena that night, behind the very railway track Guthrie had traveled on. People yelled for 'Hurricane.' The Denzel Washington movie *The Hurricane*, based on Rubin Carter's life, was playing in theaters and Dylan's 1975 song was on the sound track. Bob's spindle-leg skinniness made him appear youthful from a distance in the arena. Close-up he looked much older than his nearly fifty-nine years.

Backstage before the encore he carefully arranged his hair, teasing it with his fingers where it was thin. He stepped back on stage, waited a moment in the shadows, talking to a crew member, tensed, and then emerged into the lights. A roar went up. He strapped on his electric guitar and played 'Love Sick' and 'Rainy Day Women #12 & 35.' 'Blowin' in the Wind' was performed with acoustic guitar. He finished with 'Not Fade Away.'

It was sixty-two miles to Visalia. Bob checked into the Radisson Hotel in the early hours of the morning, heading straight to his suite on the eighth floor with his personal belongings in two beat-up metal cases. The next day was a rest day and he slept late. Band members mooched around. On television, Larry King interviewed a computer-generated Ambassador Duke from the *Doonesbury* cartoon strip, trying to inject some fun into a dull nomination race for the 2000 presidential election. An advertisement for the Apple iMac computer ran on NBC; the music was Bob singing 'Forever Young.' Downstairs some of the crew gathered in Pistachio's bar. John Denver's 'Annie's Song' played on the PA system.

The Visalia Convention Center was a concrete box with chairs set out for three thousand. The audience drifted up on a beautiful spring evening. They ranged from teenagers to people of Bob's generation. Mike Naylor, a forty-five-year-old peach farmer from Dinuba – NAYLOR'S PEACHES, WORLD'S BEST – rediscovered his youthful interest in Bob's music when his seventeen-year-old son, Matt, began downloading music for him from the Internet. 'I started listening to it, and I started liking Bob Dylan,' says Matt. Perhaps surprisingly 'The Times They Are A-Changin',' a song written years before Matt was born, coming out of an era he knew only through history books and perhaps his father, was a favorite. Larry and Pearl Montgomery of nearby Hanford found that going to a Bob Dylan concert was something they could also do with their teenaged sons. 'I like his lyrics. They're funny,' says Jeff Montgomery, aged seventeen. 'I'm hopin' [the show is] kinda loud.'

Not many big-name acts stopped in Visalia, usually bypassing the town for Fresno or Bakersfield, and the bar of the convention center nearly hummed with the excitement of a special event. When the lights went down, a deep voice asked the ladies and gentlemen to 'please welcome Columbia recording artist – Bob Dylan.' When Bob came on stage, a woman screamed: 'Get up and dance, Visalia!' and the people went crazy. At the back of the hall, teenagers bopped about to 'Tangled Up in Blue.' When Bob began the somber 'Not Dark Yet,' hundreds of people spontaneously streamed toward the stage and stood still, listening intently to the lyrics.

After the show, Bob was driven north through the farmland of the San Joaquin Valley and over the hills into Santa Cruz, a funky beach city between Monterey and San Francisco. Bob was due to play two concerts on successive nights at the small Civic Auditorium. The shows were sold out weeks in advance, but people milled around in the forlorn hope of obtaining a spare ticket. A heavyset woman with sunburned face and gappy teeth sat all day opposite the auditorium, asking passersby for a ticket. She was also hopeful of catching a glimpse of Bob at sound check, and had already called around the local hotels asking if Robert Zimmerman had booked in.

'That's his real name, you know.'

What would she do if she got through to him?

'Show him around Santa Cruz.'

That night the average age of the audience seemed a good bit older than previous shows on the tour. Instead of teenagers, the place was packed with the middle-aged, gray hair in ponytails, wearing Grateful Dead T-shirts, shorts, and sandals. The theater was Spanish-style and intimate, about the size of the auditorium at Hibbing High where headmaster Kenneth Pederson had long ago curtailed Bob's juvenile rock 'n' roll antics by pulling the curtain on his act. Bob was still capable of surprising.

The first night he sang the Willie Dixon blues 'Hootchie Cootchie Man,' with screaming guitar breaks by Charlie Sexton. Bob seemed to delight in the lyric. 'I ahm a hootchie cootchie maann,' he sang with a leer. 'Evrabaddy knows I aahmm.' As he worked through the show, sweat gathered at the end of his large nose and dripped onto the stage boards. Bob slowly twisted his body as he played, his hoary eyebrows sometimes shooting up in comedic mock-surprise.

The following evening he entertained the audience with a rare performance of 'Highlands.' He grinned as he told the story of the Boston waitress, making the crowd laugh. Almost everybody seemed to know the song. In the bleachers, a dark-haired woman became carried away and emitted piercing, orgasmic shrieks of pleasure repeatedly until she could be heard above the music. Two middle-aged men came in late, one promptly falling asleep on the other's shoulder. A man in a wheelchair spun around in the dance pattern of an excited bee. It was a weird audience and Bob seemed to like it. 'I wish we could play this place every night,' he said. 'We've got enough songs to.'

Fans in front yelled: 'Yeah!'

Bob stopped and yelled back, very loudly: 'YEAH!'

As the audience applauded the closing chords of 'Not Fade Away,' Bob stepped from the stage, through a loading door, and into his bus. He was rolling down Highway 17 before the audience left the hall.

It was a long nighttime drive through the Bay area and over the snow-capped Sierra Nevada mountains into the gambling city of Reno, Nevada. The giant electric display board outside the monolithic Reno Hilton flashed its attractions as Bob's bus descended into the desert.

LET'S GO BOWLING
The Best Champagne Brunch Is Back!
Happy Hour/Free Food
Bob Dylan – Two shows on sale now

Bob was playing an early show and a late show. A little before 7:30 P.M. on March 17 the audience made its way past the gaming tables and noisy slot machines of the casino floor to the Reno Hilton theater. It was decorated in whorehouse red. The walls were red. The carpets were red, with red Naugahyde booths and red tablecloths. Anything not red was painted to look like gold. Before the show, cigarette girls sold packs of Marlboros and plastic flowers that lit up. Waitresses took orders for drinks, which were served strong in plastic beakers. Some members of the audience were older, gamblers whiling away time before returning to the tables. There were younger people, too, who had traveled from the surrounding area just to see the show, many families – some with teenaged children who were learning Bob's songs because they were taking up music themselves – and the veteran fans who followed Bob from town to town.

Bob began the first show with a traditional song, 'Duncan and Brady.' It was an appropriate choice for a western, gambling town with its lyrics 'gonna shoot somebody just to see him die.' For the late show he opened with the even more apposite 'Roving Gambler.' He bowed low at the end, looking tired but exuding dignity, put on his snow-white Stetson hat, and walked from the stage. People ask why Bob Dylan chooses to tour in this way, playing so many shows, and often in small theaters. To those who know him well, it is clear that there is nothing else he wants to do. 'He will go as long as he can. He's practicing his practice. He's doing his *job*,' says Carole Childs. 'This is his trade. This is the troubadour in him. This is what troubadours did. This is what vaudevillians did. This is what burlesque people did. This is what you do. You entertain people.'

After the show, the shiny tour buses snaked out of the Reno Hilton car park, past the Aqua Golf course, and onto the freeway to Pocatello, Idaho, and beyond, through Washington, Montana, and Wyoming, way out into the heart of America and on around the world.

BIBLIOGRAPHY

Newspaper and magazine articles referred to are too numerous to list, but direct references are attributed in the detailed source notes that follow. The most useful Bob Dylan fanzines were: *Isis; On the Tracks*; John Bauldie's *The Telegraph* (now defunct); and the series of tour booklets compiled by Mike Wyvill and John Wraith, privately published in the United Kingdom. Of the numerous Bob Dylan–related Web sites the most useful were: Al Aronowitz's The Blacklisted Journalist; Bob Links; The Book of Bob; and bobdylan.com.

Books used for reference include:

Baez, Joan, *And a Voice to Sing With*, Summit Books, 1987.

Baez, Joan, *Daybreak*, Dial Press, 1968.

Balfour, Victoria, *Rock Wives*, Beech Tree / William Morrow, 1986.

Bashevis Singer, Isaac, *Collected Stories*, Penguin, 1984.

Bauldie, John (editor), *Wanted Man: In Search of Bob Dylan*, Black Spring Press, 1990.

Beatles, The, *The Beatles Anthology*, Cassell, 2000.

Benson, Carl (editor), *The Bob Dylan Companion*, Schirmer Books, 1998.

Bugliosi, Vincent, *Helter Skelter*, Arrow, 1992.

Burden, Eric, *I Used to Be An Animal, But I'm All Right Now*, Faber and Faber, 1986.

Carter, Rubin "Hurricane," *The Sixteenth Round*, Warner Books, 1974.

Cash, Johnny, *Cash: The Autobiography*, HarperCollins, 1998.

Chaiton, Sam, and Swinton, Terry, *Lazarus and the Hurricane*,

St. Martin's Griffin, 1999.

Charles, Ray, and Ritz, David, *Brother Ray*, Futura, 1980.

Charters, Ann, *Kerouac*, Picador, 1978.

Cohen, J. M., and Cohen, M. J., (editors), *The Penguin Dictionary of Modern Quotations*, Allen Lane, 1980.

Collins, Judy, *Trust Your Heart*, Houghton Mifflin, 1987.

Cook, Dr. Chris (editor), *Pears Cyclopaedia (100th Edition)*, Pelham Books, 1991.

Cott, Jonathan, *Dylan*, Rolling Stone Press, 1984.

Dalton, David, *James Dean: The Mutant King*, Plexus, 1983.

Davis, Clive, *Clive: Inside the Record Business*, William Morrow, 1975.

DeCurtis, Anthony, and Henke, James, *The Rolling Stone Album Guide*, Random House, 1992.

Dorman, L. S. and Rawlins, C. L., *Leonard Cohen: Prophet of the Heart*, Omnibus Press, 1990.

Draper, Robert, *The Rolling Stone Story*, Mainstream Publishing, 1990.

Dundas, Glen, *Tangled Up in Tapes: A Recording History of Bob Dylan*, privately published, 1999.

Dylan, Bob, *Drawn Blank*, Random House, 1994.

Dylan, Bob, *Lyrics 1962–1985*, Paladin, 1988.

Dylan, Bob, *Tarantula*, St. Martin's Press, 1994.

Dylan, Bob, *Writings and Drawings by Bob Dylan*, Alfred A. Knopf, 1973.

Engel, Dave, *Just Like Bob Zimmerman's Blues: Dylan in Minnesota*, River City Memoirs, 1997.

Escott, Colin, with George Merritt and William MacEwen, *Hank Williams: The Biography*, Little, Brown, 1994.

Evers, Alf, *Woodstock: History of an American Town*, Overlook Press, 1987.

Faithfull, Marianne, with David Dalton, *Faithfull*, Penguin, 1995.

Feinstein, Barry; Kramer, Daniel; and Marshall, Jim, *Early Dylan*, Bullfinch Press, 1999.

Footman, Tim (editor), *Guinness World Records 2001*, Guinness World Records 2000.

Geldof, Bob, *Is That It?*, Penguin, 1986.

Gill, Andy, *Classic Bob Dylan 1962–1969: My Back Pages*, Carlton, 1998.

Glatt, John, *Rage & Roll: Bill Graham and the Selling of Rock*, Birch Lane Press, 1993.

Goldman, Albert, *The Lives of John Lennon*, Bantam Press, 1988.

Goodman, Fred, *The Mansion on the Hill*, Jonathan Cape, 1997.

Graham, Bill, and Greenfield, Robert, *Bill Graham Presents: My Life Inside Rock and Out*, Doubleday, 1992.

Gray, Michael, *Song and Dance Man III: The Art of Bob Dylan*, Cassell, 2000.

Gray, Michael, and Bauldie, John (editors), *All Across the Telegraph: A Bob Dylan Handbook*, Futura, 1988.

Guralnick, Peter, Careless Love: *The Unmaking of Elvis Presley*, Little, Brown, 1999.

Guralnick, Peter, *Last Train to Memphis: The Rise of Elvis Presley*, Abacus, 1995.

Guthrie, Woody, *Bound for Glory*, Plume, 1983.

Haney, Robert; Ballantine, David; and Elliott, Jonathan, *Woodstock Handmade Houses*, private edition, 1994.

Hardy, Phil, and Laing, David, *The Encyclopedia of Rock, Volume 2*, Panther, 1976.

Helm, Levon, with Stephen Davis, *This Wheel's on Fire*, Plexus, 1993.

Hentoff, Nat, *Speaking Freely*, Alfred A. Knopf, 1997.

Heylin, Clinton, *Bob Dylan: Behind the Shades—Take Two*, Viking, 2000.

Heylin, Clinton, *Bob Dylan: A Life in Stolen Moments: Day by Day: 1941–1995*, Schirmer Books, 1996.

Heylin, Clinton, *Bob Dylan: The Recording Sessions 1960–1994*, St. Martin's Press, 1995.

Heylin, Clinton, *Bob Dylan: Stolen Moments*, Wanted Man Publications, 1988.

Heylin, Clinton, *Dylan: Behind the Shades*, Viking, 1991.

Heylin, Clinton, *Dylan's Daemon Lover*, Helter Skelter, 1999.

The Holy Bible, *King James Authorized*.

Hoover, Paul (editor), *Postmodern American Poetry*, W. W. Norton, 1994.

Howard, Michael, and Louis, Roger Wm. (editors), *The Oxford History of the Twentieth Century*, Oxford University Press, 1998.

Humphries, Patrick, and Bauldie, John, *Oh No! Not Another Bob Dylan Book*, Square One, 1991.

Keats, John, *The Complete Poems*, Penguin, 1988.

Kerouac, Jack, *On the Road*, Penguin, 1979.

King, Tom, *David Geffen: A Biography of New Hollywood*, Hutchinson, 2000.

Klein, Joe, *Woody Guthrie: A Life*, Delta, 1980.

Kooper, Al, *Backstage Passes & Backstabbing Bastards*, Billboard, 1998.

Kramer, Daniel, *Bob Dylan: A Portrait of the Artist's Early Years*, Plexus, 1991.

Lee, C. P., *Like a Bullet of Light*, Helter Skelter, 2000.

Lee, C. P., *Like the Night: Bob Dylan and the Road to the Manchester Free Trade Hall*, Helter Skelter, 1998.

Levey, Michael (editor), *The National Gallery Collection*, National Gallery Publications, 1987.

Lois, George, *Covering the '60s: George Lois and the Esquire Era*, The Monacelli Press, 1996.

Marcus, Greil, *Invisible Republic: Bob Dylan's Basement Tapes*, Picador, 1997.

Marsh, Dave, *Glory Days: Bruce Springsteen in the 1980s*, Sidgwick & Jackson, 1987.

Marsh, Dave, and Swenson, John (editors), *The New Rolling Stone Record Guide*, Random House, 1983.

Matteo, Steve, *Dylan*, MetroBooks, 1998.

McFree, Faridi, *Celebrate You!*, Dolphin Books, 1982.

McGregor, Craig (editor), *Bob Dylan: The Early Years: A Retrospective*, Da Capo Press, 1990.

McLagan, Ian, *All the Rage*, Sidgwick & Jackson, 1998.

Mercer, Derrik (editor-in-chief), *Chronicle of the 20th Century*, Longman, 1988.

Miles, Barry, *Ginsberg: A Biography*, Viking, 1989.

Miles, Barry, *Paul McCartney: Many Years From Now*, Vintage, 1998.

Miller, Jim (editor), *The Rolling Stone Illustrated History of*

Rock 'n' Roll, Picador, 1981.

Norman, Philip, *Symphony for the Devil: The Rolling Stones Story*, Linden Press, 1984.

Ousby, Ian (editor), *The Cambridge Guide to Literature in English*, Cambridge University Press, 1988.

Pearsall, Judy, and Trumble, Bill (editors), *The Oxford English Reference Dictionary*, Oxford University Press, 1996.

Pickering, Stephen, *Bob Dylan Approximately: A Portrait of the Jewish Poet in Search of God*, David McKay, 1975.

Pym, John (editor), *Time Out Film Guide*, Penguin, 1995.

Rimbaud, Arthur, *A Season in Hell and Illuminations*, Dent, 1998.

Rinzler, Alan, *Bob Dylan: The Illustrated Record*, Harmony Books, 1978.

Scaduto, Anthony, *Bob Dylan*, Helter Skelter, 1996. (NB: the title of the original edition was *Bob Dylan: An Intimate Biography*).

Schumacher, Michael, *There But for Fortune: The Life of Phil Ochs*, Hyperion, 1996.

Seeger, Pete, *Where Have All the Flowers Gone: A Singer's Stories, Songs, Seeds, Robberies*, A Sing Out Publication, 1993.

Shelton, Robert, *No Direction Home: The Life and Music of Bob Dylan*, New English Library, 1986.

Shepard, Sam, *Rolling Thunder Logbook*, Penguin, 1977.

Singular, Stephen, *The Rise and Rise of David Geffen*, Birch Lane Press, 1997.

Sloman, Larry, *On the Road with Bob Dylan: Rolling with the Thunder*, Bantam Books, 1978.

Spitz, Bob, *Dylan: A Biography*, McGraw-Hill, 1989.

Stein, Georg, *Bob Dylan: Temples in Flames*, Palmyra Verlag, 1991.

Stein, Jean, and Plimpton, George, *Edie: An American Biography*, Alfred A. Knopf, 1982.

Steinbeck, John, *The Grapes of Wrath*, Penguin, 1992.

Strong, Martin C., *The Great Rock Discography*, Canongate Books, 1998.

Talevski, Nick, *The Encyclopedia of Rock Obituaries*, Omnibus

Press, 1999.

Thompson, Toby, *Positively Main Street*, Coward-McCann, 1971.

Thomson, Elizabeth, and Gutman, David (editors), *The Dylan Companion*, Macmillan, 1990.

Wallis, Ian, *The Hawk*, Quarry Press Music Books, 1996.

Warhol, Andy (edited by Pat Hackett), *The Andy Warhol Diaries*, Simon & Schuster, 1989.

Weddle, David, *"If They Move . . . Kill 'Em!": The Life and Times of Sam Peckinpah*, Grove Press, 1994.

Wexler, Jerry, and Ritz, David, *Rhythm and the Blues: A Life in American Music*, Alfred A. Knopf, 1993.

Whitburn, Joel, *The Billboard Book of Top 40 Hits*, Billboard, 1996.

Williams, Paul, *Bob Dylan: Performing Artist: Book One: 1960–1973*, Xanada, 1990

Williams, Paul, Bob Dylan: *Performing Artist: The Middle Years: 1974–1986*, Underwood-Miller, 1992.

Williams, Paul, *Dylan—What Happened?*, and books/ Entwhistle Books, 1979.

Williams, Richard, *Dylan: A Man Called Alias*, Bloomsbury, 1992.

Woliver, Robbie, *Bringing It All Back Home*, Pantheon Books, 1986.

Worrell, Denise, *Icons: Intimate Portraits*, Atlantic Monthly Press, 1989.

Zollo, Paul, *Songwriters on Songwriting*, Da Capo Press, 1997.

The author used the Microsoft Encarta Encyclopedia CD-ROM; and referred to a large collection of concert programs, press and publicity material, video and audio recordings, album liner notes, legal papers, tax records, and records of birth, death, and marriage.

SOURCE NOTES

AUTHOR'S NOTE AND ACKNOWLEDGMENTS

Page 9: Dylan's worldwide record sales from a written declaration by Jeff Rosen, the administrator and general manager of Dylan's music publishing, and president of his touring company, East-West Touring. The declaration (dated Sept 11, 1998) was filed as part of a court case, Victor Maymudes vs. East-West Touring et al. (Case #BC 189007). United States album sales for Dylan and other artists are from an RIAA league table (dated Sept 9, 2000). Worldwide sales for The Beatles are from Paul McCartney's office. As of September 2000, sales were estimated at 650 million. The sometime quoted figure that worldwide sales exceed 1,000 million is considered an exaggeration.

Page 10: SESAC, which collects Dylan's performance rights, estimated his song catalogue at approximately four hundred and fifty titles as of the summer of 2000.

Page 11: Childs quotation: interview with the author.

Page 11: 'Blowin' in the Wind' (Warner Bros., Inc., 1962).

Page 11: Dylan quotation – 'Money doesn't talk, it swears' – 'It's Alright, Ma (I'm Only Bleeding)' (Warner Bros., Inc., 1965).

Page 11: Dylan quotation – 'To live outside the law, you must be honest' – 'Absolutely Sweet Marie' (Dwarf Music, 1986).

Page 11: Dylan quotation – 'Oh, some are about four minutes . . .' – *Playboy* (March 1966). This quotation has appeared in various compendiums of quotations including *The Penguin Dictionary of Modern Quotations* (Second Edition). It was not a spontaneous answer. Questions and answers for the interview were concocted by Dylan in association with journalist Nat Hentoff.

Page 12: Carolyn Dennis: author's research, detailed in later chapters.

Page 13: Dylan quotation – 'instrument of the devil' – *Rolling Stone* (June 21, 1984).

Page 13: Bobbye Hall, percussion player in Dylan's 1978 touring band, said in an interview with the author that Dylan entertained her with card tricks on the road.

Prologue: Yesterday Is Gone, But the Past Lives On

Primary sources are the author's interviews, correspondence, and discussions with: Joel Bernstein, Liam Clancy, the late Rick Danko, Anton Fig, Nora Guthrie, John Hammond Jr., Richie Havens, Levon Helm, Carolyn Hester, Garth Hudson, Jim Keltner, Al Kooper, Tommy Makem, and Roger McGuinn.

Prologue title, 'Yesterday Is Gone, But the Past Lives On', is a phrase from the song 'Don't Fall Apart on Me Tonight' (Special Rider Music, 1983).

Page 19: Joan Baez compared the color of Dylan's eyes to the blue of robins' eggs in her song 'Diamonds and Rust'.

Page 19: The quotations, 'You're Bob Dylan!' and 'Hey, man, how are ya *doin'*?,' given as an example of a typical encounter with a fan, based on author's interviews and general background material (including encounter with fan reported in *Rolling Stone* on June 21, 1984).

Page 20: Makem quotations: author's interviews.

Page 21: Dylan quotation – 'It'll be like goin' to my . . .' – apocryphal comment from *The Telegraph* fanzine (issue 44).

Pages 21-26: Description of concert from author's interviews with participants Clancy, Danko, Fig, Keltner, Kooper, Hammond Jr., Havens, Hester, McGuinn, and Makem; also video and audio recordings of the event.

Page 22: Bernstein quotation: author's interview.

Page 22: Havens quotations: correspondence with author.
Page 23: Clancy quotations: author's interview.
Page 23: Hammond Jr. quotation: author's interview.
Page 24: McGuinn quotation: correspondence with author.
Page 24: Harrison and Young quotations: transcript of show.
Page 24: Dylan quotation – 'Thanks . . .' – transcript of show.
Page 25: Nora Guthrie quotations: author's interview.
Page 25: Fig quotation: author's interview.
Page 25: Hester quotations: author's interview.
Pages 26-30: Scene at Irish Pavilion: author's interviews with guests.
Page 26: Dylan quotation – 'I don't want . . .' – author's interview with Makem.
Page 26: Makem quotation: author's interview.
Page 26: Hester quotations: author's interview.
Pages 26-30: Dylan conversation with Clancy and Clancy quotations – 'Man, would . . .' etc. – author's interview with Clancy.
Page 28: Lyrics from 'Roddy McCorley' are traditional.
Page 28: Pub song: McLagan's memoir, *All the Rage.*
Page 29: Divorce: see chapters 9 and 10.

Chapter 1: North Country Childhood

Primary sources are author's interviews, correspondence, and discussions with: John Bucklen, Ethel Crystal, Luke Davich, George Haidos, LeRoy Hoikkala, Echo Star Helstrom, Robert Karon, Larry Kegan, Angel Marolt, the late Kenneth Pederson, B. J. Rolfzen, Howard Rutman, Lewis Stone, and Jack Zimmerman. The author also spoke with members of the Dylan family who wish to remain anonymous.
Page 31: Elvis Costello quotation: *Mojo* magazine (February 1998).
Pages 31-32: Family background: author's interviews and correspondence with family members including Crystal, Stone, and Zimmerman. *Just Like Bob Zimmerman's Blues:*

Dylan in Minnesota by Dave Engel was particularly useful for background.

Page 31: Historical background re. Odessa: *Chronicle of the 20th Century.*

Page 32: Jack Zimmerman quotation: author's interview.

Page 33: Crystal quotations: author's interview.

Page 33: Dylan's birth: birth certificate.

Pages 33-34: Duluth background: author's visit to town, and interviews with local people.

Page 34: Dylan's quotations – 'If everybody . . .' and 'If it's quiet . . .' – *No Direction Home: The Life and Music of Bob Dylan* by Robert Shelton. Shelton's interviews with Dylan's late parents were particularly helpful in this chapter.

Page 34: Beatty Zimmerman quotations – 'Our phone . . .' etc. – *No Direction Home.*

Page 35: Dylan quotation – 'Mummy, I'm going . . .' – *No Direction Home.*

Page 35: Abe Zimmerman quotation – 'People would laugh . . .' etc. – *No Direction Home.*

Page 35: Abe Zimmerman quotation – 'like an ape' – *No Direction Home.*

Page 35: Dylan quotation – 'My father never . . .' – *Biograph* liner notes (Special Rider Music, 1985).

Page 36: Dylan quotation – 'In the winter . . .' – *Playboy* (February 1978).

Page 37: Carving: author's interview with Angel Marolt, who later bought the house from the Zimmermans.

Page 37: Interior of home: author's interview with Marolt and others.

Page 38: Parties and play: author's interview with Davich.

Page 39: Bucklen quotations: author's interview.

Page 39: Poems and phrase from poem – 'real mad' – *No Direction Home.*

Page 40: Stone quotations: author's interview.

Page 40: Dylan quotation – 'I'm going to play the piano . . .' – *No Direction Home.*

Page 40: Sitting by the railroad tracks: Dylan liner notes to *Joan Baez in Concert, Part 2.*

Page 41: Mesaba Country Club: *Just Like Bob Zimmerman's Blues.*

Page 41: Zimbo: author's interview with Hoikkala.

Page 41: Bar mitzvah: Dylan interview in *Spin* (December 1985).

Page 42: Abe Zimmerman quotation – 'defiled' etc. – speech by Dylan at the Grammy Awards, February 1991.

Page 42: Dylan quotation – 'He was popular . . .' – *Mojo* (February 1998).

Page 43: In an interview published in *Songwriters on Songwriting*, Dylan said: 'To me, Hank Williams is still the best songwriter.'

Page 43: Dylan quotation – 'Late at night . . .' – *Rolling Stone* (June 21, 1984).

Page 43: Dylan quotation – 'The reason . . .' – *The* (London) *Times Magazinc* (November 15, 1997).

Page 44: Dylan dialogue – 'Do you sing?' etc. – author's interview with Bucklen.

Page 44: Bucklen quotations and background: author interview.

Page 45: Abe Zimmerman's disapproval of Bob's girlfriends: interview with David Zimmerman, in *No Direction Home.*

Page 45: Bowling: *Just Like Bob Zimmerman's Blues.*

Page 45: Hoikkala: author's interview with Hoikkala.

Page 45: Rutman quotation: author's interview.

Pages 45-46: Summer camp: author's interviews with Kegan and Rutman.

Page 45: Dylan quotation – 'Well, late . . .' – author interview with Kegan.

Page 46: Rutman quotations: author's interview.

Pages 47-48: James Dean interest: author's interviews with Bucklen and Hoikkala.

Pages 47-48: *Rebel Without a Cause* dialogue: transcript of film.

Page 48: Dylan quotation – 'When I first heard . . .' – *US* magazine (circa 1987).

Page 48: Bucklen quotations: author's interviews.

Pages 48-49: Jokers and first recording (including the television show): author's interviews with Kegan and Rutman.

Pages 48-49: Kegan quotations and accident: author's interview with Kegan.

Page 49: Dylan quotation – 'I become speechless . . .' – author's interview with Kegan.

Pages 49-50: Shadow Blasters: author interviews and background from *Just Like Bob Zimmerman's Blues* and *No Direction Home*.

Page 50: Hautala and Supro guitar: author's interview with Bucklen.

Page 50: Purchase of Sears guitar: author's interview with Bucklen; background from *No Direction Home* and Dylan interview in *Rolling Stone* (June 21, 1984).

Page 51: Glissendorf, etc.: author's interviews with Bucklen and Kegan.

Page 51: Dylan quotations – 'Say a word' etc. – author's interview with Bucklen.

Page 51: Dylan quotation – 'When we meet . . .', author's interview with Bucklen.

Page 52: Car and motorcycle accidents: *No Direction Home* (first accident, with child) and author's interview with Hoikkala (incident at railroad crossing).

Page 52: Hoikkala quotation: author's interview.

Page 52: Outsiders: author's interview with Bucklen and Hoikkala.

Pages 52-53: Background on Echo Star Helstrom: author's interview with Helstrom.

Pages 53-54: Helstrom quotations: author's interview with Helstrom.

Page 53: Davich quotation: author's interview with Davich.

Page 53: Meets Helstrom: author's interviews with Bucklen and Helstrom.

Page 54: Bucklen quotation: author's interview with Bucklen (also Ruth Bucklen quotation).

Pages 54-57: Helstrom quotations: author's interview with Helstrom.

Page 55: Dylan quotation – 'Quick . . .' etc. – author's interview with Helstrom.

Page 56: Dylan loses virginity: author's interviews with Helstrom.

Page 56: Dylan quotations – 'Hey, catch . . ' and 'Hey, I'm a . . ' – author's interview with Hoikkala.

Page 57: Jacket Jamboree: author's interviews with Bucklen, Helstrom, and Pederson. Also discussions with Rolfzen.

Page 57: Pederson quotation: author's interview.

Page 57: Dylan quotation – 'What did ya think?' – author's interview with Helstrom.

Pages 57-58: Winter Frolics: author's interview with Hoikkala.

Page 58: Hoikkala quotation: author's interview.

Page 58: 'Rock & Roll HOP' advertisement: local newspaper cutting reproduced in *Just Like Bob Zimmerman's Blues*.

Pages 58-59: Band changes: author's interview with Hoikkala. Background: *Just Like Bob Zimmerman's Blues*.

Page 59: Dylan quotation: – 'The thing about rock 'n' roll . . .' – *Biograph* liner notes.

Page 59: In an interview with the *Chicago Daily News* (November 1965), Dylan said: 'I took the name Dillon because I have an uncle named Dillion [sic]. I changed the spelling but only because it looked better.'

Page 59: Dylan quotation – 'I've got my . . .' etc. – author's interview with Helstrom.

Page 60: Bucklen quotation: author's interview with Bucklen.

Page 60: English lessons: author's interviews with Bucklen and Helstrom; also discussions with Rolfzen.

Page 60: Steinbeck interest: author's interviews with Bucklen and Helstrom.

Page 60: Dylan quotation – 'John Steinbeck is . . .' – author's interview with Helstrom.

Page 60: Beatty Zimmerman quotation – 'I was afraid . . .' – *No Direction Home*.

Page 61: Breakup with Helstrom and Dylan quotations – 'What are you doing here?' and 'What are you doing?' etc. – author's interview with Helstrom.

Page 61: Bucklen and Helstrom quotations: author's interviews.

Pages 61-62: 1959 Jacket Jamboree and Bucklen quotations:

author's interview with Bucklen.

Page 62: Buddy Holly show: speaking at the 1998 Grammy Awards, Dylan said:

'I was three feet away from [Buddy Holly] and he looked at me . . .'

Page 62: Graduation party and Beatty Zimmerman quotation – 'He was . . .' – *No Direction Home*.

Page 63: Leadbelly records: author's interview with Bucklen.

Page 63: Yearbook: *Hematite* 1959.

Pages 63-64: Bobby Vee band and Vee quotations: *All Across the Telegraph: A Bob Dylan Handbook*.

Page 64: Devereux Foundation: claim made in *Bob Dylan: Behind the Shades – Take Two* by Clinton Heylin. This is hard to verify as Devereux Foundation records are confidential; Dylan's friends have no knowledge of this happening and Kegan – who was very close to Dylan at the time – believes it unlikely.

Page 64: Beatty Zimmerman quotation – 'Don't . . .': *No Direction Home*

Chapter 2: Bound For Glory

Primary sources are the author's interviews, correspondence, and discussions with: Bonnie Beecher, Marshall Brickman, John Bucklen, Walt Conley, Luke Davich, Ramblin' Jack Elliott, Tony Glover, Tova Hammerman, Echo Helstrom, Larry Kegan, 'Spider' John Koerner, Dave Morton, Odetta, Jon Pankake, Gretel Pelto (née Hoffman, later Whitaker), Bruce Rubenstein, Howard Rutman, Pete Seeger, Harry Weber, and Dave Whitaker.

Page 66: Dylan quotation – 'out of the wilderness' – *Biograph* liner notes (Special Rider Music, 1985).

Page 66: Sigma Alpha Mu background: *Dylan: A Biography* by Bob Spitz.

Pages 66-67: Background on Dinkytown from author's interviews with Dylan's contemporaries: Glover, Koerner, Morton, Pankake, Pelto (née Hoffman), Rubenstein, Weber, and Whitaker.

Page 67: Dylan described his feelings about Dinkytown and its characters in the *Biograph* liner notes: 'it was magic . . . everyday was like Sunday . . .'

Page 67: Dylan's appearance: author's interview with Hammerman.

Page 68: Dylan quotation – 'The first thing that . . .': *Playboy* (February 1978).

Pages 69-70: Meeting and relationship with Beecher: author's interview with Beecher.

Page 70: Beecher quotations: author's interview.

Page 70: Dylan quotation – 'actress girl' – 'My Life in a Stolen Moment' (Special Rider Music, 1973).

Page 70: Dylan quotation – 'fell hard' – 'My Life in a Stolen Moment'.

Page 70: Girlfriends: author's interview with Rubenstein; background from *Bob Dylan* by Anthony Scaduto and *Dylan: A Biography*.

Page 70: Dylan quotation – 'music lessons' – author's interview with Rubenstein.

Page 71: Dylan quotation – 'dress weird' – author's interview with Helstrom.

Page 71: Helstrom quotations: author's interview with Helstrom.

Pages 71-72: Kegan hospital visits: author's interview with Kegan.

Pages 72-73: Koerner background and friendship with Dylan: author's interview with Koerner.

Pages 72-73: Koerner quotations: author's interviews.

Page 73: Hammerman friendship and Hammerman quotation: author's interview with Hammerman.

Pages 73-75: Morton friendship and Morton quotations: author's interview with Morton.

Page 74: History of racial problems: *Chronicle of the 20th Century*.

Page 75: Kegan quotation: author's interview with Kegan.

Page 75: Dylan quotation – 'disowned' – author's interview with Beecher.

Page 75: Pills: author's interview with Rubenstein.
Page 76: Beecher quotations: author's interview.
Page 76: Looking for work: author's interview with Beecher.
Page 76: Coffeehouse jobs: author's interviews with Kegan et al.; background from *Bob Dylan*.
Pages 77-81: Whitaker friendship and Whitaker quotations: author's interview with Whitaker.
Pages 77-79: Hoffman friendship and Hoffman quotations: author's interview with Pelto (née Hoffman, née Whitaker).
Page 79: Dylan quotation – 'When you . . .' – author's interview with Pelto.
Page 79: Marijuana use and politics: author's interviews with Whitaker.
Page 80: Neglects studies: author's interviews with Beecher and Whitaker.
Pages 81-82: Friendship with Pankake and Pankake quotations: author's interviews with Pankake.
Page 82: Ramblin' Jack Elliott background: author's interview with Elliott. Background from *Woody Guthrie: A Life* by Joe Klein.
Page 82: Beecher quotation: author's interview with Beecher.
Pages 83-84: Harry Smith background: booklets accompanying the Smithsonian reissue of the *Anthology of American Folk Music* and *Invisible Republic* by Greil Marcus.
Page 83: Marcus points out in *Invisible Republic* that the cuckoo is not native to the United States.
Page 84: Dylan quotation – 'That's where the wealth . . .' – *Mojo* (February 1998).
Page 84: Pankake confrontation and Pankake quotations: author's interview with Pankake.
Pages 84-88: Colorado trip and Conley quotations: author's interview with Conley.
Page 86: Dylan's comments about the Gilded Garter being a strip club were reported in *No Direction Home: The Life and Music of Bob Dylan* by Robert Shelton.
Page 86: Conley–St. John dialogue: author's interview with Conley.
Page 87: Hamil–Conley dialogue: author's interview with Conley.

Page 87: Dylan quotation – 'I was kicked out of Denver' – *No Direction Home.*

Pages 87-88: Dylan snubs Conley: author's interview with Conley.

Page 88: Helstrom incident: author's interview with Helstrom.

Page 88: Desire for children: author's interview with Beecher.

Pages 88-89: Literary scene: author's interviews with Glover, Morton, Whitaker et al.

Page 89: Weber quotations: author's interview with Weber.

Page 89: Morton quotation: author's interview with Morton.

Pages 89-90: Guthrie quotations – 'that bright crackling . . .' and '. . . stealers, dealers . . .' and 'you're too lowdown . . .' – *Bound for Glory* by Woody Guthrie.

Page 90: Dylan quotation – 'Don't ask me nothin' about nothin' – 'Outlaw Blues' (Warner Bros., Inc. 1965).

Pages 90-91: Background on Guthrie: author's interviews with Nora Guthrie, Guthrie's manager Harold Leventhal, and Pete Seeger. Also *Woody Guthrie: A Life.*

Page 90: Beecher quotation: author's interview.

Page 91: Dylan quotation – 'I'm coming out there' etc. – author's interviews with Morton.

Page 91: Dylan quotation – 'No, I'm gonna master . . .' – author's interview with Beecher.

Pages 91-92: Glover quotation: author's interview.

Pages 92-93: Tapes: author's interview with Beecher.

Page 92: Dylan quotation – 'If the Library . . .' – author's interview with Beecher.

Page 93: Background on Odetta: author's interview with Odetta.

Page 93: Illness and meeting with Odetta: author's interviews with Beecher and Hammerman.

Pages 93-94: Haircut and trip home: author's interview with Beecher.

Page 94: Abe Zimmerman quotation – 'He wanted to be a folksinger, an entertainer . . .' – *Duluth News Tribune* (circa 1963).

Page 94: Rutman quotation: author's interview with Rutman.

Page 94: Dylan quotation – 'Why don't you . . .' – author's interview with Bucklen.

Page 94: Davich quotation: author's interview with Davich.
Page 95: Christmas: author's interview with Beecher.
Page 95: Dylan leaving town and quotation – 'I'd spent . . .' – *Biograph* liner notes.
Page 95: Men looking for Dylan and Gretel Whitaker quotations: author's interviews with Pelto and Whitaker.
Page 96: Dylan quotation – 'in the mercy of the world' – *Biograph* liner notes.
Page 96: Kegan quotation: author's interview with Kegan.
Page 96: Madison visit and Brickman quotations: author's interview with Brickman.
Page 97: Stayed with Lauderbach: Eve McKenzie interview with *The Telegraph* (issue 56).
Page 97: Attends Seeger concert and Seeger quotations: author's interviews with Seeger.
Page 98: Berger irritated by singing: B*ob Dylan: Behind the Shades – Take Two* by Clinton Heylin.
Page 98: Dylan described his thoughts upon entering New York for the first time in the *Biograph* liner notes.

CHAPTER 3: CITY OF DREAMS

Primary sources are the author's interviews, correspondence, and discussions with the following: Oscar Brand, Hamilton Camp, Anna Chairetakis (née Lomax), Liam Clancy, John Cohen, Erik Darling, Manny Dworman, Ramblin' Jack Elliott, Bob Engelhardt, Mimi Fariña, Nick Gravenites, Wavy Gravy (aka Hugh Romney), Sally Grossman, Arlo Guthrie, Nora Guthrie, John Hammond Jr., Echo Helstrom, John Herald, Carolyn Hester, John Lee Hooker, Pete Karman, Bruce Langhorne, Harold Leventhal, Tommy Makem, Bobby Neuwirth, Odetta, Tom Paxton, Gretel Pelto (née Hoffman), Jahanara Romney (aka Bonnie Beecher), Carla Rotolo, Suze Rotolo, Pete Seeger, Roy Silver, Mark Spoelstra, Noel Paul Stookey, Happy Traum, Dave Van Ronk, Dave Whitaker, Peter Yarrow, and Israel 'Izzy' Young.

Pages 100-102: Greenwich Village background: author's interviews with club owners Dworman and Engelhardt; musicians and background from books including *Bringing It All Back Home* by Robbie Woliver. Bauldie's essay in *The Telegraph*, reprinted in *Wanted Man: In Search of Bob Dylan*, was also a useful source of background information on Dylan's early months in New York.

Pages 101-102: Dworman quotation: author's interview with Dworman.

Page 102: Brand quotation: author's interview with Brand.

Page 102: Date (January 24): various sources including *Bob Dylan: A Life in Stolen Moments: Day by Day: 1941–1995* by Clinton Heylin.

Page 102: Dylan quotation – 'I been travelin' . . .' – attributed in *Bob Dylan* by Anthony Scaduto.

Pages 102-105: Guthrie visit and Arlo and Nora Guthrie quotations: author's interviews with Arlo and Nora Guthrie.

Page 103: Dylan quotation – 'I'm looking for . . .' – author's interview with Nora Guthrie.

Page 104: Date (January 29): various sources including *Bob Dylan: A Life in Stolen Moments*.

Pages 104-105: Nora Guthrie quotations: author's interview.

Page 105: Dylan postcard – 'I know him . . .' – *Bob Dylan*.

Page 105: Guthrie quotation – 'I ain't dead yet' – author's interview with Spoelstra.

Pages 105-107: Meeting Spoelstra and Spoelstra quotations: author's interview with Spoelstra.

Page 107: Traum friendship and Traum quotations: author's interview with Traum.

Page 107: Neil friendship: author's interviews with Spoelstra.

Pages 107-108: Attitude toward homosexuality: author's interviews with Spoelstra.

Page 108: Dylan quotation – 'We would make . . .' – *No Direction Home*.

Page 108: Gleasons: *Bob Dylan*.

Page 108: Dylan quotation – 'Mom' – *Bob Dylan*.

Pages 108-109: Beecher meeting and quotations: author's

interview with Beecher.

Page 109: Guthrie quotation – 'Pete Seeger's a . . .' – attributed in *Bob Dylan*.

Page 109: Leventhal quotations: author's interview with Leventhal.

Page 109: Seeger quotation: author's interview with Seeger.

Page 109: Dylan said in an interview for *Sing Out!* (Oct–Nov 1962) that he wrote 'Song to Woody' 'in New York City in the drug store on 8th Street.'

Page 110: Nora Guthrie quotation: author's interview with Nora Guthrie.

Page 110: Guthrie lyric – '. . . we come with the dust and we go with the wind' – 'Pastures of Plenty' (TRO-Ludlow Music, Inc).

Page 110: Guthrie speech: author's interview with Nora Guthrie.

Page 110: Marjorie Guthrie quotation – 'You gotta . . .' – author's interview with Nora Guthrie.

Page 111: Gerde's background: author's interviews; *Bringing It All Back Home*.

Page 111: Paxton like police officer: Gravy in *Bringing It All Back Home*.

Page 111: Paxton quotation: author's interview with Paxton.

Pages 111-113: Van Ronk friendship and quotations: author's interview with Van Ronk.

Page 112: Dworman quotation: author's interview with Dworman.

Page 114: McKenzie meeting and quotation: Eve McKenzie's interview with *The Telegraph* (issue 56). Also: 'He's gone!'

Page 114: Dylan quotation – 'Well, here I am!' – McKenzie interview in *The Telegraph*.

Pages 114-115: Spoelstra walks with Dylan and quotation: author's interview with Spoelstra.

Pages 115-116: Elliott meeting and Elliott quotations: author's interview with Elliott.

Pages 116-117: Clancy meeting and Clancy quotations: author's interviews with Liam Clancy. Additional background on The Clancy Brothers, including the reference to

Paddy being a member of the Irish Republican Army – liner notes to *The Clancy Brothers and Tommy Makem* (Tradition, 1961). Dylan spoke about Clancy being the best ballad singer he ever heard in a radio interview recorded at Slane Castle, Ireland, in 1984 (printed in *All Across the Telegraph*).

Page 117: Makem quotation: author's interview.

Page 118: Porco quotations: *Bringing It All Back Home.*

Page 118: Dylan dialogue – 'With who?' etc. and 'I ain't got no mother' etc. – Porco's recollections in *Bringing It All Back Home.*

Page 118: Dylan quotation – 'The first time . . .' – *Bob Dylan.*

Page 118: Dylan quotation – 'The more hair you have . . .' – *No Direction Home.*

Page 119: Chaplinesque: various, including *No Direction Home.*

Page 119: Brand quotation: author's interview with Brand.

Page 119: Hooker quotations: author's interview with Hooker.

Page 120: Dylan quotation – 'I didn't plan . . .' – *No Direction Home.*

Pages 120-121: Beecher meeting and quotations: author's interview with Beecher.

Page 120: Dylan quotation – 'Okay, I get it' – author's interview with Beecher.

Pages 121-122: Gravy friendship and Gravy quotations: author's interviews with Gravy.

Page 122: Stookey friendship and quotations: author's interview with Stookey.

Page 122: 'Toilet Man' nickname: attributed to Van Ronk in *Bringing It All Back Home.*

Page 122: 'Talkin' Central Park Mugger Blues': author's interview with Paxton.

Page 123: Details of Dylan's association with Silver: author's interview with Silver; papers in the court case Albert B. Grossman et al. vs. Bob Dylan (Case #14403/81). Dylan's opinions of Silver are drawn from his depositions in relation to this lawsuit.

Pages 123-124: Rotolo background: author's interviews with Karman and Carla Rotolo et al.

Page 124: Lomax and Anna Lomax quotations: author's

interviews with Anna Chairetakis (née Lomax).

Page 124: Dylan quotation – 'What do you think?' – author's interview with Spoelstra.

Page 124: Dylan quotation – 'fawn in the forest' – '11 Outlined Epitaphs' (Special Rider Music, 1964).

Page 125: Herald friendship and quotations: author's interview with Herald.

Page 126: Dylan quotation – 'Everything about that . . .' – *Mojo* (February 1998).

Page 126: Spoelstra on Baez: author's interview with Spoelstra.

Page 127: Mimi Baez quotation: author's interview.

Page 127: Baez quotations from her memoir, *And a Voice to Sing With*.

Page 127: Attempts to get record deal: author's interviews with Spoelstra, Young et al.

Page 127: Dylan quotation – 'I did terribly' – author's interview with Spoelstra.

Page 128: Background on Hammond: author's interview with Hammond Jr.

Pages 128-129: Hester friendship and Hester quotations: author's interview with Hester.

Page 129: Gerde's concert: author's interview with Herald et al. Also Shelton's *New York Times* article (September 29, 1961).

Page 130: Hammond quotation – 'Dylan thought . . .' – *Bringing It All Back Home*.

Page 130: Dylan quotation – 'It was one of the most . . .' – *Biograph* liner notes (Special Rider Music, 1985).

Page 130: Dylan quotation – 'What are *you* doin'?' – and other conversation with John Cohen: author's interview with Cohen.

Page 131: Four percent: Columbia contracts.

Page 131: Dylan quotation – 'I was just so happy . . .' – Dylan deposition on October 6, 1981, regarding lawsuit Albert B. Grossman et al. vs. Bob Dylan law suit (Case #14403/81).

Page 131: Dylan quotation – 'Hey, man, I gotta . . .' – author's interview with Clancy.

Pages 131-133: Background on Grossman's early career:

author's interviews with Camp, Gravenites, Sally Grossman, and Silver. The author also consulted former clients of Grossman including The Band, Odetta, Noel Paul Stookey, and Peter Yarrow; court documents; Grossman's *Rolling Stone* obituary (March 13, 1986); and *The Mansion on the Hill* by Fred Goodman. Bob Spitz reported in *Dylan: A Biography* that Grossman was dismissed from the Chicago Housing Authority for 'gross irregularities'.

Page 131: Rotolo quotation about Grossman – 'old man' – *The Mansion on the Hill.*

Page 132: Gravenites quotation: author's interview.

Page 132: Odetta quotation: author's interview with Odetta.

Page 133: Van Ronk comment: author's interview with Van Ronk.

Page 133: Seeger quotation: author's interview with Seeger.

Page 133: Silver dealings with Grossman: author's interview with Silver; court records (Case #14403/81).

Pages 133-134: Young concert: author's interview with Young.

Page 133: Dylan comments and quotations – 'a nothing little town' etc. – Young's notebooks, reprinted in *The Telegraph* (issue 56).

Pages 134-135: Brand show and Brand quotations: author's interview with Brand.

Page 134: Dylan dialogue on air – 'Ah-I was raised . . .' etc. – transcript of WNYC program, *Folk Song Festival*, from tape made available by Brand.

Pages 135-136: Carnegie Chapter Hall show: author's interview with Young.

Page 136: Dylan quotation – 'green pastures of Harvard University' – *Bob Dylan* (Columbia, 1961).

Page 136: Van Ronk comment – 'butchered' – author's interview with Van Ronk.

Page 137: Grossman–Camp dialogue: author's interview with Camp.

Page 137: Dylan quotation – 'Hey, kiddo . . .' – author's interview with Camp.

Page 137: Dylan complaints about bookings: Dylan comments in case #14403/81.

Page 137: Silver quotation: author's interview.

Pages 137-138: Trip back to Minnesota: author's interviews with Beecher et al.

Page 138: Dylan quotation – 'I'll be standin' on my feet' – 'Hard Times in New York Town' (Duchess Music Corporation, 1962, 1965).

Page 138: Helstrom quotations: author's interviews with Helstrom.

Page 139: Mary Rotolo views and quotation – 'I didn't trust him . . .' – *Dylan: A Biography.*

Page 139: Dylan quotation – 'Carla-in-law' – author's interview with Carla Rotolo.

Page 139: Dylan quotation – 'You really blew . . .' – author's interview with Spoelstra.

Page 139: Dylan quotations – 'I'm sort of . . .' – Young's notebooks, reprinted in *The Telegraph*.

Page 140: Background on Emmett Till: *The Telegraph* (issue 44).

Page 140: Clancy meeting and quotations: author's interviews with Clancy and Makem.

Page 140: Dylan quotation – 'Only ten . . .' – author's interview with Clancy.

Page 141: Peyote: author's interview with Spoelstra.

Page 141: Marijuana: author's interview with Herald.

Page 141: Dylan quotation – 'You ever . . .' – author's interview with Herald.

Page 142: Background on Ochs: *There But for Fortune: The Life of Phil Ochs* by Michael Schumacher.

Pages 141-142: Seeger meeting and quotations: author's interview with Seeger.

Page 142: Dylan quotation – 'Hope I don't find out anything . . . great God!' – 'Talkin' John Birch Paranoid Blues' (Special Rider Music, 1970).

Page 142: Paxton quotation: author's interview with Paxton.

Page 143: Spivey quotations: *Bob Dylan* by Anthony Scaduto. Background from *No Direction Home; Bringing it All Back Home*; and *The Encyclopedia of Rock Obituaries.*

Page 143: Dylan quotation – 'gorgeous creature' – Spivey's

comments in *Bob Dylan*.

Page 144: Arlo Guthrie quotations: author's interview with Guthrie.

Page 144: *Village Voice* review – 'explosive country-blues debut' – April 26, 1962 issue.

Page 145: Dylan described how he wrote 'Blowin' in the Wind' in the *Biograph* liner notes.

Page 145: Dylan quotation – 'It was just another song . . .' – *Biograph* liner notes.

Page 145: Lorre Wyatt story: *Newsweek* (November 4, 1963).

Page 145: Seeger quotation: author's interview with Seeger.

Page 145: Paxton quotation: author's interview with Paxton.

Pages 145-146: Van Ronk quotations: author's interview with Van Ronk.

Page 146: Dylan asks Leventhal and Leventhal quotation: author's interview with Leventhal.

Pages 146-150: Dylan's relationship and business dealings with Silver and Grossman: author's interviews with Sally Grossman and Silver, and papers in the case Albert B. Grossman et al. vs. Bob Dylan (Case #14403/81), filed in New York in 1981.

Page 147: Odetta quotation: author's interview with Odetta.

Page 147: Dylan quotations – 'did some good things . . .' and 'I was probably easy . . .' – sworn deposition by Dylan, made in Los Angeles on October 15, 1984, in the Albert B. Grossman et al. vs. Bob Dylan lawsuit (Case #14403/81).

Page 147: Dylan quotation – 'Well, I don't think . . .' – deposition by Dylan made in New York on October 6, 1981, in regard to the lawsuit (Case #14403/81).

Page 147: Dylan quotation – 'Grossman first gained my trust and confidence . . .' – sworn deposition by Dylan, made in Los Angeles on October 15, 1984, in the Albert B. Grossman et al. vs. Bob Dylan lawsuit (Case #14403/81).

Page 148: In the 1962 management agreement between Dylan and Grossman clause 5a makes it clear that 'the Artist' agrees to pay 'the Manager': 'Twenty-five (25) percent of the gross compensation of the Artist, received on account of his performances or services in connection with the production or distribution of any motion picture, or recording of any kind.'

Page 148: Peter, Paul and Mary: author's interviews with Paxton, Stookey, Yarrow et al.

Page 148: Paxton quotation: author's interview.

Page 149: Dylan quotation – 'I'm hot for you . . .' – *Sing Out!* (Oct–Nov 1962).

Page 149: Dylan quotation – 'Tin Pan . . .' – *Biograph* liner notes.

Pages 149-150: Witmark deal: papers in case #14403/81.

Page 150: Dylan quotation – 'a secret deal' – sworn deposition by Dylan, made in Los Angeles on October 15, 1984, in the Albert B. Grossman et al. vs. Bob Dylan lawsuit (Case #14403/81).

Page 150: Phrase – 'willfully and maliciously' – answer by Dylan's attorneys to complaints by Grossman (Case #14403/81).

Page 151: Spoelstra quotations: author's interview with Spoelstra.

Pages 151-152: 'Don't Think Twice, It's All Right' (Warner Bros., 1963).

Page 152: Dylan quotation – 'endless highway' – 'Tomorrow Is a Long Time' (Warner Bros., 1963).

Page 152: Langhorne quotation: author's interview with Langhorne.

Page 152: Spoelstra quotations: author's interview with Spoelstra.

Page 153: Dylan quotation – 'a song of desperation . . .' – original *Freewheelin' Bob Dylan* liner notes reprinted in *The Telegraph* (issue 8).

Page 153: Gravy quotation: author's interview with Gravy.

Page 153: Camp quotation: author's interview with Camp.

Page 154: Seeger quotation: author's interview with Seeger.

Page 154: Arlo Guthrie quotation: author's interview with Arlo Guthrie.

Page 154: Dylan quotation – 'The songs are there . . .' – *Sing Out!* (Oct–Nov 1962)

Page 154: Paxton quotation: author's interview with Paxton.

Page 155: Dylan quotation – 'So people don't recognize me' – author's interview with Gretel Pelto (née Hoffman, later Whitaker).

Page 155: Carnegie Hall concert: author's interviews with Pelto and Whitaker.

Chapter 4: Apotheosis

Primary sources are author's interviews, correspondence, and discussions with: the late Steve Allen, Al Aronowitz, Eve Baer, Stanley Bard, Theodore Bikel, Oscar Brand, John Bucklen, Hamilton Camp, Nancy Carlen, Jones Cullinan (née Alk), Mimi Fariña (née Baez), Barry Feinstein, Lawrence Ferlinghetti, Dana Gillespie, Wavy Gravy (aka Hugh Romney), Sally Grossman, John Hammond Jr., Bill HeckeRoth, Echo Helstrom, John Herald, Carolyn Hester, Horace Freeland Judson, Pete Karman, Daniel Kramer, Bruce Langhorne, Harold Leventhal, Peter Lownds, Maria Muldaur, Bobby Neuwirth, Anne Noznisky, Jeffrey Noznisky, Odetta, Bernard Paturel, Mary Lou Paturel, Tom Paxton, D. A. Pennebaker, Kenny Rankin, Jean Ritchie, B. J. Rolfzen, Jahanara Romney (aka Bonnie Beecher), Carla Rotolo, Suze Rotolo, Howard Rutman, Ed Sanders, Philip Saville, John Sebastian, Peggy Seeger, Pete Seeger, Mark Spoelstra, Yvonne Staples, Noel Paul Stookey, Jane Traum, Peter Yarrow, and William D. Zantzinger.

Page 156: Details of the Braun/CBS legal tussle and Braun's quotation: 'I thought it was a violation . . .': Braun deposition on November 21, 1981, in the case Albert B. Grossman et al. vs. Bob Dylan (Case #14403/81.) Background on Braun, including the quotation 'next Frank Sinatra,' profile in *Rolling Stone* (October 4, 1979).

Page 157: Dixieland band: *Bringing It All Back Home* by Robbie Woliver and *No Direction Home: The Life and Music of Bob Dylan* by Robert Shelton.

Page 157: Hammond Jr. quotation: author's interview with Hammond Jr.

Pages 157-160: Background on the 1962–63 visit to London from the author's interview with Saville. The quotation – 'any motion picture, or recording of any kind' – Dylan's 1962 management agreement with Albert Grossman. Additional background: the Martin Carthy interview published in *The Telegraph* (issue 42); the Dylan interview published in *Scene* magazine (January 26, 1963); and Saville's interview in *The Dylan Companion*.

Page 158: Saville quotations: author's interview.

Page 159: Peggy Seeger meeting and quotations: author's interviews.

Pages 159-160: Trip to Rome and Odetta quotations: author's interview with Odetta.

Page 160: In an interview with the author, Carolyn Hester said she believed 'Boots of Spanish Leather' was about Suze Rotolo.

Page 160: Dobell's: interview with former Dobell's manager Ron Gould published in *The Telegraph* (issue 49).

Page 160: Anthea Joseph, a friend of Dylan, is quoted on the subject of Dylan's drunkenness at the Troubadour in *Dylan: Behind the Shades* by Clinton Heylin.

Pages 160-161: 'Girl from the North Country': author's interviews with Beecher and Helstrom.

Page 160: Dylan quotation – 'coat so warm' – 'Girl from the North Country' (Warner Bros., Inc. 1963).

Page 161: Dylan quotation – 'This is dedicated to . . .' – March 1963 show for WNBC radio, tape supplied by Brand.

Page 161: Staples story: author's discussions with Yvonne Staples. Background: *No Direction Home*, and an essay by Shelton in *The Dylan Companion*.

Page 161: Dylan quotation and dialogue – 'Pops, can I marry Mavis?' – author's discussions with Yvonne Staples.

Page 161: Rotolo quotation – 'When I came back from Italy . . .' – interview by Balfour in *Rock Wives*, reprinted in *The Dylan Companion*.

Page 162: Background on *The Freewheelin' Bob Dylan* cover: author's discussions with Suze Rotolo, and *The Telegraph* issue 50).

Page 162: Rotolo quotations: discussions with author.

Page 162: Dylan comments at Town Hall: recording of performance.

Page 163: Jane Traum quotations: author's interview.

Page 163: Trip to Hibbing: author's discussions with Rolfzen.

Page 163: Dylan quotation – 'This is called . . .' – recording of the October 26, 1963, Carnegie Hall concert on *The Bootleg Series, Volumes 1–3* (Sony Music, 1991).

Pages 163-164: Background on changes to *The Freewheelin' Bob Dylan*: various, including Bob Dylan: *Behind the Shades – Take Two* by Clinton Heylin.

Pages 164-165: Background on Ritchie's claim to the melody of 'Masters of War': author's interview with Ritchie. Shelton wrote in *No Direction Home* that Dylan thought Judy Collins's truncated version of the song 'blunted his intent.'

Page 165: Ritchie quotation: author's interview with Ritchie.

Page 165 Mimi Fariña quotations: author's interview.

Page 165: Foreman quotation – 'Are you still fucking . . .' – author's interview with Karman.

Pages 165-166: Dylan quotation – 'Although I didn't know it . . .' – Dylan's October 15, 1984, deposition in the case Albert B. Grossman et al. vs. Bob Dylan (Case #14403/81).

Page 166: Dylan quotation – 'Country'll grow' – 'I Shall Be Free' (Warner Bros., Inc. 1963, 1967).

Pages 166-167: Conversation between Bikel and Grossman: from an interview with Bikel by the author. Background on the Greenwood, Mississippi, rally is from the author's interviews with Seeger and Bikel and a report in the *New York Times* (July 7, 1963).

Page 167: Bikel quotations: author's interview.

Page 167: Seeger quotations: author's interview.

Page 168: Dylan donation: author's interviews with Bikel and Van Ronk.

Page 168: Yarrow quotations: author's interview with Yarrow.

Page 168: Stookey quotation: author's interview.

Page 168: Dylan reaction to $5,000: *Biograph* liner notes (Special Rider Music, 1985).

Page 169: Paxton quotation: author's interview.

Page 170: Gassing incident: Carla Rotolo spoke about her sister's apparent suicide attempt and termination. Suze Rotolo declined to talk about the incidents. Bob Spitz (*Dylan: A Biography*) places the timing of the apparent suicide attempt after Newport 1963, when Dylan told Rotolo he was touring with Baez.

Page 170: Carla Rotolo quotations: author's interview.

Page 170: Brand quotations: author's interviews.

Page 170: Baez quotation – 'Would you like . . .' – from the recollection of concertgoer Eve Baer.

Page 170: Baer quotation: author's interview.

Page 171: Baez quotation – 'There's a boy wandering . . .' – Bob Dylan by Anthony Scaduto.

Page 171: Mimi Baez quotation: author's interview.

Page 171: Baez quotations – 'dragging my . . .' – *And a Voice to Sing With*.

Pages 171-172: Camp quotations: author's interview.

Page 172: Rolls-Royce road trip: based on Barry Feinstein's introduction to *Early Dylan*.

Pages 172-173: Background on Dylan in Bearsville: *And a Voice to Sing With*.

Pages 173-174: Paturel friendship and quotations: author's interviews with Bernard and Mary Lou Paturel.

Page 174: Dylan quotation – 'fishes will laugh' – 'When the Ship Comes In' (Warner Bros., Inc. 1963, 1964).

Page 174: Gravy quotation: author's interview.

Page 174: Karman quotations: author's interview.

Page 175: Scandalized Baez: *And a Voice to Sing With*.

Page 175: Earle Hotel: *And a Voice to Sing With*.

Pages 175-176: Carmel: author's interview with Carlen; *And a Voice to Sing With*.

Page 176: Dylan quotation – 'Now's the time for your tears' – 'The Lonesome Death of Hattie Carroll' (Warner Bros., Inc. 1964, 1966).

Page 176: Background on the Hattie Carroll–William Zantzinger case comes from essays published in *The Telegraph* (issue 42) and from the book *Classic Bob Dylan 1962–1969: My Back Pages*. Also author's interview with Zantzinger.

Page 176: Zantzinger quotations: author's interview.
Page 177: Dylan quotation – 'I don't know . . .' – *Newsweek* (November 4, 1963).
Page 177: David Zimmerman quotations – 'We were kind of close . . .' – *Newsweek* (November 4, 1963).
Pages 177-178: Shelton in *No Direction Home* writes that Dylan almost screamed at him about the *Newsweek* article, and had 'sniped at his parents' for talking to the press.
Pages 178-179: ECLC speech from the transcript published in *No Direction Home*.
Page 179: Dylan quotations – 'I saw a lot of myself in Oswald . . .' and 'I'm gonna . . .' – *The New Yorker* interview by Hentoff (October 24, 1964).
Pages 180-181: Maymudes's background: author's interview with mutual friends including Elliott and Muldaur, and Maymudes's website, 'It Is Good to Look Back.'
Pages 181-184: Road trip: author's interview with Karman.
Pages 181-184: Karman quotations: author's interview.
Page 182: Background on 'Mr. Tambourine Man': author's discussions with Langhorne; Dylan's comments in the *Biograph* liner notes. Also an essay about Dylan's interest in the work of Lord Buckley in *On the Tracks* (issue 15).
Page 182: Dylan quotation – 'big as a wagon wheel . . .' – *Biograph* liner notes.
Page 182: Langhorne quotations: author's interview with Langhorne.
Page 182: Dylan quotation – 'In the jingle jangle morning I'll come followin' you' – 'Mr. Tambourine Man' (Warner Bros., 1964, 1965).
Page 182: Dylan quotation – 'Drugs never played a part in that song . . .' – *Biograph* liner notes.
Page 183: Closed up: *Bob Dylan*.
Page 183: Kerouac quotation – 'the great buzzing and vibrating . . .' – *On the Road*.
Pages 183-184: Karman quotation: author's interview.
Page 184: Aronowitz quotations: author's interview.
Page 184: Ginsberg quotations – 'I thought he was just . . .' – Ginsberg by Barry Miles.

Page 184: Ferlinghetti quotations: author's interview.

Page 185: Gleason's review – '. . . another New York Jew . . .' – *San Francisco Chronicle* (February 24, 1964). His previous comments about the Monterey Festival from *The Rolling Stone Story*, by Robert Draper.

Page 186: Neuwirth quotation: discussion with author. 'Tacos-to-Go' nickname from author's interview with a confidential source.

Page 186: Aronowitz quotation: author's interview.

Page 186: Steve Allen show: author's correspondence with Allen; recording of the show.

Page 187: Rutman quotation: author's interview.

Page 187: Muldaur quotations: author's interview (also drive to Hollywood).

Page 187: Dylan quotation – 'Man, was that . . .' – author's interview with Muldaur.

Page 189: Rotolo termination and breakup: author's interview with Carla Rotolo. Suze Rotolo declined to talk about these matters.

Pages 189-190: Carla Rotolo quotations: author's interview.

Page 190: Dylan quotation – 'I don't write . . .' – *Biograph* liner notes.

Page 190: Suze Rotolo quotations: discussions with author.

Page 191: Sebastian quotations: author's interview.

Pages 191-193: Bucklen reunion and quotations: interview with Bucklen. The Bucklen visit has been previously reported as happening in 1965. This is incorrect, as Bucklen had left the air force by then and returned to the United States.

Page 191: Harrison quotation – 'We just played it, just wore it out' – *Mojo* magazine (December 1993).

Page 192: Rothchild story: *Dylan: A Biography*.

Page 192: Dylan quotation – 'I never . . .' – *Rolling Stone* (June 21, 1984).

Page 192: Alk drug user: author's interviews with Jones Cullinan (née Alk).

Pages 192-193: Dylan quotation – 'What do you . . .' – author's interview with Bucklen.

Page 193: Background on Nico friendship: *Dylan: Behind the Shades* by Clinton Heylin.

Page 193: Background on European vacation: interview with Hugues Aufray published in *The Telegraph* (issue 39).

Page 194: Use of Mayfair notepaper: *Bob Dylan Behind the Shades – Take Two.*

Page 194: Dylan quotation – 'color of the sun cut flat' – 'Mama, You Been on My Mind' (Warner Bros., Inc. 1964, 1967).

Pages 194-195: Background on *Another Side of Bob Dylan* sessions and Dylan quotation – 'I'm gonna . . .' – *The New Yorker* (October 24, 1964); author's interviews with Aronowitz; *Bob Dylan: The Recording Sessions* 1960–1994 by Clinton Heylin.

Page 195: Dylan quotation – 'The could-be . . .' – 'Ballad in Plain D' (Warner Bros., Inc. 1964).

Page 195: Dylan quotation – 'I begged . . .' – *Biograph* liner notes.

Page 196: Dylan quotation – 'i used t'hate enzo' – 'Some Other Kinds of Songs . . .' (Special Rider Music, 1973).

Page 196: Silber quotation – 'I saw at Newport . . .' – *Sing Out!* (November 1964).

Page 196: Cash wrote about his meeting with Dylan – 'like kids' etc. – in his memoir, *Cash: The Autobiography.*

Page 197: Beecher meeting and quotations: author's interview with Beecher.

Page 197: Beatles meeting: author's interview with Aronowitz and Aronowitz Web site The Blacklisted Journalist.

Page 198: Beatles, Dylan, and marijuana: *The Beatles Anthology*; author's discussions with Aronowitz and McCartney's publicist, Geoff Baker; interviews in *Mojo* magazine (December 1993); *Paul McCartney: Many Years from Now* by Barry Miles; and Cherri Gilham interview in the (London) *Observer* (September 10, 2000).

Page 199: Aronowitz quotation: author's interview with Aronowitz.

Pages 199-201: Background on Sara Lownds (née Shirley Marlin Noznisky): author's interviews with members of the Noznisky family; Sara's stepson Peter Lownds; members of the Dylan family, who wish to remain anonymous; and friends of Sara including Sally Grossman. Also birth and marriage certificates; a contemporaneous press report (the *Daily Local News*, Westchester, PA, November 1956) of the killing of Isaac Noznisky; and the *Wilmington Morning News* obituary of Bessie Noznisky (May 1961). Sara Dylan declined to speak to the author.

Page 200: Peter Lownds quotations: author's interview.

Page 200: Dylan meeting Sara: author's interview with Lownds and Sally Grossman.

Page 201: Sally Grossman–Sara Lownds friendship: author's interviews with Sally Grossman.

Pages 201-202: Hotel Chelsea stay and background: author's interview with Stanley Bard, who has managed the Hotel Chelsea since 1961.

Page 202: Dylan quotation – 'Here comes the Armenian . . .' – author's interview with Herald.

Page 202: Herald quotations: author's interview.

Page 202: Beecher quotations: author's interview.

Pages 202-203: Background on Edie Sedgwick: author's interview with Gerard Malanga, and *Edie*, by Jean Stein and George Plimpton.

Page 203: Dylan quotation – 'America should put statues . . .' – *TV Guide* (September 1976).

Pages 204-206: Background on *Bringing It All Back Home*: author's interviews with Langhorne, Rankin, and Sebastian.

Page 204: Rankin quotations: author's interview.

Page 205: Maggiore's Farm story related to author by poet and musician Ed Sanders, a longtime Woodstock resident and acquaintance of Dylan. The pump story related by another Woodstock resident, Tim Schussler.

Page 205: Dylan quotation – '. . . she's true, like ice, like fire' – 'Love Minus Zero/No Limit' (Warner Bros., Inc, 1965).

Page 205: Dylan quotation – 'I was ridin' on the Mayflower' – Bob Dylan's 115th Dream' (Warner Bros., Inc, 1965).

Page 205: Langhorne quotation: author's interview.

Page 206: Dylan quotation – 'I've written some . . .' – *New York Times* (September 28, 1997).

Pages 206-207: *Bringing It All Back Home* cover: author's interviews with Kramer and Grossman.

Pages 206-207: Kramer quotations: author's interview.

Page 207: Dylan quotation – 'I had a banana band . . .' – *Village Voice* (March 25, 1965).

Page 208: Dylan quotation – 'It's just a little story . . .' – *Melody Maker* (March 27, 1965).

Pages 208-209: Background on U.K. tour and *Dont Look Back*: author's interviews with Cullinan (née Alk), Grossman, Pennebaker et al.; the film, *Dont Look Back* (Pennebaker Hegedus Films, Inc. 1967); recordings of press conferences; *Like a Bullet of Light* by C. P. Lee; *Mojo* magazine (December 1993); and Gillespie's interview with the *News of the World* (August 31, 1980).

Pages 208-209: Pennebaker quotations: author's interview.

Pages 209-210: Dylan quotations – 'Keep a . . .' and 'Who threw . . .' etc. – *Dont Look Back*.

Page 209: Dylan quotation – 'They ask the wrong questions . . .' – *Darts* (May 1965).

Page 209: Dylan quotation – 'The Eye' – *Sing Out!* (Oct–Nov 1968).

Page 209: Grossman's quotation – 'You're one of the dumbest assholes . . .' – *Dont Look Back*.

Page 210: Paxton quotation: author's interview.

Page 210: Neuwirth dialogue: *Dont Look Back*. (NB: except 'I think Bob Dylan is a true artist . . .' which is from a discussion with the author.)

Page 210: Mimi Fariña quotations: author's interview.

Page 211: Carlen quotation: author's interview.

Page 211: Marianne Faithfull: *Faithfull*.

Page 211: Gillespie friendship and quotations: author's interview with Gillespie.

Page 212: Dylan quotation – 'I just didn't . . .' – *Dont Look Back*.

Pages 212-213: Pennebaker quotations: author's interview.

Page 213: Dylan quotation – 'You're going to . . .' – *Dont Look Back*.

Page 213: Judson quotations: author's correspondence with Judson.
Page 213: Dylan quotation – 'I feel . . .' – *Dont Look Back*.

CHAPTER 5: FULL POWER

The primary sources are author's interviews, correspondence, and discussions with: Theodore Bikel, Oscar Brand, Wayne 'Doc' Butler, Kenny Buttrey, Liam Clancy, Jones Cullinan (née Alk), the late Rick Danko, Ramblin' Jack Elliott, Lawrence Ferlinghetti, Dana Gillespie, Tony Glover, Nick Gravenites, Sally Grossman, John Hammond Jr., Ronnie Hawkins, Levon Helm, Echo Helstrom, Garth Hudson, Bob Johnston, Mickey Jones, Larry Keenan, 'Spider' John Koerner, Sandy Konikoff, Al Kooper, Alan Lomax,* Gerard Malanga, Michael McClure, Charlie McCoy, Roger McGuinn, Wayne Moss, Maria Muldaur, Bernard Paturel, D. A. Pennebaker, Hargus 'Pig' Robbins, Robbie Robertson, John Sebastian, Pete Seeger, P. F. Sloan, Mark Spoelstra, Noel Paul Stookey, Henry Strzelecki, Jonathan Taplin, Dr. Ed Thaler, Selma Thaler, Bill Waterous, Charlie Wolven, Peter Yarrow, and Israel 'Izzy' Young.
Pages 215-216: Details about the purchase of Hi Lo Ha are from tax and real estate records held at Woodstock town offices. Additional background on Dylan's blind corporations from a deposition by his employee, Naomi Saltzman, given in New York on December 17, 1981, in the case Albert B. Grossman et al. vs. Bob Dylan (Case #14403/81).
Page 216: Dylan quotation – 'long piece of vomit' – interview with the Canadian Broadcasting Company (February 20, 1966).
Page 216: Dylan quotation – 'very vomitific' – *No Direction Home*.
Page 216: Dylan quotation – 'a rhythm thing . . .' – Siegel interview in the *Saturday Evening Post* (July 30, 1966).

*Via his daughter, Anna Chairetakis.

Page 217: Gravenites quotations: author's interview.

Page 217: Personnel list on 'Like a Rolling Stone' is based on Kooper's recollection of the session, rather than studio records, which seem to be inaccurate.

Page 217: Dylan quotation – 'How does it feel' – 'Like a Rolling Stone' (Warner Bros., Inc., 1965).

Page 218: Dylan quotation – 'Hey, now don't tell me . . .' etc. – *Backstage Passes & Backstabbing Bastards* by Al Kooper.

Page 218: Springsteen quotation – 'I knew that I was listening to . . .' – Springsteen's speech at Dylan's induction into the Rock 'n' Roll Hall of Fame (January 20, 1988).

Page 218: McCartney quotation – 'It seemed . . .' – *Mojo* magazine (December, 1993).

Pages 218-222: The 1965 Newport Festival is recreated from author's interviews with Bikel, Gravenites, Sally Grossman, Kooper, Lomax, Seeger, Spoelstra, Stookey et al.; and concert footage. In an interview with the author, Theodore Bikel described Pete's conversation backstage after the performance: 'Pete was really shaken by this. He said, "You know, I feel like smashing that guitar."' The Lomax quotation was supplied by Lomax's daughter, Anna Chairetakis, who spoke to her father on behalf of the author. Yarrow's comments from stage – 'He will do . . .' – are from a transcript of an audio recording of the show.

Page 219: Sally Grossman quotation: author's interview

Pages 219-220: Taplin quotations: author's interview.

Page 219: Gravenites quotations: author's interview.

Page 220: Spoelstra quotations: author's interview.

Pages 220-221: Seeger quotations: author's interview with Seeger.

Page 221: Lomax quotation: author's questions via Lomax's daughter.

Page 221: Brand quotation: author's interview.

Page 221: Stookey quotations: author's interview.

Page 221: Yarrow comments from stage: recording of show.

Page 221: Bikel quotation: author's interview.

Page 222: Dylan quotation – 'Thank you very much' – from transcript of comments from the stage.

Page 222: Dylan's reaction: author's interviews with Bikel, Seeger, Stookey et al.

Pages 222-223: Muldaur quotations: author's interview with Muldaur.

Page 223: Dylan quotation – 'I'd dance with you . . .' – author's interview with Muldaur; Fariña quotation – 'Why don't you go over and ask Bob to dance?' – author's interview with Muldaur.

Pages 223-224: Background on *Highway 61 Revisited*: author's interviews with Kooper, Johnston, and McCoy.

Pages 223-224: Johnston background and quotations: author's interviews with Johnston.

Pages 224-225: Kooper quotations: author's interview with Kooper.

Page 225: Dylan quotation – 'paralyzed' – 'Positively 4th Street' (Warner Bros., Inc., 1965).

Page 226: Jonathan Taplin was present at the meeting with Grossman and Dylan when Dylan said he wanted to tour with an amplified band. In an interview with the author, Taplin says: 'Albert made him compromise that he would play half the set acoustic and half the set electric.'

Page 226: Dylan quotation – 'You wanna . . .' – author's interview with Sebastian.

Page 226: Sebastian quotation: author's interview.

Page 227: Hawkins quotations: author's interviews.

Page 227: Background on The Band: author's interviews with Danko, Helm, Hudson, and Robertson; *This Wheel's on Fire* by Levon Helm; and *The Hawk* by Ian Wallis.

Page 227: Dylan quotation – 'Oh, God, listen to that . . .' – author's interview with Hammond Jr.

Page 227: Dylan quotation – 'Just us' – *This Wheel's on Fire.*

Page 228: Robertson quotations: author's interview with Robertson.

Page 228: Kooper notes: *Backstage Passes & Backstabbing Bastards.*

Pages 228-229: Dylan quotations – 'Thanks for having lunch . . .' and 'Get P. F. Sloan . . .' – *Backstage Passes & Backstabbing Bastards.*

Page 229: Sloan meeting and quotations: author's interview with Sloan.

Page 229: Dylan quotation – 'I gotta big problem . . .' – author's interview with Sloan.

Page 230: Danko quotation: author's interview with Danko.

Page 231: Robertson quotations: author's interview with Robertson.

Page 231: Hudson quotation: author's interview with Hudson.

Pages 231-232: Helm quotation: author's interview with Helm.

Pages 232-233: Background on wedding: author's interviews with Sally Grossman and Dylan family members.

Page 233: Exchange with Elliott: author's interview with Elliott.

Page 233: Dylan quotations – 'What for?' etc. – author's interview with Elliott.

Page 233: Dylan quotation – 'Get out, Ochs . . .' – *Bob Dylan* by Anthony Scaduto; background from *There But for Fortune: The Life of Phil Ochs* by Michael Schumacher.

Page 234: Johnston quotations: author's interview.

Page 234: Konikoff quotations: author's interview.

Pages 234-237: Background on San Francisco section: author's interviews with Danko, Ferlinghetti, Keenan, Konikoff, and McClure. Ginsberg's singing: Miles's biography *Ginsberg*.

Page 235: Dylan quotation – 'Two-wheeled gypsy queen' – 'Gates of Eden' (Warner Bros., Inc., 1965)

Page 235: Baez described Dylan as the 'Dada King' in her book *Daybreak*.

Pages 235-238: McClure quotations: author's interview.

Page 235: Baez's December 14, 1965, letter to McClure: McClure archive, Simon Fraser University, British Columbia.

Pages 236-237: Keenan quotations: author's interview.

Page 236: Dylan quotations – 'Okay, cool . . .' and 'Bear vomit . . .' – author's interview with Keenan.

Page 236: Ferlinghetti quotations: author's interview.

Page 237: Dylan quotation – 'I'll have tea' – author's interview with Keenan.

Page 238: Dylan quotation – 'Well, I've got a monkey wrench . . .' – Beverly Hills press conference (September 4, 1965).

Page 238: Konikoff quotations: author's interview.

Pages 238-239: Details on the Dwarf Music agreement from the Dwarf contract of January 1, 1966, and documents in the case Albert B. Grossman et al. vs. Bob Dylan (Case #14403/81).

Page 239: Dylan quotation – 'I signed the papers . . .' – Dylan's deposition, on October 15, 1984, in Los Angeles, in the case Albert B. Grossman et al. vs. Bob Dylan (Case #14403/81).

Page 239: Birth of Jesse: birth records and assistance from Dylan family members.

Page 239: Warhol meeting and Malanga quotations: author's interview with Malanga.

Pages 239-240: Details of the exchange of the Warhol painting and sale price: author's interviews with Sally Grossman. Background: *The Andy Warhol Diaries*. Also Warhol's comments in *All Across the Telegraph: A Bob Dylan Handbook*, edited by Michael Gray and John Bauldie.

Page 240: Dylan quotations – 'I don't want this . . .' and 'practical' – author's interviews with Sally Grossman.

Pages 240-246: Background on *Blonde on Blonde*: author's interviews with Butler, Buttrey, Johnston, Kooper, McCoy, Moss, Robbins, Robertson, and Strzelecki.

Pages 240-241: Johnston quotation: author's interview with Johnston.

Pages 241-243: McCoy quotations: author's interview with McCoy.

Page 241: Kooper quotation – 'like a human cassette machine' – *Backstage Passes & Backstabbing Bastards*.

Page 241: Robertson quotation: author's interview with Robertson.

Pages 241-245: Buttrey quotations: author's interviews with Buttrey.

Page 242: Moss quotations: author's interview with Moss.

Page 242: The sequence in which the tracks on *Blonde on Blonde* were recorded is confusing. Musicians have contradictory memories and their recollections differ from studio records, which are not wholly reliable. Although there is evidence, from studio records, that work was done on songs before 'Sad-Eyed Lady of the Lowlands,' McCoy maintains this was the first song, and his fellow musicians consider McCoy to have the best memory.

Page 242: Dylan quotation – 'flesh like silk . . . face like glass' – 'Sad-Eyed Lady of the Lowlands' (Dwarf Music, 1966).

Page 243: Carlen view: author's interviews with Carlen.

Pages 244-245: Strzelecki quotations: author's interview.

Page 244: Dylan quotation – 'What do you guys do here?' – author's interview with Moss.

Pages 244-247: Moss quotations: author's interview.

Page 245: Robbins quotation: author's interview.

Page 245: Butler quotation: author's interview.

Page 245: Dylan quotation – 'Everybody must get stoned' – 'Rainy Day Women #12 & 35' (Dwarf Music, 1966).

Page 245: Dylan quotation – ' 'Rainy Day Women . . .' – author's interview with Buttrey.

Page 246: Ricks quotation: *Lyrics 1962–1985* by Bob Dylan.

Page 246: Dylan quotation – 'that thin, that wild . . .' – *Playboy* (February 1978).

Page 246: Dylan quotation – 'In this room . . .' – 'Visions of Johanna' (Dwarf Music, 1966).

Page 246: Kooper quotations: author's interview.

Page 246: Helstrom view: author's interviews with Helstrom.

Page 247: Moss quotations: author's interview.

Page 247: Johnston quotations: author's interview.

Page 247: Konikoff quotations: author's interview.

Page 248: Dylan quotation – 'You be . . .' – author's interview with Danko.

Page 248: Danko quotations: author's interview.

Page 249: Dylan quotation – 'Sara . . .' – *Saturday Evening Post* (July 30, 1966).

Page 249: Konikoff interview: author's interview.

Page 249: Dylan quotation – 'I wouldn't advise anybody to use drugs . . .' – *Playboy* (March 1966).

Page 249: Dylan quotation – 'It takes a lot . . .' – *No Direction Home*.

Page 250: Dylan quotation – 'No, not the writing . . .' – *Rolling Stone* (November 29, 1969).

Page 250: Drug raid and Jones quotations: author's interviews with Jones.

Page 250: Stockholm arrival: author's interviews with Danko, Jones et al.

Page 250: Danko quotation: author's interview.

Page 250: Jones quotations: author's interview.

Page 250: Dylan quotations – 'Um . . . er . . .. God . . . No, I'm not going to . . .' – transcript of Stockholm press conference (April 28, 1966).

Pages 251-252: Details of the signing of the Dwarf Music agreement in Sweden – including Braun's quotations – 'Had we known a little . . .' – documents in the Albert B. Grossman vs. Bob Dylan file (Case #14403/81), including David Braun's November 17, 1981 deposition.

Pages 252-253: Background on *Eat the Document*: author's interviews with various participants including Jones Alk, Pennebaker, and Robertson; interview with Pennebaker in *The Telegraph* (circa 1984). Pennebaker quotations: author's interview.

Page 253: Lennon quotation – 'very high and stoned' – Lennon's 1979 interview with 102.7 WNEW radio in New York.

Page 253: Dylan quotation – 'Oh! Oh! . . .' – *Eat the Document*.

Pages 253-254: Background on the deaths of Dylan's friends: author's interview with Mimi Fariña (death of her husband); author's interview with Clancy (deaths of his friends Clayton and La Farge); death of Foreman is from *Dylan: A Biography* by Bob Spitz and *No Direction Home*. Also reference books, including *The Encyclopedia of Rock Obituaries*.

Pages 253-254: Clancy quotations: author's interview.

Page 254: Dylan quotation – 'Man, how can I be responsible? . . .' – author's interview with Clancy.

Page 254: Vincent Doyle review of the Dublin concert appeared in *Melody Maker* (May 14, 1966).

Pages 254-255: Johnston quotations: author's interview.

Page 255: McCartney quotation – 'Dylan was influencing us . . .' – *The Beatles Anthology*.

Page 255: Dylan quotations – 'This is um . . .' – recording of the Manchester Free Trade Hall concert released as *Live 1966: The 'Royal Albert Hall' Concert* (Sony, 1998).

Page 255: Background on the Manchester Free Trade Hall: author's interviews. The identity of the 'Judas!' heckler: *The* (London) *Independent* newspaper (January 23, 1999). Further background from *Like the Night: Bob Dylan and the Road to the Manchester Free Trade Hall* by C. P. Lee.

Pages 256-257: Paris show and Robertson quotations: author's interview.

Page 256: Background on the Carnegie Hall protest concert from Young and press reports in *New York Post* (September 25 and 26, 1965).

Page 257: Hudson quotation: author's interview.

Pages 258-259: Pennebaker quotations: author's interview.

Page 258: *Eat the Document*: author's interview with Pennebaker. Background: *Like a Bullet of Light* by C. P. Lee.

Pages 259-261: Details of the motorcycle accident are drawn from author's interviews with Sally Grossman, Pennebaker, former Woodstock constabulary officers (Richard Ostrander, Bill Waterous, and Charlie Wolven), and a confidential source. The Sara Dylan quotation – 'Keep away . . .' – author's interview with Sally Grossman. The author also spoke with Dr. Thaler and his wife, Selma.

CHAPTER 6: COUNTRY WAYS

The primary sources are author's interviews, correspondence, and discussions with: David Amram, Al Aronowitz, Byron T. Bach, Victor Basil, Danielle Beeh, Kenny Buttrey, John Cohen, Jones Cullinan (née Alk), Charlie Daniels, the late Rick Danko, Luke Davich, Bruce Dorfman, Delores Edgin,

Solie Fott, Ray Foulk, Tony Glover, Dennis A. Good, Wavy Gravy, Sally Grossman, Levon Helm, Echo Helstrom, Garth Hudson, Gayle Jamison, Bob Johnston, Larry Kegan, Doug Kershaw, Millie Kirkham, Harold Leventhal, Angel Marolt, Michael McClure, Charlie McCoy, Martha McCrory, Bob Moore, Odetta, Bernard Paturel, Mary Lou Paturel, Tom Paxton, D. A. Pennebaker, Robbie Robertson, Monique Sampas (née Paturel), Tim Schussler, Noel Paul Stookey, Jonathan Taplin, Dr. Ed Thaler, Selma Thaler, Jane Traum, Happy Traum, Gary Vanosdale, Bill Walker, Bill Waterous, and Charlie Wolven.

Page 262: Dylan quotation – 'I was pretty wound up . . .' – *Spin* (December 1985).

Page 262: Dylan has given an account of his injuries in various interviews, including the interview with Scott Cohen of *Spin* magazine (December 1985). Dylan's convalescence is based on author's interviews with Dr. Ed Thaler, Selma Thaler, Odetta, Pennebaker, and others. Woodstock neighbor Bruce Dorfman revealed that Dylan received ultrasound treatment following the accident (interview with the author). Various friends and colleagues, including 1978 band member Billy Cross, describe Dylan swimming in the years following the accident to ease back pain.

Pages 262-263: Thaler quotations: author's interviews.

Page 263: Odetta quotations: author's interview.

Page 263: Background on M.G.M. deal: *No Direction Home: The Life and Music of Bob Dylan* by Robert Shelton.

Page 263: Dylan quotation – 'I just . . .' – *Newsweek* (February 26, 1968).

Pages 263-264: Background on Hi Lo Ha: author's interviews with Dorfman, Paturel, Traum et al.; Woodstock town records. Additional background: *No Direction Home.*

Pages 263-264: Pennebaker quotations: author's interview.

Page 264: Danko quotation: author's interview.

Page 264: Dylan quotation – 'Mr. Tim' – author's interview with Pennebaker.

Page 265: Hudson quotation: author's interview.

Pages 265-269: Background about the Basement Tapes

sessions: author's interviews with Danko, Hudson, and Robertson; and reference to the complete set of Basement Tapes recordings. All quotations from author's interviews, except Robertson's phrase 'reefer run amok,' which is from *Invisible Republic* by Greil Marcus.

Page 267: Background on Schmidt's house: author's interviews with Hudson; also *Woodstock* by Alf Evers and *Woodstock Handmade Houses* by Robert Haney et al.

Page 268: Stookey quotation: author's interview

Pages 268-269: Goldstein review – '. . . the man who defined his generation' – *New York Times* (October 22, 1967).

Page 269: Album sales are from the Recording Industry Association of America (RIAA). Certified sales in the United States of America only.

Page 269: Details of 1967 agreement with CBS: contract between Dylan and CBS, dated July 1, 1967. In his memoir *Clive: Inside the Record Business*, Davis wrote, 'it was worth' paying the money to 'keep Dylan.' Background on the Columbia deal is from Davis's memoir; *The Mansion on the Hill* by Fred Goodman, and *No Direction Home*.

Page 270: Dylan quotation – '. . . a very indulgent . . .' – radio interview with Marc Rowland (September 23, 1978) reprinted in *Dylan: Behind the Shades* by Clinton Heylin.

Pages 270-272: Background on *John Wesley Harding*: author's interviews with Buttrey, McCoy, and Johnston.

Page 270: Johnston quotation: author's interview.

Page 271: McCoy quotations: author's interviews.

Page 271: As reported in Barry Miles's biography of McCartney, *Paul McCartney: Many Years From Now*, the *Sgt. Pepper* sessions began on November 24, 1966, and ended five months later, on April 21, 1967.

Page 271: Buttrey quotations: author's interviews.

Page 271: Stookey quotation: author's interview.

Page 271: Dylan quotation – 'Do you ever . . .' – author's interview with Stookey.

Page 272: Sally Grossman quotation: author's interview.

Page 272: Dylan quotation – 'my little bundle of joy' – 'Down Along the Cove' (Dwarf Music, 1968).

Page 272: Birth of Anna Dylan: birth records, and assistance from members of Dylan family.

Page 272: Leventhal quotation: author's interview.

Page 273: Helm wrote in his autobiography, *This Wheel's on Fire*, that Dylan and Grossman were not speaking at the Guthrie tribute.

Page 273: Dakota party: *No Direction Home*.

Page 273: Dylan quotation – 'I won't be giving any concerts for a while . . .' – *Newsweek* (February 26, 1968).

Page 273: Dylan quotation – 'Just came . . .' – and all subsequent conversations with Dorfman: author's interviews with Dorfman.

Pages 273-279: Dorfman quotations: author's interviews with Dorfman.

Page 276: Beatty Zimmerman was quoted as saying the Byrdcliffe house was overflowing with books in *Positively Main Street*, by Toby Thompson (Coward-McCann, 1971).

Page 276: Aronowitz quotation: author's interview.

Page 276: Cadillac: author's interview with Paturel.

Pages 277-278: Background on the death of Abe Zimmerman: family friends in Hibbing, including Hoikkala and Angel Marolt, who bought the Zimmerman home from Beatty Zimmerman; family members who wish to remain anonymous; friends of David Zimmerman and Leventhal. Paturel described the day Dylan received news of his father's death. Additional background: *No Direction Home* (including Dylan's comment to Leventhal, 'I never knew my father.').

Page 278: Kegan quotation: author's interview.

Pages 278-279: Dylan quotation – 'How was school . . .' – *Sing Out!* (Oct–Nov 1968).

Page 279: With McClure: author's interview with McClure.

Pages 279-280: Birth of Samuel Dylan from birth records; interview with McClure; assistance from members of Dylan family. Conversation with Naomi Saltzman, background on Naomi Saltzman, and her quotation ('He couldn't believe it . . .'): her December 17, 1981, deposition, made in New York, in the case Albert B. Grossman et al. vs. Bob Dylan (Case #14403/81).

Page 280: Dylan quotation – 'I went to the only lawyer that I knew' – Dylan's October 15, 1984, deposition in the case Albert B. Grossman et al. vs. Bob Dylan (Case #14403/81).

Pages 280-281: Thanksgiving and the Dylan and Dorfman quotations: author's interviews with Dorfman. (Hoffenberg story was related to the author by Jonathan Taplin.)

Page 282: Background on Preminger meeting from *The Mansion on the Hill* by Fred Goodman, author's interviews with Seeger, and Seeger's book *Where Have all the Flowers Gone*.

Pages 282-284: Background on *Nashville Skyline*: author's interviews with Buttrey, Daniels, Johnston, and McCoy.

Page 282: Dylan quotation – 'Bongos' – author's interview with Buttrey.

Page 283: Dylan quotation – 'I begged and pleaded with him . . .' – *Biograph* liner notes (Special Rider Music, 1985).

Page 283: Johnston quotations: author's interviews.

Page 284: McCoy quotation: author's interview.

Page 284: Background on Big Sky Music: papers in the Albert B. Grossman et al. vs. Bob Dylan case file (Case #14403/81). Braun's quotations – 'kind of a palliative' etc. – are from his November 17, 1981, deposition in this case.

Page 285: Johnston quotation: author's interview.

Page 285: Daniels quotation: author's interview.

Page 285: Dylan quotation – 'joke' – *Rolling Stone* (June 21, 1984).

Page 285: Dylan quotation – 'It was just as well' etc. – Dylan's October 6, 1981, deposition in the case Albert B. Grossman et al. vs. Bob Dylan (Case #14403/81).

Page 286: Edgin quotation: author's interview.

Page 286: Presley background: author's interviews with Edgin, Johnston, Kirkham, and Moore.

Page 286: Johnston quotation: author's interview.

Page 286: Dylan–Lewis dialogue – 'Man, maybe we could do . . .' – author's interview with Johnston.

Pages 286-287: Cash show: author's interviews with Buttrey, Kershaw, and Walker.

Page 287: Walker quotations: author's interviews.

Page 287: Buttrey quotations: author's interviews.

Pages 287-289: Problems with fans in Woodstock were described in interviews with the author by former members of the Woodstock constabulary, including Bill Waterous and Charlie Wolven, and friends of Dylan, including Dorfman and Paturel. Additional background from Dylan's comments in *Spin* (December 1985).

Page 288: Paturel quotation: author's interview.

Page 288: Dorfman quotations: author's interviews.

Page 288: Dylan quotation – 'What are . . .' – author's interview with Dorfman.

Page 288: Waterous quotations: author's interviews.

Page 289: Wolven quotations: author's interviews.

Page 289: Dylan quotation – 'big brass bed' – 'Lay, Lady, Lay' (Big Sky Music, 1969).

Pages 289-290: Ohayo Mountain Road house: Woodstock town records; author's interviews with neighbor Beeh; author's tour of house courtesy of current owner.

Page 290: Beeh quotation: author's interview.

Pages 290-291: The Band: author's interviews with The Band; background from *This Wheel's on Fire*.

Page 291: Helm quotation: author's interview.

Page 291: Diet Coke deal was reported in *Rolling Stone* (April 21, 1994). Background on The Band copyrights comes from court documents in the case Albert B. Grossman et al. vs. Bob Dylan (Case #14403/81) and author's discussions with members of The Band and their advisers.

Page 291: Danko quotation: author's interview.

Pages 291-292: Background on bootlegging of Basement Tapes: *Rolling Stone* articles (June 22, 1968; September 20, 1969); *Invisible Republic* by Greil Marcus.

Page 292: Quotation from bootlegger Patrick is from *Rolling Stone* magazine (September 20, 1969). Rosen, general manager of Bob Dylan's publishing, confirmed in a declaration for a legal case the extent of the problem of pirating of Dylan work (Victor Maymudes vs. East-West Touring Company et al., Los Angeles Superior Court/Case

#BC 189007). In support of the defense of this case, Frank Creighton, a senior executive at the RIAA, made a statement about Dylan being the most bootlegged artist in the history of the music industry.

Page 292: In *This Wheel's on Fire*, Helm writes about Robertson overdubbing guitar parts on the *The Basement Tapes*, as released by Columbia in 1975.

Page 293: Glover quotation: author's interview.

Page 293: Dylan quotation – 'outrageous' – *Biograph* liner notes.

Pages 293-294: The Fire Island stories: author's interviews with Amram and Paxton.

Page 294: Hibbing reunion and quotes: author's interviews with Davich, Helstrom, and Marolt.

Page 294: Chart Busters and Jack Smith story revealed by Dylan in his October 6, 1981, court deposition (Case #14403/81).

Page 295: Victor Basil salon: author's discussion with Basil.

Pages 294-296: Background on the Woodstock Festival: interviews with local people, stars of the festival, and passages in Woodstock and *The Rolling Stone Illustrated History of Rock 'n' Roll.*

Page 295: Waterous's quotation: author's interview.

Page 295: Dorfman-Dylan quotations – '*I'm* not . . .' – author's interviews with Dorfman.

Page 296: Dylan quotation – 'That Woodstock Festival . . .' – *Rolling Stone* (June 21, 1984).

Page 296: Gravy quotations: author's interviews.

Pages 296-299: Background on the Isle of Wight concert comes principally from author's interviews with Aronowitz, The Band members, Foulk, and Paxton. The London *Daily Sketch* reported (August 16, 1969) that the Dylan family had been due to sail on the QE2 the previous day; the author also spoke with a confidential source. The *Daily Express* reported (August 14, 1969) that Dylan would play for three hours. *The Morning Star* (August 30, 1969) suggested musicians including members of The Rolling Stones might join him on stage. The couple making love and '*Freaky*, baby!' were reported in *Rolling Stone* (October 4, 1969).

Page 297: Taplin quotation: author's interview.

Page 298: Dylan quotations – 'That is a great idea' etc. – author's interview with Foulk.

Page 299: Foulk quotation: author's interview.

Page 300: Birth of Jakob Dylan is from birth certificates, and assistance from members of the Dylan family.

Chapter 7: On The Road Again

Primary sources are author's interviews, correspondence, and discussions with: David Amram, Joel Bernstein, Ronee Blakley, Henry 'T-Bone' Burnett, Kenny Buttrey, John Cohen, Paul Colby, Ron Cornelius, Charlie Daniels, the late Rick Danko, Bruce Dorfman, Ramblin' Jack Elliott, Barry Feinstein, Erik Frandsen, Dana Gillespie, Robert F. Goheen, Gary Goldstein, Nick Gravenites, Sally Grossman, Arlo Guthrie, Ronnie Hawkins, Levon Helm, Jim Horn, Neil Hubbard, Garth Hudson, Bob Johnston, Al Kooper, Bruce Langhorne, Harold Leventhal, Jacques Levy, George Lois, David Mansfield, Paul Martinson, Michael McClure, Charlie McCoy, Roger McGuinn, Jim Mullen, Gloria Naftali, Bobby Neuwirth, Tony O'Malley, Peter Ostroushko, Bernard Paturel, Billy Peterson, Larry Poons, Scarlet Rivera, Robbie Robertson, Arthur Rosato, Ed Sanders, Sam Shepard, Larry 'Ratso' Sloman, Steven Soles, Patrick Stansfield, Maeretha Stewart, Rob Stoner, Jonathan Taplin, David C. Towbin, Happy Traum, Dave Van Ronk, Bill Walker, and A. J. Weberman.

Pages 301-302: Details of the July 1970 Agreement are from a copy of the agreement. Additional background from papers in the case Albert B. Grossman et al. vs. Bob Dylan (Case #14403/81).

Page 302: Dylan quotation – 'I was willing to enter into the July 1970 . . .' – Dylan's October 15, 1984, deposition in the case, Albert B. Grossman et al. vs. Bob Dylan (Case #14403/81).

Page 302: Lectern: author's interview with Paturel.

Page 302: Details of Braun's break with Grossman are from his November 17, 1981, deposition in Albert B. Grossman et al. vs. Bob Dylan (Case #14403/81). He said: 'Bob was unhappy that I was doing some work [for] Albert, and asked me to make a choice.' Braun quote – 'I don't think . . .' – *The Mansion on the Hill* by Fred Goodman.

Pages 302-303: Gravenites quotation: author's interview.

Page 303: Details of the Peter Yarrow court case are from court reports in the (London) *Evening News* (September 15, 1970) and *News of the World* (September 20, 1970).

Pages 303-308: Background on *Self Portrait–New Morning* sessions: author's interviews with musicians including Buttrey, Cornelius, Daniels, Kooper, McCoy, Stewart, and Walker.

Page 303: McCoy quotation: author's interview.

Page 303: Buttrey quotation: author's interview.

Page 304: Walker quotation: author's interview.

Page 304: Daniels quotation; author's interview.

Page 304: Harrison: It has been claimed, in *Bob Dylan: Behind the Shades – Take Two* by Clinton Heylin and elsewhere, that Harrison plays on 'Went to See the Gypsy' on *New Morning.* But others dispute this and there is no credit on the album. In an interview with the author, Daniels said Harrison had a visa problem that meant he could not be seen to be contributing to the project.

Page 305: Cornelius quotations: author's interviews.

Pages 305-306: Details of the Princeton ceremony are from the author's correspondence with Robert F. Goheen. Crosby told *The Telegraph* in 1993 (issue 45) that he was the man whose head was exploding: 'I got Dylan incredibly high on some killer weed.'

Page 306: Dylan quotation – 'head was exploding' – 'Day of the Locusts' (Big Sky Music, 1970).

Page 306: Dylan quotation – 'concrete world full of souls' – 'Three Angels' (Big Sky Music, 1970).

Page 306: Daniels quotation: author's interview.

Page 306: Stewart quotation: author's interview.

Page 306: Dylan was quoted in *Rolling Stone* (June 21, 1984) saying *Self Portrait* was a 'joke'.

Page 306: Marcus quotation – 'What is this shit?' – *Rolling Stone* (July 23, 1970).

Page 307: Johnston quotation: author's interview.

Page 307: Dylan–Cohen conversation: author's interviews with Cornelius and a confidential source.

Page 307: Cornelius quotations: author's interviews.

Page 308: Gleason review of *New Morning: Rolling Stone* (November 26, 1970).

Page 308: Dylan quotation – 'I wasn't going to fall for that . . .' – *Bob Dylan* by Anthony Scaduto.

Pages 309-315: Information on Weberman (and quotations from Weberman) are principally from author's interviews with Weberman. The exchanges between Dylan and Weberman are from the profile of Weberman published in *Rolling Stone* (March 4, 1971). The author consulted various articles by and about Weberman, including his essay in *International Times* (January 1971); the essay by Roberts in *The Telegraph* (issue 51); and the John Bauldie essay in *All Across the Telegraph*. Dylan was quoted in *No Direction Home: The Life and Music of Bob Dylan* by Robert Shelton as saying he had loaded his garbage with dog excrement and mousetraps. Weberman quotation – 'Dylan's sold out!' – *No Direction Home.*

Page 309: 'Bookleg' quotation from *The Telegraph* (issue 51).

Page 309: Colby quotation: author's interview.

Page 310: Dylan quotation – 'bundle of joy' – 'Down Along the Cove' (Dwarf Music, 1968).

Page 313: Dylan quotations – 'I doubt if they'd really . . .' and 'pure journalese' – *Jerusalem Post* (June 4, 1971).

Page 313: Leventhal quotation: author's interview.

Page 313: Dorfman quotation: author's interview.

Pages 313-314: Background on the *Concert for Bangladesh*: articles in *International Times* (October 21, 1971); *New York Times Magazine* (November 28, 1971); and *Rolling Stone* (September 2, 1971). Also live recordings and concert footage.

Page 314: Horn quotation: author's interview.

Page 315: Neighbor problems and Naftali quotation: author's interview with Naftali.

Page 316: Ginsberg apartment: author's interviews with Amram, who reported Ginsberg's quote: 'Bob, the key of G!'

Page 316: Amram quotations: author's interviews.

Pages 316-317: Ginsberg sessions: author's interviews with Amram, Sanders, and Traum.

Page 316: Sanders quotation: author's interview.

Page 316: Traum quotations: author's interviews.

Page 317: Grateful Dead meeting: author's interview with Weir.

Page 318: Mariposa and Cohen quotations: author's interview with Cohen.

Pages 318-320: Background on *Pat Garrett & Billy the Kid* and Kristofferson's quotation: *'If They Move . . . Kill 'Em!': The Life and Times of Sam Peckinpah* by David Weddle. Dylan described his wife's unhappiness in Mexico in the *Biograph* liner notes (Special Rider Music, 1985).

Page 320: Langhorne quotation: author's interview.

Page 321: Background on the Geffen deal and Tour '74: depositions in the Albert B. Grossman et al. vs. Bob Dylan court case (#14403/81); Robertson quotes are from author's interview. The Geffen quote 'This event . . .' is from *Newsweek* (January 14, 1974); ticket sales are from *Rolling Stone* (February 14, 1974) and *Time* (January 21, 1974). Also *This Wheel's on Fire* by Levon Helm, in which Helm writes about the investments. Geffen quote – 'Bob Dylan has . . .' – *Rolling Stone* (December 12, 1974). Background on Geffen: *David Geffen: A Biography of New Hollywood*, by Tom King; *The Rise and Rise of David Geffen* by Stephen Singular; and *The Mansion on the Hill.*

Page 321: Hudson quotation: author's interview.

Page 321: Dylan spoke in *Biograph* liner notes about writing 'Forever Young' for one of his sons.

Page 322: Keats quotation – 'For ever panting . . .' – 'Ode on a Grecian Urn.'

Page 322: Dylan quotation – 'babies one, two . . .' – 'Wedding Song' (Ram's Horn Music, 1973, 1974).

Page 322: Dylan quotation – 'I hate myself . . .' – 'Dirge' (Ram's Horn Music, 1973, 1974).

Page 323: Dylan quotation – 'One foot . . .' – improvised lyric to 'Hero Blues' (Warner Bros., Inc., 1963) reported in *No Direction Home.*

Page 323: Robertson quotations: author's interview.

Page 324: Feinstein quotation: author's interview.

Page 324: Dylan described his feelings of deflation after Tour '74 in *Biograph* liner notes.

Pages 325-327: Details of Dylan's property at Point Dume are principally from the author's interview with David C. Towbin; also from Los Angeles County Assessor's Records. Dylan was quoted in *Playboy* (February, 1978) saying, 'The copper dome is just so I can recognize it when I come home.' I also referred to interviews with various visitors to the house.

Page 326: Dylan quotations – 'I want my . . .' and 'ride a horse . . .' – author's interview with Towbin.

Pages 327-329: Taplin quotation: author's interview.

Pages 327-328: Primary information on Raeben is from the author's interview with Levy. Background and Raeben's reported speech: Cartwright's essay in *Wanted Man: The Search for Bob Dylan.*

Page 328: Levy quotation: author's interview.

Page 328: Dylan quotations – 'more powerful . . .' and 'I went home after . . .' – *Dallas Morning News* (November 27, 1978) reprinted in *Wanted Man.*

Page 328: Friends of Chile benefit: author's interviews with Guthrie, Seeger, and Van Ronk.

Page 328: Guthrie quotation: author's interview.

Page 329: Bernstein's relationship with Bob Dylan, when they met, her age, and the reference to Ashtabula: *Bob Dylan: Behind the Shades – Take Two.* References to Bernstein's relationship with Dylan also appear in other books by Heylin, including *Dylan: Behind the Shades* and *Bob Dylan: The Recording Sessions 1960–1994.*

Pages 329-330: Tyrangiel's alleged relationship with Dylan: 1995 lawsuit Ruth Tyrangiel vs. Bob Dylan filed at Los

Angeles Superior Court (Case #BC 115656). The author also spoke with Tyrangiel's former attorney, Gary Goldstein, and her palimony adviser Marvin Mitchelson. Tyrangiel's quote – 'nurse, confidante . . .': is from a deposition she gave on April 4, 1995. Tyrangiel's case was dismissed.

Page 330: Background on farm: author's interviews with confidential family sources.

Page 331: Dylan spoke about the painterly songwriting method in various interviews, and *Biograph* liner notes (in which he also denies the songs were about his own marriage).

Page 331: Dylan quotation – 'as the evening sky . . .' – 'Simple Twist of Fate' (Ram's Horn Music, 1974, 1975).

Page 331: Dylan quotation – 'Like a corkscrew . . .' – 'You're a Big Girl Now' (Ram's Horn Music, 1974, 1975).

Page 331: Dylan quotation – 'lucky' – 'Idiot Wind' (Ram's Horn Music, 1974, 1975).

Page 331: Ashtabula: Bob Dylan: *Behind the Shades – Take Two*.

Page 332: Dylan quotation – 'sinkin' like a ship' – 'Tangled Up in Blue' (Ram's Horn Music, 1974, 1975).

Pages 332-334: Background on Minneapolis *Blood on the Tracks* sessions: author's interviews with Martinson, Ostroushko, and Peterson.

Page 333: Dylan said in *Biograph* liner notes that the *Blood on the Tracks* songs were not autobiographical. Jakob Dylan's quotation – 'my parents . . .' – *Rolling Stone* (June 12, 1997).

Page 333: Dylan quotation – 'You have a nice way . . .' – author's interview with Martinson.

Page 333: Peterson quotation: author's interview.

Pages 333-334: Ostroushko: author's interview.

Page 334: Dylan quotation – 'There's a kind . . .' – author's interview with Ostroushko.

Page 334: Dylan told Mary Travers in a 1975 radio interview that he could not understand how people enjoyed the pain of *Blood on the Tracks*.

Page 334: Gillespie show: author's interview with Gillespie.

Page 334: Sara at San Francisco benefit: author's interview with Tim Drummond, who played guitar with Dylan on stage.

Page 335: Oppenheim quotation – 'completely despairing . . .' – *4th Time Around* (issue 1), reprinted in *Dylan: Behind the Shades*.

Pages 335-336: Levy meeting and quotations: interviews with the author.

Page 336: Dylan quotations – 'You know, I'd like . . .' and 'Would you like . . .' – author's interview with Levy.

Pages 336-338: Background about the Rubin Carter case comes from author's interviews with Lois; *Lazarus and the Hurricane* by Sam Chaiton and Terry Swinton, and Carter's memoir *The Sixteenth Round*. The quotation 'cop-hating, cracker-hating' is from *The Sixteenth Round*.

Page 338: Dylan quotation – 'champion of the world' – 'Hurricane' (Ram's Horn Music, 1975).

Page 339: Rivera meeting and quotations: author's interviews with Rivera.

Page 339: Dylan quotation – 'Can you play . . .' – author's interviews with Rivera.

Pages 339-340: Background on the *Desire* sessions is from author's interviews with Frandsen, Mullen, Rivera, and Stoner; and information in *Tangled Up in Tapes* by Glen Dundas (identifying that it was Studio 'E'). The Don De Vito quote – 'Okay, guys . . .' – is from author's interviews with members of Kokomo.

Page 339: Mullen quotation: author's interview with Mullen.

Page 340: Dylan quotation – 'Don't ever leave me . . .' – 'Sara' (Ram's Horn Music, 1975, 1976).

Page 340: Levy quotation: author's interview.

Page 341: Stoner quotations: author's interviews.

Pages 341-355: Background on Rolling Thunder Revue: author's interviews with Blakley, Burnett, Colby, Elliott, Hawkins, Levy, Mansfield, McGuinn, Poons, Rivera, Shepard, Sloman, Soles, and Stoner. Additional background on The Rolling Thunder Revue is from articles by Hentoff and Sloman in *Rolling Stone*, and books by

Shepard and Sloman. Baez wrote in her memoir, *And a Voice to Sing With*, that she learned 'Never Let Me Go' as a child. She also wrote about wanting more money on the second leg of the tour; about Dylan kneeling before his wife in a state of distress; about her friendship with Sara Dylan; and about Bob wanting to keep the tour going.

Page 341: Dylan quotation – 'Bobby and I were talkin' . . .' – author's interview with Elliott.

Page 342: Poons loft and quotations: author's interview with Poons.

Page 342: Burnett quotations: author's interviews.

Page 342: Soles quotation: author's interview.

Page 343: Mansfield quotation: author's interview.

Page 343: Lois quotation: author's interview.

Page 343: Dylan quotation – 'We don't have to make any connections . . .' – *Rolling Thunder Logbook* by Sam Shepard (and dialogue with Dylan).

Pages 343-344: Shepard quotation: author's interview.

Page 344: Ratso nickname: author's interview with Sloman.

Page 345: Van Ronk quotation: author's interview.

Page 345: Blakley quotation: author's interview.

Page 345: Gordon Lightfoot fire: author's discussion with Neuwirth.

Page 345: Stoner and Elliott on cocaine: author's interview.

Page 346: Sloman quotation: author's interview.

Page 346: Dylan quotation – 'Yeah, but will . . .' – author's interview with Joel Bernstein.

Page 346: Levy quotations: author's interview.

Page 347: Burnett quotation: author's interview.

Page 347: Rivera quotation: author's interview.

Page 347: Dylan quotation – 'about a marriage' – recording of the December 4, 1975, show in Montreal.

Page 347: Dylan quotation – 'Yes!' – 'Isis' (Ram's Horn Music, 1975, 1976), as improvised at the Montreal show.

Page 347: Stoner quotation: author's interview.

Page 348: Blakley quotation – 'this goddamn movie' – interview with *The Telegraph* (issue 41).

Page 348: Rivera quotation: author's interview.

Page 349: Dylan quotation – 'Who's this guy . . .' – author's interview with Stoner.

Page 349: All record sales are from the Recording Industry Association of America, and are sales in the United States only.

Page 350: Blakley–Ronson dialogue: author's interview with Blakley.

Page 350: Rivera on Dylan: author's interview.

Page 350: Blakley quotation: author's interview.

Page 350: Background on Dylan's marital problems is from interviews with various friends. Mel Howard wrote an article in *The Telegraph* (issue 46) making reference to Dylan's failing marriage.

Page 350: Hawkins conversation and other *Renaldo & Clara* dialogue: transcribed from *Renaldo & Clara* (Lombard Street Films, Inc., 1977).

Page 351: In correspondence with the author, Sara Dylan's cousin Anne Noznisky said Dylan named Lombard Street Films after the street where Sara was born.

Page 351: Dylan quotation – 'I married . . .' – *Renaldo & Clara.*

Page 351: Figures for the benefit concerts: *Rolling Stone* (March 24, 1977).

Page 352: Lois quotation: author's interview.

Page 352: Tent story is from interviews with Clapton and Ronnie Wood for *The Telegraph*, reprinted in *Wanted Man.*

Pages 352-353: Elliott quotation: author's interview.

Page 353: Baez money: *And a Voice to Sing With.*

Page 353: Decline and death of Ochs is based on author's interviews with Colby, Van Ronk, and others; also *There But for Fortune: The Life of Phil Ochs* by Michael Schumacher.

Page 353: Sonny Ochs quotation – 'If Dylan really . . .' – *Bringing It All Back Home* by Robbie Woliver.

Page 353: Stoner quotation: author's interview.

Page 354: Buffington is identified as being one of Dylan's girlfriends in *Bob Dylan: Behind the Shades – Take Two.*

Page 354: Dylan and Sara: *And a Voice to Sing With.*

Page 354: Levy revealed the fight between the Dylans in New Orleans; background from the interview with Revue staff member Mike Evans in *The Telegraph* (issue 49). Additional background material is from *The Telegraph* (issues 33, 42, 45, and 49) and *On the Tracks.*

Pages 354-355: Mansfield quotations: author's interview.

Page 355: Joel Bernstein related the story about Dylan writing the lyrics of 'Lily, Rosemary and the Jack of Hearts' on his cuff.

Pages 356-357: Backstage details of *The Last Waltz* are from author's interviews with members of The Band. Also: Bernstein, Hawkins, McClure, Stansfield, and Taplin, who related the Neil Young story (also reported in *This Wheel's on Fire*).

Chapter 8: Faith

Primary sources are author's interviews, correspondence, and discussions with: Mary Alice Artes, Joel Bernstein, Joanna Bull, Henry 'T-Bone' Burnett, Billy Cross, Jones Cullinan (née Alk), Ethel Crystal, Tim Drummond, Pastor Bill Dwyer, Debi Dye-Gibson, Harvey Goldsmith, Pastor Kenn Gulliksen, Bobbye Hall, Jo Ann Harris, Ronnie Hawkins, Bob Johnston, Larry Kegan, Jim Keltner, Mark Knopfler, Al Kooper, Danny Kortchmar, Tony Lane, Harold Leventhal, David Mansfield, Faridi McFree, Marvin M. Mitchelson, Maria Muldaur, Dewey Lyndon 'Spooner' Oldham, Graham Parker, Alan Pasqua, Regina Peoples, Ted Perlman, Chuck Plotkin, Scarlet Rivera, Arthur Rosato, Howard Rutman, Janine Signorelli, Steven Soles, Patrick Stansfield, Rob Stoner, David C. Towbin, Ian Wallace, Jennifer Warnes, Dave and Ubi Whitaker, and Monalisa and Terry Young.

Page 358: Cost of remodeling the Point Dume house was given by architect David C. Towbin. Dylan's lawyer, Braun, described the incident in which black paint was sprayed on the windows in a court deposition (January 1, 1977). The incident was also reported in *Rolling Stone* (May 5, 1977). The lawsuit brought by the Dylans' neighbors at Point Dume is from the case papers of Stanley R. Primmer and Maria Primmer vs. Robert Dylan and Sarah [sic] Dylan. (Case #C173237) filed on September 10, 1976, at the Los Angeles Superior Court. The case was dismissed in 1978.

Pages 358-363: Details of Dylan's divorce from Sara Dylan are from the author's interviews with Marvin M. Mitchelson and Faridi McFree and the judgment and case register of Dylan vs. Dylan (Case #WED31404) held at the Superior Court of Los Angeles County, Los Angeles, California. Sara Dylan's allegations and quotations on the subject are from a statement she made in application for a restraining order against Dylan. The statement was made available to the press and reported in *Rolling Stone* (May 5, 1977) and elsewhere. The author also referred to reports of the case in the *New York Times*, *San Francisco Chronicle*, and other publications. Mitchelson related his conversation with Geffen, who declined to be interviewed.

Pages 359-365: Mitchelson quotations: author's interviews.

Page 360: Alk quotation – 'I realized he . . .' – author's interview with Joel Bernstein.

Pages 360-366: McFree background and quotations: author's interviews.

Page 361: Dylan quotation – 'No, I'm not . . .' and subsequent quotes in relation to McFree: author's interview with McFree.

Page 362: Considered suicide: author's interview with McFree.

Pages 362-363: Soles quotation: author's interview.

Page 363: Dylan quotation – 'I had a breakdown . . .' – *Melody Maker* (July 29, 1978).

Page 365: Normal life for Dylan children: author's discussions with family members and friends including a former school friend of Maria Dylan, Janine Signorelli.

Page 365: Dylan quotation – 'Marriage was a failure . . .' – *Rolling Stone* (June 12, 1997).

Page 365: Details of the incident involving Burke were reported in *Dylan: A Biography* by Bob Spitz.

Pages 365-366: Jakob Dylan quotation – 'I can honestly say . . .' – *Rolling Stone* (June 12, 1997).

Pages 366-367: Details on the release of *Renaldo & Clara* are from various interviews Dylan gave in January 1978 to promote the film. Pauline Kael's review – 'overpoweringly present . . .' – *The New Yorker* (February 13, 1978). The $1.25 million cost of *Renaldo & Clara* was reported in the *Los Angeles Times* (January 22, 1978).

Page 366: Dylan quotation – 'It's about the essence . . .' – *Playboy* (February 1978).

Page 367: Dylan quotation – 'I've got a few . . .' – *Los Angeles Times* (May 28, 1978).

Pages 367-377: Background on 1978 tour: author's interviews with Cross, Dye-Gibson, Hall, Harris, Mansfield, Soles, Stansfield, Stoner, and Wallace.

Page 367: Stansfield quotation: author's interview.

Page 367: Bobbye Hall pay: author's interview.

Page 368: Dye-Gibson quotations: author's interview.

Pages 368-370: Cross quotation: author's interview.

Pages 368-369: Bernstein quotations: author's interview.

Page 369: Dylan quotation – 'Can you cook and sew . . .' – 'Is Your Love in Vain?' (Special Rider Music, 1978). Parody lyric: author's interview with Dye-Gibson.

Page 369: Dylan quotation – 'street' – author's interviews with Dye-Gibson.

Page 370: Ra Aranga relationship: *All Across the Telegraph.*

Page 370: Hall quotation: author's interview.

Page 371: Soles quotation: author's interview.

Page 371: Stoner firing: author's interview

Page 371: Dye-Gibson leaves tour: author's interviews.

Page 371: Background on Dennis is from interviews with her friends, and family records. The quotation – 'I have [to] say . . .' – *Follow that Dream International* (December 1992), a Bruce Springsteen fanzine, posted on the Internet.

Page 371: The fact that *Street-Legal* was the first in Dylan's new contract with Columbia is reported in *Bob Dylan: Behind The Shades – Take Two* by Clinton Heylin.

Page 372: Napoleon cafe: author's interview with owner, Shawn Nadery.

Page 372: Formation of Special Rider Music is from

documents in the case Albert B. Grossman et al. vs. Bob Dylan (Case #14403/81).

Page 372: In an interview with the author, Debi Dye-Gibson said she thought 'New Pony' was about Springs.

Page 373: Dylan quotation – 'long-distance train rolling . . .' – 'Where Are You Tonight? (Journey Through Dark Heat)' (Special Rider Music, 1978).

Page 373: Pasqua quotation: author's interview.

Page 373: Marcus review – 'utterly fake' – *Rolling Stone* (August, 1978), as reported in *Dylan: A Biography*.

Page 373: Goldsmith quotation: author's interview.

Page 373: Vicious meeting: author's interview with Stoner.

Page 374: Jones quotation: author's interview with Jones.

Page 374: Mansfield quotation: author's interview.

Page 374: Audience figures for Blackbushe are from the author's interview with promoter Goldsmith and reflect tickets sold rather than estimates of the crowd size as reported in the press.

Page 374: Dylan quotation – 'I really love that song . . .' – author's interview with Parker.

Page 375: Parker quotation: author's interview with Parker.

Page 375: Wallace quotations: author's interview.

Pages 375-376: Stansfield quotations: author's interview.

Page 376: Harris quotations: author's interview.

Page 376: Hall quotation: author's interview.

Page 377: Wallace quotation: author's interview.

Pages 377-381: Background on Dylan's conversion is from author's interviews with his pastors Dwyer and Gulliksen; author's conversation with Artes; and interviews with various band members and friends.

Page 377: Springs spoke about telling Dylan about prayer in an interview printed in *Wanted Man: In Search of Bob Dylan*.

Page 377: Burnett quotation: author's interview.

Page 378: Ubi Whitaker: author's interviews with Dave and Ubi Whitaker.

Page 378: Dylan spoke about the San Diego show in 1978 during an address to the audience in San Diego on November 27, 1979. The fact that he played 'Slow Train Coming' on

December 2, 1978, is reported as part of a set list in *Tangled Up in Tapes* by Glen Dundas.

Page 378: 'Slow Train Coming': author's interview with Cross.

Page 378: Dylan quotation – 'this *vision and feeling*' – *Los Angeles Times* (November 25, 1980).

Pages 378-381: Vineyard Fellowship background and Gulliksen quotations: author's interviews with Gulliksen.

Page 379: Myers quotations – 'Sometime in the next . . .' – letter by Myers reprinted in *On the Tracks* (issue #4/ Fall 1994).

Page 379: Artes quotation: author's discussion with Artes.

Page 380: Dylan quotations – 'I couldn't believe . . .' and 'I truly had . . .' – *Los Angeles Times* (November 25, 1980). NB: Dylan denied using the phrase 'born-again' in his interview with *Rolling Stone* (June 21, 1984).

Page 380: Dwyer quotation: author's interview with Dwyer.

Page 380: Dylan quotation – 'The songs are . . .' – *Sing Out!* (Oct–Nov 1962).

Page 381: Crystal quotation: author's interview.

Page 381: Dylan children: author's interview with confidential source.

Pages 381-384: Background on *Slow Train Coming*: author's interviews with Drummond and Knopfler.

Pages 381-382: Wexler quotation – 'You're dealing . . .' – *Rolling Stone* (November 27, 1980).

Page 382: Dylan said in an interview with the *Los Angeles Times* (November 25, 1980) that he considered giving the *Slow Train Coming* songs to Dennis.

Page 382: Knopfler quotations: author's interview.

Page 382: Dylan quotation – 'Mark does me . . .' – *Rhythm and the Blues* by Jerry Wexler.

Page 382: Dylan quotation – 'a thousand miles . . .' – 'I Believe in You' (Special Rider Music, 1979).

Page 383: 'Man Gave Names to All the Animals': Havis's interview in *On the Tracks* (issue 18).

Page 383: Gulliksen quotation: author's interview.

Page 383: *Slow Train Coming* cover and Lane quotation: author's interview with Lane.

Page 383: Wenner review – 'Faith is the message . . .' – *Rolling Stone* (September 20, 1979).

Pages 383-384: Drummond told the author that Wexler did not want 'Gotta Serve Somebody' on the album. Album sales are from the Recording Industry Association of America. Single chart positions are from *The Billboard Book of Top Forty Hits*.

Pages 384-386: Keltner quotations: author's interviews.

Page 384: Tour band background: author's interviews with Drummond, Keltner, Oldham, and the Youngs.

Page 384: Oldham quotation: author's interview.

Pages 384-385: Monalisa Young related to the author the story about praying for Dylan's sore throat.

Pages 385-386: Description of the Warfield shows are drawn from interviews with band members – principally Keltner – and from Paul Williams's account in his book *Bob Dylan: Performing Artist (The Middle Years)*; Joe Selvin's review of the Fox Warfield shows appeared in the *San Francisco Chronicle* (November 3, 1979). The readers' letter is from the November 9 edition.

Page 386: Dylan quotation – 'I went out on tour . . .' – Spin (December,1985).

Pages 386-387: Muldaur meeting and quotations: author's interviews.

Page 387: Gulliksen quotation: author's interview.

Page 388: Dylan quotation – 'filthy . . .' – *Biograph* liner notes (Special Rider Music, 1985).

Page 388: Dylan quotation – 'higher learnin' people' – remarks to audience in Toronto, Canada (April 20, 1980).

Page 388: Dylan quotation – 'rock 'n' roll . . .' – remarks to audience in Tempe, Arizona (November 26, 1979).

Page 388: Dylan quote – 'End Times' – comments made at the Santa Monica Civic Auditorium in 1979, reported in *Dylan: Behind the Shades* by Clinton Heylin.

Page 389: Dylan quotation – 'What are they standing . . .' – author's interviews with Drummond.

Page 389: Dylan quotation – 'I didn't . . .' – transcript of 1980 Grammy Awards.

Page 389: Leventhal quotation: author's interview.

Page 390: Rutman quotations: author's interview.

Page 390: Dylan quotation – 'Howard, I'm . . .' – author's interview with Rutman.

Page 391: Ronnie Wood said in an interview reprinted in *Wanted Man: In Search of Bob Dylan* that Richards referred to Dylan's Christian period as his 'prophet of profit' days.

Page 391: Hawkins quotation: author's interview.

Page 391: Dylan quotation – 'You don't hear much about God . . .' – *Village Voice* (May 19, 1980).

Page 391: Dylan quotation – 'working all kinds . . .' – reported in *Bob Dylan: A Life in Stolen Moments: Day by Day: 1941–1995* by Clinton Heylin.

Page 392: Dylan was quoted in *Songwriters on Songwriting* saying 'Every Grain of Sand' is 'in that area where Keats is . . . That's a good poem set to music.'

Page 392: Warnes quotation: author's interview.

Page 392: Dylan quotation – 'Okay, let's try . . .' – author's interview with Warnes.

Page 393: Bloomfield quotation – 'Give me two weeks . . .' – related to the author by Drummond.

Page 393: Background on the deaths of Bloomfield and Lennon: *The Encyclopedia of Rock Obituaries*.

Page 393: Perlman quotation: author's interview.

Page 393: Drummond quotation: author's interview.

Pages 394, 400-403: Information about Carmel Hubbell, aka Carmel Dylan, and her quoted remarks are drawn from a petition for injunction against harassment and temporary restraining order (Case #C373003) brought against Carmel Hubbell by Dylan and employees of his Music Touring Co., Inc., in 1981, together with associated statements, exhibits, and correspondence. The file is held at Los Angeles Superior Court. Dialogue between Helena Springs and Carmel Hubbell is from a June 21, 1981, L.A. Sheriff's Department police report of threatening phone calls to Ms. Springs's home.

Page 394: Dylan quotation – 'I've made a lot of . . .' – author's interview with Plotkin.

Page 395: Dylan quotation – 'I get chills . . .' – *Biograph* liner notes.

Page 395: Dylan described his thoughts behind 'Caribbean Wind' in *Biograph* liner notes.

Page 396: Studio 55 sessions: author's interviews with Drummond.

Page 396: Dylan quotation – 'I'm gonna . . .' – author's interview with Drummond.

Page 396: Dylan quotations – 'Do you know . . .' and 'Would you . . .' – author's interview with Plotkin.

Pages 396-400: Clover sessions and Plotkin quotations: author's interview.

Pages 396-397: Dylan talked about the reasons Blackwell did not continue with the album in *Biograph* liner notes.

Pages 398-399: Keltner quotation: author's interview.

Page 399: Writing of 'Lenny Bruce': author's interview with Danny Kortchmar.

Page 399: Dylan quotations – 'Let me just . . .' and 'I didn't like . . .' – author's interview with Plotkin.

Pages 400-403: Information about Carmel Hubbell, aka Carmel Dylan, and her quoted remarks from papers in Case #C373003. This includes police records of conversation between Springs and Hubbell. The file is held at Los Angeles Superior Court. The author also referred to the case Jeanette Hanisee et al. vs. Carmel Dylan (Case #WEC O69637) filed at the Superior Court of the State of California, July 3, 1981.

Page 403: Dylan quotation – 'You have been paid enough' – October 6, 1981, deposition in the case Albert B. Grossman et al. vs. Bob Dylan (Case #14403/81). Background on the court case (Case #14403/81) is from the court papers. Grossman's quote – 'what I deserve' – is from Dylan's October 6, 1981, deposition in the case.

Page 404: Connolly's review – 'the greatest . . .' – (London) *Daily Mail* (June 16, 1978). Author also attended one.

Page 404: Avignon deaths and Stansfield quotations: author's interview with Stansfield.

Page 405: Dylan quotations – 'Bob Dylan, the writer,'

'something sneaky was going on,' 'I don't know, sir,' and 'It's a lot of money, huh?' – Dylan's October 6, 1981, deposition in the case Albert B. Grossman et al. vs. Bob Dylan (Case #14403/81).

Page 406: Kooper quotation: author's interview with Kooper.

Page 406: Kegan quotation: author's interview with Kegan.

Pages 406-408: Rosato quotations: author's interview with Rosato.

Pages 407-408: Information on Alk's death is from his death certificate, which states he died from 'acute heroin-morphine intoxication / injection of overdose'; and author's interviews with Rosato and Alk's first wife, Jones Alk.

Page 408: Jones Alk quotation: author's interviews

Chapter 9: Glimpses

Primary sources are author's interviews, correspondence, and discussions with: Kenny Aaronson, David Amram, Arthur Baker, William 'Bucky' Baxter, Louise Bethune, Peggi Blu, Oscar Brand, Nancy Carlen, Carole Childs, Liam Clancy, Carolyn Dennis, Sly Dunbar, Harvey Goldsmith, Wavy Gravy, 'Mean' Willie Green III, Sally Grossman, Arlo Guthrie, Ronnie Hawkins, J. J. Holiday, Steve Jones, Jim Keltner, Mark Knopfler, Al Kooper, Tony Lane, Harold Leventhal, George Lois, Angel Marolt, Maria Muldaur, Ted Perlman, Charlie Quintana, Susan Ross, Carole Bayer Sager, Paul Schrader, Gary Shafner, Sam Shepard, Larry 'Ratso' Sloman, Patrick Stansfield, Noel Paul Stookey, Brian Stoltz, Mick Taylor, Dave Van Ronk, Ian Wallace, Winston Watson, Bob Weir, and Dave Whitaker.

Page 409: David Amram and Oscar Brand described the Songwriters Hall of Fame evening.

Pages 409-410: Nancy Carlen described Dylan's meeting with Baez.

Page 410: Details of the Dylan-Grossman legal battle are from documents in the case (Case #14403/81) plus related documents filed in Los Angeles on March 23, 1982, (Case #WEC 072905).

Page 410: Dog attack story is from the lawsuit, John Reames vs. Robert Dylan et al. (Case #WEC 75836), filed in Los Angeles on October 5, 1982, and dismissed on April 4, 1983.

Pages 410-411: Childs meeting and quotations: author's interviews with Childs.

Page 411: MTV figures: *The Mansion on the Hill* by Fred Goodman.

Page 411-415: Background on *Infidels* sessions from author's interviews with Dunbar, Knopfler, Sloman, and Taylor.

Page 412: Dunbar quotations: author's interview.

Page 413: Dylan quotation – 'Because they . . .' – *Rolling Stone* (December, 1987).

Page 413: In 1983 there were press reports – (London) *Evening Standard* (June 10, 1983) and *Sun* (September 26, 1983), etc. – that Dylan had joined the Lubavitcher Hasidic sect in New York. Rabbi Kasriel Kastel quotation – 'As far as we're concerned . . .' – *Christianity Today* (1983), reprinted in *Dylan – Behind the Shades* by Clinton Heylin.

Page 414: Knopfler quotation: author's interview.

Page 414: Dylan quotations – 'Didn't make it' etc. – author's interview with Sloman.

Page 414: Dylan quotations – 'recorded it right' – *Rolling Stone* (June 21, 1984).

Pages 414-415: 'Jokerman' video: author's interviews with Lois and Sloman.

Pages 414-415: Dylan quotation – 'I know they're . . .' and 'When I saw the videos . . .' – *Rolling Stone* (December 5, 1985).

Page 415: Lois quotation: author's interview.

Pages 415-418: Background on Point Dume sessions and Letterman show: author's interviews with Holiday and Quintana. (Also quotations from Holiday and Quintana.)

Pages 415-416: Background on Point Dume estate: author's interviews with various visitors.

Pages 416-418: Holiday quotations: author's interview.

Page 416: Striptease show: Holiday interview with *The Telegraph* (issue 44).

Page 417: Dylan quotation – 'look cute and punky' – author's interview with Holiday.

Page 417: Letterman's quotation – 'a fine piece of work' – transcript of March 22, 1984, broadcast of *Late Night with David Letterman*.

Page 418: Taylor quotations: author's interview.

Page 418: McLagan wrote in his memoir, *All the Rage*, that the band had only a sketchy idea of the songs Dylan wanted to play.

Page 419: Dylan quotation – 'Wow, you got . . .' – *And a Voice to Sing With* by Joan Baez.

Page 419: Background on British and Irish shows: author attended.

Page 419: Goldsmith quotation: author's interview.

Pages 419-420: Dylan said in an interview for *Biograph* that the version of 'Tangled Up in Blue' on *Real Live* was closer to what he had originally intended.

Pages 420-423: Background on *Empire Burlesque*: author's interviews with Baker, Keltner, Kooper, Perlman, and Taylor.

Page 420: Film imagery: *Bob Dylan: Performing Artist: The Middle Years: 1974–1986* by Paul Williams. Drawing on an article in *The Telegraph* magazine, Williams identified film dialogue in various lyrics.

Pages 420-422: Baker quotations: author's interview.

Page 421: Baker told the author that Dylan thought the original version of 'When the Night Comes Falling from the Sky' sounded too much like Springsteen.

Page 421: Dylan quotation – 'I finally figured . . .' – *Icons* by Denise Worrell.

Page 421: Dylan quotation – 'a million faces' – 'Dark Eyes' (Special Rider Music, 1985).

Page 422: Keltner quotation: author's interview.

Page 422: Dylan quotation – 'We mixed the . . .' is from the author's interview with Arthur Baker.

Page 422: Dylan quotation – 'these films lying . . .' – author's interview with Schrader.

Pages 422-423: Schrader quotations: author's interview.

Page 422: Dylan told *Spin* magazine (December 1985) that 'Tight Connection to My Heart (Has Anybody Seen My Love)' was 'a very visual song . . . of all the songs I've ever written, that might be one of *the* most visual.'

Page 424: Dylan quotation – 'I just did something . . .' – author's interview with Perlman.

Pages 424-426: Background on Live Aid is from author's interviews with Baker, Bernstein, Goldsmith, Stansfield, Stookey, and other interviewees. Nicholson's introduction – 'Some artists' work . . .' – was transcribed from videotape of Live Aid. Geldof's quotation – 'displayed a . . .' – is from his autobiography, *Is That It?*

Page 424: Stansfield quotation: author's interview.

Page 424: Stookey quotation: author's interview.

Page 424: Drinking: author's interview with Baker.

Page 425: Dylan quotation – 'I'd just like to say . . .' – videotape of Live Aid.

Page 426: Background on Farm Aid: author's interview with backing singer Peggi Blu.

Pages 426-427: Visit to Hibbing and quotations: author's interview with Marolt.

Page 426: Dylan quotation – 'Well, I was . . .' – author's interview with Marolt.

Page 428: Drawing gift: author's interview with Leventhal.

Pages 428-429: Childs quotation: author's interview.

Pages 428-429: Ross meeting and quotations: author's interview with Ross.

Pages 428-429: Elizabeth Taylor meeting and Perlman quotation: author's interview with Perlman.

Pages 429-430: Muldaur quotations: author's interview.

Page 430: Primary information as to the birth of Desiree Gabrielle Dennis-Dylan and the marriage, separation, and divorce of Bob Dylan and Carolyn Y. Dennis: author's interviews with numerous sources, including friends of the couple and a member of the family who wishes to remain anonymous. Desiree's parentage is proven by her birth certificate.

Page 430: Dylan quotation – 'I couldn't live . . .' – Sydney press conference (February 10, 1986). Author attended.

Page 430: Amelia Caruana claimed during a libel case in Sydney, Australia, in May 1987 that she had been Dylan's lover during his Australian tour. Press reports of the case appeared in editions of the London newspapers the *Sun*, *Daily Mail*, and *Daily Star* in May 1987.

Pages 430-431: Manuel's death: *This Wheel's on Fire* by Levon Helm; Manuel's obituary in *Rolling Stone* (April 24, 1986); and author's interviews with friends and associates.

Page 431: The Dylan–Dennis marriage certificate was filed as a 'confidential marriage,' but the existence of the marriage certificate, and names of the parties involved, were confirmed to the author by the County of Los Angeles Registrar-Recorder / County Clerk as a 'verification'.

Page 431: Perlman quotation: author's interview.

Pages 431-432: Childs quotation: author's interview. Childs confirmed that Dylan established her in the Oak Pass Trust home. Reference was also made to Los Angeles County Assessor's records, and to a copy of the articles of the Oak Pass Trust, being one of the documents in the case Victor Maymudes vs. East-West Touring Company, Bob Dylan et al. (Case #BC 189007), establishing how the trust works.

Page 432: Dennis quotation: discussion with author.

Page 433: Bethune joins tour: author's interview.

Page 433: Bethune quotation: author's interview.

Page 434: Background on *Knocked Out Loaded*: author's interviews with Burnett, Kooper, Bayer Sager, and Shepard.

Page 434: Perlman quotation: author's interview.

Page 434: Bayer Sager quotation: author's interview.

Pages 434-435: Shepard quotations: author's interviews.

Page 435: Dylan quotation – 'If the records . . .' – *Rolling Stone* (summer 1986).

Pages 435-436: The supposed $1 million fee for *Hearts of Fire* was alluded to in the court case between Ruth Tyrangiel and Dylan (Case #BC 115656).

Page 436: Marquand's quotation – 'stardom and whether . . .' – London press conference, as reported in *The Guardian* (August 18, 1986).

Page 436: Dylan quotations – 'very real with . . .' etc. – BBC Omnibus film *Getting to Dylan.*

Page 437: Wanderings: author's interviews with various sources.

Page 437: Perlman meeting: author's interviews with Perlmans.

Page 437: Dylan quotations – 'I wanted to . . .' and 'Do I sound . . .' – author's interview with Perlman.

Pages 437-438: Jones meeting and quotations: author's interview with Jones.

Pages 438-439: With Wavy Gravy: author's interviews with Gravy.

Page 439: Dylan quotation – 'Better men than you . . .' – author's interviews with Gravy.

Pages 439-441: Dealings with The Grateful Dead: author's interviews with Gravy, Weir, and confidential Dead source. Garcia quotation – 'What am I going to do . . .' – is from the latter source.

Pages 439-440: Weir quotations: author's interview.

Page 439: Dylan quotation – 'Well, the Fender . . .' – author's interview with Weir.

Pages 441-442: Dylan / Grossman settlement is from the case papers (Case #14403/81), and the author's interviews with Sally Grossman. The Sally Grossman quote 'stonewall' is from a deposition she gave on January 23, 1987. The quote 'procrastination, obstructionism and . . .' is from plaintiff's papers filed in New York in 1987. Background: Grossman's obituary in *Rolling Stone.* The date of death is from Sally Grossman's deposition – January 26, not January 25, as reported in the press.

Page 442: Campbell quotation – 'We've learned you . . .' – *Wanted Man: In Search of Bob Dylan.*

Page 442: Dylan quotation – 'You don't . . .' – *Los Angeles Times* (September 20, 1987).

Page 442: Shafner affair was recounted by various interviewees, and the author spoke with Shafner (who refers to his former girlfriend as Brita Lee). Background on Britta Lee Shain [*sic*] appears in *Bob Dylan: Behind the Shades* –

Take Two by Clinton Heylin.

Page 443: Background on *Hearts of Fire* premiere: author attended.

Page 443: Dylan quotation – 'I saw you . . .' – author's interview with Goldsmith.

Page 443: Goldsmith quotations: author's interview.

Page 444: Springsteen quotation – 'There isn't a soul . . .' – and Arlo Guthrie's quotation: transcript of speeches at the Rock 'n' Roll Hall of Fame (January 20, 1988). The author also spoke with Guthrie.

Pages 444-446: Background on Wilburys: author's interviews with Keltner and interviews with Harrison and Lynne published in *Wanted Man: In Search of Bob Dylan.*

Page 445: Perlman told the author that Dylan grumbled to him about feeding the Wilburys.

Page 446: Dylan quotations – 'I had [the singers] up there . . .' and 'I'm determined to stand . . .' – *Newsweek* (October 6, 1997).

Page 446: Dylan used the phrase 'Never-Ending Tour' in an interview with *Q* magazine (December, 1989).

Page 447: Aaronson quotation: author's interview.

Page 447: Dylan was quoted in *Newsweek* (October 6, 1997) saying '. . . you're one cut above a pimp. That's what everybody who's a performer is.'

Pages 448-449: Background on *Oh Mercy* sessions: author's interviews with 'Mean' Willie Green III and Brian Stoltz. (Also quotaton from Green.)

Page 448: Dylan quotation – 'So what is this . . .' – author's interview with Stoltz.

Page 449: Dylan quotation – 'from the Tree of Life . . .' – *Songwriters on Songwriting.*

Page 449: Links between 'Man in the Long Black Cloak' and 'House Carpenter' are noted by Heylin in *Dylan's Daemon Lover.*

Page 449: Lanois quotation – ' "Series of Dreams" was a . . .' – *Wanted Man: In Search of Bob Dylan.*

Pages 449-450: Tarzana house: research was undertaken at the County of Los Angeles Registrar-Recorder's office in

Norwalk, California, and elsewhere into Los Angeles County property records, and Los Angeles County Assessor's records (property tax), relating to Carolyn Y. Dennis, Bob Dylan, and Fifth Floor Realty. These established ownership, the date that 5430 Shirley Avenue was purchased by Fifth Floor Realty, the date transferred to Dennis, and its value.

Page 450: Aaronson quotation: author's interview.

Page 450: Elliot Roberts story: various sources. Roberts declined to be interviewed. Jeff Kramer did not respond to requests for an interview.

Page 451: Dylan becomes a grandfather: birth certificate of child.

Page 451: Dylan quotation – 'The Devil is . . .' – author's interview with Van Ronk (and Van Ronk quotation).

Page 451: Keltner quotation: author's interview.

Page 452: Kooper quotation: author's interview.

Page 452: David Was quote – 'You know, there was a . . .' – radio interview reprinted in *On the Tracks* (issue 17).

Page 452: Fable: in an interview with *The Telegraph* (Issue 37), Don Was said Dylan told him the song 'Under the Red Sky' was about growing up in Hibbing.

Pages 453-454: Hawkins meeting and quotations: author's interviews with Hawkins.

Page 453: Dylan quotation – 'What d'ya think, Hawk?' – author's interviews with Hawkins.

Page 454: Whitaker meeting and quotations: author's interviews with Whitaker.

Page 455: Smith was contacted by the author, but declined to speak about Dylan.

Page 455: Wallace quotations: author's interviews.

Pages 455-456: Dickinson case was reported in the *Guardian* (April 23, 1992).

Pages 455-456: Fans: author's interviews with various band members and associates of Dylan.

Page 456: Aaronson quotation: author's interview.

Pages 456-459: Wallace quotations: author's interview.

Page 457: Dylan quotation – 'defiled' – transcript of comments at 1991 Grammy Awards.

Page 457: Dylan quotation – 'If it was worth . . .' – *Time* (November 25, 1985).

Pages 457-458: Weisbard article: *Sing Out!* (January 13, 1998).

Page 458: Transfer of property: Corporation Quitclaim Deed (#91-818249) transferring the property from Fifth Floor Realty (President Marshall Gelfand) to Dennis.

Page 458: Drinking: author's interviews with various sources; background: *Bob Dylan Behind the Shades – Take Two.*

Page 458: Dylan quotation – 'what they are . . .' – *Los Angeles Times* (February 9, 1992).

Page 458: Baxter quotations: author's interviews.

Page 459: Clancy quotation: author's interview.

Page 460: Trust deed: deed of trust (#92-1528153) Dylan signed in August 1992 giving Dennis control over part of his Point Dume estate, guaranteeing the divorce settlement. This document is also held by the County of Los Angeles Registrar-Recorder.

Page 460: Numbers of concerts: *Tangled Up in Tapes* by Glen Dundes.

Chapter 10: Not Dark Yet

Primary sources are author's interviews, correspondence, and discussions with: Bucky Baxter, Bob Britt, Henry 'T-Bone' Burnett, Cindy Cashdollar, Carole Childs, Ethel Crystal, the late Rick Danko, Ramblin' Jack Elliott, Dana Gillespie, Wavy Gravy, Carolyn Hester, Garth Hudson, Jim Keltner, Al Kooper, Harold Leventhal, Jacques Levy, Peter Lownds, Michael McClure, Augie Meyers, Maria Muldaur, 'Duke' Robillard, Jahanara Romney (aka Bonnie Beecher), Susan Ross, Carole Bayer Sager, Mike Seeger, Patrick Stansfield, Lewis Stone, Ian Wallace, Winston Watson, and Bob Weir. Also: Dylan family members; the principal and staff of the Page Park School, Rockford, Illinois; and the Montgomery and Naylor families who attended the Dylan show in Visalia, California, on March 14, 2000.

Page 461: Details about Sara Dylan are from interviews with relatives, including Dylan family members. It was reported in the (London) *Sun* on August 26, 1983, that Bob and Sara might remarry. Jennifer Warnes told the author about Sara dating David Blue. (David Blue's date of death is from *The Encyclopedia of Rock Obituaries.*) Harold Leventhal spoke about Sara going out in public.

Pages 461-464: Details of the marriages of Dylan's children, the births of his grandchildren, and trust funds are from sources including: birth and marriage certificates and Los Angeles property and property taxation records. Business details relating to Jesse Dylan are from press reports and Hoover's online. Additional information from Dylan family members who wish to remain anonymous.

Pages 461-462: Lownds quotation: author's interview.

Page 463: Dylan quotation – 'My initial thought was . . .' – *Mojo* (February 1998).

Page 464: Jakob Dylan quote – 'The world's as big as the block you . . .' – (London) *Daily Telegraph Magazine* (Oct. 7, 2000). An additional source of background material was Jakob Dylan's interview with *Rolling Stone* (June 12, 1997).

Page 464: Details of Tyrangiel's alleged relationship with Dylan come from the 1995 lawsuit Ruth Tyrangiel vs. Bob Dylan filed at Los Angeles Superior Court (Case #BC 115656). The author also spoke with Tyrangiel's former attorney, Gary Goldstein, and his adviser Marvin M. Mitchelson. The rose and mandarin story comes from a press report of the Tyrangiel case in the (London) *Express* (June 1, 1997).

Page 465: King background: author's interviews with various sources. King declined to speak to the author.

Page 465: Childs and Oak Pass Trust: author's interviews with Childs and Los Angeles County Assessor's Records.

Page 465: Ross background: author's interview with Ross.

Page 466: Childs breakup and quotations: author's interviews.

Page 466: Wallace firing and quotation: author's interviews with Wallace.

Page 467: Seeger recording and quotation: correspondence with author.

Page 467: Dylan expressed his disillusionment with the modern recording process in an interview with the *New York Times*, reprinted in the (London) *Daily Telegraph* (October 5, 1997).

Page 467: Dylan quotation – 'the music that's . . .' – (London) *The Times* (November 15, 1997).

Pages 467-469: Background on *Good As I Been to You* and *World Gone Wrong*, and about Frank Hutchison, from the following sources: *World Gone Wrong* liner notes (copyright Bob Dylan, 1993); the *Anthology of American Folk Music* booklets; *Invisible Republic* by Greil Marcus; and *Song and Dance Man III: The Art of Bob Dylan* by Michael Gray (the reference to Reverend Gary Davis singing 'You're Gonna Quit Me'). Song lyrics quoted are traditional.

Page 468: Dylan quotation – 'the New Dark Ages' – liner notes to *World Gone Wrong*.

Page 468: Smith quotation – 'THEFT OF STETSON HAT CAUSES DEADLY DISPUTE' – *Anthology of American Folk Music* (Smithsonian Folkways Recordings, 1997).

Page 469: Keltner quotation: author's interviews.

Pages 469-470: Details of the Page Park School donation are from the author's interviews with the staff of the school – principal Nancy Adamany and secretary Sharon Anderson – and former P.T.O. president Kim Marchione.

Page 470: Birth of Levi: birth certificate.

Pages 470-471: Woodstock '94: author's interview with Stansfield.

Page 470: $600,000 fee for Woodstock '94 reported in *Isis* (issue 56).

Page 471: Stansfield quotations: author's interview.

Page 472: Watson quotation: author's interviews.

Page 472: Dylan quotation – 'The record company . . .' – *USA Today* (May 5, 1995).

Page 472: Dylan quotation – 'vaguely get . . .' – *Drawn Blank* by Bob Dylan.

Page 473: Sixty people: interview with former Dylan roadie

Cesar Diaz (*Isis*, issue 84).

Pages 473-474: Relationship with Maymudes: author's interviews with mutual acquaintances including Beecher, Childs, Gravy, and Muldaur.

Page 473: Childs quotation: author's interview.

Pages 473-474: Beecher quotation: author's interview.

Page 474: Beecher and Harrison story: author's interview with Gravy.

Page 474: Elliott incident and quotation: author's interview.

Page 475: Details of the S.E.S.A.C. deal: *Billboard* (February 4 and 11, 1995).

Page 475: Nomura show: (London) *Sunday Times* (May 11, 1997).

Page 475: Use of 'Times They Are A-Changin'' for a Coopers & Lybrand commercial: *Rolling Stone* (April 21, 1994). Also Brian Carty quotation.

Page 476: Grateful Dead shows and quotation: confidential Dead source.

Page 476: Dylan quotation – 'There's no way to measure his greatness . . .' – eulogy released to the press (August 10, 1995). Background on Garcia death: *The Encyclopedia of Rock Obituaries*.

Pages 476-477: Dylan's comments about the Rock 'n' Roll Hall of Fame: *Fort Lauderdale Sun Sentinel* (September 29, 1995). Background on the Rock 'n' Roll Hall of Fame concert: *Rolling Stone* (October 19, 1995).

Page 477: Rickles quotation – 'You know . . .' – is from *Rolling Stone* (January 25, 1996).

Page 477: Ricks quotation – 'If the question . . .' – and Ball quotation: 'The point is . . .' – (London) *Guardian* (cutting undated; circa 1996).

Page 477: Motion's quotation – 'one of the great artists . . .' – *New York Times* (January 9, 2000).

Page 478: Dylan quotation – 'Work while the day . . .' – *New York Times*, reprinted in the (London) *Sunday Telegraph* (October 5, 1997).

Page 478: Wood was quoted in the (London) *Daily Telegraph Magazine* (July 4, 1998) regarding Dylan's stay at his home: '. . . he'd be tearing up cigarette packets, anything, and writing on them.'

Page 478: Lanois quotation – 'The words were . . .' – speech at the 1998 Grammy Awards.

Pages 477-482: Background on *Time Out of Mind* sessions: author's interviews with Baxter, Britt, Cashdollar, Keltner, Meyers, Robillard, and Watson. Additional background: Jim Dickinson interview in *On the Tracks* (February 15, 1998). Dickinson told the story about Dylan laughing on the Erica Jong line in 'Highlands'; Lanois comments reported in *On the Tracks* (June 15, 1998).

Pages 478-481: Meyers quotations: author's interview.

Page 478: Dylan quotation – 'I'd like you to play . . .' and 'some sketches' – author's interview with Meyers.

Page 479: Robillard quotation: author's interview.

Page 479: Baxter quotation: author's interview.

Page 479: Dylan quotation – 'I can't sing that' – author's interview with Britt.

Page 480: Dylan quotation – 'almost like . . .' – 'Cold Irons Bound' (Special Rider Music, 1997).

Page 480: Gray pointed out the similarity between the lyrics of 'Moonshiner' and 'Standing in the Doorway' in his book *Song and Dance Man III: The Art of Bob Dylan.*

Page 480: McClure quotation: author's interview.

Page 480: Dylan quotation – 'I've been all around the world, boys' – 'Tryin' to Get to Heaven' (Special Rider Music, 1997).

Page 480: Hutchison lyric: 'Worried Blues' – transcribed in *Invisible Republic.*

Page 481: Dylan quotation – 'but it's getting there' – 'Not Dark Yet' (Special Rider Music, 1997).

Page 481: Dylan quotation – 'You think so?' – author's interview with Meyers.

Pages 481-482: Dylan talked about the Charley Patton influence on 'Highlands' in an interview with the *Los Angeles Times* (December 14, 1997).

Page 483: Watson quotation: author's interview.

Pages 484-485: Background on Dylan's illness from author's interviews with a member of the Dylan family, and from friends whom he has spoken to about it including Dana Gillespie and Al Kooper. Medical definitions: Association of State and Territorial Directors of Health Promotion and Public Health Education.

Page 485: Mintz quotation – 'a potentially fatal infection' – *USA Today* (May 29, 1997).

Page 485: Dylan quotation – 'I'm just glad to be feeling better . . .' – statement to press on June 2, 1997.

Page 485: Watson quotation: author's interview.

Pages 485-490: Maymudes incident and subsequent court case: papers in the case Victor Maymudes vs. East-West Touring Co. et al. (Case #BC 189007) filed in Los Angeles Superior Court 1998.

Pages 486-487: 18th Street Coffee House: author's visits to cafe; Los Angeles County Assessor's Records.

Page 487: Dylan quotations – 'You're outta here!' etc. – declaration in the case Victor Maymudes vs. East-West Touring Company and Bob Dylan (Case #BC 189007).

Page 488: Childs quotation: author's interview.

Page 488: Value of Point Dume estate is from the Los Angeles County tax roll, 1999–2000.

Pages 489-490: Rosen quotations – 'Mr. Dylan has always taken . . .' – declaration of September 11, 1998, in case #BC 189007.

Page 489: 'Highway 61' leather wallet ('the perfect way to store your loot'): Dylan official merchandise catalogue distributed at concerts in 1999–2000.

Page 489: $5 billion industry and Creighton quotation: declaration by Creighton in the case Victor Maymudes vs. East-West Touring Co. et al. (Case #BC 189007).

Page 490: Dylan quotation – 'I'm still taking medication . . .' – *USA Today* (August 27, 1997).

Page 491: Pope John Paul II quotation – 'You say the answer is . . .' – (London) *Times* (September 29, 1997). The author spoke to a confidential source about Bob Dylan's feelings on this occasion.

Page 491: Cashdollar quotation: author's interview.

Page 491: Levy quotation: author's interview.

Page 491: Dylan quotation – 'the dread realities of life . . .' – (London) *Times* (November 15, 1997).

Page 491: Marcus quotation – 'shocking in its bitterness . . .' – *Mojo* (February 1998).

Page 492: Dylan quotation – 'It is a spooky record . . .' – *Newsweek* (October 6, 1997).

Pages 492-493: Background on The Wallflowers is from the author's interview with producer Henry 'T-Bone' Burnett, Dylan family members, and articles about the band in *Rolling Stone* (June 12, 1997, and January 22, 1998).

Page 492: *Bringing Down the Horse* sales: RIAA.

Page 492: Burnett quotation: author's interview.

Page 492: Jakob Dylan quotation – 'I get asked all . . .' – *Rolling Stone* (June 12, 1997).

Page 493: Jakob Dylan quotation – 'He's in an exceptional . . .' – (London) *Daily Telegraph Magazine* (October 7, 2000).

Page 493: Dylan told *The* (London) *Times* (November 15, 1997) that 'It took me by surprise when they responded like they knew it.'

Page 493: An article by R. Emmett Tyrrell, Jr., in the *American Spectator* (February 1998), mocked Dylan being honored with the Kennedy Center medal by 'the country's first boomer president.'

Pages 493-494: Turns down the award on previous years: author's interview with Ethel Crystal.

Pages 493-494: Crystal quotations: author's interview.

Page 494: Background on Portnoy and quotation – 'kind of this dense . . .' – *On the Tracks* (June 15, 1998).

Page 495: Dylan quotations – 'just every old buddy' etc. – transcript of Dylan's speech at the Fortieth Grammy Awards.

Page 495: Tyrangiel case and quotations: 1995 lawsuit Ruth Tyrangiel vs. Bob Dylan filed at Los Angeles Superior Court (Case #BC 115656). The author spoke to Tyrangiel's former attorney, Gary Goldstein, and his adviser Marvin M. Mitchelson.

Pages 495-496: Ross case: author's interview with Ross, her interview in the (London) *Daily Mail* (May 16, 1998).

Page 496: 'thing about Carols': (London) *Sunday Mirror* (March 22, 1998).

Page 497: 'The Most Intriguing People of the Century' was a *People* special edition published in 1998.

Page 497: Dylan quotation – 'especially while you are still alive' – *Los Angeles Times* (December 14, 1997).

Page 497: Dylan–Simon at Madison Square Garden: author attended.

Pages 497-498: Baxter quotation: author's interview.

Pages 498-501: Background on Duluth show: author attended.

Pages 498-500: Shepard quotations: author's interview.

Page 499: Dylan quotations – 'You know . . .' – author's notes of comments made at July 3, 1999, concert in Duluth.

Page 500: Dylan quotation – 'How does it feel?' – 'Like a Rolling Stone' (Warner Bros., Inc., 1965).

Page 501: Grateful Dead story: author's interview with Weir.

Page 501: Background on the death of Sahm: author's interview with Augie Meyers, and the obituary in *Mojo* (February 2000).

Pages 501-502: Danko and Hudson touring: the author traveled with Danko and Hudson on a road trip to Philadelphia a few weeks before Danko's death. Background on Danko death from obituary in *Mojo* (February 2000).

Page 502: Background on the death of Beatrice Rutman: author's interviews with family members including her brother Lewis; Mrs. Rutman's obituary in the *Minnesota Star Tribune* (January 27, 2000).

Page 502: Lewis Stone quotation: author's interview.

Page 502: Childs quotation: author's interview.

Page 502: Beatrice Rutman quotation: *Duluth News Tribune* (July 3, 1999).

Pages 502-507: Description of shows on spring tour and remarks from stage and audience remarks: author attended.

Page 503: Dylan quotation – 'if the Bible is right, the world will explode' – 'Things Have Changed' (Special Rider Music, 1999).

Pages 504-505: Montgomery and Naylor quotations: author's interviews.

Page 506: Dylan quotations – 'I wish we could play this place . . .' – author's notes of comments at Santa Cruz (March 16, 2000).

Page 507: 'Duncan and Brady' quotation: traditional.

Page 507: Childs quotation: author's interview.

INDEX